GREATEST OBSERVER OF

DYSFUNCTION

HUMAN

Copyright

Greatest Observer of Dysfunction
Author: **Human**
Publisher: **Notion Press**
booksbyhuman@gmail.com

Copyright © 2025 Human. All rights reserved.

Publisher's Note

This book is a work of nonfiction and represents the author's analysis, commentary, and criticism. The opinions expressed in this book are those of the author and do not necessarily reflect the views of the publisher. Factual references to historical and public figures, events, and organizations are based on publicly available information. The Fair Use Doctrine and freedom of expression protect the critiques, interpretations, and opinions of this work. However, the author and publisher disclaim liability for any errors or omissions.

Legal Disclaimer

We intend the use of names, likenesses, or mentions of public figures for the purposes of criticism, review, and scholarly discussion. Fair use principles legally protect this use; it does not aim to defame or harm anyone's reputation. We encourage readers to verify the accuracy of historical claims independently.

Book Design and Formatting

Editing, Indexing, Proofreading: Books by Human
Interior, Cover design: Books by Human

First Edition: 2025

Disclaimer

This book, "Greatest Observer of Dysfunction," presents observations, opinions, and interpretations of the author based on personal experiences, research, and analysis. This book serves informational, educational, and reflective purposes only. Author and publisher disclaim any liability for use or interpretation of material within this book. This book does not provide professional advice in any field, including, but not limited to, psychology, sociology, medicine, law, or finance. Readers should seek advice from qualified professionals before making decisions based on this book. The author has made every reasonable effort to ensure the accuracy of the information shared in this book. However, the author makes no guarantees regarding the timeliness, completeness, or reliability of the material. The book is not a substitute for expert analysis, and readers are responsible for verifying any claims or data independently. The discussions of dysfunctions in human behavior, societal systems, organizations, or relationships reflect the author's subjective interpretations and observations. These are not definitive judgments or accusations. Any resemblance to specific individuals, companies, or organizations, unless explicitly stated, is purely coincidental. The book does not intend to harm reputations or suggesting any wrongdoing. Certain chapters in this book may address topics related to emotional, gender, mental, or societal dysfunctions that some readers might find sensitive or triggering. The content is not a substitute for therapy or professional mental health care. If you are experiencing distress, please seek support from a licensed mental health professional or counselor. If the book examines legal, ethical, or regulatory dysfunctions, such analysis represents the author's personal opinion and interpretation. It is not legal advice or an authoritative assessment of any legal system, case, or entity. Readers are encouraged to consult legal experts for guidance on related matters. This book may critique institutions, systems, or ideologies as part of its analytical framework. We present this critique in good faith, and it falls under the fair use doctrine to foster critical thinking and discussion. The author and publisher are not liable for interpretations or actions taken by readers based on this critique. The book may include references to third-party entities, events, or studies to illustrate certain points. We provide these references for context and they do not constitute endorsements. We anonymized any case studies or examples unless explicitly stated, and carefully protected privacy. The author and publisher disclaim any liability for loss, damage, or injury caused by the use or interpretation of the content within this book. The readers assume full responsibility for how they apply the information shared. Any decisions, actions, or outcomes based on this material are the sole responsibility of the reader, not the author or publisher. The author reserves all rights to this book. Neither the author nor the publisher permit reproduction, distribution, or transmission of any part of this publication without their prior written consent, except as allowed by applicable copyright laws. By engaging with this book, readers acknowledge that they understand and accept the terms of this disclaimer.

Dedication

To my maternal great-grandfather, to my mother, to my father, to my cousin and to my sibling, for their love and support throughout many years.

Contents

PART V: Technology—Savior or Destroyer?

Introduction

"The world will not be destroyed by those who do evil,
but by those who watch them without doing anything."

– ALBERT EINSTEIN

While I write these words, I feel more burdened than proud, more frustrated than inspired. This is not a book of solutions. Nor is it a guide for immediate answers. It is a survival guide for humankind's future. It mirrors the dysfunctions we humans observe daily, yet choose to ignore. In every field—from relationships to geopolitics—we witness patterns of failure. Our history, genetics, and the very systems we depend upon create these failures. We are acutely aware of these dysfunctions. They jeopardize not only our future but the very survival of our species. Yet, like spectators at a tragic play, we do little to alter the script. Like many others, I've been passive, just another person watching from the sidelines. I feel helpless as I try to make sense of the chaos, frustrated because I can't fix it. I feel unable to act, and it stays with me, reminding me how hard it all seems.

If I believe we lack immediate solutions, why write this book? Because I believe in hope. Not blind optimism or naive faith, but the kind of hope that arises from awareness and action. My goal is not to offer answers but to provoke thought. I will consider it a success if even one person who reads this book chooses to educate their children about scientific inquiry over religious dogma. Prioritizing critical thinking over blind obedience is key. Only through instilling curiosity and a forward-thinking mindset in the next generation can we cultivate experts. These experts will address the monumental challenges we face. My hope lies in believing that humanity's best minds are yet to be born. Our task is to create an environment where they can thrive.

The ideas I explore here—tailored technocracy, data economies, and even sustainable agricultural revolutions—might seem like glimmers of hope. Indeed, these could be humanity's best bets in a post-resource world. As natural oil reserves deplete, we must rely on innovation for survival. Challenges fill the road to these utopias. Even the most brilliant minds lack a comprehensive plan. They struggle to navigate the political, ethical, and logistical minefields such transformations would demand. What we call progress often carries unintended consequences. While these concepts may inspire hope, they also underline staggering limitations. Our current systems and collective imagination fall short.

Throughout this book, I have dissected the dysfunctions not out of cynicism but out of necessity. If we are to survive as a species, we must first understand the forces that threaten us. We must accept our current trajectory. Whether it causes environmental collapse, sparks nuclear war, or erodes truth itself, it cannot endure. While I do not claim to have the answers, I believe this: the first step toward change is recognizing the depth of the problem.

Evolution has shaped us into creatures of contradiction. Traits that once ensured our survival—mate guarding, tribalism, and the drive for dominance—now manifest as dysfunctions. They plague our relationships, societies, and global systems. The same instincts that bind lovers can tear them apart. The same tribal loyalty that unites small groups can ignite global conflicts. These behaviors are not inherently malicious; they are the remnants of an ancient survival strategy, misplaced and dysfunctional in a modern context. And yet, while our instincts bind us to the past, our intellect offers us a path forward. We will not repeat history if we confront it honestly.

Our understanding of evolutionary traps inherent in our genetic makeup highlights a distinct and complex decision. Will we hold on to religious dogma shape the future of the next generation? Or will we choose scientific curiosity—the driving force behind humanity's greatest achievements? I am not against spirituality as a form of personal reflection or leisure. But I oppose any ideology that prioritizes blind faith over critical thinking, division over unity, or the past over the future. If humanity hopes to overcome its dysfunctions, it must shed the mental chains holding it back. We must nurture thinkers, problem-solvers, and innovators to build the next generation.

Writing this book has been an exercise in both desperation and hope. The problems we face are vast and deeply rooted, and that is why we are desperate. I believe in humanity's potential to rise above its failures. That belief gives me hope. I also find hope in the power of education. I believe it can ignite meaningful change. While I am just one observer, no different from you, I am choosing to act within my limitations by writing this book. Through these words, I am doing what I can to spark change and contribute to the conversation. I know the collective action of many has the power to alter the course of history. Together, we can confront our challenges and shape a better future.

And so, I leave you with a question that is as simple as it is profound: Who is God? Is it the all-powerful deity described in ancient texts, the architect of the universe, watching from above? Or could God be something far more connected to us—something interlaced into the very fabric of our existence?

It's a question without a straightforward answer, but one that invites us to look not just outward to the heavens, but inward—toward ourselves, and the role we play in shaping our future.

Through the pages of this book, we will search for answers—not just to this question, but to the deeper truths about ourselves, our systems, and the world we have created. Perhaps, by understanding our dysfunctions for survival, we will glimpse what an omnipotent savior might be and uncover who GOD is.

Part I

The Dysfunctional Human Condition

"Time and Money Blur the Lines of Connection"

Relationships are supposed to be the heart of human connection,
yet here we are—arguing about who did the dishes, defining gender over dinner
debates, and hiding behind "I'm fine" when our mental health is a disaster.
From romantic entanglements to identity battles to the silent crisis of the mind,
this part exposes the dysfunctions that leave us confused, lonely, and laughing
nervously at memes. It's funny, it's tragic, and it's us.

1

Breakdown of Relationship

"It is the time you have wasted for your rose
that makes your rose so important."

– ANTOINE DE SAINT-EXUPÉRY

Love is, at its core, a dazzling extension of the brain's reward system—a symphony of neurological sparks that can both bring us joy and leave us heartbroken. Picture offering a dog a biscuit: the simple gesture sets off a wave of tail-wagging and pure devotion. The dog's reward center lights up from that little biscuit, creating a loop of affection. Now, swap the dog for a person and the biscuit for a compliment, a warm hug, or an act of kindness. The process isn't so different. The essence of love remains the same—a delicate dance of chemicals—even though layers of culture and emotion wrap around human relationships. Each gesture, whether big or small, acts as a key. It unlocks the reward centers in our brains to strengthen bonds. When those gestures are missing, however, the bonds can quietly unravel.

But what is love, really? How does it begin? How does it sustain itself? And, perhaps most hauntingly, how does it fade? Love's journey deeply intertwines with the fluctuating stimulation of our brain's reward system. Love is a roaring 100% when stimulation peaks, fueled by acts of kindness, affection, and shared joys. It's passionate, consuming, all-encompassing. Somewhere around 50%, love finds balance—a steady partnership where affection and stability coexist. Below that threshold, cracks begin to form. Arguments, jealousy, neglect, and resentment act as agents, chipping away at the neural circuitry that once linked us to another so powerfully. If love falls to 0%, it isn't merely gone; it's replaced—perhaps with indifference, perhaps with bitterness, or simply with the hollow absence of connection.

In this gentle balancing act, the most potent fuel for love is time. Quality time—uninterrupted, intentional, meaningful—serves as the foundation for nurturing relationships. It's the silent architect behind those 100% moments, the quiet buffer that keeps 50% from slipping away. Yet, quality time isn't a limitless resource. In our modern lives, it competes with the demands of work, financial pressures, and the digital noise of endless distractions. For many, financial instability becomes the most insidious thief of time. Survival through long hours, multiple jobs, or relentless striving leaves little energy for love. The rhythm of connection falters, and relationships often find themselves casualties of the pursuit of economic stability.

Quality time is the lifeblood of any lasting relationship, yet its meaning varies profoundly between men and women. For women, quality time often centers on emotional intimacy—moments of undivided attention where conversations flow naturally, and they share and validate feelings. For men, quality time may lean toward shared activities, whether watching a film, cooking together, or engaging in hobbies that foster a sense of teamwork and connection. Despite these differences, the essence of quality time lies in creating moments where both partners feel seen, valued, and prioritized. Yet in today's relentless world, these opportunities are becoming increasingly scarce.

The demands of modern life erode quality time. Careers, household responsibilities, and the endless distractions of technology all chip away at the moments couples might otherwise spend together. Financial stress, however, is perhaps the most insidious thief of time. In a world where money ties directly to survival, couples often work longer hours or juggle multiple jobs to make ends meet. This relentless pursuit of financial stability leaves little room for leisure, connection, or intimacy. Instead of enjoying time with their partners, individuals often find themselves drained, preoccupied, and resentful of the very system that keeps them apart.

These financial pressures are fertile ground for conflict, and they often manifest as arguments between partners. Men may blame women for financial difficulties, perceiving them as too focused on spending or material comfort. Women may accuse men of prioritizing work over the relationship or failing to provide sufficient financial stability. These accusations are rarely about money alone—they are symptoms of deeper frustrations. Financial disagreements undermine trust, as one partner may believe the other prioritizes money over love. They erode communication, as fear of conflict leads to avoidance or resentment. They even cast doubt on commitment, making one or both partners question whether genuine emotion or pragmatic convenience builds the relationship.

Over time, these unresolved conflicts create a toxic spiral. Arguments, bitterness, and misunderstandings consume moments that should rebuild trust and foster connection. Quality time morphs into futile time—a period spent together physically but marked by emotional distance. This breakdown does not occur in isolation. Systemic failings that stretch far beyond individual relationships exacerbate the problem.

At the heart of the issue, is the modern world's unrelenting focus on tying time to money. The more we work, the more we earn to fund the perfect life—dream vacations, beautiful homes, and lavish weddings. Yet the pursuit of these ideals robs us of the time to actually enjoy them. This paradox creates a relentless cycle where love and survival are constantly at odds. The world's governance structures, meant to provide stability and opportunity, have instead perpetuated inequality and insecurity. A system pushes couples to put their relationships aside for the sake of economic survival when it prioritizes profit over well-being. Humanity has failed to create a governance model that ensures a stable standard of living for all. This failure has left us trapped in a contradiction. The quest for financial stability erodes the very foundation of love.

The solution lies not in simply "working harder" on relationships, but in addressing the systemic issues that make maintaining them so difficult. A world that ties financial survival to endless labor leaves little room for the emotional labor that love requires. To cherish long-term relationships, humans must envision and demand a governance structure that prioritizes well-being over profit. A system that ensures both financial security and time for leisure would allow couples to nurture the bonds of love without the constant shadow of economic anxiety. Until we achieve such a balance, relationships will continue to break down. This reflects not just personal shortcomings, but the collective failure of humanity. We have yet to create a world where love and survival can coexist. In the chapters ahead, we'll explore how to fix this imbalance, driven by political dysfunctions and societal inequalities, once and for all to secure our future. But for now, let's focus on what we can control in this current world by understanding the core of what love to humans is. We'll uncover how to navigate love in a world where time and money are constantly at odds.

To understand why relationships falter, we must first examine the foundations that build them. Men and women, shaped by evolutionary legacies and cultural expectations, often approach love with contrasting needs and desires. These differences are not just sources of conflict, but clues to how relationships can thrive. We'll investigate the nuances of gender roles and what men and women really want from each other.

1. MAN VS. WOMAN

The battle of the sexes is as old as humanity itself, yet beneath the surface lies a symphony of strategies fine-tuned by evolution. Men and women, guided by millennia of survival pressures, often seek unique qualities in their partners. But these distinctions are neither rigid nor insurmountable. Instead, they reveal the shared human quest for connection, security, and meaning—a delicate balance that shapes how relationships begin, flourish, and sometimes fail.

The dynamics of human relationships are complex. Few topics capture the essence of who we are more than the question of what men and women seek in a partner. At first glance, the answers may seem simplistic—men value physical attractiveness, while women prioritize emotional connection. But the truth is far more nuanced. The evolutionary currents that have shaped our species for millennia deeply embed it. To understand these dynamics is to unravel the threads of biology, culture, and personal aspiration that govern our choices in love.

For men, physical attractiveness often takes center stage in the initial stages of desire. This is not merely a superficial preference, but a deeply rooted evolutionary strategy. For thousands of generations, a woman's physical features served as markers of health, fertility, and reproductive potential. Signs of youth, symmetry, and vitality were cues that her genes—and the offspring they might create—would stand a better chance of survival. Beyond mere aesthetics, however, men also seek stability and resource potential, qualities that hint at a partner's ability to nurture a long-term bond and ensure shared prosperity. It is the duality of male desire: the immediate allure of physical beauty balanced against the pragmatic need for enduring partnership.

Women, on the other hand, face a more intricate set of evolutionary challenges. Throughout history, women bore the brunt of raising children, a task that demanded resources, protection, and emotional support. As a result, their desires became multidimensional. Kindness and dependability signaled a partner's willingness to stay through the trials of child-rearing. Emotional stability offered assurance that the relationship could weather life's inevitable storms. Yet women, too, valued resource potential—not out of materialism, but because it increased the odds of survival for both mother and child. In this light, what may seem like "romantic preferences" are, in fact, adaptations born of necessity, interlaced into the very fabric of human nature.

One of the more intriguing differences between the sexes lies in the realm of sexual fantasies. For men, these are often highly visual, centered on physical attributes that capture the imagination and ignite desire. Women's fantasies, however, are less tethered to physical appearance and more focused on emotional connection. This divergence reflects deeper psychological imperatives. Men's visual focus aligns with their evolutionary goal of identifying fertility cues. Women's emotional fantasies, on the other hand, reflect their need for trust and intimacy. These elements are crucial for forming long-term bonds.

Yet these tendencies do not remain fixed. Human behavior is remarkably flexible, shaped by personal experience and cultural norms. Modern societies, with their complex social dynamics, often blur these distinctions. The digital age, for instance, bombards both men and women with images and ideals that reshape how they perceive attraction. Still, the underlying patterns remain: men's fantasies often align with the immediate and tangible, while women's focus on the abstract and relational.

With emotional investment, the contrast between men and women becomes particularly striking. Women are often more willing to pour their emotions into a relationship, viewing it as a cornerstone of their identity and happiness. This deep investment fosters bonding and intimacy, both of which serve to strengthen the relationship. Men are more strategic in their emotional engagement, often exercising restraint to maintain flexibility for other life goals. This disparity can create tension, as one partner seeks closeness while the other values independence.

These strategies are not accidental but adaptive responses to evolutionary pressures. Women's emotional investment ensures a stable environment for raising children. Men's restraint reflects a historical need to pursue multiple opportunities, whether in mating, status-building, or resource acquisition. This doesn't mean men are less committed. Rather, competing priorities often shape their approach to relationships.

Perhaps the most fascinating aspect of human relationships is their fluidity. What men and women desire can shift dramatically depending on context. Men may prioritize physical attractiveness in short-term relationships but seek stability and resource potential for long-term commitments. Women, similarly, adapt their preferences based on life circumstances. A young woman might prioritize passion and chemistry, while later in life, emotional stability and dependability become paramount. These changes highlight the human capacity for adaptation, a trait that has allowed our species to thrive in ever-changing environments.

Even physical appearance, though universally significant, plays a different role across genders. For men, it can heavily influence perceptions and interactions, often serving as the primary gateway to deeper connection. For women, appearance is important but seldom stands alone. It works in tandem with other traits to maintain romantic interest and ensure compatibility. In this gentle dance, both genders find themselves navigating a complex web of priorities, weighing appearance, personality, and shared values in their search for a lasting bond.

Relationships, at their core, are not just about love—they are also about competition. For men, the mating market can feel like a high-stakes poker game, where emotional restraint and strategic negotiation are essential tools. Women, however, approach the game with a different mindset, often focusing on enhancing their attractiveness and analyzing interactions to gauge a partner's intentions. This asymmetry reflects a fundamental truth: men and women are not just choosing partners; they are also competing for the best possible match in a competitive landscape.

Despite these differences, both sexes are united by a shared goal: to forge a connection that transcends biology and fulfills the deeper human longing for companionship. In this sense, the strategies men and women employ are not oppositional but complementary. These strategies meet the challenges of life and love in unique ways.

While evolutionary biology provides a compelling framework for understanding relationships, it is not the entire story. Culture, personality, and individual experiences all play a role in shaping what we desire and how we pursue it. The interplay of these factors is dynamic, adding depth and richness to human connections. Men and women may approach relationships from different angles, influenced by biology and shaped by societal expectations, yet at their core, they share a common humanity. They seek connection, meaning, and the chance to build a life with someone who understands them—a yearning as old as humanity itself.

Beyond the surface differences, relationships thrive on shared values and mutual respect. It is in our imperfections and vulnerabilities that we find the true strength of love. Misunderstandings may arise, but they offer opportunities to grow closer by fostering patience and compassion. Every relationship is a journey, marked by moments of joy, conflict, and resolution that deepen the bond between two people.

In the end, the differences between men and women are not obstacles but opportunities. They remind us that love is not a static equation to be solved, but an ever-evolving journey to be navigated together. It is a dance between individuality and unity, where both partners grow stronger by embracing their unique perspectives. Through understanding and empathy, we can bridge the gaps. We can discover what it truly means to love—and to be loved—in a world as complex and beautiful as the human heart itself.

While evolutionary pressures shape the framework of attraction, it's the fireworks of chemistry that ignite love. The rush of a new romance, the butterflies, and the sleepless nights are more than poetic metaphors—they are the handiwork of brain chemistry in overdrive. But what happens when the spark dims? Let's explore the science of romantic chemistry and its evolution over time.

2. ROMANTIC CHEMISTRY

Love feels magical, but its roots are deeply biological. From the dopamine-fueled highs of infatuation to the oxytocin-driven bonds of long-term attachment, romantic chemistry is a masterclass in evolution's cunning. It binds us together long enough to overcome challenges and build a future. Yet, this same chemistry often leaves us unprepared for love's natural transitions, sowing confusion where we need clarity most.

Love, often described as the pinnacle of human emotion, has long been the subject of poetry, philosophy, and art. It has inspired acts of great courage, driven people to despair, and served as the foundation for countless human connections. Beneath the layers of cultural and historical narrative lies a scientific reality. Love is not just an abstract feeling. It is a phenomenon deeply rooted in brain chemistry and evolutionary design. By examining the interplay between biology and psychology, we can better understand how love ignites, evolves, and sometimes fades.

At its core, romantic love is a survival mechanism, sculpted by evolution to ensure reproduction and continue our species. Men and women, shaped by different adaptive pressures, have developed complementary strategies for selecting partners. Men historically valued physical attributes that signaled fertility and health, while women prioritized qualities like emotional stability and resource potential, which promised safety and security for offspring. These preferences, though rooted in ancient challenges, remain deeply embedded in our behaviors and choices today.

However, love transcends these evolutionary imperatives. It is more than a mating strategy—it is also an emotional experience influenced by brain chemistry. Dopamine, norepinephrine, serotonin, and oxytocin, the so-called "chemicals of love," drive the feelings of euphoria, excitement, and bonding that define romantic relationships. These neurotransmitters activate brain regions associated with reward, motivation, and social connection, offering a glimpse into how love becomes the powerful force it is.

Falling in love is akin to a neurochemical storm. Dopamine, the key player in the brain's reward system, surges when we are with someone we adore. It creates a sense of euphoria and compels us to seek their presence. Functional MRI studies have shown that romantic love lights up areas of the brain like the caudate nucleus, which are responsible for motivation and goal-directed behavior. This is why people in love often feel as though their partner is the center of their universe.

Norepinephrine amplifies this effect, heightening emotional responses and making memories of romantic encounters vivid and intense. Meanwhile, serotonin levels drop, mirroring patterns seen in obsessive-compulsive disorder. This biochemical change explains why past love often feels all-consuming, with thoughts of the beloved occupying every waking moment. Love, in this stage, resembles an addiction, with the partner acting as both the source of reward and the object of obsession.

But love is not just about passion—it is also about connection. Oxytocin, released during physical touch and intimacy, fosters trust and strengthens bonds. Known as the "love hormone," oxytocin cements relationships by making partners feel secure and emotionally close. These processes ensure that love moves beyond mere attraction, creating the foundation for long-term companionship.

Love, like all aspects of human experience, is dynamic. What begins as passionate infatuation evolves over time into a deeper, more stable connection—or, in some cases, fades away. Changes in brain chemistry mark this transition. Dopamine levels, which drive the intense highs of past love, begin to normalize, reducing the feelings of euphoria that initially fueled the relationship. Similarly, the effects of oxytocin may diminish as partners become more familiar with one another, leading to a reduction in perceived excitement and bonding.

This shift is not inherently negative—it is an adaptive process designed to foster long-term attachment. Passionate love, with its all-consuming intensity, is unsustainable. Instead, relationships evolve into companionate love, characterized by mutual respect, shared goals, and emotional stability. Different brain mechanisms govern this phase. They allow couples to build a life together based on trust and commitment, rather than the transient highs of early attraction.

However, this evolution does not happen automatically. For some, the fading of passion feels like a loss, particularly if external stressors, like financial difficulties or communication breakdowns, disrupt the transition to companionate love. Stress hormones like cortisol, which may initially elevate in new love, can either normalize or spike in response to challenges, impacting how connected partners feel. When these stressors overwhelm the relationship, the bond may weaken, leading to disconnection or heartbreak.

To understand the complexities of love, researchers have turned to tools like functional MRI to study its effects on the brain. One groundbreaking study, initiated in 1996, scanned the brains of individuals experiencing love, ranging from those in the throes of passion to those grappling with romantic rejection. Using the Passionate Love Scale—a questionnaire designed to measure the intensity of romantic feelings—researchers correlated self-reported emotions with observable brain activity. They found that love activates brain regions linked to reward, motivation, and even addiction, underscoring its powerful grip on human behavior.

Interestingly, the study also revealed the neurological impact of rejection. Participants who had recently experienced heartbreak showed activation in brain areas associated with physical pain, highlighting the profound emotional toll of hopeless love. This finding lends scientific weight to the idea that heartbreak is more than a metaphor—it is a real, visceral experience rooted in our biology.

While the reward and bonding systems dominate the early stages of love, the prefrontal cortex plays a critical role in managing the complexities of long-term relationships. Responsible for planning, decision-making, and evaluating social interactions, this brain region helps individuals navigate the emotional investments required for sustaining love. It allows partners to strategize their approaches to intimacy, assess compatibility, and adapt to the evolving dynamics of their relationship.

Cultural and historical perspectives also shape our understanding of love. Throughout time and across societies, people have celebrated, constrained, and redefined love. From the passionate poetry of the Renaissance to the pragmatic unions of arranged marriages, romantic relationships have always reflected the values of the societies that nurture them. By situating love within this broader narrative, we see that while the brain's chemistry is universal, its expression is infinitely diverse.

Love is a remarkable convergence of evolution, chemistry, and human will. It begins with the brain's reward system, driven by dopamine and norepinephrine, which creates the intoxicating highs of passion. Over time, oxytocin and other bonding mechanisms transform that passion into lasting attachment, laying the groundwork for long-term partnership. Yet love is not solely a product of biology. Culture, personal history, and conscious choices also shape it.

Understanding the science of love offers profound insights into why we feel the way we do and how relationships evolve. But it also highlights love's enduring mystery. For all our knowledge of neurotransmitters and brain circuitry, love remains more than the sum of its parts. Love is a force that binds us to one another. It gives meaning to our lives and, even in its most painful moments, reminds us of what it means to be human. In the end, love is not just about the chemistry of the brain—it is about the alchemy of the heart.

People often regard romantic love as one of the most profound human experiences. People celebrate it across cultures and generations as a force that binds individuals, ignites passion, and drives personal growth. Yet, beneath the poetry and artistry inspired by love lies a complex interplay of biology, psychology, and evolutionary purpose. Love is not merely an emotion; it is a deeply ingrained motivational system, one that has evolved over millennia to serve critical functions in human survival. It compels individuals to seek connection, form partnerships, and establish the bonds necessary to nurture offspring. At its heart, love is both a biological imperative and a deeply human phenomenon, blending instinct with the transformative power of choice and culture.

The origins of romantic love lie in our evolutionary past, where survival often depended on forming reliable and enduring bonds. For early humans, raising children in a harsh and unpredictable environment required cooperation and mutual support, making love a critical mechanism for fostering these partnerships. Romantic love acted as a motivator. It drove individuals to focus their energy and attention on a single partner. This ensured the stability needed to provide for and protect their offspring. While the expressions of love have varied across cultures and eras, its biological roots are universal.

At a neurological level, love is a phenomenon driven by a powerful cocktail of brain chemicals. Dopamine, the neurotransmitter associated with reward and motivation, plays a central role in the early stages of romantic love. When individuals fall in love, their brains flood with dopamine. This creates feelings of euphoria, heightened energy, and an almost obsessive focus on the beloved. This explains why past love often feels exhilarating and all-consuming; the brain is effectively "rewarding" the individual for their attention to the partner. This chemical surge activates brain regions such as the caudate nucleus, responsible for goal-directed behavior, ensuring that the beloved becomes the center of focus.

However, romantic love is not solely about passion and excitement. It also involves building trust and emotional security. Oxytocin, often called the "bonding hormone," plays a crucial role in fostering these deeper connections. Released during physical intimacy, such as hugging, kissing, or sexual activity, oxytocin strengthens the sense of trust and closeness between partners. This chemical encourages long-term attachment, transforming the initial spark of passion into a more stable and enduring bond. The interplay between these chemicals—dopamine for excitement and oxytocin for bonding—ensures that romantic relationships form and sustain over time.

Yet, love is not static. It evolves, moving through distinct phases that reflect changes in brain chemistry and emotional dynamics. The fiery passion of new love, fueled by dopamine and norepinephrine, eventually transitions into a calmer, more enduring form of connection. This shift is not a failure of love, but an adaptive process. Passionate love is intense but unsustainable; its purpose is to bring partners together. Once partners form a bond, the relationship enters a phase of companionate love. Mutual trust, shared goals, and emotional intimacy define this phase. Oxytocin and other bonding hormones become more prominent during this stage, allowing partners to build a life together based on stability and cooperation.

However, this natural progression can pose challenges. As the intensity of past love diminishes, couples may feel a sense of loss, mistaking absent passion for absent love. Without understanding the biological and emotional shifts at play, this period can lead to dissatisfaction or stagnation. Long-term relationships often require intentional effort to maintain connection and rekindle the spark of romance. Engaging in novel experiences together, fostering open communication, and prioritizing physical and emotional intimacy are effective strategies. They help partners navigate these changes and keep their relationship vibrant.

People do not experience love uniformly; it manifests differently across individuals and relationships. Factors such as personal history, attachment styles, and cultural influences shape how individuals feel and express love. Some people may experience love as a consuming passion, while others may find it a steady and grounding force. Cultural norms and societal expectations complicate these dynamics further. They influence everything from partner selection to how individuals communicate emotions. Despite these variations, the underlying biology of love remains consistent, serving as a universal foundation for human connection.

Love's challenges extend beyond its evolution over time; heartbreak and rejection also leave a profound impact on the brain and body. Studies have shown that romantic rejection activates the same brain regions associated with physical pain, underscoring the deep psychological and physiological toll of unrequited love. The emotional pain of heartbreak can disrupt brain chemistry, leading to feelings of loss, despair, and even withdrawal-like symptoms. These experiences highlight the resilience required to navigate the complexities of love and emphasize emotional support during times of loss.

Love is not just a personal experience; it is a force that shapes societies and influences human behavior on a broader scale. It fosters cooperation, builds communities, and inspires some of humanity's greatest achievements. From literature and art to family structures and social networks, love is a foundational element of human life, reflecting both our biological imperatives and our cultural aspirations.

Ultimately, love is a dynamic and multifaceted phenomenon, blending the raw power of brain chemistry with the complexities of human emotion and social connection.

Love is a journey. It begins with the thrill of passion, deepens through the bonds of attachment, and evolves into a partnership built on trust and shared purpose. Understanding the science behind love offers valuable insights into its nature, but it also reminds us of its enduring mystery. Love is both a biological drive and a deeply personal choice. It is a force that connects us to one another and to the essence of what it means to be human.

If the chemistry of love binds us together, the loss of it can tear us apart. The end of a relationship isn't just an emotional storm; it's a biological and psychological upheaval. Breakups, rejection, and betrayal bring us face-to-face with the darkest corners of our psyche. But what can these moments of heartbreak teach us about resilience and renewal?

3. LOST LOVE

There's nothing quite like the ache of a broken heart. It gnaws at the edges of our being, leaving us questioning our worth and our choices. But heartbreak isn't just a personal tragedy—it's a universal experience, etched into our biology and culture. Understanding the journey from despair to acceptance reveals how loss reshapes not only our relationships, but also ourselves.

Romantic rejection is among the most agonizing emotional experiences, marked by a cascade of intense emotions that can feel inescapable. In the immediate aftermath, heartbreak engulfs the rejected individual, bringing with it waves of anxiety and an undercurrent of rage. These emotions are visceral and consuming, forcing the individual to confront the painful void left by a severed connection. Over time, however, the intensity of these feelings begins to wane. This transition shifts the focus inward, as the individual enters a phase of resignation characterized by hopelessness and emotional exhaustion. Here, the haunting realization of permanent loss becomes central, echoing the poetic despair captured by writers like Li Po, who described longing as an unquenchable ache.

This phase of resignation deeply intertwines with the "despair response," a psychological state marked by profound sadness and inertia. Everyday tasks, once effortless, become burdensome, as the individual struggles to navigate a world reshaped by loss. Neurochemically, rejection triggers a storm in the brain. Dopamine and norepinephrine, which once fueled the euphoria of love, now intensify obsessive thoughts about the lost partner, prolonging the agony. Simultaneously, serotonin levels drop, exacerbating anxiety and plunging the individual into a depressive state.

The result is a painful biochemical feedback loop that mirrors addiction withdrawal, underscoring the depth of love's grip on the human psyche.

Rejection is a universal experience. Across cultures and demographics, people report the searing pain of unrequited love, a testament to its profound emotional impact. Yet, while shared, the experience of rejection is deeply personal. For many, the emotions extend beyond despair to encompass waves of anger, known as "abandonment rage." This rage is complex, often misdirected. Individuals may aim these feelings at their former partner, themselves, or external circumstances. This reveals the tangled web of emotions that loss creates. The same intensity that once fueled love now turns inward, reflecting the intertwined nature of love and fury. These emotions, though natural, can be destructive if left unchecked, leading to strained relationships, diminished self-esteem, and prolonged grief.

Women often process rejection differently, tending to internalize their pain in ways that manifest as emotional withdrawal, changes in appetite, or social isolation. Many find solace in sharing their experiences with friends or loved ones, a coping mechanism that offers temporary relief but may also perpetuate rumination. This tendency for introspection underscores the nuanced ways rejection affects different individuals, shaped by biology, personality, and social context. Comparisons to the animal kingdom further highlight the primal roots of these reactions. The distress cries of abandoned infant mammals mirror the human response to loss, emphasizing the instinctual nature of attachment and the devastation caused by its severance.

Yet, within this pain lies an opportunity for growth. Depression, though suffocating, often serves as a catalyst for introspection. It forces individuals to confront their role in the relationship, reevaluate past choices, and gain insights that pave the way for healthier future connections. With the support of social networks and the healing power of time, individuals can overcome rejection. Over time, they emerge with a renewed sense of self-awareness and emotional resilience. The evolutionary purpose of this despair is evident—it encourages social bonding, fosters self-improvement, and prepares individuals for future romantic endeavors.

If rejection is the shattering of love, a breakup is its slow erosion. Relationships rarely collapse overnight; instead, they unravel under the weight of unmet expectations, resource conflicts, and emotional disconnection. Among the most significant causes of breakups is provisioning failure. Traditionally, society assigned men the role of providers, tasking them with securing economic stability for their families. When this expectation goes unmet—whether because of job loss, inadequate housing, or financial strain—it often crumbles the relationship's foundation. Cross-cultural studies reveal that financial inadequacies are a leading cause of divorce, with blame frequently falling on men. Interestingly, modern dynamics add complexity to this issue. When women out-earn their male partners, societal expectations of masculinity and resentment over role reversals often strain the relationship further.

Polygyny, a practice rooted in many cultures, introduces additional challenges. Having multiple wives creates inevitable resource competition, often neglecting emotional needs. Despite efforts to distribute resources equitably—such as allocating land or time to each wife—tensions persist and often dissolve these unions. Women, in such situations, may choose to leave when their emotional or resource needs remain unmet, highlighting the interplay between cultural practices and individual agency.

Beyond financial and resource-based conflicts, cruelty and unkindness remain universal triggers for breakups. Emotional, verbal, and physical abuse inflict lasting damage, eroding trust and intimacy. These behaviors may stem from personality traits, external pressures, or specific events like adultery or infertility. In extreme cases, one partner weaponized cruelty as a "mate ejection" strategy, intentionally inflicting pain to force the other to leave. Modern variations of this tactic, such as ghosting or manipulating social media, reflect the evolving nature of breakups in a digital age.

The aftermath of a breakup is one of life's most traumatic experiences, disrupting emotional stability, social status, and financial security. Coping mechanisms vary widely—some individuals seek comfort in friends, while others turn to retail therapy or new relationships. While these strategies can offer temporary distraction, they often fail to address the underlying grief, prolonging the healing process. Financial insecurity exacerbates this pain, creating an environment where survival takes precedence over emotional recovery.

Relationships are not static; they evolve alongside the individuals within them. Over time, personal priorities shift, external pressures mount, and the dynamics of a partnership must adapt. Evolutionary history deeply roots these changes. Humans possess psychological mechanisms that alert them to threats or opportunities within their romantic environment, motivating them to act. For instance, jealousy may arise as a response to perceived infidelity, prompting efforts to secure a partner's commitment. These mechanisms, though adaptive, can strain relationships if mismanaged, leading to insecurity and conflict.

Life stages further shape the trajectory of romantic relationships. Adolescence introduces hormonal changes that spark the initial exploration of attraction, while adulthood brings the challenge of balancing ambition, family, and intimacy. As individuals age, their perspectives on relationships often deepen, informed by wisdom and experience. Older women, in particular, gain greater control over resources and influence, which they often channel toward nurturing familial bonds. This evolution underscores the enduring nature of human connection, even as romantic love itself may fade.

Rejection, while universal, is deeply personal, shaping individuals into ways that reflect both their vulnerabilities and their capacity for resilience. Breakups, similarly, reveal the fragility of love when faced with unmet expectations and societal pressures. Yet, within these trials lies the potential for growth—an opportunity to learn, adapt, and forge deeper connections in the future. As relationships evolve, they remind us that love, in all its forms, is not a static achievement but an ongoing journey of discovery, loss, and renewal.

If heartbreak reveals love's fragility, then enduring partnerships showcase its strength. Long-term commitment is neither luck nor magic—it's a craft honed through effort, empathy, and resilience. But in a world of fleeting connections and rising distractions, how can we sustain the depth and intimacy that love requires?

4. ART OF STAYING TOGETHER

Staying together in a world that celebrates individuality and instant gratification is nothing short of revolutionary. Monogamy, once the bedrock of societal stability, now requires couples to navigate a maze of pressures—financial, emotional, and cultural. Yet, within these challenges lies the key to love's true power: the art of building something lasting amidst the chaos.

Monogamous marriage and long-term commitment are two sides of the same coin. They provide a social framework and a behavioral strategy to counteract the forces that threaten romantic stability. Monogamy, far from being a mere cultural tradition, functions as a technology that aligns individual desires with collective well-being. This structure discourages fleeting pursuits. It anchors economic and emotional investments within the family. It also creates an environment where love can evolve from fiery passion into a dependable bond. Combined with adaptive strategies for staying together, this approach offers a foundation for building relationships that withstand both internal and external pressures.

Monogamy plays a crucial role in changing the incentive structure of relationships. For men, it redirects short-term sexual impulses into the pursuit of long-term partnership. This ensures they channel their energy and resources into supporting a single partner and their shared offspring. This arrangement promotes consistent emotional and financial investment, fostering a sense of responsibility and teamwork. For women, monogamy offers security by protecting their economic interests and reducing resource competition with other potential mates. It creates a partnership where both individuals prioritize shared goals, laying the groundwork for mutual support and familial stability.

Transforming initial passion into enduring love sits at the heart of successful long-term relationships. This natural evolution allows couples to move beyond the dopamine-fueled highs of infatuation into a phase of warmth and familiarity. The intensity of past love may fade. But something deeper replaces it—a bond built on trust, shared experiences, and a commitment to navigating life's challenges together. Committed relationships offer unparalleled benefits, from complementary skills and resource sharing to creating a stable environment for raising children. A united partnership provides a buffer against external pressures, strengthening the couple's ability to weather financial difficulties, societal expectations, and the trials of daily life.

Yet, staying together is not without its challenges. Couples face adaptive problems that require deliberate strategies to resolve. Effective partnerships hinge on fidelity, economic cooperation, and attending to each other's emotional and physical needs. Shared parenting responsibilities can further solidify bonds, transforming the relationship into a collaborative enterprise centered on the well-being of their children. Resource management, open communication, and mutual acts of kindness are critical tools in maintaining satisfaction and preventing defection. These strategies, though simple in theory, demand ongoing effort, patience, and understanding in practice.

The costs of separation underscore how important these efforts are. Relationship dissolution often leads to the fragmentation of kin networks, emotional upheaval, and financial instability. For children, the impact can be particularly severe, exposing them to unstable living arrangements or less supportive stepparents. The emotional and practical investments made during the early stages of a relationship become futile if the partnership falters. This failure creates a ripple effect that extends far beyond the immediate couple.

External pressures, from infertility and illness to aging and social ostracism, further complicate the equation. These uncontrollable factors can diminish a partner's perceived value, challenging the resilience of the relationship. In such situations, individuals may find themselves drawn to alternative mates who promise to fill the gaps left by their current partnership. Evolutionary psychology suggests that this dynamic is not a failing, but a mechanism designed to ensure reproductive and emotional success. However, navigating these pressures requires awareness, empathy, and a shared commitment to the partnership's longevity.

Monogamous marriage, when combined with strategies for staying together, provides a powerful framework for addressing these challenges. It aligns individual behavior with the broader goals of stability, mutual support, and collective well-being. This model fosters emotional intimacy, resource security, and a shared sense of purpose. It encourages couples to move beyond the transient nature of passion and embrace the enduring rewards of companionship.

The journey of staying together is as much about adaptation as it is about love. Successful couples understand that relationships are not static but dynamic, requiring continuous effort and adjustment. They recognize that love, while deeply rooted in biology, also reflects culture, context, and choice. By integrating the principles of monogamy with adaptive strategies, couples can navigate the complexities of modern relationships, creating bonds that are both resilient and fulfilling.

Delving deeper into the science and sociology of human connection reveals a truth. Monogamy and commitment are not just personal choices. They are vital elements of societal stability. They offer a blueprint for enduring love, one that balances individual desires with collective responsibilities.

Sex and relationships sit at the heart of the human experience, entwined with biology, culture, and the ever-evolving narrative of societal progress. Modern life has granted unparalleled freedoms, but it has also brought unexpected consequences. The rise of sexual liberalism, once seen as a triumph over repressive norms, promised personal autonomy and empowerment. Yet, this revolution has often stripped the intimacy of its depth, reducing profound connections to fleeting encounters. The assumption that liberation equals fulfillment has left many navigating a landscape of casual sex, pervasive pornography, and disillusionment. For many—particularly women—what was meant to celebrate freedom has become a source of disenchantment, as the emotional void left by these encounters grows larger.

This discontent reflects a broader failure to address the complexities of intimacy. While the sexual revolution dismantled outdated taboos, it often discarded the wisdom embedded in older systems of connection. The dismissal of traditional norms as relics of the past—what some call chronological snobbery—has left us unmoored. We now struggle to reconcile the promises of liberation with the realities of isolation. Perhaps the past holds lessons worth revisiting. It offered structures and values that prioritized commitment, mutual respect, and the understanding that sex is not merely a physical act. It is a profound bond between individuals.

Biology, too, plays its part. Men and women are not the same, and pretending otherwise risks ignoring evolutionary truths that shape our desires and behaviors. Men's physical strength, greater predisposition to aggression, and competitive tendencies are not artifacts of culture alone. Millions of years of evolutionary pressures forge them. Women, shaped by the demands of pregnancy and child-rearing, often seek emotional security, loyalty, and stability in their relationships. These differences are neither flaws nor obstacles but complementary traits that, when understood, can lead to harmony rather than discord.

Yet, modern narratives often gloss over these realities, portraying freedom from restraint as the ultimate good. The commodification of sex—where society reduces human connection to a marketplace transaction—exemplifies this shift. Casual encounters, dating apps, and platforms like OnlyFans have transformed intimacy into a product, severing it from its emotional roots. What emerges is not liberation, but loneliness, as the abundance of choice fosters superficial relationships rather than meaningful bonds. Hyper-sexualization, bolstered by media and technology, feeds this cycle, leaving individuals desensitized and disconnected, chasing the fleeting high of physical attraction while emotional fulfillment slips further away.

The narrative of consent, while essential, often fails to address the deeper power imbalances and emotional manipulations at play. In a world that normalizes violence within intimacy—through trends like choking glamorized by pornography—consent becomes a thin veneer over acts rooted in coercion and cultural pressure. These distortions of intimacy reveal a dangerous paradox: we celebrate freedom in sexual expression while overlooking the emotional and relational damage wrought by these freedoms.

Marriage, long seen as a cornerstone of human stability, now stands at a crossroads. Historically, it provided more than companionship; it offered security, cooperation, and a foundation for raising children. Modern individualism has challenged this institution, yet its value persists. Financial independence has redefined marriage as a partnership of equals, moving it beyond a survival mechanism to a platform for mutual growth. But marriage, like all relationships, requires effort. Infidelity, societal pressures, and the allure of new partners threaten its stability. Still, the solution lies not in abandoning marriage but in reimagining it—expanding its inclusivity while preserving its core values of trust, commitment, and shared purpose.

Intimacy does not inevitably erode. Beneath the surface of disconnection lies the potential for renewal. Humanity can rediscover the power of meaningful relationships. To achieve this, we must understand the biological and cultural forces that shape us, revisit the wisdom of older systems, and resist the commodification of our most intimate selves. It requires a cultural shift—a movement that values emotional depth over superficial pleasure, commitment over convenience, and genuine connection over commodified encounters.

In the end, the challenge is not just personal but systemic. Modern society, with its relentless focus on consumption and productivity, has failed to create a framework where love and connection can thrive. The pursuit of profit, whether through dating apps or hyper-sexualized media, has turned intimacy into a commodity. To move forward, we must address these systemic failures, reorienting society toward structures that foster genuine connection and respect. The question is not whether we can rekindle the essence of love, but whether we have the will to reshape the world so that it can flourish.

But what happens when love falters, and the void it leaves feels unbearable? For some, the pain drives them to seek solace in substances, chasing an artificial high that mimics the euphoria of love. Yet this escape often deepens the wounds, complicating the journey to healing and connection.

5. NARCOTIC LOVE

When love fades, it can leave a hole so vast that nothing seems capable of filling it. For many, drugs and addiction offer a temporary reprieve, an attempt to reclaim the feelings of connection and ecstasy that love once provided. But this detour often leads to deeper isolation. Understanding the link between love and addiction reveals the profound human need for connection—and the lengths we'll go to find it.

Initially, drug use may appear to offer happiness, mimicking the connectedness and thrill once found in love. Yet, this illusion quickly gives way to chaos. Heavy drug use isolates individuals, putting their spouse and loved ones at significant emotional and physical risk. Psychiatric impairments caused or worsened by drug use make it harder for individuals to engage in other activities. They struggle to form meaningful connections, further anchoring themselves in substance dependency. The inability to function in familial roles, friendships, or professional settings amplifies the isolation, leaving them increasingly reliant on the drug.

The pursuit of drugs often drives individuals into dangerous social circles, involving criminal activity or affiliations with dealers and other illegal networks. For those with a history of delinquency or unresolved emotional trauma, the lure of drugs becomes even more potent, acting as a catalyst for destructive behaviors. Financial strain, health problems, and the inability to fulfill responsibilities deepen the disconnect from supportive relationships, leaving a trail of unhappiness and chaos.

As tolerance builds, the initial high from drug use diminishes, leaving only withdrawal symptoms and dependency. This decline in the drug's value further impedes the ability to function socially or professionally, creating a cycle of dysfunction and despair. Addiction causes indifference and tunnel vision. Individuals prioritize substance use over meaningful relationships. This effectively detaches bonds with loved ones and amplifies the sense of loss.

For those caught in the grip of addiction, the stigma surrounding drug use can act as another barrier to recovery. Shame and societal judgment prevent many from seeking help, isolating them further from the very support systems that could aid their healing. This emotional alienation only reinforces the cycle of dependency, driving them deeper into addiction.

Breaking this cycle requires more than individual effort; it demands a supportive environment that counters the isolation and despair driving addiction. Like the "Rat Park" experiment, enriched social settings reduced drug dependency. Fostering meaningful connections and a sense of purpose can help individuals find alternatives to substance use. Recognizing addiction as a symptom of deeper social and emotional pain, rather than a standalone problem, is essential for healing and restoring relationships.

Ultimately, a yearning for connection in all the wrong places marks the journey from love's fading flame to drug dependence. It highlights how important it is to address emotional pain, foster supportive relationships, and build environments where individuals find fulfillment and purpose without turning to destructive escapes.

The intersection of drug addiction and the breakdown of relationships represents one of the most complex and deeply intertwined challenges in society. To fully grasp the dynamics at play, we must consider the profound influence of psychiatric impairment. It amplifies the appeal of drug use by narrowing an individual's ability to engage in alternative activities. Addiction often becomes a vicious cycle. The neurological allure of substances like opioids or stimulants overtakes the brain's capacity to find satisfaction in other areas. This further isolates the individual and deepens their dependence. This withdrawal from normalcy creates ripple effects that devastate not just the user but their families, partners, and social connections. Understanding this cycle is essential for breaking it. Without addressing the underlying psychiatric impairments, efforts to help individuals reengage with life's broader possibilities will falter, leaving both the person and their relationships in risk.

Equally important is recognizing how addiction is often the result of social disconnection, trauma, and unmet needs. Research has repeatedly shown that the roots of addiction lie in environments of neglect, isolation, and emotional pain. Social conditions deeply influence genetic predispositions, even while they remain relevant. Individuals raised in chaotic or emotionally barren households may turn to substances as a way to self-medicate their unaddressed traumas. Such environments also make it harder for individuals to form stable, loving relationships as adults, perpetuating cycles of dysfunction. The collapse of marriages and partnerships is particularly common. Addiction creates a rift between partners, transforming what should be a source of mutual support into a battleground. Yet, the solution lies not only in individual resilience but in the broader societal response.

One of the most effective ways to counter addiction's impact on relationships is through proactive support and compassionate treatment. Programs that provide individuals with housing, employment opportunities, and access to safe, legal prescriptions have shown promise in stabilizing lives and reducing drug consumption. By granting users control over their dosages in medically supervised environments, the chaos of unregulated addiction gives way to stability and the potential for recovery. Offering access to clean needles prevents the spread of diseases such as HIV and hepatitis C, not only protecting the individual but also safeguarding their loved ones. These measures are not mere acts of harm reduction; they serve as lifelines for individuals to rebuild their relationships and reengage with their communities. However, such initiatives require a societal willingness to shift the narrative around addiction, from one of punitive judgment to one of public health and human dignity.

Trauma, particularly childhood trauma, sits at the heart of many addiction narratives, shaping how individuals relate to both substances and people. The unresolved pain of neglect, abuse, or loss often manifests as an inability to trust others or regulate emotions, making healthy relationships difficult to sustain. Addressing this issue requires a dual focus. First, heal the trauma itself through therapy, community support, and relational safety. Second, create environments that actively counteract the isolation and unpredictability that exacerbate addictive behaviors. Relational approaches that emphasize love, patience, and acceptance are not only humane but scientifically supported. Individuals struggling with addiction often experience intense self-loathing and are already hyper-critical of their failures.

Reforming our societal approach to addiction also means revisiting the way we frame its solutions. The traditional punitive model—criminalizing drug use, stigmatizing users, and prioritizing abstinence at all costs—has repeatedly proven ineffective. Decriminalizing substance use and shifting the focus to treatment and harm reduction offer more promising pathways. Providing controlled access to substances for confirmed users in supervised settings can reduce the dangers of unregulated drug markets. It also creates opportunities for individuals to seek help on their terms. Society can lower the threshold for recovery by meeting basic needs such as housing, food security, and employment. This makes recovery more accessible to those trapped in cycles of dependence. These measures not only address the immediate consequences of addiction but also prevent its long-term impact on relationships, breaking the cycle before it takes root.

At the core of these efforts lies the need to build strong, supportive relationships that buffer against addiction. Whether through partnerships, family bonds, or community connections, feeling valued and loved plays a crucial role in recovery. When individuals have a network that offers security and understanding, the grip of addiction weakens. This is not to romanticize the role of relationships in addiction recovery; even the most supportive partner or family member cannot single-handedly resolve the deep psychological and physiological hold of addiction. However, by creating a society that prioritizes connection and care, we can make addiction less appealing and recovery more attainable. This involves not only supporting the individual but also empowering their loved ones with resources, education, and guidance to navigate the complexities of addiction.

The ethical dimension of addiction management also requires careful consideration. Critics of harm reduction often argue that providing maintenance drugs or clean needles enables addiction rather than addressing its root causes. However, these critiques ignore the profound benefits such programs bring, not only to individuals but to society at large. Stabilizing an addict's life reduces the strain on healthcare systems, minimizes crime, and allows individuals to begin rebuilding their relationships. Furthermore, these programs acknowledge the chronic nature of addiction—a relapsing condition that requires ongoing management rather than a one-time cure. Viewing addiction through this lens allows us to approach it with the same compassion and pragmatism we apply to other chronic conditions like diabetes or hypertension.

Ultimately, addressing the role of drugs in the breakdown of relationships requires us to reimagine our societal priorities. Instead of punishing individuals for their vulnerabilities, we must build systems that prioritize healing, connection, and human dignity. This means investing in comprehensive addiction education for individuals and families. It requires fostering environments that reduce the initial allure of substances. Policies must treat addiction as a public health challenge, not a moral failing. By adopting this holistic approach, we can not only mitigate the damage addiction does to relationships but also empower individuals to reclaim their lives and futures. In doing so, we reaffirm the fundamental truth that no one is beyond hope or healing when given the right support.

Human relationships are perhaps the most complex microcosm of the larger dysfunctions that shape our societies. The evolutionary trait of mate guarding, which once served as a mechanism for reproductive security, has metastasized into cycles of jealousy, control, and possessiveness. The instinct to protect and dominate often leads us astray. From the simmering tension between men and women to the disillusionment of lost love, it pushes us toward conflict rather than connection.

But relationships are just the beginning. The same evolutionary wiring that shapes our romantic entanglements also dictates how we perceive and react to broader social identities. In the next Chapter 2: *Gender and Identity*, we move beyond individual relationships into the murky waters of gender, identity, and discrimination. Boundaries that once united tribes and enforced cooperation now divide us. This reveals a world where the dysfunction of relationships mirrors the dysfunction of society.

2

Gender and Identity

"It is not our differences that divide us.
It is our inability to recognize, accept, and celebrate
those differences."

– AUDRE LORDE

What defines man, woman, or other identities? For much of human history, societies have perceived gender as a binary construct tethered to the immutable realities of biology. Reproductive functions, a concept dating back to the earliest scientific inquiries classified as male and female. This view shaped societies, laws, and languages, grounding the duality of man and woman as self-evident and unquestioned. This chapter explores the complexity between gender, identity, and discrimination, uncovering how our evolving definitions of self are reshaping the human experience.

People understood sexual orientation—being lesbian, gay, or bisexual—as a separate layer of human existence. It was a complex aspect rooted in the emotional and physical attractions between individuals. But in the mid-20th century, a seismic shift redefined these foundational concepts. John Money and his colleagues introduced the term "gender" to describe the social and cultural dimensions of maleness and femaleness, decoupling it from biological sex. To Money, biology was a starting point, while culture and environment shaped the contours of gender identity.

If gender is purely cultural, why do similar roles persist across civilizations? Think about it. From Ice Age hunter-gatherers to bustling modern cities, men have often taken on the roles of providers and protectors. Meanwhile, women have traditionally stepped into caregiving and nurturing duties. These patterns repeat so consistently that it begs the question—are they just cultural traditions, or is something deeper at play? Perhaps biology or a shared human experience we've yet to fully understand.

John Money didn't dwell on such questions. He set out to free people from the rigid gender norms of his time, envisioning a world where identity could break free from biology. But his ideas didn't end the debate—they ignited it. Today, identity has shifted from a shared reality to an ideological battleground, where even defining gender remains contested.

Despite the modern framing of gender debates, history reveals that non-traditional gender expressions are far from unprecedented. Ancient Egypt, for instance, celebrated a pantheon of gods who embodied fluid gender traits, and artists depicted some pharaohs blending male and female characteristics. In other cultures, shamans, priests, and mystics often took on roles that transcended binary gender norms. These roles reflected their societies' acknowledgment of the spiritual or social significance of such identities. However, societies often contextualized these expressions within their religious or societal frameworks, making them distinct from today's personal identity politics.

The term *transgender* emerged in the 1960s, introduced by John F. Oliven in *Sexual Hygiene and pathology*. Oliven described it as distinct from transsexualism, emphasizing the psychological and social aspects of identity rather than purely biological considerations. Transgender individuals often report a profound discomfort with their assigned gender, seeking solace in assuming new roles, identities, and appearances. This pursuit, some suggest, is not unlike the intensity of religious belief— an intense, subjective conviction that reshapes an individual's reality. A religious believer might endure pain or sacrifice to honor their god. Similarly, some transgender individuals undergo surgeries or hormonal treatments to align their physical selves with their internal perceptions.

Interestingly, while religion and transgender identity share psychological parallels— both arising from deep-seated insecurities or existential longings—society treats them differently. A devout Christian, for example, might claim to commune with God, reshape their life according to divine will, or even endure stigma for their beliefs. Yet, people respect such faith, even when it defies empirical reality. Transgender individuals often face intense discrimination. This disparity may arise because religion's long-standing cultural entrenchment and its public practices, lacking overt sexual connotations, shielded it from criticism. In contrast, transgender identities challenge deeply held societal norms around sex and reproduction, provoking discomfort and resistance.

Faced with discrimination, many transgender activists have sought to assert their identities by claiming to *be* the gender with which they identify. This claim asserts that trans women *are* women and trans men *are* men. While this strategy aims to secure equal rights and societal acceptance, it has also intensified backlash, as many perceive this claim as a denial of biological reality. In trying to fit into predefined categories, transgender individuals inadvertently invite debates over semantics—"What is a woman?"—that further polarize society.

Perhaps a more productive approach is to frame transgender identity differently. It is not a claim to biological fact, but a deeply held belief akin to religious faith. A Christian identifies with Christ. A Muslim identifies with Allah. Similarly, a transgender individual might articulate their identity as a belief in alignment with another gender. This reframing—coined here as "transligion"—shifts the focus from contentious biological debates to understand identity as a personal, almost spiritual conviction.

Historically, precedents exist for this perspective. The Galli priests of ancient Rome and Greece, for example, were men who adopted female roles as part of their devotion to the goddess Cybele. Their transformation reflected not a denial of biology, but express religious and cultural identity. Similarly, modern transgender individuals might find greater societal acceptance by positioning their identity as a belief system rather than a claim to redefine reality.

This approach could also mitigate the unproductive discourse that arises from current debates. When transgender individuals claim they are women or men, it opens the door to endless disputes over definitions and boundaries. The absurdity of such debates becomes clear when extended to other scenarios: if someone identifies as a potato or a wolf, do we redefine these terms? Such rhetorical games, while provocative, distract from the core issue—the need for dignity, respect, and human rights.

Best-selling books like *What is a Woman?* hypothetical titles like *What is a Potato?* emerge from this rhetorical dilemma, generating profit for authors and media pundits but offering little resolution. By embracing a "transligion" identity, transgender individuals could transcend these debates. They assert their right to exist and express themselves without conforming to rigid or contested definitions.

Religious critics are often among the most vocal opponents of transgender rights, yet they cannot see the psychological commonality between their faith and transgender identity. Both arise from profound human needs—for meaning, security, and self-expression. If religious believers can demand respect for their faith despite its lack of empirical basis, why should transgender individuals not receive similar respect for their identities? Framing the issue in these terms could foster mutual understanding and diminish hostility.

Ultimately, the path forward lies in transcending binary thinking—whether about gender or belief. By acknowledging the psychological, cultural, and historical dimensions of identity, society can move toward a more compassionate and nuanced understanding. Transgender individuals, like all humans, seek connection, purpose, and recognition. Whether through gender, religion, or other forms of self-expression, their journey reflects the universal human quest to make sense of a complex and often alienating world.

To understand the complex web of challenges faced by transgender individuals in relationships, one must consider the deeply embedded social, psychological, and cultural forces at play. Gender identity, as an evolving concept, intersects with human relationships in ways that can amplify existing vulnerabilities while also revealing profound truths about societal norms and personal connection. These dynamics, though nuanced, stem from the age-old human struggle for acceptance, understanding, and survival within a collective.

The fear of revealing one's gender identity to a partner is, at its core, a fear of rejection—a primal dread shared across millennia. Humans, as deeply social creatures, rely on connection not merely for reproduction but for emotional sustenance and survival. For transgender individuals, disclosing their identity risks shattering this connection. A partner's reaction may validate their humanity or starkly remind them of societal biases. This fear grows knowing that such revelations might invoke confusion, prejudice, or even hostility. It's a painful reality. It mirrors historical fears of being ostracized from tribes or communities for being "different."

The stigma surrounding transgender identities exacerbates these challenges. While society has made strides in recognizing the spectrum of gender, prejudices persist, often carried by the partner's family, friends, or social circles. For the transgender individual, navigating this tangle of societal judgment feels like walking a tightrope between their truth and the expectations of others. Historically, societies have resisted change that disrupts long-standing norms, and gender nonconformity challenges one of humanity's most rigid constructs. The result is an often-exhausting endeavor to justify one's existence in the face of collective disapproval.

Communication is the lifeblood of relationships, yet, for transgender individuals, it can become a battlefield. Explaining gender-related experiences requires language and empathy that many partners may lack. The emotional labor of bridging this gap falls disproportionately on the transgender individual, often leading to frustration and feelings of isolation. When compounded by a partner's inability—or unwillingness—to understand, the relationship can falter under the weight of unmet needs and unspoken truths.

Few aspects of transgender experience are as deeply personal—and yet universally misunderstood—as body dysphoria. This disconnects between one's physical body and internal identity can create profound insecurities that ripple into intimacy. For transgender individuals, the bedroom becomes not just a space of vulnerability but a mirror reflecting their deepest struggles. Partners, too, may grapple with understanding these insecurities, creating a void where connection should flourish. This tension underscores the fragility of human relationships when individual battles with self-image test them.

A partner's understanding and support can make or break a relationship involving a transgender individual. The journey of gender identity is complex and deeply personal, yet it often demands partnership and advocacy from those closest. A lack of understanding from a partner can feel like a betrayal, compounding the loneliness already experienced in a world that often feels hostile. Society expects partners to grasp the nuances of this journey. This places a unique burden on the relationship, challenging traditional roles and assumptions about mutual support.

Transgender individuals often find themselves cast as educators in their relationships, tasked with explaining their experiences, needs, and struggles. While education is vital for fostering understanding, it can also feel like an unfair burden. Imagine navigating a personal identity crisis while simultaneously being expected to articulate it clearly and convincingly to someone else. This dual labor—self-discovery and external explanation—is emotionally draining, leaving little room for the organic growth of the relationship.

The legal and medical dimensions of transitioning add further layers of complexity. Name changes, surgeries, and other processes demand not only significant financial resources but also emotional resilience. These challenges ripple into shared finances and daily life, testing the adaptability of both partners. Historically, major societal changes—from industrial revolutions to civil rights movements—have demanded sacrifices and adjustments in personal lives. In transgender relationships, these adjustments often feel disproportionately heavy, given the societal resistance to their cause.

Intimacy, a cornerstone of most romantic relationships, becomes another arena of negotiation. For transgender individuals, body dysphoria can create barriers to physical closeness, while mismatched sexual preferences further complicate the equation. The idea of sexual compatibility is as old as human relationships. Yet, it takes on extra dimensions in gender identity. Circumstances force couples to navigate uncharted territory with patience and empathy.

Many transgender individuals persistently worry about being reduced to a fetish instead of being seen as a whole person. This dehumanization, while subtle, echoes broader societal patterns of objectifying those who are different. Transgender individuals must grapple with the fear that their partner's interest may stem more from curiosity or fantasy than genuine connection—a fear that undermines trust and intimacy.

The ultimate fear, rejection, looms large in these relationships. Whether because of the partner's discomfort, family pressures, or societal judgment, the risk of abandonment is a constant shadow. This fear is not unfounded; studies and personal accounts reveal that many relationships involving transgender individuals dissolve under the weight of external and internal pressures. Such rejection not only ends relationships but also reinforces the societal narrative that dismisses transgender identities as undeserving of love or stability.

Even with a supportive partner present, transgender individuals face scrutiny in public spaces. Stares, comments, and judgments serve as daily reminders of their perceived "otherness," placing strain on the relationship. Public perception, while intangible, wields immense power, shaping how individuals see themselves and their partnerships. For the partner, too, the experience of public judgment can unsettle, revealing the pervasive nature of societal bias.

Safety concerns further complicate the landscape. Transgender individuals and their partners often navigate a world where violence—physical, emotional, or systemic—is an actual threat. Expressing their relationship openly can invite hostility, forcing them to choose between authenticity and safety. This balancing act mirrors the broader human struggle for freedom in the face of oppression, a theme that has defined countless social movements throughout history.

The cumulative effect of these challenges often manifests in mental health struggles. Depression, anxiety, and other conditions are common among transgender individuals, exacerbated by the pressures of maintaining relationships in a hostile world. Partners may also feel the strain, with the emotional demands of supporting a transgender individual affecting their well-being. This dynamic creates a feedback loop of stress and disconnection, making the pursuit of a stable, healthy relationship even more daunting.

At its heart, the relationship challenges faced by transgender individuals are a manifestation of the larger societal struggle to embrace diversity and reject prejudice. These challenges demand a reevaluation of how we define love, partnership, and identity. They call on us to move beyond superficial acceptance and toward a deeper understanding of the human experience. By addressing these obstacles with empathy, education, and systemic change, we can create a more inclusive world. Gender identity should not define relationships, but by mutual respect, support, and genuine connection should.

To unravel the complexities of gender and identity, we must first revisit the foundations. From evolutionary biology to cultural constructs, the story of LGBTQIA+ identities reveals a profound truth: humanity's understanding of itself is as diverse as life itself. Let's begin with the origins of these identities and the linguistic evolution that mirrors humanity's quest to define and express the self.

1. VERBAL GYMNASTICS

Language shapes our perception of the world, clear in the evolving vocabulary of identity. LGBTQIA+ isn't just an acronym—it's a roadmap through the complexities of human experience, reflecting centuries of struggle, discovery, and adaptation. From the simplicity of biological reproduction to the complex spectrum of modern identities, the story of these terms captures humanity's enduring drive to articulate who we are.

The LGBTQIA+ story begins, like most human stories, with life's basic mechanics—reproduction. Life's prime directive, hard-wired into every cell, is to continue itself. In its earliest forms, life began simply: single-celled organisms reproduced asexually, splitting into two identical offspring. This efficient system worked well for survival but stagnated genetically, offering little variety of adaptation. Enter sexual reproduction, a revolutionary leap that ensured not only the survival of life but its evolution. By combining genetic material from two parents, sexual reproduction created offspring with new traits, introducing diversity that became the foundation for resilience against environmental challenges.

At the heart of this evolutionary innovation lies *oogamy*, reproduction seen in humans and many other species. In oogamy, reproductive cells, or gametes, are asymmetrical. Female gametes, or eggs, are large, stationary, and nutrient-rich, designed to nurture the early stages of life. Male gametes, or sperm, are small and mobile, tasked with traveling to the egg for fertilization. This division of labor, far from arbitrary, was an evolutionary masterpiece. The size and mobility of gametes reflect millions of years of refinement. Over time, the female's role as nurturer and the male's role as seeker of the egg became deeply entrenched. These roles define sex at its most basic level. In humans, this biological distinction persists: a male is an individual who produces sperm, while a female produces eggs. Simple, elegant, and, until recently, uncontested.

Introducing "gender" as a concept separate from biological sex disrupted this simplicity. Coined by John Money and colleagues in the 1950s, the term "gender" aimed to describe the social and cultural aspects of maleness and femaleness, independent of biological definitions. While Money's intention was to expand understanding of human identity, it also opened Pandora's box, creating a new realm of debates about identity, roles, and societal norms. Etymologically, "gender" derives from the Latin *genus*, meaning kind or sort—a term that inherently invites subjectivity. Unlike the clear-cut definition of biological sex, gender became a spectrum, influenced by cultural norms, individual experiences, and societal expectations.

To understand the complexities of LGBTQIA+, we must first explore the broader concept of sexuality itself. Sexuality, viewed through evolution, serves as a deeply ingrained survival mechanism beyond mere attraction. Take male-to-male sexual behavior, for example, which is observed across various species. In non-human animals, such behavior often serves social purposes, such as establishing dominance within a hierarchy. Among early human ancestors, similar dynamics likely played out. Within alpha male systems, sexual behavior between males may have reinforced social bonds or shown control, ensuring the cohesion and stability of the group.

Female-to-Female intimacy traces back to the communal lives of prehistoric women. In a world where survival required cooperation, women formed strong social bonds, often centered on child-rearing. These relationships naturally included emotional intimacy and physical affection. With no societal constructs like marriage or laws to restrict behavior, what we now label as lesbian, gay, or bisexual tendencies were likely common. These behaviors were not genetically fixed but evolved from environmental and social circumstances. For males, long periods of female unavailability during pregnancy may have influenced the behavior of gay sex. Same-sex interactions likely emerged as both a psychological and physical outlet—a practice still observed in many primates today. For females, shared child-rearing responsibilities and proximity created opportunities for deep emotional connections that sometimes extended into physical intimacy.

Thus, homosexual and bisexual behaviors are not genetic anomalies but adaptive behaviors shaped by necessity and social structures. These patterns, deeply rooted in our evolutionary past, are part of the psychological repertoire that humans have inherited.

Intersex, however, stands apart as a biological phenomenon. Unlike behaviors rooted in psychology and culture, intersex arises from genetic anomalies affecting sexual development. Conditions like Androgen Insensitivity Syndrome (AIS) or Congenital Adrenal Hyperplasia (CAH) result in physical characteristics that do not neatly fit male or female categories. Treatments often aim to address medical complications or societal pressures. However, intersex individuals exist and challenge simplistic binary views of sex. It reminds us of the diversity inherent in life.

The term "queer" has a long and contentious history. Originally used as an insult for those who defied societal norms, activists reclaimed it in the late 20th century as a badge of pride. Today, queer functions as an umbrella term for anyone who does not conform to traditional sexual or gender norms. For many, it is a convenient label that avoids the specificity of identifying as gay, lesbian, or bisexual. If someone feels unsure or prefers not to disclose their identity, queer offers a protective ambiguity. This term accommodates those attracted to the same sex, identify as a wolf, or reject labels altogether.

"A" in LGBTQIA+ stands for Asexual, Aromantic, or A gender, encompassing those who feel little or no attraction, romantic interest, or connection to gender norms. These identities challenge the assumption that attraction and romance are universal human experiences. For some, lacking sexual or romantic interest is as valid as experiencing it, highlighting the diverse ways humans exist.

And now, the star of our alphabet soup: transgender individuals, who face the harshest discrimination and societal misunderstanding. Desperation often pushes this community into defensive strategies that sometimes backfire, adding fuel to their detractors' fire. One strategy involves claiming to be "trapped in the wrong body," asserting identification as man, woman, or even wolf. While this claim seeks to validate their identity, it often clashes with biological realities, creating a rift between their lived experience and public acceptance.

Another strategy involves seeking scientific validation. Researchers have spent millions searching for a "transgender chromosome" or hormonal markers to prove transgender identity as a natural phenomenon. Yet, such efforts risk reducing a deeply personal experience to a biological oddity. Similarly, promoting medical interventions, such as hormone therapy for children, has sparked ethical debates about the long-term implications for society.

Why do transgender activists pursue these paths? The answer lies in survival. In a world that denies them basic human rights, these strategies aim to secure dignity, safety, and opportunity. Yet, these efforts often play into the hands of critics, particularly conservative factions, who use such claims to delegitimize the entire community.

The backlash reveals the tension between seeking validation and challenging societal norms—a tightrope walk transgender individuals navigate daily.

The acronym LGBTQIA+ has grown to reflect the expanding understanding of identity, but its length has also become a source of satire and exhaustion. Adding "+" to the end is an acknowledgment of inclusivity, but it also signals a recognition that keeping track of every identity is an impossible task. This evolution mirrors the complexity of human experience: endlessly diverse yet yearning for connection.

At its core, LGBTQIA+ represents the human struggle to define and express identity in a world that resists simplicity. Sex begins with a biological foundation, while gender emerges as a social construct. From evolutionary adaptations to personal beliefs, this alphabet soup captures the messy, beautiful complexity of being human. While debates about labels and definitions will continue, the goal remains the same: fostering understanding, respect, and the freedom to be oneself.

As we reflect on this journey, identity is both a personal and collective endeavor. Their capacity for connection, whether through reproduction, adaptation, or self-expression, united humans. This legacy began with the simplest life forms and continues to evolve in the complexity of modern society.

Now, let us delve deeper into these contentious strategies, which range from making extraordinary or implausible claims to pursuing scientific and medical avenues that often provoke backlash. These approaches stem from a desperate pursuit of dignity and rights. However, they frequently backfire. Instead of progress, they push the transgender community into deeper marginalization and jeopardize access to even basic human rights. Among these strategies are the controversial declarations of identity. Individuals may claim to be not just men or women, but also entities like wolves or other fantastical identities. This creates a rhetorical minefield that alienates allies and fuels opposition. The enlistment of psychologists to argue that transgender identity is not a mental disorder or delusion stirs significant debate. This issue intersects in complex ways with both science and advocacy. Parallel to this is the effort to find biological evidence for transgender identity. Researchers look at genetic, hormonal, or developmental factors to validate it scientifically. This quest has led to exaggerated and costly pursuits, such as searching for a so-called "transgender chromosome." Finally, promoting medical interventions, such as hormone treatments for children at the onset of puberty, raises profound ethical and societal questions. These concerns focus on long-term consequences and the potential for harm if not carefully regulated. Each of these issues merits a detailed examination to understand their implications and to evaluate whether they are advancing or hindering the broader fight for equality and acceptance.

As we grapple with the expanding lexicon of identity, another layer of complexity emerges: the deeply personal, almost spiritual conviction with which individuals embrace their truths. For transgender individuals, this conviction goes beyond biology. It enters the realm of belief—a phenomenon best understood by viewing identity through the lens of faith.

2. GOOD INTENTIONS, BAD OUTCOMES

What do religion and gender identity have in common? At first glance, they might seem worlds apart, yet both are driven by an unshakable conviction of deeply personal truths. Have you ever noticed how transgender people, like devout followers of a religion, often take deep offense when others question their beliefs about identity? Much like religious devotees, transgender individuals defend their self-defined truths with passion. Religious followers passionately protect their faith, whether it's Christianity, Islam, or another creed. Similarly, transgender individuals, from those identifying as men or women to those embracing abstract identities like rainbows or wolves, show the same protectiveness over their beliefs. For the sake of clarity and exploration, let us refer to these individuals collectively as *transligionists*—a term that acknowledges their belief system as akin to a religion. This designation isn't a slight but a lens to understand the intense, faith-like conviction many hold about their identities and the societal backlash it often provokes.

I have extensively studied surveys, research papers, and efforts to link transgender identity to genetic markers or hormonal influences. From this, I have drawn a conclusion: the term "transgender" itself is misleading and problematic. It perpetuates a false association with biological sex and contributes to the ridicule and discrimination faced by transgender from conservative factions, governments, and wider society. This term sets the stage for endless debates about gender and sex, fueling division rather than fostering understanding. It positions their identity as a matter of biology or science, opening the door to unnecessary scrutiny and pseudoscientific inquiry.

Instead, the path forward lies in reframing this conversation. Transligionists, like the religious, avoid debating factual or scientific truths. Rather, they are taking part in a belief system, one that provides confidence, security, and a sense of identity. A devout Christian finds solace in believing Jesus died for their sins, while a transligionist gains empowerment presenting as a man, woman, or reptile. These beliefs serve as coping mechanisms for deeply rooted insecurities, particularly those tied to physical attributes and self-perception.

The conversation around transligionist identity often leads to questions about sexuality, but it is vital to separate the two. Genetics does not root sexuality—there is no "gay gene" or "lesbian gene." Experiences, stimuli, and personal preferences shape it over time. For example, a male-to-female transligionist may enjoy sex with women while presenting as a woman, technically making them heterosexual. The same individual might also engage in sexual relationships with men, identifying as homosexual. In another scenario, they might feel attraction to both sexes, identifying as bisexual. This diversity in sexual preferences underscores a key point: transligionist has nothing to do with sexuality. Much like religious affiliation, it is a belief system centered on identity and self-perception, not on sexual behavior.

To put it simply, transligionists' choices in cosplaying different genders or identities do not determine their sexuality. Just as religion operates independently of sexual orientation, transligionist serves as a framework for appearance-based confidence, untethered from whom one loves or engage with intimately.

Critics often focus on the extreme measures transligionists take to transform their bodies, such as undergoing surgery to remove or alter physical features. For many, this seems extreme. But consider the parallels with religious practices: circumcision, body scarification, fasting to the point of harm, or even self-flagellation. These acts are not uncommon among devout followers seeking to align their physical selves with spiritual ideals. Transligionists cutting off their penises or undergoing surgeries are no different in principle. Both groups are driven by a belief system that provides meaning, security, and validation. If one views transligionists as delusional for such practices, then one must equally apply the same lens to religious traditions that involve bodily harm or modification.

Another misplaced effort by transligionists is their attempt to root their beliefs in science. Researchers have spent millions of dollars on studies seeking to identify a "transgender gene" or hormonal explanation for their identity. This mirrors the historical efforts of religious institutions to prove that God exists through scientific means. For centuries, scientists like Galileo and Darwin embarked on research to align science with divine truth. Religious patrons often funded their work. However, they ultimately discovered that faith and fact belong to different realms. Similarly, transligionists must accept that their identity is not a matter of biology or hard science. It is a belief—a deeply personal and subjective experience.

Efforts to "prove" transligion through genetics or brain chemistry are not only futile but counterproductive. They misplace the focus on external validation instead of embracing the inherent human need to construct identities that provide comfort and meaning. Science does not have, nor does it need, a "transligion chromosome."

Instead, the focus should shift to recognizing transligion as a belief system, one deserving of respect and protection akin to religious freedoms.

The desire to modify one's attributes to align with an inner sense of identity is not exclusive to transligionists. People undergo tattoos, piercings, extreme bodybuilding, or even plastic surgery to achieve the image they feel represents them best. Transligionists' decisions to alter their bodies—whether through surgery or hormone treatments—are part of this broader spectrum of human behavior. Individual desires, not some imagined "transgender hormone," drive these acts to align outer selves with inner realities. Evolutionarily, our brains seek acceptance, belonging, and reproductive success. These drives manifest in countless ways, from social posturing to extreme self-modifications.

However, evolution did not program humans to cut off their ears or reshape their bodies—it only gave us a brain capable of imagining, striving, and believing. The neural pathways driving a transligionist to undergo surgery exert a profound and compelling influence. They mirror the same ones that drive a religious diehard to self-sacrifice or a bodybuilder to push their physical limits. It is the capacity for belief, amplified by neurotransmitters like dopamine and serotonin, that propels humans to pursue their ideals, no matter how extreme.

Transligionists must confront a hard truth: their identity is not a scientific phenomenon but a personal belief. This acknowledgment does not diminish their humanity; rather, it reframes their struggle in a way that invites understanding and respect. By vocally aligning their experiences with belief systems like religion, transligionists can argue for their rights in a framework that society already understands and protects. "We are transligionists," they can say, "seeking confidence and peace in our appearance, much like religious individuals seek solace and purpose in their faith."

This perspective shift could dismantle much opposition they encounter. Conservatives, often staunch defenders of religious freedoms, would find it harder to attack transligionists who claim parallel rights. The debate would shift away from contentious claims of biological determinism. Instead, it would focus on shared human experiences—belief, identity, and the pursuit of security in a world that is often harsh and judgmental.

By embracing their identity as transligionists—a belief system rather than a biological imperative—these individuals can carve a path forward that is both honest and empowering. They can claim their space in society without relying on pseudoscientific validation. Instead, they advocate for universal human rights rooted in dignity, respect, and the shared humanity of belief. In doing so, they uplift themselves. They challenge society to view identity as a spectrum of faith and self-expression. It is no longer a rigid binary tied to chromosomes and hormones.

If identity is deeply personal, its collision with public domains like sports exposes fault lines in our understanding of fairness and inclusivity. Nowhere are the debates about gender more contentious than in competitive athletics, where biology and performance intersect in ways that challenge traditional classifications. Let's examine how testosterone—a hormone at the heart of the debate—redefines what it means to compete.

3. INTER-TRANS SPORTS

Competitive sports have long celebrated human potential, yet they also expose the stark realities of biological differences. Testosterone, a single molecule, exerts enormous influence over strength, speed, and endurance, shaping the outcomes of competitions. But as gender identities evolve, so too must the structures of sports. The question is no longer just about winning or losing—it's about redefining what fairness truly means in an era of blurred boundaries.

For centuries, sports have celebrated the peak of human physical performance, with male and female athletes pushing the boundaries of what the human body can achieve. Yet, the stark differences between male and female athletic records, particularly in strength and power-based sports, highlight a fundamental truth rooted in biology. The natural physiological divergence between the sexes, most notably in testosterone production, creates a playing field that is anything but level.

Testosterone, the hormone synonymous with muscle growth, strength, and recovery, is the silent architect behind these disparities. Its profound influence on fast-twitch muscle fibers, bone density, and oxygen transport efficiency gives males a decisive advantage in sports requiring explosive power. But what happens when women challenge this biological status quo? Exceptional female athletes who push closer to male world records face unique challenges. They not only battle the limits of their bodies but also endure societal scrutiny for their naturally high testosterone levels. This dynamic raises compelling questions about the essence of competition, the fairness of categorization, and the role of hormones in defining athletic excellence. Consider the case of Florence Griffith-Joyner, or Flo-Jo. Her electrifying performances in the 1988 Seoul Olympics shattered world records in the 100m and 200m sprints. Remarkably, those records still stand today. Flo-Jo's unprecedented speed and dramatic improvement in a short time sparked speculation about performance-enhancing drug use. She denied such accusations and never failed a drug test. The controversies surrounding her, set against the backdrop of doping scandals in the 1980s, epitomize the challenges faced by women who excel in sports. Flo-Jo's legacy shines brilliantly in celebration. Yet, it also highlights how exceptional female athletes often face a unique mix of admiration and suspicion. This reaction is driven by society's fixation on defining "natural" performance.

Testosterone serves as the engine of strength and endurance, fueling physical capabilities that translate directly into athletic performance. Its effects are most visible in the development and activation of fast-twitch muscle fibers—the fibers responsible for explosive movements like sprinting and weightlifting. Additionally, testosterone enhances bone density and hemoglobin levels, both critical for sustaining high-intensity efforts and minimizing injury risk. In males who produce 10–20 times more testosterone than females, these advantages accumulate into a biological edge that is difficult to bridge. The result is a consistent dominance of male athletes in strength-based sports, where raw power and recovery are paramount. This sexual dimorphism underscores why female athletic records, while extraordinary in their own right, rarely rival those of males. However, exceptional women challenge this framework. Their performances defy conventional expectations, sparking both admiration and controversy.

History is rich with examples of female athletes who have redefined the limits of human potential, from blistering sprints to jaw-dropping weightlifting feats. Yet, these achievements often spark accusations and debates about hormonal "advantages." Athletes like Caster Semenya, with naturally elevated testosterone levels, face intense scrutiny in the spotlight. Their prominence stems not only from their triumphs but also from the biological nuances that give them an edge. The controversy stems from a provocative hypothesis. To rival or surpass male records in strength-based sports, a woman's body must leverage testosterone's effects at levels comparable to male athletes. This can occur through natural genetics or artificial means. This hypothesis does more than question the fairness of current sports regulations—it invites a reexamination of the very foundations of athletic competition.

The paradox becomes even more striking when we consider the biochemical playing field. In strength-based sports, success hinges on the body's ability to produce and utilize testosterone effectively. This ability transcends traditional gender boundaries, making testosterone not just a hormone but a great equalizer. A woman seeking to outperform men in such domains must either naturally produce testosterone levels akin to males or enhance its effects through medical intervention. In this context, the distinction between male and female performance begins to dissolve, replaced by a new metric of success: hormonal optimization. The implications are profound.

If testosterone dictates performance, the binary classification of athletes into male and female categories comes into question. It becomes less about fairness and more about tradition, potentially stifling innovation and equity in sports.

This biological paradox has not gone unnoticed by sports' governing bodies, whose policies often reflect a desire to preserve traditional notions of fairness. For instance, organizations like World Athletics impose strict testosterone limits on female athletes, ostensibly to ensure fair competition within the women's category. However, these regulations can penalize athletes for their natural physiology, effectively excluding women who fall outside the "acceptable" hormonal range. This approach raises uncomfortable ethical questions. Why should regulations constrain female athletes for their hormonal profiles while male athletes compete without similar scrutiny? Such policies inadvertently reinforce the very inequalities they aim to address, perpetuating a framework that privileges certain biological attributes over others. To achieve fairness, we must redefine it to reflect the complex interplay of hormones, biology, and performance.

The disparity between male and female world records offers a stark illustration of testosterone's influence. In sprinting, the fastest male times outpace female records by significant margins, reflecting the hormone's impact on muscle power and oxygen utilization. Similar patterns emerge in weightlifting and swimming, where male dominance correlates with testosterone-driven advantages. What happens if the playing field levels? Hypothetically, female athletes with higher testosterone levels—or enhanced hormonal effects—could compete without restriction. In such cases, the gap might narrow or even disappear altogether. Such scenarios challenge the traditional narrative of gendered competition, reframing sports as a contest of biochemical efficiency rather than mere physicality.

Yet, testosterone production is only part of the story. Equally important is how the body utilizes this hormone—a process influenced by receptor sensitivity, genetic predispositions, and training regimens. Some athletes, regardless of their baseline testosterone levels, exhibit extraordinary efficiency in translating hormonal signals into physical prowess. Variability adds complexity to the debate, showing that athletic success depends as much on hormonal interaction quality as quantity. Viewed through this lens, strength-based sports shift focus. They become less about gender dichotomies and more about a biochemical arms race. The ultimate victor is the one who best optimizes their physiological toolkit.

Beyond the biological, the testosterone paradox invites profound ethical and philosophical reflections. If hormonal optimization is the key to athletic excellence, should sports continue to segregate competitors by sex? The notion of mixed-gender competition, while radical, challenges entrenched assumptions about fairness and inclusion. We cannot ignore the role of medical advancements in leveling the playing field. Should women enhance their testosterone levels to compete on equal footing with men? Or does such intervention undermine the integrity of sport? These questions echo broader societal debates about equality, innovation, and the boundaries of human potential, underscoring the interconnectedness of science, ethics, and culture.

At its core, the testosterone paradox reveals the tricky challenges of human performance. Exceptional female athletes who approach or surpass male records embody the profound influence of hormonal factors, challenging conventional wisdom about gender and competition. Their achievements compel us to rethink fairness in sports. They urge a shift from binary classifications to a more nuanced understanding of biology and excellence. Looking at the future reveals an obvious challenge. It's not about preserving outdated distinctions but embracing the complexity of human potential. We should celebrate athletes not for their gender but for their extraordinary mastery of the human body's capabilities. In doing so, we may redefine not only sports but also the very essence of competition itself.

Hormones like estrogen, cortisol, and human growth hormone (HGH) play a significant physiological role. They reveal the unique advantages women bring to certain sports, particularly those emphasizing endurance, flexibility, and technique. Estrogen, for instance, enhances fat metabolism, providing a reliable energy source during ultra-endurance events. It also improves joint flexibility and cardiovascular efficiency—key factors in activities like gymnastics and long-distance running. Cortisol steps in during prolonged physical exertion, breaking down fats and proteins to sustain energy and helping the body adapt to the stress of endurance events. Meanwhile, HGH supports recovery, muscle repair, and maintaining lean muscle mass, critical for both repetitive impacts and overall athletic performance. Together, these hormonal benefits allow women to excel in areas that emphasize efficiency, resilience, and precision. This explains why women close the performance gap with men in ultra-endurance sports. They leverage their ability to metabolize fat more effectively, withstand pain and fatigue, and execute sophisticated techniques with exceptional balance and flexibility. These attributes, rooted in hormonal and structural adaptations, enable women to redefine excellence in disciplines where power gives way to endurance and finesse.

Sports, especially those demanding strength, speed, and explosive power, traditionally follow binary male and female categories. This approach now feels increasingly inadequate. In disciplines driven largely by testosterone's physiological impact, this traditional categorization creates a mismatch between inclusivity and fairness. Testosterone, a hormone central to muscle development, energy utilization, and recovery, does not respect the boundaries of male or female as neatly as sports policies do. This presents a profound challenge: how do we craft a competitive framework that embraces intersex and transgender athletes without compromising the integrity of competition? The answer may lie not in clinging to binary labels but in rethinking the way we group athletes entirely.

One potential solution lies in shifting the focus from gender to the biochemical realities that drive performance. Testosterone, a measurable and critical determinant of athletic ability in strength-based sports, could serve as the foundation for categorization. Creating tiers based on testosterone levels would subdivide athletes into brackets such as <5 nmol/L, 5–15 nmol/L, and >15 nmol/L. This approach shifts the focus away from contentious debates over identity and toward a performance-driven model. By ensuring that all athletes, regardless of gender identity or biological sex, compete against those with comparable physiological capacities, it promotes fairness. Furthermore, the framework acknowledges that testosterone, while not the sole factor, significantly influences performance in these disciplines. It also mitigates the need for invasive tests that pry into athletes' personal identities, allowing sports to focus on the measurable aspects of ability.

Alternatively, an open category could sidestep much of the current polarization. By creating a space where athletes of any gender, hormonal profile, or physiological makeup can compete, we foster inclusivity. Such an arena would allow exceptional athletes, including transgender and intersex competitors, to showcase their abilities without sparking controversy. Traditional male and female categories could still exist for those who meet specific criteria, such as cisgender women with lower testosterone levels. The open category would include transgender athletes. It would also provide opportunities for cisgender athletes whose performance defies conventional expectations. This creates a platform for excellence unbound by traditional divisions.

A more radical yet elegant solution involves basing categorization on pure performance metrics. Imagine sprinting events grouped not by gender but by time brackets—sub-11 seconds for the 100 meters, for instance. This system eliminates the fraught debates surrounding testosterone and identity entirely, instead of celebrating raw athletic output. Performance-based brackets would require careful calibration to ensure meaningful competition, but they would refocus sports on the very essence of athletic achievement results. This method might initially disrupt deeply ingrained traditions, but it offers a pathway to fairness free from the social and biological controversies that currently plague competitive sports.

For transgender athletes, eligibility policies could adopt a science-driven approach rooted in physiological markers. Transgender women may compete in female categories if they meet certain hormonal criteria. For eligibility, general guidelines require maintaining testosterone levels below a specified threshold (e.g., <5 nmol/L) for at least a year. This policy acknowledges the physiological effects of transitioning while addressing fairness concerns from cisgender competitors. Meanwhile, transgender men, whose transition often involves testosterone supplementation, could compete in male or open categories without restriction, given that they align naturally with the male hormonal profile.

Intersex athletes, whose unique biology resists simple classification, require thoughtful and individualized consideration. Instead of forcing rigid labels, sports could adopt a more inclusive approach. Intersex individuals with testosterone levels in male ranges could compete in male or open categories. Those with lower levels who meet other criteria might still qualify for female categories. Such policies would respect the diversity of intersex experiences while maintaining competitive equity. This case-by-case approach avoids stigmatization while ensuring fairness by neither excluding nor including any athlete solely based on biological variance.

Robust scientific research must underpin all these potential frameworks. Testosterone effects are only one piece of a complex puzzle involving muscle density, bone structure, neuromuscular coordination, and receptor sensitivity. By partnering with sports scientists and medical experts, governing bodies can develop evidence-based policies that adapt as our understanding of these factors evolves. Science must lead the way, not societal pressures or political agendas, in crafting rules that are as inclusive as they are fair.

Dialog is equally essential. Athletes, advocates, and experts must contribute directly to shaping policies. Forums where stakeholders can voice concerns, share insights, and debate potential solutions will foster trust and reduce polarization. Cisgender women worried about fairness, transgender athletes seeking inclusion, and intersex individuals navigating complex identities all deserve a voice in defining the future of sports. Transparent discussions can help dismantle misconceptions, build empathy, and pave the way for policies that reflect the diversity and complexity of human athleticism.

However, implementing such changes will not come without challenges. Balancing fairness and inclusion mean confronting tough questions about natural advantages. High testosterone intersex athletes, for instance, may dominate female categories, raising concerns about competitive equity. Meanwhile, ensuring that transgender athletes feel welcome without unfairly disadvantaging cisgender competitors remains a sensitive balancing act. These challenges demand inclusive policies. They must avoid singling out any group as inherently "different" or "unfair." They should acknowledge the real physiological impacts that hormones and biology can have on performance.

Ultimately, sports must evolve beyond outdated binaries to embrace a future where gender no longer defines performance but achievement does. A testosterone-based categorization system, an open category, or performance brackets all offer ways to reimagine competition in a way that honors both fairness and diversity. These frameworks recognize that human athleticism is not a binary construct, but a spectrum shaped by countless variables. By focusing on the factors that truly define excellence, we can create a sporting world that celebrates all athletes while preserving the integrity of competition. In doing so, we affirm the true essence of sports. At their core, they go beyond simply winning. Sports push the boundaries of human potential in every form it takes.

4. FROM PUBERTY TO JURASSIC PARK

The boundaries of human identity, once considered relatively fixed, have become a frontier of exploration in the modern era. Technological advances in medicine and biotechnology, combined with evolving social norms, have made it possible to challenge, reshape, and even transcend the biological constraints of our species. Among the most controversial arenas of this transformation is the use of hormone blockers during puberty for transgender individuals. Medical professionals often frame these treatments as necessary interventions for those experiencing gender dysphoria. However, they also raise profound ethical questions. Should we intervene in the natural processes of human development? What are the potential long-term consequences for individuals and society? This debate becomes even more surreal when imagining a theoretical future. It involves using hormones derived from reptiles or other species to alter human physiology. Such a proposition stretches the boundaries of both science and ethics.

Hormone blockers, often prescribed to transgender youth, pause the physical changes associated with puberty. For individuals grappling with gender dysphoria, this pause aims to provide a reprieve. It allows time to explore their gender identity without the added stress of unwanted bodily changes. Advocates argue that these interventions can reduce mental health risks, such as depression and anxiety, which are disproportionately high in transgender youth. However, the long-term effects of hormone blockers remain insufficiently studied, raising significant concerns. Puberty is not merely a process of physical maturation, but a period of profound neurobiological and psychological development. Blocking this process could have irreversible consequences for bone density, fertility, and brain development. It may leave individuals in a state of arrested growth—not just physically, but perhaps cognitively and emotionally as well.

The ethical implications of administering hormone blockers to minors become even more contentious when considering the role of consent. A child in adolescence may struggle to grasp the long-term consequences of such a decision. This is especially true given the complex interplay of social, psychological, and biological factors involved. Parents and medical professionals often argue that the immediate relief these treatments provide outweighs the potential for regret. However, cases of detransitioners—individuals who later regret their gender-affirming medical interventions—highlight the risks. Acting too swiftly on such decisions during a tumultuous developmental phase can have lasting consequences. In a society increasingly driven by the principle of self-determination, whether such profound interventions should even be available to minors remains a deeply polarizing issue.

The philosophical and ethical dilemmas surrounding hormone blockers become even more convoluted when extended into the realm of speculative biotechnology. Imagine a future where science develops the capacity to use hormones derived from reptiles to alter human attribute and physiology. This possibility emerges not from science fiction but from advancing genetic engineering and synthetic biology. Consider a transgender person who identifies not just as a different gender but as a different species—perhaps a reptile. They may consent to using hormones to develop scales, a forked tongue, or other reptilian traits. The very idea stretches the boundaries of what it means to be human, challenging both our biological heritage and the ethical frameworks that govern medical science.

From a scientific perspective, research into using reptile hormones in humans would involve significant risks and unknowns. Reptile hormones evolved to function within entirely different biological systems, and their introduction into the human body could have unpredictable effects. These might range from benign outcomes, like minor changes in skin texture, to catastrophic ones, such as organ failure or systemic toxicity. Pursuing such research would likely demand extensive animal experimentation. This raises further ethical concerns about how humanity treats non-human species in its quest to fulfill human desires.

The ethical questions posed by this hypothetical are no less profound than the technical ones. Should society allow, or even encourage, research into modifying human physiology to align with an individual's self-identified species? People often cite autonomy—the right to decide about one's body—to support such endeavors. When a person consents, aware of the risks, who can deny them? Yet autonomy cannot be the sole determinant in such cases. The potential societal implications, including normalizing extreme body modifications and redefining humanity itself, demand careful consideration. At what point does the pursuit of individual identity begin to undermine the collective understanding of what it means to be human?

Introducing reptile hormones into human biology would challenge existing medical ethics. These ethics prioritize treatments that preserve or restore normal function. Altering the essence of an individual goes beyond these foundational principles. This shift from therapeutic to elective or transformative medicine could open a Pandora's box of demands. Individuals may begin seeking modifications that extend far beyond gender affirmation or species identity. The medical field must determine where to draw the line between feasible and frivolous, ethical and exploitative.

Opponents of such research might argue that humanity should resist the temptation to meddle with its fundamental nature. They believe it is vital to preserve the sanctity of human biology against the allure of radical transformation. They could point to the slippery slope of genetic and hormonal modification, warning that what begins as an individual choice could evolve into societal pressure. If the technology to become "reptilian" becomes available, could the next frontier be adopting traits of other species—avian wings for flight enthusiasts, or feline agility for athletes? At what point does the quest for self-expression reject the human condition itself?

Proponents, however, might frame this pursuit as the ultimate expression of human creativity and autonomy. They could argue that restricting such research stifles scientific innovation and infringes on personal freedom. In a diverse, individualistic world, why let biology's boundaries constrain imagination? For many, the idea of aligning one's physical attribute with an inner identity, however unconventional, represents liberation rather than a threat.

Society cannot ignore the broader implications of allowing such transformations. If some individuals choose to become reptilian, how would society accommodate this new diversity? Will such individuals face discrimination or gain recognition as pioneers of human evolution? How would laws and social norms adapt to accommodate those who no longer fit within traditional definitions of humanity? These questions highlight the interconnectedness of ethical, social, and scientific considerations in this emerging field.

The debate over hormone blockers and the hypothetical use of reptile hormones for transformation raises complex issues. Ultimately, it circles back to a fundamental question: how far should humanity go in its quest to transcend biological roots? As we stand on the cusp of unprecedented possibilities in medicine and biotechnology, the choices we make today will define the contours of our future. Will we embrace humanity's vision as fluid and boundless, or preserve limits to safeguard the integrity of the human experience? These questions lack simple answers yet demand rigorous debate, touching the essence of humanity in an era redefining what it means to be human.

The desire for identity is ancient. It stems from a primal need to belong, to carve out a safe space within a chaotic world. But this drive, when distorted by societal constructs and power dynamics, creates divisions that perpetuate discrimination and conflict. The evolutionary instinct to categorize "us" versus "them" becomes weaponized, morphing into verbal gymnastics and policies that, despite their good intentions, often lead to bad outcomes.

This chapter leaves us with a critical question: what happens when these identity battles turn inward? The answer lies in the realm of mental health, explored in Chapter 3: *Mental Health Crisis*. The same traits that create external divides—fear, insecurity, and the need for control—also ravage our inner worlds. They leave individuals wrestling with unseen demons born from environmental dysfunction.

3

Mental Health Crisis

"Shame is the most powerful, master emotion.
It's the fear that we're not good enough."

– BRENÉ BROWN

Imagine a world where one in eight people fights a silent, invisible enemy. It's a shadow that clouds their thoughts, drains their energy, and isolates them from others. This reflects the reality of the global mental health crisis, an epidemic as pervasive as it remains overlooked. From depression to PTSD, the struggles of millions go unnoticed, buried under the weight of stigma, inadequate care, and societal indifference. Yet, mental health is not just a personal struggle—it is a collective responsibility, entwined with the structures, values, and priorities of our world. This chapter delves into the silent epidemic, exploring its roots, manifestations, and the urgent need to rethink how we approach mental well-being.

Central to the mental health crisis is a malicious stigma that has persisted across centuries and cultures. Mental illness, unlike physical ailments, remains shrouded in shame and misunderstanding. Those struggling with depression, anxiety, or bipolar disorder often face harsh stereotypes. People often see them as weak, or attention-seeking. This stigma makes it hard for them to seek help without fearing judgment.

This stigma is not merely social but systemic, ingrained in the very structures meant to provide support. Many communities still cling to traditional beliefs that mental illness is a moral failing, a sign of spiritual deficiency, or even possession. In professional environments, admitting to mental health struggles can jeopardize careers, further silencing those in need. Society forces individuals to suppress their pain, allowing it to fester into crises that timely intervention could have prevented.

Even for those who overcome the stigma, access to mental health care often feels like an insurmountable barrier. In wealthier nations, urban areas disproportionately hold mental health services, leaving rural populations underserved. In lower-income countries, the disparity is even starker, with as few as one psychiatrist per million people. Economic factors compound this inequity. Therapy, medication, and psychiatric evaluations are prohibitively expensive for many, while insurance coverage for mental health care lags behind coverage for physical health conditions. Compounding these issues is a global shortage of mental health professionals, creating a system where those in crisis wait weeks or months for appointments. For some, the wait is fatal.

Complicating matters further are the controversial forces shaping the mental health landscape. Big Pharma often plays the role of savior and scapegoat. Pharmaceutical companies have undeniably advanced how they treat mental illness, transforming lives with their medications. Yet their profit motives have also led to the over-medicalization of mental health. The diagnostic boundaries of disorders like depression and ADHD have expanded significantly over the past few decades. Critics argue this shift stems not from newfound scientific understanding but from efforts to broaden definitions to expand drug markets. Antidepressants, heralded as a miracle cure by some, are emblematic of this tension. Millions swear by their efficacy. Others, however, question their true impact, citing studies that suggest their benefits may be no greater than a placebo—except in the most severe cases. Side effects, ranging from weight gain to emotional numbness, further fuel the debate.

In contrast, the rise of psychedelics like psilocybin and MDMA in mental health treatment has sparked cautious optimism. Preliminary studies show promise for these substances in treating conditions such as PTSD and treatment-resistant depression, often achieving results after just a few guided sessions. But this emerging field is not without its ethical and legal challenges. Psychedelics remain tightly controlled substances in most countries, and concerns about their long-term effects and potential for misuse have sparked resistance from regulatory bodies. As science advances, society faces a challenge. We must balance innovation with caution. It's essential to ensure that new therapies avoid repeating the mistakes of over-prescription and commercial exploitation.

The broader societal context further exacerbates the crisis. Social media, the defining communication tool of our time, plays a dual role in mental health. On one hand, it connects individuals with support networks and raises awareness about mental illness. On the other, its curated feeds and algorithms often amplify feelings of inadequacy, anxiety, and isolation. Young people, in particular, feel crushed under the weight of constant comparison and the fear of missing out, struggling with rising rates of depression and self-harm. Meanwhile, the criminal justice system has become an unintended catch-all for untreated mental illness. Jails and prisons now house more individuals with mental health conditions than psychiatric facilities, a grim testament to systemic failure. These institutions are ill-equipped to provide proper care, often worsening the conditions of those they detain. The intersection of mental health and gun violence adds another layer of complexity. Policymakers wrestle with addressing the mental health dimensions of mass shootings without further stigmatizing those with mental illnesses. The vast majority of individuals with mental health conditions are non-violent.

Certain populations face unique mental health challenges that demand specialized attention. Gender dynamics, for instance, shape mental health outcomes in profound ways. Men, conditioned to suppress vulnerability, often delay seeking help until they reach breaking points. Women, meanwhile, face distinct struggles, including postpartum depression and the mental toll of balancing societal expectations. For LGBTQ+ individuals, discrimination, family rejection, and societal exclusion compound mental health risks, leading to disproportionately high rates of suicide and substance abuse. In the workplace, the relentless demands of modern capitalism have given rise to widespread burnout, with employees feeling trapped in cycles of overwork and exhaustion. Employers, slow to acknowledge the human cost of productivity, are only beginning to address these issues through mental health initiatives and accommodations.

Schools, too, have become battlegrounds for mental health. Students face mounting pressures from academic expectations, social dynamics, and increasingly uncertain futures. Early intervention programs in schools, from counselling services to peer support groups, have shown great promise but remain underfunded and unevenly implemented. A failure to address mental health at this critical stage often leads to lifelong struggles, underscoring the urgency of systemic reform.

On a personal level, mental health struggles ripple through relationships, creating cycles of conflict, alienation, and despair. Romantic and familial bonds, meant to provide stability and support, can become sources of tension when mental illness enters the equation. Partners may struggle to understand or cope with their loved one's condition. Meanwhile, individuals with mental health challenges often isolate themselves, fearing they might become a burden. This feedback loop of misunderstanding and withdrawal exacerbates existing issues, leaving all parties feeling unsupported.

To address the mental health crisis, society must adopt a holistic approach that spans cultural attitudes, policy reform, and individual action. Destigmatizing mental illness is paramount, requiring public education campaigns and visible advocacy from influential figures. Expanding access to affordable, high-quality care is essential. This requires investing in training mental health professionals, integrating mental health services into primary care, and exploring innovative treatment models. We must stay vigilant against commercial exploitation and over-medicalization, ensuring patient care remains central to mental health efforts.

To understand the depth of today's mental health crisis, we must first look backward—into the historical shadows where stigma took root. For centuries, misconceptions and fears have shaped how we perceive mental illness, leaving a legacy of shame and exclusion that persists today.

1. DEMON MIND

Mental illness has always been humanity's misunderstood ghost. In ancient times, people labeled those displaying symptoms of mental distress as cursed, possessed, or morally corrupt. These interpretations, born of fear and ignorance, laid the foundation for a stigma that would evolve over centuries. From asylums that segregated the "insane" to cultural narratives that painted mental illness as a threat, society has long marginalized those who struggled. Understanding this history is essential not only to dismantle stigma but also to forge a future where societies treat mental health as a universal human experience.

The stigma surrounding mental illness is a shadow stretching back through centuries. Fear, misunderstanding, and power intertwine to incorporate this into human history. Ancient societies linked mental mysteries closely to supernatural beliefs. People often viewed mental illness as a direct manifestation of forces beyond human understanding. A person experiencing hallucinations or intense emotional distress faced harsh judgment. People quickly labeled them as possessed by demons, cursed by witches, or punished by an offended deity. These interpretations were not merely individual beliefs, but collective narratives that permeated entire communities. They justified both the isolation and the harsh treatments inflicted upon those afflicted. Exorcisms, brutal rituals, and public shaming were tools of purification. These practices reinforced the belief that mental illness was a moral or spiritual failing. Such explanations provided order in an unpredictable world, but also sowed seeds of fear and alienation that would persist for millennia.

A profound lack of medical understanding in subsequent eras preserved and compounded this stigma. For much of human history, the causes of mental illness remained obscured, cloaked in ignorance and misinterpretation. People dismissed depression as mere laziness, a failure to muster sufficient willpower, and blamed conditions like schizophrenia on personal weakness or sinful behavior. These interpretations shifted the burden of blame onto the individual. They framed mental illness as a choice rather than a condition, a character flaw rather than a health issue. Lacking scientific frameworks created a vacuum filled with superstition, judgment, and punitive measures. As medical science began to evolve, it offered some hope but also alternative forms of marginalization. In the 18th and 19th centuries, asylums became the preferred solution for dealing with the mentally ill. While intended as places of care, many facilities quickly devolved into sites of neglect and abuse. Confining individuals to institutions reinforced perceptions of them as dangerous, unpredictable, or broken. The physical isolation of asylums mirrored the societal barriers erected to keep the mentally ill at arm's length, reinforcing stereotypes that linger to this day.

Cultural and social norms have further entrenched these stigmas, shaping how societies perceive and treat mental illness. The push for conformity to "normal" behavior has often excluded those who deviate. Patriarchal societies often viewed mental illness as a stain on both the individual and the family. This perception of dishonor led to secrecy, denial, and outright exclusion, with affected individuals being barred from marriage, employment, and community life. These cultural taboos created a cycle of silence and marginalization, discouraging open conversations about mental health and preventing those in need from seeking help. The arts, which have such power to shape societal perceptions, have often done little to challenge these biases. Instead, literature, theater, and later cinema have frequently depicted the mentally ill as violent villains or comic figures to be mocked. These portrayals, repeated across generations, have etched enduring stereotypes into the public consciousness. This makes it harder for individuals with mental illness to be seen as fully human.

The fear of the unknown has been perhaps the most pervasive force driving the stigmatization of mental illness. Even as scientific understanding has progressed, the symptoms of mental illness—often unpredictable, invisible, or poorly understood—continue to evoke unease. This fear is not irrational; it stems from humanity's evolutionary past, where survival depended on quick judgments about potential threats. In early human societies, people interpreted behaviors seen as abnormal as signs of danger, whether from disease, injury, or a loss of social cohesion. Isolating individuals who exhibited such behaviors may have been a protective strategy, minimizing risk to the group. These ancient instincts were useful in a prehistoric context. However, they have outlived their purpose. Today, they often lead to discrimination and exclusion. Modern societies understand mental illness causes and treatments more effectively.

The misuse of scientific and medical authority has also played a significant role in perpetuating stigma, particularly during the dark era of eugenics. In the late 19th and early 20th centuries, mental illness was used to justify cruel policies. These included forced sterilizations, institutionalization, and other dehumanizing measures aimed at "improving" the human gene pool. These practices reduced individuals to the sum of their perceived deficits, stripping away their humanity and subjecting them to unspeakable violations of their rights. Women, in particular, bore the brunt of these attitudes. Physicians wielded conditions like hysteria as a catch-all diagnosis to dismiss legitimate health concerns, often using it to control or silence patients. These historical abuses have left deep scars, fueling mistrust in mental health systems and contributing to the gendered dimensions of stigma that persist to this day.

While modern advocacy and scientific advancements have made strides in challenging these historical biases, their echoes continue to shape how societies perceive and treat mental illness. The road to dismantling stigma requires education and systemic reform. It also demands a willingness to confront the deep cultural narratives that have shaped our collective understanding of mental health. Examining the historical roots of this stigma helps untangle the fear, misunderstanding, and prejudice that shadow countless lives. In doing so, we create the possibility of a future where mental illness is no longer a source of shame or isolation. Instead, it becomes a shared aspect of the human experience, deserving of empathy, respect, and care.

Beneath the stigma lies an even older story—one that traces back to our evolutionary roots. Shame and isolation, once essential for survival, became tools of exclusion in the realm of mental health.

1.1 SURVIVAL OF THE SHAMIEST

In the harsh realities of early human life, shame and social isolation were not just emotions, but survival strategies. The group swiftly corrected or excluded behaviors that threatened stability to protect resources and cohesion. These instincts, deeply ingrained in our psychology, helped humans thrive in resource-scarce environments. But in the modern world, these same instincts have mutated into a stigma that isolates individuals with mental health challenges, exacerbating their suffering.

From an evolutionary perspective, shame and social isolation are not arbitrary reactions. They are deeply ingrained mechanisms shaped by the relentless pressures of survival. In early human societies, where cooperation and group cohesion were paramount, behaviors that deviated from established norms threatened the delicate balance that held communities together. Shame emerged as a psychological tool; an internal alarm system designed to align individual behavior with the group's expectations. When someone strayed too far—whether through aggression, selfishness, or unpredictability—shame functioned as a deterrent, prodding them back into compliance. This emotional response was not merely punitive; it was instructive, encouraging self-correction, and reinforcing social bonds. Feeling shame offered an evolutionary advantage: it reduced the risk of social exclusion and increased access to group resources and protections. Over time, this emotional feedback loop became deeply embedded in the human psyche, an invisible thread that helped shape early social order.

Yet shame alone was insufficient to address all threats to group stability. Where individuals exhibited erratic or dangerous behavior, isolation became a necessary, albeit harsh, strategy. This was especially true when such behaviors suggested illness or impairment that could endanger the group. Early humans lacked medical knowledge to distinguish between infectious diseases and non-contagious conditions. People often viewed unusual or unpredictable behavior as a potential danger. By isolating or excluding these individuals, the group minimized the risk of spreading potential pathogens. This also reduced the chances of actions that might attract predators or disrupt critical activities like hunting and gathering. These measures, though cold, stemmed from the primal calculus of survival. The group prioritized preserving its collective well-being over fairness or compassion. The group excluded those who failed to contribute or posed risks to safeguard its survival.

This exclusionary instinct also played a key role in reinforcing social norms. When societies punished or isolated nonconformists, their exclusion served as a potent warning to others. Observing the fate of the excluded reinforced how crucial it was to adhere to group expectations, creating a shared moral framework that governed behavior. This dynamic was particularly effective in small, tightly knit groups where the consequences of deviance were immediately visible. In this way, isolating outliers strengthened the majority's cohesion, ensuring that cooperation and trust remained intact. Group survival required balance, excluding a few to safeguard the majority.

The struggle for survival in resource-scarce environments demanded efficiency. Communities prioritized contributors—those who could hunt, gather, or defend—while isolating individuals seen as liabilities. Those unable to contribute consumed resources without offering anything in return. Exclusion, though cruel by today's standards, was a calculated strategy to ensure the group's survival. Ancient societies operated with brutal pragmatism, where survival trumped altruism and sentimentality.

Shame and isolation played paradoxical roles as social signals, acting as both deterrents and invitations for connection. Displays of shame—like lowered posture, avoiding eye contact, or withdrawing—nonverbally expressed remorse or a wish to rejoin the group. These cues often drew sympathy or support, paving the way for reconciliation. Similarly, isolation sometimes spurred others to step in, especially when they interpreted the behavior as a plea for help, not a threat. These mechanisms served dual purposes, balancing punishment with restoration to strengthen group dynamics.

Moreover, certain traits associated with mental illness, though stigmatized today, may have been advantageous in early human contexts. Anxiety, for example, heightened vigilance and sensitivity to danger, traits that could protect both the individual and the group from predators or environmental threats. Many people today view hyperactivity and impulsivity as disruptive. However, in ancient times, they might have fueled exploration and innovation. These traits could have helped groups find new resources or adapt to changing conditions. These traits, while sometimes problematic, were not inherently maladaptive; their value depended on the context in which they occurred. The stigmatization of such behaviors in contemporary society reflects a mismatch between ancient evolutionary functions and modern social norms.

In modern contexts, the legacy of these evolutionary mechanisms can lead to unintended consequences. The instinct to isolate those who deviate from the norm persists, even as our understanding of mental illness has advanced. Social exclusion, once a survival strategy, now exacerbates how vulnerable people suffer. Similarly, the internalized shame felt by individuals with mental health challenges often prevents them from seeking help, perpetuating cycles of silence and stigma. Recognizing the evolutionary roots of these behaviors allows us to challenge them more effectively. It reminds us that shame and isolation were once adaptive. However, they no longer align with a world that actively understands, treats, and accommodates mental health issues.

Ultimately, how shame and isolation evolved reveals a profound truth about humanity. Our deepest instincts, forged in the crucible of survival, continue to shape societies in ways both beneficial and harmful. By understanding these origins, we can begin to rewrite the narrative, replacing exclusion with empathy and judgment with understanding. Just as early humans adapted to their environments, so too can we adapt our social norms to reflect the knowledge and values of our time. This respects past struggles while embracing the potential for a compassionate future.

Religion and culture reshaped survival instincts as human societies evolved, turning pragmatic responses into moral judgments. Mental illness was no longer just a challenge—it became a sin.

1.2 RELIGION HIJACKED SHAME

When religion entered the picture, it rewrote the narrative of mental illness. People once regarded unpredictable behavior as evidence of moral failing or spiritual corruption. Religious authorities used these interpretations to enforce social order, employing rituals like exorcisms and public shaming. The practical need to guide individuals back to the group morphed into a weapon of judgment, cementing stigma in cultural and spiritual narratives.

The evolutionary roots of shame and social isolation were not inherently cruel; they were pragmatic tools that early humans developed to navigate the harsh realities of survival. In small, tightly knit groups, people often viewed deviant or erratic behavior as a threat to cohesion or safety. Someone acting unpredictably might draw predators, disrupt communal tasks, or signal illness, potentially endangering the entire group. Isolation, therefore, was a calculated response—a way to contain risk and protect resources. Shame, too, played a critical role, serving as an internal check that guided individuals back toward accepted norms, preserving harmony within the group. These instincts, though blunt and unsparing, relied on the logic of survival. Human societies grew more complex, seeking explanations for the unexplainable. Over time, emerging religious and cultural frameworks reinterpreted, distorted, and ultimately co-opted these adaptive mechanisms.

Lacking scientific knowledge, early humans sought answers in the divine and the supernatural. They used these beliefs to explain phenomena beyond their understanding, including the strange and often frightening manifestations of mental illness. Behaviors that once triggered evolutionary instincts—erratic movement, unpredictable emotions, or unusual speech—became infused with spiritual significance. A person who acted differently was no longer just a potential threat to group safety; they were a vessel for supernatural forces. The survival-driven need to isolate such individuals transformed into a moral imperative to purify them. This marked a profound turning point. Evolutionary pragmatism gave way to a moralistic worldview, where mental illness was seen as evidence of divine punishment, demonic possession, or a curse.

Religious frameworks provided narratives that resonated with ancient communities, offering order in an unpredictable world. By framing mental illness as a moral or spiritual failure, these interpretations grounded the same exclusionary instincts in survival logic. Exorcisms, purification rituals, and public shaming became tools not just of protection but of redemption, designed to expel evil and restore cosmic balance. These practices reinforced fear and stigma, making mental illness not only a social liability but a spiritual blemish. The shame that once encouraged self-correction became a weapon wielded by the community, deepening isolation and suffering. Evolutionary instincts, stripped of their survival context, took on new roles in serving religious narratives, embedding stigma within the moral fabric of societies.

This shift had profound consequences. While evolutionary responses relied on communal logic—protect the group, preserve resources—religious interpretations added moral judgment that punished the individual. Where an ancient community might have isolated a member for practical reasons, religious frameworks painted the afflicted as inherently flawed, marked by sin or divine wrath. This moralization of mental illness entrenched stigma on a deeper level. It became not just a practical response, but judged the individual's worth or purity. The evolutionary need to warn others about potential danger took a darker turn. It justified lasting exclusion by labeling the afflicted as cursed or possessed. Society deemed them unfit for reintegration.

Humanity's search for meaning beyond survival took a wrong turn. This instinct, which sparked advances in art, philosophy, and science, also moralized behaviors once treated pragmatically. Mental illness became tied to morality, replacing survival strategies with harmful systems of judgment. Shame, meant to unite communities, instead divided them as people turned on one another in the name of spiritual purity.

The evolutionary response to deviance was once adaptive, serving group survival. Over time, religious and cultural systems hijacked this response, amplifying its harshness and stripping it of its utility. What began as a survival mechanism became a tool for discrimination, labeling the afflicted as sinners, outcasts, or vessels of evil. This shift entrenched the stigma of mental illness deep within human society. Understanding this transformation shows stigma isn't a natural law but a historical and cultural construct—one people can challenge and change.

The echoes of these historical judgments linger today, shaping modern attitudes toward mental health. But to address stigma effectively, we must confront its enduring legacy.

1.3 BLAME IT ON THE ANCESTORS

The shadows of the past cast long, unbroken lines into the present. Historical views of mental illness as weakness or sin continue to inform societal attitudes, perpetuating cycles of silence, shame, and neglect. These ancestral biases are more than historical artifacts; they are living barriers that prevent individuals from seeking help and societies from providing it.

From its origins, fear of the unknown fueled misconceptions about mental illness. People often regarded it as evidence of divine punishment or demonic possession. Over time, this stigma evolved into a pervasive force. It silences those in need, breeds shame, and discourages action. This stigma acts like an invisible cage. It locks individuals into cycles of self-doubt and fear. It isolates them from the support systems they desperately need. For centuries, people treated mental illness not as a condition deserving compassion and understanding but as a marker of moral weakness or spiritual failure. This legacy has normalized silence, forcing individuals to hide their struggles to avoid judgment or ostracism. As a result, shame festers. It often amplifies the very symptoms that need treatment. Meanwhile, societal denial of the problem ensures meaningful change remains out of reach.

This silence and shame are further compounded by the cultural, social, and systemic roots of stigma, which vary across societies but share common threads. In many cultures, mental illness is still associated with dishonor, weakness, or a threat to familial and communal reputations. Such attitudes discourage open discussions about mental health, punishing vulnerability rather than supporting it. Social norms prioritize conformity, marginalizing those who deviate from perceived standards of normality. This marginalization extends beyond individuals to their families, as the stigma often attaches itself to kinship, compounding the burden of secrecy. Meanwhile, systemic factors, such as media portrayals of mental illness as violent or erratic, reinforce these fears, embedding stereotypes into the public consciousness. Institutions, whether educational, legal, or healthcare-related, frequently reflect these biases, further alienating individuals and leaving them with few avenues for redress. The result is a society where support structures fail their purpose. Instead of helping individuals, they perpetuate marginalization. These barriers are not just structural but also psychological.

Access to mental health care represents one of the most glaring consequences of this stigma-driven system, with disparities that starkly highlight the inequities of modern societies. Geography plays a critical role, as rural and remote areas often lack even the most basic mental health services, leaving entire populations underserved. For those in urban centers, where resources are more concentrated, the high cost of care remains a formidable obstacle. Therapy sessions, medications, and specialized treatments can quickly become unaffordable, particularly for those without comprehensive insurance or sufficient income. Socioeconomic factors worsen these disparities. Individuals from lower-income backgrounds often face a double burden. They experience higher exposure to stressors like poverty and discrimination. They have fewer resources to address their mental health needs. The shortage of mental health professionals only intensifies this crisis. In many regions, trained therapists, psychiatrists, and counselors are in short supply. This shortage forces individuals to endure long waiting times or rely on overburdened systems, unable to provide adequate care.

This neglect carries staggering costs, affecting both individuals and society. Untreated mental illness contributes to cycles of poverty, unemployment, and physical health problems, creating a feedback loop that entrenches inequality. When stigma discourages action, it deprives individuals of the opportunity to seek help, exacerbating conditions that might otherwise be manageable. It also prevents society from addressing the systemic issues at the root of the crisis, leaving mental health care as an afterthought rather than a priority. Stigma carries significant historical and cultural weight. It has left a lasting imprint on how societies perceive and address mental health. This divide creates a gulf between those in need and the care they require. Bridging this gap means confronting past biases and reimagining a future that values mental health equally with physical health.

Stigma is universal, but it does not affect everyone equally. Gender, culture, and systemic inequities actively shape how people experience and address mental health, revealing the deeply personal dimensions of this crisis.

2. CRYING IS GENDER NEUTRAL

Mental health wears unfamiliar faces across genders. Women, men, and LGBTQ+ individuals each confront unique pressures, from societal expectations of beauty and strength to the stigma surrounding vulnerability and identity. Yet, beneath these differences lies a shared struggle: the universal challenge of navigating mental health in a world that often prioritizes appearances over authenticity.

Addressing gender-specific mental health issues require recognizing that cultural roles, systemic inequities, and personal circumstances deeply shape these challenges. These experiences are as diverse as the individuals themselves, yet they share common threads of stigma, silence, and systemic neglect. To foster a healthier, more inclusive society, we must examine how gender shapes mental health. It is equally vital to address the biases and structures that continue to cause suffering.

For women, the intersection of biological and societal factors creates unique mental health challenges. Conditions like postpartum depression highlight how deeply gendered experiences can affect emotional well-being. The hormonal shifts and physical toll of childbirth are immense. Societal expectations of perfect motherhood compound these challenges. Any deviation from idealized norms often invites judgment and misunderstanding. Despite its prevalence, society often dismisses or stigmatizes maternal mental health struggles, leaving many women to cope in silence. Beyond motherhood, women frequently face the mental health repercussions of gender-based violence, including domestic abuse, sexual harassment, and assault. These experiences can lead to trauma, PTSD, and long-term psychological scars, often exacerbated by societal victim-blaming and insufficient support systems. Unrealistic beauty standards and the "superwoman" syndrome add to this burden. These pressures demand that women excel in careers, maintain families, and conform to narrow definitions of femininity. These pressures create a relentless cycle of self-doubt and stress, leaving women vulnerable to anxiety, depression, and burnout.

Men, too, face significant but often overlooked mental health challenges shaped by societal expectations. The cultural mandate of stoicism equates vulnerability with weakness, silencing many men who might otherwise seek help. Society dismisses emotional struggles as a failure to meet the ideal of "manliness," fostering reluctance to address mental health issues. Societal pressures worsen this stigma. The demands to be financial providers and meet benchmarks of success create immense stress. These pressures often lead to feelings of inadequacy. Troubling statistics reflect these challenges: men are more likely to die by suicide and less likely to seek treatment for depression and anxiety. Despite these realities, mental health services often fail to engage men in ways that resonate with their unique needs, further entrenching barriers to care. The reluctance to seek help is not merely a personal failing, but reflects societal norms that prioritize silence over healing.

Layers of discrimination and exclusion shape the mental health landscape for LGBTQ+ individuals. The mental toll of homophobia, transphobia, and societal rejection is profound, creating a pervasive sense of isolation and vulnerability. Microaggressions in daily life and systemic barriers in healthcare further alienate LGBTQ+ individuals, making it difficult for them to access competent and affirming mental health services. Unique stressors amplify mental health struggles, especially for LGBTQ+ youth. These include the fear of coming out, navigating identity, and seeking acceptance. This group also faces higher rates of homelessness and unemployment.

Intersectionality compounds these challenges, as LGBTQ+ individuals who also contend with racial, ethnic, or socioeconomic discrimination experience even greater mental health disparities. Elevated rates of depression, anxiety, substance abuse, and suicidal ideation among LGBTQ+ populations underscore the urgency of providing inclusive, culturally competent care. Such care not only addresses immediate mental health needs but also affirms the identities and experiences of those it serves.

Though mental health challenges vary for women, men, and LGBTQ+ individuals, shared barriers like trauma, abuse, and systemic neglect unify them. Trauma does not discriminate by gender; its impact is universal, yet cultural and social contexts often shape how it manifests and how people address it. Access to mental health care remains a significant hurdle for all genders. Cost, stigma, and a shortage of specialized professionals worsen the problem. These barriers create inequities that disproportionately impact marginalized communities. Intersectionality further complicates these issues, as overlapping identities—such as race, socioeconomic status, and ethnicity—amplify disparities in mental health outcomes. A systemic overhaul that prioritizes inclusivity and equity is essential to ensuring everyone moves forward together.

Solutions must be as multifaceted as the challenges they address. Public awareness campaigns can play a pivotal role in breaking the stigma surrounding gender-specific mental health issues, fostering open conversations that normalize seeking help. Policy reforms are equally crucial, advocating for equal access to mental health resources and implementing workplace and institutional policies that support mental well-being. Building support networks is essential, creating spaces where individuals can share experiences and find solace in the community. Education and training, particularly for mental health professionals, must incorporate gender-sensitive approaches that recognize the diverse needs of their patients. Schools, workplaces, and healthcare systems must commit to fostering environments of inclusivity and understanding, paving the way for systemic change.

Society must move beyond the confines of outdated norms and biases to embrace a more compassionate, inclusive approach to mental health. This requires collective effort, where individuals, healthcare providers, and policymakers work in tandem to dismantle stigma and expand access to care. By addressing gender-specific mental health challenges, we not only improve individual lives but also strengthen the fabric of society itself. When society actively understands and supports mental health across genders, humanity can truly thrive.

Home may hold the heart, but the workplace often strains the mind. In the grind of modern employment, mental health frequently becomes collateral damage.

3. 9-TO-5 SURVIVAL

The workplace, once a source of purpose and community, has become a crucible for mental health struggles. Chronic stress, unrelenting deadlines, and toxic cultures are eroding well-being at an unprecedented scale. Employees, caught between professional expectations and personal needs, face mounting pressure with little support. As workplaces shape much of our waking lives, they also hold the power to transform mental health care.

Workplace mental health has emerged as a critical issue in our modern economy, reflecting the profound interconnectedness between professional environments and individual well-being. Workplace mental health refers to the mental and emotional resilience of employees within their professional lives. It is no longer an afterthought. Instead, it has become a cornerstone of thriving organizations. Research consistently underscores this, revealing alarming statistics: millions of employees worldwide grapple with stress, anxiety, depression, and burnout, often exacerbated by workplace conditions. As the boundaries between personal and professional life blur in the digital age, the role of the workplace has shifted. Now it extends beyond productivity; it's a space to nurture mental well-being. Organizations increasingly recognize how vital it is to address mental health. It's not just a moral imperative but a business necessity. Mental health directly impacts productivity, employee retention, and overall success.

The challenges of workplace mental health are multifaceted, with burnout standing out as one of the most pervasive issues. Burnout manifests as emotional exhaustion, detachment from work, and a decline in performance. It often stems from excessive workloads, lack of control over one's tasks, and a glaring absence of recognition for hard work. The impact is devastating. Individuals may experience profound disillusionment and physical symptoms, such as insomnia and chronic fatigue. Organizations also suffer, facing high turnover, reduced productivity, and eroding morale. Chronic workplace stress compounds this issue, with tight deadlines, interpersonal conflicts, and job insecurity, creating a relentless cycle of pressure. Prolonged stress spills over into physical health, contributing to conditions like hypertension and cardiovascular disease, while also intensifying mental health challenges such as anxiety and depression. In many cases, workplace structures worsen these issues. They reinforce a stigma that blocks open discussions about mental health. As a result, employees suffer silently.

Toxic work cultures, systemic neglect, and modern professional pressures form the roots of poor workplace mental health. A toxic work culture, characterized by micromanagement, favoritism, and a lack of transparencies, erodes trust and engagement, leaving employees feeling undervalued and unsupported. Digital connectivity's constant demands have erased traditional boundaries, disrupted work-life balance and drained energy with minimal time for recovery. Job insecurity, fueled by economic instability, adds another layer of stress, as employees navigate layoffs, restructuring, or underemployment with a constant fear of losing their livelihood. Compounding these issues is the widespread inadequacy of workplace support systems. Many organizations lack accessible mental health resources or fail to train managers and HR professionals to recognize and address mental health challenges effectively. This systemic neglect leaves employees without the tools or spaces they need to cope, pushing them closer to crisis.

The consequences of poor workplace mental health are far-reaching, impacting both employees and employers in profound ways. For employees, untreated mental health challenges take a heavy toll. They lead to physical and emotional decline and strain relationships. These challenges also cause absenteeism or presenteeism, where employees are present physically but mentally disengaged. For employers, the financial costs of lost productivity, high turnover, and how workplace culture deteriorates are staggering. Organizations that fail to address mental health also risk significant reputational damage and, in some cases, legal liabilities if they neglect their duty of care. The workplace, once a site of opportunity and growth, becomes a breeding ground for dissatisfaction and harm, undermining both individual potential and organizational goals.

Employers play a critical role in reversing this tide and fostering environments that prioritize mental health. Building a supportive workplace culture starts with fostering openness. This means normalizing mental health discussions. It creates an environment where employees feel safe sharing their challenges without fear of judgment or reprisal. Managers must lead by example, sharing their own experiences with mental health to break down barriers and inspire trust. Policies such as flexible work hours, remote work options, and clear performance expectations can alleviate stress and empower employees to balance their professional and personal lives. Zero-tolerance policies for workplace harassment or bullying are essential in cultivating safe and respectful environments. Providing access to mental health resources shows a tangible commitment to employee well-being. These resources include Employee Assistance Programs (EAPs), partnerships with mental health professionals, and dedicated wellness programs. Training managers to recognize signs of distress and respond empathetically can bridge the gap between struggling employees and the help they need.

Addressing burnout and stress requires proactive interventions that prioritize rest and recovery. Regular breaks, mindfulness practices, and wellness initiatives can help employees recharge. Policies like no emails after hours or mandatory vacation days enforce boundaries to protect their time and energy. Encouraging hobbies, personal growth, and engagement outside of work builds resilience, reminding employees that their worth transcends professional output. Ultimately, employees themselves play a role in promoting workplace mental health, advocating for their needs, practicing self-care, and supporting colleagues through empathy and collaboration. By cultivating a shared sense of responsibility, workplaces can transform into communities that uplift rather than diminish their members.

The future of workplace mental health lies in innovation and inclusivity. Leading companies are already implementing progressive policies like unlimited PTO, mental health days, and wellness spaces, demonstrating that well-being and productivity are not mutually exclusive. Technology provides new avenues for support, from mental health apps to AI tools that monitor workplace stress. Shifting cultural priorities— from productivity to holistic well-being—promises a humane approach to work. The time for action is now. Organizations should prioritize mental health both as a growth strategy and a commitment to their people. By addressing these challenges collectively, we can reimagine workplaces as spaces where employees thrive both professionally and personally, fostering healthier, happier societies.

Workplaces are crucial, but the mental health foundation begins much earlier. It starts in schools where children learn not only to read and write but also to cope and connect.

4. MINDS OVER MARKS

Schools extend beyond academics, functioning as emotional ecosystems that nurture mental health. Yet, academic pressures, bullying, and resource gaps have turned schools into stress incubators. The mental health of students, though vital for their success, is often overlooked, leaving many to struggle in silence during their formative years.

Addressing mental health in schools is no longer a luxury—it is a necessity. Schools are not just centers for academic instruction; they are crucibles where children and adolescents develop the emotional and social skills that will shape their futures. Yet, the mental health challenges faced by students are mounting at an alarming rate. Anxiety, depression, and behavioral disorders have become pervasive, fueled by academic pressures, social expectations, and, more recently, the isolating effects of the pandemic. Statistics paint a grim picture: mental health disorders now account for a significant portion of absenteeism, academic decline, and even school dropouts. Schools hold a unique position to play a transformative role in addressing these challenges. These environments detect early warning signs and offer the greatest potential for life-changing intervention. To fulfill this role, schools must embrace a holistic approach to mental health. This approach should recognize the profound impact of psychological well-being on learning, development, and overall success.

The mental health challenges students face are as diverse as they are complex. Academic pressure is a pervasive stressor, with students feeling the relentless weight of high expectations, competitive environments, and standardized testing. These demands often erode self-esteem, leaving students feeling inadequate or perpetually behind, no matter their achievements. Social and peer dynamics compound these pressures. Navigating friendships, bullying, and the insidious effects of cyberbullying can destabilize a student's mental health. This is especially true in an era where social media magnifies comparisons and reinforces unrealistic ideals. For many, trauma and adverse childhood experiences (ACEs)—whether stemming from abuse, neglect, family instability, or poverty—cast long shadows over their ability to thrive in school. These unresolved traumas manifest in behavioral issues, withdrawal, or academic decline, perpetuating cycles of disadvantage. Simultaneously, identity development during school years can bring its own struggles, whether related to gender, sexuality, or cultural and racial identity. The aftermath of the pandemic has exacerbated these challenges. It disrupted social connections and created widespread anxiety about academic progress. This has deepened feelings of isolation and inadequacy among students.

Despite the urgency of these issues, significant barriers prevent schools from addressing mental health effectively. Stigma remains a formidable obstacle, silencing conversations about mental health and making students reluctant to seek help for fear of judgment or labeling. Resources are another glaring issue. Many schools lack the funding to hire counselors, psychologists, or social workers, leaving students without access to professional support. The shortage of trained mental health professionals stretches available help too thin, even when accessible. Academic responsibilities already overburden teachers. Despite this, people expect them to fill the gap in mental health support. Yet, they frequently lack the training or resources needed to address their students' emotional needs. This systemic neglect not only leaves students unsupported but also creates environments where mental health challenges escalate unchecked, compounding their long-term effects.

Early intervention holds the power to break this cycle, providing a lifeline to those caught in its grip. Recognizing the warning signs of mental health struggles— such as changes in behavior, academic decline, or social withdrawal—can make a profound difference. When addressed early, these issues are less likely to develop into chronic conditions that persist into adulthood. Schools that invest in early support see improvements in attendance, academic performance, and overall student well-being. Parents and teachers are indispensable allies in this process, working together to build networks of support around students. By fostering open communication and creating safe spaces for dialog, these partnerships can help identify and address mental health concerns before they become overwhelming.

To combat these challenges, schools must implement comprehensive mental health programs that address the needs of their students holistically. Incorporating mental health education into the curriculum can demystify psychological well-being, equipping students with the knowledge and tools to navigate their emotions. On-site counseling and therapy services provide accessible support. Peer support initiatives, such as training students as mental health ambassadors, also foster empathy. Together, they create environments of mutual care. Practices like mindfulness exercises, yoga, and stress management techniques teach students how to regulate their emotions and cope with challenges. Anti-bullying campaigns, focused on building inclusivity and empathy, tackle the root causes of one of the most significant stressors in schools. These programs not only address immediate concerns but also build a foundation for lifelong resilience.

Educators play a pivotal role in this transformation. With the right training, teachers can become frontline advocates for mental health, recognizing signs of distress and responding effectively. Workshops and professional development programs equip them with the skills needed to support their students emotionally while maintaining a safe and accepting classroom environment. Teachers can foster cultures of understanding and acceptance. This encourages students to voice their concerns without fear of judgment. As a result, mental health becomes a visible and normalized part of the school experience.

Parents and communities are equally crucial in supporting student mental health. Schools can engage parents by providing resources and hosting workshops that empower families to address their children's needs. Community partnerships with local mental health organizations can expand the range of services available, ensuring that no student falls through the cracks. These collaborations create a support network that extends beyond the school walls, reinforcing the message that mental health is a shared responsibility.

Implementing mental health programs is not without its challenges. Resistance from stakeholders, often rooted in stigma or a lack of awareness, can slow progress. Funding limitations create disparities, with wealthier districts offering robust services while underfunded schools struggle to meet basic needs. Balancing these initiatives with academic goals requires careful planning and commitment from all parties involved.

Yet, schools that have prioritized mental health offer compelling examples of what is possible. Schools with dedicated wellness centers and programs incorporating mental health apps demonstrate innovation. Virtual counseling also plays a role. Together, these initiatives show how commitment can lead to measurable improvements in student outcomes.

The future of school mental health lies in technology, policy, and a shift in cultural priorities. Mental health apps and AI-driven tools can identify students in need early, offering interventions that are both timely and tailored. Policy advocacy drives change by demanding mandatory mental health education, securing increased funding, and embedding well-being into school accreditation standards. Schools can redefine success by adopting holistic approaches that integrate physical, emotional, and social wellness. Success then becomes not just academic achievement but cultivating healthy, balanced individuals.

The call to action is urgent. Educators, parents, policymakers, and students themselves must come together to prioritize mental health as an integral part of education. Increased funding, open dialog, and systemic change are essential to creating schools that nurture not only the minds but also the hearts of their students. This approach transforms schools from mere learning spaces into sanctuaries of growth, resilience, and well-being. The long-term benefits of this shift are immeasurable: healthier individuals, stronger communities, and a society that values mental health as a cornerstone of human potential.

Mental health care often begins in schools and workplaces. However, its most visible form is in the pharmaceutical industry—a controversial powerhouse of hope and complexity.

5. KINDNESS WITH A SECRET

Psychotropic drugs have revolutionized mental health care, transforming lives once deemed unlivable. But the pharmaceutical industry, driven by profit, walks a fine line between healing and exploitation. As medications provide relief to millions, they also raise ethical concerns about over prescription, affordability, and access.

The pharmaceutical industry occupies a central and contentious role in the mental health landscape, straddling the fine line between innovation and the pursuit of profit. Its contributions to modern psychiatry are undeniable—psychotropic medications have revolutionized treatment, offering relief to millions suffering from depression, anxiety, bipolar disorder, and schizophrenia. Yet, this dominance has also raised pressing ethical questions about the balance between advancing care and serving corporate interests. As the global mental health crisis deepens, the reliance on medication as the primary treatment highlights the industry's profound influence. Medications can be lifesaving for many. Yet, society often presents them as the definitive solution to complex psychological issues. This approach sidelines broader conversations about holistic care, systemic inequities, and root causes of mental health struggles. Examining this complex dynamic is crucial for creating a future where the pharmaceutical industry contributes responsibly to mental health care.

Historically, the rise of psychotropic drugs marked a pivotal shift in mental health treatment. In the mid-20th century, developing antidepressants, antipsychotics, and mood stabilizers offered hope to patients who had previously faced a lifetime of institutionalization. These breakthroughs transformed mental health care, shifting it from asylums to outpatient clinics, where medication became the cornerstone of treatment. Early milestones, such as the introduction of chlorpromazine for schizophrenia or Prozac for depression, promised liberation from the shackles of untreated mental illness. But with these advancements came an unforeseen consequence: the medicalization of human emotion. Pharmaceutical companies eager to expand their markets played a significant role in promoting new diagnostic categories. Conditions like Attention Deficit Hyperactivity Disorder (ADHD) and Generalized Anxiety Disorder (GAD) are valid in many cases. However, they have become targets for aggressive marketing campaigns. This raises concerns about pathologizing normal behaviors and overprescribing medications to increasingly broad populations.

The pharmaceutical industry's emphasis on biological explanations for mental illness closely ties to this diagnostic expansion. The widely accepted chemical imbalance theory, while simplifying complex psychiatric conditions for public understanding, has also funneled focus onto medication as the primary treatment. This perspective often neglects the social, cultural, and environmental factors that play critical roles in mental health. Rising prescription rates reflect this imbalance. In many countries, antidepressant, and antipsychotic use has surged, often without adequate exploration of alternative treatments or long-term consequences. Children and elderly populations, in particular, have seen alarming rates of medication use, raising ethical questions about whether these interventions are always necessary or beneficial. The narrative of medication as a one-size-fits-all solution has shaped patient expectations. It has also influenced prescribing behaviors. These behaviors often prioritize convenience over comprehensive care.

The tension between profit motives and patient welfare lies at the core of these issues. The pharmaceutical industry's pricing strategies often place essential medications out of reach for low-income populations, both in developed and developing countries. Cases like the EpiPen pricing controversy highlight the broader pattern of exorbitant costs, leaving vulnerable patients unable to afford the treatments they need. Patent protections further exacerbate this problem, as companies exploit legal loopholes to delay producing cheaper generic alternatives, perpetuating inequities in access. Meanwhile, aggressive marketing tactics, including direct-to-consumer advertising and financial incentives for physicians, create conflicts of interest that prioritize sales over sound medical judgment. Ethical violations, like Purdue Pharma's role in the opioid epidemic, illustrate the devastating consequences of unchecked corporate influence. The drive for profit often undermines the integrity of mental health care.

The industry's influence extends beyond pricing and marketing to the very foundations of mental health research and policy. Pharmaceutical sponsorship of clinical studies has introduced biases that often favor positive outcomes for the sponsor's products, skewing the evidence base used to guide treatment decisions. Regulatory bodies, such as those behind the DSM, have faced scrutiny. Their ties with drug companies raise concerns about potential conflicts of interest. These connections blur the line between independent scientific rigor and corporate influence, eroding patient trust in the system. Financial relationships with pharmaceutical companies' trap physicians, challenging their ability to make unbiased decisions in their patients' best interests.

International controversies further underscore the pharmaceutical industry's complex role in mental health care. The opioid crisis in the United States exemplifies the catastrophic effects of profit-driven practices. Medications originally intended for pain management fueled addiction epidemics. These have profound mental health repercussions. Similarly, the overprescription of ADHD medications in Western countries has sparked debates about long-term impacts on children and teens. Globally, disparities in access to psychiatric medications reveal stark inequities, with low-income countries struggling to secure even the most basic treatments. Organizations like the WHO promote generic antidepressants in developing regions. These efforts highlight the pressing need for equitable solutions. However, they often face resistance from pharmaceutical giants in protecting their profits.

Amid these challenges, alternative perspectives challenge the pharmaceutical dominance in mental health treatment. Critics argue that overreliance on medication overshadows psychotherapy, community-based care, and preventive approaches that address the root causes of mental illness. Countries like Norway and Finland have adopted therapy-centered mental health models. These models prioritize holistic care over pharmacological solutions. They reveal how a balanced system might function.

For psychiatrists and mental health professionals, this raises ethical dilemmas about balancing patient needs with the pervasive influence of pharmaceutical interests. Cultural differences also play a role, as varying approaches to mental health across the globe demonstrate that medication is not the only path to healing.

For patients, the consequences of this pharmaceutical dominance are profound. Dependence on medication, withdrawal symptoms, and under reported side effects erode trust in the system, leaving individuals disillusioned and vulnerable. Research links antidepressants to increased suicide risk in adolescents, a sobering reminder of risks often minimized in clinical trials. Real-life accounts of patients grappling with long-term medication use reveal the emotional and physical toll of a system that prioritizes profit over holistic care.

Solutions to these systemic issues must begin with policy reforms that prioritize transparency, accountability, and patient welfare. Stricter regulations on lobbying and advertising, coupled with increased funding for non-pharmaceutical therapies, can help create a more balanced approach to mental health care. Encouraging affordable generic drug production and expanding access to essential medications paves the way toward greater equity, offering hope to underserved communities. Investment in community-based programs and holistic treatments, from cognitive-behavioral therapy to mindfulness practices, can complement medication and address mental health challenges at their root. Education and advocacy campaigns empowering patients to make informed decisions about their treatment can further shift the paradigm toward patient-centered care.

Looking ahead, emerging trends in mental health treatment offer both hope and caution. Digital therapeutics, such as mental health apps and AI-driven tools, present new opportunities. They complement traditional approaches. However, they also invite alternative forms of commercialization and ethical dilemmas. Psychedelic therapy, once stigmatized, is now at the forefront of research into treatments for depression and PTSD, signaling a potential revolution in mental health care. However, the regulation and commercialization of these therapies will determine whether they serve patients or profits.

Ultimately, addressing the role of pharmaceutical companies in mental health requires a collective commitment to ethical reform and balanced care. Governments, healthcare providers, and patients must work together to demand transparency, prioritize affordability, and support diverse treatment options. By reimagining a mental health system where innovation and compassion coexist, we can move toward a future that truly serves the needs of all.

Amid the broader mental health crisis lies a deeply painful intersection: the role of violence, particularly rape, in shaping trauma and mental well-being.

6. RAPE

Rape transcends violence alone; it is a profound assault on mental health. Its roots lie in both biology and societal failings, blending evolutionary instincts with modern inequities. Understanding the intersection of trauma, mental health, and systemic change is essential to addressing this pervasive issue.

Humanity has spent centuries devising laws, building social norms, and cultivating systems of justice to regulate behavior and curtail the darker impulses of our species. Yet, in rape, these efforts remain frustratingly inadequate. Despite education campaigns, legal reforms, and societal condemnations, sexual violence persists, defying the best of our collective intentions. This stubborn resilience reveals an unsettling truth: we are grappling with a problem whose roots run deeper than culture, law, or even morality. Our strategies falter because they skim the surface, addressing symptoms rather than causes. To genuinely understand and combat rape, we must confront a profound and uncomfortable reality. Its origins lie not just in societal constructs but also in the very architecture of human evolution and biology.

At its core, rape is a perverse expression of evolutionary imperatives. Men's anatomy and hormonal makeup closely connect to it. Evolution, indifferent to morality, has shaped male bodies and behaviors to prioritize reproductive success above all else. Traits like aggression, dominance, and an unrelenting sexual drive once ensured the survival and propagation of genes. Today, these same traits form the underpinnings of behaviors we condemn.

The scientific observation that men think about sex, on average, 19 times a day, reflects this biological inheritance. This goes beyond a psychological quirk. Instead, it is a vestige of our evolutionary past, where reproductive urgency was key to genetic survival. This evolutionary blueprint does not excuse rape, but it demands recognition as a foundational factor if we are to understand the phenomenon fully.

The roots of this behavior trace back to the dynamics of polygynous systems. These systems have been prevalent across countless species, including early humans. In such systems, a single dominant male often mates with multiple females, maximizing his reproductive output. This arrangement provided evolutionary advantages. It allowed for the rapid spread of advantageous traits and increased genetic diversity. It also reinforced traits that enhanced male competitiveness.

However, it fostered behaviors driven by relentless sexual competition. The male imperative to reproduce at all costs often translated into aggression. Over millions of years, these pressures sculpted male anatomy and psychology. They embedded a drive that modern society now seeks to suppress.

Polygynous systems favored males who could dominate rivals and secure access to females, creating intense selection pressures. Strength, aggression, and persistence became evolutionary currencies, ensuring that only the fittest males could pass on their genes. This competition also explains the sheer scale of sperm production in males compared to the limited reproductive potential of females. Each sperm represents a chance to perpetuate a lineage, and the buildup of sperm triggers biological signals that fuel the urge for release. Combined with testosterone, which amplifies sexual drive, and dopamine, which reinforces the pursuit of pleasure, the male body becomes a vessel of constant reproductive readiness. In evolutionary terms, such readiness was an asset; in modern ethics and justice, it can manifest as a liability.

While these evolutionary dynamics explain the impulses, they also highlight the critical role of the brain, particularly the prefrontal cortex. This part of the brain, responsible for self-control, empathy, and moral reasoning, acts as a check on primal urges. It is the prefrontal cortex that prevents most men from acting on aggressive sexual impulses, aligning their behavior with societal norms. Yet, this restraint is not uniform. Factors like mental health, substance abuse, and societal influences can weaken the prefrontal cortex's control, allowing evolutionary impulses to surface in destructive ways. Rape, then, is not merely an act of individual malice but a collision of evolutionary imperatives with impaired self-regulation and a permissive environment.

The evolutionary narrative shows why laws or education alone cannot entirely eradicate rape. These measures, while essential, operate within the framework of human constructs, attempting to regulate behaviors rooted in biology. To make meaningful progress, we must address the broader contexts that amplify these impulses. Loneliness, social isolation, and unmet emotional or sexual needs exacerbate the biological drives, creating fertile ground for violence. Evolution may have wired men to seek multiple mates. However, modern society's emphasis on monogamy fails to provide equitable opportunities for relationships. This leaves many men frustrated and disillusioned. As a result, the critical balance maintained by the prefrontal cortex becomes further destabilized.

Human anatomy is not just a marvel of biological engineering but also a relentless driver of behavior, often in ways that transcend conscious control. Among the most persistent and primal of these forces is the sexual urge, a product of evolutionary refinement aimed at ensuring the survival of the species. This machinery, fine-tuned over millions of years, does not merely exist—it demands action. The relentless production of sperm begins deep within the seminiferous tubules of the testes. Here, the body creates millions of sperm cells daily. Each one is a microscopic messenger of genetic continuity.

Once produced, sperm cells embark on a journey through the epididymis, where they mature and await their eventual release. Here, they are not idle passengers but active participants in a system that accumulates pressure as time passes. The epididymis serves as the primary storage site, but as the body produces more sperm, it gradually moves them into the vas deferens, a longer-term repository. Meanwhile, fluid secretions from the seminal vesicles, prostate gland, and bulbourethral glands mix with the sperm, creating semen. This combination of cellular buildup and fluid accumulation generates physical pressure within the ducts of the reproductive tract. Stretch-sensitive nerve endings in these regions detect the mounting tension, sending urgent signals to the brain—a biological alarm system that says, quite literally, "release needed."

These signals travel via the spinal cord to the brain, which interprets them in no uncertain terms. The message strikes with clarity and force: individuals must address the buildup of sperm. This is not merely a physical sensation, but a call to action deeply intertwined with hormonal and neurological processes. Testosterone, the primary male hormone, amplifies this message by enhancing the sensitivity of the reproductive system to these signals. Meanwhile, dopamine, the neurotransmitter associated with pleasure and reward, heightens the sense of urgency and primes the individual for action. Oxytocin facilitates smooth muscle contractions within the reproductive tract. Together with other chemicals, it creates a cascade of physical and psychological responses. These responses intensify the desire for sexual release.

The brain's interpretation of these signals does not occur in isolation. External stimuli—visual cues, tactile sensations, or even thoughts—merge with the internal messages of sperm buildup to create a complex psychological experience. The result is an urge that feels both immediate and overwhelming, compelling individuals to seek release. This physiological cycle repeats itself with remarkable regularity. Men often feel mounting pressure within days of their last release. This creates a rhythm of biological demand. It operates largely outside their conscious control.

Yet this relentless drive is not merely a quirk of biology; it is a cornerstone of evolutionary strategy. By ensuring that males remain in a state of near-constant reproductive readiness, nature maximizes the chances of successful mating and genetic propagation. However, in the modern world, where societal norms, relationships, and individual circumstances impose constraints on this primal urge, the system can create tension and frustration. The anatomy and neurochemistry that ensure the continuity of life often clash with human culture. This clash leads to a range of behaviors—from the sublime to the destructive. Understanding the interplay between biology and behavior is essential. This understanding helps us navigate the challenges posed by a system that, while ancient in design, profoundly shapes our lives. Sometimes, its effects are troubling.

Understanding rape through the lens of evolution does not absolve individuals of responsibility. Rather, it underscores the urgency of systemic approaches that address the root causes. It demands that we go beyond punitive measures and embrace strategies that mitigate the triggers of violence. This includes fostering mental health, creating equitable social structures that facilitate meaningful relationships, and challenging cultural norms that glorify aggression and entitlement. Only by integrating evolutionary insights with societal reforms can we hope to diminish the prevalence of sexual violence.

In the end, the struggle against rape is a battle between our biological past and our ethical aspirations. Evolution has left us with impulses that once served a purpose in prehistoric savannahs. However, these impulses clash with the principles of justice and equality that define modern civilization. To navigate this tension, humanity must harness its greatest evolutionary gift—the ability to reason, reflect, and adapt. Only by addressing both the biological and social dimensions of rape can we hope to align our actions with the moral ideals we aspire to uphold.

At the heart of violence lies a deeper truth—loneliness and disconnection fuel behaviors that harm both individuals and society.

6.1 LONELINESS: THE SILENT TRIGGER

Loneliness, the silent epidemic of modern life, creates fertile ground for destructive behaviors. When individuals feel disconnected, their need for control, recognition, or release can manifest in harmful ways. Addressing loneliness is not just an emotional imperative but a societal one.

To address the pervasive issue of rape, society must confront how biology, psychology, and systemic failures intersect with a multidimensional strategy. Mitigating loneliness is key, as it often fuels frustration and destructive behavior. Humans, as inherently social beings, require meaningful relationships and emotional connections to maintain mental well-being. Yet, modern life—fragmented, competitive, and increasingly isolated—has eroded these connections. Many find themselves adrift, deprived of companionship, and overwhelmed by unfulfilled desires, creating a volatile state of mind that can lead to aggression, entitlement, and, in extreme cases, violence.

Global governance must step forward to ensure equitable standards of living, enabling individuals to form fulfilling partnerships and cultivate mental resilience. But while such systemic change takes root, immediate steps are necessary to address the crisis.

The first line of defense is education and awareness. Comprehensive sex education is not merely about biology; it is about fostering respect for boundaries, teaching consent, and demystifying healthy relationships. From a young age, educators must teach individuals to recognize the autonomy of others and emphasize respecting others. Workshops on gender sensitivity, anti-harassment strategies, and bystander intervention can transform schools, workplaces, and communities into bastions of awareness. Public campaigns, too, can dismantle harmful stereotypes and counter the normalization of sexual violence by challenging myths and promoting the virtues of consent and respect.

Parallel to education is the empowerment of women and vulnerable groups. Empowerment is a broad and transformative concept. It includes providing self-defense training to those at risk. It also enhances economic independence through educational and vocational opportunities. Additionally, it creates safe spaces where individuals can find shelter and support. These measures not only reduce vulnerability but also shift power dynamics, enabling women to assert their rights and protect themselves in environments historically designed to marginalize them.

Policymakers must reform the legal and law enforcement systems to function as true deterrents. Laws against sexual violence must be clear, and strictly enforced, with swift justice delivered through specialized courts. Victims must feel supported, not stigmatized, when reporting crimes. Law enforcement personnel, often the first point of contact, need thorough training to handle such cases with sensitivity and professionalism. Accountability mechanisms must ensure that no perpetrator escapes justice, regardless of their social status or influence.

Cultural and societal norms must also evolve. Patriarchy, deeply ingrained and often unacknowledged, perpetuates a hierarchy that normalizes violence and devalues women. Society must dismantle systemic inequalities to promote shared responsibilities in homes, workplaces, and governance. Media has a critical role in this transformation. By monitoring and restricting content that objectifies women or glorifies violence, and by highlighting narratives of empowerment and equality, media can reshape perceptions and inspire change.

Community-based interventions can amplify these efforts. Training individuals to recognize and intervene in potentially harmful situations fosters a collective responsibility for safety. Community watch programs and increased surveillance in high-risk areas can deter potential offenders. Engaging men and boys in conversations about consent and respect is vital. Encouraging healthy masculinity can also challenge toxic behaviors at their root. These efforts ensure that future generations grow up with a deeper understanding of equality and empathy.

Addressing mental health is equally vital. Survivors of sexual violence require psychological counseling and support to rebuild their lives. Identifying and treating individuals with tendencies toward violence can prevent repeat offenses. Rehabilitation programs for offenders, though contentious, have the potential to transform behavior when approached with the right resources and methodologies.

Technology and infrastructure can provide critical support. Safety apps enable individuals to alert authorities or trusted contacts in emergencies. These apps can save lives. Better-lit streets, secure public transportation, and surveillance in vulnerable areas also enhance overall security. Advocacy and policy changes driven by grassroots movements and NGOs can sustain momentum, pushing governments to prioritize gender equality, victim support, and education reforms.

Holding perpetrators accountable is non-negotiable. Leaders must enforce zero-tolerance policies for sexual misconduct across all sectors, from schools to workplaces. Society must end impunity, often shielded by social or political privilege. Every perpetrator, regardless of status, must face justice under the law.

Finally, data is key to understanding and combatting sexual violence. Research into the root causes, patterns, and cultural contexts of rape can inform prevention strategies. By tracking progress and adapting measures based on evidence, societies can refine their approaches and address the problem more effectively.

While these measures form a comprehensive framework, they are not a panacea. The deeper challenge lies in aligning our biological instincts and social constructs with the principles of justice and equality. Humanity can only build a world free from sexual violence by addressing its root causes. These causes include loneliness, inequality, ignorance, and systemic failures. Until then, sexual violence will remain a shadow over our collective existence.

6.2 ICELAND RAPE

In Iceland, people often regard women as queens, celebrating their equal footing in virtually every aspect of society. The Nordic nation has consistently topped global rankings for gender equality, boasting progressive policies that empower women economically, socially, and politically. Paid parental leave, wage equity, and an education system that emphasizes fairness make Iceland a beacon of feminist achievement. However, lurking beneath this utopia is a darker, more insidious problem: gender-based violence, particularly sexual assault, most often occurring within the supposed safety of homes. Despite Iceland's progressive initiatives, the country struggles to address this pervasive issue effectively. The root of the problem lies not in a lack of effort or resources, but in the ideological framework shaping their response. Iceland approaches sexual violence through a feminist-socialist lens. However, this perspective fails to confront the deeper evolutionary underpinnings of the crime. As a result, their strategies remain frustratingly ineffective.

People often refer to Iceland as a "feminist paradise," and for good reason. Women in Iceland enjoy benefits that remain aspirational for much of the world. Gender quotas ensure their representation in political and corporate spheres, while comprehensive child-care policies make it easier for women to balance professional aspirations with family life. The country's laws guarantee pays equity and parental leave for both mothers and fathers, creating a model that champions gender cooperation rather than competition. The education system fosters equality from an early age, teaching boys and girls to view each other as equals. Yet, despite these achievements, Iceland's idyllic portrayal is incomplete. The same mechanisms that empower women also leave men grappling with a profound sense of displacement and loneliness, issues that are often overlooked in the feminist narrative.

Among Iceland's progressive policies is a stringent stance on sex work. Prostitution is illegal, and the educational system heavily stigmatizes sex work, portraying it as degrading and exploitative. This approach, while well-intentioned in protecting vulnerable individuals from exploitation, inadvertently creates a social imbalance. By criminalizing prostitution and stigmatizing alternative outlets for sexual expression, Iceland inadvertently shuts down one of the few accessible pathways for men to fulfill their evolutionary drives. Biology deeply roots human sexuality, particularly male sexuality. Male sexual release transcends emotional or social desires; it is a physiological drive shaped by evolution. The inability to satisfy these urges, compounded by the power dynamics of Iceland's feminist utopia, contributes to a toxic cycle of isolation and frustration.

In this environment, many men fall into a downward spiral of loneliness. Icelandic men, navigating a society that often vilifies traditional masculinity, find it increasingly difficult to approach women. Stringent laws that make sex work inaccessible exacerbate this social alienation. As the number of lonely, disenfranchised men grows, so does the risk of violence. Research has shown that unmet sexual needs and prolonged social isolation can lead to anger, resentment, and, in extreme cases, criminal behavior. Rape, in this context, becomes a tragic and reprehensible outlet for their frustration. The feminist-socialist response focuses on education and empowerment. However, it fails to acknowledge the deeper dynamics. It treats rape as purely a societal construct rather than a multifaceted issue with biological, psychological, and social roots.

To address this crisis, Iceland's leadership must rethink their approach. The solution lies in acknowledging the evolutionary drivers of human behavior and crafting policies that balance progressive ideals with realistic accommodations for human nature. Iceland could explore regulated, consensual frameworks for sex work, designed to ensure safety and dignity for all parties involved. Providing men with outlets for biological urges may break the cycle of frustration and violence. Education must also shift from stigmatizing sex work to promoting healthy, consensual relationships that recognize the complexities of human sexuality. Iceland's leaders, including its female president, must lead to a nuanced conversation that embraces empathy and pragmatism. Only by addressing the root causes of gender violence, rather than treating its symptoms, can Iceland hope to close this glaring gap in its feminist paradise.

This does not reject the feminist ideals that made Iceland a global model. Instead, it urges inclusivity, pairing women's progress with strategies for men's struggles. By adopting these measures, Iceland can truly become a land of equality. This ensures equality not just in name but also in safeguarding all citizens' dignity.

The mind serves as sanctuary and battlefield alike. Our evolutionary programming, once designed to alert us to danger and enforce social cohesion, now traps us in cycles of shame, anxiety, and despair. Loneliness and the grind of modern life stretch the mind to its limits. This crisis reflects failures both in individuals and in the systems meant to support them.

As the cracks in mental health deepen, they begin to mirror the cracks in our political systems. Chapter 4: *Political Dysfunction* explores how personal struggles scale to governance. Leaders and institutions often reflect the same insecurities, greed, and short-term thinking that plague individuals. Mental dysfunction extends to the state, shaping our world.

Part II

The Dysfunctional Society

"Government for the Few, By the Few, Paid by Your Taxes"

Politics: the art of convincing you that
nothing is wrong while everything burns. This part uncovers how power works
(or doesn't), why wars never seem to stop, and how the economy treats your
joblessness like an investment opportunity. Add a sprinkle of corruption, and Big
Data betrayal, and suddenly "progress" doesn't feel so progressive. Get ready to
roll your eyes and think, "Well, that explains a lot."

4

Political Dysfunction

"Politics is the art of looking for trouble, finding it everywhere,
diagnosing it incorrectly, and applying the wrong remedies."

– GROUCHO MARX

Humanity has tried to govern itself since the dawn of civilization, but ambition, creativity, and frequent failure have defined the effort. From small tribal councils to massive bureaucracies, governance has always sought to balance survival, cooperation, and control. Yet, even after thousands of years, modern political systems remain fragile. Corruption, inequality, and ideological divides continue to plague societies, casting long shadows over progress.

Today, the world faces immense challenges: climate change, mass migrations, and pandemics. These crises expose the contradictions in the systems meant to sustain us. Many of these systems are buckling under their own weight.

This chapter explores the layers of political dysfunction that have shaped our history, threaten our present, and endanger our future. It asks a critical question: Can humanity evolve its systems of governance before governance itself becomes obsolete?

Throughout human history, the quest for governance has been a balancing act between survival, cooperation, and control. Early tribal societies relied on consensus-based leadership, where intimate circles made decisions rooted in shared goals and mutual trust. These systems, however, struggled to scale as populations grew, resources dwindled, and conflicts arose. When humans began practicing agriculture, it marked a turning point—tethering them to land, creating wealth disparities, and intensifying the need for structured governance. From the city-states of Mesopotamia to the dynastic empires of China, centralized power became the dominant paradigm. Leaders often cloaked their authority in divine right, reinforcing their grip through fear and superstition. Yet, these systems, for all their grandeur, were inherently fragile; they crumbled under the weight of corruption, inequality, and the relentless tides of rebellion.

The Enlightenment era promised a reprieve as ideas of democracy, individual liberty, and reason began to take root. Governance, it seemed, could separate itself from tyranny. The revolutions of the 18th century—American, French, and others—laid the foundation for modern representative systems. However, practice often compromised these ideals. Democracies fell prey to electoral manipulations, economic inequalities, and institutional biases. Campaign finance corrupted the democratic spirit, turning elections into contests of wealth rather than will. Media influence, both as a tool of enlightenment and propaganda, further distorted public perception, entrenching partisan polarization. The ideal of governance "for the people" often faltered under the pressures of populism, corporate lobbying, and short-term policymaking.

Globally, the legacy of colonialism exacerbated disparities in governance. Artificial borders drawn by imperial powers disregarded ethnic, cultural, and historical contexts, sowing seeds of conflict that persist in today's geopolitics. In the post-World War era, governance entered a new phase, where nations, no longer isolated, became entwined in the web of international alliances and rivalries. The Cold War further polarized the world, forcing countries to align with ideological extremes rather than explore governance models suited to their unique circumstances. The rise of global capitalism introduced new challenges. Markets flourished, but wealth inequality deepened. Political systems increasingly prioritized economic growth over social equity and environmental sustainability.

In the 21st century, these failures have compounded into crises of legitimacy. Gerrymandering, voter suppression, and technological vulnerabilities have weakened electoral systems, originally designed to amplify the voice of the people. Critics accuse judicial systems, meant to uphold justice, of overreach or political bias. Ideological divisions paralyze public policies, including those addressing healthcare, immigration, and climate change. Media, intended to inform and empower citizens, has become a double-edged sword—an arena where truth competes with sensationalism and manipulation. Though information flows freely, societies remain stuck in mistrust and division.

The geopolitical landscape mirrors these struggles. Nations oscillate between cooperation and confrontation, from climate accords that fail to deliver meaningful action to trade wars that disrupt global stability. The tension between national sovereignty and global interdependence has left the world without a cohesive strategy for shared challenges like pandemics, mass migrations, and technological disruption. Human governance, for all its complexity and evolution, remains inadequate.

The story of political dysfunction is not merely one of failure, but also of paradox. Nowhere is this contradiction clearer than on the global stage, where leaders envisioned institutions like the United Nations as symbols of collective morality and universal justice. Yet these very institutions often falter, revealing the compromises and inequalities baked into their foundations. To understand the fragility of global governance, we must begin with its most ambitious experiment—and its most glaring paradox.

1. AMERICAN PROXY

Born from the ashes of two world wars, the United Nations embodied humanity's hope: resolving disputes through dialog, not destruction. Its lofty charter spoke of universal rights and justice, embodying a moral compass for a fractured globe. This institution, shaped by both power and principle, tells a sobering tale. Under the shadow of its largest benefactor, the United States, the UN became an arena where actors negotiate morality, and ideals bow to influence. The paradox of global morality lies in its entanglement with the interests of those who control the funding. Echoing the idiom "don't bite the hand that feeds you," this dynamic permeates the corridors of diplomacy. Carefully navigating American interests, the UN subtly aligns its moral proclamations with the priorities of its most generous patron.

This dynamic transforms morality from an absolute into a negotiation. The United States projects itself as the defender of freedom and justice while exerting influence as both funder and arbiter. This ensures the UN rarely challenges U.S. geopolitical imperatives. The result is a paradoxical morality. The UN's dependence on powerful nations compromises its ideals, entangling it in the realities of power dynamics. While the UN may speak of universal justice, its actions often reflect the priorities of those who sustain it. This tension exposes the gap between the purity of its mission and the pragmatism of its survival.

The United Nations arose from the ruins of two world wars as humanity's boldest attempt to govern a fractured world through shared principles. Its founders envisioned a fortress to protect dialog and cooperation, shielding against cycles of aggression and despair. Yet even in 1945, as leaders signed its founding charter, contradictions emerged. The organization depends on the consensus of major powers and the financial contributions of its wealthiest members, especially the United States, creating a fragile balance between idealism and realpolitik.

This chapter examines the influence of America's disproportionate financial support on the UN's priorities. It shows how funding dynamics have skewed the institution's impartiality, limited its effectiveness, and exposed the power dynamics shaping global governance.

At its inception, the United Nations embodied lofty ideals. It promised to uphold universal human rights, deter aggression, and resolve disputes without war. Yet failures have shaped its history more than triumphs. The UN has faced significant struggles. It failed to prevent partition conflicts in India and Palestine. It remained paralyzed during genocides in Rwanda and Bosnia. These failures reveal its difficulty in reconciling moral imperatives with the geopolitical interests of its most powerful members. In each failure, the organization's structural flaws became more apparent. These shortcomings reflect an institution operating at the crossroads of power and principle. As the UN's largest financial contributor, the United States exerts outsized influence over its policies. It uses the organization as both a tool of diplomacy and a proxy for its geopolitical agenda.

The UN's financial structure remains precarious. The United States contributes more than 20% of its regular budget and an even greater share of peacekeeping funds. This funding disparity creates an implicit hierarchy where the influence of the U.S. shapes priorities, actions, and, crucially, inactions. The American veto on the Security Council frequently shields its allies, especially Israel, from international censure. It ensures initiatives counter to U.S. interests rarely gain traction. These dynamics fosters perceptions of bias, undermining the UN's credibility as a neutral arbiter of justice. In cases like the Israeli-Palestinian conflict, U.S. backing has neutralized the UN's capacity to act as a peace broker. This has reduced the organization to a platform for symbolic gestures rather than substantive interventions.

The consequences of this imbalance are starkly evident in the UN's selective interventions. In the Libyan crisis of 2011, the U.S. and its NATO allies leveraged UN resolutions to justify military action under the banner of protecting civilians. This contrasts sharply with the UN's inertia during the Syrian civil war or its muted response to Saudi-led atrocities in Yemen. The inconsistency reveals the impact of geopolitical pressures. These disparities stem not from failed will but from an institution serving its patrons' interests. The United States, by its financial influence, has often dictated the terms of engagement, leaving crises that fall outside its strategic priorities to fester.

Yet America's influence is not the sole source of the UN's failures. The institution suffers from structural deficiencies. These include its reliance on consensus among a divided Security Council, its convoluted bureaucracy, and its aversion to enforcing standards. Together, these issues leave it ill-equipped to address the complexities of the modern world. The Rwandan genocide and the Srebrenica massacre are grim reminders of what happens when neutrality becomes an excuse for inaction. In both cases, the United Nations failed to take decisive action. This failure stemmed from its own limitations and powerful members, including the U.S., who resisted committing resources or risking political capital. Chronic underfunding compounded these failures, further eroding the UN's capacity to act effectively.

The post-9/11 era brought new challenges to the UN's credibility, particularly in the realm of counterterrorism. While the United States championed global counterterrorism efforts, ambivalence, and contradiction defined the UN's response. The simultaneous election of Syria—a known state sponsor of terrorism—to the Security Council undermined Resolution 1373, hailed as a landmark in counterterrorism. This juxtaposition epitomized the UN's struggle to project moral clarity in an era defined by asymmetric threats. The organization struggles to distinguish between legitimate resistance movements and acts of terror. This failure muddies its role as a defender of international norms, leaving it open to manipulation by states pursuing their own agendas.

The UN faces critical 21st century challenges, including climate change, nuclear proliferation, and rising authoritarianism. However, it remains constrained by structural flaws and the disproportionate influence of its most powerful members. Its limitations are not merely operational, but existential, reflecting a deeper crisis in global governance. The ideals that inspired the UN's founding now appear outdated. They seem ill-suited to a world where power fragments, challenges, interconnect, and international institutions face growing scrutiny over their legitimacy.

The UN's failures are not just failures of policy or execution, but failures of imagination. The United States' outsized influence in the UN both reflects and drives this inadequacy, demanding a rethinking of global cooperation. Humanity must confront a deeper question: what should global governance look like in an age of unprecedented complexity? Only by addressing this can we break free from the cycles of inaction and inequality that define the UN's history. The answers, as this chapter will explore, may lie not in reforming the UN but in reimagining it entirely.

The United Nations emerged as the envisioned custodian of global morality and order. Yet, it often becomes entangled in the murky politics of terrorism, a realm demanding moral clarity but rarely displaying it. Terrorism is an act of calculated chaos: the deliberate targeting of civilians to inspire fear, disrupt societies, and coerce governments. Yet, the UN, with its complex web of resolutions and declarations, has struggled to articulate a unified stance that categorically rejects terrorism in all its forms. This failure stems not from a lack of legal instruments, but from a persistent ambiguity in the organization's moral and operational framework. By seeking to appease its diverse member states—many of whom hold conflicting views on what constitutes terrorism—the UN has inadvertently diluted its own authority. In doing so, it has often appeared to condone acts of violence that defy its foundational principles.

The problem lies in the UN's unwillingness to recognize that no political grievance, however profound, justifies the deliberate slaughter of innocents. Acts like suicide bombings, hijackings, and mass shootings should be beyond debate, yet the UN's equivocation of these issues has repeatedly undermined its credibility. The United States, with its insistence on moral clarity, has frequently clashed with the UN on this front. The U.S. frames its fight against terrorism not just as strategy but as principle: no neutrality exists when civilian lives are at risk. This stark perspective contrasts sharply with the UN's tendency to frame terrorism within the broader, and often murkier, context of political resistance. By attempting to straddle the line between condemnation and neutrality, the UN has allowed its position to be interpreted as ambiguous at best, complicit at worst.

The 1990s, often characterized as a decade of post-Cold War disarray, brought these contradictions to the fore. While the United Nations expanded its peacekeeping mandates and humanitarian missions, its approach to terrorism remained fragmented and inconsistent. Bombing U.S. embassies in Kenya and Tanzania, attacking the USS Cole, and the rise of Al-Qaeda highlighted the growing threat of transnational terrorism. Yet, the UN's responses to these events were tepid, marked more by rhetoric than decisive action. Critics argue that by failing to confront the states and networks that supported these acts, the UN indirectly perpetuated the conditions under which terrorism flourished.

The attacks of September 11, 2001, represented a watershed moment for global counterterrorism efforts, prompting the UN Security Council to adopt Resolution 1373. This landmark resolution called for states to criminalize terrorism, freeze assets linked to terrorist activities, and enhance international cooperation. At first glance, it seemed to signal a new era of UN resolve. However, the subsequent election of Syria—a state widely accused of sponsoring terrorism—to the Security Council revealed the deep contradictions within the organization. How could the UN claim to combat terrorism while granting leadership roles to nations implicated in its propagation? This contradiction eroded the resolution's moral weight and highlighted the geopolitical compromises that often undermine the UN's credibility.

Loopholes and ambiguities frequently undermine the effectiveness of resolutions, even when crafted with the best intentions. The lack of a universally accepted definition of terrorism has been a perennial stumbling block, allowing member states to exploit the ambiguity for their own ends. For decades, the Non-Aligned Movement—a coalition of developing nations—has argued that violent resistance against colonialism or occupation is distinct from terrorism. The historical context of anti-colonial struggles grounds this perspective. However, this precedent allows acts of violence against civilians to be justified as political resistance. Both state and non-state actors have weaponized this rationale, complicating the UN's efforts to draw a firm line against terrorism.

The influence of the Nonaligned Movement exemplifies the broader challenges of achieving consensus in a body as diverse as the UN. The UN comprises 193 member states representing diverse political ideologies, economic interests, and historical grievances. As a result, its resolutions often reflect the lowest common denominator instead of a clear moral stance. This dilution is particularly evident in the UN's enforcement mechanisms—or lack thereof. States that sponsor terrorism or provide safe havens for terrorist groups often face little more than symbolic censure. Failing to impose tangible consequences fosters a culture of impunity, emboldening those who exploit violence for political gain.

Historical events underscore the urgency of addressing these shortcomings. The bombings of U.S. embassies in Africa, the September 11 attacks, and the rise of the Islamic State are part of a broader trend. Together, they escalate global terrorism. Each attack represents a failure not only of national security but of international governance. The UN, as the supposed steward of global peace, bears a share of the responsibility for these failures. The UN struggles to act decisively. Whether imposing sanctions, mobilizing peacekeeping forces, or providing clear definitions, the UN falls short. This failure leaves the world exposed to the threats the organization aimed to address at its creation.

To fulfill its mission of maintaining international peace and security, the UN must undergo a profound transformation in its approach to terrorism. This begins with moral clarity: a categorical rejection of any act that targets civilians, regardless of the perpetrator's motives or the context of the violence. It requires the UN to resist the pressures of political expediency and reaffirm its commitment to universal human rights. Equally important is the need for effective enforcement mechanisms. Tangible consequences must back resolutions, ensuring accountability for states and entities that sponsor terrorism.

In its current form, the UN's counterterrorism efforts are a microcosm of its broader struggles: noble in intent, flawed in execution, and compromised by geopolitics. If the organization is to remain relevant in an era of asymmetric threats and globalized violence, it must confront the realities of its own shortcomings. The fight against terrorism is not merely a battle of laws and policies, but a test of humanity's capacity to uphold its most fundamental principles. Facing not just reform but survival, the UN struggles with its purpose.

The United Nations mirrors the compromises of global governance. However, political dysfunction extends beyond the international stage. The internal mechanisms of democracy—once heralded as humanity's greatest political achievement—also bear the weight of contradictions. To explore the evolution and paradox of democracy is to unravel the troubled relationship between governance and its people.

2. SPIRITUAL GOVERNANCE

Democracy's architects designed it, knowing it could never achieve perfection. Born from Enlightenment ideals, it sought to shift power from monarchs ordained by divinity to citizens endowed with reason. Its promise was as revolutionary as its flaws were inevitable. Elections, the cornerstone of democracy, emerged as both a triumph of collective agency and a stage for manipulation. Campaign finance transformed democratic contests into spectacles of wealth, while gerrymandering warped representation, turning the will of the people into a political illusion. Despite its noble aspirations, democracy often falls prey to the forces it seeks to regulate: ambition, greed, and power. Understanding democracy's paradox means questioning whether governance by the people truly serves them.

For most of history, governance stemmed not from choice but from a divine mandate. Kings ruled by the grace of gods, high priests interpreted celestial will, and societies often idealized emperors themselves. Religion provided the scaffolding for governance, granting rulers both legitimacy and the tools to enforce order. To question the ruler was to question the divine. For millennia, this system ensured stability, but at a cost, the power to govern remained concentrated, inaccessible to the majority, and rarely accountable. The Enlightenment sparked an era of questioning and reason, challenging the belief in divine will as authority's sole foundation. Governance began to transition from sacred right to secular responsibility, culminating in the democratic systems we know today. This shift, marked by revolutions and reforms, gradually affirmed that sovereignty belonged to the people, not rulers.

Democracy, described as governance "by and for the people," emerged as a radical experiment. At its heart was the idea of elections—a process by which citizens could choose their leaders. This lofty ideal has faced persistent challenges. Early elections excluded many, granting voting rights only to landowning men from elite classes. Over centuries, movements for suffrage expanded this right, pushing for inclusion across gender, race, and socioeconomic lines. Today, elections are the cornerstone of modern democracy, employing increasingly sophisticated methods. From paper ballots to electronic voting machines and blockchain-based systems, technology has attempted to bring efficiency and transparency to the process. However, these advancements have not erased the vulnerabilities of elections. Countries use various electoral systems, including first-past-the-post, proportional representation, and ranked-choice voting. Each system has its strengths and pitfalls, but none is immune to the human flaws in governance.

The issues within modern electoral systems are multifaceted. Electoral reform remains a pressing need, as many democracies continue to rely on outdated methods that fail to ensure accessibility and fairness. In some nations, voter suppression tactics—whether through restrictive ID laws or reduced polling stations—actively disenfranchise marginalized communities. Gerrymandering, where political actors manipulate electoral boundaries for gain, undermines the very principle of fair representation. Failing to address flaws turns elections into contests of who exploits the system most effectively, ignoring the people's will.

Electoral integrity is another critical challenge. The credibility of elections is under constant scrutiny, particularly in an age where technological interference is an actual threat. Cyberattacks, misinformation campaigns, and the specter of external meddling erode public trust. Political actors weaponize voter fraud, though statistically rare, to delegitimize results. Strengthening democratic institutions to ensure secure and credible elections is essential, not only to prevent fraud but to rebuild voters' confidence in an increasingly skeptical electorate.

Then there is the influence of money, an ever-present specter in modern politics. Loopholes in campaign finance laws, where they exist, allow corporate and private donors to wield disproportionate influence. Political campaigns, particularly in large democracies, require immense resources, turning elections into contests not of ideas but of funding. Those who bankroll campaigns often shape policies, which once reflected public interest. The voices of ordinary citizens, drowned out by financial powerhouses, leave democracy increasingly skewed towards the wealthy and well-connected.

Electoral deficiencies often result in unqualified or corrupt politicians. The public lacks access to clear governance information or the skills to evaluate leadership effectively. As a result, choices often hinge on charisma, identity, or empty promises. Politicians who ascend to power through these flawed systems frequently serve their benefactors rather than the people. Corruption becomes entrenched, as those in office manipulate the very structures meant to hold them accountable. Leaders craft policies for personal gain or power, ignoring public good and fueling inequality and disillusionment.

The chapter ultimately returns to the paradox of democracy. Celebrated as the most equitable form of governance, it struggles with imperfections that demand urgent attention. Without electoral reforms, enhanced integrity measures, and greater transparency in campaign financing, democracy risks devolving into a system that serves only a privileged few. Governance must evolve to reflect the people's will, addressing not only election mechanics but also societal structures shaping voting rights and behaviors.

The failures of democracy are not abstract—they manifest in the leaders it produces and the systems that empower them. The paths to power vary widely. From grassroots politics in India to campaign finance spectacles in the United States, these paths show how the foundations of governance shape outcomes. To examine these systems is to confront the fragile architecture of modern leadership.

2.1 BLUEPRINT FOR POLITICIANS

The quality of governance mirrors the pathways to power. In India, dynastic privilege, party loyalty, and grassroots identity politics shape political ascendance. In the United States, ambition, and fundraising prowess dominate, creating a system that measures influence in dollars rather than merit. Both models expose democracy's vulnerabilities, where polarization, corruption, and judicial overreach reduce governance to a transactional exercise. Politicians shaped by these systems prioritize their survival over public welfare, leaving democracies teetering under the weight of their contradictions. To reform governance, we must first reimagine the foundations of leadership.

The quality of politicians mirrors the systems that nurture them. It also reflects the values guiding them and the challenges constraining them. When comparing India and the United States, the pathways to political power reveal stark contrasts shaped by history, culture, and institutional frameworks. In India, political careers often start in student politics or grassroots movements. Allegiance to a party and its ideology frequently outweighs merit or individual vision. The weight of political dynasties is a defining feature; family connections often act as an express route to leadership roles, sidelining meritocratic advancement. In the United States, political power often hinges on personal ambition. Success requires navigating a complex web of fundraising, media influence, and public appeal. This system lets outsiders and innovators break through but also equates political capital with dollars as much as votes.

These foundational differences shape the type of leaders who emerge and the priorities they pursue once in office. In India, many politicians rise through party hierarchies or dynastic legacies. They focus on consolidating power within their networks, leveraging influence over bureaucracies and judicial appointments to maintain control. Loyalty to the party or family frequently overshadows accountability to the public. In the United States, separating powers limits interference in bureaucracy and the judiciary. However, the relentless need for campaign funding ties politicians to corporate and donor interests, often neglecting ordinary citizens. In both systems, these pathways create vulnerabilities that bring governance to its knees, eroding trust in democratic institutions.

Partisan polarization, a universal affliction in democracies, illustrates this erosion vividly. In India, polarization is frequently along religious, caste, or regional lines, weaponized by politicians to secure votes. In the U.S., ideological divides—magnified by the echo chambers of social media—create a binary worldview that treats compromise as betrayal. These divides paralyze governance, turning legislatures into battlegrounds of obstruction rather than forums for problem-solving. In both nations, misinformation acts as fuel for polarization, with politicians exploiting or even creating narratives to deepen divisions for electoral gain.

Corruption is another common thread that undermines governance. In India, systemic graft siphons public funds and drives decisions to benefit cronies rather than citizens. Political dynasties and entrenched loyalties exacerbate this, allowing corruption to become institutionalized. Transparency initiatives, like India's Right to Information Act, aim to counter corruption. However, these efforts face resistance from politicians who risk losing power with greater accountability. In the United States, overt corruption is less visible. Instead, it takes subtler forms, like lobbying and the revolving door between politics and private industry. Campaign finance loopholes allow corporate donors to exert disproportionate influence, turning governance into a transactional exercise where those who pay to play shape policies.

Corruption is one of humanity's oldest and most insidious challenges, threading through history as an ever-present shadow over governance and society. At its core, it betrays trust by wielding power for private gain rather than the common good. Corruption adapts across eras and regions. It morphs to suit the systems it inhabits, from petty bribes by local officials to grand-scale embezzlement by heads of state. Understanding corruption requires viewing it as more than isolated acts. It is a systemic phenomenon shaped by cultural norms, economic pressures, and political structures. This chapter seeks to unravel the many faces of corruption, laying the groundwork to explore its pervasive influence and humanity's enduring struggle against it.

Corruption manifests in countless forms, but analysts broadly categorize its core types. Petty corruption, often encountered by everyday citizens, involves small-scale bribes or favors exchanged for basic services. While minor, it normalizes unethical behavior and erodes public trust in institutions. Grand corruption operates at the highest levels of government. It involves vast sums of money and shapes national policies to benefit a select few. Political corruption bridges these scales, occurring when leaders exploit their positions to consolidate power, manipulate elections, or divert public resources for personal enrichment. Together, these forms of corruption create a web that entangles societies, undermining their moral and institutional fabric.

Examining its prevalence across diverse nations vividly illustrates the global nature of corruption. In Nigeria, oil wealth has become both a blessing and a curse, fueling corruption that stifles development and deepens inequality. In Peru and Indonesia, political elites often collude with corporate interests to exploit natural resources. This collusion causes devastating consequences for the economy and the environment. China and Russia offer examples of centralized power fostering systemic corruption, where the lines between state and personal wealth blur. These cases reveal that corruption spans regions and political systems, manifesting wherever power lacks accountability.

Corruption drivers vary as widely as its manifestations. Small-scale bribery thrives in environments where inefficiency and bureaucracy force individuals to "grease the wheels" for essential services. Political funding is another critical factor; the insatiable demand for campaign resources often pushes candidates and parties toward unethical practices, creating a vicious cycle of dependence on wealthy donors or illicit funds. Organized crime syndicates exploit weak institutions to forge symbiotic relationships with corrupt officials, enabling them to traffic goods, launder money, and conduct illegal trade. Large corporations, too, are complicit, manipulating markets or bending regulations to secure competitive advantages. These drivers interweave rather than exist in isolation, reinforcing one another in a self-sustaining cycle.

The consequences of corruption are profound and far-reaching. Economically, corruption siphons resources away from critical sectors like education, healthcare, and infrastructure, perpetuating poverty and inequality. Nations with high levels of corruption often struggle to attract investment, as uncertainty and inefficiency deter businesses. Socially, corruption erodes trust in institutions, breeding disillusionment and cynicism among citizens. This erosion of trust can lead to political instability, as marginalized populations—those most affected by corrupt practices—rise in protest against the status quo. Corruption also inflicts severe environmental damage, as illicit resource extraction and lax enforcement of regulations prioritize short-term profits over sustainability.

Cultural and geopolitical contexts have historically shaped attitudes toward corruption. During the Cold War, Western powers often turned a blind eye to corruption in allied nations, prioritizing anti-communist alliances over accountability. This tolerance allowed corrupt regimes to flourish, embedding practices that persist to this day. Cultural norms also play a role; some societies view corruption as a necessary evil or even a legitimate strategy for surviving in a system they perceive as inherently unfair. These attitudes complicate efforts to combat corruption, as societal acceptance blunts the impact of reform.

Despite these challenges, there are glimmers of hope in the fight against corruption. Civil society organizations, activists, and international conventions have made significant strides in promoting transparency and accountability. Initiatives like India's Right to Information Act and global frameworks such as the United Nations Convention against Corruption empower citizens to demand better governance. Courageous individuals who expose corruption often face significant risks but inspire movements for change. These efforts underscore why collective action is vital to address a problem that affects us all.

Corruption is not merely a moral failing or a product of individual greed; it is a systemic issue deeply embedded in the structures of power and governance. Understanding its complexities requires examining not just the acts themselves but the environments that enable them. This chapter lays the foundation for a deeper exploration of how corruption operates, the damage it inflicts, and the strategies needed to combat it. Addressing root causes and elevating voices of resistance can lead to a future where power serves integrity and the common good.

Judicial overreach further complicates governance in both democracies. In India, the judiciary often steps in to address executive and legislative failures, blurring how powers divide among branches. While this activism can protect citizens' rights, it also creates a precedent where unelected judges wield disproportionate influence over policy decisions. For instance, landmark rulings on issues like environmental protection or electoral reforms, while progressive, have sometimes bypassed legislative debate, raising questions about democratic accountability. In the U.S., the judiciary plays a key role in interpreting constitutional rights. This has led to landmark decisions shaping societal norms. However, increasingly politicized judicial appointments have turned courts into arenas of ideological contestation. This trend undermines the judiciary's credibility as an impartial arbiter, further eroding public trust.

The result of these systemic flaws is governance that falters under the weight of its contradictions. Politicians, shaped by systems that reward partisanship, patronage, or fundraising expertise, often lack the vision or integrity to prioritize public good over personal or party gain. In their wake, weakened institutions foster polarization, allowing corruption to thrive. The public, left disillusioned, retreats into cynicism or apathy, further diminishing the democratic process. Governance quality reflects the structures producing leaders. India and the United States show the urgent need to reform both election mechanics and the principles guiding political life.

Governance failures go beyond flawed leadership, extending into the darker intersections of politics and crime. The global drug trade, often framed as a criminal epidemic, reveals the complicity of state actors and institutions, entangling governance with shadow economies. Exploring narcotics politics reveals a stark truth: the war on drugs often serves convenience over genuine resolution.

2.2 POLITICS WITH A PINCH OF COCAINE

The global drug trade is a $500 billion enterprise that thrives not just on crime, but on complicity. Governments and institutions, publicly committed to eradicating narcotics, often find themselves entangled in its operations. The intersections of governance and drug trafficking reveal deep hypocrisies. Examples include the Iran-Contra affair, where cocaine profits funded covert wars, and Afghanistan's opium boom under Western occupation. While street-level traffickers face harsh penalties, powerful networks evade accountability, using corruption and financial systems to blur the line between legality and crime. Narcotics politics involves more than drugs; it reflects power's readiness to trade morality for profit.

The drug trade spans the globe. It runs from the coca fields of South America to Afghanistan's opium poppies and from heroin routes in Southeast Asia to synthetic drug labs in industrialized nations. This trade thrives not in isolation but through tacit complicity, implicating both state actors and institutions. Governments, often under the guise of combating drug trafficking, have historically enabled or ignored these activities, driven by motivations ranging from financial gain to geopolitical strategy.

In the 1980s, the Iran-Contra scandal exposed the depth of these connections. The Reagan administration publicly championed a "War on Drugs." It covertly facilitated weapons sales to Iran, using the proceeds to fund Contra rebels in Nicaragua. Investigations revealed that drug cartels laundered some of these funds, effectively using cocaine profits to finance covert U.S. operations. The official narrative maintained plausible deniability. However, the scandal revealed a troubling paradox: the government that demonized drug traffickers was complicit in their operations when it served broader strategic interests. The fallout from Iran-Contra showed how the drug trade could serve as a tool of statecraft. In this context, the lines between legality and criminality blur in pursuit of political objectives.

Afghanistan offers another stark example of this duality. Following the U.S.-led invasion in 2001, the country became the world's largest producer of opium, accounting for over 80% of global heroin supply. Despite the presence of NATO forces and billions of dollars invested in counter-narcotics programs, opium production surged, implicating both local power brokers and international stakeholders. The Taliban, initially ousted from power, found a lucrative source of funding in the drug trade, taxing opium farmers and traffickers to finance their insurgency. Simultaneously, reports suggested that certain Afghan government officials, including Western allies, deeply embedded themselves in the narcotics economy. Counterinsurgency efforts and counter-narcotics initiatives often clashed. Opium became both a source of income for insurgents and a bargaining chip for political actors within the U.S.-backed government.

In Mexico, the drug trade is inseparable from the country's political fabric. Cartels like Sinaloa and Jalisco New Generation have gained immense power through violence and corruption. They have also infiltrated the highest levels of government. In 2020, authorities arrested Mexico's former defense minister, General Salvador Cienfuegos, for aiding a drug cartel. This action revealed the depth of this collusion. Diplomatic negotiations secured Cienfuegos's release, underscoring how deeply intertwined state institutions and organized crime have become. Investigators accused politicians, law enforcement officials, and military leaders in providing protection to cartels, ensuring their dominance in the drug trade. Collusion perpetuates a cycle of violence, claiming tens of thousands of lives each year. Meanwhile, drug trafficking profits flow to both criminal organizations and their enablers within the state.

The economic motivations for enabling or ignoring the drug trade are significant. The global drug trade generates an estimated $500 billion annually, much of which is laundered through legitimate financial systems. Banks, real estate markets, and even stock exchanges become conduits for these funds, often with the tacit approval of regulatory authorities. In 2012, regulators fined HSBC, one of the world's largest banks, $1.9 billion for facilitating money laundering by drug cartels. Despite the hefty fine, no executives faced criminal charges, reflecting the asymmetry of accountability when powerful financial institutions are involved. This pattern extends beyond HSBC. It reflects a broader system where drug trade profits enter the formal economy, erasing the line between licit and illicit wealth.

Historical examples further illuminate this dynamic. The Vietnam War raised controversy over the CIA's alleged role in drug trafficking. This involved the Golden Triangle, a region spanning Thailand, Laos, and Myanmar. Reports suggested that the agency transported opium to finance covert operations against communist forces. While official denials followed, the accusations underscored the role of intelligence agencies in leveraging the drug trade for geopolitical purposes. Similarly, in Colombia, the rise of cartels like Medellín and Cali during the 1980s and 1990s coincided with U.S. anti-communist efforts in Latin America. The U.S. government invested heavily in combating cartels through initiatives like Plan Colombia. Yet, allegations persisted those factions within military and paramilitary groups, often aligned with U.S. interests, participated in drug trafficking.

The political motivations for turning a blind eye to the drug trade are equally compelling. In many cases, the stability of allied regimes or the pursuit of strategic objectives takes precedence over combating narcotics. In the 1990s, Myanmar's Shan State revealed this dynamic. The central government granted autonomy to ethnic militias, producing heroin for ending their rebellion. The Burmese junta, reliant on the heroin economy to sustain its power, prioritized political consolidation over counter-narcotics efforts. In Central Asia, the drug trade has become central to the informal economies of countries like Tajikistan and Kyrgyzstan. State actors often play direct roles in trafficking. Global powers, prioritizing these nations' roles as buffers against extremism or energy transit routes, frequently overlook their involvement in the narcotics trade.

The consequences of this complicity are profound, extending beyond economic distortions and political corruption to societal devastation. The global war on drugs, ostensibly aimed at eradicating narcotics, has disproportionately targeted small-scale traffickers and users while leaving the larger networks relatively unscathed. In the United States, for instance, decades of stringent drug laws have led to mass incarceration, with African American and Latino communities bearing the brunt. The flow of drugs into the country has continued unabated, with cartels adapting their methods and exploiting systemic weaknesses. This duality—harsh punishment for the powerless and impunity for the powerful—reflects the inherent contradictions of the war on drugs.

Efforts to address the nexus between governments and the drug trade face significant challenges. Corruption, entrenched interests, and the sheer scale of the industry make reform difficult. Nevertheless, there are instances of progress. In Colombia, the 2016 peace agreement between the government and the FARC guerrilla group aimed to address the root causes of the drug trade. It included provisions for transitioning coca farmers to legal crops, signaling a significant shift in strategy. In Portugal, the decriminalization of drug use and emphasis on treatment over punishment have yielded positive results, reducing addiction rates and drug-related deaths. These examples demonstrate that alternative approaches, focusing on harm reduction and socio-economic development, can offer viable paths forward.

Ultimately, the drug trade serves as a stark illustration of how illegality and power intersect. It reveals the contradictions of a global system that selectively enforces laws and subordinates' morality to expediency. The connections between governments and cartels, whether overt or covert, highlight the entanglement of economic, political, and criminal interests that sustain the narcotics economy. Addressing this issue requires more than law enforcement; it demands a rethinking of the structures and incentives that allow the drug trade to flourish. It challenges us to confront uncomfortable truths about complicity and accountability in a world where crime and governance boundaries blur increasingly.

The drug trade reveals the moral compromises of governance. Alongside, a new pattern emerges: upward wealth redistribution. Public policies enrich the few, while disadvantaged the many. This "reverse Robin Hood" effect reveals the deep ties between politics and profit, challenging the idea that governance exists to serve the public good.

2.3 WHEN POLICY MEETS PROFIT MARGINS

Governments often claim their economic policies serve the public interest, but the reality tells a different story. Public funds often flow to the wealthiest, justified as measures for stability or innovation. Examples include the 2008 financial crisis bailouts, which favored banks over families, and tax loopholes benefiting hedge funds and private equity. Defense contracts and fossil fuel subsidies further exemplify this cycle, where wealth begets influence, and influence shapes policies that consolidate wealth. This "reverse Robin Hood" effect not only exacerbates inequality but also erodes trust in governance, revealing a system designed to serve privilege over principle.

The 2008 financial crisis stands as a defining moment in this trend. Market collapses and the ensuing recession prompted governments worldwide to inject massive sums into the economy through bailouts and stimulus packages. In the United States, the Obama administration implemented an $831 billion stimulus plan, much of which was channeled into rescuing financial institutions and stabilizing markets. Policymakers framed these measures as necessary to prevent systemic collapse and save jobs. However, their execution disproportionately favored the wealthy. Institutions like Goldman Sachs, AIG, and Citigroup, among others, received billions in government aid. Later, they reported record profits and distributed bonuses to top executives. Foreclosures skyrocketed, unemployment soared, and middle-class families bore the brunt of the crisis.

This wealth transfer was not an accident but a feature of a system deeply intertwined with political connections and lobbying. Major players in finance and industry established relationships with policymakers, ensuring they influenced the crafting of bailout packages. Warren Buffett, a vocal advocate for government intervention during the crisis, made strategic investments in companies like Goldman Sachs and Bank of America. These companies later benefited significantly from federal support. Buffett's actions, while legally sound, exemplify the dual role of a public advocate for economic stability and a private profiteer benefiting from government largesse. This duality challenges the narrative of altruistic billionaires "saving" the economy.

Beyond finance, the influence of political connections extends into sectors like defense, energy, and technology. Defense contractors such as Lockheed Martin, Northrop Grumman, and Boeing have long leveraged their political ties to secure lucrative government contracts. The U.S. Department of Defense budget, which consistently exceeds $700 billion annually, funnels vast sums into these companies. A significant portion of public funds supports projects often criticized for inefficiency or irrelevance. For example, the F-35 fighter jet program has faced numerous delays and cost overruns, yet continues to receive funding. Advocates justify such expenditures by framing them in terms of national security, though the clear beneficiaries remain contractors and their shareholders.

Big Oil presents another glaring example. Subsidies and tax breaks for fossil fuel companies have persisted even as the world grapples with climate change. In the United States alone, these subsidies amount to an estimated $20 billion per year, despite the industry being among the most profitable globally. Companies like ExxonMobil and Chevron, while reporting billions in profits, receive federal support under the guise of energy security and job creation. This dynamic persists partly because of extensive lobbying efforts; in 2020, the oil and gas industry spent over $110 million on lobbying in the United States, ensuring its interests remained protected.

The role of hedge funds and private equity firms further illustrates the mechanisms of wealth concentration. These entities have mastered the art of exploiting financial regulations, often engaging in practices like tax avoidance and asset stripping. Carried interest, a tax loophole that allows hedge fund managers to pay significantly lower tax rates on their earnings, exemplifies how policy favors the ultra-wealthy. Despite bipartisan calls to eliminate this loophole, it remains intact, reflecting the power of financial lobbying. For instance, Stephen Schwarzman, CEO of Blackstone Group, has donated millions to political campaigns, ensuring that policies detrimental to his industry face significant resistance.

The symbiotic relationship between wealth and politics sustains and exacerbates these patterns. Lobbying expenditures in the United States exceeded $3.5 billion in 2022, with top contributors spanning industries from pharmaceuticals to technology. This money secures access to legislators, shapes policies, and ensures favorable regulatory environments. Cronyism becomes not an aberration but a defining feature of policymaking, where the wealthy use their resources to perpetuate their advantage. The result is a self-reinforcing cycle: wealth begets influence, influence shapes policy, and policy consolidates wealth.

We must not overlook the media's role in perpetuating this system. Mainstream coverage often frames government assistance to corporations and billionaires as necessary for economic stability or innovation. Stories of hardship among the middle and lower classes receive significant attention. However, media outlets frequently under report the mechanisms that perpetuate inequality. The public focuses on unemployment rates and rising living costs. Meanwhile, structural advantages that enable billionaires to thrive during economic downturns receive far less scrutiny. The pandemic further exposed this dynamic; while millions faced job losses and financial precarity, the collective wealth of U.S. billionaires grew by over $2 trillion between March 2020 and November 2021.

Ethical questions loom large in this landscape. These policies rely on the "trickle-down" idea, claiming that wealth at the top drives growth for all. Yet, evidence repeatedly shows that this wealth rarely trickles down as promised. Instead, it consolidates at the top, exacerbating inequality. In the United States, the top 1% of earners now control over 32% of the nation's wealth. This figure has grown over the past four decades.

The interplay of personal financial interests with public policy adds another layer of complexity. During the financial crisis, studies revealed that lawmakers with significant investments in financial institutions were more likely to vote in favor of bailouts. While such actions may not breach legal boundaries, they raise questions about conflicts of interest and the integrity of legislative decision-making. This phenomenon underscores how the lines between public service and personal gain can blur, further eroding public trust in governance.

The long-term consequences of this wealth concentration are profound. Economically, it distorts markets, reduces competition, and undermines innovation by favoring established players with the means to influence policy. Socially, it exacerbates inequality, creating a divide between the wealthy elite and the rest of society. Politically, it weakens democracy by favoring the priorities of an influential few over the majority's interests. This dynamic is not unique to the United States; it reflects globally, from Russia's oligarchs to China's tycoons, illustrating the universal challenge of balancing wealth and power in governance.

To address this imbalance, societies must implement systemic reforms. These include greater transparency in lobbying and campaign financing, stricter regulations on conflicts of interest, and policies that prioritize equitable wealth distribution. Tax reforms, such as closing loopholes like carrying interest and implementing wealth taxes, could begin to redress the disparities. Additionally, fostering a media environment that critiques the intersection of wealth and policy could empower citizens to demand greater accountability.

The story of wealth distribution in contemporary governance is not just about economics; it is a tale of power, influence, and the moral dilemmas of our time. This challenges us to consider whose interests the systems we uphold truly serve. It also asks what it means to create an economy that genuinely benefits the public good. Today's choices carry high stakes, shaping society's contours for generations.

Beneath the surface of public policies lies another layer of dysfunction: the hidden economy of secret trades. From illegal mining to smuggling networks, these operations intertwine crime with the formal economy, exploiting systemic vulnerabilities to thrive. To understand these secret trades is to uncover the shadow side of globalization.

2.4 FROM SMUGGLERS TO CEOS

Secret trades are the undercurrents of globalization, blurring the boundaries between legality and crime. They manifest in operations like Somalia's piracy, fueled by desperate economies; the DRC's conflict-driven coltan mining, sustained by global tech demands; and illegal logging in the Amazon, driven by insatiable consumer markets. These trades thrive on weak governance, secrecy jurisdictions, and institutional complicity, creating networks that evade scrutiny while devastating economies, societies, and ecosystems. Addressing secret trades demands more than regulation—it requires dismantling the global systems that perpetuate inequality and corruption.

Globalization, often hailed as the force of uniting economies and fostering development, has inadvertently amplified the scope and complexity of secret trades. Over the past three decades, global markets have integrated at an accelerated pace. This integration has opened new opportunities for trade and investment. However, it has also created loopholes for corruption and illicit transactions. Recorded and unrecorded financial flows coexist in this expanded marketplace, blurring the lines between legal and illegal trade. Multinational corporations and state actors compete for dominance. Organized crime syndicates exploit gaps in governance, creating lucrative networks. These networks thrive on weak regulations, fragmented jurisdictions, and institutional complicity. Globalization has thus become a double-edged sword—promising prosperity for some while entrenching corruption and exploitation for others.

Organized crime groups stand at the heart of secret trades, functioning as both facilitators and beneficiaries. These syndicates are adept at creating transnational networks that connect local producers, middlemen, and global markets. Their success relies on more than operational efficiency. It depends on their ability to co-opt officials and policymakers. These actors provide the protection and access needed to ensure the smooth flow of goods. The rise of piracy off the coast of Somalia offers a compelling example of how criminal networks thrive under conditions of weak governance. What began as a response to illegal fishing in Somali waters evolved into a multi-million-dollar industry, where hijacked ships and ransom demands became normalized. Far from being chaotic, these operations displayed a high degree of coordination, with the profits funneled into local economies and global markets alike.

Coltan mining in the Democratic Republic of the Congo (DRC) reveals another dimension of secret trades. Workers extract valuable resources under exploitative and often illegal conditions. Miners extract coltan, essential for producing electronic components, from regions rife with conflict and governance challenges. Rebel groups and armed factions control mining areas, using forced labor to extract the mineral while channeling profits into arms purchases and perpetuating cycles of violence. International buyers, including major corporations, indirectly sustain these operations by sourcing materials without stringent ethical oversight. This interplay between local violence and global demand embeds secret trades within larger economic systems.

Secrecy jurisdictions—or tax havens—further complicate efforts to combat secret trades and their associated corruption. These regions provide financial anonymity and minimal regulatory oversight, enabling corrupt actors to launder and conceal illicit gains. Secrecy jurisdictions form the backbone of financial flows supporting secret trades. They hide billions siphoned from state coffers in emerging markets and shelter the accounts of powerful elites. They allow wealth to be extracted from the public sphere and re-entered through legal channels, often under the guise of foreign investment or offshore holdings. Efforts to trace and recover these funds often fail. Opaque jurisdictions shield their clients under the guise of financial privacy, blocking accountability.

Manipulating trade prices, or trade mispricing, is a key driver of secret trades. This involves under- or over-invoicing exports and imports to move money across borders illicitly. Emerging markets are especially vulnerable because of weak oversight and corruption, allowing billions of dollars to be siphoned away annually. These financial outflows erode economic opportunities, public trust, and institutional credibility.

The impacts extend beyond economics, affecting social and environmental systems. Resource-rich but institutionally fragile regions suffer disproportionately. Illegal extraction of resources like timber, gold, and rare earth metals often leads to environmental degradation, biodiversity loss, and displacement of communities. For example, illegal logging in the Amazon drives deforestation, threatening climate change efforts and indigenous rights. Similar patterns in Southeast Asia and Central Africa harm ecosystems and livelihoods, hidden from end consumers.

Regulatory responses, like the Dodd-Frank Act's conflict mineral provisions, aim to increase transparency but often lack enforcement and address symptoms, not root causes. Corrupt networks continue facilitating illegal mining, logging, and fishing, depleting natural resources and worsening food insecurity. Marginalized communities face polluted land and water, further diminishing their livelihoods.

Despite these challenges, international cooperation and advocacy provide hope. Civil society groups and investigative journalists expose secret trades, while initiatives like the Extractive Industries Transparency Initiative (EITI) push for accountability. Progress depends on political will and active engagement across sectors to address these complex issues holistically.

In sum, the phenomenon of secret trades provides a lens to examine the broader dynamics of corruption and global inequality. These illicit activities deeply intertwine with the formal economy, reflecting systemic vulnerabilities and power imbalances.

Addressing secret trades requires more than piecemeal reforms; it demands a reimagining of governance, accountability, and international solidarity. This chapter reveals hidden networks fueling global inequality. It calls for an equitable and transparent economy that shares trade and development benefits broadly, avoiding concentration in the hands of a few.

The military-industrial complex shows the deep ties between governance, economics, and conflict. This system turns war into profit, perpetuating cycles of violence under the guise of security.

2.5 WHY STOP WARS WHEN THEY PAY SO WELL?

War, once a last resort of states, has become a cornerstone of economic and political strategy. The American military-industrial complex exemplifies this transformation, as defense industries and policymakers lock themselves in a symbiotic relationship. From Cold War arms races to the War on Terror, the military-industrial complex has entrenched global instability. It raises urgent ethical questions about linking economic growth to perpetual conflict.

The military-industrial complex closely ties the United States' role in global politics. This term describes the complicated web connecting the defense industry, military institutions, and government. This system shapes modern American governance and anchors how the United States engages globally. Since the mid-20th century, the military-industrial complex has shaped U.S. economic, political, and military strategies. It acts as both a driver and a consequence, influencing policymaking and the global landscape of conflict. Its influence extends across borders, forging alliances and fueling wars, while also perpetuating cycles of violence and instability that feed back into its mechanisms.

The origins of the American military-industrial complex trace back to World War II. During this time, the United States mobilized on an extraordinary scale, transforming itself into the "Arsenal of Democracy." Governments repurposed factories that once produced consumer goods to churn out tanks, airplanes, and ammunition at an unprecedented scale. This period demonstrated the economic potential of military production, setting the stage for what would become a permanent integration of industry and military strategy. When the war ended, instead of returning to a peacetime economy, the United States found itself entering a new era of geopolitical competition: the Cold War. This rivalry with the Soviet Union required sustained military preparedness and justified the continuous expansion of defense industries.

By the mid-20th century, defense contractors became central to the American economy. Lockheed Martin, Boeing, Northrop Grumman, and Raytheon rose to prominence. They produced advanced weaponry, symbols of both national pride and tools of war. These corporations relentlessly lobbied Congress. Their efforts secured lucrative contracts and ensured defense spending remained a top priority.

The growing flow of resources into defense strengthened these companies, embedding them further into the economy. This created a feedback loop: the more money allocated to defense, the harder it became to scale back military spending without causing economic disruption.

In 1961, President Dwight D. Eisenhower delivered a farewell address warning of the unchecked power of the military-industrial complex. Now it shaped American politics.

The Cold War years demonstrated how deeply the military-industrial complex could shape global politics. The United States adopted a strategy of containment, aiming to prevent the spread of communism by any means necessary. This often-involved military interventions, covert operations, and the arming of allies in regions deemed strategically important. In Vietnam, for example, the U.S. waged a protracted war that combined ideological motivations with economic imperatives. Defense contractors benefited enormously from the conflict, as the demand for helicopters, ammunition, and chemical agents like napalm skyrocketed. The Vietnam War devastated Vietnam and its neighboring countries. It also set a precedent for future U.S. conflicts. The United States leveraged its industrial and technological superiority to wage wars aimed at maintaining economic dominance as much as achieving ideological or strategic goals.

The Cold War's end in the early 1990s barely weakened the influence of the military-industrial complex. Following the Soviet Union's collapse, America emerged as the sole superpower, creating new opportunities for military expansion. In 1991, the Gulf War demonstrated the effectiveness of the U.S. military's high-tech weaponry. The U.S. military deployed precision-guided munitions, stealth bombers, and advanced communication systems on a massive scale, solidifying America's reputation as a military powerhouse.

This war also underscored the economic stakes of military engagement. During the Vietnam War, the defense industry reaped enormous profits. America's continued presence in the Middle East ensured a steady demand for arms and equipment in the years that followed.

A pivotal moment came with the September 11, 2001, attacks, which reshaped the global act of the military-industrial complex. What followed was the War on Terror, an era of perpetual warfare spanning Iraq, Afghanistan, and numerous other countries. Justifying the 2003 invasion of Iraq with false claims about Saddam Hussein's weapons of mass destruction highlighted how the military-industrial complex operates. Defense contractors secured billions in contracts, supplying everything from armored vehicles to private security personnel. American companies profited from rebuilding Iraq's infrastructure, much of it destroyed by U.S. bombing campaigns.

During this period, emerging technologies transformed the military-industrial complex. Drones, surveillance systems, and cyber weapons became pivotal to U.S. military strategy, enabling covert but highly destructive warfare. Drone strikes in Pakistan, Yemen, and Somalia erased the boundaries between war and peace, fostering a state of perpetual conflict that justified continuous military spending.

Intelligence agencies extended their reach through militarization and surveillance programs. Whistleblowers like Edward Snowden revealed how deeply these practices infiltrated governance, exposing the pervasive influence of the military-industrial complex.

The global implications of this system are profound. American foreign policy, shaped by the interests of the military-industrial complex, often prioritizes military solutions over diplomatic ones. This has led to a pattern of interventions that destabilize regions while creating new markets for arms sales. In the Middle East, the U.S. supplied weapons to allies like Saudi Arabia. Saudi forces used these weapons in conflicts like the war in Yemen, causing widespread humanitarian suffering. Similarly, the arming of rebel groups in Syria turned a civil war into a proxy conflict, with devastating consequences for the region.

The effects of the military-industrial complex are not limited to active war zones. It also shapes the global arms trade, with the United States consistently ranking as the world's largest exporter of weapons. This trade extends America's influence but also perpetuates cycles of violence, as weapons sold to one ally today can end up in the hands of adversaries tomorrow. Proliferating arms has fueled conflicts in regions like Africa and South Asia. Advanced weaponry increases tensions and prolongs wars in these areas.

Domestically, the military-industrial complex has profound implications for American democracy. Defense spending constitutes a significant portion of the federal budget, creating economic dependencies that are difficult to break. Military bases and defense contractors are often strategically located in key congressional districts, ensuring bipartisan support for high levels of military spending. The revolving door between government and industry further entrenches this system, as former military officials take lucrative jobs with defense contractors and vice versa. This dynamic blur the line between public service and private profit. It raises questions about whether decisions prioritize the nation's best interests or the financial gain of a few.

The cost of this system extends beyond economics to include moral and political consequences. Normalizing warfare as a tool of governance erodes the principles of democracy and accountability. By prioritizing short-term strategic gains over long-term stability, the system fosters a world where conflicts persist rather than resolve.

An often-overlooked consequence is the environmental impact of perpetual warfare. Producing and using military equipment contributes significantly to pollution and climate change. Furthermore, the emphasis on military solutions diverts resources from critical areas like education, healthcare, and infrastructure, perpetuating domestic inequalities. Meanwhile, the United States spends billions projecting power abroad.

As we look to the future, the role of the military-industrial complex in global politics shows no signs of diminishing. Emerging technologies like artificial intelligence, hypersonic weapons, and space-based systems are already being integrated into military strategies, creating new frontiers for conflict and competition. These developments raise profound ethical questions about the nature of war and the responsibilities of nations in an increasingly interconnected world. The rise of great power competition, especially with China and Russia, is likely to drive further military budget expansions. This will further entrench the military-industrial complex in both domestic and global affairs.

The American military-industrial complex is not merely a feature of the nation's governance; it is a defining element of its identity on the world stage. It has shaped the way the United States interacts with other nations, the way it addresses conflicts, and the way it defines its own security. Yet, this system also comes with profound costs—costs that are often borne by the most vulnerable, both at home and abroad. To understand America's role in global politics, one must confront a system where war machinery functions as both means and ends. It drives conflict to maintain power as much as to address threats. This system raises urgent questions about the world we are building and the choices shaping security, prosperity, and influence.

From wars and wealth to illicit economies and political flaws, the challenges of governance are vast and interconnected. To overcome these challenges, humanity must move beyond the past and embrace bold innovations to redefine how societies govern themselves.

Politics, at its best, should serve the collective good. Leadership driven by ego and systems designed for exploitation makes dysfunction inevitable. The evolutionary need for power and dominance disrupts more than relationships do. It drives nations, turning politics into survival for a few at the many's expense. Proxy wars, corrupt policies, and profit-driven governance are merely extensions of the same instinctual behaviors that fracture our personal lives.

This leads us directly to the economy, explored in Chapter 5: *Economic Inequities.* When political dysfunction prioritizes profit over people, the global economy becomes a stage for inequality and exploitation. The wealth gap continues to widen, and resources dwindle. Survival becomes a privilege, not a right. This stark reality reminds us that governance dysfunction has dire consequences for humanity's future.

5

Economic Inequities

"An imbalance between rich and poor is the oldest and
most fatal ailment of all republics."

– PLUTARCH

A historical examination reveals a fundamental link between the accumulation of wealth and the exertion of power. It's easy to think of today's billionaires as one-of-a-kind success stories. They appear to rise through hard work, brilliance, and some luck. The reality behind the luxury is far less glamorous. The opulent palaces of the elite aren't just symbols of success—they are the products of carefully crafted systems. These systems extract, concentrate, and protect wealth, using colonial conquest, industrial power, or today's digital empires. Beneath the glittering surface of luxury yachts and record-breaking stock valuations lies a stark truth: inequality isn't accidental—it's engineered. Policies, rules, and global institutions work behind the scenes to funnel resources upward. This isn't just capitalism running wild; it's the result of deliberate choices, wrapped in stories of progress and inevitability. But as wealth concentrates at the top, the cracks in these stories become impossible to ignore. This forces us to confront a critical question. What is the true cost of this growing disparity? It impacts billions left behind and the stability of societies.

In the financial pages of Forbes and Bloomberg, the Top 10 billionaires always command attention. It's not just for their wealth, but for the dynamic power play that defines their rankings. Some strive fiercely for the coveted top spots, leveraging innovation, influence, and strategy to ascend the ladder. Their ascent is not simply a tale of entrepreneurial brilliance. It is the direct outcome of a system engineered to concentrate wealth and power in the hands of a select few. The stark truth is that the 1% at the apex of the global economic hierarchy controls more wealth than the bottom 99% combined. This is not an accident or an anomaly; it culminates from centuries of systemic inequality, a phenomenon rooted in our earliest civilizations. The gap between those who have and those who struggle to survive shapes far more than material conditions. It shapes the intimate fabric of human relationships, as we explored in Chapter 1. When most of the population struggles to meet basic needs, ripple effects follow. These include how time, trust, and emotional connection erode over time. Such impacts resonate across generations.

This concentration of wealth and the resulting social fractures are not unknown phenomena; they are the result of a continuous process that began in prehistoric times. Early hierarchical societies, from tribal chieftains to empires, relied on systems that rewarded a few at the expense of the many. Over millennia, these structures evolved but never disappeared. Today, the methods of maintaining this concentration of power are more sophisticated, cloaked in economic jargon, political spin, and technological advancement. Yet, the goal remains the same: to ensure the perpetuation of privilege among those who already possess it. Interconnected systems, not just individual malice, maintain this tradition. Elites carefully craft these systems to preserve and deepen inequality.

Consider the historical context. Colonialism, slavery, and feudalism created vast disparities that persist even in post-colonial societies. The descendants of those who benefited from these exploitative systems continue to hold sway over modern economies. These entrenched elites have adapted to capitalism, which, while a driver of innovation, inherently prioritizes profit over equality. Corporations, financial institutions, and policymakers engineer systems to entrench the wealthy. Through tax loopholes, deregulation, and wage suppression, they ensure wealth flows upward. Meanwhile, the majority work harder for diminishing returns.

Politics, too, plays its role. Governments often serve the interests of the powerful. They enact legislation that disproportionately benefits the elite—through tax cuts for the rich or corporate subsidies disguised as economic development incentives. Lobbyists and special interest groups write the rules of the game. They ensure these rules favor those who are already ahead. Globalization, while touted as a force for good, has often exacerbated these inequalities. International trade agreements and supply chains exploit labor in low-income countries, funneling profits to multinational corporations headquartered in wealthier nations. This dynamic not only widens the gap between countries but also within them, as blue-collar workers in developed nations see their jobs outsourced and their wages stagnate.

Even education, often seen as an equalizer, perpetuates inequality. Access to quality learning remains limited to those who can afford it. Underfunded public schools, skyrocketing college tuition, and privatized education systems ensure that the cycle of poverty continues. Meanwhile, systemic discrimination—based on race, gender, caste, or religion—creates additional barriers for marginalized groups, limiting their opportunities for upward mobility. The digital age has introduced additional dimensions to these disparities, as tech billionaires amass unprecedented control over wealth and data, further skewing how resources flow to different groups.

The financialization of modern economies has transformed profit-making, shifting the focus from producing tangible goods and services to speculative investments. This trend disproportionately benefits hedge funds, banks, and wealthy investors while leaving workers and small businesses vulnerable to economic instability. Corruption exacerbates the issue, diverting public resources meant for collective benefit into the hands of the few. The media further reinforces these inequalities, often normalizing wealth concentration by promoting consumerism or sensationalizing distractions from systemic issues. Together, these forces create a cycle where inequality is perpetuated, economic instability grows, and the divide between the privileged and the majority deepens.

What emerges from this complex web of historical, economic, political, and cultural forces is a picture of a world engineered to perpetuate inequality. Each actor—be it governments, corporations, or media—contributes knowingly or unwittingly to this dynamic. But these systems, while deeply entrenched, are not immutable. Change requires a fundamental redistribution of power and resources, along with a shift in values that prioritize equity over endless accumulation.

Modern systems do not merely produce wealth as a byproduct; they concentrate it as their raison d'être. Across centuries, the machinery of inequality has evolved to ensure that the privileges of the elite remain impervious to societal upheaval. From colonial conquests to corporate globalization, the mechanisms have grown more sophisticated but no less ruthless. The void between those who thrive and those who survive has become impossible to ignore today, as the top 1% command nearly half the planet's resources. Understanding the roots of this inequality requires a journey into the world of the elite, where privilege is not just inherited but endlessly fortified.

1. ELITE PLEASURE

The elite are not merely beneficiaries of inequality—they are its architects. For centuries, the wealthy have perfected systems that transform scarcity into abundance for themselves while maintaining it for others. Colonial empires laid the foundation, funneling resources from the Global South to enrich a select few in Europe. The industrial age followed, creating fortunes on the backs of exploited labor. Today, the tools of wealth concentration have become less visible but no less potent. Trade agreements, tax havens, and financial markets operate like invisible hands, ensuring the wealth of the elite grows even in times of global crises. These mechanisms have created a world where a small fraction of humanity enjoys unimaginable privilege while billions struggle to secure basic necessities.

The story of wealth concentration is not just about numbers; it is about the architecture of human societies and the forces that shape them. Global wealth concentration refers to the staggering reality that a minuscule fraction of the population—the so-called 1%—controls nearly half of all global wealth. This figure is not a fluke of modern economics but a testament to the enduring systems that have enabled this inequality. The richest individuals and families—from tech moguls to oil tycoons—sit atop a pyramid of wealth. Centuries of systemic privilege, exploitation, and innovation build this pyramid. Elites intentionally design these systems to protect elite status. Beneath them lies a vast expanse of humanity, struggling to access the resources, opportunities, and dignity needed for a decent life. This imbalance is not merely a statistic; it is a defining feature of our world, shaping the opportunities of nations, the policies of governments, and the relationships of individuals. This chapter explores the mechanisms that sustain this disparity. Political collusion, exploitative trade practices, the military-industrial complex, and other pillars of inequality ensure that wealth flows upward and remains concentrated.

Why does this matter? Wealth concentration is not simply an economic phenomenon—it is a political, social, and ethical crisis. When wealth concentrates disproportionately in the hands of a few, the effects are profound. The very principles of democracy and fairness begin to collapse. Those who control the majority of wealth also wield disproportionate influence over political systems, shaping legislation and policy to protect their interests. This creates a feedback loop, where the systems designed to serve society at large are instead co-opted to preserve the privilege of the elite. The impact on global inequality is profound. Billions struggle to meet basic needs, even as the wealthy enjoy the fruits of compounding privilege—access to education, healthcare, and leisure. This disparity slows economic growth, weakens social cohesion, and fosters a sense of alienation that can erupt into political instability and social unrest.

But this is not a problem that emerged in isolation or suddenly. It is the outcome of a historical trajectory that stretches from feudalism to colonial empires, from the rise of industrial capitalism to the digital age. In every era, concentrated wealth drives innovation. Yet, it also serves as a force of exclusion, ensuring progress remains unevenly distributed. The systems that perpetuate inequality are as old as civilization itself, but they have evolved into forms that are subtler, more efficient, and harder to dismantle. This chapter will explore both the historical roots and contemporary examples of these mechanisms. It sets the stage for a deeper understanding of persistent disparities. The focus now shifts to how and why they endure—and what actions might address them.

The roots of modern wealth inequality trace back to the age of colonial empires. It was then that human exploitation and resource extraction reached a scale previously unimaginable. Colonial powers built their fortunes not through mutual exchange or partnership, but through the systematic plundering of lands, labor, and lives. The British East India Company, for example, drained India of its wealth through aggressive taxation, forced cultivation of cash crops, and outright resource extraction. This wasn't merely an economic endeavor; it was an imperial project that reshaped entire societies, leaving local economies in ruins and their people impoverished. King Leopold II of Belgium turned the Congo into a personal fiefdom. He extracted vast quantities of rubber under brutal conditions. The inhumanity was so severe that entire communities faced destruction. These incidents did not occur in isolation. They were part of a larger, recurring pattern. They were part of a larger system where European powers divided the world into zones of extraction and exploitation. This laid the foundation for the stark economic disparities we see today between the Global North and South. Colonialism not only transferred wealth to the imperial centers, but also entrenched power structures that continue to favor those nations long after their empires dissolved.

The Industrial Revolution, heralded as a triumph of human ingenuity, introduced another layer of inequality, this time within nations. It was a period that created unprecedented wealth, but it concentrated that wealth in the hands of a new class of industrial magnates. Figures like Rockefeller, Carnegie, and Vanderbilt emerged as titans of industry, amassing fortunes so vast they rivaled the GDP of smaller countries. Their wealth came at a cost. Exploited laborers toiled in dangerous factories, earning meager wages to build this success. Cities grew into industrial hubs, but they also became epicenters of poverty, disease, and unrest as the working class bore the brunt of rapid urbanization. The captains of industry basked in the opulence of gilded mansions. Meanwhile, the vast majority of people lived in squalor, their lives reduced to endless cycles of work and survival. This class divide solidified structural inequalities that capitalism perpetuates: those who control capital continue to compound their advantages, while labor providers stagnate.

World War II's devastation reshaped the global economic order once again. This time, the United States took the lead. The Bretton Woods Agreement of 1944 established institutions like the International Monetary Fund (IMF) and the World Bank, ostensibly to promote global stability and development. However, these systems cemented the economic dominance of the United States and its allies. The U.S. dollar became the world's reserve currency, a status that gave the country unparalleled influence over international trade and finance. Meanwhile, programs like the Marshall Plan funneled billions of dollars into rebuilding war-torn Europe, but they largely excluded the poorer nations of Asia, Africa, and Latin America. These regions, still grappling with colonial legacies, faced abandonment. Western economic powerhouses left them to fend for themselves in a dominated world.

This period of reconstruction in the Global North deepened the divide between wealthy and poor nations. Much of the Global South remained trapped in cycles of poverty and dependence, even as Europe and the U.S. experienced unprecedented economic growth and technological advancement. The mechanisms of inequality had evolved but remained as effective as ever, ensuring that wealth and power continued to flow toward the centers of historical privilege. These historical processes—from colonial extraction to post-war economic systems—show a harsh truth. Inequality is not merely a byproduct of progress, but often its engine. It is a system deliberately designed to concentrate wealth in the hands of a few while leaving the majority behind.

Many celebrate elite opulence as a testament to human ingenuity. Yet, this narrative often masks deeper inequalities. But this celebration obscures a darker truth: their wealth is not the product of merit alone. It is the result of systems designed to protect and perpetuate privilege. To see this clearly, one must examine how modern billionaires have mastered the art of extracting more from a system that offers less to everyone else.

1.1 RICH GET RICHER, YOU GET POORER

Many hail 21st century billionaires as visionaries. Yet, their success stems as much from systemic advantages as it does from individual brilliance. Figures like Elon Musk and Jeff Bezos have leveraged not just innovation but also tax loopholes, financial speculation, and exploitative labor practices to build their empires. Governments lose significant revenue because of corporate tax avoidance, resulting in underfunded public infrastructure and weakened social safety nets. This is not accidental. This system channels wealth upward. It rewards those who already hold the reins of power. The ultra-rich consolidate their dominance while the majority falls further behind. They grapple with stagnating wages, rising costs, and diminishing opportunities. This dynamic threatens the very fabric of society.

Humanity's relationship with wealth has always been complex. Yet, the modern era has birthed an unprecedented phenomenon: a tiny elite concentrating unimaginable fortunes. The rise of billionaires in the 21st century symbolizes both the triumph of capitalism and its darkest contradictions. As economies globalize and technologies advance, the barriers to creating vast wealth have diminished. This change favors the select few who possess the right mix of innovation, timing, and access to resources. However, this concentration of wealth has revealed systemic flaws. Exploitative economic structures and tax evasion schemes leave billions of ordinary citizens burdened with the costs of progress. Meanwhile, the wealthiest escape accountability. The result is a world where the top 1% control more wealth than the rest of humanity combined. This stark inequality challenges the very foundations of modern governance and morality.

The sheer scale of wealth amassed by today's billionaires is staggering. In 2023, there were 2,640 billionaires globally, collectively holding $12.2 trillion—more than the GDP of most countries. Their dominance spans industries that define the modern economy, particularly technology, finance, and luxury goods. Figures like Elon Musk and Jeff Bezos epitomize the tech-driven surge of wealth. Musk, with his Tesla empire and ventures into space exploration through SpaceX, has reached extraordinary heights of wealth. He has become not only the world's richest person but also a symbol of how innovation and speculative investments can catapult individuals into the stratosphere of fortune. Bezos, founder of Amazon, reshaped global commerce, creating a company so vast and influential that it has redefined supply chains, labor markets, and even cloud computing. Together, Musk and Bezos illustrate the unparalleled power of the tech boom. Consumer dependence, market speculation, and technological disruption combine to create fortunes on an almost mythical scale.

The luxury goods market, while less visible in the tech-centric discourse of wealth, has similarly fueled the rise of billionaires like Bernard Arnault, CEO of LVMH. By commanding brands synonymous with prestige—Louis Vuitton, Dior, and Moët Hennessy—Arnault has leveraged the aspirational desires of global consumers to build an empire worth over $200 billion. His ascent underscores the enduring allure of exclusivity and the global appetite for luxury, even in times of economic uncertainty. These examples demonstrate that modern wealth is not merely about utility or productivity but about capturing cultural narratives and commanding consumer loyalty across borders.

Global financialization underlies the rise of these billionaires. Wealth increasingly comes not from producing goods or services. Instead, people generate it by manipulating capital itself. Stock markets, hedge funds, and investment vehicles have transformed wealth accumulation into an abstract game, accessible only to those with the capital to play. This system disproportionately benefits the wealthy, who can afford to invest in complex financial instruments while enjoying protections unavailable to ordinary citizens. The 2008 financial crisis exemplifies this disparity. When global markets collapsed because of risky financial practices, governments acted quickly. They rushed to bail out major banks and financial institutions with taxpayer money, injecting trillions into the system to prevent a total economic meltdown. Millions of ordinary citizens faced foreclosures, job losses, and evaporated savings. The crisis exposed a harsh truth. Those at the top rig the rules of financial systems. These rules ensure they maintain their position of advantage. These systems ensure that the wealthy remain insulated from the consequences of their own failures.

This dynamic is further entrenched by the use of tax havens, a shadowy but critical component of modern wealth accumulation. The world's wealthiest individuals and corporations routinely exploit loopholes in international tax laws to shield their fortunes from public scrutiny and taxation. Revelations like the Panama Papers in 2016 and the Pandora Papers in 2021 pulled back the curtain on this secretive world. They exposed how global elites use offshore accounts, shell companies, and legal loopholes to hide trillions of dollars. The Panama Papers implicated high-profile figures—from politicians to celebrities. They revealed how the world's wealthiest siphon money away from the public purse. Ordinary citizens, meanwhile, shoulder the burden of funding infrastructure, healthcare, and education. Similarly, the Pandora Papers documented how leaders—including kings and presidents—used secretive financial structures to amass and conceal wealth. These revelations raise serious questions about the moral and political integrity of those entrusted with governance.

The implications of these practices extend far beyond individual fortunes. Governments suffer when billionaires evade taxes or manipulate financial systems to their advantage. This deprives them of the resources needed to address pressing societal challenges—from poverty and healthcare to climate change. This exacerbates inequality, creating a cycle where public services deteriorate, and economic disparities deepen. Meanwhile, the wealthy continue to profit, their fortunes growing exponentially as the rest of society struggles to keep pace.

This system of modern wealth accumulation also raises ethical questions about the very nature of success in a globalized economy. People often celebrate billionaires as innovators, disruptors, and visionaries. They frame their success as the product of hard work and ingenuity. Yet, this narrative obscures the systemic advantages they enjoy—access to capital, networks, and policies tailored to protect their interests. The same system that rewards billionaires penalizes those without the resources to navigate its complexities, perpetuating inequality and fostering resentment.

The rise of the 1% is not just a story of economic triumph but reflects deeper structural flaws in the global economic system. It is a tale of how the pursuit of wealth, unchecked by accountability or ethics, can erode the social fabric and undermine the promise of democracy. Addressing these disparities requires systemic reforms. We must close tax loopholes and increase financial transparency. It's time to rethink how we create and distribute wealth in our interconnected world. Without such changes, the gulf between the ultra-wealthy and the rest of humanity will continue to widen, threatening the stability and cohesion of societies around the globe.

For every billionaire minted, there are countless workers who bear the weight of their success. These individuals toil in factories, warehouses, and fields, often for poverty wages, under conditions that maximize profit at their expense. To understand inequality, one must look beyond the boardrooms and into the lives of those who make the system function.

1.2 DEMOCRACY FOR SALE

Democracy, often celebrated as the great equalizer, has become a tool for entrenching inequality. In theory, democratic systems empower the many, but they frequently serve the few. Campaign finance laws, lobbying, and deregulation allow corporations and the ultra-rich to wield outsized influence over policy, shaping it to their advantage. Trade agreements favor multinationals over local economies, while tax policies protect wealth at the expense of public welfare. The result is a system where governance extends elite interests, undermining its very premise of equality and representation.

Throughout history, governments have often portrayed themselves as the protectors of the people, arbiters of justice, and defenders of equality. Yet, a closer examination reveals a pattern of collaboration with the elite. The powerful forge these alliances not to serve the many but to preserve their power and wealth. The modern era, with its intricate webs of lobbying, tax policies, and global trade agreements, provides a masterclass in how these partnerships operate. Beneath the surface of democracy and economic progress lies a hidden system. Influence flows upward, and decisions favor the powerful. Meanwhile, the majority struggle in an economy rigged against them. This partnership between governments and elites is not merely a symptom of corruption; it is the design of a world where power sustains itself by merging governance with wealth.

One of the most glaring mechanisms through which elites shape government policy is lobbying. Lobbying, once seen as a tool for advocacy and representation, has transformed into a billion-dollar industry. Corporations and the ultra-wealthy now dominate it, ensuring their voices drown out those of ordinary citizens. The 2010 Citizens United v. Federal Election Commission decision in the United States epitomizes this dynamic. By allowing unlimited corporate contributions to political campaigns under the guise of free speech, the ruling opened the floodgates for unprecedented corporate influence in politics. Elections became less about public will and more about financial muscle, with billions spent to shape outcomes favorable to big business. The pharmaceutical industry spent over $300 million on lobbying in 2022 alone. This ensured that legislation on drug pricing, patents, and healthcare reform aligned with its interests. Similarly, oil giants like ExxonMobil and Chevron have poured billions into lobbying efforts to block climate legislation, preserve fossil fuel subsidies, and undermine renewable energy initiatives. These industries exemplify how lobbying transforms democracy into a transactional affair, where the highest bidder dictates policy.

Elites don't stop at shaping policies through lobbying. Their influence extends far beyond that. It extends deeply into tax and regulatory frameworks. The 2017 U.S. The Tax Cuts and Jobs Act reveals how tax policies often benefit the wealthy. It serves as a simple case study. Marketed as a boon for middle-class families, the law disproportionately advantaged corporations and high-income earners. Lawmakers slashed corporate tax rates from 35% to 21%. This move saved companies billions but added to the national debt. The wealthiest individuals saw reductions in estate taxes and caps on deductions that primarily benefited the middle class. The act's long-term effects have been stark: while corporate profits soared, wage growth for ordinary workers remained stagnant, and income inequality deepened. This pattern is not unique to the U.S. Around the globe, tax policies protect wealth rather than redistribute it. The rich pay less, even as their fortunes grow.

Deregulation serves as another pillar of the government-elite partnership, often under the guise of fostering innovation and reducing bureaucratic red tape. Yet, deregulation has repeatedly led to disastrous consequences for the broader public. The 2008 global financial crisis offers a sobering example. Years of financial deregulation, including the repeal of the Glass-Steagall Act in 1999, allowed banks to engage in risky speculative practices. Complex instruments like mortgage-backed securities and credit default swaps became ticking time bombs, and when they exploded, the fallout devastated the global economy. Governments rushed to bail out the very banks that caused the crisis. They injected trillions into the financial system while millions of ordinary people lost their homes, jobs, and savings. Deregulation privatized profits for the financial elite while socializing the costs of their failures. It serves as a stark reminder of how governments prioritize the interests of the few over the welfare of the many.

Global trade agreements expose yet another frontier. Here, the collaboration between governments and elites becomes evident. Agreements like NAFTA were championed as engines of economic growth. They promised prosperity through the free flow of goods, services, and capital across borders. However, the reality for many workers and communities has been far bleaker. In the United States, NAFTA led to the loss of over 700,000 manufacturing jobs. Companies relocated production to Mexico to take advantage of lower wages and weaker labor protections. While corporations reaped the benefits of reduced costs and expanded markets, displaced workers faced declining wages, job insecurity, and diminished bargaining power. Similar patterns have played out worldwide under the rules of the World Trade Organization (WTO), which frequently favor multinational corporations over local economies. By enforcing intellectual property laws that protect corporate interests and imposing trade rules that restrict government support for local industries, the WTO has entrenched global economic inequalities. Developing nations, often forced to open their markets to foreign competition, struggle to protect their domestic industries and workers, leaving them vulnerable to exploitation.

The partnership between governments and elites is not a conspiracy, but a structural reality of modern governance. It is a system where the tools of democracy—lobbying, taxation, regulation, and trade—are co-opted to serve the interests of the powerful. These alliances don't persist because of apparent corruption alone. They exist because the fabric of power incorporates them. The results are visible everywhere. Soaring corporate profits stand alongside stagnant wages. Markets expand for the few while communities face economic decline. Policies prioritize wealth accumulation over the well-being of the many. Addressing these dynamics requires more than piecemeal reforms; it demands a fundamental rethinking of how governance and economics intersect. Without such change, the collaboration between governments and elites will continue shaping a world defined by inequality, instability, and eroding democratic ideals.

When people compromise institutions meant to safeguard equality, the effects ripple outward. The consequences go far beyond economic disparity. Eroding democracy does not just embolden the wealthy; it disenfranchises the masses, breeding unrest and destabilizing societies. Yet, the structure of democracy remains intact, concealing the vast machinery that serves the elite.

1.3 WAR: THE ULTIMATE STARTUP

War has always been profitable for the few and catastrophic for the many. From the industrialists of World War II to the modern defense contractors of the Iraq and Afghanistan conflicts, the military-industrial complex operates as a self-sustaining system. Companies like Lockheed Martin and Halliburton profit immensely from prolonged conflicts, lobbying for policies that ensure perpetual military spending. These wars devastate regions, displace millions, and destabilize economies, yet they also generate trillions for private contractors. This cycle—where war fuels profit and profit fuels war—reveals the true cost of systems designed to prioritize economic gain over human life.

The military-industrial complex is more than just a phrase. Popularized by President Dwight D. Eisenhower in his 1961 farewell address, it serves as a cautionary tale. It warns of the unchecked alliance between governments, defense contractors, and military institutions. Eisenhower warned of a system where economic and political incentives would prioritize perpetual military expansion, even at the expense of genuine national security. Eisenhower's foresight emerged in the shadow of World War II. The conflict not only reshaped global power dynamics, but also entrenched the defense industry as a cornerstone of the U.S. economy. Over the decades, this complex has evolved into a sprawling network. It entangles political leaders, private corporations, and international strategy in a feedback loop of spending and influence. The scale of its growth has surpassed anything Eisenhower could have imagined.

Today, the U.S. defense budget exceeds $850 billion annually, surpassing the combined military spending of the next 10 nations. This immense sum funds everything from salaries and benefits for service members to the research and development of cutting-edge technologies like autonomous drones and laser weapons. But a significant portion of this budget doesn't stop at government institutions; it flows directly into the coffers of private corporations. Companies like Lockheed Martin, Boeing, and Raytheon dominate defense contracting, their fortunes tied to producing fighter jets, missiles, and warships. These corporations don't merely profit from existing conflicts; they actively shape the policies that ensure their continued relevance. Through lobbying, campaign contributions, and the infamous "revolving door" of personnel moving between government and private industry, these firms wield enormous influence over decisions about military spending.

Governments cloak the motives for such expenditures in the national security language. Yet, economic interests often lurk beneath the surface. Leaders framed the Iraq War as a mission to combat terrorism and promote democracy. Yet, it also conveniently aligned with securing access to oil reserves and enriching private contractors like Halliburton. In Afghanistan, the prolonged conflict generated billions in profits for companies providing logistical support, weapons, and infrastructure. These examples are far from anomalies. These examples reveal a broader truth. Wars do not occur for geopolitical reasons alone. An economic system sustains wars because it rewards their continuation.

The reach of the military-industrial complex extends far beyond U.S. borders. American companies sell weapons to authoritarian regimes. This fuels conflicts and repression across regions like the Middle East and Southeast Asia. In Africa, resource-rich nations plagued by instability often find themselves caught in a militarized scramble for control over rare earth minerals critical to modern technology. These dynamics perpetuate cycles of violence. They displace communities and deepen global inequality. They enrich arms manufacturers and maintain the geopolitical dominance of nations like the United States.

Yet, even as the defense industry amasses wealth and power, questions about its efficiency and morality persist. The Pentagon has failed repeated audits, unable to account for billions of dollars in assets and expenditures. Costs for weapons systems, like the troubled F-35 fighter jet, balloon into the trillions, while critical domestic needs—such as education, healthcare, and infrastructure—go underfunded. The prioritization of military might over societal well-being reveals a deep paradox. The military-industrial complex promises security through strength. Yet, it often delivers insecurity through neglect, mismanagement, and global instability.

The result is a self-perpetuating system, where economic interests dictate policy and policy sustains economic interests. Defense contractors ensure their survival by strategically placing operations in key congressional districts, creating jobs that politicians are loath to jeopardize. Meanwhile, lawmakers, some of whom hold stock in these very companies, face conflicting incentives when allocating budgets. The cycle continues, driven not by clear threats or rational strategy but by the systemic inertia of a machine built to expand itself. This dynamic is immensely profitable for a select few. However, it raises profound questions about its long-term consequences.

What does it mean for global peace, democracy, and allocating resources in a world desperate for solutions beyond the battlefield?

Wars, though devastating for nations and individuals, often serve as unparalleled opportunities for profit in the corporate world, particularly for companies deeply embedded within the military-industrial complex. These corporations thrive because conflict remains normalized and prolonged. War generates demand for weapons systems, logistics, and much more. Leaders publicly frame wars as national defense or humanitarian intervention. A closer look, however, reveals a system where profit drives decisions. The Iraq and Afghanistan wars provide vivid case studies. They show how corporate interests intertwine with military strategy. This creates a feedback loop where economic benefits for a select few come at the expense of countless lives and global stability.

The Iraq War, initiated in 2003 under the pretext of eliminating weapons of mass destruction and promoting democracy, became a massive economic windfall for private contractors. Between 2003 and 2011, the U.S. government spent an estimated $2 trillion on the war, including direct combat operations and the long-term care of veterans. A significant portion of this expenditure flowed to private companies, with Halliburton and its subsidiary, KBR, among the primary beneficiaries. The U.S. government awarded KBR contracts totaling over $39 billion during the conflict to provide logistical support, such as building bases, supplying troops, and transporting fuel. Investigations later revealed instances of over-billing, fraud, and substandard work, including reports of unsafe facilities and contaminated water supplied to U.S. soldiers. Yet, these practices barely dented the company's profitability, as the sheer volume of funds allocated to the war effort overshadowed any accountability measures.

Similarly, the defense contractor Lockheed Martin reaped immense rewards from the Iraq War, particularly through its production of precision-guided munitions and advanced weaponry. The use of Lockheed's Hellfire missiles, for example, soared during the conflict, as did demand for its C-130 Hercules transport aircraft and satellite systems. The company's stock value doubled between 2003 and 2008, a period that coincided with peak military operations in Iraq. These profits were not an incidental outcome but the result of a business model that views war as a reliable market. Lockheed Martin's lobbying efforts reflect this reality, with the company spending over $14 million annually to ensure continued congressional support for defense spending.

The war in Afghanistan, the longest in U.S. history, offers another illustration of how conflict becomes an engine of corporate profit. Between 2001 and 2021, the U.S. spent approximately $2.3 trillion on the war, much of which flowed to private contractors. Of this, an estimated $107. The U.S. allocated $9 billion to reconstruction efforts, aiming to rebuild Afghanistan's infrastructure and institutions. Reports from the Special Inspector General for Afghanistan Reconstruction (SIGAR) revealed massive waste and misuse of these funds. Corruption, mismanagement, and lack of oversight plagued many projects. People often abandoned facilities or rendered them unusable shortly after completion.

Private military contractors played a particularly prominent role in Afghanistan, with companies like DynCorp International and Academi (formerly Blackwater) taking on roles traditionally reserved for government forces. These firms provided security, training, and operational support, often at a premium cost. At the height of the war, contractors outnumbered U.S. troops in Afghanistan, with over 100,000 personnel on the ground. These companies argued that they offered cost-effective solutions. Critics, however, noted their profit-driven motives often led to ethical lapses, including documented cases of human rights abuses and civilian casualties.

The profits generated by these wars extended beyond the battlefield to the development and procurement of advanced military technology. The F-35 fighter jet program, a centerpiece of U.S. military spending, exemplifies how defense contractors capitalize on prolonged conflicts to justify massive investments in weapons systems. Developed by Lockheed Martin, the F-35 has become the most expensive weapons program in history, with a projected lifetime cost of $1.7 trillion. The jet played a limited operational role in Iraq and Afghanistan. Yet, the program's funding was repeatedly justified. The reason? The need to maintain technological superiority in ongoing and future conflicts. Critics argue that the program's costs far outweigh its strategic benefits. Nevertheless, the project continues to receive substantial funding because of the political and economic influence of its corporate backers.

Beyond individual companies, wars benefit the broader defense industry by driving sustained increases in military budgets. The U.S. defense budget surged during the Iraq and Afghanistan wars, from $287 billion in 2001 to $721 billion in 2010. Even as troop deployments decreased in the 2010s, the budget remained inflated, largely because of the influence of defense contractors. Companies directed a significant portion of these funds toward research and development, enabling them to innovate technologies marketed as essential for future conflicts. Military forces initially deployed drones in limited roles in Afghanistan. Since then, they have become a cornerstone of modern warfare. Companies like General Atomics and Boeing have profited immensely from their expanded use.

The influence of defense contractors extends into policymaking, ensuring that military spending remains a priority even during peacetime. The so-called "revolving door" between government and the private sector facilitates this dynamic, with former military officials frequently joining defense firms as executives or consultants. In 2020 alone, over 600 individuals transitioned from government roles to positions in the defense industry, leveraging their insider knowledge to secure lucrative contracts. This close relationship blurs the line between public service and private profit. The system allows economic interests to shape decisions about war and peace rather than strategic necessity.

Globally, war profits extend far beyond the borders of the U.S.S. companies. The arms trade, dominated by firms in the United States, Russia, and Europe, flourishes in conflict zones worldwide. Authoritarian regimes, often supported by weapons supplied by Western manufacturers, perpetuate violence that sustains demand for military goods. For instance, the Saudi-led intervention in Yemen, backed by U.S.-made weapons and logistical support, has turned the country into a humanitarian disaster while enriching arms manufacturers.

Wars, then, are not merely tragic events but lucrative enterprises for those positioned to exploit them. Defense contractors, private military firms, and reconstruction companies all benefit from prolonged conflicts. This often comes at the expense of the very goals these wars claim to achieve. The profits generated by the Iraq and Afghanistan wars highlight a deeper truth. The military-industrial complex is a system designed to perpetuate itself, prioritizing economic gain over human lives and global stability. As long as these incentives remain entrenched, the cycle of war and profit will continue, leaving devastation in its wake.

Even in times of peace, inequality finds new avenues to assert itself. Promises of innovative solutions like Universal Basic Income (UBI) offer hope but often mask deeper systemic failures.

1.4 UBI: A BAND-AID FOR A BROKEN SYSTEM

Universal Basic Income, with its promise of providing financial security for all, seems like a progressive solution to the challenges of automation and inequality. Yet beneath its utopian allure lies a troubling reality. UBI is often championed by the same elites who benefit most from the status quo, distracting from systemic reform. While it offers temporary relief, it does little to address the root causes of inequality, such as exploitative labor practices, tax avoidance, and concentrating wealth. Without deeper structural changes, UBI risks becoming a Band-Aid on a broken system, pacifying discontent while leaving the underlying dynamics untouched.

Inequality in the modern world is more than wealth amassed by the 1%. It is also about the mechanisms used to pacify the remaining 99%—a delicate balance of distraction, token gestures, and outright resistance to meaningful change. In this precarious arrangement, Universal Basic Income (UBI) emerges as an alluring mirage, a policy proposal designed to inspire and captivate disillusioned masses. Many advocate for UBI as a silver bullet to address inequality and the destabilizing effects of automation. It promises a future where everyone receives a guaranteed income, ensuring dignity and survival irrespective of employment. Beneath its utopian allure lies a stark reality. UBI is both economically impractical and politically manipulative. It often serves as a diversionary tactic that sustains the very systems it claims to challenge. Its feasibility falters under scrutiny, revealing a tool not for empowerment but for maintaining the status quo.

To understand the appeal and pitfalls of UBI, one must first grasp the context of modern inequality. The top 1% of the global population controls nearly 50% of the world's wealth, a disparity that grows with each passing year. In the United States alone, the combined wealth of billionaires surged by $1.7 trillion during the pandemic, while millions of workers struggled to make ends meet. Governments disguise policies like tax cuts for the rich and corporate subsidies as economic imperatives, perpetuating wealth concentration. Advocates propose UBI as a countermeasure in this context. It aims to redistribute wealth and provide a safety net for those excluded from the gains of globalization and automation. Yet, the very elites who benefit most from inequality often champion UBI. They do so not out of altruism but to deflect attention from structural reforms. These are reforms that would directly challenge their dominance.

At its core, UBI seems deceptively simple: provide every citizen with a regular cash payment, no strings attached. Proponents argue that it would alleviate poverty, empower individuals to pursue education or entrepreneurial ventures, and buffer against the job losses caused by technological disruption. Trials in various countries, such as Finland's experiment from 2017 to 2018, sought to test these claims. The Finnish trial provided 2,000 unemployed citizens with €560 per month, regardless of whether they sought work. The results were mixed. While recipients reported greater happiness and reduced stress, the experiment failed to boost employment significantly or address broader economic disparities. Moreover, the limited scope and funding of such trials highlight the difficulty of scaling UBI to a national or global level.

The economic challenges of implementing UBI on a meaningful scale are monumental. To provide every U.S. adult with a modest $1,000 monthly payment—a commonly cited benchmark—would cost approximately $3.8 trillion annually, nearly equivalent to the entire federal budget. Financing such a program would require unprecedented tax increases, likely targeting the same wealthy individuals and corporations that wield significant political influence. History shows that efforts to tax the rich often face fierce resistance, as seen in the backlash against wealth tax proposals by Bernie Sanders and Elizabeth Warren. Their plans aimed to impose a 2-6% annual tax on fortunes exceeding $50 million. Economists projected that this tax would generate trillions over a decade. Yet, it faced vehement opposition from billionaires like Jeff Bezos and Elon Musk. Without substantial taxation of the wealthy, UBI would either necessitate unsustainable deficits or come at the expense of existing social programs, undermining its promise of universal support.

Even if governments could fund UBI, its effectiveness in addressing inequality remains questionable. Critics argue that it risks becoming a replacement for targeted welfare programs, providing a uniform benefit that fails to account for varying needs. A flat payment might lift some individuals out of poverty. However, it does little to close the wealth gap. It also fails to address systemic issues like housing affordability and access to healthcare. Furthermore, UBI does not inherently challenge the structures that perpetuate inequality, such as exploitative labor practices, tax avoidance, and political corruption. By focusing on redistribution without addressing production and power dynamics, UBI risks becoming a band-aid on a hemorrhaging system.

The support for UBI among some members of the elite raises further suspicions about its true purpose. Figures like Mark Zuckerberg and Elon Musk have publicly endorsed UBI, framing it as a necessary response to job displacement caused by automation. Yet, their companies are among the most aggressive in automating labor and resisting unionization. The paradox is clear: the very forces driving economic disruption are now positioning themselves as benevolent visionaries offering solutions. In this context, UBI functions as a diversionary tactic. It stabilizes social unrest without challenging corporate profit-maximizing practices or the wealth accumulation of the 1%. It is a strategy designed to placate rather than empower, ensuring that calls for systemic change remain diluted and fragmented.

While UBI captures headlines and dominates policy debates, grassroots movements continue to fight for alternatives that address inequality at its roots. Occupy Wall Street, which erupted in 2011, responded viscerally to concentrated wealth and power in the hands of the few. Its rallying cry—"We are the 99%"—highlighted the stark divides created by decades of neoliberal policies. Although the movement lacked concrete demands, it sparked a global conversation about inequality and inspired subsequent activism, from labor strikes to climate protests. In France, the Yellow Vests movement brought millions to the streets. They protested fuel taxes that disproportionately burdened the working class. This highlighted the tension between environmental policies and economic justice.

Labor strikes, too, have seen a resurgence, with workers demanding fair wages, better working conditions, and a greater share of corporate profits. In 2021, the U.S. experienced a wave of labor actions dubbed "Striketober," as workers across industries pushed back against decades of stagnant wages and growing workloads. These movements emphasize collective action and structural change, challenging the very systems that enable inequality rather than accepting piecemeal solutions like UBI.

Proposed solutions rooted in structural reform offer more promise than the illusions of universal cash payments. Wealth taxes, for instance, directly target concentrated resources among the ultra-rich. Proposals like Warren's and Sanders's wealth taxes could generate trillions, funding not only poverty alleviation but also investments in education, healthcare, and infrastructure. Internationally, organizations like the United Nations have called for action to close the global wealth gap. They advocate for progressive taxation, corporate accountability, and global cooperation on climate change and human rights. While these initiatives face significant political and logistical hurdles, they represent a more comprehensive approach to equity than the blunt instrument of UBI.

The fight against wealth concentration and the search for alternatives center on power—who holds it, how they wield it, and how society can redistribute it. UBI, despite its progressive rhetoric, fails to challenge the entrenched hierarchies that perpetuate inequality. It offers relief without empowerment, stability without justice. The fight for equity requires more than redistribution; it demands a reimagining of economic and political systems to prioritize collective well-being over individual gain. One transformative solution involves wealth capping for elites, where a panel of experts assesses and fixes a cap on personal wealth needed to sustain their organizations, future research, and luxury lifestyles. Any surplus, along with profits generated beyond this cap, would be redirected into a global pool managed by a United Nations body. This pool would fund initiatives akin to a Y Combinator for Humanity, investing in research, innovation, and projects tackling global challenges like poverty, education, and climate change. Grassroots movements, wealth taxes, and international collaboration may lack the simplicity of UBI. Yet, coupled with wealth capping, they offer a path toward genuine transformation—a world where prosperity is not a privilege, but a shared right.

The challenges of UBI highlight a broader pattern: systems designed to appear equitable while protecting elite interests. Nowhere is this dichotomy more apparent than in the intersection of governance and finance, where lawmakers tasked with ensuring fairness often exploit their positions for personal gain. This unholy alliance of public roles and private profits erodes trust and deepens inequality, revealing the moral rot within democratic systems.

1.5 PUBLIC ROLE, PRIVATE PROFIT

At the heart of democratic governance lies a fragile but essential contract: that those entrusted with power serve the public good. Lawmakers routinely betray this contract when they exploit insider knowledge to enrich themselves. The practice of elected officials trading stocks, often aligned with privileged information, is a glaring conflict of interest that undermines public trust. High-profile examples abound. Congressman Spencer Bacchus profited during the 2008 financial crisis. Senator Richard Burr made well-timed sales before the COVID-19 crash. Nancy Pelosi's household investments suspiciously aligned with major policy shifts. While reforms like the 2012 STOCK Act aimed to curb these abuses, their weak enforcement and trivial penalties have done little to deter such practices. This intertwining of governance and financial gain not only compromises the integrity of institutions but also fosters widespread cynicism among citizens. Trust in Congress has plummeted to historic lows, leaving democracy vulnerable to collapse under the weight of its own contradictions.

Insider trading laws form a web of technicalities. Yet one truth cuts through the complexity: trust in democratic institutions is eroding. Not through outright legal violations, but through practices that are legal, morally dubious, and damaging to public confidence. At the heart of this erosion is a broken system. It allows those in positions of power—elected officials entrusted to govern—to leverage privileged information for personal financial gain. The rules of insider trading are stringent for CEOs and corporate insiders, but for the lawmakers who craft these rules, the boundaries are remarkably porous. This is not just a story of financial transactions; it is a saga of democracy's fragility in the face of unbridled self-interest and the slow corrosion of the social contract that holds societies together.

On September 19, 2008, Republican Congressman Spencer Bacchus placed a bet against the stock market, shorting the market with precision timing. His investment, which increased in value as the NASDAQ fell, was no random gamble. Just a day earlier, Bacchus had attended a classified meeting with senior officials from the U.S. Treasury and Federal Reserve. In that room, he was privy to stark warnings about an imminent global financial meltdown. Armed with this knowledge, he placed his trade, doubling his investment as the market spiraled downward. While millions of Americans watched their savings evaporate, Bacchus profited from foreknowledge of their pain. Remarkably, his actions were entirely legal. A glaring loophole in the system allowed those with insider knowledge to profit from impending disaster—as long as they were lawmakers and not corporate executives.

Bacchus's story is not unique. During the 2008 financial crisis, at least 34 lawmakers altered their investment portfolios within days of private briefings with administration officials, making 166 stock trades between them. These trades often foreshadowed market movements, raising uncomfortable questions about whether these elected representatives were acting in the public interest or their own. When pressed for answers, many, like then-House Minority Leader John Boehner, refused to discuss their financial activities. The optics were damning: as ordinary Americans lost jobs, homes, and savings, the political elite seemed immune, even opportunistic. Yet, lawmakers did not break any laws. The very individuals responsible for regulating markets had exempted themselves from the rules they imposed on others.

Legislators heralded the STOCK Act's passage in 2012 as a breakthrough. It aimed to curb abuses by prohibiting lawmakers from using insider information for personal gain. It also required disclosure of their trades. The law, with its catchy acronym—Stop Trading on Congressional Knowledge—seemed a step toward accountability. But its impact was superficial at best. Authorities responded to STOCK Act violations with minimal fines, often as low as $200, offering little deterrence when fortunes were at stake. Enforcement was virtually nonexistent. Over 78 documented violations of the STOCK Act occurred in the decade following its enactment, yet not a single lawmaker faced significant consequences. The legislation became a paper shield, more symbol than substance.

Consider Senator Richard Burr. As chairman of the Senate Intelligence Committee, officials briefed him in January 2020 about the impending severity of the COVID-19 pandemic. While publicly reassuring Americans of the country's preparedness, Burr privately sold over $1 million in stocks, shifting his investments to safe treasury securities. Within weeks, the market plunged. Burr's trades, meticulously timed, shielded him from losses while millions of Americans saw their retirement accounts decimated. His defense? He acted on public information—a claim difficult to disprove but harder still to believe. Investigations by the FBI and SEC ultimately went nowhere, underscoring the difficulty of enforcing insider trading laws against lawmakers.

Nancy Pelosi's financial dealings, while not as overtly suspicious, illustrate another facet of the problem. As Speaker of the House, Pelosi wielded immense influence over legislation, yet her household's stock trades routinely aligned with major policy shifts. During the pandemic, the Pelosi family's net worth soared by 60%, largely because of investments in companies directly impacted by legislation she oversaw.

For example, her husband, Paul Pelosi, purchased millions in Tesla stock as Congress debated electric vehicle subsidies. Investors copying Pelosi's trades would later celebrate the move. While no direct evidence of insider trading has surfaced, the optics are undeniable. When public servants consistently outperform the market by margins that would make Warren Buffett envious, skepticism is inevitable.

The conflicts of interest extend beyond individuals to the systemic interplay between lawmakers and the industries they regulate. Senator David Perdue served on the Senate Banking, Housing, and Urban Affairs Committee. He traded stocks in financial institutions like JPMorgan Chase and Bank of America while overseeing their regulatory framework. Similarly, trades in cybersecurity firm FireEye occurred while Perdue sat on a cybersecurity panel privy to classified information. These patterns reveal a troubling dynamic: lawmakers are often both players and referees in the economic arenas they regulate, creating an inherent conflict of interest.

The problem extends beyond the United States. Globally, the intertwining of political power and financial gain is a persistent issue. In some nations, corruption is apparent, with politicians directly enriching themselves through graft. In others, the methods are subtler but no less corrosive. The use of privileged information, opaque financial disclosures, and regulatory loopholes undermines trust in democratic systems worldwide. This erosion of trust has far-reaching consequences. Democracy relies on believing in fairness, the view that elected officials serve the public rather than themselves. When that belief falters, the entire system is at risk.

The consequences of this erosion are not abstract. Trust in American institutions has been steadily declining for decades. A 2022 Gallup poll showed only 7% of Americans expressed confidence in Congress. This was the lowest of any institution surveyed. This cynicism feeds disengagement, voter apathy, and polarization, creating a feedback loop that further entrenches dysfunction. The perception that lawmakers operate by different rules, profiting while the public struggles, fuels resentment and weakens the social contract.

Efforts to reform these practices face significant obstacles, not least because the people tasked with enacting change are the beneficiaries of the status quo. Proposals to ban stock trading by lawmakers have gained traction in recent years, with bipartisan support in principle but little action in practice. Cynics argue that self-regulation is unlikely when it conflicts with personal financial interests. The challenge is not just legal but cultural: shifting the norms that have allowed these practices to flourish requires sustained public pressure and political will.

The broader implications of insider trading in Congress go beyond financial ethics. They touch on the very nature of governance and the role of elected officials in society. When lawmakers prioritize personal gain over public service, they betray the principles of democracy and deepen the divides that threaten its survival. Trust, once broken, is difficult to restore. In an era of unprecedented challenges—from climate change to economic inequality—the need for transparent, accountable leadership has never been greater. Yet, as the stories of Bacchus, Burr, Pelosi, and others reveal, the gap between rhetoric and reality remains vast.

History teaches us that systems built on inequality and distrust eventually collapse under their own weight. The question is whether modern democracies will address these challenges proactively or succumb to the forces of disillusionment and decline. The stakes are nothing less than the future of governance itself. As long as those in power profit from their privileged positions, the promise of democracy will remain unfulfilled. It becomes a beacon dimmed by the shadow of self-interest. Only by confronting these realities head-on can society begin to rebuild the trust and integrity on which lasting progress depends.

The story of wealth is often told through the lens of human ingenuity and ambition. Yet, beneath this narrative lies a primal truth: wealth begins with control over the Earth's resources. Elites derive their power not just from innovation but from controlling oil wells in the Middle East and cobalt mines in Africa. It rests on a monopoly over what nature provides. This shift from innovation to domination reveals an unsettling truth. A small elite has systematically hoarded natural resources— water, minerals, land, and energy. This creates global disparities that extend far beyond economics. We will see into this uneasy relationship between humanity's consumption and the Earth's limits, revealing how natural depletion has become the keystone of inequality.

2. NATURAL DEPLETION

Beneath the surface of modern progress lies a simple yet staggering reality: the world's wealthiest individuals owe much of their power to the Earth itself. Oil, minerals, and land have shaped the trajectory of human history as much as the great wars and revolutions they have funded. However, this is not a story of mutual benefit between humanity and the planet but of extraction, exclusion, and exploitation. Governments and corporations plan to turn the natural wealth of nations into private profits. Local populations, however, bear the brunt of environmental and economic costs. This systemic hoarding of resources fuels global inequality and accelerates depleting the very resources on which humanity depends. As we dig deeper into this interplay, the way we manage—or mismanage—the Earth's bounty will define the trajectory of our collective future.

Concentrating wealth in the hands of the 1% is not a coincidence. Nor is it a natural evolution of economic systems. It results from deliberate actions and strategies, many revolving around the control and exploitation of natural resources. At its core, wealth ties back to the earth itself. The oil beneath its surface. The minerals locked in its crust. The forests, rivers, and fertile lands that sustain life. Elites have mastered the art of shaping economies around natural resources. They ensure that extraction, ownership, and trade funnel profits upward. Most people, however, receive little more than the remnants. This dominance over natural resources is not just a marker of wealth. It is a cornerstone of power. Policies, legal frameworks, and global systems work together to favor the elite.

The story of concentrated wealth begins with the way governments and corporations collaborate to seize and monopolize natural resources. Consider the global oil industry, where a handful of corporations—such as ExxonMobil, Shell, and Chevron—control much of the world's production and distribution. These companies often operate with the full support of governments, which provide subsidies, tax breaks, and even military interventions to secure access to oil-rich regions. The Iraq War, for instance, was not just a geopolitical conflict; it was also a means of opening Iraq's vast oil reserves to Western corporations. The U.S. government spent billions of taxpayer dollars on military operations, only for the resulting contracts and profits to flow to private oil companies and their shareholders. Meanwhile, the people of Iraq, whose land was the source of this wealth, faced displacement, economic instability, and environmental degradation.

This pattern extends far beyond oil. In mining, companies like Glencore and Rio Tinto dominate global markets for essential minerals such as cobalt, lithium, and gold. These resources are critical to modern technologies, from smartphones to electric vehicles, and their extraction often occurs in developing countries under exploitative conditions. Governments, eager to attract foreign investment, frequently offer mining companies generous terms, including low taxes and lax environmental regulations. Corporations export the profits, leaving local communities to face polluted landscapes, health crises, and minimal economic benefit. In the Democratic Republic of Congo, cobalt mining has become a multibillion-dollar industry. Yet, miners often work in dangerous, informal conditions. They earn a little more than poverty wages.

The process of funneling resource wealth to the elite also involves reshaping economies to prioritize resource extraction over other forms of development. Many resource-rich nations become heavily dependent on exporting raw materials, a phenomenon known as the "resource curse." This dependency creates a fragile economic system where a few elites control the wealth generated by resource exports, while the broader population remains excluded from the benefits. Governments often enforce this dynamic through privatization, selling off public resources to corporations under the guise of efficiency and modernization. This transfer of ownership ensures that profits flow to private hands rather than being reinvested in public goods like education, healthcare, or infrastructure.

Elites manipulate natural resources, extending to land itself, using legal and financial systems to amass vast tracts of agricultural or urban land. In many countries, a small percentage of individuals control the majority of arable land, concentrating ownership. This concentration forces small farmers and indigenous communities off their lands, either through legal dispossession or coercive practices. Once in control, elites use the land for industrial agriculture, real estate development, or speculative investments, further consolidating their wealth. In Brazil, land grabs in the Amazon have allowed agribusinesses to expand. This expansion happens at the expense of indigenous peoples and the rainforest itself. A global network of investors profits while ecosystems and livelihoods face destruction.

Governments play a critical role in maintaining this system, acting as intermediaries between the elite and the general population. Taxation policies, trade agreements, and legal frameworks ensure that resource wealth concentrates in the hands of the few instead of being distributed. Tax incentives and subsidies for resource industries are often justified as necessary for economic growth, yet they disproportionately benefit large corporations. Governments tax ordinary citizens on labor and consumption, forcing them to bear the financial burden of maintaining systems that exclude them. Trade agreements like NAFTA or WTO rules further reinforce this dynamic by prioritizing the interests of multinational corporations over local economies and labor rights.

The ultimate source of wealth, then, lies not in abstract financial instruments or entrepreneurial genius but in the earth itself. The control of natural resources, facilitated by governmental and corporate collusion, is the signature of elite power. This system not only generates immense profits for the 1% but also ensures a steady flow of wealth by locking the 99% out of ownership and decision-making. This fundamental imbalance shapes the global economy, using natural resources as the foundation to build and perpetuate inequality. Without addressing this exploitation at its root, efforts to create a more equitable world will remain incomplete.

If the control of natural resources underscores the dynamics of inequality, the relentless consumption of these resources paints an even bleaker picture. Every drop of water, ounce of cobalt, or barrel of oil extracted feeds a system that thrives on scarcity and imbalance. But as the demands of humanity grow, the Earth's capacity to sustain this exploitation is faltering. The first challenge is to confront the scale of the crisis: a planet straining under the weight of human consumption.

2.1 EARTH CAN'T KEEP UP!

The Earth is groaning under the weight of humanity's appetite. Industries pump billions of gallons of water from aquifers each year, depleting them faster than they can replenish. Miners extract millions of tons of rare minerals each year, sacrificing ecosystems. Industries burn fossil fuels with little regard for their devastating climatic impact. This relentless consumption has brought the planet to a tipping point. Crises like Cape Town's "Day Zero" and California's recurring droughts offer sobering reminders of water scarcity. Meanwhile, cobalt and lithium extraction for tech industries leaves behind environmental devastation and human suffering. Yet, amidst these challenges, the seeds of innovation emerge. From advanced water reclamation to recycling metals from e-waste, humanity has glimpsed solutions that could rewrite this bleak trajectory. But will we act in time, or will the Earth's breaking point become our own?

The state of the world's natural resources is a stark reminder that humanity's voracious consumption has pushed the planet to its limits. Water, minerals, and fossil fuels—resources that have sustained civilizations for centuries—are now under immense pressure, teetering on the edge of depletion or collapse. This crisis is not merely a distant threat; it is a lived reality for billions of people today, reshaping economies, societies, and even geopolitics. As the global population grows and resource demand accelerates, the strain on critical elements of life becomes ever more acute. This exposes the fragility of our systems and highlights the urgent need for a sustainable reimagining of their use.

Water, the essence of life, is now a source of scarcity for over 2 billion people globally. This crisis extends beyond arid regions and underdeveloped nations. Even some of the most advanced cities have come perilously close to running dry. Cape Town, South Africa, captured global attention in 2018 when "Day Zero" approached, threatening to cut off municipal water supplies entirely. Severe drought, compounded by overuse and mismanagement, left the city's reservoirs critically depleted. Officials forced residents to ration water to 50 liters per person per day. In the United States, California's recurring droughts have become emblematic of a broader crisis, with reservoirs like Lake Mead and Lake Powell shrinking to historic lows. Agriculture, industry, and domestic use compete fiercely for dwindling supplies, while climate change accelerates the crisis by disrupting rainfall and increasing evaporation. The crisis reveals not just a shortage of water but a failure to manage it equitably and sustainably.

Depleting minerals and metals essential for modern technology presents another pressing concern. Cobalt and lithium, critical components of batteries for electric vehicles and renewable energy storage, are at the heart of this challenge. The surging demand for these materials has created a race to extract them, often at great environmental and social cost. In the Democratic Republic of Congo, which produces over 70% of the world's cobalt, mining operations have led to widespread deforestation, soil degradation, and water contamination. The human toll is staggering, with tens of thousands of workers, including children, laboring in hazardous conditions. Lithium extraction, concentrated in countries like Chile, Argentina, and Bolivia, poses similar challenges. The process requires vast amounts of water, leading to conflicts with local communities and ecosystems in already arid regions. As reserves dwindle and demand continues to climb, the race for these critical materials threatens to deepen global inequalities and ecological destruction.

Fossil fuels, the backbone of the industrial era, are another resource under immense strain. While reserves of oil and natural gas have not yet run dry, their extraction is becoming increasingly complex and costly, pushing humanity into ever riskier endeavors. Offshore drilling in deep-sea environments, fracking in shale-rich regions, and tar sands extraction in Canada are emblematic of this trend, each with severe environmental consequences. These methods disrupt ecosystems and exacerbate climate change, as burning fossil fuels remains the largest contributor to greenhouse gas emissions. The International Energy Agency (IEA) expects global demand for oil to peak within the next two decades. However, the environmental cost of reaching that peak is already being felt. The melting Arctic stands as a stark warning. Oil companies now eye its untapped reserves, a sign of the extent humanity will go to sustain its fossil fuel addiction.

These crises connect deeply with broader global patterns; they are deeply interconnected. The overuse of water, minerals, and fossil fuels reflects a broader pattern of unsustainable resource exploitation that prioritizes short-term gains over long-term resilience. As reserves shrink and environmental damage grows, the burden will fall unequally. Developing nations, often rich in resources but poor in capital, are disproportionately affected, bearing the brunt of environmental degradation and resource conflicts. Meanwhile, the global elite continue to extract profits, leaving the majority to grapple with the consequences. The precarious state of natural resources highlights an urgent need for transformation. Humanity must shift how it manages its relationship with the planet. A shift that values sustainability and equity over consumption and profit.

The quest for sustainability in a world of dwindling resources has spurred remarkable advancements in technologies for resource reuse. From reclaiming water to recycling metals and recovering energy from waste, humanity is developing tools that could redefine its relationship with the planet. These innovations are not just incremental improvements; They signal a shift from linear consumption to circular systems, where people regenerate resources instead of simply using and discarding them. These technologies hold great promise. They can address resource shortages, reduce environmental harm, and build resilience as global demand grows.

Water reclamation and desalination have emerged as critical solutions to the global water crisis. Technologies like reverse osmosis, which uses semi-permeable membranes to filter out salt and impurities from seawater, have become the cornerstone of modern desalination plants. These facilities, such as the Carlsbad Desalination Plant in California, provide potable water to millions, offering a lifeline in drought-stricken regions. However, reverse osmosis is energy intensive, and its high costs and environmental impacts—such as brine discharge—highlight the need for more efficient alternatives. Emerging technologies, like graphene-based filters, hold immense promise. Graphene, a material only one atom thick, can desalinate water at a fraction of the energy cost of conventional methods, potentially revolutionizing water management. Such advancements could make water reclamation accessible even in resource-poor regions, transforming how humanity navigates scarcity.

Recycling metals is a critical frontier in the fight against resource depletion. This is especially true as demand for materials like cobalt, lithium, and rare earth elements continues to surge. The sheer volume of electronic waste—estimated at 53.6 million metric tons in 2019—represents both a challenge and an opportunity. Advanced recycling techniques now extract valuable metals from discarded smartphones, laptops, and industrial machinery. Methods such as hydrometallurgical processing, which uses chemical solutions to dissolve and recover metals, are increasingly efficient. Companies like Umicore, a leader in precious metal recycling, have developed facilities capable of extracting up to 95% of metals from e-waste. Automobiles and industrial equipment also offer rich sources of recyclable materials. Innovations in shredding and magnetic separation enable the recovery of steel, aluminum, and copper, reducing the need for virgin mining and its associated environmental costs. Scaling these technologies globally could significantly offset resource depletion, turning waste into a renewable treasure trove.

Energy recovery from waste plays a critical role in sustainable resource management, turning what people once discarded into a valuable power source. Technologies like pyrolysis and anaerobic digestion convert organic and non-organic waste into energy, reducing landfill volumes and greenhouse gas emissions. Pyrolysis, a process that heats waste without oxygen, produces synthetic fuels and biochar to enrich soil. This method is particularly effective for plastic waste, addressing one of the most persistent environmental pollutants. Anaerobic digestion, on the other hand, uses microorganisms to break down organic waste, generating biogas that can power homes, vehicles, and industries. Countries like Sweden have embraced anaerobic digestion on a large scale, converting food and agricultural waste into energy that fuels entire cities. These technologies not only mitigate the environmental impact of waste but also contribute to energy security, offering a sustainable alternative to fossil fuels.

Together, these innovations in water reclamation, metal recycling, and energy recovery illustrate the potential of human ingenuity to tackle the pressing challenges of resource depletion. Yet, their success depends on scaling them globally, integrating them into existing systems, and ensuring equitable access. As these technologies advance, they offer a compelling vision of the future. A world where humanity thrives without exhausting the planet. People perpetually regenerate resources rather than merely consuming them, sustaining ecosystems and humanity for generations.

As Earth's resources dwindle, one constant remains: the wealth they generate rarely benefits everyone equally. Instead, the profits flow upward, creating pipelines of power and privilege that allow select elites to dominate. The systems that enable this inequity—corporate monopolies, government collusion, and legal loopholes— deserve scrutiny as we uncover the stark realities behind the world's economic elite.

2.2 ELITE ZONE: TRESPASSERS PROSECUTED

Across the world, corporations and governments cloak natural resources in barbed wire—both literal and figurative—to ensure their wealth stays in elite hands. From the timber laws in Brazil to the water rights in Australia, the pattern is unmistakable. Governments grant multinational corporations and state-backed entities unfettered access to the Earth's bounty. Small-scale miners, farmers, and communities, however, face severe penalties for even attempting to share in it. The cobalt mines of Africa, the pipelines of Nigeria, and the oil reserves of Russia all tell the same story of exclusion and control. By criminalizing access and deploying state power to protect elite interests, these systems deepen inequality and transform the planet's resources into tools of oppression. The laws that govern these practices may be legal, but they are far from just.

The mechanisms by which governments regulate natural resources deeply entrench wealth within the hands of the 1%. States around the world have built a system that favors large corporations and penalizes individual access. Legal frameworks ensure that a few elites monopolize resources and the immense wealth they generate. Corporations and governments often present this system as necessary for sustainable development, national security, or economic stability. However, a closer examination reveals its true purpose. It solidifies inequality by ensuring that the 99% remain excluded from meaningful ownership or benefit.

Consider Brazil's logging industry, regulated under the Environmental Crimes Law (Law No. 9.605/1998). This law ostensibly protects the Amazon from illegal deforestation. Yet, its enforcement disproportionately targets small-scale operators, indigenous communities, and local farmers. Vast swathes of forest remain accessible to large certified corporations with government ties. These companies secure permits for "sustainable logging," yet their operations often result in large-scale deforestation and ecological harm. The penalties for unauthorized logging are severe. Fines and imprisonment of up to four years ensure that profits from Brazil's vast timber resources remain concentrated among a select few corporations. Meanwhile, local communities who depend on the forest for their livelihoods face criminalization for minor infractions.

In Russia, the Federal Law on Subsoil Resources restricts oil extraction to companies granted government licenses. Governments typically award these licenses to corporations with close political ties, like Rosneft and Gazprom, creating an oligopoly. Unauthorized extraction, even by small-scale operators, is punishable by fines and up to five years of imprisonment. This tightly controlled system ensures that wealth from Russia's massive oil reserves flows to a handful of state-aligned entities and their shareholders. Ordinary citizens, meanwhile, see little benefit. The result is a stark divide between the wealth concentrated in Moscow's elite circles and the widespread poverty in oil-producing regions.

In Nigeria, a country where oil accounts for over 90% of export revenue, the Petroleum Industry Act grants exclusive rights to national and multinational oil companies. Tampering with oil pipelines can result in imprisonment for up to 21 years. It is often a desperate act, carried out by impoverished communities seeking access to the wealth flowing beneath their feet. This legal framework ensures that Nigeria's oil wealth enriches a small political and corporate elite while leaving the majority of Nigerians in poverty. Despite being Africa's largest oil producer, over 40% of Nigeria's population lives below the poverty line, a glaring testament to the inequities perpetuated by these laws.

Indonesia's Law No. 4 of 2009 on Mineral and Coal Mining illustrates a similar dynamic in the mining sector. The law grants licenses to large corporations, often backed by the military or government officials. Small-scale or informal miners often lack the resources to navigate the licensing process. Authorities criminalize them, imposing fines of up to 10 billion IDR and imprisonment for up to 10 years. These penalties funnel profits from Indonesia's abundant mineral wealth—coal and gold—to large corporations like PT Freeport Indonesia. Local communities, meanwhile, grapple with environmental degradation and economic exclusion.

South Africa's Mineral and Petroleum Resources Development Act also underscores how mining laws favor elite interests. Major corporations dominate extracting gold, platinum, and diamonds, resources forming the backbone of the country's economy. Unauthorized mining, often undertaken by desperate individuals in abandoned mines, is punishable by imprisonment of up to 10 years. This system consolidates wealth among a small group of mining magnates. Millions of South Africans live in poverty. They have limited access to the wealth generated by their nation's resources.

The legal frameworks extend beyond minerals and oil to other critical resources. In Australia, the Water Act 2007 governs allocating water rights, prioritizing agricultural and industrial use by corporations over community needs. Water theft, often a survival tactic by drought-stricken farmers, is punishable by heavy fines and imprisonment. These penalties ensure that corporations like Murray-Darling Basin Authority maintain control over water resources. These resources are critical to both life and agriculture. Similarly, in India, the Environment Protection Act, 1986 restricts sand mining to government-leased operations, penalizing informal miners with fines and imprisonment. Sand, essential for construction and infrastructure, has become a lucrative resource for companies with government backing, leaving small-scale miners vulnerable to exploitation and legal action.

Even in resource-rich countries like Zambia and the Democratic Republic of Congo (DRC), the story is the same. The DRC's Mining Code and Zambia's Mines and Minerals Development Act of 2015 grant cobalt mining rights to multinational corporations like Glencore and China Molybdenum. Authorities impose severe penalties, including imprisonment and asset forfeiture, for smuggling or informal mining. These laws ensure that cobalt, a resource critical to the global tech industry, benefits companies like Tesla and Apple. Local miners earn poverty wages and endure hazardous working conditions.

In the United States and Canada, natural resource laws similarly favor corporate entities. The Energy Policy Act in the U.S. grants drilling and extraction permits to corporations like ExxonMobil, with penalties for unauthorized activities varying by state. In Canada, sustainable forestry laws require logging permits that are predominantly issued to large corporations, criminalizing small-scale logging with fines and imprisonment of up to 10 years.

Across the globe, these laws form a web of regulations designed to exclude the majority from accessing natural resources. Governments criminalize small-scale activities and prioritize corporate interests, ensuring that the wealth from these resources concentrates among the 1%. This system sustains the economic dominance of elites. It perpetuates a cycle of inequality, where resources that should benefit, everyone are instead used to solidify the power and wealth of a select few.

Amidst the barriers and inequities of resource control lies an undeniable truth: scarcity is also a catalyst for innovation. When pushed to the brink, humanity's capacity for ingenuity has often turned crises into opportunities. The challenge now is to leverage this potential not for profit alone, but for the collective good of a planet and its people.

3. STAY UNEMPLOYED

Many discuss unemployment as a grim statistic or cyclical inevitability, but in reality, the global economy intentionally constructs and embeds it. For elites, unemployment is not a problem to be solved, but a feature to be leveraged. A jobless workforce suppresses wages, weakens collective bargaining, and ensures a steady supply of desperate labor—all of which translates to record profits for corporations. Industries that prey on economic despair, such as payday loans and for-profit education, thrive in this fertile ground of insecurity. Governments, far from countering this trend, often perpetuate it, using unemployment as a tool to stabilize economies for the wealthy at the expense of the vulnerable. In truth, the billionaire business model doesn't just tolerate unemployment—it depends on it.

The pressure of high unemployment exerts a gravitational pull-on wages. When there are more people seeking jobs than available positions, employers gain the upper hand in negotiating terms. Desperate for income, workers accept lower pay, longer hours, and precarious contracts. This dynamic is especially evident in industries that rely on low-wage labor, such as manufacturing, retail, and gig work. Companies like Amazon thrive in environments where job scarcity ensures a steady supply of workers willing to endure grueling conditions for minimal compensation. The result is not only higher profit margins for corporations but also a downward spiral for wages across the board, further concentrating wealth at the top.

Unemployment also erodes the bargaining power of unions and organized labor, which historically have been the most effective tools for challenging inequality. When jobs are scarce, the threat of being replaced looms large, deterring workers from demanding better pay or conditions. This enables corporations to bypass collective demands, secure favorable contracts, and implement cost-cutting measures with little resistance. In sectors like logistics and agriculture, weakened unions allow companies to maintain razor-thin operating costs while reaping enormous profits. The irony is that the very fear of unemployment—a fear born of scarcity—is what enables the wealthy to accumulate more, as workers become increasingly expendable.

Moreover, the unemployed are not merely passive victims; their existence fuels industries that profit from economic despair. Payday loan companies, credit card providers, and rent-to-own schemes prey on those who lack steady income, charging exorbitant interest rates that trap people in cycles of debt. These financial instruments, while marketed as lifelines, ultimately enrich the lenders, many of whom are subsidiaries of major financial institutions. In 2022 alone, the U.S. payday loan industry generated over $9 billion in revenue, much of it extracted from communities with high unemployment rates. Similarly, for-profit educational institutions and retraining programs target the unemployed, offering costly courses that promise to increase employability but often deliver little value. These industries capitalize on the desperation of those seeking a way out, converting their struggle into revenue streams for shareholders and executives.

The unemployed also serve as a tool to maintain societal stability in favor of the elite. Governments, under pressure from corporations, often implement minimal social safety nets that keep the unemployed on the edge of survival without empowering them to demand systemic change. Governments design programs like unemployment benefits or food assistance to prevent rebellion while maintaining dependence on a system that perpetuates exclusion. This precarious existence creates a divided workforce. Employed workers live in constant fear of losing their jobs. Those who are unemployed remain too burdened by immediate needs to challenge the broader system.

At a macroeconomic level, policymakers often weaponized unemployment as a tool to curb inflation and protect the interests of capital. Central banks, in their pursuit of "stable" economies, prioritize low inflation over full employment. Policymakers tolerate—even engineer—higher unemployment because it reduces consumer demand and keeps prices stable. Yet this stability overwhelmingly benefits the wealthy, who hold most assets and escape the hardships of joblessness. For example, during periods of high unemployment, stock markets often thrive as companies report lower labor costs and improved profit margins, boosting returns for investors. In this way, the very existence of unemployment becomes a driver of wealth for those at the top.

Even automation, often touted as a solution to labor inefficiencies, plays into this dynamic. Replacing human workers with machines exacerbates unemployment while enhancing the productivity and profitability of corporations. The gains from automation rarely trickle down to the displaced workers. Instead, shareholders and executives absorb the benefits. In industries like logistics and manufacturing, robotics, and AI have driven record profits for companies like Amazon and Tesla. Meanwhile, companies replace workers, leaving them to fend for themselves.

The cycle is self-reinforcing. High unemployment ensures a cheap, compliant labor force, which maximizes profits for the elite. These profits are then used to lobby for policies that maintain the status quo. These policies favor deregulation, weaken social safety nets, and prioritize corporate interests over public welfare. Meanwhile, the unemployed, though excluded from the system, remain its silent enablers, their desperation fueling the very conditions that keep the elite at the top. This system turns suffering into wealth and ensures that inequality not only persists but deepens with each economic cycle.

In the vast and teeming public maidans of India, dust swirls with the shouts of restless crowds. An extraordinary phenomenon unfolds whenever a celebrity or politician graces the stage. Unemployed men and women, many facing the crushing weight of economic uncertainty, flock to these events with a dedication that defies logic. They climb towering mast lights and precariously dangle from rooftops. They risk life and limb for a fleeting glimpse of a figure whose life is worlds apart from their own. These celebrities and politicians, ensconced in luxury and power, become deities in the eyes of the struggling masses. For those in the crowd, this moment is not just entertainment; it is a desperate attempt to touch something larger than themselves, a fleeting escape from the monotony of their daily struggles.

But this spectacle is more than mere adulation—it is a mirror held up to society's inequalities. Why would a person risk their life just to see someone who exists in a stratosphere of unimaginable privilege? The answer lies in the architecture of disenfranchisement. The elites who command the wealth and resources of the nation have built a system that feeds off this desperation. By denying millions the opportunities for education, employment, and dignity, they create a void in which the promise of transcendence becomes irresistible. For the unemployed and disenfranchised, these gatherings offer a rare chance of feeling connected to something grand. They affirm that they too are part of a shared narrative—even if that narrative is designed to exploit their aspirations.

Organizers meticulously construct these events, turning them into spectacles rather than organic celebrations of stardom or leadership. Celebrities and politicians, aware of the power dynamics at play, rely on these throngs to fuel their own egos and maintain their relevance. The size of the crowd becomes a metric of their influence, a visual testament to their ability to command attention. But what are these displays without the laboring masses? If the elite were to create a society where every individual had access to meaningful work and economic security, the crowds would dwindle. The unemployed would no longer have the time or the emotional need to participate in these orchestrated gatherings, robbing celebrities and politicians of their human props.

In this framework, the unemployed are not just victims of systemic inequality—they are pawns in a game designed to sustain the power structures of the elite. These gatherings, far from celebrating talent or leadership, stage the disenfranchised as background characters in someone else's story. The tragedy is not just the risk they take by climbing precarious heights to catch a glimpse of the stage. Their labor and attention serve as the scaffolding that builds these grand illusions. As long as elites prioritize their egos over societal progress, the maidans will remain crowded. The mast lights will continue to bear the weight of desperate climbers, and the cycle of exploitation will persist—cloaked in the guise of adoration.

Policymakers have systematically reshaped unemployment from a societal ill into a calculated advantage. History reveals a consistent pattern of exploiting joblessness to consolidate wealth and suppress dissent, turning what should be an aberration into a cornerstone of economic policy. To understand this phenomenon, we must first examine how the machinery of capitalism intentionally creates and sustains a reservoir of the unemployed.

3.1 JOBLESS ON PURPOSE: PROFITS FIRST!

The Industrial Revolution transformed humanity's relationship with labor, but its promises of progress came at a heavy price. As factories replaced fields, industrialists displaced millions, creating a desperate workforce willing to accept any wage. This "reserve army of labor," as Marx described it, founded a system designed to maximize profits at the expense of dignity. In the Great Depression, mass unemployment justified policies that concentrated wealth and marginalized workers further. Post-war strategies institutionalized unemployment as a tool to suppress labor movements and stabilize inflation, ensuring the continued dominance of economic elites. Far from being accidental, elites weaponized unemployment to serve their interests.

Many view unemployment as a temporary setback, a fluctuation in economies striving for equilibrium. Yet, it is a far more complex phenomenon, encompassing a range of forms: cyclical unemployment, which rises and falls with the ebb and flow of economic activity; structural unemployment, where technological advancements or shifts in industry render certain skills obsolete; and frictional unemployment, the brief interlude as individuals transition between jobs. Beyond these definitions lies a more provocative reality: sustained high unemployment is not merely a byproduct of economic mismanagement or inevitable technological progress. It can, and often does, serve the interests of the economic and political elites. For those at the top of the wealth pyramid, unemployment offers tools of control, pathways to profit, and mechanisms to consolidate their position. This paradox, in which jobless individuals suffer while the powerful grow richer, runs deeply through the history of modern economies.

This dynamic traces its roots to the seismic shifts of the 18th and 19th centuries, when agrarian economies transformed into industrial powerhouses. The Industrial Revolution, often celebrated for its innovations, introduced mass unemployment as a new and permanent feature of society. As machinery replaced manual labor on farms and in small workshops, millions found themselves displaced, wandering newly industrialized cities in search of work. For the emerging capitalist class, this surplus labor force was less a problem and more an opportunity. The unemployed created a reserve army of labor—a pool of workers so desperate for wages that they would accept long hours, low pay, and inhumane conditions. This arrangement not only maximized profits for factory owners but also suppressed wages across industries, as workers competed against one another for the few jobs available. Unemployment, far from being an accident of progress, became a lever that elites could pull to maintain economic dominance.

The 1930s brought the phenomenon into stark relief during the Great Depression, a global economic collapse that saw unemployment in the United States rise to nearly 25%. For millions, joblessness meant destitution and despair, but for political and economic elites, it was both a challenge and an opportunity. On one hand, mass unemployment fueled radical political movements, from labor strikes to socialist uprisings, that threatened elite control. On the other hand, it provided a rationale for consolidating wealth and power under the guise of recovery. Programs like the New Deal provided jobs and stabilized the economy. Yet, they also reinforced corporate dominance through public-private partnerships that funneled resources into large-scale infrastructure projects. Even in crisis, the elite found ways to benefit, using unemployment to justify policies that preserved their wealth while offering minimal concessions to the broader population.

The post-World War II era ushered in economic policies aimed at balancing full employment with elite wealth preservation. In capitalist democracies like the United States, the Cold War fueled efforts to project economic dominance over the Soviet Union. Initiatives such as the GI Bill integrated millions of soldiers into the workforce, promoting education and home ownership to bolster the post-war economy. However, unemployment remained a strategic tool for economic management. Influenced by Keynesian theories, policymakers maintained just enough unemployment to suppress inflation and avoid unrest, institutionalizing this approach through central bank policies.

Defense and infrastructure spending enriched elites, particularly those tied to military and industrial sectors. President Eisenhower's warning about the military-industrial complex underscored how public funds generated private profits. Despite lower unemployment, wealth concentration persisted, with elites capturing the majority of economic gains.

From the Industrial Revolution onward, unemployment evolved into a calculated feature of economic systems, both a threat to stability and a tool for control. Policymakers weaponized it, using the lack of work to reinforce inequality and maintain power structures.

Elites engineered the machinery of unemployment, while economic theories provided a layer of justification. From Keynesian interventions to neoliberal austerity, these frameworks shaped policies that perpetuated inequality. To understand how this intellectual evolution cemented unemployment as a systemic feature, we turn to the ideological roots of modern economic management.

3.2 TURNING JOB LOSS INTO LOAN GAINS

For the modern corporation, unemployment is not merely an external condition, but an integral part of its strategy. High joblessness suppresses wages, allowing giants like Amazon and Walmart to maximize profits. Financial institutions profit from the fallout, as unemployed workers turn to personal loans and credit cards to make ends meet. Governments, influenced by corporate lobbying, deregulate labor markets and privatize public assets, further entrenching inequality. Globally, multinational corporations exploit high unemployment in developing nations to set up low-wage operations, ensuring astronomical profits at the expense of local communities. This calculated manipulation of joblessness not only enriches the elite but destabilizes societies, making unemployment a cornerstone of modern capitalism's exploitative machinery.

Unemployment is not merely a symptom of economic downturns or market inefficiencies; it is a calculated feature of modern economies that disproportionately benefits the elite. By keeping a significant portion of the workforce unemployed, corporations, and financial institutions maintain control over labor markets, political systems, and even global trade dynamics. This dynamic feeds a vicious cycle. Unemployment suppresses wages and erodes worker rights. It also creates financial opportunities that further enrich those at the top, particularly in industries tied to banking and natural resource extraction.

High unemployment exerts downward pressure on wages, giving corporations the upper hand in labor negotiations. When millions of workers compete for scarce jobs, their ability to demand better pay or working conditions diminishes. This dynamic allows companies to keep wages low while boosting profit margins. During the 2008 financial crisis, U.S. unemployment peaked at 10%. This created an environment where companies could restructure their labor forces, reduce benefits, and automate jobs without significant pushback. Between 2009 and 2012, while workers struggled with stagnant wages and precarious employment, corporate profits soared by over 40%. Companies like Walmart and Amazon, which thrive on low-wage labor, capitalized on this dynamic, expanding their operations and reaping record-breaking profits. The wealth generated through this labor exploitation flowed directly into the hands of shareholders and executives, further widening the gap between the 1% and the rest.

The banking sector also plays a critical role in profiting from unemployment, particularly through the mechanics of lending and debt. When unemployment rises, individuals, and governments alike turn to loans to survive economic hardships. For banks, this creates an opportunity to issue credit at high interest rates, expanding their influence over both private and public sectors. Consider the aftermath of the 2008 crisis. As unemployment surged, household debt in the United States hit $14 trillion by 2010. Millions relied on credit cards, mortgages, and payday loans to cover basic expenses. After receiving taxpayer-funded bailouts, banks became flush with liquidity and eager to lend. This increased reliance on debt tied households to a cycle of repayments, effectively transferring wealth from the unemployed to financial institutions.

Governments facing unemployment crises often resort to taking large loans from international banks or financial institutions like the International Monetary Fund (IMF). These loans, ostensibly intended to fund job creation programs or stabilize economies, come with stringent conditions that often exacerbate inequality. For example, many loans require privatizing state-owned assets, including natural resources, which corporations then purchase at discounted rates. This dynamic is particularly visible in resource-rich developing countries. In Zambia, where unemployment hovers around 11%, the government has repeatedly borrowed from international institutions to stabilize its economy. In exchange, it has privatized industries like copper mining, allowing multinational corporations to control the country's most valuable resource. Corporations repatriate the profits from these operations to headquarters in developed nations, leaving local communities impoverished.

Unemployment also enables the elites to manipulate political systems, ensuring policies that perpetuate their dominance. High unemployment creates fertile ground for calls to deregulate labor markets under the guise of "job creation." Deregulation often leads to temporary increases in employment but at the cost of worker protections and long-term job stability. Elites, through lobbying and campaign contributions, influence governments to enact these policies, ensuring labor remains cheap and expendable. In India, recent labor reforms have made it easier for companies to hire and fire workers. Businesses celebrated this move, but unions decried it as a step toward precarious employment. Policymakers pushed these reforms through during a period of high unemployment exacerbated by the COVID-19 pandemic, showcasing how elites leverage crises to advance their interests.

The implications of unemployment extend beyond economics, shaping social and political landscapes in ways that further entrench inequality. High unemployment widens income gaps, as those at the bottom struggle with stagnant wages while the wealthy accumulate capital. According to OECD data, the top 10% of earners in developed nations now earn nearly ten times more than the bottom 10%. Joblessness has only exacerbated this disparity. Unemployment also fuels political instability, as disillusioned citizens turn to populist leaders promising radical change. However, these leaders often serve elite interests under the guise of opposing them. The rise of populist governments in countries like Brazil and Hungary has led to troubling policies. These governments dismantle labor protections and prioritize corporate interests, deepening the inequalities they claim to address.

Global trade practices further illustrate how unemployment benefits the elite, particularly in developing countries. High unemployment creates leverage for developed nations and their corporations to negotiate trade agreements that favor their interests. In regions like Southeast Asia, high joblessness forces governments to accept unfavorable terms in the hope of attracting foreign investment. Corporations like Foxconn, a major supplier for Apple, exploit this dynamic. They establish factories in areas with high unemployment, where workers accept low wages and grueling conditions. This arrangement ensures high profits for multinational corporations while offering minimal economic development for the host countries.

In this system, unemployment is not an unfortunate byproduct of capitalism but a deliberate tool wielded to maintain and expand elite power. It suppresses wages, inflates corporate profits, and drives financial dependence, all while destabilizing social and political structures to the benefit of those at the top. Debt, deregulation, and trade imbalances create a dangerous cycle. Unemployment sustains a system where many suffer to enrich the few, ensuring the wealthy remain unchallenged at the top of the global economy.

Compassion is often highlighted during economic crises. Policymakers present bailouts as salvation for the economy, but a closer look reveals who truly benefits. As workers lose their livelihoods, the elite secure their wealth, leveraging crises to consolidate power. The final section examines how this cycle plays out during moments of supposed recovery.

3.3 RESCUE PLANS: ELITE'S BONUS ROUND

Economic crises are moments of upheaval, but for the elite, they are also opportunities. During the 2008 financial crisis, corporations secured massive bailouts that enriched executives while workers faced foreclosure and poverty. In Europe, austerity measures turned public suffering into private gain, as corporations acquired assets at bargain prices. In developing nations, joblessness fueled industries that thrive on exploitation, from sweatshops to debt servitude. These crises are not exceptions to the rule but features of a system that ensures recovery for the wealthy while deepening despair for the vulnerable. Policymakers do not design rescue plans to heal; they design them to reward.

Unemployment, often lamented as a tragedy of modern economies, carries an under-explored dimension: its role as a silent architect of elite dominance. While it disempowers millions, leaving them vulnerable and voiceless, it simultaneously empowers the few, enabling them to consolidate wealth and control. This duality is not accidental but a recurring feature of economic systems that prioritize profit over people. Unemployment has visibly served elite interests in global crises over the past decades. Governments and corporations have maneuvered to transform economic downturns into opportunities for their own enrichment. This phenomenon exists across economies as disparate as the United States, the European Union, and developing nations like India and China. It reveals a pattern of exploitation that sustains the privilege of the few at the expense of the many.

Elites weaponized unemployment during the 2008 financial crisis in the United States to consolidate their wealth. In the wake of the collapse of Lehman Brothers and the ensuing financial meltdown, unemployment in the U.S. skyrocketed, peaking at 10% in October 2009. Over 15 million Americans lost their jobs, their homes, and their savings. The crisis exposed the fragility of an economy built on speculative finance. Ordinary citizens bore the brunt of the fallout. Yet Wall Street emerged stronger than ever. The federal government, under the guise of stabilizing the economy, injected $700 billion into the financial system through the Troubled Asset Relief Program (TARP). These funds primarily bailed out banks deemed "too big to fail," such as Goldman Sachs and Citigroup, whose risky practices had precipitated the crisis.

Far from being held accountable, these institutions used the bailout funds to consolidate their dominance. Executives rewarded themselves with bonuses, totaling over $18 billion in 2008 alone, even as unemployment lines lengthened across the country. Wealth concentration reached unprecedented levels during the recovery, with the top 1% capturing 95% of income gains from 2009 to 2012. Meanwhile, the unemployed faced a labor market flooded with job seekers, suppressing wages and eroding bargaining power. This dynamic created a perfect storm for corporations, which could exploit the desperate for lower wages while reaping record profits. Wall Street's gains, built by devastating Main Street, were not an anomaly but a stark reminder of how unemployment reinforces existing hierarchies.

Across the Atlantic, the European Union's response to the same crisis tells a parallel story. Following the economic downturn, austerity measures became the policy prescription of choice for nations like Greece, Spain, and Italy. These measures, ostensibly aimed at reducing government debt, often took the form of drastic public spending cuts and tax hikes. The consequences were devastating: unemployment soared to over 27% in Greece and 24% in Spain by 2013, with youth unemployment surpassing 50% in some regions. Policymakers rendered entire generations jobless, sacrificing their futures on the altar of fiscal responsibility.

Yet, even as unemployment crippled households and widened inequality, austerity proved a boon for elites. European corporations capitalized on the crisis by acquiring distressed assets—factories, infrastructure, and land—at rock-bottom prices. For example, German multinationals expanded their foothold in Southern Europe, leveraging the weakened economies to outsource production and slash labor costs. Financial institutions also benefited, earning lucrative fees from restructuring national debts while profiting from privatizing public assets. The disparity between the sacrifices demanded of ordinary citizens and the profits reaped by the wealthy revealed a harsh reality. Unemployment and economic hardship were not just unfortunate side effects. They were integral to a system that perpetuated elite dominance.

In developing economies like India and China, unemployment serves as both a symptom of structural inequality and a tool of corporate exploitation. Multinational corporations, lured by cheap labor and minimal regulation, have transformed these nations into hubs of global production. The dynamic is simple yet ruthless: high unemployment creates an oversupply of labor, enabling companies to dictate wages and working conditions. In India, the garment industry employs millions under exploitative terms. Workers earn as little as $3 a day in conditions often described as modern-day slavery. Similarly, in China, the manufacturing sector thrives on the backs of workers in sprawling factories like those operated by Foxconn, a major supplier for Apple. These workers endure grueling hours for meager pay, with their lack of alternatives ensuring compliance.

The profits generated by these labor practices flow not to the workers or even their host nations but to corporate executives and shareholders in the Global North. The wealth extracted from sweatshops and factories finds its way into stock markets and offshore accounts, further enriching the elite class. Meanwhile, the unemployed in these countries remain trapped in cycles of poverty, unable to break free from the exploitative systems that rely on their desperation. This dynamic underscores a grim irony: while unemployment devastates individuals and communities, it is an essential ingredient in the recipe for corporate profit and elite wealth accumulation.

The global interplay of unemployment and elite power highlights a troubling paradox. In theory, unemployment is a problem to be solved—a blemish on the otherwise smooth functioning of capitalist economies. It often functions as a feature of the system, a tool that concentrates wealth and cements inequality. The story is the same everywhere. Financial manipulations of Wall Street, austerity-driven policies in the European Union, and the exploitative practices of multinational corporations in developing nations fuel the same cycle. Unemployment, far from being an aberration, integrates into the fabric of modern economies, allowing those at the top to secure their dominance.

Understanding this dynamic requires more than outrage or resignation. It demands that we reevaluate how economic systems operate and whose interests they serve. As long as unemployment continues to be used as a tool for consolidating power and wealth, the promise of equitable progress will remain elusive. The challenge is twofold. It lies not just in addressing unemployment as a statistic but also in dismantling the structures that exploit it. Only then can economies serve the many rather than the privileged few.

Unemployment is often lamented as a societal failure, but the evidence suggests it is anything but accidental. It is a tool wielded by elites to suppress wages, erode rights, and maximize profits. From the Great Depression to the gig economy, elites have weaponized joblessness to concentrate wealth and entrench power. Each cycle of unemployment deepens inequality, leaving millions in despair while the 1% reap the rewards. Addressing this systemic issue requires more than superficial solutions—it demands a fundamental rethinking of how economies prioritize profit over people. The next frontier, the data economy, promises to perpetuate these dynamics unless we confront and dismantle the systems that sustain them.

If unemployment is the cornerstone of modern inequality, data is its emerging frontier. Tech corporations have commodified human behavior, replicating the exploitative systems of the past and creating new avenues for wealth concentration. As we transition to the digital age, the dynamics of power and privilege take on an unprecedented form.

Economics is the art of distributing resources, but in a world governed by greed, it becomes the art of hoarding them. The instinct to gather and protect—so vital in early human history—has created an economic system where the elite flourish while the majority struggle. From depleting natural resources to commodifying human labor, the economy mirrors the same dysfunctions that govern our relationships and politics.

Economic inequality extends its consequences far beyond bank accounts. They seep into education, explored in Chapter 6: *Education in chaos*. When wealth controls access to knowledge, future generations inherit a world that locks away tools for change, perpetuating cycles of privilege and ignorance. The dysfunction of the economy becomes the dysfunction of the classroom, shaping the future before it even begins.

6

Education in chaos

"Education is the most powerful weapon
which you can use to change the world."

– NELSON MANDELA

People often celebrate education as the great equalizer, the cornerstone of progress, and the foundation of a thriving democracy. Yet, scratch beneath the surface of these lofty ideals, and you'll uncover a far grimmer reality. Around the world, classrooms have become the frontline in a battle not for enlightenment, but for control. While public education falters under the weight of systemic neglect, private institutions thrive, not as sanctuaries of opportunity but as fortresses of privilege. Millions lack critical thinking skills. This prevents them from challenging the world they inherit. As a result, power stays concentrated in the hands of a select few. This chapter ventures into the heart of this paradox. It reveals how elites weaponize education to reinforce hierarchies rather than dismantle them.

The modern discourse on the data economy highlights a key barrier. This barrier is the lack of breakthrough technologies for data storage. Such technologies could revolutionize how we store, process, and access information. However, achieving such innovation doesn't happen in isolation; it demands a future generation enamored with science and critical thinking, driven to solve these grand challenges. A revolutionary breakthrough would have profound implications. It could liberate society from the grip of economic elites. It could also dismantle entrenched systems of social inequality. The vision is tantalizing. It envisions a world where people disperse knowledge and opportunity. Humanity thrives collectively, rather than dividing into a privileged few and an underserved many.

But let us consider what this revolution might disrupt. The elites, whose power hinges on controlling resources—be they material, financial, or intellectual—stand to lose the most. Their empires, built on the foundations of scarcity and exclusivity, would crumble if access to high-quality education and the resulting technological empowerment became universal. It begs a sobering question: would these elites, who so tightly guard their status and influence, truly endorse equal access to quality education for all? The answer, veiled in the machinations of policy and funding priorities, appears dishearteningly clear. Genuine equality in education would undermine their hegemony, making it unlikely that they would voluntarily champion such a transformative cause.

Quality education requires more than ideals. Meeting these demands requires tangible resources. This includes billions in funding for infrastructure and the training and retention of expert educators. It also involves establishing systems that foster critical thinking in even the most neglected corners of society. Yet, governments seem unwilling or unable to muster such an investment. Their priorities are starkly different. They focus on the military-industrial complex. They pursue space-faring capabilities and Mars colonization. This becomes an escape route for the elites. These pursuits, touted as humanity's next great leap, starkly contrast with the glaring deficiencies in educational systems worldwide. The irony is thick; while they proclaim to save humanity, their actions reveal a vested interest in saving themselves.

Consider Elon Musk, the celebrated entrepreneur, who has openly criticized the failures of traditional education systems. He founded Ad Astra, a school for his children. It has unique features, including no rigid grade levels. It focuses on individual strengths and interests. Its teaching methods encourage genuine engagement. It's a model that, at first glance, seems to embody the ideals of innovation and personalized learning. A privileged few confine such a model to themselves, but why? Why not extend this vision to the broader population? The exclusivity of Ad Astra mirrors a broader pattern, one we see reflected in the world's most prestigious educational institutions—MIT, Stanford, Harvard, and the like. These institutions, while ostensibly open to the brightest minds, remain accessible to a mere fraction of the population, often favoring those already ensconced in privilege. Elites and governments consciously limit access to transformative education. Only approximately 0.0067% of the global population can attend Ad Astra-style institutions. These filter out the intellectual elite to serve their interests. Meanwhile, the majority remains without access.

This exclusivity is not accidental; it is a conscious strategy. By filtering out the brightest scientific and critical thinking minds, the elites ensure a steady supply of intellectual capital to sustain their dominance. These hallowed halls train individuals to maintain the status quo. They design systems, technologies, and frameworks that perpetuate inequality rather than dismantle it. This is not education in the service of humanity; it is education in the service of power.

Meanwhile, the rhetoric of space exploration and colonization serves as a convenient distraction. Governments and corporations funnel billions into these endeavors. They aim to ensure humanity's survival as a multi-planetary species. In reality, these investments prioritize the survival of a select few. The rest of humanity grapples with underfunded education systems. They face widening inequalities and devastation from war and ecological collapse. The hypocrisy is glaring. Governments and trillionaires talk about building a future among the stars. They neglect the foundational work of equitable education on Earth.

The result is a grim paradox. Elites co-opt systems like education, innovation, and equitable resource distribution. Instead of uplifting humanity, these systems entrench existing power structures. Elites invoke the promise of a better future to obscure their self-serving agendas. This promise reveals itself as a mirage. Future chapters will explore how elites systematically block these movements. Under the guise of saving humanity, elites secure their dominance. Meanwhile, the rest of us fend for survival in a fractured world.

Education, hailed as the great equalizer, has always been a battleground for power. For centuries, elites have understood its transformative potential—not just to uplift individuals, but also to threaten established hierarchies. In this understanding lies their strategy: to manipulate educational systems, bending them to perpetuate their dominance rather than liberate the minds of the masses. The narrative sold to the public promises' opportunity and meritocracy. Beneath this veneer, however, lies a calculated effort. This effort suppresses critical thinking and restricts intellectual empowerment to an elite minority. Education, instead of a ladder out of inequality, becomes a tool to reinforce it.

This chapter probes into the mechanisms by which elites maintain their grip on power through education. It examines how elites systematically block democratizing access to quality science education. They ensure that resources, infrastructure, and teaching needed for genuine innovation remain elusive for the majority. Elites propagate private schools and institutions. These schools appear to prioritize excellence. However, they subtly discourage critical thinking that could question the status quo. Exclusive "Ad Astra"-style schools cater to the privileged. Policymakers deliberately underfund public education. The aim is clear: to filter out the brightest minds to serve elite interests, leaving the rest to navigate systems that perpetuate their disadvantage.

Through these carefully curated systems, the elites protect their hegemony, ensuring that scientific advancement serves their agendas rather than humanity. But this manipulation comes at a cost—a society where inequality deepens, and the vast potential of millions is squandered in service of a few. By exploring these themes, we uncover the tactics elites employ. We also reveal the societal implications of a world where education is a controlled privilege, not a universal right. The stakes are high: the future of progress, equity, and human flourishing hangs in the balance.

If education is a battlefield, then the elites have long claimed the high ground. For centuries, they have honed their ability to dictate who learns what—and who learns nothing at all. Their strategy is neither random nor subtle; it's a meticulous system of control designed to preserve dominance. From the policies they champion to the institutions they build, every choice reflects a singular goal: to shape education into a tool of suppression rather than liberation. Elite institutions like MIT, Stanford, and Harvard cultivate privilege and systematize inequality.

1. ELITE ASTRA

Imagine a school designed not to educate the many but to serve the few. These institutions groom students to sustain systems of power. They learn to view inequality not as a problem to solve but as a hierarchy to maintain. These institutions, from exclusive private academies to billion-dollar tech initiatives, are more than schools— they are incubators of privilege. Elite Astra serves as a prime example of this principle. It serves as a case study in how the powerful redefine what education is. They use it as a tool to entrench dominance while presenting it as the pinnacle of progress.

Education has always been a double-edged sword: a tool with the potential to enlighten and equalize but also a weapon to divide and control. Throughout history, those in power have understood this dichotomy well. They have used education not as a universal right but as a privilege, carefully distributed to reinforce existing social hierarchies. In ancient societies like India, the caste system dictated every aspect of life, including education. The Brahmins, positioned at the top of the social order, monopolized learning and knowledge, ensuring that their grip on power remained unchallenged. Society systematically excluded the lower castes and "untouchables" from formal education. This design relegated them to ignorance. Authorities forbade access to sacred texts like the Vedas. They imposed harsh penalties on those who breached these barriers. The ruling classes restricted access to knowledge. This ensured compliance from those at the bottom of the hierarchy. They remained unable to conceive of a reality beyond the imposed one.

This pattern of exclusivity persisted as societies strengthened, finding new expressions in different contexts. In medieval Europe, the birth of universities marked a significant milestone in the institutionalization of education. Yet, these centers of learning were far from egalitarian. Founders established the earliest universities—like Bologna, Oxford, and Paris—to serve the clergy and nobility. Their doors were closed to peasants and commoners, who constituted the overwhelming majority of the population. Education at these institutions was not about fostering critical thinking or promoting upward mobility; it was about preserving the power of the elite class. The curriculum itself reflected this aim, focusing on theology, law, and classical texts—subjects that reinforced the divine right of kings and the sanctity of existing social orders. Those who emerged from these institutions were not agents of change but gatekeepers of tradition, entrusted with maintaining the status quo.

Even in societies that prided themselves on enlightenment and progress, the exclusivity of education was a consistent theme. Take the colonial period as an example. Colonizers established schools across Africa, Asia, and the Americas. Colonial powers did not design these schools to uplift local populations. Instead, they created a small, loyal class of intermediaries—clerks, administrators, and translators—to serve colonial interests. Colonial authorities introduced Western-style education in British India through institutions like Calcutta's Hindu College in the 19th century. Thomas Macaulay described its aim as creating a "class of persons, Indian in blood and color, but English in taste, in opinions, in morals, and in intellect." This system of education carefully excluded the vast majority of Indians. It assimilated a select few into a colonial worldview that upheld the British Empire's dominance.

The historical legacy of education as a tool for maintaining power is not an abstract concept; it is a reality with deep roots, visible in the structures of inequality that persist today. Caste-based restrictions, medieval exclusivity, and colonial manipulation reveal a clear pattern. Those who control education control the narrative. Through that, they shape the very fabric of society. This understanding is crucial as we examine how modern elites continue to wield education as a means of preserving their dominance. The institutions may look different, and the rhetoric may have grown, but the underlying dynamics remain remarkably unchanged.

At the heart of this elite-controlled system lies a paradoxical curriculum. While it claims to champion innovation and critical thinking, it often does the opposite. By controlling the narratives taught, the elite ensure that education serves their interests, manufacturing compliance rather than cultivating revolutionaries. To truly understand the mechanisms of this control, one must first examine the foundation: the curriculum itself.

1.1 THE PRIVILEGE CURRICULUM

Educators carefully craft curricula as blueprints for society. They are not mere collections of lessons. Elite institutions design these blueprints to do more than impart knowledge. They shape ideologies, suppress dissent, and perpetuate the status quo. Across the globe, this approach manifests in subtle but insidious ways, from sanitizing history to obscuring critical analysis. By tailoring education to reflect their vision of the world, the elite ensure that the system itself becomes an accomplice in their quest for power.

Society often heralds the modern era as an age of democracy and equal opportunity. Yet, elite influence over education remains pervasive. It now operates in more sophisticated guises. Today, educational manipulation no longer relies on evident exclusionary practices, like those in medieval universities or colonial schools. Instead, it operates through indirect forms of policy manipulation and curriculum control. These mechanisms ensure that education remains a tool for preserving elite dominance. Elites wrap it in the language of progress and choice. However, it is designed to limit genuine empowerment for the majority.

Policy manipulation has become a cornerstone of elite influence in modern education. In many countries, this begins with the systematic defunding of public schools under the guise of fiscal responsibility. The United States offers a striking example. Over the past few decades, lobbying efforts by corporations and wealthy individuals have significantly shaped the discourse around education funding. Organizations like the American Legislative Exchange Council (ALEC), backed by corporate sponsors, have promoted legislation that redirects public funds into private and charter schools through voucher programs. The result is a starved public education system where underfunded schools struggle to provide even the basics, disproportionately affecting low-income and minority communities. Meanwhile, private schools—often accessible only to the affluent—flourish, perpetuating a cycle where quality education becomes a privilege rather than a right. This mirrors the colonial tactic of investing in a select few intermediaries, leaving the majority to languish without resources or opportunities.

Elites extend their control over education beyond funding to include the content students learn. Elites exert significant influence over curricula to ensure that schools produce obedient workers rather than critical thinkers. Textbook selection processes, for instance, have become battlegrounds for ideological dominance. In states like Texas, the State Board of Education wields considerable power. Conservative committees tailor textbook content to reflect their agendas. It often downplays systemic inequality, labor history, or the darker aspects of colonialism. By shaping what students learn, elites craft a narrative that justifies existing power structures while discouraging questions that might challenge them. Elites do not limit this control to one country. In India, nationalist government pressures have changed history textbooks. These changes erase or downplay events like the caste system's brutality or communal violence. They promote a sanitized version of history aligned with elite and political interests. The goal requires no complexity: to produce citizens who accept the status quo without questioning it.

Elites manipulate education systems in ostensibly progressive nations to serve their agendas. Take the rise off for-profit educational institutions, which are marketed as opportunities for upward mobility, but often saddle students with crushing debt while delivering subpar outcomes. Companies like Pearson, a multinational education corporation, have monopolized educational resources and assessments, turning learning into a commodified industry. Corporations backed by elite investors profit enormously. They offer the best resources to those who can afford them. The rest navigate overcrowded classrooms and outdated materials, reinforcing inequality.

Such tactics are not new but represent how historical strategies evolve to maintain control. Where once elites used caste laws or royal decrees to restrict access, they now leverage policy frameworks, economic incentives, and ideological control. The methods may have changed, but the objective remains the same: to ensure that education perpetuates their dominance rather than dismantling it. Elites use these mechanisms to control knowledge carefully and shape the world. It becomes a resource parceled out to sustain their hold on power, rather than a tool for liberation.

Elites must not only dictate what schools teach; they must also control how students learn. The emphasis on rote memorization over analytical thinking isn't just a quirk of pedagogy; it's a deliberate strategy. By discouraging questioning and rewarding compliance, these systems create graduates who excel at maintaining hierarchies but falter at challenging them. Nowhere is this more apparent than in the private institutions catering to the privileged few.

1.2 MEMORIZE, DON'T ANALYZE

Private schools promise excellence, prestige, and opportunity—but for whom? Beneath the glossy brochures and elite networks lies a chilling truth: these institutions exist not to level the playing field but to ensure it remains tilted. Their graduates emerge as gatekeepers of privilege, armed not with the tools to transform the world but with the skills to preserve it. The emphasis on compliance over critique ensures that the cycle of inequality continues uninterrupted.

Society heralds the rise of private educational institutions as a triumph of choice and competition. These institutions offer families the freedom to select schools aligning with their values and aspirations. But beneath this celebratory narrative lies a troubling reality. These schools, while marketed as hubs of excellence, often serve as instruments of social stratification, perpetuating privilege rather than dismantling it. Catering primarily to affluent families, private schools have proliferated in response to the perceived inadequacies of public education. Their genuine appeal does not lie in providing a superior education for all. Instead, it lies in exclusivity. This exclusivity acts as a badge of status for those who can afford it. Elite boarding schools like Eton College in the United Kingdom and posh academies in New York and Mumbai have a simple function. They act less as centers of learning and more as gateways to a world reserved for the wealthy.

Many private schools design their curricula to discourage critical thinking and produce compliant students. The emphasis is often on rote learning, drilled repetition, and standardized testing—methods that reward memorization over innovation. In the United States, the rise of "prep schools" in the 20th century epitomized this trend. These institutions promised entry into prestigious universities, focusing narrowly on test scores, grade point averages, and polished extracurricular resumes. Educators often sideline critical thinking because it disrupts authority and imagines alternative systems. Teachers train students to navigate existing structures with precision. They learn to fit seamlessly into the corporate, political, or academic upper echelons. This training avoids challenging the frameworks that sustain those structures. In South Korea, education is synonymous with grueling college entrance exam preparation. Private academies, known as "hagwons," dominate the landscape. They produce students' proficient at solving problems within rigid boundaries but rarely encourage stepping outside them.

These institutions are also notorious for their exclusionary practices. High tuition fees act as the first line of defense against inclusivity, ensuring that only those from affluent families can access their resources and networks. Some schools go even further, employing legacy admissions policies that give preference to children of alumni—a practice that entrenches generational privilege. In the United States, preparatory school pipelines closely link elite universities like Harvard and Princeton. They admit a disproportionately high number of legacy students. This practice often excludes equally or more qualified candidates from underprivileged backgrounds. Families in developing countries increasingly view private schools as a ticket out of poverty. However, many cater exclusively to the wealthy. This creates parallel educational systems that deepen societal divides instead of bridging them.

The propagation of such private schools underscores a deliberate effort by elites to preserve their dominance. Educators do not design these schools to democratize education or empower all children equally. These schools reinforce a system where access to opportunity depends on wealth and heritage. These schools groom their students to perpetuate the status quo. The promise of private education as a panacea for failing public systems is, at its core, a mirage—an illusion carefully constructed to obscure the inequities it sustains. Examining these schools' curricula, policies, and societal roles reveals the machinery of exclusivity. This mechanism polishes pathways of privilege while leaving the vast majority outside, looking in.

While elite institutions thrive, public education faces a slow, deliberate erosion. Nowhere is this more evident than in science education, where underfunded programs leave students unprepared for the challenges of a modern, tech-driven economy. This disparity is no accident; it's a calculated effort to keep critical thinking—and the potential for disruption—firmly out of reach for the majority.

1.3 FUNDING FADES, SCIENCE CRASHES

Science has long been humanity's great equalizer, a field where ideas, not status, are supposed to reign supreme. But access to quality science education remains a privilege reserved for the few. Across underfunded public schools, outdated equipment and overwhelmed teachers strip students of the chance to engage with innovation. Elites monopolize progress, excluding millions from the industries shaping our future.

The barriers to equal access to science education in the modern world are not merely byproducts of systemic neglect; they are deliberate constructs that serve to maintain the gap between privilege and disadvantage. Policymakers systematically undermine public science programs once hailed as beacons of opportunity. This leaves many students without the resources to explore or excel in scientific fields. Budget cuts across the United States have closed thousands of school science labs. This has turned what was once a hands-on, exploratory subject into a dry, theoretical exercise. In 2019, Detroit Public Schools faced a stark reality: only 25% of its high schools had functioning science labs, and even those lacked up-to-date equipment. Extracurricular programs that once nurtured future scientists—robotics clubs, science fairs, and field trips to observatories—have become luxuries that public schools can no longer afford. Elite private institutions invest millions in cutting-edge technology and expert faculty. Meanwhile, public schools grapple with outdated textbooks and overcrowded classrooms. Elites ensure the majority loses the spark of curiosity.

Geographical disparities compound these inequities, particularly in rural and underprivileged urban areas, where access to quality science education is practically nonexistent. In rural India, a 2017 survey revealed concerning statistics. Over 75% of secondary schools lacked a dedicated science teacher. Untrained instructors taught the students. Even in wealthier nations, such as the United Kingdom, urban schools in low-income neighborhoods often lack adequate facilities for teaching STEM subjects. A 2020 report found that over 40% of schools in economically disadvantaged areas of England had no functional chemistry or physics labs. These gaps are not incidental; they are indicative of a system that prioritizes efficiency and cost-cutting over the intellectual and professional future of millions. Students in these areas lack access to quality education in foundational scientific fields. This locks them out of careers in technology, engineering, and medicine. These are the very fields driving the modern economy.

The digital divide is yet another frontier where inequality in science education is starkly visible. As classrooms increasingly rely on technology to teach and engage students, those without access to the internet or modern devices find themselves excluded from these opportunities. During the COVID-19 pandemic, this divide became glaringly apparent. In the United States alone, an estimated 17 million students lacked home internet access, leaving them unable to participate in online learning. For science education, this gap was devastating. Students in affluent areas engaged in virtual lab simulations, coding workshops, and webinars with scientists. In contrast, disadvantaged peers relied on printed worksheets and received minimal guidance. In sub-Saharan Africa, the disparity is even more severe, with less than 10% of households having reliable internet access. This technological exclusion not only limits immediate educational opportunities but also reinforces long-term economic disparities, as digital literacy becomes an increasingly essential skill in the global workforce.

Elites systematically undermine public science programs. They perpetuate geographical disparities and allow the digital divide to persist. This ensures that access to science education remains a privilege rather than a right. This deliberate stratification serves to maintain their dominance, as innovation and critical thought become the domain of an increasingly narrow segment of society. The dream of democratizing science education becomes a mirage. Elites keep the tools needed to realize it just out of reach for those who need them most.

Systemic inequities in education extend beyond funding or curriculum. Authorities codify them in the metrics used to measure success. Standardized tests, often touted as neutral arbiters of merit, have become one of the most effective tools for perpetuating privilege. Their biases serve to reinforce the barriers that already exist, ensuring that opportunity remains out of reach for most.

1.4 STANDARDIZED TESTS, STANDARDIZED PRIVILEGE

Institutions present tests as the great equalizer, claiming to measure potential without prejudice. Yet, in reality, they are anything but. From costly preparation programs to built-in cultural biases, standardized testing has become a system designed to privilege the privileged. Far from promoting equity, these tests deepen divides, turning education into yet another mechanism for maintaining inequality.

Suppressing equitable education is not an abstract theory but a tangible reality, manifesting in ways that systematically disadvantage those outside elite circles. One of the clearest examples is the inherent bias of standardized testing, a mechanism that purports to measure merit but reinforces pre-existing inequalities. Critics have long accused the SAT, a cornerstone of U.S. college admissions, of favoring students from affluent families. Numerous studies reveal a strong correlation between SAT scores and household income, with students from wealthier families consistently outperforming their less privileged peers. The reasons are as clear as they are troubling. Wealthier families can afford private tutors, test preparation courses, and multiple retakes of the exam to optimize scores. Meanwhile, low-income students often lack access to such resources, relying on overburdened public schools to provide limited guidance. The result is a system where people believe merit skews access to prestigious universities—and the opportunities they provide—toward those who already hold advantages.

Charter schools, often championed as a solution to failing public education systems, reveal another layer of educational suppression. Critics accuse many charter schools of perpetuating segregation and exacerbating inequalities, even as some provide innovative learning environments. In the United States, data shows that a significant number of charter schools lack diversity, serving predominantly white or affluent student populations. For example, a 2017 study found that 17% of charter schools were "hyper-segregated," with more than 90% of students belonging to a single racial or ethnic group. This trend is not coincidental. Admission policies at some charter schools, such as requiring parents to complete extensive applications or commit to volunteer hours, implicitly favor families with greater socioeconomic resources. These practices exclude many low-income and minority families, ensuring that charter schools serve as enclaves of privilege rather than engines of opportunity. They replicate the exclusivity of elite private schools under the guise of public accessibility.

The control over curricula provides yet another avenue for educational suppression, particularly in how educators teach—or omit—scientific topics. Educational policymakers in regions driven by ideological or political agendas often exclude or distort crucial scientific concepts. A glaring example excludes evolution from biology curricula in parts of the United States. Policymakers in Tennessee and Texas modified textbooks. They downplay or omit the theory of evolution. Creationist narratives or vague references to "intelligent design" often replace scientific explanations. This censorship extends beyond the United States; in countries like Turkey, authorities curtail efforts to teach evolution, framing it as controversial or incompatible with national values. Such omissions deprive students of a foundational understanding of biology, limiting their ability to engage with modern scientific discourse. The implications of such education extend beyond the classroom. Students enter a world defined by scientific and technological advancements. However, they remain ill-equipped to participate in or contribute to those fields.

Elites manipulate educational systems to maintain societal hierarchies, as illustrated by these real-world examples. Standardized tests ensure that pathways to success are disproportionately accessible to the privileged. Charter schools, despite their promise, often deepen divides rather than bridge them. And curriculum censorship stifles critical thinking and scientific literacy, leaving generations unable to question or challenge established power structures. These mechanisms create a tightly controlled educational landscape. Access, knowledge, and opportunity remain privileges rather than rights. Elites design this landscape to protect the few rather than empower the many.

Behind every standardized test lies a seductive myth: the promise of meritocracy. This idea—that hard work and talent can overcome systemic barriers—is a cornerstone of modern education rhetoric. But for most, the ladder of opportunity is less a path to progress and more a carefully rigged system designed to keep them exactly where they are.

1.5 CLIMBING A RIGGED LADDER

Meritocracy is a comforting illusion, a story we tell ourselves to justify inequality. Yet, for millions, the promises of education—upward mobility, equality, opportunity—

remain unfulfilled. Wage gaps, systemic biases, and entrenched barriers expose the hollow core of this narrative, revealing a system designed not to uplift but to maintain the status quo.

The promise of a brighter future—one built on the principles of meritocracy and boundless opportunity—has been one of the most enduring myths of modern society. It is a comforting story, one that assures individuals that success is within their grasp if only they work hard enough. Yet, the reality beneath this narrative is far less inspiring. The very structure of the educational framework, often touted as the great equalizer, systematically undermines this ideal. Studies consistently show that upward mobility is elusive for marginalized groups, even for those who attain higher education. In the United States, society heralds a college degree as the ultimate gateway to economic stability and success. However, for Black and Latino graduates, the wage gap compared to their white counterparts persists, reflecting a system where race and socioeconomic status continue to shape outcomes. Similar phenomena extend beyond the United States. Across the globe, marginalized communities encounter invisible ceilings, where their achievements fail to translate into equal opportunities. The myth of meritocracy becomes a cruel joke. It blames individuals for their lack of progress. Meanwhile, it ignores the structural barriers designed to hold them back.

Elites have become masters of weaving narratives that obscure these inequalities, crafting tales of progress and innovation to distract from the persistent realities of exclusion. Political rhetoric frequently glorifies technological advancements and scientific breakthroughs, presenting them as evidence of a collective march toward a better future. Yet, these triumphs often benefit a narrow segment of society, leaving the majority grappling with the same systemic inequities. Consider the global celebration of advancements in artificial intelligence or space exploration. Society heralds' figures like Elon Musk and Jeff Bezos as visionaries. People laud their efforts to colonize Mars or perfect autonomous systems as the pinnacle of human achievement. Elites conveniently ignore glaring disparities in access to basic education and resources. Governments and corporations in the United States pour billions into private space programs. Over 30% of public schools lack funding to update outdated textbooks. They also cannot provide students with functioning computers. The juxtaposition is stark: humanity gazes at the stars while inequality shackles its feet to uneven terrain.

This narrative strategy is not accidental but carefully crafted to maintain the status quo. By focusing public attention on a promised utopia, elites divert scrutiny away from the systems they have built to secure their dominance. Progress often serves as a smokescreen, obscuring the systemic barriers that deny millions access to the tools needed for this supposed future. Wrapped in the myth of technological salvation, society numbs itself to the enduring inequalities embedded within the education system and beyond. While alluring, the promise of a better tomorrow is ultimately hollow when today's foundations remain deeply fractured.

Dissecting this mirage of a promised future reveals an uncomfortable truth. Narratives of progress often serve as a means of control, rather than liberation. They offer hope while withholding change, ensuring that the structures of inequality remain intact. The challenge is not simply to critique these narratives. It is to dismantle the systems they protect. We must replace them with a reality where progress is a shared inheritance for all, not the privilege of the few.

The educational inequalities we've explored are not random; they are deliberate. They are part of a larger system in which elites use their influence to shape not only schools but societies. By controlling who gets elected, they ensure that these systems remain in place, perpetuating their dominance under the guise of democracy.

1.6 ELECTED TO EXPLOIT

Education does not exist in a vacuum. The systems of power that govern our world are intimately tied to it. From media narratives to campaign funding, elites have mastered the art of manipulating democracy itself. By controlling who leads, they ensure that education remains a tool for inequality, suppressing critical thinking and innovation for all but a select few.

The elites have perfected the art of sustaining their dominance, suppressing humanity's collective voice against their monopolization of resources and wealth. They wield tools both overt and subtle, ensuring that their hegemony remains unchallenged. Elites manipulate democratic processes as one of their most insidious methods. They convince the masses to elect politicians repeatedly. These politicians safeguard elite interests under the guise of serving the public. By controlling media narratives, funding political campaigns, and shaping public discourse, the elites make choice appear illusory. A cornerstone of this strategy lies in the rigging of education systems, designed to trap the majority in a feedback loop of ignorance. By stifling critical thinking and underfunding public schools, they ensure that large swaths of society lack the analytical skills necessary to challenge propaganda or scrutinize elite-driven agendas. Elites deliberately keep the majority in intellectual darkness, turning democracy into a hollow mechanism. Historical examples of elite influence abound. During the Gilded Age in America, industrial magnates bought political influence to maintain monopolies. Today, billionaires bankroll election campaigns to ensure tax policies favor the ultra-rich. These cycles repeat endlessly. Leaders' dangle promises of reform before the public. Leaders abandon those promises once they secure power. This perpetuates a system rigged to protect wealth and power.

The consequences of this manipulation are stark, beginning with the widening gap between socioeconomic classes. Education, ostensibly a ladder of opportunity, has instead become a mechanism for reinforcing inequality. Studies consistently show a strong correlation between education levels and income inequality. For example, data from the OECD highlights that countries with the greatest income disparities also suffer from unequal access to quality education. In the United States, the gap between public and private education exacerbates this divide. Affluent families secure a head start for their children through elite schools and tutoring. Meanwhile, low-income families struggle to access basic educational resources. Over generations, these disparities compound, creating entrenched class systems where upward mobility becomes an exception rather than a norm. This inequality permeates every aspect of society, from access to healthcare to political representation, deepening the divide between the haves and the have-nots.

Beyond economic disparities, suppressing critical thinking within education has stifled societal innovation. Elites limit the diversity of thought. They focus curricula on rote memorization and standardized tests. This ensures that the next generation of problem-solvers stays tethered to conventional frameworks. History illustrates the transformative power of diverse perspectives. The scientific revolution of the Renaissance and technological breakthroughs of the 20th century are prime examples. These were often driven by individuals who challenged orthodoxy. Today, however, the marginalization of underprivileged communities from quality education narrows the pool of innovative thinkers. Consider the tech industry, which thrives on innovation yet remains dominated by individuals from a narrow socioeconomic background. The lack of diverse perspectives hampers creativity. It produces solutions catering to the elite. These solutions neglect global challenges, such as poverty, climate change, and equitable resource distribution. Suppressing critical thinking is not just a loss for the marginalized; it is a collective failure for humanity.

Perhaps most alarming is how the eroding education system undermines the very foundations of democracy. A poorly educated populace is more susceptible to manipulation, less likely to question authority, and less equipped to engage in informed decision-making. This erosion is evident in voter turnout trends, particularly in undereducated communities where participation in democratic processes is often low. For instance, in the 2016 U.S. presidential election, voter turnout in counties with lower education levels was significantly lower than in more educated regions. This disengagement allows elites to consolidate power further, as political discourse becomes dominated by those who can afford to influence it. Democracy, stripped of its informed electorate, becomes a hollow exercise—a layer of participation masking the reality of oligarchic rule.

The elites have succeeded in creating a society where the systems that should empower the many instead serve to entrench the privileges of the few. The widening socioeconomic gaps, suppression of innovation, and erosion of democratic principles are not accidents but deliberate outcomes of a system designed to maintain their hegemony. Elites cloak this manipulation in the language of progress and choice. It traps humanity's collective potential within structures. These structures prioritize preserving power over pursuing equity and advancement.

People often describe education as the cornerstone of democracy, innovation, and equality. But as we've seen, forces of control often overshadow the fight for empowerment, turning education into a battleground. The systems that could uplift millions are instead used to entrench inequality, ensuring that power remains concentrated in the hands of a privileged few. Yet, this story is not without hope. Change is possible, but it requires a collective reimagining of education's purpose—not as a means of control, but as a tool for liberation. Only then can we unlock its true potential and chart a path toward a future where knowledge is a shared treasure, not a guarded privilege.

Peel back the layers of any education system, and you'll find a blueprint for society itself. What we teach—or fail to teach—our children reflects not only our values but also our fears, biases, and ambitions. Gender, a construct woven into the fabric of every culture, looms large in these blueprints. Boys and girls are not just students; they are future workers, citizens, and leaders, shaped by lessons that either liberate or confine them. To understand the role of education in perpetuating inequality, we must first confront the ways it reinforces gender roles, stifling individuality under the weight of tradition.

2. ADAM AND EVE

The gender divide in education is not an accident; it is a carefully maintained legacy. For centuries, societies have used education to mold boys into providers and protectors, and girls into caretakers and homemakers. This divide is not merely historical—it persists in dropout rates, biased curricula, and societal expectations that push boys toward competition and girls toward compliance. The result is a system that stifles potential on both sides, locking children into roles they never chose. Unraveling inequality requires closely examining how education perpetuates stereotypes. This includes the erasure of women's achievements in textbooks. It also involves the glorification of rigid masculinity.

Education, often celebrated as the cornerstone of progress and equality, is far from a universal solution in its current state. Boys and girls worldwide face a labyrinth of challenges within educational institutions. These challenges are not incidental. They are deeply entrenched in cultural, political, and economic systems. For girls, barriers often start before they even step into a classroom. Societal norms and economic pressures prioritize their domestic roles over their education. Boys often grapple with systems that stigmatize emotional expression. These systems box them into rigid definitions of masculinity. This leaves them ill-equipped to adapt to a transforming world. These struggles are not abstract; they manifest in dropout rates, mental health crises, and long-term disparities in opportunities. Together, they reveal the many faces of inequality that permeate global education.

This section explores these multifaceted issues, beginning with inspecting gender disparities and how systemic biases either limit or distort opportunities for boys and girls. We explore curriculum controversies. These include the erasure of women's contributions in history. It also examines how gender stereotypes in textbooks shape societal attitudes and expectations. Religious influences, used as tools of control, complicate education further. Certain belief systems dictate what children can or cannot learn. This is especially true for topics like gender and sexuality. This section addresses psychological and behavioral tolls caused by these systems. Boys and girls face mental health challenges. An education system that prioritizes conformity over compassion worsens these challenges. By unpacking these interconnected issues, we aim to illuminate how education, rather than leveling the playing field, often reinforces the very inequalities it claims to dismantle.

Nowhere is the gender divide more pronounced than in the question of access. Societal forces shape children's educational journeys before they even set foot in a classroom, deciding who belongs and who does not. For millions of girls around the world, education remains a distant dream, blocked by traditions that prioritize marriage over learning. Economic demands and outdated expectations of strength and self-reliance push many boys out of school. Access, then, is not just a logistical challenge but a moral question—one that asks who deserves a future.

2.1 BRIDES BEFORE BACHELORS

Imagine a girl with a brilliant mind, one that could someday unlock the mysteries of the universe or revolutionize her community. Imagine a girl forced out of school at age 12 to become a child bride. A tradition that values her as a wife more than a thinker extinguishes her potential. This is not an isolated story; it is the reality for millions of girls across the globe. But gendered barriers to education do not stop there. Boys, too, are victims of a system that views their education as secondary to their immediate economic utility. For both, the loss is incalculable—not just for them, but for the societies that never benefit from their untapped potential.

Education, often regarded as a fundamental human right, reveals stark inequalities when examined through the lens of gender. For centuries, cultural and social norms have erected barriers to girls' education, particularly in regions where patriarchal traditions dominate. Across parts of South Asia, Sub-Saharan Africa, and the Middle East, former marriage remains one of the most pervasive obstacles. In Niger and Bangladesh, child marriage rates exceed 40%. Societal pressures force young girls to abandon their studies. They take on domestic and maternal roles instead. This practice denies these girls the opportunity to acquire knowledge and skills, perpetuating a cycle of dependency and poverty. Historical parallels are striking: in 19th century England, educators trained middle-class girls only to become "accomplished" for marriage prospects, while they denied working-class girls' education entirely. The echoes of these disparities persist, with millions of girls today still excluded from classrooms simply because of entrenched societal expectations.

Even when families prioritize girls' education, safety concerns often present insurmountable hurdles. The lack of secure transportation and gender-sensitive facilities in schools discourages attendance, especially in rural areas. In India, a 2018 survey revealed a significant barrier for girls. Over 20% of adolescent girls dropped out of school because of a lack of separate toilets. This caused heightened vulnerability and embarrassment during menstruation. Similar stories unfold across Sub-Saharan Africa, where girls must often walk long distances to reach schools, exposing them to the risk of harassment or assault. These barriers not only inhibit academic participation but also reinforce the perception that educating girls is an unwise investment, further entrenching gender inequalities.

Economic pressures compound these challenges. In impoverished households, where resources are scarce, education often becomes a zero-sum game. Families prioritize boys' schooling, viewing them as future breadwinners, while they relegate girls to household chores or informal labor. In regions like West Africa, this phenomenon becomes especially pronounced as families force girls as young as 10 to work in domestic servitude to support them. The global scale of this inequity is staggering. UNESCO estimates that 129 million girls worldwide remain out of school. Economic hardships disproportionately targeting their gender exclude many girls from education.

Such practices not only rob these girls of their potential but also deprive societies of the innovation and leadership they could bring.

While the barriers faced by girls are well-documented, boys, too, encounter distinct challenges within educational systems, albeit rooted in different social dynamics. In many regions, boys are more likely to drop out of school because of economic pressures that force them into the workforce. Across Latin America and parts of Southeast Asia, boys leave school early to contribute to family incomes, particularly in agricultural or industrial sectors. Historical patterns reveal similar trends; during the Great Depression in the United States, young boys often left school to work in factories or on farms, prioritizing immediate survival over long-term aspirations. Today, this reality persists, with boys in low-income families disproportionately bearing the burden of supporting their households, often at the expense of their education.

Societal expectations about masculinity further complicate boys' relationships with education. Many cultures view academic achievement as incompatible with traditional notions of masculinity. Peer pressure, particularly during adolescence, discourages boys from excelling in school, branding studiousness as "uncool" or effeminate. In countries like Jamaica, studies have shown that boys often underperform academically because prevailing norms devalue educational success as a masculine trait. These stereotypes perpetuate a cycle of disengagement, where boys, feeling alienated from the system, withdraw further, leading to higher dropout rates. Such pressures not only harm individual boys but also contribute to broader social stagnation by limiting their potential contributions to society.

These gendered disparities reveal the systemic failures of educational systems worldwide. Girls face overwhelming barriers rooted in cultural norms, safety concerns, and economic pressures, while boys grapple with societal expectations and the weight of economic responsibilities. Addressing these challenges requires a holistic approach—one that dismantles harmful traditions, invests in infrastructure, and redefines societal values to create an education system that truly serves all.

Access to education is just the beginning. What happens within classrooms—the lessons imparted and the ideologies that are reinforced—plays a crucial role in shaping the thinkers and citizens children will grow into. This becomes particularly evident in the ongoing clash between science and ideology. In certain classrooms, creation myths are taught in place of evolutionary theory, and religious dogma takes precedence over empirical evidence. In such environments, education turns into a battleground for ideological control, rather than serving as a pathway to intellectual growth and societal progress. This highlights the crucial role of unbiased, evidence-based education.

2.2 SCIENCE? LET'S PRAY ON IT

The clash between science and ideology is as old as human civilization. But in today's classrooms, this ancient conflict takes on new urgency. From the U.S. to Saudi Arabia, curricula are being rewritten. These changes prioritize dogma over discovery. This leaves students ill-equipped to tackle modern challenges. Whether it's omitting evolution or distorting climate science, these ideological battles are not just about knowledge—they are about power. By controlling what children learn, societies ensure that the next generation inherits their biases, perpetuating ignorance in the guise of tradition.

The controversy over teaching evolution in schools vividly demonstrates how education becomes a battlefield for ideological supremacy. In numerous regions, policymakers systematically erase or distort the theory of evolution—a cornerstone of modern biology—in favor of creationist narratives rooted in religious doctrines. The United States, a nation at the forefront of scientific innovation, has repeatedly found itself embroiled in this debate. In 1925, the Scopes Trial gained fame. Authorities in Tennessee prosecuted a high school teacher for teaching evolution. A state law prohibited any material contradicting the biblical account of creation. Though the trial ended with a conviction for John Scopes, the case ignited a national dialog about the role of religion in education. Yet, nearly a century later, the controversy persists. In Texas and Kansas, conservative textbook committees dilute or omit references to evolution. They frame it as "just a theory" instead of recognizing it as a foundational scientific principle. This struggle is not a relic of history but an ongoing issue. Religious advocacy groups push for "intelligent design" in science curricula. This is a thinly veiled attempt to reintroduce creationism under a modern guise.

The consequences of such curricular censorship extend far beyond the classroom, undermining the scientific literacy of entire generations. Students educated without a robust understanding of evolution find themselves ill-prepared to engage with higher education in biological sciences, medicine, or environmental studies. The implications ripple through society, diminishing the pool of qualified professionals capable of addressing complex challenges like climate change, pandemics, and biodiversity loss. Consider the case of Turkey, where in 2017 the government removed evolution from its high school biology curriculum, citing its complexity and alleged incompatibility with cultural values. The decision sparked outrage among scientists and educators, who warned that it would erode the nation's scientific competitiveness. These fears are not unfounded. Nations restricting access to critical scientific concepts risk falling behind in global innovation. Students from these systems struggle to meet higher education's rigorous demands. They also face challenges in international research collaborations.

This suppression of evolution reflects a broader tension between modernity and tradition, where education becomes a proxy for larger cultural battles. In countries like Saudi Arabia and Iran, authorities strictly regulate teaching evolution, aligning curricula with Islamic theology. These policies shape not only what students learn but also how they perceive the relationship between science and faith. Deliberately omitting or distorting evolution fosters a problematic worldview. It prioritizes dogma over evidence. This stifles critical inquiry and reinforces societal norms that discourage questioning authority.

The broader impact of these controversies is a society less equipped to grapple with the complexities of the modern world. By excising evolution from curricula, educational systems fail their primary mission: to prepare students for a future grounded in understanding and innovation. Instead, they perpetuate ideological conformity, ensuring that education serves as a tool of control rather than enlightenment. Eroding scientific literacy is not just an academic issue; it is a societal one, shaping how nations confront—or fail to confront—their most pressing challenges. The battle over evolution is a microcosm of a larger struggle for education's soul. It reflects a conflict between those who view education as liberation and those who use it as an instrument of power.

Religion has always been a powerful force in shaping societies, and education is no exception. Across the globe, classrooms reflect the struggles of their societies to reconcile faith with inquiry. In some places, religious teachings dominate, leaving little room for critical thinking or diverse perspectives. In some countries, authorities enforce secularism so rigidly that it alienates people seeking to express their faith. The result is often the same: a generation caught between tradition and modernity, uncertain of its place in the world.

Religion's influence in education is among the oldest and most contentious societal intersections. The sacred and the secular compete for dominance in shaping young minds. Around the world, policymakers integrate religious texts into school curricula, often sacrificing inclusivity and critical inquiry. In some countries, such as Pakistan and Saudi Arabia, public schools routinely incorporate Islamic scriptures and teachings into what is ostensibly a secular education system. For example, in Pakistan, the government-mandated Islamiat curriculum requires all students, including non-Muslims, to learn passages from the Quran and hadiths as part of their schooling. While proponents argue that such integration preserves cultural and religious values, the impact on inclusivity is profound. Classroom policies that exclude or invalidate their beliefs often alienate non-Muslim students who already face societal discrimination. Medieval Europe shows historical parallels, where the Church monopolized education and based all learning on religious doctrine. The exclusionary nature of these systems ensured that only those aligned with dominant religious ideologies could fully participate in intellectual and societal life.

This tension between religious influence and inclusivity becomes even sharper when viewed through the lens of secularism. Debates over the role of religion in education have sparked fierce legal and cultural battles, particularly in democracies that pride themselves on pluralism. In the United States, the Supreme Court has repeatedly ruled on prayer in public schools. The landmark Engel v. Vitale (1962) case declared school-sponsored prayer unconstitutional. Despite this, controversies persist, with some communities continuing to push for Bible studies or moments of silence that subtly reintroduce religious practices into public education. These debates underscore the delicate balance between respecting religious freedom and separating church and state—a principle foundational to American democracy yet perennially challenged.

Globally, approaches to balancing religion and education vary dramatically, offering insights into the complexities of this relationship. In France, the policy of laïcité (secularism) bans religious symbols, such as hijabs or crucifixes, from public schools. Enacted to preserve state neutrality, the policy has sparked significant controversy, with critics arguing that it disproportionately targets Muslim students and stifles personal expression. On the other end of the spectrum, countries like India face a distinct challenge. They grapple with managing a pluralistic society. In such societies, cultural heritage deeply intertwines with religious identity. Indian schools often footstep a fine line. They incorporate religious festivals and teachings to reflect diversity. They attempt to avoid favoritism. This balance is frequently upset by political and communal tensions.

History, like science, is susceptible to manipulation and control. It becomes a powerful tool for shaping societal memory through sanitized textbooks and deliberate omissions of truth. When history prioritizes fostering obedience and pride over presenting facts, it loses its essence as a field of inquiry. Instead, the classroom transforms into a factory of conformity, steering students away from critical thinking. Such manipulation aims to influence how societies remember and forget, serving the agendas of those in power. By controlling narratives, history is no longer about truth but about molding perceptions to maintain control.

2.3 HISTORY REWRITTEN BY COMMITTEE

History is the story we tell ourselves about who we are and where we come from. Educators around the world often manipulate this story to serve political agendas. From India's romanticized depiction of its freedom struggle to China's carefully curated accounts of the Communist Party, history textbooks are less about education and more about indoctrination. By rewriting the past, those in power shape the future, ensuring that students grow up not as critical thinkers but as loyal subjects.

Curricula are not neutral documents; they are deeply political tools, often shaped to serve the agendas of those in power. Around the world, governments have used education to promote specific ideologies, rewriting history and suppressing critical thinking to maintain control over the narrative. Nationalistic curricula are among the most potent examples of this manipulation, designed not to inform students but to indoctrinate them. Consider the case of India, where the portrayal of Mahatma Gandhi in school textbooks reflects selective hagiography. People rightly celebrate Gandhi's contributions to India's independence. However, his personal experiments, such as his practice of celibacy, remain controversial. Writers often omit or gloss over details like Gandhi sleeping beside young women, including his daughter-in-law. A curated narrative ensures Gandhi's position as the "Father of the Nation" remains unchallenged. It reinforces his symbolic value as a unifying figure. This narrative avoids complexities that might provoke dissent or reevaluation of his legacy.

This practice is not unique to India. President Recep Tayyip Erdoğan's administration in Turkey revised history textbooks. They glorify the Ottoman Empire. They downplay the secular reforms of Mustafa Kemal Atatürk, the founder of modern Turkey. These changes reflect Erdoğan's broader ideological agenda of reintroducing Islamic conservatism into Turkish identity. Similarly, in China, the Communist Party has meticulously curated the story of Mao Zedong. Textbooks extol his leadership in founding the People's Republic. They minimize the catastrophic failures of policies like the Great Leap Forward and the Cultural Revolution. These policies led to millions of deaths. In doing so, these curricula serve to consolidate nationalist pride while suppressing any critical analysis that might question the legitimacy of current regimes.

Suppressing critical thinking naturally extends these efforts. Educational systems that prioritize rote memorization over analytical skills do so not out of pedagogical necessity but as a deliberate strategy to produce compliant citizens. North Korea entirely subordinates its education system to the regime's propaganda. North Korean authorities deny students access to global perspectives. Instead, students spend years memorizing the accomplishments of the Kim dynasty and learning songs and slogans extolling their leaders. The North Korean government actively discourages critical thinking because it threatens their reliance on absolute control.

Even in democracies that ostensibly celebrate freedom of thought, educators continue to emphasize rote learning. Standardized testing regimes, such as those in the United States, reward students for recalling information rather than engaging with it critically. This focus is not accidental; it mirrors the interests of a system designed to produce a workforce adept at following instructions but ill-equipped to challenge the status quo. Historical precedents illustrate the danger of such systems. Nazi Germany weaponized education to produce loyal citizens and soldiers. Nazi officials rewrote textbooks to propagate Aryan superiority, twisting scientific theories like Darwinism to justify eugenics. The Nazi regime discouraged and punished critical inquiry into these ideas. This ensured generations of Germans grew up with a distorted worldview. That worldview aligned with the regime's goals.

Manipulating curricula and suppressing critical thinking serve a dual purpose. They control how citizens understand the past. They also limit their ability to question the present. By shaping education in their image, governments and elites ensure that their narratives dominate, rendering dissent difficult and innovation stifled. The classroom, which should be a place of liberation and intellectual growth, becomes instead a site of conformity and control. The consequences of this are profound, as societies built on unquestioning obedience are ill-prepared to navigate the complexities of a transforming world.

If history and science can be tools of control, then religion is perhaps the oldest and most potent weapon in the arsenal. The intersection of faith and education is fraught with tension, as societies struggle to balance tradition with modernity. What happens when classrooms become battlegrounds for sacred beliefs versus secular ideals?

2.4 PENCILS FIGHTING JIHAD

In Afghanistan, a girl carrying a pencil is not just a student; she is a revolutionary. For decades, opposing forces of progress and oppression have caught the country's education system in their crossfire. From the modernization efforts of the 1960s to the Taliban's relentless bans, the classroom has become a symbol of both hope and resistance. Governments may shutter schools and silence dreams, but advocates persist in their fight for education. The belief that learning is not just a privilege but a fundamental human right fuels this perspective.

Education in Afghanistan tells a haunting tale of interrupted progress. Cycles of war, ideology, and oppression disrupt its potential. This underscores the transformative power of knowledge and the enduring efforts to suppress it. The story begins in the pre-Taliban era, a time when Afghanistan was making strides toward modernization. In the 1960s and 1970s, government reforms and international aid led to a burgeoning education system. Enrollment rates surged, and for the first time, Afghan women attended universities in significant numbers, pursuing careers in medicine, law, and teaching. Kabul University, once a vibrant hub of learning, symbolized these advancements. Yet, this progress was fragile, undermined by the Soviet invasion in 1979. The conflict decimated the nation's infrastructure, including schools, as violence engulfed cities and displaced millions. Teachers fled, classrooms crumbled, and what had been a symbol of hope became another casualty of war.

The power vacuum left by the Soviet withdrawal in 1989 sowed the seeds for the rise of the Taliban. Emerging from the chaos of civil war in the early 1990s, the Taliban framed themselves as a force of order and morality. Drawing upon conservative interpretations of Islamic law, they imposed a rigid ideology that prioritized strict gender roles and societal control. Education became one of their primary battlegrounds, with a vision that relegated women to the domestic sphere. The Taliban justified banning girls from schools as a means of preserving morality, claiming that Western-style education corrupted Islamic values. By 1996, their rule institutionalized these restrictions, closing girls' schools, dismissing female teachers, and turning education into a tool for indoctrination.

Under Taliban rule (1996-2001), the impact on girls' education was catastrophic. Literacy rates among Afghan women plummeted to single digits, a stark reversal of the progress made decades earlier. The infrastructure of education deteriorated further, with schools repurposed as military outposts or left to decay. For Afghan girls, the consequences were profound: isolation from knowledge compounded by societal pressures to marry early, often as a means of economic survival. This erasure of education denied an entire generation the opportunity to dream beyond survival, leaving a legacy of psychological trauma and hopelessness.

The fall of the Taliban in 2001 ushered in a period of cautious revival. International intervention brought resources and renewed attention to rebuilding Afghanistan's education system. NGOs and UN agencies established schools for girls, and by 2020, millions of Afghan girls were once again in classrooms. Literacy rates began to rise, and with them, a glimmer of hope returned. Yet, persistent challenges remained. Security concerns loomed large, as insurgent attacks targeted schools and teachers, deterring families from sending their children to learn. In 2018, for instance, more than 1,000 schools were closed because of threats from extremist groups, impacting over 500,000 students. Cultural resistance, particularly in rural areas, further hindered progress, as conservative communities often viewed girls' education with suspicion.

The Taliban's return to power in 2021 reignited fears for Afghanistan's fragile progress. Despite initial promises to respect girls' education "within Islamic law," reality soon betrayed their words. Authorities closed secondary schools for girls across most provinces and dismissed female educators once more. The international response was swift and condemnatory, with sanctions and aid reductions targeting the Taliban regime. However, these measures also deepened Afghanistan's humanitarian crisis, straining the resources needed to keep schools open.

The impact of these policies reverberates far beyond the classroom. For individual Afghan girls, the denial of education represents the shattering of aspirations—to become doctors, teachers, or leaders. Psychological trauma intensifies as society defers dreams and replaces them with feelings of worthlessness and anxiety. For communities, the consequences are equally dire. Economically, restricting girls from education reduces the potential workforce, stifling productivity and growth. Health outcomes also suffer, as studies consistently link maternal education to lower mortality rates and improved community well-being.

Yet, amid despair, resistance persists. Underground schools, often hidden in homes, continue to operate despite the risks. Teachers and students alike face threats of violence, yet they defy oppression to keep the light of education alive. International and local organizations play a vital role, providing online resources and campaigning tirelessly for global attention. Platforms like social media amplify the voices of Afghan girls, sharing their stories and rallying support across borders.

The story of education in Afghanistan is a stark reminder of the broader implications of denying this basic right. It affects not only individual lives but the trajectory of entire nations. As Afghan girls continue to fight for their right to learn, the global community faces an ethical imperative to support them. The world must act through diplomacy, advocacy, and innovative solutions. Education in Afghanistan must become a promise fulfilled for all, not a privilege for the few. This struggle, emblematic of the broader fight for equality and progress, reflects humanity's enduring hope: that knowledge, once ignited, can never be entirely extinguished.

People often describe education as humanity's greatest hope to break cycles of poverty, challenge injustice, and create a more equitable world. Yet, as this chapter has shown, it is also one of our greatest battlegrounds. From gender divides to ideological control, the forces shaping education reflect the broader struggles of our societies. But amidst the darkness, there is light. Whether in underground schools in Afghanistan or classrooms challenging tradition, the fight for education continues. It is a fight not just for knowledge but for the future itself—a future where every child, regardless of gender or circumstance, can learn, grow, and dream.

Every adult has survived puberty, yet few understand its profound impact on the human journey. It is a chrysalis phase, where the boundaries between child and adult blur, and the fragile threads of identity begin to weave together. But this transformation is not just internal. Societal norms, cultural expectations, and external pressures conspire to shape how each individual emerges from this chaotic, beautiful process. To understand the modern adolescent experience, we must examine the "puberty flower." This includes its biological roots, emotional highs and lows, and the social dynamics that surround it.

3. PUBERTY FLOWER

Puberty is the great equalizer of humanity—an experience so universal yet so unique that it defies easy definition. For centuries, people treated it as a simple biological fact: a time of physical change transforming children into adults. But as we peer closer, puberty reveals itself as much more. It is a crucible of identity, a storm of hormones, and a battlefield of societal expectations. The whispers of tradition and the shouts of social media shape adolescence today with both ancient and modern forces. This subsection unpacks puberty's multifaceted nature, exploring not only the science behind the transformation but also the emotional and cultural currents that define it.

Puberty is a metamorphosis that is both universal and deeply personal, a liminal phase where childhood dissolves into adulthood, leaving behind an irrevocably changed individual. It is a time of unparalleled growth and discovery, but also one rife with confusion, insecurity, and vulnerability. Historically, societies have marked this transition with rituals, ceremonies, and structured guidance, acknowledging its profound importance in shaping identity and roles within the community. Yet today, in our hyperconnected and rapidly changing world, the path through puberty has become increasingly complex and fraught. Modern adolescents must navigate not only the timeless challenges of hormonal turbulence and self-discovery but also unprecedented pressures stemming from technology, growing social norms, and cultural conflicts. The result is a generation caught between the promise of boundless potential and the weight of overwhelming expectations.

Puberty is no longer solely about physical changes, though these remain as startling and significant as ever. Hormonal surges, which once equipped young people for survival and reproduction, now function in a world vastly different from the one where these mechanisms first evolved. Testosterone and estrogen act as ancient architects of the human body. They trigger a cascade of changes. These changes affect muscles, skin, and reproductive organs. They also influence emotions, cognition, and social behavior. Growth spurts, acne, mood swings, and the sudden awakening of sexual desire collide in a symphony of transformation. For many, this phase feels as though something violently invades the self, making their bodies and minds feel no longer entirely their own. This biological process unfolds and varies dramatically across cultures, genders, and social contexts.

Issues of identity increasingly entangle with puberty in today's world. For some, the question of "Who am I?" is straightforward; for others, it is a journey fraught with complexities. LGBTQ+ adolescents, in particular, often face an additional layer of challenges as they explore questions of gender and sexuality in environments that may be anything but supportive. In some parts of the world, Gay-Straight Alliances in schools provide a safe space. They offer a lifeline to those grappling with internalized shame or fear of rejection. But in many places, societal norms remain rigid, and the simple act of coming out can provoke hostility, ostracism, or even violence. A 2021 study by The Trevor Project revealed a shocking statistic. It found that 42% of LGBTQ+ youth in the United States seriously considered suicide in the previous year. This underscores the dire need for inclusive support systems. These young people are not just finding themselves—they are doing so in a world that often refuses to accept them.

As society grapples with questions of identity, medical science has opened new doors and sparked heated debates. The use of puberty blockers, once a little-known intervention for rare medical conditions, has become a focal point of the cultural and political battleground surrounding gender identity. For transgender adolescents, these treatments offer a reprieve from the distress of undergoing physical changes misaligned with their sense of self. Proponents argue that delaying puberty allows young people the time and space to make informed decisions about their future without irreversible consequences. Yet critics warn of potential long-term health risks and question whether adolescents possess the maturity to make such profound choices. This debate reflects broader tensions between autonomy and protection, between individual rights and societal norms.

Some adolescents navigate the deeply personal terrain of gender and sexuality. Others grapple with a lack of guidance on basic aspects of human relationships and reproduction. Sex education, a topic as old as human civilization, remains a patchwork of progress and failure. Experts credit comprehensive programs in Sweden that emphasize inclusivity and critical thinking with lowering rates of teenage pregnancy and sexually transmitted infections. Meanwhile, abstinence-only curricula in parts of the United States have left generations of young people ill-prepared for the realities of adult relationships. The consequences of inadequate sex education are stark. The World Health Organization reports that over 1 million sexually transmitted infections are acquired daily worldwide. Many of these infections are preventable through basic education. The lack of open dialog about sexuality creates more than physical risks. It perpetuates shame, stigma, and misunderstandings. Society leaves young people to navigate this critical aspect of life without a compass.

But puberty is not just about relationships and reproduction; it is also a time of immense emotional turbulence. Adolescents today face a mental health crisis on an unprecedented scale. According to UNICEF, one in seven 10-to-19-year-olds worldwide experiences a mental health disorder, and suicide is the fourth leading cause of death among this age group. Social media, once heralded as a tool for connection, has exacerbated these issues, providing a relentless stream of comparison, criticism, and curated perfection that can erode self-esteem. The pressure to project an idealized image online often clashes with the messy reality of adolescence. This leaves young people feeling isolated, even though they are more connected than any previous generation. Addressing this crisis requires not only access to mental health resources but also a cultural shift that values authenticity over appearance and connection over competition.

Yet even as young people battle internal struggles, external threats loom large. In the United States, gun violence has transformed schools from sanctuaries of learning into sites of fear and tragedy. Officials report over 300 school shootings annually. Active shooter drills have become a grim routine. Students and teachers must grapple with the psychological toll of constant vigilance. The March for Our Lives movement, led by survivors of the Parkland school shooting, has shone a spotlight on the urgent need for gun control reform. But progress remains stalled by political polarization and the outsized influence of the gun lobby. For today's adolescents, growing up in the shadow of violence adds yet another layer of complexity to an already challenging period.

Despite these myriad challenges, adolescence is also a time of boundless potential. The same hormonal surges that fuel mood swings also ignite creativity and ambition. The same social struggles that test resilience can forge empathy and connection. But realizing this potential requires a reimagining of the systems that shape adolescence, from education to healthcare to community support. Schools, in particular, must evolve beyond their traditional focus on rote memorization and standardized testing. A modern education system must equip young people with key skills. These include critical thinking, emotional intelligence, and adaptability in a complex, interconnected world. Training must equip educators to impart knowledge and recognize the emotional and social needs of their students.

Supporting adolescents through this transformative phase also demands that society confront its own discomfort with change. Puberty is a period of disruption. Bodies change, relationships shift, and identities emerge. For some, this disruption is exhilarating; for others, it is disorienting. But for all, it is an opportunity—a chance to grow, to question, to redefine. How society responds to this disruption will determine not only the trajectory of individual lives but also the future of humanity. Adolescents are not just the inheritors of the world we create; they are the architects of the world to come. By investing in their growth, supporting their struggles, and embracing their potential, we can build a future defined not by inherited challenges but by collective solutions.

At the heart of puberty is a powerful force: hormones. These chemical messengers have the ability to transform bodies, shape minds, and stir emotions in ways that are both exciting and overwhelming. To fully grasp puberty's effect on identity and society, we must first explore this biological process—a process that can foster growth but also lead to turmoil. Understanding this intricate balance is key to understanding the broader impact of puberty on the individual and the world around them.

3.1 PAUSE BUTTON FOR PUBERTY

Puberty doesn't wait for anyone. Once it begins, its relentless march can feel overwhelming—especially for transgender adolescents grappling with mismatched physical and emotional realities. Enter puberty blockers, a medical intervention designed to hit the pause button, offering time for exploration without irreversible changes. While hailed as a lifeline by many, these treatments spark fierce debate, raising questions about health risks, adolescent autonomy, and societal acceptance of fluid identities. Exploring this emerging frontier reveals the complexities of modern adolescence. It highlights the value of empathy and informed dialog in guiding young people through their journeys.

Hormone blockers have brought hope and controversy to adolescent identity. They offer a medical means to delay puberty for those questioning their gender. These medications stop producing sex hormones temporarily. They provide a temporary reprieve from the physical changes of puberty. These changes include breast development or the deepening of the voice. Proponents emphasize the potential of hormone blockers. They give adolescents time to explore their gender identity. This happens without the additional distress of bodily changes that may feel incongruent with their inner sense of self. Medical guidelines emphasize a cautious approach to hormone blockers. The World Professional Association for Transgender Health (WPATH) requires thorough evaluations and consent before initiating these treatments. For many youths experiencing gender dysphoria, this intervention can be life-changing, offering a bridge to greater self-understanding.

Yet, the use of hormone blockers has sparked significant debate, exposing the ethical and medical complexities of intervening during such a formative stage of life. Advocates argue that these treatments can alleviate profound distress, improving mental health and allowing young people the breathing space to make informed decisions about their future. Critics, however, raise concerns about potential risks, such as decreased bone density and the unknown long-term effects of halting puberty. Ethical considerations further complicate the picture: How much autonomy can adolescents truly exercise when making such life-altering choices? Historical cautionary tales remind us of the unintended consequences of early medical interventions, urging a balance between compassion and prudence.

One alternative to the often-polarized discourse around gender identity is the idea of "transligion." This framework conceptualizes transgender identity not as a biological certainty but as a belief system rooted in a deeply personal journey of self-expression. Transligion is similar to religious practices aligning with one's spirituality. It lets individuals celebrate their chosen gender through symbolic and emotional connections. This approach avoids insisting on biological or legal reclassification. Someone might express their gender identity through clothing, behavior, or a chosen name. This is similar to how adherents of a faith adopt rituals and symbols resonating with their spiritual identity. By framing gender identity in this way, society can foster acceptance without demanding wholesale changes to legal and biological frameworks, reducing friction and emphasizing personal agency.

This perspective challenges the prevailing notion that individuals possess an inherent "transgender gene" that biologically dictates their identity. Instead, it suggests that feelings of gender incongruence may arise from insecurities or discomfort with one's appearance, societal roles, or personal style. These feelings are valid and deserve empathy, but they need not demand claims such as "I am biologically a woman" or require a wholesale redefinition of gender. In transligion, cosplaying a favorite gender is self-expression and confidence-building. It resembles how individuals in other belief systems adopt practices to connect with their inner selves. This approach reframes gender identity not as a rigid binary or a demand for legal recognition but as a dynamic and deeply personal belief system.

The question of detransitioning further underscores the value of careful consideration when introducing medical interventions like hormone blockers. Detransitioning—when individuals who have transitioned to another gender later decide to return to their birth-assigned identity—is a reminder of the fluid nature of identity, particularly during adolescence. Personal accounts of detransitioning often reveal a mix of factors, including growing self-awareness, societal pressures, or dissatisfaction with medical outcomes. Advocates often describe hormone blockers as reversible, but their long-term effects, such as potential fertility issues or permanent physical changes, complicate the picture. These experiences highlight the need for an approach that prioritizes exploration and self-expression over irreversible decisions during puberty.

Ultimately, the debate surrounding hormone blockers, gender identity, and medical ethics reflects broader societal struggles to reconcile individuality with shared norms. Transligion offers a path forward, one that emphasizes self-discovery and personal belief while avoiding the polarizing demands for rigid legal and biological categorization. Society can support adolescents by fostering environments that encourage expression and exploration. This avoids binding them to premature decisions that might not align with their future selves. This approach, grounded in empathy and respect, offers a way to navigate one of the most complex challenges of our age.

Even as adolescents navigate their identities, society often leaves them adrift in understanding their bodies, relationships, and boundaries. Sex education, meant to be a compass, often reflects society's discomfort with open dialog. From myths to misinformation, the gaps in this education leave young people vulnerable. It's time to examine what happens when the manual is missing.

3.2 SEX ED: THE MISSING MANUAL

If adolescence is a maze, then sex education should be its map. Yet, for millions of young people, this map is incomplete—or entirely absent. From abstinence-only programs to outdated curricula, sex education often fails to address the realities of modern adolescence, leaving questions unanswered and vulnerabilities exposed. The result is a generation navigating relationships and sexuality with little more than guesswork. By reimagining sex education as an inclusive, empowering foundation, we can equip young people with the knowledge and confidence to make informed choices, transforming confusion into clarity.

The state of sex education across the globe presents a fractured and often inadequate response to one of humanity's most fundamental aspects: sexuality. Curricula vary wildly, reflecting a patchwork of cultural values, political priorities, and societal taboos. Countries like Sweden and the Netherlands start comprehensive sex education early. This includes discussions on relationships, consent, and LGBTQ+ inclusivity. Students benefit from these informed and progressive frameworks. In stark contrast, abstinence-only programs dominate parts of the United States. Sex education often focuses on warnings about premarital sex. It lacks practical knowledge about contraception or healthy relationships. Even within countries, the disparity is glaring; affluent urban schools may offer robust programming while rural or underfunded districts receive little more than outdated lectures laced with shame and silence. This inconsistency leaves millions of young people navigating their sexual maturity with partial, biased, or entirely absent guidance.

The gaps in sex education have profound consequences, manifesting in both personal and societal crises. One of the most measurable impacts is the correlation between inadequate education and rates of unintended pregnancies and sexually transmitted infections (STIs). The statistics are sobering. In the United States, states with abstinence-only education consistently report higher rates of teen pregnancies and STIs compared to those with comprehensive programs. For example, Mississippi, which emphasizes abstinence in its curricula, has among the highest rates of teen births in the country. These numbers are not unique to one region or ideology but reflect a global trend: where education fails, health crises follow. Yet the problem goes beyond numbers. Myths and misconceptions flourish when accurate information is absent, leading to behaviors that exacerbate risks. Surveys in countries with poor sex education reveal alarming misunderstandings, such as the belief that certain home remedies can prevent pregnancy or that contraceptives are universally harmful.

The barriers to implementing effective sex education are deeply entrenched, reflecting a collision of logistical, cultural, and ideological obstacles. A significant challenge lies in the shortage of trained professionals equipped to deliver these lessons. Many educators, untrained in the subject or uncomfortable discussing it, resort to vague or overly clinical language that fails to engage students meaningfully. A 2018 study in the United States revealed a troubling statistic. Nearly 40% of teachers responsible for sex education felt unprepared. This mirrors global trends in under-resourced schools. The content often suffers as a result, with teachers skipping critical topics like consent or LGBTQ+ issues to avoid controversy.

Religious and cultural opposition further hampers progress. Advocacy for abstinence-only education, often rooted in moral or religious beliefs, remains a powerful force, particularly in conservative societies. These groups argue that comprehensive sex education undermines traditional values, framing it as an invitation to promiscuity rather than a tool for empowerment. This resistance is not new. Institutions throughout history have cloaked sexuality in taboo to control knowledge and regulate behavior. Victorian England deemed discussions of sexual health inappropriate, leading to widespread ignorance and preventable suffering. Today's battles over curricula echo these historical tensions, as communities clash over what young people should know and when they should know it.

The inadequacies of sex education are a stark reminder of the broader failures in preparing young people for adulthood. Without accurate information and supportive frameworks, society leaves adolescents vulnerable to health risks, misinformation, and exploitation. Addressing this gap requires not just policy changes but a cultural shift— one that values open dialog over silence, inclusivity over exclusion, and knowledge over fear. By confronting these challenges, society can move toward a future where sex education is not a battleground but a foundation for healthier, more empowered lives.

Puberty is not just about biology; it's also about relationships—platonic, romantic, and everything in between. Adolescents often feel caught between traditional education's expectations and social connections' allure. This creates a unique and often tumultuous mix of learning and living.

3.3 FROM BOOKS TO BREAKUPS

For many adolescents, the schoolyard is less a place of academic rigor and a more social arena. Friendships, crushes, and heartbreaks dominate the landscape, competing with textbooks for attention. In this swirl of emotions and experiences, young people often lack the tools to navigate relationships with empathy and self-awareness. By understanding this dynamic, we can help adolescents balance their educational and emotional worlds, fostering growth in both.

The modern education system, designed to cultivate curiosity and prepare students for life, often fails to engage its audience meaningfully. With its emphasis on standardized tests, rote memorization, and outdated curricula, schools can become places of profound boredom for students. The monotony of repetitive lectures, irrelevant assignments, and rigid structures alienates many young learners. Instead of being captivated by the joy of discovery, students turn their attention elsewhere, seeking stimulation and fulfillment in areas that promise immediate gratification. The classroom transforms into a backdrop for socializing rather than a space for intellectual exploration. Clubs, parties, and past relationships become the center of attention, with the education system's original purpose—fostering learning and equipping students with life skills—fading into the background. Education-driven boredom has led to a cultural shift. Schools have become social hubs. In these hubs, the pursuit of knowledge is secondary to connection and entertainment.

Changing social norms around relationships and sexuality compound this shift. Modern society often celebrates casual sexual encounters and fluid relationships as markers of liberation. Popular media and culture play a significant role in shaping these attitudes. Shows like Euphoria or iconic figures like Carrie Bradshaw in Sex and the City portray youthful exploration and sexual experimentation as rites of passage. However, this cultural normalization often glosses over the psychological complexities of such experiences. For some, casual relationships can provide a sense of freedom and empowerment. Yet for others, they bring unintended emotional consequences, such as feelings of regret, attachment, or exploitation. These dynamics mirror broader societal shifts. They echo moments like the 1960s sexual revolution. This era challenged traditional norms but sparked debates on morality, emotional well-being, and responsibility.

Central to navigating these relationships is the concept of consent—an area where education often falls glaringly short. Consent is not merely when "no" is absent, but when clear, informed, and enthusiastic agreement is present. Teaching this nuance is crucial, yet many schools fail to address it adequately. Consent education should cover not only the legal definitions but also the interpersonal skills needed to navigate boundaries and communication. Programs like those piloted in Scandinavian countries, which emphasize mutual respect and emotional intelligence, stand as rare examples of success. However, in many parts of the world, consent education is either nonexistent or overshadowed by cultural taboos, leaving students ill-equipped to handle complex interactions. Lacking this critical knowledge perpetuates cycles of misunderstanding and harm.

This gap becomes particularly troubling when examining the prevalence of sexual violence among youth. Statistics reveal a grim reality: college campuses report alarmingly high rates of sexual assault, with one in five women experiencing such violence during their time at university. High school environments are similarly fraught, with many young people encountering harassment or coercion before they even reach adulthood. Historical patterns show a tendency to ignore or minimize harmful behaviors. Examples include Victorian silence on marital abuse and mid-20th century workplace harassment dismissals. These persist today as institutional negligence and inadequate support systems. Survivors often face significant barriers in seeking justice or healing, relying on underfunded hotlines, overburdened counseling services, or an unsympathetic legal system.

At its core, failing to recognize the emotional and relational dimensions of human sexuality roots the problem. The narratives surrounding sex and relationships often glorify liberation and experimentation without addressing their deeper implications. This is especially evident in the sociosexuality gap, where societal norms encourage men to pursue casual sex while stigmatizing women for the same behaviors. This double standard not only perpetuates gender inequality but also distorts the dynamics of relationships, leaving individuals—particularly women—feeling disempowered and emotionally unfulfilled. As argued in "cads and dads," society's celebration of fleeting encounters often overlooks the value of emotional connection and mutual respect.

Within this landscape, the dichotomy of "cads and dads" emerges as a lens through which to understand male sexuality and its societal glorification. Popular culture often celebrates cads, characterized by their promiscuity and emotional detachment, as symbols of freedom and allure. From James Bond to countless rom-com protagonists, media romanticizes the cad archetype, shaping young men's aspirations and young women's expectations. In contrast, society often undervalues dads—who represent commitment, stability, and emotional investment—seeing them as dull or overly traditional. This skewed narrative distorts perceptions of masculinity, encouraging boys to equate their worth with conquest rather than connection.

The consequences for women navigating this cultural dynamic are profound. In a social marketplace that prizes fleeting encounters over meaningful relationships, women often face conflicting pressures. Society encourages them to embrace casual relationships as markers of liberation and empowerment. On the other, they frequently bear the emotional fallout of interactions shaped by detachment and misaligned expectations. The glorification of cads leaves many women feeling unfulfilled. It pressures them to conform to a framework valuing quantity over quality. People dismiss meaningful relationships with emotionally present "dads" as outdated or unexciting.

This dichotomy feeds directly into the larger challenges of navigating sexual relationships and consent. A culture that rewards superficial connections rarely equips young people with tools to engage in meaningful communication about boundaries and desires. Societal narratives that prioritize immediacy over mutual understanding often overshadow the need to understand and respect consent—clear, informed, and enthusiastic. The result is a landscape rife with misunderstandings and, in worse cases, harm. Programs designed to teach consent and respect, while promising, remain sporadic and unevenly implemented, leaving many young people to learn these critical lessons through trial and error.

Addressing this imbalance requires redefining masculinity and prompting a broader cultural shift. By challenging the glorification of the cad and elevating the values embodied by the dad, society can foster a healthier, more supportive environment for relationships. This redefinition is not just about men; it benefits women and the wider social fabric by prioritizing emotional intimacy and mutual respect over the fleeting allure of casual encounters. In the classroom, this transformation must begin with an education system that goes beyond academics to address the complexities of relationships and identity. By teaching communication, empathy, and self-awareness, schools can prepare students to navigate the nuances of human connection—offering them not just knowledge, but wisdom for life.

The solution lies in transforming the education system to prioritize engagement, empathy, and relevance. Schools must go beyond simply delivering academic content to address the broader challenges young people face in navigating relationships, identity, and consent. By creating a curriculum that values communication, emotional intelligence, and self-reflection, education can reclaim its role as a foundation for meaningful growth. By doing so, educators can guide students toward healthier, more fulfilling paths in both their personal lives and the broader society they will shape.

Adolescence brings intense pressures that lead many young people to turn to distractions for comfort—some harmless, others destructive. These coping methods, ranging from short-lived relationships to substance abuse, highlight deeper issues within our education and support systems. By exploring the intersection of love and addiction, we gain insight into the challenges facing today's youth. Let's take a closer look at the consequences when youth spiral from breakups to drugs.

3.4 CUPID MEETS COCAINE

The pursuit of connection and escapism is as old as adolescence itself. Yet, today's youth face unprecedented challenges, from the glorification of casual relationships to the easy availability of substances. These coping mechanisms, while temporarily satisfying, often mask deeper struggles like anxiety, loneliness, and unmet expectations. To break the cycle, we must address the root causes, offering young people meaningful engagement, emotional support, and a sense of purpose.

The modern education system, with its relentless focus on standardized testing and rigid curricula, often fails to capture the curiosity and creativity of its students. The monotony of traditional schooling, combined with the lack of meaningful engagement, leaves many adolescents feeling disconnected and uninspired. For some, this disengagement manifests as truancy or academic underperformance. For others, the boredom becomes a gateway to risky behaviors, as they seek excitement and escape outside the classroom. The allure of past relationships, parties, and substances offers a temporary respite, making freedom from the confines of school life appear illusory. However, these distractions often spiral into patterns of instability, heartbreak, and a deeper sense of inadequacy. Social environments often expose adolescents to drugs. Many initially view these substances as coping mechanisms. They help with anxiety and depression stemming from failed relationships or unmet expectations.

This cycle has repeated through generations, tracing its roots to the early drug epidemics of the 20th century. California in the 1960s, for instance, became synonymous with the counterculture movement and the widespread use of LSD and marijuana. By the 1980s, the crack cocaine crisis devastated communities, disproportionately affecting marginalized groups. Remnants of these crises are visible today. Sprawling tent encampments line the streets of cities like San Francisco and Los Angeles. They house individuals trapped in addiction and poverty cycles. Authorities often temporarily clear these encampments during high-profile visits, only for them to reappear once the spotlight fades. This recurring pattern of neglect highlights society's inability—or unwillingness—to address the root causes of addiction and its links to disillusionment and trauma.

For many young people, substance use begins as an escape from the emotional fallout of violent or unstable relationships. Early heartbreaks, coupled with the stress of navigating adolescence, leave deep scars that are difficult to heal. Drugs offer a seductive promise: temporary relief from the pain and anxiety that haunt them. Over time, this reliance evolves into dependency, as the substances become not just a coping mechanism but a means of survival. Even when opportunities for rehabilitation arise, many choose to remain in the cycle, as sobriety threatens to unearth the traumas they are desperate to forget. This particularly affects those whose insecurities from failed relationships, societal pressures, and alienation have eroded their self-esteem.

The prevalence of substance abuse among youth today is alarming. Vaping, once marketed as a safer alternative to smoking, has surged in popularity among teenagers, introducing many to nicotine addiction. Opioids, overprescribed in the late 1990s and early 2000s, have left a devastating legacy. Many adolescents succumbed to addiction through peer pressure or self-medication for mental health issues. Data from the National Institute on Drug Abuse shows a growing concern. Nearly 10% of U.S. high school seniors report misusing prescription drugs. Alcohol and marijuana remain staples of adolescent experimentation. Similar patterns appear worldwide, extending beyond the United States. Globally, young people increasingly turn to substances to numb modern life's pressures. Economic uncertainty, social isolation, and social media exacerbate these pressures.

Underlying these behaviors are deeper mental health challenges, such as anxiety, depression, and feelings of inadequacy. The rise of social media has amplified these struggles, offering constant comparisons and unattainable ideals that erode self-esteem. Platforms that promise connection often deliver loneliness, as curated images and highlight reels create a distorted reality. A mental health crisis is emerging. Rising rates of adolescent depression and anxiety reflect this crisis. Studies show a clear link between social media use and declining mental well-being. Yet, barriers to treatment persist. Stigma surrounding mental health prevents many from seeking help, while a lack of access to affordable and effective services exacerbates the problem. In schools, where early intervention could make a significant difference, a shortage of counselors and resources leaves many students to navigate these challenges alone.

The cycle of academic disengagement, substance abuse, and untreated mental health issues creates a pervasive sense of hopelessness for many young people. These challenges, while deeply personal, are also systemic, reflecting the failures of institutions to address the needs of their most vulnerable members. Breaking the cycle requires a fundamental shift. Education systems must prioritize engagement and relevance. Mental health services should be accessible and destigmatized. Society must address addiction and despair's root causes. Without these changes, more people will fall through the cracks. Their stories will fill the streets, testifying to a society that failed to care for its own.

While adolescence brings its share of personal challenges, external dangers increasingly dominate the landscape. Gun violence in schools, a uniquely modern crisis, has turned classrooms into places of fear rather than learning. How can young people thrive when their safety is constantly at risk?

3.5 SAFETY FIRST, LEARNING LATER

Educators design schools to serve as sanctuaries of growth and learning. Yet, for millions of students, they have become sites of fear and trauma, haunted by the specter of gun violence. From active shooter drills to the psychological toll of constant vigilance, the impact is devastating. Addressing this crisis requires not just policy change but a cultural reckoning, one that prioritizes the safety and well-being of our youngest citizens.

Gun violence has cast a long and dark shadow over educational institutions, transforming places of learning into sites of fear and tragedy. School shootings, once unthinkable, have become a grim reality in many nations, particularly in the United States. Statistics paint a harrowing picture. In 2023, the U.S. experienced over 300 school shootings annually. These incidents ranged from targeted violence to accidental discharges on school grounds. Each school shooting leaves behind a trail of devastation. It causes immediate loss of lives, fractures communities, and leaves survivors with enduring trauma. Columbine High School in 1999 marked a turning point, searing school shootings into the public consciousness. Despite public outcry, the frequency of school shootings has increased. Events like Sandy Hook Elementary in 2012 and Marjory Stoneman Douglas High School in 2018 reignited debates but led to little systemic change.

For students, the psychological toll of living under the constant threat of gun violence is profound. Active shooter drills, once unimaginable, are now a routine part of school life, forcing children as young as kindergarteners to rehearse survival scenarios. While these drills aim to prepare, they also instill a pervasive sense of hypervigilance and anxiety. Many students report feeling unsafe at school, their minds divided between academic pursuits and an undercurrent of fear. Cold War-era nuclear drills offer historical parallels, with existential threats looming over every classroom. Unlike the distant fear of a nuclear strike, gun violence feels immediate and intimate. It erodes the foundational sense of security schools are meant to provide.

At the heart of this crisis lies the intricate web of the military-industrial complex and the influence of the gun lobby. The gun industry wields significant economic and political power. Manufacturers and advocacy groups like the National Rifle Association (NRA) shape policies that prioritize profit over public safety. Lobbying efforts, often backed by millions of dollars, ensure that even modest gun control measures face staunch opposition. Lawmakers wrote the Second Amendment in a vastly different historical context. It has become a rallying cry for those resisting regulation. Gun control has become a deeply polarized battle, with resistance stymying progress at every turn. Legislative efforts face repeated obstruction because of partisan divisions and the financial influence of the gun lobby. The enduring legacy of this dynamic mirrors other instances where economic interests have overridden public welfare, such as the tobacco industry's decades-long denial of smoking dangers.

Despite these challenges, advocacy and prevention efforts have emerged as powerful counterforces. Student-led movements, most notably March for Our Lives, have galvanized young people to demand change. The 2018 shooting in Parkland, Florida, sparked this initiative. It has brought urgency to the gun control conversation. Social media has been used to organize protests, advocate for policy reform, and challenge complacency. These movements reflect a broader historical pattern of youth activism driving societal change, from the Civil Rights Movement to anti-war protests. Their voices, however, often collide with the entrenched barriers of political inertia and corporate interests.

Policy proposals aimed at reducing gun violence range from universal background checks to mental health screenings and secure storage laws. While these measures enjoy broad public support, their implementation remains elusive in the face of political gridlock. Countries like Australia enacted sweeping gun reforms after the Port Arthur massacre in 1996. These examples show that change is possible. However, they contrast starkly with the U.S., where ideology, money, and power paralyze progress.

The epidemic of gun violence in schools is not just a crisis of safety but a failure of societal priorities. It reflects a world where corporations prioritize profits over people, leaving the youngest and most vulnerable to bear the brunt of political dysfunction. Addressing this issue requires more than policy changes; it demands a cultural reckoning, a reimagining of values that places the well-being of children above all else. Only then can schools reclaim their purpose as sanctuaries of learning and growth, free from the specter of violence.

Society designs education to act as the great equalizer and a key to a better future. Yet it has become another casualty of dysfunction, a system skewed by privilege and outdated ideals. From curricula that stifle critical thinking to institutions that serve only the wealthy, the classroom reflects the broader inequalities of society.

But ignorance is not just a personal tragedy—it becomes a public health crisis, as explored in Chapter 7: Healthcare Fails. Misinformation and withholding critical knowledge weaken healthcare systems, leaving humanity vulnerable to both disease and exploitation. The dysfunction of education feeds directly into the dysfunction of healthcare, where the human body becomes yet another battlefield for profit and power.

7

Healthcare Fails

"Of all the forms of inequality, injustice in healthcare
is the most shocking and inhumane."

– MARTIN LUTHER KING JR.

Healthcare is one of humanity's crowning achievements—a system designed to heal, preserve, and enhance life. Vaccines have eradicated diseases that once decimated populations, antibiotics have turned fatal infections into minor inconveniences, and modern surgeries routinely achieve feats previously deemed miraculous. Yet, lurking in the shadows of these triumphs is a paradox. The same system that saves lives also prioritizes profit over healing. This leaves millions without access to essential care. Pharmaceutical companies, often regarded as the engines of medical innovation, have evolved into entities where the bottom line eclipses their attempt to save lives. From eye-watering drug prices to monopolistic practices that stifle competition, healthcare today has become a commodity rather than a universal right. As the world marvels at its medical advances, it must also confront the uncomfortable truth that wealthy interests rig the system to prioritize profits over well-being.

The story of global healthcare is a tale of contradiction. On one hand, humanity has achieved unprecedented advancements in medicine, from vaccines that have eradicated deadly diseases to life-saving treatments that once seemed like science fiction. On the other hand, the institutions driving these breakthroughs—large pharmaceutical companies collectively referred to as "Big Pharma"—embody a stark tension. They stand between the promise of public health and the pursuit of profit. These entities, ostensibly devoted to improving human well-being, operate within a framework of market incentives that often prioritize financial gain over equitable access to care. As a result, the very tools designed to heal have become instruments of exclusion, benefiting those who can afford them while leaving billions underserved.

Historical forces deeply entrenched the roots of this tension. In the 20th century, pharmaceutical companies emerged as key players in the fight against diseases like polio, tuberculosis, and malaria. However, alongside their contributions to public health, their profit-driven practices became apparent. The 1950s saw the rise of blockbuster drugs like antibiotics, which revolutionized medicine but also heralded a new era of pharmaceutical dominance. By the 1980s, as neoliberal policies deregulated industries worldwide, Big Pharma cemented its role as a global powerhouse. This era also saw the notorious rise of pharmaceutical pricing scandals. One striking example was the astronomical cost of AZT, the first drug approved for treating HIV/AIDS. Initially priced at $10,000 per year in the late 1980s, it sparked outrage as activists highlighted how the exorbitant cost effectively condemned poorer patients to death. Despite the public outcry, the pattern of prioritizing profits over accessibility persisted, laying bare the ethical quandaries at the heart of Big Pharma's operations.

The interplay between Big Pharma and the broader healthcare system reveals a web of influence spanning legal, media, and political domains. Legally, pharmaceutical companies wield patents as weapons, creating monopolies that prevent cheaper generic alternatives from entering the market. The story of insulin in the United States is a case in point. Discovered over a century ago, insulin remains prohibitively expensive, with prices skyrocketing in recent decades despite minimal changes to its production. This is not a mere coincidence, but the result of a calculated strategy to maximize profits. Patents and regulatory loopholes ensure that even life-sustaining drugs remain out of reach for many, perpetuating cycles of dependency and despair.

In the media, the pharmaceutical industry's influence shapes public narratives about health, often obscuring systemic issues. Advertising budgets for prescription drugs run into billions annually. These campaigns saturate television and digital platforms with messages. They frame health care as a matter of individual responsibility rather than systemic reform. This strategy, coupled with aggressive lobbying, creates a political environment where policies align with corporate interests rather than public needs. One need only look at the opioid crisis to understand the consequences. Beginning in the late 1990s, companies like Purdue Pharma aggressively marketed opioids, such as OxyContin, downplaying their addictive potential. The result was a nationwide epidemic that claimed hundreds of thousands of lives, all while generating billions in profits. Despite the devastation, courts have imposed limited legal accountability, with settlements often amounting to a fraction of the revenue generated.

These dynamics are not unique to one country but represent a global pattern of inequity. In developing nations, systemic issues magnify the challenges. During the HIV/AIDS epidemic of the 1990s and early 2000s, Big Pharma's insistence on enforcing patents prevented the widespread distribution of affordable antiretroviral drugs in Africa. The refusal to lower prices or allow generics led to millions of preventable deaths, even as governments and activists pleaded for action. Only sustained international pressure, including protests and high-profile legal battles, pushed companies to make generic versions available, albeit years too late for many.

Understanding the role of Big Pharma requires scrutinizing the systems that enable its dominance. This chapter explores how legal frameworks, media strategies, and political lobbying intersect to maintain the industry's monopolistic grip. It also considers the broader societal implications, particularly the ways these practices reinforce existing inequalities. As we navigate the intersection of health and profit, one question looms large: how can a system designed to heal also become a mechanism for harm? The answer lies not only in the actions of corporations, but in the structures that allow them to thrive. This dynamic demands scrutiny if we are to envision a future where healthcare serves humanity rather than the market.

The relationship between Big Pharma and the world of drugs—both legal and illicit—is a complex dynamic with profit motives, political maneuvering, and societal impact. At its core lies a striking paradox: while pharmaceutical companies produce life-saving medications, they also engage in practices that blur the lines between healing and harm. The journey of prescription drugs, from laboratory development to becoming substances of abuse on the streets, reveals many layers of complicity. These involve Big Pharma, foreign drug cartels, and policymakers.

One need look no further than the opioid epidemic to see how pharmaceutical companies inadvertently—or in some cases knowingly—contributed to the rise of street-level drug addiction. In the late 1990s, Purdue Pharma aggressively marketed OxyContin, a powerful opioid painkiller, as a safe and effective solution for chronic pain. By downplaying its addictive potential, Purdue and other companies flooded the market with prescriptions, particularly in economically depressed regions like

Appalachia. The overprescription of these drugs created a pipeline from pharmacies to black markets. As prescriptions became harder to obtain because of mounting regulations, individuals turned to cheaper and more accessible alternatives. These included heroin and illicitly manufactured fentanyl, often supplied by international drug cartels. This convergence of corporate greed and the shadowy operations of foreign drug mafias created a public health crisis. Over 500,000 opioid-related deaths occurred in the United States alone between 1999 and 2019.

The story of medical marijuana and broader drug legalization policies adds another layer of intrigue to this narrative. Cannabis, long vilified by prohibitionist policies, has emerged as a potential alternative to traditional pharmaceutical treatments for conditions such as chronic pain, anxiety, and epilepsy. This shift poses a significant threat to pharmaceutical companies, whose profits often rely on patented medications for pain management, such as opioids. Unsurprisingly, some pharmaceutical firms have actively lobbied against cannabis legalization. During California's Proposition 64 campaign to legalize recreational marijuana in 2016, revelations exposed that Insys Therapeutics, a company producing fentanyl-based medications, contributed $500,000 to anti-legalization efforts. Their reasoning barely concealed the truth: cannabis represented a direct competitor to their products.

Yet, the relationship between Big Pharma and cannabis is not purely antagonistic. As legalization spreads, pharmaceutical companies have sought to stake their claim in this burgeoning market. Researchers have developed and approved synthetic cannabinoids, such as Marinol and Epidiolex, for specific medical uses. This allows companies to profit from cannabis-derived treatments while maintaining control over their production and distribution. This dual strategy—opposing broad legalization while investing in pharmaceutical alternatives—underscores Big Pharma's ability to adapt to and manipulate evolving drug policies to its advantage.

The broader implications of drug legalization extend beyond cannabis. In states where marijuana is legal, studies show a decline in opioid prescriptions, suggesting that cannabis serves as a safer alternative for pain management. However, this trend also poses a financial threat to pharmaceutical companies that depend on the lucrative opioid market. To counteract this shift, some companies have funded research that emphasizes the risks of cannabis use, including its potential for dependency or cognitive impairment. While such concerns are valid, the selective focus on cannabis risks reveals a strategic effort. This contrasts with decades of efforts to minimize the dangers of opioids, shaping public perception to maintain market dominance.

The role of Big Pharma in shaping drug policy debates is both overt and covert. Funding for research, advocacy campaigns, and political lobbying allows these companies to steer conversations about drug efficacy and safety. For instance, some pharmaceutical firms have supported studies highlighting the benefits of long-term opioid therapy for chronic pain. This happened despite mounting evidence of its role in the addiction and overdose crises. These companies fund anti-legalization campaigns that frame marijuana and other substances as dangerous or untested. This selective narrative control shapes' public opinion and policy outcomes, often prioritizing corporate interests over public health.

The collusion between pharmaceutical companies and foreign drug cartels further complicates the landscape. In regions like Mexico, cartels control much of the illicit drug trade. There is growing evidence of overlapping networks that divert pharmaceutical opioids to black markets. Cartels capitalize on the demand created by prescription drug dependency, supplying heroin and synthetic fentanyl to communities ravaged by addiction. While direct links between Big Pharma and cartels are rare, their shared interest in sustaining demand creates a symbiotic relationship. This relationship exploits the vulnerabilities of addicted populations.

For handling these kinds of issues, Big Pharma often faces opposition rooted in arguments that draw from ancient or pseudo-practices like Ayurveda, homeopathy, and natural medicine. Government bodies often amplify this inclination as they seek to secure vote banks, offering tacit or overt support to alternative practices. Yet, in promoting these alternatives, we risk neglecting the critical importance of the golden hour of treatment—where every minute counts in saving lives. Delays caused by reliance on such pseudo-practices can lead to irreversible consequences, as patients may seek modern medicine only when it is no longer effective. In this dance between tradition and modernity, the underlying forces remain unexamined. These include the commodification of health, the mistrust in scientific systems, and the cultural narrative that pits ancient wisdom against contemporary innovation. This friction reveals a broader societal struggle, where identity, politics, and profit often entangle choices about healing, sidelining evidence and outcomes.

The story of healthcare inequity extends beyond boardrooms and corporate strategies, deeply affecting the realm of reproductive health. In this space, the personal struggle for autonomy clashes with Big Pharma's profit-driven strategies, transforming matters of life and choice into an economic battleground. Examining this intersection reveals a harsh truth: the fight for reproductive rights is not merely a moral issue but also an economic one, where the drive for profit often undermines the fundamental rights and choices of individuals.

1. BABY RIGHTS ARE OUTSIDE

Society often frames the right to make decisions about one's body as a cornerstone of freedom. Yet, the harsh realities of economics increasingly undermine this ideal. In the world of reproductive health, access to contraceptives and abortion medications can mean the difference between freedom and fear for millions. Big Pharma's shadow stretches over every choice, every clinic, and every patient. Pharmaceutical companies determine who can access these life-changing drugs, how much they cost, and the conditions for their use. For marginalized communities, this often translates into limited options, higher risks, and devastating health consequences. Rather than empowering individuals, the commodification of reproductive healthcare has turned it into a privilege accessible only to those who can afford it. This perpetuates cycles of inequality under the guise of progress.

Public discourse often frames the debate surrounding reproductive health and abortion rights as a moral or philosophical contest. Beneath the surface lies the intricate and powerful influence of economic interests, particularly those of pharmaceutical companies. Big Pharma, with its substantial lobbying power and market dominance, plays a pivotal role in shaping the legislative and social landscape of reproductive health. This influence complicates the narrative, intertwining public health needs with corporate strategies designed to maximize profit.

Take, for example, the pharmaceutical industry's influence on abortion legislation. While many companies publicly align themselves with reproductive rights to signal social responsibility, their lobbying efforts often tell a more nuanced story. In countries where abortion stirs political contention, pharmaceutical firms often fund political campaigns on both sides of the debate. For instance, companies with investments in contraceptive development may support abortion restrictions to drive demand for their products. Conversely, those producing medical abortion drugs like mifepristone and misoprostol advocate for laws that ensure accessibility. However, this often comes with a focus on maintaining high pricing and profit margins. The interplay of these forces ensures that the conversation around reproductive rights remains not only ethically charged but also economically lucrative.

The pricing and availability of abortion medications further reveal the role of Big Pharma in perpetuating inequality. In the United States, the cost of a medical abortion can range from $500 to $800. This is a stark contrast to countries where government-subsidized health care significantly lowers the price. These disparities highlight the pharmaceutical industry's ability to exploit regulatory environments, setting prices that prioritize profit over accessibility. This dynamic extends beyond abortion drugs. A few companies patent contraceptives, particularly long-acting reversible contraceptives (LARCs) like IUDs, creating monopolies that stifle competition and inflate prices. In low-income regions, this pricing strategy limits access, forcing millions of women to rely on less effective or riskier methods of birth control.

The intersection of pharmaceutical interests and sex education adds another layer to this complex picture. In some cases, pharmaceutical companies sponsor educational materials distributed in schools, subtly promoting their products under the guise of public health initiatives. This practice raises questions about the impartiality of the information provided to young people. For example, materials funded by manufacturers of LARCs may downplay the benefits of condoms. They may also emphasize abstinence in ways that align with corporate interests rather than comprehensive public health strategies. Such efforts shape societal attitudes toward reproductive health, ensuring that the pharmaceutical industry remains a gatekeeper of knowledge and access.

The story becomes even more entangled when considering how these dynamics intersect with broader drug policies and the black market. The high cost and restricted access to legal abortion pills and contraceptives often drive desperate individuals toward unregulated alternatives. In regions that criminalize abortion, black markets flourish, offering counterfeit or unsafe medications that endanger lives. Ironically, some of these black-market supplies originate from overproduction or illicit diversion of products by pharmaceutical manufacturers themselves. Foreign drug cartels, sensing an opportunity, step in to fill the void, blending legitimate medical products with their own operations to exploit vulnerable populations.

This intersection of corporate control, regulatory frameworks, and illicit markets perpetuates social inequality, disproportionately affecting marginalized communities. While wealthy individuals navigate restrictive systems through private clinics or overseas travel, those with fewer resources face limited, often dangerous, options. This stark disparity underscores how the commodification of reproductive health prioritizes the interests of elites, ensuring that their dominance remains unchallenged.

By examining the economic forces behind reproductive health, the debate is not solely about personal morality or political ideology. It also revolves around power— who wields it, who profits from it, and who misses out on its benefits. In this light, the fight for reproductive rights extends beyond individual autonomy to encompass broader questions of equity, access, and justice. Recognizing and dismantling these structural barriers is essential. This is the path to creating a society where reproductive health is a universal right, not a privilege reserved for those who can afford it.

Complex ethical, legal, and societal arguments deeply embed the debate over abortion. Yet, the pro-choice perspective consistently emphasizes a foundational principle: the autonomy and rights of women must take precedence. Assertions by pro-life advocates often rest on oversimplified or rigid interpretations of science, morality, and law that fail to account for the lived realities of pregnancy. For example, the claim that human life begins at conception assumes a definitive moral and scientific consensus that does not exist. Life, in biological terms, is a continuum. Sperm and eggs exist before conception, yet society does not treat their destruction as morally equivalent to ending a pregnancy. This perspective ignores the essential question of personhood—a complex social and philosophical concept that varies across cultures and legal systems.

At the core of the pro-choice stance is the principle of bodily autonomy. The idea that a fetus's right to life can override a woman's autonomy presumes that one person's dependence on another justifies infringing on their rights. Such logic, applied elsewhere, would demand forced organ donation or compelled medical interventions—actions widely regarded as violations of individual liberty. History offers grim examples of the dangers of denying bodily autonomy. Examples include the forced sterilizations of marginalized women in 20th century America and restrictive abortion laws. Such laws have endangered countless lives by driving individuals to unsafe procedures. Together, these injustices highlight the urgent need to protect reproductive rights as an integral part of broader human rights.

Moreover, pro-life rhetoric often relies on idealized notions of morality and responsibility while overlooking the realities of unintended pregnancies. Advocates argue that alternatives like adoption negate the need for abortion, yet this perspective ignores the profound physical, emotional, and economic toll of pregnancy itself. Carrying an unwanted pregnancy to term is not a morally neutral act; it demands that women endure significant risks and sacrifices, often if their mental and physical health, financial stability, and personal aspirations are at stake. In failing to address these realities, such arguments prioritize potential life over actual lives, placing an undue burden on women.

The notion that abortion devalues human life also falls short when viewed in a societal context. Countries with strong reproductive rights, such as Sweden and the Netherlands, often exhibit higher standards of living. They also have lower rates of unintended pregnancies. This success is thanks to comprehensive sex education, accessible contraception, and robust social support systems. These societies affirm life by ensuring that children are born into circumstances where they can thrive. They allow women to make decisions that align with their well-being and capabilities.

Conversely, restrictive abortion laws often correlate with higher maternal mortality rates and unsafe procedures, exposing the hypocrisy of policies that claim to protect life while endangering it.

Religious arguments further complicate the discourse, as they often impose specific theological interpretations on a pluralistic society. In nations founded on principles of religious freedom, such as the United States, laws rooted in particular doctrines violate the principle of separating church and state. While individuals have the right to practice their faith, using these beliefs to curtail others' rights infringes on the freedoms of those with differing values. The imposition of religious morality through abortion restrictions reveals an unsettling trend: the prioritization of ideological conformity over individual agency.

Pro-life advocates wield scientific advancements and public opinion to bolster their case, yet these reveal inconsistencies. While advancements in fetal imaging provide valuable insights into development, they do not determine legal personhood or resolve ethical debates about autonomy. Public opinion, often cited to justify restrictive laws, divides deeply and depends on context, making it an unreliable foundation for universal rights. True democracy safeguards personal freedoms against the tyranny of the majority, ensuring that individuals retain control over decisions that affect their bodies and lives.

The debate over reproductive health often pivots around the question of when life—and thus individual rights—begins. This conversation is not just philosophical; biological factors deeply root this issue. From the complicated mechanics of a fetus's circulatory system to the monumental moment of the first breath, this transition is profound. It offers a compelling lens through which to examine the interplay of science, ethics, and rights.

1.1 BREATHING INTO HUMAN RIGHTS

The moment a newborn takes its first breath is both miraculous and ordinary—a biological marvel that unfolds thousands of times each day around the world. Inside the womb, a fetus's circulatory system bypasses the lungs, which are inactive until birth. Specialized structures like the foramen ovale and ductus arteriosus ensure that blood flows efficiently, sustaining life in an environment devoid of oxygenated air. At birth, this system undergoes a dramatic transformation. The newborn's first cry forces fluid from the lungs, allowing them to fill with air. Hormonal surges trigger the closure of fetal structures and initiate independent respiration. This physiological shift marks not just survival but the start of self-sustenance. Viewed through the lens of rights, this moment offers a biologically grounded basis for defining how dependency transforms into individuality. It challenges societies to reconcile scientific realities with ethical considerations.

At birth, humanity witnesses one of nature's most breathtaking transitions. It is the moment a fetus, reliant on every beat of its mother's heart for survival, suddenly breaks free. It takes a sharp, shuddering inhale, signaling the fragile but unmistakable start of independence. This event is not merely symbolic; it represents an intricate symphony of physiological, biochemical, and environmental changes that are both miraculous and meticulously orchestrated. Before this moment, the fetus exists in a unique state of dependency, supported by specialized structures and mechanisms that bypass the lungs entirely. It is only after successfully navigating this transformative process that the fetus achieves a level of independence. This marks the point where the concept of individual human rights can meaningfully begin.

Inside the womb, a fetus's circulatory system is an elegant design of adaptation. Lacking functional lungs, the fetus relies on the placenta and umbilical cord to exchange oxygen and nutrients. Structures such as the ductus venosus, which shunts blood away from the liver, and the foramen ovale, which directs oxygen-rich blood between the heart's atria, exemplify this tailored system. The ductus arteriosus, another critical pathway, reroutes blood from the pulmonary artery directly to the aorta, bypassing the inactive lungs. This setup ensures that vital organs receive oxygenated blood, but it cannot sustain life outside the womb.

The journey from dependence to independence begins with the newborn's first exposure to the outside world. Upon delivery, environmental stimuli—a sudden drop in temperature, tactile stimulation, and the release from uterine pressure—activate the newborn's respiratory system. A cascade of signals travels to the brainstem's medulla oblongata, triggering the first inhalation. This initial breath is a monumental physiological effort. The diaphragm contracts, creating negative pressure that draws air into fluid-filled lungs. As the alveoli expand, surfactant—a lipid-rich substance produced late in fetal development—reduces surface tension, preventing the lungs from collapsing. Without this critical adaptation, the newborn would struggle to oxygenate blood, underscoring why premature infants, often lacking sufficient surfactant, require medical intervention.

Simultaneously, the cardiovascular system undergoes a dramatic transformation. With the first breaths, oxygen floods the lungs, prompting pulmonary vessels to dilate and decreasing pulmonary vascular resistance. Blood that previously bypassed the lungs now flows through them, facilitating oxygenation. Pressure shifts within the heart close to the foramen ovale, while the ductus arteriosus constricts in response to rising oxygen levels and declining prostaglandin concentrations. The umbilical cord's clamping halts blood flow through the ductus venosus, redirecting circulation entirely through the newborn's body. Within hours, these fetal shunts permanently close, leaving behind vestiges like the ligamentum arteriosum and ligamentum venosum as reminders of the fetus's previous dependency.

This transition is further supported by biochemical and hormonal responses. The birth process triggers a surge of catecholamines, such as epinephrine, which stabilize blood glucose levels and adapt the cardiovascular system to postnatal demands. Cortisol, released in the last weeks of pregnancy, prepares the lungs for fluid absorption and primes the body for thermoregulation. Even thyroid hormones play a role, increasing metabolic activity to meet the energy-intensive needs of independent life.

Yet, it is the first cry that encapsulates the newborn's transformation. This cry, often seen as an emotional milestone, is a physiological marvel. It expels remaining fluid from the airways, ensures full inflation of the alveoli, and serves as an auditory indicator of the newborn's vitality. This act completes the transition, marking the newborn's entry into a world where it can sustain itself without the placenta's lifeline.

From a philosophical and ethical perspective, the newborn's achievement of physiological independence provides a compelling basis for defining the onset of individual rights. Before this transition, the fetus's life is inextricably bound to the mother, incapable of surviving without her support. The intricate, stepwise adaptation from fetal circulation to neonatal respiration underscores the complexity of this transformation. Only when the newborn successfully breathes and circulates blood independently does it attain a status distinct from its prior dependence.

This understanding has profound implications for how we define and protect life at its earliest stages. It compels us to consider the continuum of development not as a binary event but as a journey marked by critical milestones. Recognizing these transitions can enrich ethical debates and inform policies. These policies balance respect for potential life with the rights and autonomy of the living, sentient individuals who sustain it.

In conclusion, the pro-choice perspective champions the nuanced realities of reproductive health, prioritizing women's autonomy and rights in the face of oversimplified and often contradictory pro-life arguments. It advocates for safe and legal access to abortion as an integral component of comprehensive health care, recognizing that such decisions are deeply personal and situational. Upholding these rights affirms not only the dignity and agency of women but also the broader societal values of freedom, equity, and compassion. As we examine this issue, the conversation must evolve beyond moral absolutism to embrace the complex interplay of individual circumstances, public health, and human rights.

The pursuit of health and happiness has long been entangled with the pursuit of profit. Nowhere is this tension more poignant than in the realm of reproduction. The journey to parenthood, filled with hope and vulnerability, has become fertile ground for exploitation. Fertility clinics, promising miracles, often steer patients toward costly interventions not because they are necessary but because they are lucrative. To understand how commodification works, we must first examine how the healthcare system transforms, creating life into a business model. This system leaves countless families behind.

2. MONEY HONEY

Few experiences are as deeply personal—or as emotionally charged—as the desire to create life. For many couples, this journey begins with fertility treatments, a field where science and hope intertwine. Yet, behind the glossy brochures and compassionate promises of fertility clinics lies a stark reality: an industry driven by financial incentives rather than patient outcomes. Hypothyroidism or polycystic ovary syndrome (PCOS)—disorders that, while disruptive, are frequently treatable with carefully managed hormone therapies. These treatments, involving medications like clomiphene or letrozole, stimulate ovulation and could allow conception within months at a fraction of the cost of more invasive methods. Yet, many couples never hear these options. Instead, clinics swiftly usher them into the high-cost, high-tech world of in vitro fertilization. IVF, while revolutionary, has become the cornerstone of a business model that prioritizes profit over affordability. Patents and proprietary technologies inflate prices, making treatments inaccessible to all but the wealthiest. The exploitation extends to surrogacy, where vulnerable women bear both the physical and ethical burdens of a system that commodifies the act of giving life. This dynamic reveals a healthcare model not built to serve but to extract, turning the miracle of parenthood into a privilege rather than a right.

For women with hormone imbalances, the road to conception often begins with a promise of medical solutions. A straightforward diagnosis might reveal conditions like hypothyroidism or polycystic ovary syndrome (PCOS)—disorders that, while disruptive, are frequently treatable with carefully managed hormone therapies. These treatments, involving medications like clomiphene or letrozole, stimulate ovulation and could allow conception within months at a fraction of the cost of more invasive methods. Yet, many couples never hear these options. Instead, clinics swiftly usher them into the high-cost, high-tech world of in vitro fertilization (IVF).

The shift from simpler treatments to IVF is not accidental but calculated. Fertility clinics, often run as profit-driven enterprises, frame IVF as the optimal solution, emphasizing its success rates and "time sensitivity." This narrative is compelling to couples, particularly those who feel the clock of biology ticking loudly in their ears. What they may not realize is that the financial incentives for hospitals and clinics to recommend IVF far outweigh their commitment to exploring more affordable alternatives. IVF cycles generate thousands of dollars in revenue per patient, with added costs for medications, embryo freezing, and genetic screening. Hormone therapy, in contrast, is relatively inexpensive and offers limited profit margins. This economic disparity drives many clinics to overprescribe IVF. It subtly steers patients away from options that could achieve the same results with greater patience and less financial strain.

The mechanisms of profit extend beyond the clinics themselves, into the realm of proprietary technologies and patents. Pharmaceutical companies patent the drugs used in IVF, from ovarian stimulants to hormone support medications, enabling them to set exorbitant prices. Companies similarly protect cryopreservation technologies and embryo culture systems, ensuring that each IVF cycle remains a lucrative endeavor. Hospitals and clinics, beholden to these proprietary systems, pass the costs onto patients while appearing that these systems are necessary. The narrative of cutting-edge science becomes a smokescreen for financial exploitation, with couples unaware that their journey to parenthood is being monetized at every turn.

The consequences of this system extend globally, creating a gap between those who can afford advanced reproductive technologies and those who cannot. In wealthier nations, marketers promote IVF as the ultimate solution for infertility, while they downplay or dismiss the lower costs of simpler treatments. In developing countries, the disparities are starker. Here, many struggle to access even basic reproductive healthcare, while clinics reserve IVF for the wealthy elite. Clinics in these regions frequently exploit the lack of public awareness, offering loans or installment plans that entangle financially vulnerable couples in debt cycles. For every successful IVF story, there are countless untold tales of families left drained emotionally and economically. These families have invested everything in a system designed to prioritize profits over results.

Surrogacy, another facet of reproductive technology, mirrors these inequities. Where legal, advocates often present it as the last hope for couples facing infertility. Clinics emphasize their success rates while glossing over their ethical and financial complexities. Surrogates, typically women from economically disadvantaged backgrounds, enter contracts that offer financial relief but often expose them to significant health risks. The commodification of reproduction, whether through IVF or surrogacy, underscores a stark reality: the business of fertility thrives not on equitable solutions but on perpetuating inequalities.

Patents further exacerbate these divides, creating monopolies over reproductive technologies that drive up costs and stifle competition. Instead of democratizing access, these patents ensure that only a privileged few can afford state-of-the-art treatments. Companies weaponized the promise of innovation to justify exorbitant pricing, forcing those without means to dream of parenthood from the sidelines. This system, designed to maximize profits, commodifies one of humanity's most intimate desires—creating life.

The narrative woven by fertility clinics and pharmaceutical companies is one of hope and technological progress, but beneath this surface lies a troubling truth. The reproductive healthcare industry operates as a marketplace where corporations package and sell hope, setting prices based on profit rather than medical necessity. Couples, desperate for a child, find themselves caught in a web of misinformation and manipulation, with their trust exploited in the pursuit of profit. To confront these systemic issues, society must demand transparency, ethical practices, and equitable access to reproductive healthcare. This approach ensures that all people, not just the highest bidders, can dream of parenthood as a real possibility.

The commodification of healthcare extends far beyond fertility treatments. Chronic conditions, often manageable through lifestyle changes, have become another lucrative frontier for profit-driven medicine. Among these, the case of fatty liver disease stands as a stark reminder. It shows how healthcare systems exploit vulnerability by offering expensive interventions in place of affordable, effective alternatives.

2.1 LIVER GRADES FOR PROFITS

The reality of fatty liver treatment starkly contrasts the narrative sold by these institutions. Grade 1 fatty liver, the most common and benign stage, involves fat deposits that rarely impair liver function. Even Grade 2, where fat infiltration becomes more pronounced, does not inherently signal liver failure or severe risk. Studies consistently show that lifestyle changes—adopting a Mediterranean diet, reducing sugar intake, and engaging in moderate exercise—can reverse the condition in weeks or months. Yet, healthcare providers rarely encourage patients to prioritize these sustainable solutions. Instead, providers push expensive pharmaceutical options, many of which lack robust clinical approval or demonstrated efficacy. The medications often come from Big Pharma, which aggressively markets them despite their limited role in addressing the root causes of fatty liver.

Misrepresenting fatty liver disease highlights the broader dynamics of prescription drug pricing and access. Healthcare companies frequently inflate the cost of medications prescribed for such conditions, leveraging patients' fear and trust to justify exorbitant prices. This mirrors the case of insulin. In the United States, its prices have soared by over 600% in two decades, despite the drug being over a century old. The pricing strategies employed by pharmaceutical companies hinge on market monopolies, which are sustained through patents and regulatory loopholes. With fatty liver, these medications often rely on tenuous claims of efficacy. Complex patent systems shield these drugs from competition and delay when generics can enter the market.

Patent extensions, known as "evergreening," are a common tactic. Companies make minor modifications to existing drugs—changing a dosage form or combining ingredients—to secure additional years of market exclusivity. This practice not only keeps prices high but also stifles innovation, as companies divert resources from developing genuinely novel treatments to manipulating the patent system. For patients in developing countries, the situation is even grimmer. International trade agreements, often influenced by pharmaceutical lobbying, restrict access to affordable generics, exacerbating healthcare inequities. The lawsuits filed by major drug companies against generic manufacturers further reinforce these monopolies, ensuring that millions of patients remain dependent on high-cost branded medications.

Overpriced medications impose financial burdens not only on individual patients but also across society. Many patients, unable to afford prescriptions, compromise on adherence, skipping doses or halting treatment altogether. This leads to poorer health outcomes, increased hospitalizations, and higher long-term healthcare costs. Data reveals that over 25% of patients in the U.S. struggle to afford their prescribed medications. This figure underscores the systemic failure to balance innovation with accessibility.

The exploitation of fatty liver patients, coupled with the global manipulation of drug pricing and patents, reflects a healthcare industry deeply entangled with profit motives. While advocates uphold the narrative of medical progress to justify high costs, the system often prioritizes financial gain over genuine patient care. For conditions like fatty liver, this means the perpetuation of unnecessary treatments and the neglect of simpler, more effective solutions. Unraveling this dynamic requires transparency in medical recommendations, the dismantling of monopolistic patent practices, and a shift toward healthcare policies that prioritize accessibility and equity.

Until then, patients remain vulnerable to a system designed to profit from their fears rather than address their needs.

Healthcare exploitation extends far beyond prescription pads and patent filings. It seeps into the very fabric of society, preying on the vulnerable at every stage of life. Among the most affected are adolescents, whose boredom and disillusionment with uninspired systems make them prime targets for exploitation. From sterile schools to the allure of nightlife, the calculated manipulation of youth creates fertile ground for addiction, fueling both the global drug trade and elite profiteering.

2.2 CARTELS LOVE BORED TEENS

Teenagers, caught in the turbulence of puberty and societal expectations, often find themselves searching for meaning and escape. In a world where schools fail to inspire and media glorifies instant gratification, the lure of nightlife and substance use becomes irresistible. This isn't a coincidence—it's the result of a system that thrives on disempowerment. From shadowy cartels to polished pharmaceutical companies, the global drug trade profits from engineered chaos, drawing young people into cycles of dependency. The societal toll is staggering: fractured families, destabilized communities, and overwhelmed healthcare systems. Beneath this devastation lies a calculated agenda, where addiction serves as a tool for control and profit. To confront this reality is to challenge the systems that commodify disillusionment, turning vulnerable lives into a marketplace for exploitation.

The trajectory of a teenager's life in modern society often begins with a profound disillusionment within the walls of their school. Designed ostensibly as spaces for critical thinking and intellectual growth, many educational institutions have devolved into sterile environments devoid of engagement, creativity, or purpose. Instead of fostering curiosity, schools emphasize rote memorization and standardized testing, leaving students feeling alienated. This boredom, coupled with the intense social pressures of adolescence, transforms schools into breeding grounds for social escapism. Parties and clubs—initially casual social diversions—become havens where teenagers seek belonging and excitement, often experimenting with substances to escape the monotony and anxiety of their lives. The elites, through their calculated influence on education policy and media, perpetuate this cycle, steering young minds away from self-awareness and toward chaos. By making schools uninspiring and framing nightlife as the epitome of freedom and expression, they pave the way for a harmful culture. This culture feeds directly into the machinery of global drug trade and cartel economics.

The transformation begins in puberty, a stage of heightened vulnerability and identity exploration. Media bombard adolescents, grappling with the physiological and emotional upheaval of puberty, with portrayals that glamorize wild lifestyles and instant gratification. Films, music videos, and social media influencers frequently present partying, clubbing, and substance use as rites of passage. Meanwhile, schools—underfunded, overcrowded, and often disengaged from their students' realities—fail to offer meaningful alternatives. Critical thinking, civic engagement, and self-reflection are conspicuously absent from curricula. Instead, the classroom becomes a perfunctory prelude to the "real" education that awaits in the social scene. This includes navigating relationships, mastering the art of fitting in, and, increasingly, finding access to drugs.

This engineered chaos is no accident. Beneath the surface lies a darker agenda driven by elites whose financial empires thrive on the destabilization of human potential. The global drug trade, worth hundreds of billions annually, thrives on the young, particularly those who enter the cycle of substance use during adolescence. Cartels and drug syndicates operate with frightening precision, targeting teenage party-goers with drugs that promise temporary relief from their insecurities and depressions. Dealers introduce cocaine, MDMA, and increasingly, synthetic opioids like fentanyl, under the guise of enhancing the party experience. What begins as experimentation often spirals into dependency, creating lifelong consumers for the drug industry. Behind the scenes, powerful interests profit from this trade, using offshore networks and shell companies to launder money while maintaining plausible deniability.

The connection between drug cartels and global politics is equally insidious. Historically, the drug trade has intertwined with international power dynamics. The 1980s, for instance, saw the CIA's involvement in covert operations funded by drug trafficking, as revealed in the Iran-Contra affair. Similar patterns persist today, with cartels wielding influence over local governments and law enforcement, often operating with impunity for financial and political leverage. These dynamics perpetuate cycles of violence, corruption, and dependency, ensuring that the drug trade remains an integral—if shadowy—pillar of the global economy.

Pharmaceutical companies also play a role in this ecosystem, although with a coating of legality. The opioid epidemic, one of the most devastating drug crises in modern history, began not in dark alleys but in doctors' offices. Companies like Purdue Pharma aggressively marketed opioids like OxyContin as safe and non-addictive, despite internal knowledge of their high addiction potential. Doctors, incentivized by lavish conferences, promotional gifts, and misleading data, prescribed these medications at unprecedented rates. By the mid-2000s, millions of Americans struggled with addiction, and overdose deaths soared. The parallels between this crisis and the party culture targeting teenagers are striking: both exploit human vulnerability for profit, feeding addiction while externalizing the societal costs.

The societal toll of these intertwined crises is staggering. Adolescents lured into substance use often face lifelong struggles with addiction, mental health issues, and economic instability. Addiction tears families apart, destabilizes communities, and overwhelms public health systems. In 2020 alone, over 90,000 Americans died from drug overdoses, a grim milestone that reflects both the scope of the problem and the failure of current interventions. Meanwhile, the elites at the top of this system—pharmaceutical executives, cartel leaders, and complicit policymakers—reap immense financial rewards. Settlements, such as Purdue Pharma's $4.5 billion agreement, barely scratch the surface of the profits these entities accumulate, often leaving victims with inadequate resources for recovery.

The commodification of teenage chaos serves a dual agenda for societal elites. On one level, it generates immediate profits through drug sales, pharmaceutical prescriptions, and the rehabilitation industry. More troublingly, it creates a disempowered generation, distracted by substance use, mental health struggles, and escapism, incapable of challenging systemic inequalities. This method of control isn't new. From 19th-century opium dens used by colonial powers to those engineered by British colonial interests to weaken the Qing Dynasty in China to the crack epidemic in 1980s America, substance dependency has historically been a tool of exploitation. Today, the stakes are even higher. Teenagers face a precarious future, and society risks losing its collective humanity to forces that thrive on division and despair. Recognizing and dismantling these systems is crucial to safeguarding not just individual futures but the fabric of society itself.

While addiction and chronic illnesses expose one side of healthcare's profit-driven dynamics, treating rare diseases reveals another: the monopolization of hope. Corporations have co-opted groundbreaking medical advancements, once celebrated as triumphs of innovation. Pharmaceutical giants price life-saving treatments beyond the reach of those who need them most.

2.3 RICH REMEDIES

Rare diseases, affecting small but often desperate patient populations, have become a lucrative frontier for the pharmaceutical industry. Treatments for conditions like Spinal Muscular Atrophy (SMA) exemplify the troubling interplay between innovation and exploitation. Drugs like Biogen's Spinraza, priced at $375,000 annually, and Novartis's

Zolgensma, with a staggering $2.1 million price tag, highlight how pharmaceutical companies capitalize on desperation. While companies defend these costs by pointing to research and development expenses, the reality often reveals vast profit margins and monopolistic practices. Corporations have twisted orphan drug laws, intended to incentivize rare disease research, into tools for profit maximization rather than equitable access. Families face impossible choices, turning to crowdfunding or debt to save their loved ones, while patients in low-income countries have no options at all. Addressing these injustices requires bold solutions. Non-profit pharmaceutical models, price controls, and reforms in patent laws must prioritize humanity over profit. These measures ensure that life-saving treatments become a universal right rather than a privilege reserved for the wealthy.

The pharmaceutical industry's relationship with rare diseases like Spinal Muscular Atrophy (SMA) reveals a complex web. This web involves profit motives, scientific breakthroughs, and moral dilemmas that define modern medicine. At the heart of this dynamic are elite investors—venture capitalists, institutional stakeholders, and affluent individuals—who have identified the pharmaceutical sector as a lucrative opportunity for wealth generation. The health care system prices life-saving medications not based on accessibility or societal need but on maximizing returns for shareholders. Nowhere is this more evident than in the development and pricing of orphan drugs, treatments designed for rare diseases affecting small patient populations. These drugs promise extraordinary medical advancements but at costs that exacerbate global inequality.

Consider SMA, a devastating genetic disorder that progressively destroys muscle function and often leads to early mortality. For families affected, treatments like Biogen's Spinraza or Novartis's Zolgensma represent hope—yet that hope comes at a staggering financial cost. Spinraza's annual price of $375,000 (after an initial $750,000 in the first year) and Zolgensma's $2.1 million price tag—the highest for any drug worldwide—illustrate a troubling reality. They show how the pharmaceutical industry monetizes desperation. Pharmaceutical companies defend these prices by citing the significant research and development (R&D) costs involved. However, closer scrutiny reveals a vast gulf between production costs and sale prices. Spinraza's development benefited from publicly funded research, yet Biogen reaps enormous profits, with stock values surging after the drug's approval. Such cases epitomize a system where the financial burden of innovation falls disproportionately on patients and public funds, while the rewards flow to private investors.

These exorbitant prices are not accidents but outcomes of deliberate strategies underpinned by monopolistic practices. Patents and intellectual property laws grant companies exclusive rights to their treatments, effectively barring competitors from introducing cheaper alternatives for years, sometimes decades. Practices like "evergreening," where minor modifications to drugs extend patent protections, further entrench monopolies. Zolgensma's groundbreaking gene therapy represents a monumental leap in treating SMA. Yet, its market exclusivity ensures Novartis can dictate terms, leaving patients and governments with little recourse but to pay or go without. In developing countries, where health care budgets are already stretched thin, such pricing models prevent many patients from accessing these treatments, entrenching global disparities.

The legislative landscape surrounding rare diseases contributes to this imbalance. Corporations have co-opted orphan drug laws, originally designed to incentivize treatments for conditions affecting small populations, to maximize profits. Pharmaceutical companies enjoy tax credits, market exclusivity, and expedited regulatory pathways, but they rarely couple these incentives with requirements to ensure affordability. Instead, these benefits bolster profit margins, reinforcing the industry's financialization at the expense of public health.

The elite investors backing these companies play a pivotal role in sustaining this system. Venture capital firms and institutional investors prioritize therapies with high market potential, often steering research toward expensive treatments rather than widespread health needs. The allure of double-digit returns overrides ethical concerns, perpetuating a framework where wealth dictates access to life-saving medicine. This dynamic reflects a broader historical pattern: just as landowners, once profited from food shortages, modern elites profit from the scarcity of affordable treatments.

This profit-driven paradigm has profound implications for patients and families. Stories of parents crowdfunding to afford Spinraza or Zolgensma underscore the emotional and financial strain imposed by the industry's practices. In the United States, where insurance coverage is patchy and co-pays can be prohibitive, families face impossible choices. They must mortgage their futures, rely on charity, or forgo treatment entirely. Globally, the situation is even bleaker. While patients in affluent nations grapple with high out-of-pocket costs, those in low-income countries face even harsher realities. Economic and geographic disparities effectively exclude them from accessing these therapies and cementing health inequities.

Governments and media play a significant role in this ecosystem, shaping its dynamics in profound ways. Pharmaceutical lobbying exerts immense influence on health care policies, ensuring that it dilutes or delays reforms addressing pricing or accessibility. The industry spends billions annually on lobbying efforts and political contributions, shaping legislation to safeguard its interests. Media narratives, meanwhile, often portray drug pricing controversies as isolated incidents or frame high costs as the necessary price of innovation. This framing obscures the systemic nature of the problem, deflecting scrutiny from the underlying power dynamics that perpetuate inequality.

The ethical questions surrounding high drug prices are as urgent as they are complex. Advocates argue that pricing must account for the long-term benefits of treatments and the R&D investments they require. Yet this rationale collapses under scrutiny when profits vastly exceed costs, forcing patients to bear the financial burden. The World Health Organization increasingly recognizes access to essential medicines as a fundamental human right. However, the current model prioritizes shareholder interests over human lives, raising profound questions about the morality of commodifying health care.

Potential solutions exist, but they require a radical reimagining of pharmaceutical development and distribution. Non-profit pharmaceutical initiatives, such as the Institute for OneWorld Health, demonstrate that affordable innovation is possible. Public funding for research, coupled with price regulations, could shift the focus from profit maximization to public welfare. Collaborative efforts like patent pools or compulsory licensing can break monopolies and expand access to life-saving treatments. Countries with successful price control mechanisms, such as the UK's National Institute for Health and Care Excellence (NICE), offer models for balancing innovation with affordability.

Ultimately, the pharmaceutical industry's approach to rare diseases epitomizes the broader inequalities that define modern capitalism. By prioritizing profit over accessibility, elites consolidate wealth and power while leaving millions to suffer. Addressing this injustice requires confronting the systems that enable it—from patent laws and lobbying practices to the financialization of health care. It is a moral imperative to reimagine a pharmaceutical landscape where innovation serves humanity rather than profits, ensuring that life-saving treatments are a right, not a privilege.

2.4 HEALTHCARE: NOT FOR SALE

The story of modern medical technology is one of profound contradictions. On one hand, we celebrate the marvels of advanced diagnostic tools, like CT scanners and MRIs, that can peer into the human body with astonishing precision. On the other hand, these very machines epitomize the complex web of economic interests that place profit above accessibility. At their core, these devices are not merely products of engineering ingenuity; they also reflect an economic system where the many shoulder the cost of innovation while the few enjoy the rewards. The research and development of scanning machines, for instance, are often driven by private corporations. Wealthy elites fund these corporations, viewing healthcare not as a service, but as a lucrative investment. Developing these technologies involves teams of scientists, expensive materials, and years of trial and error—efforts funded to anticipate high returns. When the machines finally roll off the production line, their price tags reflect more than the cost of creation. They also include hefty profit margins demanded by investors and manufacturers.

Hospitals, caught in the middle of this economic chain, must purchase these machines at exorbitant prices. They must do this to remain competitive and deliver care marketed as the "best" for their patients. For a hospital, acquiring a state-of-the-art CT scanner might cost several million dollars—a financial burden that does not end with the purchase. Maintenance, upgrades, and training staff to operate these devices add to the ongoing costs. To recoup this investment, hospital administrators often find themselves adopting a return-on-investment mindset, subtly or explicitly instructing doctors to maximize the usage of these machines. As a result, economic factors sometimes influence the decision to send a patient for a scan beyond medical necessity. It can also be driven by the imperative to justify the machine's cost. Patients trusting the system to act in their best interests are often unaware of the economic forces shaping their healthcare experience.

This paradigm raises an uncomfortable question: should the development and distribution of life-saving technologies be driven by profit motives at all? History offers us alternative models that hint at more equitable approaches. For example, during the post-World War II era, governments around the world invested heavily in public health infrastructure and scientific research. In nations like the United Kingdom, the state established the National Health Service and took on a significant role in funding medical advancements. Policymakers grounded these initiatives in the principle that healthcare is a public good, not a commodity. While not without flaws, these systems demonstrated that technocratic governance—when adequately funded and insulated from the influence of private wealth—could produce remarkable results.

Imagine a world where public institutions develop medical technologies and fund them through a capped wealth redistribution model. In this framework, elites could still contribute their resources, but the system would cap their returns. The system would redirect excess profits back into funding further innovation and ensuring affordability. Without the pressure to generate profit for shareholders, research priorities could shift from market-driven concerns to addressing the most pressing health challenges. This would not only democratize access to medical technologies but also ensure that ethical considerations take precedence over economic ones.

The current profit-driven model, while fueling rapid advancements, has a dark side: it perpetuates inequality and incentivizes overuse. When healthcare becomes an industry, humanity becomes secondary to profitability. Breaking free from this cycle requires a fundamental rethinking of how we approach innovation. Shouldn't the ability to diagnose a disease early, to save a life, be a universal right rather than a privilege reserved for those who can afford it? The answer lies not in abolishing private enterprise, but in reimagining its role within a system that values human well-being above all else.

3. DATA MONOPOLY

The relationship between Big Pharma and patient data is one of quiet exploitation. Clinical trials, heralded as cornerstones of scientific progress, increasingly serve as gateways for companies to secure indefinite rights to participants' health information through convoluted consent forms. Partnerships with tech titans like Google's DeepMind amplify this trend, creating vast data ecosystems that prioritize profit over privacy. Even seemingly innocuous tools like wearable fitness trackers and health apps blur the boundaries of consent, gathering detailed health metrics under the guise of user benefit. This systematic commodification of personal health data raises critical questions about ethics and governance in the digital health era. Corporations have co-opted what was once a public good—a resource for advancing medicine and improving lives—into a private asset. This shift excludes patients from decisions about how organizations use their most personal information.

Health care data emerging as a strategic asset is a revolution. It is reshaping the medical landscape while quietly becoming one of the most lucrative commodities of the modern era. As diagnostic tools, electronic health records (EHRs), and wearable devices generate vast quantities of health information; this data transcends its original purpose of improving patient care. It becomes a resource to be mined, analyzed, and monetized. Pharmaceutical companies leverage it to design precision medicines, identify patient populations for clinical trials, and predict market trends. Health care data is a map, a treasure trove of human vulnerabilities and needs, guiding Big Pharma and elite investors to the next profit vein. Yet the individuals who generate this data—patients seeking care—rarely benefit from its exploitation. Instead, they unwittingly fuel a system that prioritizes corporate profit over their own health equity.

Elites and their corporate empires anticipated this shift long before it became mainstream knowledge. Recognizing the potential of data-driven health care, they orchestrated a quiet acquisition of the infrastructures necessary to control this new economy. In 2018, Roche, a pharmaceutical giant, acquired Flatiron Health for $1.9 billion. Ostensibly, this was a move to enhance cancer care by using Flatiron's oncology-specific EHR platform. But beyond the altruistic layer lay a more calculated intent: securing exclusive access to troves of oncology data to bolster Roche's dominance in the oncology drug market. This acquisition exemplified how corporations and their investors positioned themselves to capitalize on a resource more valuable than oil in the 21st century—data.

The inherent value of healthcare data lies in its ability to facilitate innovation, but this innovation is often a double-edged sword. For instance, by analyzing EHRs, pharmaceutical companies can tailor clinical trials with unprecedented precision, targeting only the most likely responders to a drug. While this accelerates drug approval processes, it also creates a system where health care becomes ever more segmented and inaccessible. Drugs designed for niche markets, based on granular data insights, come with eye-watering price tags justified by their specificity. The benefits of these advancements, therefore, disproportionately favor those who can afford them, perpetuating existing inequalities.

But what makes this data economy truly insidious is the mechanism behind its creation: organizations collect patients' data without their explicit understanding or compensation. Governments, often under the guise of promoting digital health initiatives, play a key role in enabling this exploitation. Consider the case of NHS England's controversial plan to share patient data with private firms. In 2021, the program faced backlash for its lack of transparency, with patients unknowingly having their medical histories aggregated and offered to third parties. While proponents argued this would spur medical innovation, critics highlighted how it effectively turned citizens' health information into a commodity without their informed consent.

Manipulating data economies extends beyond collection to controlling their narrative and use. Organizations shape healthcare data to serve specific interests rather than merely storing it. Pharmaceutical companies sponsor studies that rely on proprietary data sets, skewing research outcomes in favor of their products. By owning the data and funding the analysis, they effectively control the narrative of what works and why. This monopolistic control marginalizes competing narratives—whether about cheaper generics or alternative treatments.

The interplay between government complicity and corporate ambition underscores the ethical vacuum in this new frontier. Governments, eager to appear progressive in adopting digital health solutions, partner with private entities that promise innovation but deliver profit extraction. These partnerships blur the lines between public good and private gain, leaving patients with little recourse. The rhetoric of "innovation" becomes a smokescreen for systemic exploitation, and the commodification of health care data deepens the gap of global inequality.

Acquiring health care data by elites and Big Pharma is not just a story of market dominance; it is a testament to the structural inequalities that define the modern world. By manipulating the data economy and enlisting government complicity, they have transformed health care from a domain of healing to one of profit. In doing so, they have not only enriched themselves but also shaped a troubling future. Wealth and influence, rather than need or merit, gate access to innovation. The story of data in health care is a cautionary tale. It shows how unchecked ambition and systemic collusion can hijack even the most human of pursuits: the quest for health and well-being.

Transforming healthcare into a data economy didn't happen overnight. It began with noble intentions: improving patient care, accelerating research, and streamlining medical systems. But behind these promises lies a more troubling reality. The partnerships between pharmaceutical companies and tech giants have turned patient data into a commodity. Organizations extract, monetize, and control information with little regard for the individuals at its core. To understand how this dynamic unfolded, we must explore the intricate web of collaboration and exploitation that defines the modern healthcare data economy.

3.1 PARTNERS IN DATA CRIME

The alliance between pharmaceutical giants and tech companies has redefined the landscape of healthcare, turning patient information into the lifeblood of a sprawling data economy. Clinical trials, once celebrated as founding medical progress, now serve a different purpose. They have become entry points for corporations to secure unfettered access to participants' health data through opaque consent forms. Tech behemoths like Google, through ventures such as DeepMind, amplify these efforts, gaining access to vast datasets under the guise of innovation. Wearable devices and health apps further blur the boundaries of consent, collecting sensitive health metrics while burying their intentions deep within dense user agreements. This ecosystem of data exploitation operates with a troubling lack of transparency. Corporations leverage patient trust and exploit legal loopholes to transform health information into a private asset. What emerges is a system where the commodification of data trumps the ethical imperative to protect the very individuals it is supposed to serve.

The strategies employed by Big Pharma to collect and monopolize health care data reveal a systematic exploitation of modern technology, patient trust, and legal loopholes. At the forefront of this operation are clinical trials. These trials, ostensibly designed to evaluate the safety and efficacy of new drugs, increasingly serve as a treasure trove for data harvesting. Participants, often motivated by hope for treatment or altruism, sign complex consent forms that stretch far beyond the immediate scope of the trial. These documents, buried in dense legal jargon, often grant companies indefinite rights to use the collected data for purposes unrelated to the original study. The narrative of informed consent, a cornerstone of ethical medical research, becomes a disguise for corporate overreach. Once corporations acquire this data, they rarely return it to the public domain, effectively privatizing knowledge that could benefit society at large.

The scale of data collection grows exponentially through partnerships between pharmaceutical giants and health tech companies, leveraging cutting-edge tools to access unprecedented levels of patient information. A striking example is the 2015 collaboration between Google's DeepMind and the UK's National Health Service (NHS). Ostensibly, this partnership aimed to develop AI tools for early diagnosis and patient management. However, it was soon revealed that DeepMind had accessed the personal health records of 1.6 million patients without their explicit consent. The backlash forced regulators to scrutinize the agreement. However, the incident highlighted a pervasive issue. When tech and pharma collaborate, patient data becomes a bargaining chip, often traded without public transparency. These partnerships, marketed as vehicles for innovation, reveal a troubling reality where corporations treat health data as corporate capital rather than a public resource.

Mobile health apps and wearable devices have added another layer of complexity to Big Pharma's data collection strategies. Promising users' insights into their fitness, sleep, or chronic conditions, these tools subtly extract vast amounts of personal health information. For instance, a diabetes management app developed by a pharmaceutical company might track glucose levels, dietary habits, and physical activity. While this data ostensibly helps patients manage their condition, companies also monetize it, contributing to marketing strategies, drug development, and even insurance pricing models. The allure of convenience blinds users to the deeper implications of such data collection. This includes a loss of control over personal health information and its commodification by entities whose primary loyalty lies with shareholders, not patients.

These strategies converge to form a mosaic of corporate dominance over health data, revealing a pattern of systemic disregard for individual autonomy and ethical transparency. Clinical trials exploit participants' hope; tech collaborations erode trust in public institutions; and consumer-friendly apps disguise surveillance as service. The exploitation of health data is not merely a technical or legal issue. It is a profound moral dilemma. It raises questions about the boundaries of consent, the ownership of personal information, and the role of profit in the sacred sphere of health care. The story of Big Pharma's data collection is a cautionary tale about the costs of technological progress when governance and ethical oversight fail to keep pace.

While partnerships and technological advancements create the framework for data collection, the real profits lie in monetization. Companies anonymize and sell health records, framing their actions as progress while obscuring the ethical compromises that underpin them. This practice reveals a deeper systemic issue: the shift from patient care to data control, where health information becomes currency in a marketplace of exploitation.

3.2 YOUR DATA, THEIR GOLD

Imagine your most intimate health details being traded without your knowledge, let alone your approval. Incidents like Google's Project Nightingale, where corporations accessed millions of patient records without consent, expose their ethical failings in prioritizing data control over transparency. Companies like IMS Health, now IQVIA, have built billion-dollar businesses monetizing anonymized health data, even as re-identification techniques make such assurances increasingly hollow. These practices erode trust in healthcare systems, shift the focus from patient care to profit, and expose individuals to significant risks. As corporations reframe data exploitation as innovation, the healthcare industry must confront a stark reality. Its foundations are shifting from compassion to control, creating a system where profit, not patients, takes center stage.

The exploitation of health data by corporations has unfolded through a series of chilling incidents, each illuminating the precarious intersection of innovation, ethics, and privacy. In 2019, Google's Project Nightingale demonstrated the audacity with which tech giants maneuver to acquire sensitive health information. Partnering with Ascension, a sprawling U.S. health system, Google gained access to over 50 million patient records. This included lab results, diagnoses, and hospitalization data—all without informing patients or their doctors. This covert operation was justified as an effort to develop advanced AI tools for health care, but its secrecy triggered an outcry. The revelation prompted an investigation by the Department of Health and Human Services' Office for Civil Rights. It underscored public fears of data misuse in an era where trust in tech companies was already eroding. The sheer scope of data collected and its potential for commercial exploitation raised uncomfortable questions about the future of patient privacy in health care.

The saga of IMS Health (now IQVIA) adds another layer to this troubling narrative. Specializing in aggregating prescription data from pharmacies, IMS Health transformed what seemed like innocuous transactions into a goldmine of actionable intelligence for pharmaceutical companies. Without obtaining consent from patients, the company collected and anonymized prescription records, selling them to drug manufacturers eager to refine their marketing strategies. The anonymization process, touted as a safeguard, did little to assuage concerns that this practice commodified deeply personal health information. Pharmaceutical firms used this data to tailor advertising campaigns and influence physicians' prescribing habits, perpetuating a system where patient health was secondary to corporate profit. IMS Health's model epitomized the quiet monetization of health data, a phenomenon that has grown into a multi-billion-dollar industry operating largely in the shadows.

In 2018, Facebook's ambitious plan to collect anonymized health data from hospitals highlighted how even non-health companies saw gold in the growing health data economy. Facebook proposed combining hospital data with user information to identify patterns that could improve patient care, presenting this initiative as a benevolent foray into health innovation. However, the timing could not have been worse. Just as the Cambridge Analytica scandal exposed Facebook's reckless handling of user data, its health care ambitions sparked public outrage. Critics argued that even anonymized data, when combined with Facebook's vast troves of personal information, could reveal identities, leading to potential misuse. Authorities swiftly paused the project. However, the episode revealed the tech giant's intentions to infiltrate yet another dimension of human life, leveraging health data as a strategic asset.

These incidents reveal a systemic trend: corporations prioritize data monetization over individual rights. Whether it is Google, IQVIA, or Facebook, the exploitation of health data operates on a similar blueprint—masking profit-driven initiatives as technological progress while sidelining ethical considerations. The collective impact of these practices is profound. They erode public trust in health systems, exacerbate disparities in access and outcomes, and reshape health care. In this new domain, the currency of care is not compassion, but control over data. This trajectory raises urgent questions about governance, accountability, and the moral responsibilities of corporations in the digital age.

This systemic prioritization of data monetization over individual rights sets the stage for a deeper issue: the illusion of informed consent. While corporations exploit data under the guise of progress, patients are often misled into believing they retain control over their personal information. This deception is embedded in the very systems designed to protect them. As we transition to examining consent practices, it becomes clear that the complexity of legal frameworks is not accidental—it is a deliberate tool to obscure rights, consolidate power, and perpetuate inequities in modern healthcare.

3.3 SIGN HERE TO CONFUSE YOURSELF!

Modern healthcare deceives patients by making them believe they are giving informed consent. Consent forms, filled with impenetrable legal jargon, give patients the false impression of choice while allowing companies unrestricted access to their data. This parallels historical practices where complexity served to consolidate power, leaving the public disempowered. Frameworks that allow organizations to share de-identified data worsen the issue, despite growing evidence showing that such information allows others to identify individuals. Exclusive agreements between pharmaceutical companies and healthcare providers further entrench these inequities. They stifle collaboration and perpetuate a system where health data fuels corporate monopolies rather than public benefit. As these practices continue, they erode trust, amplify disparities, and raise fundamental questions about fairness in the data economy.

Manipulating consent and controlling health data by elites and pharmaceutical giants reveals a troubling pattern. It involves using power and complexity to obscure the true extent of data collection and usage from the individuals it impacts. One of the most insidious tactics involves the convoluted nature of consent processes. Consent forms, often adorned with impenetrable legal jargon and excessive length, give the false impression that patients have made informed choices. In reality, they function more as shields for corporate and institutional interests than as tools for patient empowerment. The average patient, confronted with dense text and ambiguous language, is unlikely to fully grasp the implications of their agreement. They may unknowingly permit the sale, sharing, or long-term storage of their sensitive health information. This is not an unknown phenomenon but reflects how practices evolve, using complexity to consolidate power. In medieval times, legal codes written in Latin served a similar purpose, keeping the populace reliant on intermediaries for understanding. Today, the legal language of consent forms has replaced Latin, but the effect remains the same—disempowering the individual while granting expansive permissions to those in control.

Exploiting legal frameworks is another avenue through which elites assert dominance over health data. Companies frequently invoke the concept of de-identification, enshrined in many privacy laws, to justify data sharing without consent. They claim that anonymized data cannot harm individuals. However, this assertion crumbles under scrutiny. Advances in analytics and the growing availability of public datasets have made it increasingly possible to re-identify individuals from supposedly anonymized data. A striking example comes from studies demonstrating that de-identified genetic information can be cross-referenced with public genealogy databases to pinpoint specific individuals. In one widely discussed case, researchers could identify participants in genetic studies by comparing their anonymized DNA data with open-access family tree databases. This ability to re-identify data raises urgent questions about the adequacy of existing safeguards and the ethical obligations of those collecting and sharing health information.

Another powerful manipulation tactic is the use of exclusive agreements to restrict access to critical health data. Pharmaceutical companies and research institutions often enter into contracts with hospitals and other healthcare providers, securing exclusive rights to patient data for their own research. While these agreements can drive innovation and lead to medical breakthroughs, they also create silos of information, limiting broader scientific access and collaboration. For instance, a pharmaceutical firm might agree with a major hospital network to collaborate. This grants them privileged access to vast amounts of patient data while excluding independent researchers or competitors. This practice mirrors the historical monopolies of trade routes or raw materials, where control over a key resource became a means of amassing power. Just as these monopolies stifled competition and concentrated wealth, exclusive health data agreements risk privileging corporate interests over collective progress.

Government policies further complicate the landscape, often acting as both enablers and inadequately equipped regulators of this data-driven ecosystem. Many countries lack comprehensive legislation to protect health data, leaving citizens vulnerable to exploitation. The European Union's General Data Protection Regulation (GDPR) offers a stark contrast to weaker regulations in other regions. It sets a high standard for data protection and individual rights. Yet, even the GDPR faces challenges in enforcement, as regulators often struggle with limited resources and the sheer scale of non-compliance by powerful entities. Elsewhere, lacking robust laws creates a regulatory vacuum, enabling corporations to operate with impunity. Penalties for data breaches or misuse, when they occur, are frequently too small to deter terrible actors. They amount to a minor cost of doing business rather than a meaningful consequence.

Meanwhile, governments actively encourage data sharing to spur economic growth, sometimes prioritizing innovation over individual rights. Initiatives like the U.S. Precision Medicine Initiative aims to collect vast amounts of health data to advance medical research and economic competitiveness. While such programs hold the promise of groundbreaking discoveries, they often overlook fair compensation for the individuals whose data makes these advances possible. This echoes earlier industrial revolutions, where the labor and resources of many fueled the wealth of a few. In the emerging economy of health data, patients' information becomes the raw material, while the profits accrue disproportionately to corporations and governments.

These dynamics reflect a broader pattern of power imbalances. The complexity of systems, the exploitation of legal loopholes, and inadequate oversight allow elites to manipulate and benefit from resources that should serve the public good. They also underscore the enduring challenge of ensuring that innovation and progress do not come at the cost of fairness, equity, and trust. As societies navigate these dilemmas, they must address an underlying question. Who ultimately benefits from the systems we create, and who bears the hidden costs?

The exploitation of health data has evolved from isolated incidents to systemic patterns, turning breaches of privacy into normalized features of modern healthcare. The consequences of this shift extend far beyond the individual, threatening the integrity of healthcare systems worldwide.

Healthcare, like education, should be a universal right. But in a world where profits take precedence over people, it has become a luxury for the privileged. From data exploitation to systemic neglect, the dysfunctions of healthcare mirror those of every other institution shaped by human greed and shortsightedness.

These failures echo those of religion, explored in Chapter 8: *Religion and Hypocrisy*. Just as healthcare commodifies the body, religion commodifies the soul. The institutions meant to provide meaning and morality have often become tools for division and control. They perpetuate cycles of dysfunction that reach deep into the fabric of society.

Part III

Institutional Dysfunctions

"God Said It, the Media Sold It, Justice Denied It"

What happens when ancient faith meets modern hypocrisy?
When truth becomes an option, and justice is just a privilege for the rich?
This part shines a light on the absurdities of organized religion, media
manipulation, and a legal system that feels like a VIP club for the elite.
We question everything, not out of disrespect but out of necessity—because
blind trust can be the most dangerous dysfunction of all.

8

Religion and Hypocrisy

"Religion is regarded by the common people as true,
by the wise as false, and by the rulers as useful."

– SENECA

The role of religion in shaping societal structures throughout history is significant, acting as both a moral guide and a mechanism for consolidating power. Religious institutions intertwine with education and healthcare systems to maintain social hierarchies. They often do so under the guise of altruism and spiritual duty. This dynamic is not incidental but a deliberate strategy employed by elites to perpetuate their dominance. Ruling classes align with religious authorities to co-opt the moral authority of faith. They use it to legitimize their wealth and privilege, embedding inequality in institutions meant to nurture and heal. Religion hijacking schools and hospitals is not just about spiritual influence. This story reflects calculated control, where elites wield salvation and care to uphold societal stratification.

The use of religion in education offers one of the most striking examples of this interplay. In medieval Europe, the Catholic Church dominated educational institutions, teaching doctrines that reinforced the divine right of kings and the natural order of feudal hierarchies. Schools run by the clergy prioritized the study of theology and Latin, training young men—predominantly from the elite class—to serve as priests, scribes, or bureaucrats. Religious institutions limited lower-class education to basic instruction, emphasizing obedience and humility. This bifurcated system ensured that knowledge—and thus power—remained concentrated in the hands of a select few, while the masses internalized a worldview that justified their subjugation. The elite's control of education extended into the colonial period, where missionaries established schools across Africa, Asia, and the Americas. These institutions ostensibly aimed to "civilize" indigenous populations, but their curricula systematically undermined local cultures and reinforced the superiority of European norms. In India, British missionaries used Christian schools to propagate the ideology of the "White Man's Burden." They taught Indians to accept their subservience to colonial rule as divinely ordained.

Healthcare, too, has been a potent arena for religious control and elite dominance. Monasteries and religious orders often attached hospitals to their domains, framing care as charity rather than a human right. While this arrangement provided essential services, it also allowed religious institutions to exert moral and social influence over the sick and vulnerable. Charitable hospitals subjected the poor to sermons and moral lessons while providing care. These reinforced the idea that their suffering was a test of faith or punishment for sin. This dynamic persisted into the colonial era, where missionary hospitals served as extensions of imperial power. In Africa, missionary hospitals provided care but also became centers for religious conversion. Patients often had to participate in Christian rituals or renounce indigenous beliefs to receive treatment. Colonial governments and wealthy patrons funded these hospitals to project an image of benevolence. They ensured the moral authority of religion supported their dominance.

Religion and elites continue to forge alliances, transcending the distant past. In the 20th century, Christian fundamentalist schools, and hospitals rose in the United States. Wealthy donors funded them to promote conservative values and oppose social reforms. Private Christian schools, called "segregation academies," resisted public school integration by establishing themselves during the civil rights era. These institutions, funded by affluent white families, used religious rhetoric to justify segregation, perpetuating racial and economic inequalities under the banner of divine order. In healthcare, organizations like the Catholic Health Association have wielded significant influence over public policy, often opposing reproductive rights and LGBTQ+ healthcare access. These positions, while framed as matters of religious conscience, frequently align with the interests of elites who benefit from maintaining traditional power structures.

This study seeks to unravel the mechanisms by which religion has been used to entrench social inequalities through education and healthcare. Examining incidents like medieval monastic hospitals and colonial missionary schools reveals patterns. These illuminate how elites co-opt religious institutions for their gain. The methodology involves a comparative analysis of primary and secondary sources, including historical texts, archival records, and contemporary case studies. By focusing on specific incidents across different cultures and time periods, the research aims to uncover patterns of control that transcend geographic and temporal boundaries.

Ultimately, the narrative of religion's entanglement with education and healthcare is one of moral ideals subverted for material gain. People have manipulated faith and charity, despite their potential to inspire progress, to justify oppression and inequality. Delving into this dynamic reveals the challenge of disentangling the spiritual from the structural. It raises questions about both historical motives and persisting systems. Moral authority and material dominance connect in sobering ways. For centuries, trusted institutions have served as battlegrounds for power, where elites leverage faith to secure control.

1. ELITES ARE DIVINE

Imagine a world where the rulers were not merely human but god-like, their every decree imbued with divine will. In ancient Egypt, the Pharaoh was not just a king; he was Horus incarnate, a living god bridging the realms of mortals and the eternal. This divine status transformed governance into a sacred duty, enshrining obedience not as a civic responsibility but as a spiritual necessity. This narrative of sacred rule, however, was no isolated phenomenon. It echoed through medieval Europe, where the "Divine Right of Kings" cloaked monarchs in heavenly legitimacy, quashing dissent and entrenching hierarchies. Religion, far from being a force for equality, became the scaffolding for systemic oppression, ensuring that questioning authority meant defying both state and God.

The notion of divine rule transcended cultures and epochs, finding a particularly enduring expression in medieval Europe through the doctrine of the "Divine Right of Kings." This principle held that monarchs derived their authority directly from God, placing them above earthly accountability. Elites wielded this belief in the Middle Ages to weaponize heresy accusations and silence political opposition. The coronation rituals of European kings, often conducted in grand cathedrals and presided over by the Church, were theatrical affirmations of this divine connection. The anointing of Charlemagne by Pope Leo III in 800 CE solidified his rule. It also reinforced the

Church's role as the arbiter of divine will. Monarchs invoked their God-given authority to justify oppressive policies and wars. The Crusades, framed as holy missions, also consolidated power and wealth for the elite. Religious authority and royal power are intertwined, creating a feedback loop. The legitimacy of one bolstered the other, entrenching a rigid social order with little room for mobility or reform.

Religion's role in maintaining feudal hierarchies extended far beyond the throne. The medieval Church was not merely a spiritual institution, but a formidable economic and political power, owning vast tracts of land and amassing immense wealth. In feudal societies, where land was the primary measure of power, the Church was often the largest landowner, second only to the monarchy. This wealth enabled it to wield significant influence over both the peasantry and the nobility. The Church's alignment with the ruling class was evident in its teachings, which emphasized obedience, humility, and the divine justification of the existing social order. The doctrine of the "Great Chain of Being" depicted a hierarchical universe, with God at the top, followed by kings, clergy, nobles, and, finally, the common people. Sermons, art, and literature reinforced this worldview, embedding it deeply in society's consciousness.

Feudal lords and the clergy worked in tandem to maintain this order. While the nobility provided military protection for the Church, the clergy offered spiritual legitimacy for feudal exploitation. Religious teachings told peasants their suffering was God's plan, promising them rewards in the afterlife. Tithes, a mandatory payment to the Church, further drained the meager resources of the peasantry, channeling wealth upward while reinforcing the Church's dominance. The medieval monastery system also exemplified this dynamic. Ostensible centers of charity and learning, many monasteries became hubs of elite control, stockpiling wealth and serving as advisors to kings and lords. Institutions like Cluny Abbey in France wielded immense influence, shaping political decisions under the guise of spiritual guidance.

These historical foundations of elite control over religion highlight a recurring theme: the use of divine narratives to justify and maintain systemic inequality. Elites positioned themselves as intermediaries between humanity and the divine to consolidate power. Elites framed challenges to their authority as both political insubordination and spiritual transgressions. This fusion of religion and power has left an indelible mark on human history, shaping the structures of society and perpetuating disparities that endure to this day.

The divine justification for elite dominance was only part of the equation. To maintain their grip on power, elites relied on a subtler, yet equally potent, strategy: division. Through education and religion, they carved societies into fragmented units, ensuring that solidarity among the oppressed was an unattainable dream. Religious education sowed seeds of division under the guise of enlightenment, showcasing this strategy clearly.

1.1 DIVIDE AND RULE

In colonial India, schools built by British missionaries served a dual purpose: spreading Christian values and creating an elite class loyal to the Empire. These institutions, while promising progress, systematically eroded indigenous knowledge systems and widened societal divides. This tactic was far from unique. In the Islamic world, madrassas often served as ideological factories, reinforcing theological rigidity and aligning with elite interests. And in Northern Ireland, segregating Protestant and Catholic schools entrenched sectarian identities, fueling decades of conflict. Religious education emerged as a tool for moral instruction and a weapon for perpetuating inequity. This raises profound questions about its role in shaping societies.

Religious education has long served as a powerful tool for perpetuating social hierarchies, shaping minds and cultures to sustain existing power structures. In colonial India, British elites systematically used missionary schools to instill Western Christian values, disrupting indigenous knowledge systems and reinforcing the colonial hierarchy. These schools, often established by missionary societies but supported by the colonial administration, framed education as a benevolent offering to the colonized population. However, the curriculum was designed to prioritize the English language, Christian theology, and British history, subtly embedding the notion of British cultural and moral superiority. Indigenous traditions, literature, and scientific advancements were either ignored or actively undermined, relegating local knowledge systems to the margins. The British education system in India disconnected English-educated elites from their cultural roots and aligned them with colonial interests. Figures like Thomas Macaulay openly championed creating a class of Indians. He advocated for Indians who were "Indian in blood and color, but English in taste, opinions, morals, and intellect." This strategy succeeded in producing a cohort that facilitated colonial governance. However, it deepened social divisions and eroded traditional systems of knowledge and control that had previously bound communities together.

In the Islamic world, madrassas have historically played a central role in education, social cohesion, and religious instruction. However, the influence of elites in shaping the ideology and reach of certain madrassas reveals how religious education can be co-opted to serve political or economic agendas. In the 20th century, elites in countries like Saudi Arabia began funding madrassas abroad to promote a particular interpretation of Islam aligned with their own interests. These schools, often established in impoverished regions of South Asia and Africa, provided free education, meals, and stipends, making them attractive options for disadvantaged families. However, the curriculum often prioritized theological teachings over critical thinking or broader subjects like science and the arts. This narrow focus not only limited students' opportunities for economic and intellectual advancement but also aligned them ideologically with the interests of their benefactors. Local elites and international actors, including the U.S., co-opted madrassas into geopolitical strategies during the Cold War. These schools became breeding grounds for ideologies that destabilized regions or maintained authoritarian rule. They perpetuated cycles of poverty and dependence while cementing elite sponsors' influence.

The role of religious education in reinforcing social and cultural divides is particularly stark in regions with entrenched sectarian conflicts, such as Northern Ireland. Northern Ireland's education system segregates Protestant and Catholic children into separate schools, perpetuating division. While these schools ostensibly exist to provide religious instruction, they also perpetuate deep-seated sectarian divisions that have fueled violence and mistrust. Protestant schools often emphasize British identity, unionist politics, and loyalty to the Crown, while Catholic schools focus on Irish identity, nationalist aspirations, and opposition to British rule. This segregation extends beyond the classroom, shaping social interactions and community affiliations. During the Troubles in the late 20th century, educational divisions mirrored and worsened societal conflict. Generations of children grew up with little meaningful interaction with the opposing community. The educational divide acted as both a symptom and a cause of the region's enduring sectarianism. It reinforced the power structures and political agendas of elites on both sides.

Across these diverse contexts, religious education emerges as a double-edged sword. People have wielded religion as a mechanism for control, despite its potential for moral guidance and social stability. Elites shape curricula and control access to education through religious schools. They promote ideologies that align with their interests, ensuring power structures and inequality remain intact. Religious education has shaped the social fabric in ways that perpetuate division and hierarchy. This includes colonial missionary schools of British India, elite-sponsored madrassas of the Islamic world, and sectarian schools of Northern Ireland. These systems show how religion, education, and power intersect to influence societies. They raise questions about education's role in challenging or upholding inequities.

While education served as a battleground for ideological control, healthcare became a stage for moral and cultural domination. Religious institutions, cloaked in charity, used medical care to influence bodies and minds. They extended their reach into the most intimate spheres of human life.

1.2 IN GOD, WE TREAT

Religious doctrine governs medical care in many Catholic hospitals across the United States, often unnoticed by patients. Yet, the refusal to provide contraceptive services or abortion is a stark reminder of how deeply faith can dictate healthcare decisions. This is not an unknown phenomenon. Missionary hospitals in colonial Africa once paired medical treatment with cultural assimilation, blurring the lines between healing and proselytization. Today, the legacy persists, with religious ideologies shaping medical ethics, educational curricula, and even access to care. This dynamic forces us to confront a troubling question: How can healthcare uphold universal rights when it is beholden to religious restrictions?

Elites have leveraged healthcare institutions as tools to influence societal norms and consolidate control. Religious hospitals, under the guise of charity, embed doctrines reflecting benefactors' interests. These doctrines sometimes conflict with patient autonomy and comprehensive care. In the United States, Catholic hospitals form one of the largest networks of healthcare providers, accounting for a significant portion of hospital beds nationwide. While these institutions provide essential services to millions, their adherence to religious doctrines often restricts access to certain medical procedures, including contraception, abortion, and sterilization. Hospitals impose these restrictions on patients regardless of their religious affiliation. They apply universally, regardless of individual beliefs or circumstances. In cases of emergency, such as ectopic pregnancies, the refusal to perform life-saving procedures has sparked widespread debate about the balance between religious freedom and medical ethics. By controlling access to care through religious hospitals, elites impose their moral frameworks on society. Marginalized communities, reliant on these institutions, are often disproportionately affected.

The historical role of missionary hospitals in colonial Africa offers another poignant example of healthcare being wielded as a tool for influence. Established by European elites and funded by colonial governments or wealthy patrons, these hospitals ostensibly aimed to address the health needs of colonized populations. However, their primary mission was often religious conversion rather than medical care. Patients were frequently required to attend religious services or accept Christian teachings as a condition for receiving treatment. In the late 19th and early 20th centuries, missionary hospitals in East and Central Africa erased cultural traditions.

They framed traditional healing practices as "pagan" or "backward." This approach undermined indigenous medical knowledge and positioned Western medicine—and by extension, Western culture—as superior. The support of colonial authorities for these hospitals further entrenched this dynamic, as healthcare became a means of legitimizing imperial rule. European elites presented themselves as benevolent providers of health and salvation. They used missionary hospitals to subjugate local populations, intertwining physical care with spiritual and cultural domination.

Control of medical education has also been a critical avenue through which religious institutions influence healthcare practices. Religiously affiliated medical schools often shape curricula to align with their doctrines, limiting the scope of training for future healthcare professionals. In the mid-20th century, Catholic medical schools in Europe and the Americas omitted or minimized reproductive health topics. They framed contraception and abortion as morally unacceptable instead of medically necessary. This educational gap extended into clinical practice, where graduates of such institutions were less likely to offer comprehensive reproductive services, regardless of patient needs. This limitation not only impacts individual healthcare outcomes but also perpetuates systemic disparities, as entire regions may lack providers trained in certain essential services. Debates about including topics like gender-affirming care or assisted dying in medical education persist today. They highlight tensions between religious ideologies and evolving healthcare standards. Religious medical schools influence healthcare systems by deciding what to teach and omit. They steer these systems toward doctrinally acceptable practices at the expense of broader patient care.

Across these contexts, healthcare institutions emerge as arenas where religious authority intersects with social and political power. Catholic hospitals deny specific services, missionary hospitals provide conditional care, and religiously affiliated medical schools impose doctrinal limitations. Together, these systems align healthcare with particular moral and cultural frameworks. This intersection affects individual lives and reinforces broader inequality. Access to comprehensive and equitable care often depends on navigating religiously influenced systems. The enduring legacy of these institutions underscores the need to examine faith's role in healthcare critically. It challenges the balance between religious expression and the universal right to health.

Just as religion shaped healthcare and education for the masses, it also molded the upper echelons of learning. Universities, the supposed bastions of enlightenment and merit, were long entwined with religious power, cementing hierarchies under the banner of divine blessings.

1.3 DEGREES WITH DIVINE BLESSINGS

People romanticize Oxford and Cambridge as intellectual hubs, but these institutions originally served religious and elite interests. Yet, their origins tell a more sobering story. Established to educate clergy and reinforce elite dominance, these universities excluded the masses, embedding privilege into their foundations. Their curricula, steeped in theology and classical studies, mirrored the priorities of the ruling classes rather than the needs of society. Even as these institutions evolved, their legacy of exclusion persisted through mechanisms like legacy admissions, ensuring that the privileges of a few endured across generations. These dynamics compel us to rethink the narrative of higher education as a purely meritocratic endeavor.

Universities, often seen as bastions of knowledge and progress, have historically been instruments for maintaining elite dominance, particularly when intertwined with religious foundations. Institutions like Oxford and Cambridge exemplify this dynamic, their origins steeped in the traditions of the Church. Elites established these medieval universities to educate clergy and fulfill administrative and religious needs. Their curricula emphasized theology, canon law, and classical studies, reinforcing the intellectual framework that justified the existing social hierarchy. Universities restricted access to wealthy, high-status individuals, ensuring education stayed exclusive. Scholarships tied to religious patronage reinforced the Church's and elites' influence in higher education. Oxford and Cambridge became synonymous with privilege, producing graduates who dominated ecclesiastical and political institutions. These graduates formed insular networks of power, perpetuating social and economic dominance across generations.

The control of academic freedom by religious authorities further demonstrates how universities were used to maintain doctrinal conformity and suppress challenges to elite hegemony. The Galileo affair of the 17th century is a stark example of this tension. Galileo's support for helio-centrism—an idea that the Earth revolves around the Sun—challenged the geocentric worldview endorsed by the Catholic Church. This was more than a scientific dispute; it threatened the Church's authority. The Ptolemaic system, integrated into theological teachings, emphasized humanity's centrality in God's creation. Galileo's findings, supported by observations through his telescope, were groundbreaking, yet the Church viewed them as heretical. The Roman Inquisition tried him, forced him to recant his views, and placed him under house arrest. The Church's suppression of Galileo's work delayed scientific progress, illustrating how religiously affiliated institutions could wield their power to stifle dissent and maintain intellectual control. This incident reflects a broader historical pattern. By controlling universities and intellectual output, elites ensured knowledge reinforced power structures instead of challenging them.

Even beyond their theological origins, elite religious universities perpetuate inequality by cultivating exclusive alumni networks that consolidate social capital. Institutions like Harvard, Princeton, and Yale, originally founded with religious missions, evolved into secular powerhouses, but their role in maintaining elite dominance remains unchanged. Their alumni networks function as gateways to influence, linking graduates to opportunities in politics, business, and academia. The Rhodes Scholarship, established to bring promising students to Oxford, promotes academic excellence. However, it has also become a symbol of privilege, connecting recipients to a global power network. These networks often operate behind the scenes, creating opportunities and advantages for insiders while excluding those without access. Legacy admissions policies further entrench this exclusivity, ensuring that the children of wealthy and influential families maintain their place within these institutions. Higher education benefits and promises of mobility remain concentrated disproportionately within elite circles.

Through their religious foundations, control of intellectual discourse, and cultivation of exclusive networks, universities have historically served as pillars of elite dominance. Despite advancing knowledge, universities have perpetuated inequality, a role society cannot overlook. These institutions restrict access, shape curricula to align with dominant ideologies, and foster connections that sustain power structures. Universities reinforce hierarchies they originally aimed to transcend. This legacy challenges the notion of universities as purely meritocratic spaces. It reveals them as arenas where knowledge and power intersect to serve the interests of the few over the many.

Education and healthcare were not the only domains where religion upheld inequality. In some societies, religion became the very blueprint for social stratification. The caste system in India offers a stark illustration of how faith can sanctify and perpetuate inequity, embedding oppression into the fabric of daily life.

1.4 HOLY ORDER

The caste system in India, rooted in ancient Hindu texts, represents one of history's most rigid frameworks of social hierarchy. Framing inequality as divinely ordained, this system placed entire communities in positions of unassailable privilege or perpetual subjugation. Temples, as centers of spiritual authority, became fortresses of exclusion, denying marginalized groups access to rituals and sacred spaces. Even as reform movements challenged these practices, entrenched caste systems through religion proved a formidable barrier, revealing the enduring power of faith to define and divide.

The caste hierarchy, rooted in ancient texts like the Manusmriti and reinforced by Hindu scripture interpretations, divided society into rigid categories. This system included Brahmins, Kshatriyas, Vaishyas, and Shudras, relegating Dalits as "untouchables." This division was not merely social but sacralized, with the caste order presented as divinely ordained. Temples, the spiritual, and cultural hubs of Indian society, became the epicenters of this stratification. Upper castes restricted religious rituals, education, and access to sacred texts. This ensured knowledge, wealth, and power remained concentrated in their hands. This religious sanctioning of inequality transformed the caste system into an immutable institution, embedding discrimination into the spiritual fabric of the society. Religious elites portrayed caste divisions as part of cosmic law. They framed any challenge to the hierarchy as blasphemy. This strategy effectively suppressed dissent for centuries.

Religious leaders weaponized institutions by denying Dalits temple entry, reinforcing caste divisions. Even in modern times, instances of exclusion have served as stark reminders of this systemic inequality. In 1932, elites barred Dalits from using roads leading to Kerala's Vykom Temple. They were not even allowed to enter. This led to the Vykom Satyagraha, a protest movement spearheaded by reformers like Mahatma Gandhi and Periyar E.V. Ramasamy, who sought to challenge caste-based discrimination. Despite widespread support, the resistance faced intense backlash from upper-caste elites and temple authorities, who argued that allowing Dalits to enter the temple would desecrate sacred spaces. Protests at the Kalaram Temple in Maharashtra during the 1930s, led by B.R. Ambedkar, highlight resistance to caste reform. Dalits demanded entry, exposing entrenched inequality within religious institutions. These movements exposed deep ties between religious authority and social control. Temples functioned not only as places of worship but as fortresses of privilege, denying equality to the marginalized.

Upper-caste elites played a central role in sustaining this system. By controlling religious institutions, they ensured that the caste hierarchy remained unchallenged. Temple management committees, historically dominated by Brahmins and other upper-caste elites, wielded significant influence over economic resources, education, and social rituals. Collecting temple donations and land revenues provided a steady stream of wealth that further consolidated their power. Additionally, these elites used their control over religious education to perpetuate narratives that justified caste-based discrimination. By interpreting and disseminating scriptures in ways that emphasized the sanctity of caste divisions, they ensured that the system remained self-perpetuating. Dalit reformers and anti-caste movements faced violent suppression or co-option when challenging dominance. Elites intertwined religious authority with economic and political power, creating barriers to social mobility. This reinforced a cycle of exclusion that persists today.

The intersection of the caste system and religious institutions in India demonstrates how faith can be used to entrench inequality, transforming societal divisions into divine mandates. By controlling access to temples, scriptures, and rituals, upper-caste elites ensured their dominance while marginalizing entire communities. These practices reveal the dual role of religion as both a source of spiritual solace and a tool of systemic oppression. India has made strides toward legal and social reform. Yet, religiously sanctioned inequalities continue to shape its social fabric, underscoring challenges of dismantling hierarchies rooted in faith and tradition.

Religion's role in reinforcing societal divides reached new heights when it aligned itself with conquest. From the Americas to Africa, faith became the banner under which empires expanded, subjugating cultures and rewriting histories in the name of divine providence.

1.5 CONQUEST: A DIVINE AFFAIR

Colonialism in Latin America was not just a political and economic endeavor; it was a profoundly spiritual one. The Catholic Church, wielding the Doctrine of Discovery, transformed conquest into a divinely sanctioned mission. It declared the subjugation and conversion of indigenous peoples as acts of salvation. This fusion of faith and empire erased ancient cultures and spiritual traditions, replacing them with structures designed to consolidate European dominance. From forced labor systems like the encomienda to the reshaping of indigenous identities, the Church's role in conquest laid the foundation for enduring inequalities. Yet, this legacy is far from monolithic.

In Latin America, the Catholic Church has historically been a pivotal force, intertwined deeply with the colonial and post-colonial power structures that shaped the region. When Spanish and Portuguese conquistadors arrived in the 15th century, the Church allied with colonial elites. It legitimized their rule and aided in the subjugation of indigenous populations. Missionary orders, such as the Jesuits and Franciscans, accompanied military expeditions, presenting Christianity as both a spiritual salvation and a justification for conquest. The Doctrine of Discovery, endorsed by papal bulls like Inter Caetera in 1493, declared a divine mandate for European powers. They were to claim lands and convert non-Christian populations. Under this framework, the Church not only facilitated the expropriation of indigenous territories, but also justified the forced labor and cultural erasure that followed. The encomienda system, which granted Spanish settlers' control over indigenous labor for their Christianization, exemplified this collusion. The clergy positioned themselves as spiritual shepherds of colonized peoples, gaining influence and wealth. They consolidated a religious hierarchy, mirroring colonial social and economic inequalities.

In the 20th century, movements like Liberation Theology emerged within the Church, challenging these entrenched hierarchies and advocating for social justice. Liberation Theology, rooted in the teachings of Gustavo Gutiérrez and Oscar Romero, emphasized the preferential option for the poor. It called on the Church to align with marginalized communities instead of elite interests. However, this movement met fierce resistance from both conservative factions within the Church and the ruling classes it threatened. Elites, fearing the empowerment of the poor and the potential destabilization of their dominance, actively worked to suppress Liberation Theology. Governments in countries like Brazil, El Salvador, and Chile targeted clergy who preached its principles, labeling them as subversives or communists. Right-wing forces assassinated Archbishop Oscar Romero of El Salvador in 1980 while he said Mass. He was a prominent advocate for the poor and critic of state-sponsored violence, and right-wing forces aligned with elites orchestrated his death. The Vatican itself, under Pope John Paul II, distanced the Church from Liberation Theology, fearing its association with Marxist ideology. Elites curtailed the Church's revolutionary potential, suppressing efforts to address systemic inequalities.

The Church's historical alignment with elite interests has also had enduring implications for indigenous rights and social equality in Latin America. Throughout the colonial period and into the modern era, the Church acted as a gatekeeper of cultural legitimacy. It marginalized indigenous traditions and reinforced European norms' dominance. The forced conversion of indigenous peoples frequently involved destroying their sacred sites and imposing Christian practices, erasing centuries of cultural heritage. In many cases, church officials were complicit in or directly responsible for policies that stripped indigenous communities of their autonomy and access to resources. Some factions of the Church advocated for indigenous rights in the late 20th century. However, the institutional legacy of its colonial alliances continued to hinder meaningful progress. Land disputes, access to education, and recognition of cultural traditions remain contentious issues, with indigenous communities often excluded from decision-making processes dominated by elite-controlled institutions.

The Church's role in Latin America encapsulates a paradox. It professes to serve society's spiritual and moral needs, but has also maintained inequality and elite dominance. Its complicity in colonial conquest, resistance to reformist movements like Liberation Theology, and marginalization of indigenous voices have left an indelible mark on the region's social fabric. The Church has undeniably contributed to education, healthcare, and community building. However, its actions often reflect a desire to preserve the status quo, showing the enduring tension between faith and power. Latin America faces the challenge of reconciling deeply ingrained religious traditions with the need for justice and equality. The region still grapples with profound disparities.

Religious complicity in conquest and subjugation extends beyond history books. In the modern age, faith continues to be wielded as a powerful tool of influence— this time not through colonization but through political manipulation. Religion's entanglement with power persists in its ability to shape policies, mobilize voters, and consolidate wealth, often favoring the elite at the expense of equity.

1.6 HOLY VOTES FOR SALE

Modern democracies, idealizing freedom and equality, still see religion dividing and privileging certain groups. Religious lobbying groups in the United States wield immense influence, shaping legislation on healthcare, taxation, and education to protect elite economic interests. Evangelical mega-churches and Catholic organizations often frame universal healthcare or progressive taxation as threats to religious freedom or moral values. They rally congregations to support agendas that widen societal inequities. Media networks like TBN and CBN amplify this narrative, blending theology with conservative ideologies to shape public opinion. Prosperity preachers like Kenneth Copeland and Joel Osteen amass vast fortunes under the guise of spiritual leadership. This deepens economic divides within their congregations. These dynamics reveal how religion, far from being an equalizer, frequently perpetuates systems that privilege the few while exploiting the many.

Religion's influence on political, media, and economic systems underscores its enduring role as a vehicle for elite power, often working against broader societal equity. In the United States, religious lobbying has become a formidable force in shaping policies that often serve the interests of the privileged few. Powerful evangelical and conservative Catholic organizations, for instance, have consistently lobbied against universal healthcare and progressive taxation. Framing these issues as moral or ideological battles, these groups argue that government intervention in healthcare undermines personal responsibility and religious freedom. Behind this rhetoric lies the reality that these policies align with wealthy elites' economic interests. They benefit from low taxes and privatized healthcare systems. The Affordable Care Act, which sought to expand healthcare access, faced staunch opposition from religious organizations claiming it infringed on religious liberties by mandating contraceptive coverage. This lobbying not only undermines reforms aimed at reducing inequality, but also exploits faith-based narratives to sway public opinion, effectively aligning religious agendas with elite economic priorities.

The control of media by religious institutions and their elite backers further amplifies this influence, shaping public opinion to reinforce their agendas. Religious broadcasting networks like Trinity Broadcasting Network (TBN) or the Christian Broadcasting Network (CBN) wield immense power in framing cultural and political narratives. Owned and operated by wealthy religious figures, these networks promote messages that often blend theology with conservative ideology, advocating for policies that maintain traditional hierarchies. During election cycles, such platforms become pivotal in mobilizing voters, particularly around contentious issues like abortion, LGBTQ+ rights, and taxation. Political groups carefully craft messages to appeal to religious values while endorsing pro-elite policies. The rise of televangelism in the late 20th century epitomized this dynamic. Charismatic preachers like Jerry Falwell and Pat Robertson gained massive followings and leveraged their platforms to shape political discourse. Their influence extended beyond the pulpit and into the halls of power. They created a media ecosystem that perpetuated viewing society as favoring the wealthy and powerful under the guise of religious righteousness.

Accumulating wealth by religious leaders further illustrates how religion can perpetuate social inequalities. Figures like Kenneth Copeland, Joel Osteen, and Creflo Dollar built vast empires under the banner of faith. They amassed fortunes through donations, book sales, and lucrative speaking engagements. Prosperity theology, a doctrine equating material wealth with divine favor, is central to their ministries. It encourages followers to donate generously, promising spiritual and financial blessings. These leaders live in opulent mansions, fly private jets, and wield enormous cultural influence. Meanwhile, their financially struggling congregations provide the funds that sustain their lifestyles. Investigations reveal how religious exemptions from taxation entrench disparities. They allow religious institutions to operate as de facto businesses while avoiding financial scrutiny. This phenomenon is not unique to modern televangelists; history is replete with examples of clergy accumulating wealth, from medieval bishops who controlled vast landholdings to contemporary mega-church leaders whose operations rival multinational corporations.

Together, these dynamics paint a picture of how religion, far from being merely a source of spiritual guidance, functions as a potent instrument of control and inequality.

Religious lobbying shapes policy to favor elite interests. Religious media influences' public opinion to align with conservative agendas, while the wealth of religious leaders highlights economic disparities in these systems. This fusion of faith and power perpetuates structures benefiting a privileged few. Religious leaders frame these outcomes as divinely ordained, masking inequalities under moral authority. The enduring challenge is disentangling genuine faith from exploitative mechanisms of control. This requires confronting the deep-rooted intersections of religion, politics, and wealth.

2. SUFFERING: NOW IN HOLY FORMAT

Religion's capacity to hijack the human mind in the name of a higher power is profound and unsettling. It remains one of history's most remarkable phenomena. Religions use intricate systems of belief, rituals, and moral codes to tap into human psychology. They transform fear, hope, and social instincts into instruments of devotion. At its most extreme, this influence compels acts that defy reason or self-preservation. These range from ascetic fasting that endangers life to ritualistic mutilations that permanently harm the human form. Communities frame these practices as tests of faith, loyalty demonstrations, or pathways to divine reward. The allure of transcending the ordinary, aligning with a cosmic order, or securing eternal salvation is potent. It makes pain, suffering, and even death seem insignificant by comparison. In these moments, the line between faith and fanaticism blurs, exposing how malleable the human mind becomes under the influence of religious fervor.

Religious systems co-opted and amplified evolutionary traits once crucial for survival to exploit human susceptibility. Humans evolved as social creatures, deeply dependent on group cohesion and shared belief systems for protection and survival. The need to conform, to trust authority, and to signal loyalty to the group ensured that individuals could thrive within tightly knit communities. Rituals and sacrifices, even in their most extreme forms, often served to reinforce these bonds, creating a sense of belonging and collective purpose. The human capacity for imagination enabled ancestors to envision tools, strategies, and future scenarios. This same trait gave rise to abstract concepts like gods, spirits, and afterlives. While this imaginative capacity fostered creativity and innovation, it also made humans uniquely prone to adopting and acting on delusions that promise transcendence or ultimate meaning. The interplay of these evolutionary traits—social cohesion, trust in authority, and a boundless imagination—creates fertile ground for extreme practices, particularly when framed as divine imperatives.

Elites throughout history have recognized and exploited this psychological orientation for their own advantage, hacking these instincts to maintain control and perpetuate inequality. By positioning themselves as intermediaries between humanity and the divine, they transform devotion into a tool of dominance. In medieval Europe, the Church wielded the fear of eternal damnation to extract tithes and consolidate power, demanding unquestioning obedience under the guise of spiritual salvation. Similarly, in some societies, leaders have encouraged extreme body mutilation practices to demonstrate piety or tribal allegiance, using these customs to enforce conformity and loyalty. The Indian caste system, reinforced by religious doctrine, justified centuries of discrimination, while colonial powers exploited local faiths to cement their authority. Elites understood that controlling religious narratives and rituals redirected human energy. It steered people away from questioning inequality or self-determination and toward acts that reinforced dominance.

Recognizing this loophole in human psychology is essential if we are to break free from the cycles of exploitation that these systems perpetuate. As a species, we must critically examine how faith, ritual, and tradition are used to manipulate our actions and our sense of purpose. This does not mean rejecting spirituality or cultural practices altogether, but interrogating the ways they intersect with power and control. Fostering critical thinking and prioritizing human rights can reclaim agency over our lives. It redirects evolutionary traits that bound us to oppressive systems toward building societies rooted in equity and empathy. Only then can we truly honor the richness of our shared humanity, free from the chains of delusion that have too often been mistaken for divine truth.

2.1 CIRCUMCISION

Circumcision, a practice with deep cultural, religious, and historical roots, may trace its origins to the evolutionary behaviors of early human ancestors. In the prehistoric period, long before Homo sapiens developed complex societies, environmental conditions, and social dynamics likely played a role in shaping this practice as it emerged. During water scarcity, maintaining hygiene was particularly challenging. Communities might have viewed smegma accumulation as an infection sign because of its odor and irritation. In the hierarchical alpha-male group systems common among early hominins, younger males often lacked access to mating opportunities, leading to prolonged periods of sexual inactivity. Without the regular cleaning mechanisms afforded by abundant water or mating behaviors, smegma buildup could have become prevalent. Primitive groups observing these issues might have adopted circumcision as a solution. They used sharp stones or basic tools to remove the foreskin and address hygiene concerns. Circumcision began as a practical response to environmental and social pressures. Societies codified circumcision into cultural and religious practices, carrying it forward despite changing conditions.

As human civilizations advanced, circumcision became imbued with symbolic meanings far removed from its hypothetical origins. Priestly and elite classes in ancient Egypt practiced circumcision, symbolizing purity and divine connection. The practice spread to neighboring Semitic peoples, where it took on religious significance. In Judaism, circumcision became a central rite. Religious tradition codifies the covenant of circumcision, or Brit Milah. Jews perform Brit Milah on the eighth day of a male child's life. This act serves as a sign of the pact between God and Abraham. In Islam, circumcision (Khitan) serves as a rite of purification, marking the entry of boys into the faith and adherence to the teachings of the Prophet Muhammad. These religious interpretations transformed circumcision from a pragmatic act into a sacred ritual, ensuring its endurance across centuries and geographies.

Beyond religious contexts, circumcision has also been integral to cultural practices in various societies. Among the Xhosa people of South Africa, circumcision is part of a broader rite of passage into manhood. Young men undergo the procedure as part of an initiation ceremony known as ulwaluko, which includes a period of seclusion and instruction in cultural values. These rituals reinforce group identity and social cohesion. However, without proper medical oversight, they carry risks like infection or, in extreme cases, death. Such practices highlight the duality of circumcision: a revered tradition with profound symbolic weight, yet one that can carry significant physical and ethical concerns.

In modern times, the health implications of circumcision remain a topic of debate. Proponents argue that circumcision reduces risks of certain infections, like urinary tract infections and sexually transmitted diseases, including HIV. This is especially true in regions with limited healthcare access. The World Health Organization (WHO) has supported circumcision initiatives in high-HIV-prevalence areas as a preventative measure. Critics argue that the health benefits of circumcision are overstated, particularly in societies with access to clean water and hygiene facilities. Regular washing often manages infections related to smegma buildup. This raises ethical questions about non-consensual circumcision, particularly when performed on infants who cannot make an informed decision. Activist movements, such as Intactivism, advocate against routine infant circumcision, emphasizing bodily autonomy and questioning whether the procedure is necessary in modern contexts.

For individuals living in areas where water scarcity persists, alternative hygiene practices offer viable solutions to issues like smegma buildup without resorting to circumcision. Regular cleaning using minimal water, such as damp cloth wipes, can effectively maintain genital hygiene. Public health campaigns focusing on education about these methods can empower communities to address hygiene concerns while respecting individual bodily integrity. Personal narratives further illuminate the diversity of perspectives on circumcision. Some see circumcision as essential to their cultural or religious identity. Others reflect on its physical and emotional implications, whether performed with or without consent.

As society continues to evolve, circumcision remains a deeply polarizing practice, embodying a complex interplay of history, religion, culture, and medicine. Understanding its origins and current debates requires balancing respect for tradition with critical engagement on issues of health, ethics, and autonomy. By fostering dialog and prioritizing informed choice, humanity can navigate this ancient practice in a way that honors both its historical significance and the rights of individuals.

2.2 FGM

Female Genital Mutilation (FGM) is a deeply entrenched practice that starkly illustrates the intersection of tradition, control, and the subjugation of women's bodies. Defined by the World Health Organization (WHO), FGM encompasses all procedures involving partial or total removal of external female genitalia for non-medical reasons. Authorities classify FGM into four types, with Type I involving partial or total removal of the clitoris. Type II, excision, extends to the removal of the clitoris and the labia minora, sometimes including the labia majora; Type III, infibulation, involves narrowing the vaginal opening by cutting and repositioning the labia; and Type IV includes all other harmful procedures, such as pricking, piercing, or cauterizing. Cultural and religious beliefs root these procedures, evolving them over centuries and gaining resilience through societal norms.

FGM origins trace back thousands of years to ancient African and Middle Eastern societies. It predates the major religions that later adopted or tolerated the practice. Ancient Egyptians practiced FGM, linking it to chastity and purity according to historical evidence. Inscriptions on temple walls and writings from Greek historians like Herodotus reference the practice, suggesting its deep cultural roots. Over time, it spread across regions, adapting to local customs and becoming intertwined with patriarchal structures. In some communities, it became a rite of passage, marking the shift from girlhood to womanhood. This cultural embedding ensured its survival, even as broader societal norms evolved.

The reasons for practicing FGM are diverse and complex, often rooted in deeply held beliefs about purity, marriageability, and social acceptance. Communities often see FGM as necessary for marriage to ensure chastity and fidelity. People believe FGM reduces sexual desire, preserving moral and familial honor. Others view it as a religious obligation, despite the fact that neither the Quran nor the Bible explicitly mandates it. This conflation of cultural norms with religious edicts creates a powerful justification for the practice, making it resistant to external criticism. Somali and Sudanese communities see FGM as indispensable to a girl's upbringing, with prevalence exceeding 90%. Communal ceremonies often celebrate the procedure, reinforcing its perceived importance.

FGM is geographically widespread, with prevalence concentrated in regions of Africa, the Middle East, and parts of Asia. Countries like Somalia, Egypt, and Indonesia have particularly high rates of FGM, though the practice varies in form and prevalence even within these regions. In Somalia, FGM is nearly universal. Type III infibulation is the most common form, highlighting the extreme nature of the practice in certain cultural contexts. In Egypt, nearly 87% of women aged 15–49 have undergone FGM. Medical professionals often perform FGM, a trend referred to as the "medicalization" of the practice. FGM in Indonesia is less invasive, but remains prevalent. Cultural and religious justifications drive this practice. Migration has also spread FGM to diasporic communities in Europe, North America, and Australia, raising global awareness but also complicating efforts to address the issue.

Authentic stories like that of Waris Dirie bring the brutal reality of FGM into sharp focus. Born in Somalia, Dirie underwent infibulation at the age of five, a traumatic experience that left her scarred physically and emotionally. As she grew older, Dirie escaped her rural upbringing, eventually becoming an internationally renowned model and later a UN special ambassador to eliminate FGM. Her autobiography, Desert Flower, chronicling her harrowing journey, helped spotlight FGM as a global human rights issue. Dirie's activism galvanized international efforts, providing a platform for survivors to speak out against the practice and challenging the cultural norms that sustain it.

The health implications of FGM are profound and devastating. In the short term, the procedure often results in severe pain, excessive bleeding, infection, and even death. Long-term consequences include chronic pain, complications during childbirth, reduced sexual pleasure, and psychological trauma, such as anxiety, depression, and post-traumatic stress disorder (PTSD). Survivors frequently experience social stigma if complications render them unable to bear children or satisfy cultural expectations tied to FGM. These consequences highlight the irreparable harm inflicted by a practice that is, at its core, an act of control and subjugation.

Efforts to combat FGM have gained momentum over the past few decades, driven by a growing recognition of its violation of human rights. Internationally, the United Nations has adopted resolutions condemning FGM, and campaigns like UNICEF's Joint Programme on Female Genital Mutilation work toward eradicating the practice. Many countries have enacted laws banning FGM, including Kenya, Egypt, and Senegal, though enforcement often remains inconsistent because of cultural resistance and weak legal infrastructure. Grassroots movements, particularly those led by survivors, have played a crucial role in advocating for change, challenging the stigma surrounding FGM, and fostering dialog within practicing communities.

Understanding perspectives from within these communities is essential for meaningful progress. While many women who have undergone FGM oppose it, others continue to support the practice, seeing it as integral to their identity and culture. For some, rejecting FGM feels like rejecting their heritage. This ambivalence underscores the need for culturally sensitive approaches that respect traditions while emphasizing the health risks and human rights violations associated with FGM. By engaging with community leaders, fostering education, and amplifying survivor voices, it is possible to dismantle the societal norms that perpetuate this harmful tradition.

FGM reflects the complex interplay of tradition, power, and control, sustained by cultural and religious beliefs that resist change. Efforts to eradicate FGM require addressing cultural roots and empowering those affected despite progress. Global collaboration and community-driven efforts can make this violation of women's rights a relic of the past. Societies can spare future generations from enduring harm by ending FGM.

2.3 ASHURA

Ashura, the tenth day of Muharram, holds profound significance in Islam, representing both a day of mourning and spiritual reflection. For Sunni Muslims, Ashura commemorates the deliverance of the Prophet Moses and the Israelites from Pharaoh's tyranny, marked by fasting as an act of gratitude to God. For Shia Muslims, Ashura is a day of immense sorrow. It centers on the martyrdom of Imam Hussain, the grandson of the Prophet Muhammad, at the Battle of Karbala in 680 CE. Yazid I's forces slaughtered Hussain and his followers, symbolizing ultimate sacrifice. It represents resistance in the face of tyranny and injustice. The memory of Karbala permeates Shia's identity, evoking themes of resistance, loyalty, and the struggle for moral integrity. Over centuries, Ashura has evolved into a cornerstone of Shia practice, with rituals designed to channel grief into collective expressions of devotion and solidarity.

The historical context of the Battle of Karbala is central to understanding Ashura's resonance. The Umayyad Caliph Yazid I demanded allegiance from Hussain, a move seen by many as an attempt to legitimize an unjust and corrupt regime. Hussain's refusal marked a pivotal moment in Islamic history, embodying the principle that moral truth must prevail over political expediency. Yazid I's forces denied Hussain and his followers' water and subjected them to brutal violence. On the plains of Karbala, Hussain's martyrdom became a defining moment for Shia Islam, establishing him as a paragon of virtue and resistance. Vivid retellings of this event through sermons and poetry, known as majlis, preserve its emotional and spiritual impact. They ensure Karbala's legacy remains an enduring force in Shia's consciousness.

Ritual practices associated with Ashura, particularly in Shia communities, reflect deep mourning and solidarity with Imam Hussain. Tatbir, or self-flagellation, is among the most striking practices. Participants strike themselves with blades or chains to draw blood as a symbolic act of shared suffering. Mourners pound their chests, chant elegies, and engage in bloodletting during Ashura processions. This iconic sight is especially common in Iran, Iraq, Pakistan, and Lebanon. Participants see these acts as physical manifestations of grief and offerings of pain to commemorate Hussain's suffering. Processions in Karbala itself are especially powerful, drawing millions of pilgrims who retrace the steps of Hussain's last journey. The sea of black-clad mourners converging on the shrine of Imam Hussain during Ashura epitomizes collective devotion, transforming personal grief into a profound communal experience.

However, tatbir and other forms of ritual self-harm have sparked significant controversy within and beyond the Shia community. Critics argue that such practices perpetuate a negative image of Islam and distract from the ethical and spiritual lessons of Karbala. Religious scholars and community leaders have called for reforms, emphasizing alternative commemorations that honor the memory of Hussain without self-inflicted violence. Blood donation campaigns channel the symbolism of sacrifice into tangible acts of benefit. They align with the values of compassion and altruism represented by Imam Hussain's legacy. This shift reflects an ongoing effort to reconcile tradition with modern sensibilities, ensuring that Ashura remains a relevant observance.

However, there is a growing call to reconsider some of the more extreme practices associated with Ashura, particularly those involving self-harm, which can overshadow its central message. Shifting focus to community service, education, and peaceful commemoration can help future generations uphold Ashura's essence. This approach aligns with its ethical teachings and modern sensibilities. Moving away from harmful rituals creates opportunities to emphasize broader spiritual and moral lessons of Hussain's legacy. This fosters a more inclusive, forward-thinking approach. The next generation can honor the spirit of Ashura by advocating for justice and unity. They can inspire positive change while ensuring participant safety and well-being.

2.4 FINGER CUTTING

Practices like finger amputation or self-inflicted wounds, represent visceral and profound expressions of emotion and cultural identity. Such acts, often tied to grief, devotion, or rites of passage, symbolize the relationship between the body and intangible realms of spirit and community. In various cultures, the body serves as a medium for expressing deep emotions that defy words. Removing a body part symbolizes an offering, sacrifice, or release. Though these practices are startling to outsiders, for the communities that uphold them, they carry profound meaning, embedding personal loss and communal values into the flesh.

In the remote highlands of Papua, Indonesia, the Dani tribe practices finger-cutting, or ikipalin, as a mourning ritual to honor deceased relatives. For the Dani, the fingers are not merely physical appendages but representations of interconnectedness and familial bonds. When a loved one dies, amputating a fingertip, often by women, manifests emotional pain. It symbolizes the severing of a shared life. Each missing finger tells a story of loss, transforming grief into a visible and permanent marker of devotion. Older female relatives, such as mothers or grandmothers, historically performed this practice, bearing physical reminders of family members they outlived. Finger-cutting is increasingly rare because of government bans and external influences. However, it remains a potent symbol of the Dani's cultural heritage and their way of grappling with mortality.

The Dani worldview deeply roots the symbolic meanings behind these acts of self-alteration. The community externalizes grief as a shared force. They do not internalize grief. Finger amputation channels this grief into a concrete form. The act reflects their belief. Physical pain mirrors emotional suffering. It can also help alleviate it. By sacrificing a part of themselves, mourners honor the memory of the deceased, ensuring that their connection endures beyond death. This physical expression of loss reinforces communal bonds, as the collective participation in mourning rituals fosters solidarity and mutual support among surviving family members. In this way, ikipalin transcends the individual, becoming a shared acknowledgment of life's fragility and the ties that bind.

Dani people carry out finger-cutting procedures with a mixture of solemnity and practicality. Practitioners traditionally perform the amputation using a sharp stone or blade, often without anesthetic. Ceremonial elements, including prayers or chants, accompany the act to honor the deceased and seek spiritual protection. Practitioners treat the wound with plant-based remedies or ash after severing the fingertip to promote healing and prevent infection. Generations of empirical knowledge inform these traditional methods, making them integral to the ritual. Families often bury or preserve the severed fingertip as part of mourning, symbolizing the departed's enduring presence.

The health and safety concerns associated with these practices are significant, given the risks of infection, excessive bleeding, and long-term complications. Traditional methods of care, while effective in some cases, lack the safeguards of modern medical practices, leaving participants vulnerable to complications. Healthcare initiatives reaching the Dani and similar communities have initiated efforts to reduce ritual risks. Cultural perceptions view physical sacrifice as an essential ritual aspect, often clashing with interventions.

The ethical discussions surrounding body-altering rituals like ikipalin reveal a complex tension between cultural preservation and human rights. Critics argue that practices involving self-harm, especially those performed under social pressure, violate fundamental principles of bodily autonomy and well-being. Others, however, emphasize respecting cultural traditions, viewing them as expressions of identity and resilience against homogenizing forces. Anthropologists and human rights advocates debate preserving, modifying, or eradicating such practices. This raises questions about who defines the boundaries of tradition and modernity. For the Dani, losing such rituals could erode a cultural framework that has sustained them for generations.

Personal accounts from Dani tribe members provide invaluable insight into the practice and its evolving significance. Some elders speak of ikipalin with reverence, describing it as a necessary and honorable act that brings closure to grief. Others express relief that the practice is fading, noting the physical and emotional toll it takes. A Dani woman who underwent the ritual as a teenager recalled the pain as unbearable yet transformative. She emphasized the pride she felt in fulfilling her cultural duty. Meanwhile, younger Dani individuals, exposed to modern education and values, often view the practice with skepticism, questioning its relevance in a changing world. These testimonies highlight the diversity of perspectives within the community, reflecting the dynamic interplay of tradition and modernity.

The practice of finger-cutting among the Dani tribe serves as a poignant reminder of how cultures navigate grief, identity, and continuity. However, as the world becomes more interconnected, it is essential to prioritize the well-being and safety of individuals over the perpetuation of harmful traditions. Communities should respectfully discontinue this practice and focus on preserving grief and remembrance through symbolic alternatives. Transitioning away from physical harm allows the community to honor its heritage while promoting health and dignity. This ensures cultural identity remains a source of strength, not harm.

2.5 TOURISM TANGLES TRADITIONS

The human body, both resilient and fragile, has long served as a canvas for cultural expression. Yet, many traditional practices that alter or harm the body—whether through cutting, stretching, or binding—raise urgent ethical and health concerns. These rituals, celebrated for their symbolic richness, often exact a steep physical and psychological toll on the individuals who undergo them. Scarification, lip stretching, and neck elongation, for instance, may cause chronic pain, mobility issues, or social stigmatization in a globalized world. Even practices like tooth filing or circumcision, performed without modern medical safeguards, carry risks of infection, permanent injury, or trauma. These rituals, deeply embedded in cultural and spiritual frameworks, demand scrutiny for the harm they inflict. Global movements call for prioritizing health and human rights over tradition.

Modern media and tourism have complicated the conversation around these practices by often exploiting them for profit rather than promoting understanding or change. Travel documentaries and social media platforms romanticize indigenous rituals, packaging them as exotic spectacles for consumption by Western audiences. Tourists eager for unique experiences flock to communities like the Kayan villages in Thailand or Maasai regions of Kenya. They often treat participants as relics of a vanishing world. This commodification pressures individuals to continue harmful traditions, not for cultural preservation, but to attract tourism revenue. Even volunteer agencies, often run by elites, capitalize on these spectacles under the guise of cultural preservation or development work. These organizations frequently funnel profits into private coffers while perpetuating cycles of poverty and dependence among the very communities they claim to help. The global marketplace commodifies culture, leaving those bearing its marks voiceless.

Globalization and modernization have both disrupted and reinforced traditional body modification practices. Westernization has introduced alternative beauty standards and modern medical ethics, leading many younger individuals to reject customs like foot binding or lip stretching. The influence of global human rights movements has also played a role, with international campaigns highlighting the harm caused by practices such as female genital mutilation (FGM). However, globalization has also provided a platform for traditional practices to resurge in altered forms, often stripped of their original meaning. For example, scarification or stretched earlobes are now popular among Western body modification enthusiasts, divorced from their cultural roots and marketed as fashion statements. This dual impact reflects the complex interplay between cultural preservation and the homogenizing forces of modernity.

Media and tourism have further amplified the tension between tradition and change. Films, documentaries, and online content have exposed indigenous customs to global audiences, often reducing them to entertainment or sensationalism. This exposure can both erode and reinforce practices, depending on the context. Tourism creates economic incentives to continue traditions that might otherwise fade, but often at the cost of distorting their meaning. In Bali or Ethiopia, rituals once performed for spiritual or communal reasons now cater to tourist expectations. Performers modify or exaggerate ceremonies for dramatic effect. The result dilutes cultural authenticity, with practices increasingly shaped by external demand rather than internal significance.

Legal interventions have sought to address these challenges, with varying degrees of success. Organizations like UNICEF and the United Nations work to outlaw harmful practices like FGM, child marriage, and extreme scarification. They frame these as violations of human rights. Local governments, influenced by these efforts, have enacted bans or restrictions, though enforcement is often uneven. In some cases, laws clash with deeply entrenched traditions, sparking resistance from communities who view them as external impositions. Efforts to balance legal measures with cultural sensitivity remain fraught, requiring ongoing dialog between governments, activists, and the communities affected.

The debate between preservation and change lies at the heart of these issues. Advocates for cultural heritage argue that body modification practices represent invaluable links to history and identity, deserving protection in a rapidly homogenizing world. Others contend that traditions causing physical or psychological harm should evolve or fade, particularly when they conflict with modern understandings of health and human rights. Initiatives to bridge this divide include reinterpreting rituals in less harmful ways. Examples include replacing self-flagellation with blood donations during Ashura or promoting symbolic alternatives to circumcision. These efforts demonstrate the potential for traditions to adapt without sacrificing their core values.

The health implications of harmful body modifications are significant and often lifelong. Infections, scarring, and chronic pain are common outcomes, particularly in practices performed without medical oversight. Women with bound feet in imperial China suffered limited mobility and debilitating pain. Those undergoing FGM face complications like childbirth difficulties and long-term psychological trauma. Men participating in rituals like the Sun Dance endure physical strain that can lead to permanent injuries. These health risks underscore the need for informed consent and modern medical interventions, particularly as communities grapple with the future of these traditions.

Human rights perspectives increasingly see harmful or coercive practices as incompatible with dignity and autonomy. UNICEF's campaigns against FGM and child marriage highlight the role of education and advocacy in combating these practices, particularly by empowering women and young people. Critics of these campaigns argue for rooting solutions in dialog and cultural understanding, cautioning against a one-size-fits-all approach. Programs that prioritize education and community leadership, rather than external mandates, have proven more effective in fostering sustainable change.

Success stories highlight how communities can transition from harmful practices to healthier alternatives. In Senegal, grassroots efforts led by local women have significantly reduced rates of FGM, showcasing the power of community-driven reform. Similarly, initiatives in Kenya have encouraged the Maasai to reinterpret traditional rites of passage without physical harm. These examples demonstrate that engaging communities as partners, not targets, fosters change while respecting traditions.

Examining harmful body modification practices reveals the need to balance cultural preservation with transformation. While rituals often embody rich cultural heritage, their potential harm requires ethical reflection. As globalization reshapes societies, respecting traditions must not shield them from scrutiny. Through education, advocacy, and dialog, humanity can navigate this complex interplay, ensuring the body becomes a symbol of empowerment rather than suffering.

3. HOLY SCANDALS

The sexual abuse scandals in the Catholic Church are one of the most devastating breaches of trust. They reveal systemic abuse, cover-ups, and an entrenched culture of silence. Allegations of sexual misconduct by priests have surfaced globally, tracing back decades or centuries. They implicate not just offenders but also the institutions overseeing them. These cases show how an organization professing moral authority often prioritizes its reputation. It does so over the safety and dignity of its most vulnerable members—its children. What started as whispers grew into a global reckoning. Survivors, journalists, and investigators exposed the crisis, challenging one of the world's most powerful religious institutions.

In the U.S., the scandal reached a tipping point in 2002. The Boston Globe's Spotlight team published an investigation exposing widespread sexual abuse by Catholic priests in the Boston Archdiocese. The reports revealed dozens of priests molested hundreds of children over decades. Church officials covered up the crimes by reassigning offenders to new parishes instead of reporting them. Cardinal Bernard Law, the archbishop of Boston, emerged as a central figure in the scandal, resigning in disgrace but avoiding legal repercussions by relocating to Rome. The investigation's fallout triggered similar revelations nationwide. It resulted in thousands of lawsuits, billions in settlements, and several dioceses declaring bankruptcy. The Boston case prompted policy reforms in the Church, like stricter background checks and review boards for allegations. However, questions about the sufficiency of these measures persist.

The revelations in Boston inspired inquiries worldwide, with Ireland emerging as another epicenter of abuse scandals. The 2009 Ryan Report, a five-volume investigation commissioned by the Irish government, unveiled horrific accounts of abuse in Catholic-run schools, orphanages, and industrial homes. Clergy and staff subjected thousands of children to physical, emotional, and sexual abuse over several decades. The report detailed both the abuse and the culture of impunity that allowed it to flourish. Church officials often dismissed complaints or intimidated victims into silence. Public outrage over the findings led to apologies from senior Church figures and the Irish government, as well as financial compensation schemes for survivors. However, the revelations also accelerated the secularization of Irish society, with many citizens questioning the moral authority of an institution so deeply implicated in systemic wrongdoing.

Australia's reckoning with abuse in the Catholic Church reached its zenith with the case of Cardinal George Pell, one of the Vatican's most senior figures. Authorities convicted Pell in 2018 for abusing choirboys in the 1990s. However, Australia's High Court overturned the verdict in 2020 because of insufficient evidence. Pell's case, though, was just a small part of a widespread pattern of abuse. The government established the Royal Commission into Institutional Responses to Child Sexual Abuse in 2013. It investigated allegations across religious, governmental, and community organizations. The report painted a damning picture of the Catholic Church. Survivors accused over 7% of Australian priests of abuse between 1950 and 2010.

The commission's findings sparked widespread calls for accountability. One major proposal was mandatory reporting laws for clergy. This clashed with the Church's stance on the sanctity of confession.

Across all these cases, a chilling pattern emerged: rather than confronting abusers and protecting victims, Church leaders often prioritized the institution's reputation. Church officials quietly moved offending priests to new parishes, where they frequently reoffended, while dismissing, shaming, or coercing victims into silence. Legal protections afforded to religious institutions, coupled with the Church's influence in many societies, enabled this culture of impunity to persist for decades. This systemic failure not only compounded the harm to victims but also eroded public trust in the Church as it instituted moral guidance.

The impact on victims has been profound, with many survivors recounting lives marked by psychological trauma, substance abuse, and strained relationships. Efforts to seek justice have often been fraught with challenges, as victims face powerful institutional resistance, lengthy legal battles, and the emotional toll of revisiting their abuse. Yet, the courage of these survivors in coming forward has been instrumental in driving the global conversation around accountability and reform.

In response to these scandals, the Vatican, and local dioceses have implemented measures aimed at preventing future abuse. Pope Francis has called for zero tolerance toward abuse, convening a global summit on the issue in 2019 and instituting guidelines to investigate allegations. Dioceses worldwide have established child protection offices and mandated training programs for clergy and staff. However, critics argue that these reforms often fall short, lacking transparency and independent oversight. Survivors and advocates continue to demand more substantial changes, including the full disclosure of records and prosecuting complicit Church leaders.

Sexual misconduct spans beyond the Catholic Church and extends across other Christian denominations, revealing a broader crisis of accountability and institutional failure. In Protestant churches, particularly within the Southern Baptist Convention (SBC), allegations of abuse have exposed deep flaws in oversight and transparency. In 2019, The Houston Chronicle and San Antonio Express-News revealed over 700 sexual abuse cases. These involved leaders and volunteers in SBC-affiliated churches over two decades. Victims included children and adults. The report highlighted inaction, where church leaders failed to report allegations or let accused pastors move between congregations. This revelation spurred calls for reform, including establishing a centralized database to track accused clergy. While some within the SBC embraced these measures, others resisted, citing the denomination's decentralized structure and concerns over autonomy. The scandal underscored the challenges of addressing abuse within loosely organized religious systems that lack the hierarchical oversight of the Catholic Church.

Evangelical communities, known for their emphasis on charismatic leadership, have also faced scandals involving high-profile figures and youth leaders. Televangelists commanding vast followings and financial resources exploit their congregants' trust in cases of sexual misconduct. In a notable case, church secretary Jessica Hahn accused Jim Bakker, a prominent 1980s televangelist, of sexual assault. Bakker ultimately went to prison for financial fraud, not assault allegations. The case highlighted congregants' vulnerability in evangelical settings with weak accountability structures. Similarly, numerous cases have emerged involving youth pastors in evangelical churches, exploiting their roles to prey on minors under their care. Some churches have responded with internal investigations and resignations. Others minimized public scrutiny, reflecting a tension between victim protection and institutional reputation.

The Orthodox Church, with its own traditions and hierarchies, has also grappled with reports of sexual misconduct, though these cases often receive less public attention. In regions such as Eastern Europe and the Middle East, cultural taboos, and deference to religious authority have contributed to under reporting and a lack of institutional accountability. Notable incidents, such as allegations against senior Orthodox clergy in Greece and Russia, have exposed similar patterns of abuse and cover-up seen in other denominations. In some cases, church leaders have issued public apologies and committed to internal reforms, but systemic change remains slow. The Orthodox Church's ties to national identities and governments complicate addressing misconduct. Religious leaders' political influence often stifles or dismisses accusations.

Across denominations, the response to sexual misconduct has varied, but common threads of denial, cover-up, and resistance to accountability emerge repeatedly. Institutions designed to provide spiritual guidance have instead, in many cases, enabled harm by prioritizing their reputation over the welfare of their members

The scandals within Protestant, evangelical, and Orthodox communities reveal that no branch of Christianity is exempt from these issues. These incidents underscore the urgent need for cross-denominational collaboration to address abuse. Establishing transparent systems of accountability and rebuilding trust are crucial for addressing the harm done to congregants. Such cases highlight that institutional change requires more than just policy reforms; it demands a cultural shift and a deep commitment to justice, dignity, and the well-being of all individuals involved. Only through this transformation can true healing and progress be achieved within these communities.

3.1 SEX SCANDALS IN ISLAM

Sexual abuse and misconduct in Islamic contexts are troubling yet under-discussed. Cultural taboos and systemic barriers often shroud these global abuse scandals. In many Islamic educational institutions, or madrasas, cases of abuse have exposed a dark underside to establishments revered for religious instruction. Reports from Pakistan and Bangladesh reveal sexual misconduct by madrasa teachers. The cases often involve young boys living on-site, separated from their families. In 2021, a case in Pakistan involving the abuse of a teenage boy by a prominent religious scholar garnered national outrage, leading to the scholar's arrest. Societal stigma frequently hinders such cases, as families avoid reporting incidents to prevent dishonor and ostracism. Delays and influence from powerful religious networks often obstruct legal proceedings, leaving victims without closure or justice.

High-profile cases involving imams or clerics accused of misconduct further illuminate the challenges of addressing abuse in Islamic communities. In some instances, these religious figures leverage their authority to exploit vulnerable congregants, using their positions of trust to silence accusations. Authorities in the UK convicted an imam in 2017 for abusing multiple children during Quran lessons. The case, which only came to light after years of silence, highlighted the reluctance within some communities to confront allegations against revered figures. Communities have responded with both swift action and backlash in some cases, while others have shielded perpetrators from accountability. Deep respect for religious leaders in many Islamic societies fosters a culture of impunity, dismissing accusations as slander or conspiracy.

Cultural and legal challenges compound these issues, making it even harder for victims to seek justice. Concepts of honor and shame play a significant role in many Islamic societies, where families may prioritize protecting their reputation over addressing the abuse. Victims, especially women and girls, face trauma, and societal judgment. Accusations often turn against them, questioning their morality and behavior. Legal systems in many countries further exacerbate these difficulties, as laws rooted in religious interpretations or patriarchal structures can place insurmountable hurdles in the path of justice. In some jurisdictions, a woman's testimony carries less weight than a man's. The burden of proof in sexual abuse cases is unreasonably high, deterring victims from coming forward.

Despite these challenges, advocacy, and reform efforts are emerging to protect victims and promote accountability. Organizations like Sahil in Pakistan work to document cases of child sexual abuse and provide support services to victims, including counseling and legal aid. In Bangladesh, campaigns led by activists and NGOs have pushed for stricter oversight of madrasas and harsher penalties for abusers. Globally, the #MeToo movement has inspired survivors within Islamic communities to share their stories, challenging entrenched norms and sparking conversations about abuse in religious contexts. These efforts, while still in their infancy in many places, signal a growing awareness of the need to address sexual misconduct within Islamic institutions.

Sexual abuse and misconduct in Islamic contexts underscores the universal nature of these crimes and the systemic failures that allow them to persist. While cultural and legal barriers add layers of complexity, the courageous efforts of survivors, activists, and reformers demonstrate that change is possible. Addressing this crisis demands legal and institutional reform. It also requires a cultural shift prioritizing dignity and safety over reputation or authority. It is a difficult but essential path toward justice and accountability in religious communities worldwide.

3.2 SEX SCANDALS IN HINDUISM

Sexual misconduct in Hindu religious institutions reveals the dark underbelly of faith-based hierarchies and the unchecked power wielded by some spiritual leaders. Among the most infamous cases is that of Asaram Bapu, a self-proclaimed godman who amassed millions of followers over decades, wielding immense influence across India's socio-political landscape. Authorities accused Asaram in 2013 of raping a 16-year-old girl at his ashram in Rajasthan, sparking outrage nationwide. The trial exposed not just the crime but also a sprawling network of enablers who threatened witnesses and attempted to obstruct justice. The court convicted Asaram in 2018 and sentenced him to life imprisonment despite significant hurdles. It was a rare victory in a system criticized for failing to hold powerful religious figures accountable. However, his case highlighted the harm caused by such leaders. Investigations revealed more abuse allegations and financial impropriety, leaving a trail of devastated lives.

Another prominent case involved Swami Nithyananda, a controversial figure accused of multiple counts of sexual abuse and exploitation, including assaulting female devotees at his ashram. Videos allegedly showing him in compromising situations with followers went viral, leading to widespread condemnation and legal scrutiny. Despite mounting evidence and legal proceedings, Nithyananda fled India in 2019, reportedly establishing a self-declared "nation" called Kailaasa, further complicating efforts to hold him accountable. These incidents show how spiritual leaders exploit trust and authority. They use religious doctrine and fear of divine retribution to silence victims and control communities.

The problem extends beyond individual leaders to encompass broader issues within Hindu religious institutions, including ashrams and temples. Reports of abuse at pilgrimage sites and within cloistered religious communities paint a troubling picture of systemic exploitation. Predators claiming to offer spiritual guidance often prey on vulnerable groups, including women, children, and impoverished devotees. Several accounts from pilgrimage centers like Varanasi and Tirupati detail sexual harassment. These involve temple staff or resident priests over the years. The insularity of these communities, combined with their deeply ingrained hierarchies, creates an environment where abuse can flourish unchecked.

Societal reactions to these scandals vary, reflecting outrage, denial, and resistance to change. High-profile cases like those of Asaram and Nithyananda have sparked massive public protests and extensive media coverage, forcing authorities to take action. Yet, victims often face significant challenges in coming forward. Fear of ostracization, coupled with the immense influence of accused figures, acts as a deterrent. Devotees, deeply invested in their spiritual leaders, sometimes rally to their defense, branding accusations as conspiracies to undermine faith. These dynamics create a hostile environment for survivors, who must not only navigate a legal maze but also contend with public skepticism and threats from loyal followers.

The Indian legal system's handling of sexual misconduct in religious institutions reflects progress and indicts persistent systemic weaknesses. High-profile convictions, such as that of Asaram, demonstrate that justice is possible, but such outcomes remain exceptions rather than the norm. Delays in legal proceedings, combined with insufficient protection for witnesses and victims, often allow powerful figures to evade accountability. Moreover, laws governing religious institutions are fragmented and poorly enforced, leaving significant gaps in oversight. Initiatives like preventing sexual harassment at the workplace and enforcing child protection laws offer recourse. However, inconsistent application in religious spaces calls for stronger frameworks.

3.3 SEX SCANDALS IN OTHERS

Sexual abuse scandals extend beyond major religions like Christianity, Islam, and Hinduism, permeating other religious contexts where power and secrecy combine to shield perpetrators and silence victims. In Buddhism, allegations against prominent Tibetan Buddhist teachers have forced a reckoning within a tradition often idealized for its emphasis on compassion and nonviolence. One of the most high-profile cases involved Sogyal Rinpoche, a renowned teacher, and author of The Tibetan Book of Living and Dying. Sogyal faced accusations of sexual abuse, manipulation, and assault over decades. Followers ignored his misconduct, unwilling to question his authority or stature. In 2017, after an independent investigation confirmed allegations, he resigned from the Rigpa organization. This left a community grappling with betrayal and the need for systemic change. Some Buddhist institutions have initiated reforms for transparency and accountability. However, Tibetan Buddhism's hierarchical and teacher-centric structure poses challenges to addressing abuse.

In the Jehovah's Witnesses community, allegations of sexual abuse have centered not only on the acts themselves but also on the organization's policies that critics say enable cover-ups. A key contention is the "two-witness rule." This doctrine requires accusations of wrongdoing to have at least two witnesses for validity. In cases of sexual abuse, where witnesses are rarely present, this policy effectively silences victims and protects perpetrators. Investigations in Australia and the U.S. revealed extensive abuse within the community. Some elders discouraged victims from reporting crimes, prioritizing the organization's reputation over justice. Legal actions, including multimillion-dollar lawsuits and government inquiries, have pressured the leadership to revise its policies, but reforms have been slow and met with resistance. These cases highlight the tension between religious doctrines and the demands of modern legal and ethical standards.

The Orthodox Jewish community has also faced its share of abuse scandals, with cases emerging from insular enclaves in the United States, Israel, and elsewhere. These communities strictly adhere to religious law and mistrust secular authorities. They often handle allegations internally via rabbinical courts instead of civil justice systems. This approach frequently results in inadequate responses, as rabbinical courts lack the investigative tools and impartiality needed to address criminal behavior effectively. High-profile cases in ultra-Orthodox schools in Brooklyn or religious leaders in Jerusalem expose the pressure on victims to remain silent. Fear of ostracism, concerns about family reputations, and religious prohibitions against reporting fellow Jews to secular authorities—known as mesirah—compound the difficulties faced by survivors seeking justice. Grassroots advocacy groups like Jewish Community Watch and Za'akah are breaking the wall of silence. They support victims and push for greater transparency in Orthodox institutions.

Cases across Buddhism, Jehovah's Witnesses, and Orthodox Judaism show common institutional failures. Insular structures, reverence for authority, and doctrinal rigidity enable abuse to thrive. The impact on victims is profound. They face trauma from abuse and additional barriers from their communities' resistance to accountability. Legal actions, advocacy, and awareness have driven some progress. However, these entrenched issues require sustained efforts to dismantle systems protecting abusers.

Religious institutions grappling with scandals must confront an uncomfortable truth. Religious leaders must earn moral authority through integrity, transparency, and justice.

4. BESANT DETOUR

The human mind, capable of profound rationality and boundless curiosity, also harbors a peculiar inclination: a need to reconcile what it discovers with what it believes. In this duality lies the seed of self-defeat. When a scientist harbors belief in the supernatural as a "benefit of doubt," it creates an existential contradiction, conflicting with their pursuit of evidence and reason. It is akin to charting the vast, uncharted seas with a compass of logic while clutching, in the other hand, the comforting charm of superstition. A dual stance may seem noble to some, but history and logic show it begins a self-defeating journey that undermines the purpose of science.

Modern examples of scientists who attempt to harmonize science with religious belief illustrate this dilemma. Guy Consolmagno, an American research astronomer and director of the Vatican Observatory, speaks of the universe's beauty and rationality as reflections of a creator's personality. William Daniel Phillips, a Nobel laureate in physics, intertwines his Christian faith with his scientific pursuits, seeing the natural world as a divine gift meant for exploration. Similarly, Jennifer Wiseman, an astrophysicist deeply involved with the Hubble Space Telescope, views her study of the cosmos as an act of worship. These individuals, celebrated for their contributions to science, also articulate views that blend the empirical with the theological. Yet, their attempts to bridge this divide often dilute the scientific message, veering into territory that undermines the rigor and universality of the scientific method. Their faith-infused perspectives shift the goalposts of inquiry, often precluding the need for further questioning by invoking the divine as an ultimate explanation.

To understand why such detours are perilous, one can draw parallels to a historical figure whose ideological trajectory exemplifies this pitfall: Annie Besant. Besant's early life was a mixture of shifting beliefs. Born into a religiously inclined household, she was deeply immersed in Christian doctrine as a child. During her teenage years, she embraced intellectual rebellion. By her troubled marriage and subsequent divorce, Besant became a fierce advocate for atheism. Her speeches and writings championed reason over superstition, railing against the oppressive structures of organized religion. For a time, her mission was clear; her trajectory aligned with progress and emancipation.

But then came the detour. Besant's rigid atheism gave way to philosophical agnosticism, a position she embraced under the guise of open-mindedness. This shift, subtle at first, led her to Theosophy, a mystical blend of spiritualism and Eastern philosophies. She abandoned her rationalist crusade, immersing herself in esotericism by the end of her life. Her legacy, once firmly tethered to secularism and progress, became muddled with spiritual and religious undertones. The Indian National Congress, which she had influenced significantly, mirrored this trajectory. Initially rooted in progressive, secular ideals, the party drifted into religious symbolism as it countered the influence of right-wing Hindu nationalism. The Congress party's attempts to appease religious groups have frequently compromised its secular image, resulting in ideological inconsistency.

The lesson here is stark. When individuals or institutions take a detour from atheism or secular rationalism to adopt agnosticism or religious accommodation, they unwittingly pave the way for extremism. The initial concession, made in the name of inclusivity or humility, often snowballs into full-fledged capitulation. Annie Besant's ideological trajectory illustrates this with painful clarity, as does the Congress party's strategic shift in response to Narendra Modi's brand of Hindu nationalism. In both cases, what began as a philosophical or political compromise ended with foundational principles eroding.

The same danger looms for scientists who allow religious belief to coexist with their scientific endeavors. By entertaining the possibility of a divine hand, they anchor their work to an endpoint that precludes further exploration. History suggests that when this happens, the progress of discovery often halts, leaving others to strip away the bias of belief and start anew. Religious dogma frequently constrained early strides in understanding the natural world. Secularizing science was essential to unleashing its full potential. When a scientist attributes a discovery to God or divine will, they limit inquiry and leave further exploration to those willing to go beyond such confines.

In this context, the coexistence of science and religious belief is not only ineffective but contrary to the essence of science itself. Similar to Annie Besant's shift from atheism to Theosophy, such compromises lead to stagnation and confusion, forcing others to recover what little progress remains. To advance humanity's pursuit of knowledge, it must avoid reconciling the rational with the mystical. Each step taken in this direction diverts from the true path of scientific progress, hindering the clarity and focus necessary for discovery and understanding. Only by maintaining a clear distinction between science and belief can true advancement be achieved.

5. TRANSLIGIOUS TERRORIST

The concept of "transligion" introduces a framework where individuals openly acknowledge their identity or lifestyle as a belief system rather than a biological or innate characteristic. From this perspective, a transgender individual might claim to believe in cosplaying as a gender or form, like a reptile, aligning with their personal confidence or aesthetic. This approach seeks to reframe identity debates by focusing on individual belief and expression, acknowledging the psychological or stylistic roots of such choices. This approach offers a middle ground where personal identity focuses on affirming belief systems, similar to religion's role in shaping values and practices. The shift could foster societal recognition, granting "transligion" protections and freedoms akin to those of religious systems, including expression and discrimination safeguards.

Like religion, transligion would come with rights and challenges that mirror those of established belief systems. Transligious people could expect the same legal protections as religious groups, including freedom of speech, assembly, and exemption from certain obligations that conflict with their beliefs. However, with these rights also come potential conflicts related to broader societal norms and human rights. Religious practices often intersect with issues of governance, law, and societal equality, and similar intersections could arise with transligion. For instance, claims of discrimination might emerge from transligious expressions clashing with secular or scientific frameworks, creating a need for nuanced legal and ethical boundaries. Societies balance religious freedoms with harms like discrimination; transligion would navigate similar challenges to avoid infringing on public good.

The proposal to exclude transligious individuals from technocratic governance arises from concerns that personal beliefs could bias rational, evidence-based decisions. Technocracy roots governance in scientific knowledge, empirical evidence, and logical reasoning, requiring decision-makers to act free from personal ideologies. A religiously motivated technocrat might prioritize faith-based policies over data-driven solutions, potentially endangering public welfare, as seen in debates over evolution, climate change, or reproductive rights. Similarly, a transligious technocrat might prioritize policies influenced by their personal belief system, skewing rational discourse in favor of subjective ideologies. Both cases introduce risks of policy disruption, governing the process in a way vulnerable to belief-based biases rather than objective considerations.

The harm caused by religious extremism offers a stark cautionary tale. Throughout history, religious terrorists have used their belief systems to justify violence and disrupt societal stability. From the Crusades to modern extremist groups like ISIS, leaders weaponize religious ideologies to impose dogma through terror, undermining governance and creating widespread suffering. Hypothetically, a transligious extremist could similarly weaponize their belief system, advocating for disruptive or harmful policies under the guise of personal or collective validation. Imagine a hypothetical transligious terrorist group erasing biological distinctions in public records and demanding recognition of individuals only by chosen identities. Such a movement could lead to societal confusion, legal disputes, and eroding evidence-based policies in healthcare, education, or criminal justice. While such scenarios remain speculative, they highlight the potential risks of integrating deeply belief-driven individuals into systems designed to operate on empirical principles.

To protect technocratic governance, it must remain grounded in rational, objective decision-making, separate from ideological influences, whether religious or transligious. This ensures governance stays unbiased, much like secularism shields policymaking from religious interference, fostering rationality amid ideological conflicts.

6. FRAUD AMMA

As people grow older, they often face significant challenges, particularly when they feel neglected by their families. This neglect can stem from the busy nature of modern life, physical distance, or strained relationships. Left feeling lonely and vulnerable, many elderly individuals search for connection and belonging. This is where charismatic spiritual leaders, often known as god-men or god-women, step in.

These figures appear warm and welcoming, offering the love and community the elderly crave. However, behind this outward appearance often lies a calculated plan to exploit their vulnerability. By filling the emotional gap left by family, these leaders create a sense of dependency, gradually isolating the elderly from their loved ones. In many cases, this manipulation leads the elderly to transfer their assets and wealth to the religious trusts these leaders' control. Over time, this practice has helped these spiritual elites build vast material empires, all under the guise of offering care and compassion.

Consider the case of Mata Amritanandamayi, affectionately known as Amma, whose global following is estimated in the millions. Amma's approach is emblematic of this phenomenon. Her ashram, the Mata Amritanandamayi Math, offers refuge and a sense of family to countless devotees, many of whom are elderly individuals seeking the warmth of community. However, behind the spiritual outward appearance, allegations have surfaced regarding the methods employed to encourage devotees to bequeath their assets to the organization. Critics argue that the ashram's environment fosters a sense of obligation among the elderly, leading them to believe that transferring their wealth to the trust is a noble act of devotion. This practice has significantly contributed to the ashram's vast accumulation of wealth and property, raising questions about the ethical implications of such asset transfers.

In parallel, the Waqf Boards in India present another dimension of this issue. Established to manage endowments for religious and charitable purposes within the Muslim community, these boards oversee substantial properties across the nation. However, the administration of these assets has not been without controversy. Instances have emerged where authorities or entities have actively claimed properties, including those owned by elderly individuals, as Waqf assets, leading to legal disputes and familial discord. The lack of transparency and allegations of mismanagement within some Waqf Boards have further complicated matters, leaving many elderly individuals and their families entangled in protracted battles over property rights.

These scenarios underscore a broader societal concern: the exploitation of the elderly under the guise of religious devotion. The emotional and psychological manipulation employed by some religious organizations not only deprives families of their rightful inheritance but also sows seeds of discord and mistrust. The government's role in this context becomes crucial. While the state is responsible for safeguarding the welfare of its senior citizens, the intersection of religious privilege and political influence often hampers effective intervention. Regulatory oversight of old age homes and religious trusts is imperative to prevent such exploitation. However, the deep entanglement of religion and politics in India poses significant challenges to implementing and enforcing such measures.

The narratives of Mata Amritanandamayi and the Waqf Boards illustrate the complex interplay between spirituality, exploitation, and governance. This emphasizes the need for stronger laws to protect the rights and assets of elderly people. Such measures would ensure they can live their later years with dignity and security, safe from those who seek to exploit them for financial gain.

Religion is humanity's oldest narrative; a system of beliefs meant to unite and inspire. Yet leaders often twist it into a tool for power, using it to divide rather than connect. From holy scandals to commodifying faith, religion mirrors evolutionary traits like control, dominance, and tribalism that drive other human dysfunctions.

These same traits find a new stage in the media, explored in Chapter 9: *Media and Truth*. Where religion once dictated morality, the media now dictates truth. The dysfunctions of faith evolve into those of information, as leaders manipulate narratives and trade facts for influence.

9

Media and Truth

"The truth is rarely pure and never simple."

– OSCAR WILDE

For as long as humans have told stories, the elites have understood the power of controlling the narrative. From ancient empires to modern nation-states, rulers have relied on the tools of communication to shape reality, bending truth to serve their purposes. Consider the priests of ancient Mesopotamia, who inscribed divine edicts onto clay tablets, presenting them as the immutable will of the gods. These proclamations—often conveniently aligned with the desires of the ruling class—were used to justify taxation, labor conscription, and even war. The divine authority bestowed by these texts made disagreement, not just traitorous but blasphemous. A farmer resisting unfair grain levies was no longer defying a king, but offending the gods themselves. By embedding power within sacred narratives, the elites of ancient civilizations ensured not only compliance but devotion, a tactic that would echo throughout human history.

Religious principles became the perfect vehicle for controlling truth, cloaked in the guise of moral and cosmic order. In medieval Europe, the Catholic Church mastered this art with astonishing efficiency. Its monopoly on literacy and scripture allowed it to dictate not only spiritual life but also temporal power. Kings ruled by divine right, a concept sanctified by the Church and reinforced through sermons and scripture. The clergy painted vivid depictions of heaven and hell, promising an eternal reward for obedience and unspeakable torment for rebellion. When Galileo challenged the geocentric model of the universe, he was not merely debating science; he was threatening the Church's carefully constructed narrative of celestial hierarchy. The truth was secondary to control. Galileo's forced recantation under threat of heresy highlights the power of institutions. They used truth as a tool of domination, shaping both beliefs and the boundaries of imagination.

Inventing the printing press in the 15th century briefly upended this dynamic, democratizing access to information. But even this revolutionary technology was quickly co-opted. Martin Luther's 95 Theses, nailed to a church door in 1517, became one of the first viral media events, igniting the Protestant Reformation. Yet, as religious factions splintered and competed for followers, they weaponized the same printing presses to churn out propaganda. Catholic and Protestant authorities alike produced lurid pamphlets accusing their rivals of everything from witchcraft to sexual depravity. These texts didn't aim for theological precision. Their purpose was to stir emotions. They sought to ignite passions and rally the faithful. Media had become a battlefield, and truth was often its first casualty.

By the 20th century, the relationship between media, power, and truth had reached new heights of sophistication. Totalitarian regimes like Nazi Germany and Stalinist Russia transformed propaganda into a science. Joseph Goebbels, Hitler's minister of propaganda, understood that repetition was more potent than reason. Through radio broadcasts, films, and posters, the Nazi Party constructed a narrative of Aryan supremacy, portraying Jews, communists, and other minorities as existential threats. The lies were not incidental; they were the foundation upon which the regime built its policies of genocide and war. Stalin, for his part, erased political rivals not only from life but from photographs and history books. By controlling the media, he controlled memory itself, crafting a version of the past that served his future ambitions.

In modern times, the techniques of truth manipulation have become subtler, but are no less pervasive. The rise of mass media—television, radio, and later the internet—offered elites unprecedented opportunities to shape public opinion. During the Cold War, media narratives amplified the fear of communism in the United States. These narratives painted the Soviet Union as an omnipresent threat. Hollywood joined the effort, producing films and shows that glorified American values while vilifying the Red menace. This manufactured consensus justified an arms race that enriched defense contractors and entrenched the military-industrial complex. In the Middle East, elites seeking power cultivated religious extremism. They used carefully curated sermons and media broadcasts to spread their influence. The Saudi monarchy-controlled Wahhabi clerics and media outlets to portray its rule as divinely ordained. This strategy suppressed dissent, cloaking it under the guise of religious unity.

The digital age has only amplified these dynamics. Social media platforms, hailed initially as democratizing forces, have become tools for manipulation on a scale unimaginable to ancient priests or medieval popes. Algorithms prioritize sensationalism over accuracy, spreading misinformation faster than any printing press could. Religious and political elites exploit these platforms to reinforce tribal identities and polarize societies. Consider the rise of ISIS, which used social media to recruit followers and propagate its ideology. Slickly produced videos and viral hashtags presented the group not as barbaric extremists but as righteous warriors defending their faith. The medium lent credibility to the message, making it all the more seductive.

Even in secular democracies, those controlling the media shape the truth. Billionaire media moguls like Rupert Murdoch wield immense influence, framing political debates to serve their interests. News outlets become echo chambers, amplifying narratives that align with the agendas of their owners. In the United States, partisan networks like Fox News and MSNBC construct parallel realities, each presenting its audience with a curated version of the truth. Religious narratives still play a role, albeit in modernized forms. Prosperity gospel preachers use television and social media to promise divine blessings in return for donations. They merge ancient promises of salvation with modern marketing techniques.

Throughout history, the elites have understood a simple truth: whoever controls the narrative controls the people. They maintain dominance by twisting truth and spreading misinformation. This has occurred through divine decrees of empires, church dogmas, or Silicon Valley algorithms. The challenge for humanity is not just to recognize these patterns, but to dismantle them. Global crises like climate change, pandemics, and democracy's erosion shape the world today. Discernment of truth from manipulation is no longer just personal enlightenment.; it is a prerequisite for collective survival.

1. MEDIA POLITICS

Throughout history, elites have strategically intertwined their wealth and influence with political leadership and media ownership to shape public narratives and maintain dominance. This symbiotic relationship between affluence and authority is evident across various nations, where financial power translates into political clout and control over information dissemination.

In Indian politics, religion, media influence, and polarizing, narratives intertwine so tightly that disentangling them feels nearly impossible. Northern India, with its mosaic of communities, languages, and faiths, has long been a battleground for ideologies. In the last decade, this battleground has shifted dramatically. Narratives steeped in religion dominate, spread by political leaders and amplified by media channels and social platforms. Narendra Modi, the charismatic leader of the Bharatiya Janata Party (BJP), emerged as a maestro of this orchestration. Modi's ability to invoke Hindu pride, coupled with his persona of being a "chaiwala who rose to power," created an emotional resonance with the masses. His appeals were not just about policies but about identity, cleverly blending Hindu nationalism with economic aspirations. Meanwhile, Rahul Gandhi, representing the Congress party, seemed initially out of depth in this theater. His image as an elite, disconnected leader rendered him ineffective against Modi's grassroots appeal. Media narratives painted Rahul as weak and ideologically scattered, further cementing his early failures.

In a twist emblematic of Indian politics, Rahul Gandhi has rebranded himself. He now appears as a devout religious follower, a "bhakt" navigating terrain traditionally held by the BJP. This shift was deliberate and strategic. It aimed to reclaim the Hindu vote bank that had moved to the BJP under the saffron banner. Rahul Gandhi carefully calculates his temple visits, rituals, and Brahmin heritage declarations. They align with the cultural and religious sentiments of the majority. Congress, traditionally seen as centrist or leaning left, has visibly nudged itself toward the right, adopting a more overtly religious rhetoric. This strategy aims to undermine the BJP's exclusivity over Hindu nationalism by presenting an alternative that is equally devout, yet ostensibly more inclusive.

This rebranding, however, has unleashed a recent wave of political maneuvering. BJP supporters and media outlets, adept at controlling narratives, have begun painting Congress as "pseudo-right," accusing it of pandering to Hindu sentiments without ideological conviction. The strategy is dual-pronged: to alienate hardcore BJP loyalists from this "new Congress" while confusing centrist and left-leaning voters. The narrative is no longer about policies or governance, but a competitive display of who can appear more devoutly Hindu. This contest reduces political discourse to a shallow spectacle. Issues of economy, education, and healthcare lose focus to temple visits and religious symbolism.

The consequences of this shift are far-reaching and troubling. India, a secular democracy at its core, finds its political fabric fraying under the strain of religious polarization. The media, far from being a neutral observer, actively shapes and intensifies these divisions. News channels, owned or influenced by powerful corporate entities with political affiliations, amplify the rhetoric of Hindu nationalism or the alleged hypocrisy of Congress's newfound religiosity. Social media platforms, rife with bots and paid campaigns, add fuel to the fire, spreading half-truths and deepening societal fractures. Public discourse is no longer about debating policies but about defending identities, with religion wielded as a weapon rather than a personal belief.

This descent into religiously driven politics has revealed the rot within India's democratic institutions. As religion tightens its grip on society, political leaders find it easier to appeal to faith than to logic, to division rather than unity. The cost of this approach is profound, not just to erode secular values but also in the way it stunts progress. Critical issues like climate change, economic inequality, and gender justice take a backseat. Public and political energy shifts to debates over which party embodies the "true Hindu ethos." What began as a strategy to consolidate votes has evolved into a dangerous game that risks destabilizing the delicate pluralism that has long defined India. In this game, the lines between religion, politics, and media blur, leaving the country grappling with an identity crisis that threatens to overshadow its democratic ideals.

Beneath the spectacle of religious politics, money pulls the true levers of power. Political donations, shrouded in secrecy and riddled with controversy, have become the lifeblood of India's electoral machinery. These funds dictate who wields influence, amplifies certain voices, and dominates narratives. In the murky world of political funding, the realities of wealth and power test democracy's promises.

1.1 INDIA: POLITICAL DONATIONS

Observers often hold up India's political system, with its vibrant elections and debates, as a model of democratic resilience. Yet behind this facade lies a financial architecture that fuels campaigns and consolidates power: political donations. Electoral bonds, introduced with promises of transparency, have instead fostered opacity, turning the act of donation into a secretive transaction that undermines public trust. The staggering sums exchanged—₹10,000 crore between 2018 and 2022—reveal the sheer scale at which wealth influences governance. The lion's share flows to the ruling BJP, raising troubling questions about impartiality and the extent to which state institutions are co-opted to sustain this flow. This financial tide shapes policies, biases narratives, and marginalizes critical issues, leaving the citizenry to wonder: Whose democracy is this, really?

Political donations now fuel electoral campaigns in Indian democracy's grand theater. Money, not ideas, increasingly dictates the contours of power. The introduction of electoral bonds in 2018 significantly changed how donations funnel into political campaigns. Framed as a reform to enhance transparency, the reality has been far from its promise. These bonds—bearer instruments sold by the State Bank of India—allow individuals, corporations, and other entities to donate unlimited sums anonymously to political parties. Supporters claim this system reduces black money's role in politics. Critics argue it does the opposite, hiding donors in secrecy and amplifying wealth's influence on elections.

The scale of donations made through electoral bonds is staggering. Between 2018 and 2022, reports show sellers moved bonds worth over ₹10,000 crore. A significant majority of these funds went to the ruling BJP. The opaque nature of these transactions has raised alarms among activists and opposition parties, who argue that the system disproportionately benefits the incumbent government. The bonds are purchasable only through the State Bank of India. Critics allege that the government uses this access to donor data to enable favoritism and target rivals. The misuse of state institutions to consolidate power erodes the fairness that democracy purports to uphold.

The controversy deepens when one examines how these bonds bypass safeguards that were traditionally in place to prevent unchecked financial influence in politics. Previously, donations above ₹20,000 had to be declared with details of the donor. Electoral bonds dismantled this transparency by allowing anonymous contributions, essentially legalizing secretive funding. Even the Reserve Bank of India expressed reservations, warning that these bonds could undermine India's currency system by introducing instruments outside regulatory control. The Election Commission of India also raised concerns about how the scheme undermines its ability to monitor election financing. Authorities disregarded these objections and implemented the program with little public debate.

Adding to the murkiness are allegations of malpractices by the State Bank of India. Reports indicate that the SBI has sold electoral bonds outside designated windows, allegedly under pressure from the government, violating its own guidelines. For instance, banks sold bonds during critical election periods despite no scheduled windows, raising questions about their independence. Such instances suggest that the lines between state machinery and political power have become dangerously blurred, with public institutions being co-opted to serve partisan interests.

Despite the magnitude of the issue, media coverage has been conspicuously subdued. Major news outlets, many owned or influenced by corporate entities with political affiliations, have largely refrained from investigative reporting on electoral bonds. Instead, discussions are often limited to surface-level debates or government press releases lauding the scheme's benefits. Social media trends, often orchestrated by powerful interests, divert attention by focusing on peripheral issues or amplifying unrelated controversies. This media strategy ensures that the public remains unaware of the scheme's implications, allowing it to persist unchallenged.

The judiciary, often seen as a counterbalance to political overreach, has also faced criticism for its handling of the issue. Courts delayed verdicts on multiple petitions, challenging the constitutionality of electoral bonds. Interim orders provided little clarity. Activists argue that these delays serve the interests of the powerful by allowing the system to continue unabated, even as questions about its legality remain unanswered. The lack of urgency in addressing this matter highlights a broader systemic inertia for holding the powerful accountable.

The broader implications of widespread political donations and the electoral bond scheme are profound. By prioritizing the flow of money over the voice of the electorate, the system undermines the foundational principles of democracy. Political parties, reliant on large donors, become beholden to corporate interests, skewing policy decisions in favor of the wealthy elite. Issues critical to the common citizen—employment, education, healthcare—take a backseat to the agendas of those who fund campaigns. This creates a vicious cycle where the gap between the ruling class and the governed widens, eroding trust in democratic institutions.

The media's complicity in downplaying these issues exacerbates the problem. In a country where news channels are often more focused on sensationalism than substance, critical stories about electoral bonds rarely make it to prime time. Coverage often frames the narrative to minimize criticism. Proponents portray the scheme as well-intentioned but flawed rather than a structural threat to democracy. This selective reporting reflects the growing influence of political and corporate interests over the fourth estate, reducing its role as a watchdog of democracy.

The story of electoral bonds is not just about one policy; it is a window into the systemic issues plaguing Indian democracy. It reveals how leaders consolidate power, co-opt public institutions, and control media narratives. The stakes are not just political but societal, affecting the very fabric of democracy and governance. If these issues remain unaddressed, the promise of government "by the people, for the people" will grow hollow. Money, not votes, will shape the nation's destiny.

If donations fuel campaigns, media ownership projects, and preserve this power. In today's world, information is currency. Corporate elites controlling narratives raise critical questions about journalism's independence and the integrity of public discourse. Moving from the mechanisms of political funding, we now enter the realm of media ownership—a battleground where truth is often the first casualty.

1.2 INDIA: MEDIA OWNERSHIP

Indian democracy should value every voice. Yet, a handful of corporate empires wield outsized influence over what the nation hears, sees, and believes. Media ownership, long a contentious issue, has reached new heights of consolidation, with giants like Reliance Industries and the Adani Group dictating editorial priorities. This concentration of power isn't merely a business strategy; it's a political weapon, aligning corporate interests with government narratives and reshaping public opinion to favor the elite. As journalism becomes propaganda, it erodes the democratic ideal of an informed electorate. It commodifies truth and stifles dissent.

In India, the entanglement of economic elites, political leadership, and media ownership is a powerful triad that shapes the nation's policies and public narratives. This nexus has profound implications, often skewing governance to favor the powerful while deepening social and economic inequalities. Political funding, media control, and lobbying reveal how leaders exert influence and maintain dominance in a rapidly evolving democracy.

The role of media as a narrative-controlling apparatus is central to this dynamic. Mukesh Ambani's Reliance Industries Limited acquired Network18 in 2014. Network18 operates prominent outlets like CNN-News18 and Money control, which reach millions of viewers. This consolidation of media ownership raised alarms about the potential for editorial bias, as the interests of RIL—India's largest private sector company—intersected with political and economic discourses. NDTV, once protecting independent journalism, illustrates the broader trend. In 2022, the Adani Group, under Gautam Adani, acquired a controlling stake in the channel, sparking concerns about dwindling spaces for dissenting voices. Critics feared that this acquisition could dilute NDTV's critical reporting, further aligning media narratives with the interests of political and corporate elites.

The implications of such ownership extend beyond shaping opinions; they influence policy-making itself. Reliance and Adani Group dominate telecommunications, energy, and infrastructure. Their business strategies often align with government initiatives like energy, self-reliance, and infrastructure expansion. For instance, the Adani Group's rapid expansion into renewable energy aligns with national policies promoting sustainability, a synergy that some argue affords the conglomerate preferential treatment. Observers frequently cite tariff approvals and environmental clearances as examples of policies benefiting powerful entities disproportionately. Critics cite swift approvals for projects like Adani's Carmichael Coal Mine in Australia. Such cases exemplify the global influence these conglomerates wield, both in India and abroad.

The consequences of this power concentration are stark. As of 2023, the top 1% of India's population controls over 40% of the nation's wealth, as reported by Oxfam. This extreme wealth concentration, fueled in part by policies that favor large businesses, has exacerbated income disparities, leaving small and medium enterprises struggling to compete. Employment practices further widen the gap: large corporations increasingly embrace automation, prioritizing efficiency over job creation. This shift often displaces low- and middle-income workers, compounding the vulnerabilities of India's labor market.

The interplay between wealth, politics, and media in India illustrates how elites maintain their dominance by crafting policies and narratives that reinforce their position. Combining anonymous political funding, media consolidation, and policy influence perpetuates social inequality and erodes public trust in democratic institutions. While economic growth driven by large conglomerates is undeniable, the challenge lies in ensuring that this growth translates into equitable opportunities rather than entrenching existing disparities. India's experience is a cautionary tale of unchecked elite influence. It reminds us that democracy's strength lies in balancing power and safeguarding all citizens' interests, not just the privileged few.

The media may be the messenger, but behind the message lies a deeper, more entangled relationship between power and wealth. The nexus between political leadership and corporate giants like the Adani Group reveals a troubling pattern of favoritism, regulatory leniency, and unchecked growth. From infrastructure to energy, this relationship casts a long shadow over governance and public welfare. It is time to unpack the Adani-Modi complex—a case study in the perilous intersection of corporate ambition and political patronage.

1.3 INDIA: ADANI - MODI COMPLEX

Few alliances in modern India have sparked as much intrigue and controversy as the one between the Adani Group and Prime Minister Narendra Modi. It is a partnership that has transcended traditional boundaries of business and governance, with allegations of land grabs, environmental violations, and opaque financial practices.

The muted response of regulatory institutions and the complicit silence of mainstream media only deepen the concern. This isn't merely about one corporation's rise; it's about the systemic vulnerabilities that allow concentrated power to flourish unchecked.

Allegations against the Adani Group unravel complex economic and political intersections. They raise concerns about prioritizing corporate gain over public and environmental welfare. Accusations against Adani span land acquisition, environmental mismanagement, airport privatization, and coal imports. They include favoritism in contracts, tax evasion, and using shell companies, intertwining corporate growth with political influence. The silence of mainstream media, coupled with orchestrated online trends, has further muddled public discourse, reducing the visibility of systemic issues that demand scrutiny.

The alleged land scam in Gujarat sets a stark precedent. During Narendra Modi's tenure as Chief Minister, Adani reportedly acquired land for industrial projects at rates significantly lower than competitors. K Raheja Corp bought land at ₹470 per square meter, and Maruti Suzuki at ₹670. Yet, Adani secured parcels for as little as ₹1 to ₹32 per square meter. This disparity, documented in reports such as a 2014 article in Business Standard, raises red flags about potential favoritism and systemic manipulation of pricing mechanisms. Further investigations revealed that authorities altered the classifications of forest land in Gujarat to benefit Adani's Mundra Port project. Officials downgraded land classified as Eco-Class 2 to Eco-Class 4. This allowed Adani to bypass stricter environmental regulations, causing an estimated loss of ₹586.7 million in public funds. These actions represent not just financial irregularities but also a profound disregard for environmental accountability.

Forest land misutilization extends beyond Gujarat. In Maharashtra, the government approved clearing 370 acres of forest for Adani's coal power plant. Promised jobs seemed disproportionate to the ecological cost. Proponents cited 350 jobs—100 direct and 250 indirect—as justification for the project. In 2018, BJP-led governments at both state and central levels cleared an additional 142 acres, justifying environmental compromises with meager economic returns. Such cases show a pattern of trading ecological losses for minimal economic gains. They raise ethical concerns about development priorities in a nation facing environmental crises.

Airport privatization represents another critical dimension of these allegations. In 2018, the Indian government privatized six profitable airports, all awarded to Adani despite the company's lack of prior experience in managing such facilities. The Public-Private Partnership Appraisal Committee controversially removed key criteria. These included prior airport management experience and restrictions on bidding for multiple airports. These changes paved the way for Adani. They bypassed concerns from the Finance Ministry and NITI Aayog about financial and operational risks of inexperienced operators handling critical infrastructure. Despite these objections, Adani emerged as the winner for all six contracts, marking a significant consolidation of airport operations under one corporate entity.

The takeover of Mumbai Airport further highlights the intertwining of corporate strategies and state mechanisms. In 2020, the GVK Group, controlling the Mumbai Airport faced Enforcement Directorate raids. Shortly after, Adani acquired a 74% stake in the airport. Critics allege that these raids exerted undue pressure on GVK to relinquish its hold, enabling Adani to secure a strategic asset under questionable circumstances. Such incidents reinforce concerns about the potential use of regulatory agencies to facilitate corporate acquisitions, blurring the lines between governance and business interests.

Coal imports reveal another layer of alleged corporate favoritism. After Adani started exporting coal from controversial Australian mines, the Indian government took significant steps. It slashed import duties from 2.5% to 0% and mandated power plants to use imported coal blends. These policy shifts disproportionately benefited Adani, with imported coal reportedly priced 10 times higher than domestic alternatives. Authorities compelled public-sector companies to purchase this expensive coal blend, imposing additional costs on taxpayers. These policies intertwining with Adani's business interests reveal a troubling pattern. Regulatory frameworks are often skewed to favor specific players, harming public and economic welfare.

Allegations of favoritism extend beyond domestic borders, with the Adani Group securing high-profile contracts in Sri Lanka, Bangladesh, and Israel. In Sri Lanka, the government canceled a trilateral deal involving India, Japan, and Sri Lanka for the East Container Terminal. Adani then emerged as the sole private player in the restructured West Container Terminal deal. Critics argue that Adani's close ties with the Indian Prime Minister enabled these deals. This creates the impression that state diplomacy directly drives the corporation's success. Such perceptions erode trust in the impartiality of governance, raising concerns about the intersection of corporate influence and foreign policy.

Tax evasion and financial mismanagement form another critical component of the allegations. The Directorate of Revenue Intelligence accused Adani of inflating import costs and funneling money through Mauritius-based shell companies to evade taxes. Reports estimate that these practices resulted in tax losses of approximately ₹10 billion. Despite the severity of these allegations, adjudicating authorities dropped the charges, leading to suspicions about the robustness of regulatory oversight when powerful entities are involved. Additionally, allegations of substantial loans from public-sector banks, totaling approximately ₹2.48 trillion, have raised questions about the risk to public funds. Critics say such debts, along with bad loans and write-offs, expose a precarious financial system. Public institutions often shoulder the liabilities of a few corporations.

The role of shell companies in the Adani Group's financial dealings amplifies these concerns. Mauritius-based entities allegedly linked to Adani insiders have routed billions into the group, raising questions about money laundering and opaque investment practices. Opposition leaders have demanded investigations into these shell companies, arguing that their operations undermine financial transparency and accountability. The lack of substantial responses from regulatory authorities further complicates efforts to address these allegations, leaving critical questions unanswered.

Media outlets have kept coverage conspicuously muted throughout this unfolding saga. Rather than investigating the specifics of these allegations, mainstream outlets often highlight Adani's contributions to infrastructure and economic growth, sidelining critical analysis. Public discourse is further diluted by orchestrated social media campaigns, such as the #IStandWithAdani trend, which deflects attention from substantive issues. This dynamic reflects a broader challenge in Indian democracy, where media and public institutions increasingly struggle to hold powerful entities accountable, allowing corporate narratives to dominate.

These allegations, taken together, paint a troubling picture of systemic imbalances. The recurring theme of policy manipulation, regulatory compromises, and media complacency underscores the need for greater transparency and accountability in governance. At stake is how people view one corporation and the broader integrity of India's economic and political institutions. The silence surrounding these issues is as significant as the allegations themselves, revealing the challenges of sustaining democratic values in the face of concentrated power.

The story of the Adani Group reveals a striking example of the unchecked power that corporate and political alignments can wield in India. However, the tale does not end there. In Mukesh Ambani, we encounter a figure who has mastered the art of influence—not through overt controversies, but through a more nuanced, pervasive strategy of silent domination. Adani's rise involves controversies and bold expansion, while Ambani quietly and strategically controls governments, industries, and narratives. From energy to telecommunications, his imprint is ubiquitous, and his approach far more insidious. This next section probes into Ambani's complex network of power and the silent reshaping of India's economic and political landscape.

1.4 INDIA: AMBANI, GOD OF SILENT CORRUPTION

In the annals of Indian capitalism, Mukesh Ambani's name looms large—not just for his staggering wealth but for the breadth of his influence. As the chairman of Reliance Industries, Ambani embodies a new era of corporate power that seamlessly intertwines with political authority and media control. Unlike others who make headlines with controversies, Ambani operates in the shadows, ensuring his dominance across sectors while evading scrutiny. From the KG-D6 gas scandal under the UPA to Reliance Jio's rise under the NDA, his journey shows an uncanny ability. He aligns business interests with the agendas of successive administrations. Beneath the surface of corporate success is a troubling reality. Policies tailored for profit, a media landscape favoring him, and a growing divide between corporate gains and public welfare define it. This section unpacks the silent yet profound ways in which Ambani's empire has shaped India's political and economic systems.

In the sprawling narrative of India's economic and political evolution, few names evoke as much power and influence as Mukesh Ambani. The head of Reliance Industries, Ambani, is not just a businessman; he is an institution unto himself, his fortune intertwining seamlessly with the very machinery of governance in India. His unmatched skill in navigating successive governments is evident. Be it the Congress-led UPA or the BJP-led NDA, political ideologies often appear secondary to corporate loyalty. Ambani's success story is as much about entrepreneurship as it is about his remarkable capacity to align his business interests with the priorities of those in power.

Ambani's relationship with Indian political parties is less about affiliations and more about access. Reliance Industries has consistently benefited from policies tailored to its needs, regardless of which party is in power. During the UPA regime, Reliance's KG-D6 gas fields became a focal point of controversy. Allegations arose that the government had allowed Ambani's company to inflate production costs, which directly impacted the revenue share owed to the government. The Comptroller and Auditor General (CAG) pointed to losses amounting to ₹10,000 crores, sparking debates about how policies seemed curiously favorable to Reliance's operations. During the Congress era, Ambani expanded investments in telecommunications and petrochemicals, benefiting from regulatory frameworks critics argued favored Reliance.

When the political tides shifted in 2014 and Narendra Modi's BJP swept to power, Ambani's fortunes continued to rise unabated. Under Modi's regime, Ambani's ventures not only expanded but often appeared to align seamlessly with government initiatives. The rollout of Reliance Jio, for instance, revolutionized India's telecommunications sector. While groundbreaking technology and pricing strategies drove success, regulators timing on certain changes raised eyebrows. In 2016, Jio received approvals that significantly reduced its operational costs, including a controversial waiver for license fees on spectrum use, effectively saving Reliance Industries billions. Critics argued that the government's push for digital India dovetailed so perfectly with Jio's launch that the lines between policy and private enterprise blurred. The result? Jio rapidly became a telecommunications behemoth, disrupting competitors and reshaping the industry in less than a decade.

Perhaps what sets Ambani apart is his ability to balance relationships across the political spectrum. Unlike other corporate magnates who tie their fortunes to a single party, Ambani cultivates alliances with all major political players. People perceive his relationship with the BJP as strong, yet his connections to Congress remain significant. The Ambani family's longstanding ties with the Gandhi family are well documented, with past business partnerships and shared social circles. This balancing act ensures that Reliance Industries thrive irrespective of electoral outcomes. UPA-era gas exploration policies or NDA's digital and infrastructure initiatives have benefited him. Ambani positions himself as essential to any government's economic vision.

Ambani strengthens his ability to straddle political divides by controlling India's media landscape. Through ownership stakes in major news networks like Network18 and its subsidiary CNN-News18, Reliance wields considerable influence over public narratives. Critics claim Ambani and Reliance use their media presence to shield themselves from scrutiny. Controversies surrounding Reliance, be it regulatory concessions, environmental violations, or allegations of monopolistic practices, often receive muted coverage. Instead, the focus shifts to framing Ambani as a nation-building entrepreneur whose ventures align with India's developmental aspirations. This selective reporting not only shapes public perception but also ensures that deeper investigations into policy favors rarely see the light of day.

The muted coverage of the Reliance KG-D6 gas controversy under the UPA is a striking example. Similarly, Jio's regulatory benefits under the NDA highlight this media strategy. While independent journalists and activists raised alarms, these stories were largely absent from prime-time debates. Instead, the media spotlight consistently portrayed Reliance as a trailblazer in transforming India's economic landscape, from the "Digital India" narrative to its contributions to retail and petrochemicals. Reliance-controlled platforms amplify pro-development rhetoric, drowning out opposition leaders who raise questions about Reliance's influence.

Ambani's dominance reflects a symbiotic relationship between business and politics in India, beyond corporate acumen. Successive governments have embraced him as a partner in their economic visions, whether it's building refineries, expanding retail networks, or digitizing the nation. His adaptability to political shifts, cross-party relationships, and media control shows the enduring power of corporate influence in shaping policy.

This dynamic has troubling implications for India's democracy. When policymakers favor one conglomerate, they erode the promise of a level playing field for businesses and citizens. Smaller enterprises struggle to compete, while the public bears the brunt of regulatory decisions that prioritize corporate profits over broader economic equity. Media's complicity in downplaying these issues further weakens democratic accountability, creating an environment where power consolidates in the hands of a few. Ambani's story is not just about one man's success. This reflects how deeply business and politics intertwine. Ordinary citizens face a system that increasingly values corporate clout over democratic ideals.

As the narrative of corporate and political interplay unfolds in India, the dynamics of wealth, power, and media influence transcend borders. From Mukesh Ambani's quiet dominance to the Adani Group's overt entanglements, India teaches profound lessons. Elite influence can erode democratic values. Yet, these challenges are not uniquely Indian. Across the globe, another democracy—the United States—grapples with its own entanglement of economic power and political control.

The American stage, however, operates on a different scale and with its own set of rules. Landmark decisions like *Citizens United* have institutionalized the role of money in politics, turning elections into billion-dollar contests. Media moguls like Rupert Murdoch and tech titans such as Elon Musk wield enormous influence over public opinion, mirroring and amplifying the priorities of the elite. Lobbyists and Super PACs, often hidden in plain sight, transform legislative halls into marketplaces of influence. In the United States, democracy risks becoming a commodity. This raises a question: Can the American Dream endure the corrosive effects of unchecked wealth and power?

1.5 US: POLITICAL DONATIONS

In the United States, political donations have transcended their original purpose of enabling democratic participation, becoming a powerful tool for consolidating influence. The landmark Supreme Court decision in *Citizens United v. FEC* opened the floodgates, allowing corporations and billionaires to channel unlimited funds into political campaigns through Super PACs. Figures like Michael Bloomberg and the Koch family exemplify how wealth translates into outsized political clout, shaping policies that often prioritize elite interests. While proponents argue that such donations are an exercise in free speech, critics contend they undermine the principle of equal representation. The staggering sums involved—billions in each election cycle—highlight a troubling reality: the louder the voice of money, the quieter the voice of the average voter. This section unpacks how the nexus of wealth and politics skews democracy toward privilege and power.

In the United States, economic elites, political leaders, and media owners wield power and perpetuate it through a symbiotic relationship. This nexus reveals how significant wealth and influence can shape policy-making, control narratives, and maintain social inequality. The elite secures dominance through campaign contributions, lobbying, and media ownership. Governance aligns with their interests, while the broader populace struggles with systemic inequities.

Elites choreograph their roles in American politics while concealing much of their influence. The nexus of wealth and power has long shaped the nation's political landscape, with campaign contributions serving as the lifeblood of influence. The turning point came with the 2010 Supreme Court ruling in Citizens United v. FEC, which redefined the political financing game. This decision flooded the political system with money. It legitimized Super PACs, which can raise unlimited funds for campaigns, provided they stay independent of candidates. Corporations and ultra-wealthy donors flooded the political landscape with money, eroding the notion of one person, one vote. The figures are staggering: during the 2020 election cycle alone, Super PACs amassed over $2.1 billion, with a significant portion emanating from an elite cadre of billionaires.

Among the major players, Michael Bloomberg, the media mogul and former New York City mayor, stood out for his unprecedented financial largesse. In 2020, Bloomberg spent over $1 billion on his own Democratic presidential campaign—a figure that dwarfed the entire campaign budgets of most of his rivals. This cash infusion secured Bloomberg a debate stage spot. It also raised questions about how personal wealth can bypass traditional political hurdles. On the Republican side, Sheldon Adelson and his wife, Miriam became kingmakers. They donated $218 million to Republican campaigns and Super PACs in one election cycle. Their largesse ensured that their priorities, particularly those aligned with their casino empire and staunchly pro-Israel policies, resonated within GOP platforms.

The influence of the Koch brothers, particularly Charles Koch, highlights a more systemic approach to elite dominance. Through a vast network of think tanks, advocacy groups, and Super PACs, the Koch family has funneled hundreds of millions of dollars into American politics. In the 2018 midterm elections alone, the Koch network announced plans to spend $400 million, primarily to support conservative and libertarian causes. Their financial power extends beyond elections, shaping policy debates on issues ranging from tax cuts to climate change. The Kochs leave their fingerprints on legislative initiatives that deregulate industries, cut corporate taxes, and roll back environmental protections to align with their interests.

The impact of such contributions is profound, creating a political ecosystem where access and influence are commodities. Wealthy donors gain entry to exclusive fundraisers, closed-door meetings, and personal audiences with policymakers. This access often translates into tangible policy outcomes. Martin Gilens and Benjamin Page's 2014 study revealed striking findings. Economic elites and business interests disproportionately shape U.S. policy, while average citizens have negligible influence. The study concluded that the U.S. operates more like an oligarchy than a democracy, with policy outcomes often favoring the affluent over the majority.

This confluence of wealth and politics reveals a troubling reality: those funding the system write its rules. Campaign finance laws, tax codes, and regulatory frameworks often reflect the interests of elite donors, perpetuating a cycle of inequality. By strategically investing in candidates and causes, America's wealthiest individuals and corporations ensure that the levers of power remain firmly in their grasp. Using money in politics corrupts democratic ideals. This reflects a systemic flaw in politics. It prioritizes wealth over representation, leaving citizens to deal with policies shaped by elites.

If money decides the winners in politics, media decides the narratives. The interplay between wealth and media ownership is a story of who gets to frame the public discourse, who gets heard, and whose interests are served. From traditional news outlets to social media empires, magnates consolidate media power with profound implications for democracy. Shifting from donations to media control, we see a startling truth. Media ownership influences not just what we know, but also how we think.

1.6 US: MEDIA OWNERSHIP

Media is often called the fourth estate, a pillar of democracy tasked with holding power accountable. Yet, in the United States, this pillar leans heavily toward elite interests. Figures like Rupert Murdoch and Jeff Bezos epitomize a new era of media ownership, shaping narratives to align with corporate priorities and political leanings. Fox News, under Murdoch, drives conservative agendas, while Bezos' Washington Post navigates the murky waters between journalistic independence and Amazon's corporate influence. Digital platforms led by Elon Musk and Mark Zuckerberg have concentrated power. They are redefining the boundaries of free speech and information control. Consolidating media power blurs journalism, corporate advocacy, and political manipulation. It traps the public in a labyrinth of half-truths and hidden agendas.

The intertwining of elite influence and media ownership in the United States is a story of subtle control and overt manipulation. From traditional news outlets to modern digital platforms, the ability to shape public opinion and steer political discourse has become an indispensable tool for the powerful. Rupert Murdoch embodies this trend. His vast media empire spans News Corp and Fox Corporation, owning outlets like The Wall Street Journal, New York Post, and Fox News. Fox News alone averaged 2.5 million prime time viewers in 2020, making it a juggernaut in conservative circles. Its editorial slant has often mirrored the interests of its owner and political allies, serving as a crucial mouthpiece for Republican agendas. From promoting deregulation to framing climate change skepticism as rational discourse, the network's narratives reflect the priorities of the elites it represents.

The story of Jeff Bezos and The Washington Post offers a different, though no less compelling, perspective on elite media ownership. When Bezos acquired the newspaper for $250 million in 2013, he transformed it into a digital powerhouse. Under Bezos, The Washington Post adopted a more robust digital strategy, bolstering its reach and influence. Jeff Bezos claims editorial independence for the Washington Post. Yet, his roles as a media owner and Amazon founder with lobbying power raise questions. Critics observe that coverage of Amazon's labor practices, antitrust cases, and taxes often footsteps lightly. This highlights the tension between journalism and corporate interests.

A handful of powerful conglomerates dominate media ownership in the U.S., overshadowing individual magnates. Comcast Corporation, controlled by the Roberts family, owns NBCUniversal, which includes networks like NBC News and MSNBC, shaping liberal and centrist narratives. Until recently, AT&T owned Warner media, including CNN, a leading voice in global news dissemination. This consolidation of media ownership raises concerns about homogeneity in news perspectives and the marginalization of dissenting voices. These outlets portray themselves as independent arbiters of truth, but their ownership structures consistently amplify narratives favorable to elite stakeholders.

The role of digital platforms in this ecosystem has become even more significant. Social media giants like Facebook (Meta Platforms) and Twitter (now X Corp.) wield unprecedented power over the flow of information. These platforms, overseen by figures like Mark Zuckerberg and, more recently, Elon Musk, do not merely host conversations; they curate, amplify, and suppress content, often aligning with their owners' ideological and financial interests. Twitter, in particular, played an outsized role in shaping political discourse during Donald Trump's presidency. Trump's prolific use of the platform—his tweets reaching tens of millions of followers—transformed it into a digital town square. He bypassed traditional media to connect directly with his base. This positioned him as an anti-establishment figure, despite supporting policies favoring corporate elites.

The dramatic shift came when Twitter banned Trump following the January 6, 2021, Capitol riots, citing concerns about incitement to violence. This decision marked a watershed moment, illustrating the immense power of tech platforms to regulate political speech. Enter Elon Musk, whose purchase of Twitter in 2022 for $44 billion reignited debates about free speech, platform moderation, and political influence. Musk, a vocal critic of the Biden administration and its tax policies, framed his acquisition as a move to restore free speech. Yet, Musk's leadership shows selective reinstatements of controversial figures, like Trump, and decisions reflecting his personal and political biases, according to critics. Musk moved Tesla's headquarters from California to Texas, citing regulatory and tax frustrations under Biden. This aligns him with those favoring corporate autonomy over social equity.

The concentration of media power among elites allows them to control narratives that safeguard their interests. The boundaries between journalism, corporate agendas, and political advocacy blur, creating a mediated reality shaped by a few powerful actors. Platforms like Twitter, once seen as democratizing, now reflect elite battles where algorithms and ownership shifts dictate what billions see and believe. The interplay between Trump, Musk, and digital media highlights how elites wield technology to maintain dominance and reshape influence. This raises pressing questions: Who controls the narrative, and who benefits from the constructed version of truth?

2. MEDIA GEOPOLITICS

After securing local politics via media and manipulation, elites turn to geopolitics. Here, fortunes, resources, and global influence are at stake. This transition is not merely a strategy of expansion but a calculated playbook rooted in destabilization. By entering international arenas, elites aim to secure access to resources—oil, gas, minerals—at prices that favor their interests. Acquiring these resources cheaply often disrupts existing governance structures in resource-rich regions. To achieve this, they employ an age-old tactic: sowing division and unrest among local populations and their governments. Elites combine media narratives, covert operations, and diplomatic maneuvering to orchestrate instability, undermining sovereign control and creating a buyers' market for resources.

The story of Iraq in the early 21st century is emblematic of this approach. The country, home to one of the largest proven oil reserves globally, became a focal point of geopolitical machinations following the U.S.-led invasion in 2003. Ostensibly launched to remove Saddam Hussein and eliminate weapons of mass destruction—claims that were later discredited—the invasion fractured Iraq's political and social fabric. Behind the public rationale lay a more pragmatic motive: control over oil. As insurgencies and sectarian violence engulfed Iraq, oil production faltered, and prices plummeted, allowing Western firms to negotiate extraction deals under favorable terms. Companies like ExxonMobil and BP gained footholds in Iraq's energy sector, reaping enormous profits amid the chaos. This sequence of events illustrates the pattern: destabilize a resource-rich region, delegitimize its governance, and then capitalize on the resulting economic desperation.

In achieving this destabilization, the media plays a pivotal role, crafting narratives that justify intervention while demonizing the target state. U.S. media outlets amplified the drumbeat for war in Iraq, as corporate elites with military-industrial stakes influenced coverage. Stories of weapons of mass destruction and links between Saddam Hussein and Al-Qaeda dominated headlines, shaping public opinion and international consensus. Years later, as officials debunked these claims, Iraq suffered irreversible damage. It became destabilized, its infrastructure shattered, and its oil market exploited. Such media-driven campaigns demonstrate how narratives can create a pretext for intervention, turning public opinion into a tool for resource acquisition.

Elites adapted the same playbook for regions like Venezuela, which possesses the world's largest oil reserves. In recent years, economic sanctions, diplomatic isolation, and narratives of authoritarianism have painted the Venezuelan government as a pariah. While domestic policies and governance issues contributed to Venezuela's crises, external pressures exacerbated the situation, leading to hyperinflation, mass migration, and civil unrest. The resulting instability devalued the country's oil industry, making it ripe for potential foreign exploitation. International media framed Venezuela's crisis as socialism's failure. They often omitted how sanctions and external manipulation deepened the collapse. This selective framing serves to delegitimize local leadership while paving the way for external actors to extract concessions under the guise of aid or stabilization.

In Africa, a continent rich in minerals and hydrocarbons, the destabilization strategy manifests through proxy conflicts and strategic alliances. The Democratic Republic of Congo, rich in cobalt and critical minerals, faces decades of violence and instability. Multinational corporations reliant on cobalt for electronics and batteries benefit from this instability, as weak governance allows for exploitative contracts and unregulated mining. Local militias, often supported by external funding, perpetuate cycles of violence, ensuring that the central government remains too fractured to enforce resource sovereignty. Meanwhile, narratives in global media emphasize the DRC's corruption and inefficiency, deflecting attention from the role of foreign powers and corporations in sustaining the conflict.

The geopolitical tactic of destabilization extends beyond physical conflicts to economic manipulation. Governments use sanctions, embargoes, and trade restrictions to weaken resource-rich nations. Iran, for example, has faced decades of sanctions that cripple its economy while driving down the cost of its oil exports in black markets. Western powers, backed by media narratives framing Iran as a nuclear threat, have maintained these sanctions despite periods of compliance with international agreements. This economic pressure benefits global oil markets, keeping prices stable while constraining Iran's ability to profit from its resources. The result is a weakened state that cannot challenge how global elites dominate the energy sector.

The last layer of this strategy lies in fostering inter-state rivalries that distract from elite exploitation. By framing resource-rich regions as arenas of ideological or sectarian struggle, elites ensure that local populations remain divided and unable to resist external interference. The Gulf States' rivalry with Iran, stoked by arms deals and strategic alliances, ensures a steady flow of weapons into the region while keeping oil markets volatile. In Africa, narratives of ethnic divisions perpetuate conflicts that hinder unified governance, allowing foreign interests to extract resources with minimal resistance. These divisions are not organic but carefully nurtured through a mix of historical grievances, economic dependencies, and media manipulation.

The blueprint is clear: control local politics, enter the geopolitical stage, and destabilize resource-rich regions through narratives of division and conflict. By the time the dust settles, the elites stand to gain—whether through lucrative extraction contracts, weakened competitors, or favorable market conditions. For the nations and populations at the center of these conflicts, the result is often poverty, instability, and a loss of sovereignty. This cyclical exploitation underscores the systemic nature of elite dominance, where local manipulation seamlessly transitions into global control.

2.1 THE ART OF SELLING CONFLICT

Selling a war to the American people requires more than just military strategy; it is an exercise in narrative engineering, fear-mongering, and systematic manipulation of public opinion. The 2003 Iraq invasion shows how political motives, media, and intelligence manipulation turn geopolitical agendas into justified moral crusades.

The Bush administration crafted dual narratives. One was for public consumption, and another for power circles, as seen in the Downing Street Memo. This narrative discrepancy highlights how modern democracies market wars with precision.

The origins of the Iraq invasion lay not in the aftermath of September 11, 2001, but in pre-existing plans to reshape the Middle East. Just weeks after the attacks on the World Trade Center and Pentagon, Deputy Secretary of Defense Paul Wolfowitz had already identified Iraq as a target. Saddam Hussein, once a U.S. ally during Iraq's war with Iran in the 1980s, had outlived his geopolitical usefulness. His defiance, including expelling UN inspectors in the 1990s, gave the U.S. a pretext to reassert dominance in the oil-rich region. Wolfowitz's memo to Donald Rumsfeld made it clear: the U.S. needed to "build momentum" for regime change in Iraq. The terrorist attacks of 9/11 became the perfect excuse to connect Saddam Hussein to global terror networks, even though no evidence linked him to Al-Qaeda.

Leaders could not wage war without gaining the support of the American people. Thus began one of the most sophisticated influence campaigns in modern history. The administration's first step was to frame Iraq as an existential threat. Weapons of mass destruction (WMDs) became the centerpiece of this narrative. Between late 2001 and mid-2002, officials like Dick Cheney and Donald Rumsfeld repeatedly claimed Iraq had chemical and biological weapons stockpiles. President George W. Bush warned of Saddam's pursuit of nuclear weapons, famously invoking the image of a "mushroom cloud" as the potential cost of inaction. Investigators later discovered that these statements relied on conjecture, faulty intelligence, and deliberate falsehoods.

Media outlets amplified the administration's claims, often without scrutiny. Newspapers like The New York Times ran front-page stories based on leaks, alleging mobile biological labs and aluminum tubes for uranium enrichment. Officials cited these stories in press briefings, creating a feedback loop that reinforced the narrative. The tactic was brilliant in its simplicity: plant the story, repeat it through trusted media, and present it as common knowledge. By the time doubts about the evidence surfaced, the narrative had already swayed public opinion.

The Downing Street Memo, leaked in 2005, revealed just how far the administration was willing to go to "fix" the facts around its decision to invade Iraq. According to MI6 chief Richard Dearlove, U.S. officials were determined to remove Saddam Hussein "no matter what." Officials manipulated intelligence to fit a predetermined conclusion and dismissed UN inspections as mere formalities. Dearlove met with Tony Blair to explain the Bush administration's rationale for war. Officials fabricated claims of Iraq's WMDs to gain support.

Selling the war to Congress required an ultimate step: the release of the National Intelligence Estimate (NIE) in October 2002. Rushed and riddled with errors, the NIE claimed that Iraq possessed stockpiles of WMDs and was pursuing nuclear weapons. These assertions were based on outdated intelligence and heavily influenced by political pressure. Yet, this report became the foundation for Congress's authorization of military force against Iraq. Even members of Congress who were initially skeptical voted in favor of the resolution, unwilling to appear weak on national security.

Internationally, the Bush administration sought to legitimize its actions through the United Nations. Resolution 1441, passed in November 2002, demanded that Iraq comply with renewed weapons inspections. Hans Blix, the head of the UN inspection team, conducted over 900 inspections at more than 500 sites, finding no evidence of WMDs. Still, the administration dismissed these findings, accusing Saddam of hiding his weapons and obstructing the inspectors. In February 2003, Colin Powell gave a dramatic UN presentation. Using satellite images and communications, he claimed Iraq was in "material breach" of obligations. Critics later discredited Powell's speech, but it convinced many that war was the only option.

By March 2003, the Bush administration had achieved its goal. A majority of Americans supported the invasion, Congress had authorized it, and key allies like the United Kingdom were on board. The invasion began on March 20, 2003, with promises to disarm Iraq, free its people, and defend the world from grave danger. Yet, as history would show, Iraq had no WMDs, no significant links to Al-Qaeda, and no ongoing nuclear program. The war, founded on lies, caused the deaths of over 500,000 Iraqis and thousands of coalition troops. It destabilized the region, giving rise to insurgencies and extremist groups like ISIS, and left a lasting stain on U.S. credibility.

The Iraq War is not merely a cautionary tale about flawed intelligence or poor planning. It is a case study in how power operates in modern democracies. Leaders control narratives, use fear, and exploit trust to manufacture consent. These actions serve narrow interests at great human cost. The Downing Street Memo and similar documents reveal this process. They warn of unchecked authority and truth's fragility under propaganda.

In Chapter 13, we will dissect the anatomy of these conflicts, revealing the hidden hand of elites behind the layers of geopolitics. From lithium battles in Latin America to water disputes in South Asia, resources today are not just commodities but powerful weapons. We will explore how these competitions provoke not only wars but also humanitarian crises, laying bare the interplay between greed, violence, and human suffering. The stakes are clear: if unchecked, this ruthless competition will define the next chapter of our shared history, leaving a legacy of division and despair.

As humanity has evolved, so too have the tools of influence. From political donations to corporate lobbying, from media empires to state propaganda, power has always sought new mediums to consolidate control. But in the digital age, the battleground has shifted. Social media, once heralded as the great equalizer, has become a weapon of mass manipulation, amplifying division and exploiting vulnerability. In the next section, we delve into the story of Facebook—a platform built on the promise of connection yet corrupted by its pursuit of profit. In Myanmar, engagement-optimized algorithms turned into engines of hate. The resulting destruction has impacts far beyond its borders.

3. FAKEBOOK

In the early 21st century, the promise of technology to unite humanity seemed limitless. Social media platforms, particularly Facebook, envisioned themselves as the architects of a more connected world. But in Myanmar, this vision unraveled into a grim dystopia, revealing how unchecked technology can become a catalyst for division, violence, and even genocide. The Rohingya story, marked by ethnic cleansing amplified by Facebook's algorithms, reminds us of technology's danger when used irresponsibly.

Myanmar, once sealed off under a military junta, emerged into the digital age almost overnight. After decades of isolation, the country opened its doors to the global market in the 2010s. This opening brought a flood of mobile phones and internet access. It was driven by government deals with foreign firms eager to exploit a vast user base. By 2016, internet penetration had soared from virtually zero to 40%, and for most citizens, Facebook was the internet. Pre-installed on phones and offered as a data-free platform by local providers, it quickly became the primary source of news for nearly 38% of the population.

But this digital awakening coincided with simmering ethnic tensions. The Buddhist majority in Myanmar harbored longstanding animosity toward the Rohingya, a Muslim minority historically marginalized and denied citizenship. Enter Ashin Wirathu, a Buddhist extremist who had previously used pamphlets to disseminate hate but now found an exponential reach through Facebook. His virulent propaganda painted the Rohingya as existential threats—foreign invaders plotting to overrun Myanmar. The Facebook algorithm, designed to prioritize engagement, amplified his hate-filled posts, spreading them to millions who reacted with outrage and fear.

The consequences were catastrophic. In 2012, a series of Facebook-fueled rumors about alleged crimes by Rohingya individuals triggered mob violence, with Buddhist mobs burning Rohingya villages and displacing tens of thousands. While this initial outbreak predated Facebook's peak influence, it set a precedent for how digital platforms could escalate tensions. By the time Facebook had become ubiquitous in Myanmar, these patterns of misinformation had entrenched themselves in the public consciousness.

Between 2012 and 2017, the spiral of violence worsened. Nationalists weaponized every minor altercation involving Rohingya individuals into a narrative of impending danger. Fabricated stories and doctored images flooded Facebook, many of them orchestrated by military officials posing as ordinary users. One rumor alleged that Saudi Arabia backed Rohingya insurgents by helping them stockpile weapons, inciting mass panic and intensifying anti-Rohingya sentiment. Civilian mobs, emboldened by these narratives, began carrying out organized attacks on Rohingya communities, often with tacit support from the military. Attackers burned villages, slaughtered families, and forced survivors into makeshift camps.

The military, however, was not merely a passive observer. Recognizing the platform's potential, they co-opted Facebook as a tool of psychological warfare. Posing as news outlets and lifestyle pages, they disseminated propaganda that dehumanized the Rohingya and legitimized violence against them. When Rohingya insurgents launched retaliatory attacks in 2016 and 2017, these narratives escalated, culminating in a campaign of "clearance operations" by the military. More than 700,000 Rohingya fled to Bangladesh. Attackers burned their villages, prompting the UN to label it a textbook ethnic cleansing case.

Amid this carnage, Facebook remained inert. Researchers and human rights activists repeatedly warned the company about the role its platform was playing. One alarming report revealed that Facebook employed just one Burmese-speaking content moderator for a country of over 50 million people. Despite these warnings, Facebook prioritized growth and user engagement, making only superficial efforts to address the rampant hate speech and misinformation on its platform.

The aftermath of the Rohingya genocide laid bare the devastating power of algorithm-driven disinformation. In 2018, Facebook finally banned accounts linked to Myanmar's military leadership, acknowledging its platform's role in enabling violence. However, by then, the damage was done. Violence destroyed villages, claimed lives, and turned nearly a million Rohingya into stateless refugees living in sprawling camps across the border. Even today, Facebook's efforts to combat hate speech in

Myanmar remain inconsistent, with reports of inflammatory ads continuing to slip through the cracks.

This tragedy is not just about Myanmar. A parable for the modern world, it reveals how unregulated technology can exacerbate divisions, turning prejudice into policy and rumor into violence. By maximizing engagement, algorithms warp reality, creating echo chambers that thrive on fear and rage. This story serves as a powerful reminder of the unintended consequences of our digital age. Myanmar's story is a warning that in the age of social media, the line between virtual discourse and real-world atrocities is very thin.

As we look ahead, the global implications are clear. Platforms like Facebook wield immense power over information ecosystems, yet their governance often lags behind their influence. Myanmar was an early, tragic case, but the mechanisms of algorithmic radicalization—amplifying conspiracies, polarizing communities, and enabling violence—are universal. The question is whether humanity can learn from this lesson before the next tragedy unfolds in another corner of the digital world.

Myanmar's tragedy exposed the dark side of social media, where platforms once meant to inform and unite now mislead and divide. Algorithmic amplification of hate and falsehoods extends beyond geopolitical violence, distorting truth and reshaping collective memory. From Facebook-driven ethnic cleansing to viral conspiracy theories, the same exploitative mechanism persists, profiting from human vulnerabilities. Next, we explore conspiracy theories, where weaponized algorithms twist curiosity and skepticism into unreality. A prime example is the moon landing conspiracy, illustrating how misinformation can erode trust in humanity's greatest achievements.

4. HOUSTON, WE HAVE A GREEN SCREEN

Conspiracy theories, fueled by the algorithms of modern social platforms, have demonstrated a remarkable capacity to distort reality and undermine public trust. Conspiracy theories' power is not logical but psychological. They exploit our love of mystery, distrust of authority, and desire for simple answers in a complex world. The moon landing conspiracy persists despite overwhelming evidence. This shows how deeply misinformation can take root when amplified by modern media. But beneath this phenomenon lies a more sinister truth: unchecked misinformation is not just a societal irritant; it is a powerful tool in the hands of elites, enabling control over narratives, resources, and even the trajectory of human progress.

The moon landing, one of humanity's most celebrated achievements, has long been the target of conspiracy theorists. They posit an elaborate hoax—one orchestrated by the U.S. government, allegedly aided by Hollywood directors like Stanley Kubrick—to fake a lunar landing on a soundstage. This narrative grew during the Cold War. America's space race victory over the Soviet Union was not only a scientific achievement but also an ideological triumph. Despite exhaustive scientific rebuttals and the physical evidence of moon rocks, conspiracy theorists persist, claiming everything from doctored photographs to fabricated moonwalk footage. Such theories thrive in the digital age, where algorithms prioritize engagement over accuracy, feeding users content that inflames emotions and confirms biases.

For elites, such platforms offer a potent mechanism to manipulate public perception and policy. Consider the nascent field of space exploration and its growing commercial stakes. Companies like SpaceX and Blue Origin, led by billionaires Elon Musk and Jeff Bezos, dominate the narrative surrounding humanity's interstellar ambitions. On the surface, their stories inspire hope: colonizing Mars, mining asteroids, and securing humanity's future. Yet beneath this grand narrative lies a familiar pattern. The control of information allows these entities to obscure the environmental risks, economic monopolies, and political influence that come with privatizing space.

Asteroid mining, for instance, holds the promise of unimaginable wealth. Precious metals like platinum, found in asteroids, could revolutionize industries on Earth. The rhetoric around space often ignores key issues. The narrative avoids addressing who will control resources, how profits will circulate, and the environmental costs of exploiting extraterrestrial bodies. Social platforms, rife with misinformation, allow these questions to be drowned out by speculative theories and exaggerated claims of technological salvation.

The danger grows when these elites compete for dominance. Space exploration may soon echo the geopolitical resource battles of Earth, with misinformation campaigns used to justify territorial claims and economic exploitation. Conspiracy theories have undermined environmental protections and discredited climate science. Similar tactics could obscure the ethical and legal challenges of space colonization.

Conspiracy theories are not anomalies; they are products of systems designed to prioritize profit over truth. They thrive because they tap into fundamental human vulnerabilities, but they endure because they serve powerful interests. Unchecked misinformation spreads, destabilizing societies and consolidating power, often invisibly affecting those impacted. With space exploration, the stakes are planetary—or even interplanetary.

Unchecked misinformation is a modern Pandora's box, its consequences far-reaching and often irreversible. If humanity fails to counter its spread and address enabling systems, the dream of a unified, informed global society will remain a dream. In the hands of the powerful, conspiracy theories are more than diversions; they are weapons, shaping narratives and ensuring that the elite remain unchallenged, whether on Earth or beyond.

The moon landing in 1969 marked a pinnacle of human achievement, a moment when humankind extended its reach beyond Earth. Skeptics shrouded this milestone in conspiracy theories, claiming it was an elaborate hoax staged on Earth. This narrative, persistent and alluring, sheds light on the complexities of trust in institutions, the human fascination with hidden truths, and the potent dynamics of misinformation. To understand how the moon landing conspiracy theory gained traction, we must explore the cultural, political, and psychological forces that sustain such ideas.

The Cold War was a geopolitical rivalry between the U.S. and the Soviet Union. It unfolded in technological races, proxy wars, and ideological battles. The space race became a key arena for proving supremacy. By the late 1950s and early 1960s, the Soviets were leading, having launched Sputnik, the first satellite, and sent Yuri Gagarin, the first human, into orbit. President Kennedy set a daring goal: land a man on the moon and bring him back safely. Exploration was only part of the goal. Ambition drove the mission, proving what humanity could achieve through daring dreams. Beyond that, it sought to assert ideological dominance. Winning the space race would symbolize the triumph of democracy and capitalism over communism.

Amidst this backdrop, NASA embarked on the Apollo program, marshaling the efforts of more than 400,000 engineers, scientists, and technicians. After setbacks, including the tragic Apollo 1 fire in 1967, the program culminated in the Apollo 11 mission. On July 20, 1969, Neil Armstrong and Buzz Aldrin walked on the lunar surface. Networks broadcast this historic feat live to an estimated 600 million viewers. The mission appeared to be a unifying moment for humanity, but within a year, doubts began to surface.

In 1974, ex-Navy officer Bill Kaysing published We Never Went to the Moon. The book, America's Thirty Billion Dollar Swindle, laid the foundation for the moon hoax theory. He argued that the U.S., desperate to fulfill Kennedy's promise, faked the landing using Hollywood-style staging. Kaysing pointed to alleged anomalies in moon photos and videos. These included missing stars, strange astronaut movements, and the flag's apparent fluttering in a vacuum. His theories resonated with a public growing skeptical of government narratives, particularly after events like the Vietnam War and the Watergate scandal.

The conspiracy theory gained new life in the 1970s and 1980s, fueled by films like Capricorn One (1978), which depicted a faked Mars landing. By the 2000s, cable documentaries and the internet brought the theory to new audiences. Fox

News aired a 2001 special titled Conspiracy Theory: Did We Land on the Moon? which rehashed old arguments and lent the theory an air of legitimacy. The rise of the internet proliferated theories, creating echo chambers that merged skepticism of authority with distrust of science.

Key elements of the theory rely on a misunderstanding of scientific principles. Camera settings excluded stars from appearing in lunar photos. Engineers optimized the cameras for the bright lunar surface, not the faint light of distant stars. The flag's apparent motion was because of the horizontal rod holding it aloft and the vibrations from its placement in the lunar soil. The astronauts' "unnatural" movements were the result of the moon's lower gravity and the cumbersome space suits. Conspiracy theorists often dismiss these explanations as part of the supposed cover-up.

Psychologically, conspiracy theories appeal to the human tendency to seek patterns and hidden meanings, especially in complex or unsettling events. The moon landing, an extraordinary accomplishment requiring unprecedented coordination and technology, can seem too monumental to believe. Coupled with the allure of being privy to "hidden truths," conspiracy theories offer a sense of empowerment to their adherents. They frame believers as part of a select group who see through the deception, reinforcing mistrust in mainstream narratives.

Even as these theories persist, overwhelming evidence supports the moon landing. The Apollo missions brought back 842 pounds of lunar rocks, studied and verified by scientists worldwide. Independent space agencies, including the Soviet Union's, tracked the Apollo missions and acknowledged their success. More recently, high-resolution images from lunar orbiters have captured the landing sites, including equipment left behind and even the astronauts' footprints.

The moon landing conspiracy exemplifies how misinformation thrives in an environment of mistrust and limited scientific literacy. This underscores why fostering critical thinking in science's methods is vital, especially in an age of rampant misinformation. The Apollo missions showcased human ingenuity. However, the skepticism they face underscores the challenge of building trust in knowledge and exploration institutions.

The moon landing conspiracy feels like a relic of a simpler era, when people indulged mistrust of institutions with few tangible consequences. But in the modern age, misinformation operates on a far more dangerous scale, influencing not just perceptions but lives and policies. The COVID-19 pandemic exemplifies this phenomenon. Scientific uncertainty and political agendas collided, sparking debates about the virus's origins. Theories about lab leaks and zoonotic spillovers spread like the virus itself. This creates a maze with intellectual and existential stakes, affecting global trust, health, and governance.

5. COVID-19 PLAN-DEMIC

Where COVID-19 originated is a key question of our time. It's significant not only for the pandemic's global impact but also for the scientific and political quagmire it exposed. Theories surrounding the virus's origins are a collision of hard science, international politics, and media narratives. Two main hypotheses dominate the debate. The spillover theory suggests the virus jumped naturally from animals to humans. The lab leak theory claims it accidentally escaped from a Wuhan research facility. Each offers compelling circumstantial evidence, but the lack of direct proof keeps humanity grappling with uncertainty.

Precedent anchors the spillover hypothesis. Historically, most pandemics, from the 1918 flu to more recent outbreaks like SARS and MERS, have originated when animal viruses adapted to infect humans. COVID-19 fits this mold at first glance, with its closest genetic relatives found in bats. Scientists first focused on a Wuhan wet market as the epicenter. They theorized the virus moved from bats to an intermediary host, possibly pangolins, before infecting humans. Early media reports reinforced this idea, presenting the market as the undeniable source of the outbreak. However, as investigations progressed, this certainty eroded. Chinese authorities admitted that the first known cases of COVID-19 had no connection to the market, and searches for infected animals in the market yielded no results.

Despite its shaky foundation, the spillover hypothesis persisted because of its alignment with prior knowledge and the reluctance to consider alternative explanations. However, the lab leak hypothesis, dismissed early as a fringe conspiracy, began gaining traction as evidence mounted. Wuhan houses the Wuhan Institute of Virology (WIV). The facility studies coronaviruses and conducts controversial gain-of-function research to enhance infectivity in humans. This coincidence, that the outbreak began in the same city as one of the world's leading coronavirus research centers, raised eyebrows. A leaked cable from U.S. diplomats in 2017 revealed concerns about WIV's safety protocols, warning that the lab lacked properly trained personnel to handle high-risk research. In hindsight, this memo feels ominously prescient.

The lab leak theory gained traction after reports surfaced. Reports claim WIV researchers entered hospitals with COVID-like symptoms in November 2019, weeks before the first recorded cases. These claims remain unverified, but they underscore the need for transparency. China's reluctance to allow an independent investigation further fuels suspicion. Beijing retaliated economically against calls for accountability, such as Australia's demand for a thorough inquiry, escalating international tensions.

Initially, the lab leak theory faced an uphill battle, not because of a lack of plausibility but because of political polarization. During the early days of the pandemic, the Trump administration's aggressive rhetoric, including terms like "China virus," politicized the debate. Critics dismissed the lab leak theory as xenophobic propaganda. The media largely echoed this sentiment, downplaying the hypothesis and labeling it a conspiracy theory. This narrative shaped public opinion, silencing scientists who considered the theory viable. It wasn't until political tensions eased and unknown voices emerged that the hypothesis gained credibility.

Scientific inquiry, ideally guided by evidence and free from bias, has not been immune to these dynamics. Some scientists with professional ties to the Wuhan lab, such as Peter Daszak, publicly dismissed the lab leak theory, citing conflicts of interest. Daszak's involvement in a WHO-led investigation further complicated matters. Critics accused the inquiry of being cursory and unbalanced, and even the WHO's director-general acknowledged its shortcomings, calling for a more extensive investigation.

As of now, neither hypothesis has conclusive evidence. The spillover theory relies on historical precedent but lacks a direct link to infected animals. The lab leak theory relies on circumstantial evidence, like the outbreak's location and safety concerns at WIV. However, it lacks definitive proof. The Batwoman, a leading researcher at WIV, examined the lab's samples and found no match for COVID-19. While this offered some reassurance, skeptics argue that self-reported findings from a researcher tied to the lab are insufficient.

The stakes of understanding COVID-19's origins extend beyond scientific curiosity. Knowing how the pandemic began is crucial for preventing future outbreaks. If the virus spilled over naturally, efforts should focus on regulating wildlife trade and improving zoonotic surveillance. If it escaped from a lab, authorities must enforce stringent international standards for research and biosafety. Yet, geopolitical rivalries, media narratives, and human aversion to ambiguity complicate the path forward.

COVID-19's origin story warns against the dangers of certainty without proof. It reveals how political agendas, media biases, and institutional conflicts of interest can distort the pursuit of truth. As the world recovers from the pandemic, its origins remain unclear. This reflects our struggle to reconcile science, politics, and the need for clarity.

The COVID-19 pandemic was not only a global health crisis but also a seismic event in the realm of information warfare. The disease itself was devastating, claiming millions of lives and disrupting the fabric of society. Yet, an equally insidious phenomenon accompanied it: the parallel pandemic of misinformation. Conspiracy theories, pseudo-scientific remedies, and conflicting advice from authorities spread like wildfire across the digital world, undermining public trust and skewing the response to the virus. Misinformation, from bioweapon theories to miracle cures, shaped public health policies and eroded cohesion. It exposed the fragility of systems against coordinated narratives.

Early in the pandemic, people widely speculated that authorities had planned COVID-19 as biological warfare. The virus's origins in Wuhan, combined with its devastating global spread, seemed to align with the logic of a weaponized pathogen. Some pointed to China's strategic interests, alleging that unleashing the virus could weaken adversarial economies while sparing China's own. Others speculated about accidental leaks from laboratories, a narrative that gained some legitimacy when questions arose about safety practices at the Wuhan Institute of Virology. Despite circumstantial evidence fueling these theories, no definitive proof confirms that anyone engineered or intentionally released COVID-19. Scientific consensus still leans toward natural zoonotic spillover, a hypothesis supported by the historical precedent of diseases like SARS and MERS.

Yet, it's unsurprising that the bioweapon narrative persists. Such theories thrive in the fertile ground of uncertainty and mistrust, amplified by the geopolitical rivalries of the 21st century. Social media platforms played a crucial role in disseminating these ideas, often outpacing efforts by governments and health organizations to provide accurate information. Such theories proliferated, undermining public health, fostering vaccine hesitancy, resisting mask mandates, and polarizing pandemic responses. Nations grappled with not only the virus itself but also the social fragmentation exacerbated by competing truths in the information ecosystem.

The pandemic also offered a grim preview of the future of warfare. If COVID-19 had been a deliberate act, it would have exemplified the potential of biological warfare to destabilize the modern world. Unlike traditional warfare, which relies on visible conflict and physical destruction, a biological attack is insidious, spreading invisibly through populations while leaving economies and governments reeling. The response to such an attack would require unprecedented global coordination, something the COVID-19 pandemic has shown we are far from achieving. COVID-19 chaos, even without clear bioweapon evidence, may spark more interest in bio-weapons. This underscores the need for stronger international biosecurity measures.

Looking ahead, the future of warfare is unlikely to resemble the battles of the past. Instead, it will combine biological, cyber, and psychological dimensions, targeting the infrastructure of societies rather than their armies. Information manipulation will play a central role, as seen during the pandemic, where disinformation campaigns amplified confusion and division. Cyberattacks on healthcare systems, for instance, could coincide with the release of pathogens, creating multi-layered crises that overwhelm governments and erode public trust. The lines between war and peace will blur, with adversaries engaging in constant, low-intensity conflicts aimed at weakening rivals without triggering outright retaliation.

The response to these threats requires a paradigm shift. Nations must invest not only in military hardware but also in digital literacy, public health resilience, and international collaboration. The COVID-19 pandemic revealed a powerful modern weapon. It's not missiles or guns but the ability to manipulate truth itself. The pandemic was more than a health crisis. It was a rehearsal for future conflicts, where the battlefield is our minds and the stakes are societal stability.

The COVID-19 pandemic laid bare a fundamental truth about our interconnected world: the power to manipulate information is as potent as any weapon. The pandemic revealed vulnerabilities in traditional media, the influence of digital platforms, and how easily people lose trust. Yet, in this chaos lies an opportunity to rethink the role of media in society. If the media of today often amplifies division and misinformation, what might a reimagined media landscape—one focused on expertise, neutrality, and public good—look like?

In the digital age, the media has replaced the pulpit as humanity's primary storyteller. But when truth becomes a commodity, it loses its power to unite. Manipulating information reflects the same instincts that shaped religious and political systems: a drive to influence and control.

This dysfunction reaches its zenith in the justice system, explored in Chapter 10: *Justice Denied*. Manipulating truth causes justice to falter. Greed and power skew fairness and distort all institutions. A broken system forces humanity to face its consequences.

10

Justice Denied

"The law is like a spider's web, that catches the weak and the poor,
but lets the strong and the rich break through."

– ANACHARSIS

The judiciary has been considered throughout history as the final arbiter of justice and the ultimate safeguard against abuses of power by those in authority. However, this noble ideal often gives way to harsh realities, as manipulation and bias distort the judiciary, turning it into a tool that serves the very elites it was meant to hold accountable. This phenomenon is as old as the concept of law itself; it is not new. Ancient kings ruled as sovereigns and judges. Modern legal systems, tangled in politics, often mold the judiciary to protect power, shield elites from accountability, and reinforce inequalities. Manipulating the judiciary reveals a story of strategic dominance—an elaborate game where the law serves as a tool for control, not justice.

In ancient Mesopotamia, people celebrated the Code of Hammurabi as one of the earliest codified systems of justice. Etched into stone for all to see, it proclaimed principles of fairness and retribution. But behind the grand declarations of justice, a closer reading reveals its inherent bias toward the elite class. Penalties for crimes varied by social status. An injury to a wealthy noble brought harsher punishment than one to a commoner or slave. Far from being impartial, lawmakers designed the system to maintain the social order and ensure that the powerful remained unchallenged. Similar patterns emerged in ancient Rome, where patricians wielded control over judicial decisions. Roman leaders ostensibly created the Twelve Tables, a foundational legal document of the Republic, to protect plebeians from elite exploitation. Officials selectively interpreted these laws. Patrician landowners benefited, using influence to maintain control over economic and legal power.

The interplay between law and elite power did not remain confined to the ancient world. In medieval Europe, the judiciary became an arm of divine authority, often manipulated by monarchs and the Church to suppress dissent and consolidate control. The Inquisition serves as a chilling example of this manipulation. Framed as preserving religious orthodoxy, this process became a weapon. It targeted political rivals, heretics, and wealthy families for asset seizures. Trials were often based on coerced confessions extracted through torture, and verdicts served not justice but the interests of the powerful institutions overseeing them. The veneer of legality masked a deeper agenda: silencing opposition and reinforcing the supremacy of those in power.

The Enlightenment brought promises of legal reform and separating powers, but elites continued manipulating the judiciary, albeit in subtler forms. In the 19th century, colonial powers used the legal system as an instrument of subjugation. In British India, laws like the Rowlatt Act allowed arrests without trial. Officials claimed it maintained order but used it to suppress independence movements. Courts, staffed by colonial officers, rarely sided with indigenous plaintiffs, reinforcing the hierarchy between colonizers and the colonized. The system perpetuated economic exploitation and social inequalities, ensuring that challenges to imperial authority were swiftly and legally neutralized.

In modern times, elites manipulate the judiciary by leveraging media narratives, financial influence, and fabricated evidence to escape accountability. In the United States, the Gilded Age saw industrial magnates like John D. Rockefeller and Andrew Carnegie use the courts to suppress labor unions and maintain monopolies. Through strategic legal battles and hefty campaign contributions, these tycoons ensured favorable rulings that upheld their dominance. Antitrust laws aimed to curb power but saw selective enforcement. Judges deferred to economic stability arguments crafted by the elites under scrutiny.

Even in democracies where the judiciary is ostensibly independent, its susceptibility to influence remains a persistent issue. In the 20th century, the Civil Rights Movement in the United States exposed the deeply entrenched biases within the legal system. Courts eventually became venues for landmark victories like Brown v. Board of

Education, but these rulings were hard-won against systemic obstructionism. State and local courts, controlled by segregationist elites, routinely upheld Jim Crow laws, perpetuating racial inequalities for decades. Selective justice reveals how judicial systems maintain the status quo. They protect dominant groups while marginalizing communities.

Today, manipulating the judiciary has evolved into a sophisticated operation, often cloaked in legality and procedural integrity. High-profile cases involving corporate malfeasance, environmental violations, or political corruption frequently demonstrate how elites use their resources to shape outcomes. In India, the intersection of wealth, politics, and media has skewed judicial impartiality. Major conglomerates often delay cases for years and secure favorable verdicts through lobbying, media campaigns, and selective evidence presentation. Corporate elites acquiring media outlets worsen this trend. They shape narratives to discredit opposition and sway public opinion for the accused.

Perhaps the most striking example of judicial manipulation in the digital age arises from proliferating misinformation. By strategically disseminating false narratives, elites can delegitimize critics, obscure facts, and even influence juries and judges. The trial of Julian Assange highlights this dynamic. Some see Assange as a transparency crusader. Others call him a criminal threat. His legal battles hinge on media perception as much as legal arguments. Elites use leaked documents, selective reporting, and vilification of whistleblowers. They escape accountability and suppress exposers of their actions.

The judiciary, like any human institution, is not immune to the forces of power and manipulation. Its very design—to uphold justice impartially—makes it an attractive target for those who seek to bend it to their will. Ancient tablets favored elites with laws. Modern courtrooms face media and corporate lobbying influence. The judiciary's story remains a struggle between fairness and control. The promise of justice remains tantalizingly close, yet persistently out of reach for those on the margins. In a complex, interconnected world, we must expose manipulations. The judiciary must act as a bulwark against inequality, not perpetuate it.

1. AMERICA'S COURTROOM CIRCUS

The U.S. legal system ideal claims equality before the law. This vision emphasizes fairness and impartiality as guiding principles. Yet, history shows that inequality and influence often overshadow this aspiration, with wealth and power subtly shaping legal outcomes. Courts have long treated elites and ordinary citizens unequally, a disparity that is not unique to modern times. It is an enduring legacy of societal stratification that has persisted despite centuries of reform and progress. Through high-profile cases and public controversies, this tension between principle and practice has become an enduring question in the American conscience.

1.1 DONALD TRUMP'S EGYPTIAN TALE

Trump's financial impropriety allegations and judicial shielding offer a case study. They highlight power, influence, and democracy's vulnerabilities. The trail began with a $10 million withdrawal in Egypt, a cash-strapped campaign, and a sudden financial influx into Trump's campaign. Each piece of evidence suggested a narrative in which foreign influence may have greased the wheels of an American election. Yet, this story's true intrigue lies not in who proves the claims but in how powerful actors harnessed the judicial system to shield the accused from scrutiny.

The FBI's investigation into a potential Egyptian bribe to Trump's campaign represents a textbook example of elite manipulation of the judiciary. The agents uncovered credible evidence that Egypt's intelligence services withdrew $10 million in cash just days before Trump's inauguration. This aligned suspiciously with Trump's unexpected decision to loan his campaign $10 million, a reversal of his previous refusals to self-fund. Political appointees strategically wielded their authority to obstruct every step toward uncovering a concrete link, despite sufficient evidence. Attorney General Bill Barr, appointed by Trump, intervened to restrict the FBI's access to Trump's financial records, characterizing the investigators as overzealous and imposing bureaucratic roadblocks.

This elite shielding is not an isolated incident but part of a broader pattern in which powerful individuals bend institutions to their advantage. Historical precedents abound: from the Watergate cover-up to corporate executives dodging accountability after the 2008 financial crisis. In Trump's case, the Department of Justice transformed from a guardian of the law into a partisan shield. Officials sidelined career prosecutors pushing for further investigation. Loyalists shut down the inquiry, citing insufficient evidence they had blocked from collection.

The ramifications of such actions ripple far beyond Trump or this case. They erode public trust in the judiciary, reinforcing perceptions that justice bends to wealth and political connections. The legal system, designed to uphold accountability, becomes a tool of the powerful, fostering cynicism and deepening societal divides. In office, Trump released billions in military aid to Egypt. He invited its president to the White House and praised a regime criticized for human rights abuses. These actions heightened perceptions of transactional politics. But without an impartial, fully empowered investigation, the truth remains cloaked in doubt.

This case exemplifies how elites weaponized delays, institutional gatekeeping, and public narratives to insulate themselves. It underscores the need for judicial reform, particularly mechanisms that insulate investigations from political interference. Yet, as the judicial system falters, it sows the seeds of ingroup-outgroup dynamics, fueling resentment and polarization—a fertile ground for nationalism. The next chapter explores globalization's intertwining with these dynamics. Nationalism reacts to elite failures while complicating global cooperation. The struggle to reconcile localized identities with interconnected challenges becomes the next frontier in understanding the modern world.

1.2 O.J. SIMPSON AND DREAM TEAM

The 1995 O.J. Simpson trial combined celebrity culture, wealth, and America's legal system. This sensational case seemed to shift justice's boundaries. O.J. Authorities accused Simpson, a former NFL star and actor, of brutally murdering his ex-wife Nicole Brown Simpson and her friend Ronald Goldman. When allegations surfaced, the trial became a global media spectacle. It exposed the stark interplay of wealth, fame, and the judicial process.

Simpson's defense team, famously known as the "Dream Team," was a powerhouse of legal acumen. Johnnie Cochran led a team with Robert Shapiro, F. Lee Bailey, and Alan Dershowitz. Their influence and expertise were beyond most people's reach. This elite legal machinery, reportedly costing millions, meticulously deconstructed the prosecution's case, undermining the evidence with relentless precision. Cochran's phrase, "If it doesn't fit, you must acquit," referenced ill-fitting gloves. It became a cultural touchstone. Yet, beneath the theatricality of the trial lay profound questions: Would an ordinary citizen, devoid of Simpson's wealth and celebrity, have received the same caliber of defense? Would the jury, swayed by arguments of systemic racism within the Los Angeles Police Department, have reached the same verdict for someone less famous?

The trial's outcome—Simpson's acquittal in the criminal court—provoked national debate, dividing public opinion along lines of race, class, and access to justice. For many, it revealed the extent to which wealth could tilt the scales of justice. The defense successfully framed the case as not just about Simpson but about centuries of racial injustice, leveraging public mistrust of the LAPD to their advantage. Critics claimed the trial shifted to systemic racism rather than the murders. Simpson's celebrity acted as both shield and weapon. For others, the trial was emblematic of a broader truth: that in America, the courtroom often favors those who can afford to shape the narrative.

The Simpson trial underscored how elites can leverage the legal system to their advantage, not through direct manipulation but by harnessing its inherent complexities and inequalities. Simpson's wealth funded a defense team that overwhelmed prosecution resources. It created reasonable doubt unreachable for less affluent defendants. The case left an indelible mark on the legal and cultural landscape, illustrating how power and privilege can intertwine to challenge notions of equality before the law. Afterward, debates about money's role in justice deepened. The fundamental question remained: When the law serves the powerful, can justice ever be impartial?

1.3 JEFFREY EPSTEIN

The Jeffrey Epstein case stands as a chilling example of how wealth, connections, and the shadowy corridors of influence can warp the mechanisms of justice. Epstein, a financier linked to powerful figures in politics, business, and entertainment, faced mid-2000s investigations for sexually abusing minors—a crime whose exposure should have brought severe penalties. Instead, the judicial outcome was a stunning testament to the privileges of the elite. In 2008, Epstein negotiated a plea deal with federal prosecutors, agreeing to plead guilty to minor state charges of soliciting prostitution from a minor. The deal spared him federal prosecution for trafficking and abuse allegations. He received a 13-month county jail sentence with daily work release privileges. For the victims, it was a staggering betrayal; for the public, it raised unsettling questions about the justice system's susceptibility to power.

At the heart of this plea deal was an extraordinary confluence of influence and secrecy. Epstein's legal team featured prominent attorneys like Alan Dershowitz and Kenneth Starr. These figures skillfully navigated the legal system to benefit their high-profile client. Beyond the courtroom, Epstein's connections reached into the upper echelons of politics and society. Epstein kept ties with powerful figures like former President Bill Clinton, Prince Andrew, and business magnate Leslie Wexner, whose wealth rivaled his own. These associations created an aura of invincibility around Epstein, making it all the more difficult to separate the man from his network.

Alexander Acosta, later Trump's Secretary of Labor, led federal prosecutors who brokered Epstein's non-prosecution agreement. The deal shielded him from severe accountability. This agreement, made without notifying many of the victims, included provisions that granted immunity to Epstein's alleged co-conspirators. It was an arrangement so lenient that it later sparked investigations and widespread condemnation. Critics claimed Epstein's wealth and connections let him manipulate the system. He secured a deal unthinkable for ordinary defendants. Acosta later defended the decision by suggesting Epstein's legal team had "intimidated" prosecutors, an admission that underscored the asymmetry of power at play.

Epstein's 2008 plea deal exemplified how wealth and influence create a parallel system of justice for elites, where authorities grant severe crimes disproportionate leniency. But his story did not end there. In 2019, federal authorities arrested Epstein on sex trafficking charges after renewed investigations and public outrage. This time, the sheer weight of evidence threatened to unravel not just Epstein's predatory empire but also the complicity of those within his network. Epstein's suspicious death in a Manhattan jail cell, officially ruled a suicide, left the truth elusive. Speculation grew about powerful allies intervening to protect themselves.

The Epstein case is not just the story of one man but a microcosm of how elite privilege can subvert accountability. It exposes a justice system that, when confronted with the wealthy and connected, too often fails to serve its highest ideals. For the victims, Epstein's light sentence and mysterious death denied them the full measure of justice. The case revealed how elites evade consequences. It left distrust in institutions and a haunting question: How many like Epstein operate with impunity, hidden by influence and power?

1.4 OPERATION VARSITY BLUES

The 2019 Operation Varsity Blues scandal laid bare the mechanisms through which wealth and influence can corrupt even the most ostensibly meritocratic systems. For decades, prestigious universities in the United States had marketed themselves as sanctuaries of fairness and intellectual achievement, where admission hinged on talent, determination, and merit. This image shattered when federal prosecutors exposed a sprawling conspiracy. Dozens of wealthy parents, college coaches, and administrators manipulated admissions with bribery, fraud, and deception. The scandal exposed not only individual acts of greed but also the structural inequities that allowed privilege to masquerade as ability.

At the heart of the operation was William "Rick" Singer, a college admissions consultant who masterminded the schemes. Singer exploited his access to elite institutions, orchestrating fraudulent pathways into colleges for the children of affluent families. In many cases, this involved bribing university coaches to designate students as athletic recruits, even if the applicants had no experience in the sports in question. Singer's network also included complicit administrators and standardized test proctors who altered exam scores or took tests on behalf of students. These schemes bypassed the competitive admissions process, securing spots for students whose qualifications often paled in comparison to those of their peers.

The list of implicated parents read like a who's who of American privilege: Hollywood actors, CEOs, investors, and other wealthy elites. Among the most prominent figures were actresses Lori Loughlin and Felicity Huffman, whose cases became emblematic of the scandal. Loughlin and her husband, fashion designer Mossimo Giannulli, paid $500,000 to have their daughters falsely designated as crew recruits for the University of Southern California. Huffman, meanwhile, paid $15,000 to have her daughter's SAT scores fraudulently inflated. The sums were staggering, highlighting a harsh reality. In merit-based systems, the ultra-wealthy often find ways to buy influence and manipulate outcomes.

The scandal was not merely a tale of parental desperation, but a symptom of deeper societal inequities. Elite families viewed college admissions as a gateway to maintaining generational privilege. A degree from a prestigious institution, they believed, was not just an educational credential but a signal of status, ensuring access to elite social and professional networks. These parents' actions revealed their lack of faith in their children's abilities. They felt entitled to bypass rules that applied to others. For families without such wealth, the scandal was a gut-wrenching reminder of how skewed the playing field truly was.

Public outrage was swift, and the judicial response varied widely. Some parents, like Huffman, received short prison sentences, with Huffman serving just 11 days. Others, including Loughlin and Giannulli, faced harsher penalties, though still far less severe than the sentences routinely handed down for less egregious crimes committed by lower-income individuals. Many of the implicated families could mitigate consequences through high-powered legal teams and media strategies that framed them as misguided but well-intentioned parents. Critics noted that the scandal exposed the dual justice system in the United States, where wealth could often shield individuals from the full weight of accountability.

Beyond individual prosecutions, the scandal forced society to reckon with the broader role of money in higher education. The revelations exposed a system full of inequities. Legacy admissions favored alumni children, while massive donations secured naming rights and policy influence. Operation Varsity Blues merely highlighted the most brazen abuses within an ecosystem where privilege and access were long-standing currencies. Universities scrambled to distance themselves from the scandal, tightening policies and auditing admissions practices, but the damage to their reputations was done.

Operation Varsity Blues served as a microcosm of the broader societal forces that allow wealth to erode meritocracy. Moneyed interests hollowed out institutions designed to reward talent, perpetuating cycles of inequality. For millions of struggling students and families, the scandal confirmed a bitter truth. Equal opportunity remains a fragile illusion, easily undermined by the wealthy who rewrite the rules. The judicial outcomes, while varied, left lingering questions about whether justice could ever be truly impartial in a society so deeply stratified by wealth and power.

2. PIL TO LOL: MADE IN INDIA

India's judicial system, a cornerstone of its democratic framework, aspires to uphold the principles of justice and equality. Its storied history reveals moments when these ideals faced tests, particularly in cases involving the nation's elite. Wealth, influence, and the sprawling networks of power have often intersected with the legal process, prompting debates about fairness and impartiality. Direct evidence of judicial manipulation is elusive and rarely proven. Yet, outcomes of some high-profile cases make the public question judicial neutrality under social and political pressure.

2.1 SALMAN KHAN BUCK

The 2002 Salman Khan hit-and-run case shows how wealth, fame, and justice collide. It illustrates how elite influence shapes legal outcomes, testing public faith in the system. In September 2002, Salman Khan, a top Bollywood star, allegedly drove his SUV into a group of homeless individuals sleeping on a Mumbai sidewalk. The accident resulted in the death of one person and injuries to four others. What followed was a legal saga spanning over a decade, marked by controversies, delays, and the shadow of celebrity privilege.

The initial days after the incident set the tone for what would become a contentious legal battle. Ravindra Patil, a police constable assigned as Salman Khan's bodyguard, was present in the vehicle and immediately identified Khan as the driver. Patil gave damning testimony, claiming Khan ignored his warnings to slow down while intoxicated. This statement should have served as a critical piece of evidence. Instead, it became a flashpoint of controversy as Patil faced immense pressure, both personal and systemic, during the trial. By 2007, he had died under distressing circumstances, destitute and ostracized, a development that many saw as emblematic of the power imbalance at play. The loss of such a key witness left a gaping hole in the prosecution's case.

Significant delays and procedural twists characterized the trial. Witnesses changed testimonies, the defense questioned evidence management, and alternative theories about the driver's identity emerged. The defense argued that it was Salman Khan's driver, not Khan himself, who had been behind the wheel. This claim gained traction despite initial testimonies pointing directly at the actor. The trial meandered, with each twist increasing public speculation about the effectiveness of India's justice system when dealing with immense wealth and fame.

By 2015, the case reached a dramatic turning point. A lower court convicted Khan of culpable homicide not amounting to murder and sentenced him to five years in prison. The conviction appeared, briefly, as a moment of accountability. Yet, within months, the Bombay High Court overturned the ruling, acquitting Khan of all charges. The court cited insufficient evidence and procedural lapses, including discrepancies in witness accounts and failing to establish beyond a reasonable doubt that Khan was the driver. This acquittal not only absolved the actor, but also reignited debates about the influence of celebrity and wealth in India's judiciary.

The case deeply polarized public perception. Salman Khan's supporters, including many in Bollywood, celebrated the acquittal as vindication for a beloved star. Critics, however, saw the outcome as a glaring example of systemic inequity. The trial's lengthy duration, Ravindra Patil's fate, and investigative inconsistencies highlighted a judicial process skewed toward the powerful. For many, the case showed how fame and money shield individuals from legal consequences, especially in a society where the disenfranchised struggle for basic accountability.

The Salman Khan case is more than a high-profile trial. By offering a lens to examine justice, privilege, and power in India, it sheds light on the structural challenges in prosecuting individuals whose social and economic capital place them far beyond the reach of ordinary citizens. Moreover, it highlights the societal tendency to conflate celebrity with virtue, enabling figures like Khan to craft narratives of generosity and philanthropy that obscure their legal entanglements.

In history, the case reflects a recurring theme: elites manipulating judicial systems that falter under their influence. From ancient monarchs above the law to modern corporate tycoons, legal battles often play out in public opinion as much as in courtrooms. The patterns remain strikingly consistent. The Salman Khan saga, with legal ambiguity and societal fascination, reminds us of the difficulty of achieving justice when facing the immense pull of fame and fortune.

2.2 BHOPAL GAS TRAGEDY

The 1984 Bhopal Gas Tragedy is one of industrial history's darkest chapters. It revealed the devastating cost of corporate negligence and justice's limits against powerful entities. On December 2–3, 1984, methyl isocyanate gas leaked from UCIL's Bhopal plant, releasing a toxic cloud over the sleeping city. The disaster killed over 3,000 people immediately and injured tens of thousands more, leaving many to grapple with chronic illnesses and disabilities. The tragedy unfolded in hours, leaving lasting suffering. Justice has been slow, uneven, and mired in controversy over compromised accountability.

In the days following the disaster, attention quickly turned to Union Carbide Corporation (UCC), the American parent company of UCIL, and its CEO, Warren Anderson. Reports of lax safety standards, inadequate maintenance, and cost-cutting measures painted a grim picture of corporate indifference to risk. Investigators revealed that officials at the Bhopal plant deactivated or failed to repair safety systems to save money, ignoring warnings about potential hazards. The gas leak did not happen by accident but culminated from systemic negligence driven by profit motives. Anderson, as the head of UCC, became the symbol of this corporate recklessness.

India's response to the disaster initially appeared resolute. Authorities arrested Warren Anderson after his visit to Bhopal but released him on bail within hours. He left the country, reportedly under diplomatic and corporate pressure. This began a pattern where justice faltered in the face of power. In 1987, India charged Anderson and UCC executives with culpable homicide. The U.S. denied repeated extradition requests, leaving Anderson a fugitive under Indian law. He lived in the U.S. without standing trial. Many viewed this as emblematic of the accountability gap between nations and their hosted corporations.

The Indian government, representing the victims, settled with UCC in 1989 for $470 million in compensation. Critics widely condemned this amount, though significant on paper, as grossly inadequate given the disaster's scale and its enduring impact on victims. Critics argued that the government had prioritized expediency and corporate appeasement over securing meaningful redress for those affected. The funds, when distributed, amounted to paltry sums for individual victims, a stark contrast to the lifelong medical and social costs they continued to bear.

Indian courts focused legal proceedings on UCIL's Indian executives, accusing them of negligence. In 2010, nearly three decades after the tragedy, the court convicted eight former UCIL employees and sentenced them to two years in prison. The court quickly stayed the sentences and released the convicted individuals on bail, prompting outrage among victims' groups and activists. For many, the convictions felt like a symbolic gesture rather than a substantive effort to deliver justice. Foreign executives like Anderson evaded Indian law. UCC avoided accountability through corporate maneuvers, including its 2001 acquisition by Dow Chemical.

The legal and political handling of the Bhopal Gas Tragedy exposed deep flaws in the mechanisms of accountability for multinational corporations operating in the Global South. The power disparity between UCC and Indian victims highlighted global inequities. Corporate influence often overrides national sovereignty and justice systems. The United States hesitated to extradite Anderson, despite mounting evidence of UCC's culpability, highlighting state actors' complicity in shielding corporate elites.

Public perception of the case remains one of profound injustice. Lenient sentences for Indian executives, lack of foreign trials, and inadequate compensation deepened victims' and advocates' sense of betrayal. The Bhopal Gas Tragedy became more than a case of industrial disaster; it became a symbol of the systemic imbalance that allows the powerful to evade responsibility while the marginalized bear the brunt of their actions. For the survivors, justice remains elusive, their lives a testament to a world where corporate interests often trump human lives.

2.3 SANJAY DUTT

Sanjay Dutt Arms Act case stands out in India's legal history as a complex interplay of celebrity, crime, and the justice system. After the 1993 Mumbai bomb blasts killed over 250 and injured hundreds, Bollywood actor Sanjay Dutt's arrest shocked the nation. The investigation revealed a murky connection between Dutt and members of the underworld responsible for orchestrating the attacks. Authorities alleged that Dutt obtained illegal weapons, including an AK-56 rifle and hand grenades, through individuals tied to the blasts. Dutt insisted that he obtained the weapons solely for personal protection during communal unrest, but the case took on larger implications as it unfolded.

Dutt's arrest in 1993 under the stringent Terrorist and Disruptive Activities (Prevention) Act (TADA) initially painted him as a figure entangled in a larger conspiracy. The TADA charges suggested a potential link to the conspirators behind the bomb blasts, a claim that carried grave implications for his public image and legal fate. However, after years of protracted legal proceedings, the TADA court acquitted Dutt of terrorism-related charges, determining that he was not directly involved in the conspiracy. The court convicted him under the Arms Act for illegally possessing the weapons. In 2007, the court sentenced him to six years in prison. In 2013, the Supreme Court upheld the decision but reduced it to five years.

Throughout the case, Dutt's celebrity status loomed large, raising questions about whether it influenced the legal process. His defense argued he was a victim of circumstances. As an actor, he acted out of fear and made poor decisions during Mumbai's tumultuous period. Public sentiment, divided between sympathy and skepticism, often reflected his dual identity as a beloved film star and a convicted criminal. Supporters highlighted his charitable work and transformation since the incident, framing him as a man who had learned from his mistakes. Critics, however, pointed to the relatively lenient treatment he seemed to receive, particularly during his imprisonment.

The controversy deepened during Dutt's incarceration. His frequent paroles and furloughs—granted on grounds of medical needs and family obligations—sparked widespread debate. Between 2013 and 2016, authorities granted Dutt leave from prison multiple times, far exceeding what most inmates in similar circumstances could expect. Prison authorities defended these decisions as legal. However, many questioned if Dutt's fame and connections secured these privileges. His paroles often coincided with his film releases or family events. This timing led many to believe his celebrity status reduced the severity of his punishment.

Dutt's release in 2016, after serving his sentence with allowances for remission, marked the end of a long legal saga. Yet, the case continued to resonate in public discourse as an example of how wealth, influence, and fame can intersect with the justice system. It highlighted the uneven experiences of high-profile individuals versus ordinary citizens within India's legal framework. The disparity lay not in his conviction but in the process. Delays, privileges, and public sympathy highlighted elite preferential treatment.

The Sanjay Dutt case encapsulates the challenges of ensuring equal justice under the law in a society where celebrity culture holds immense sway. It also reflects broader concerns about accountability and privilege in high-profile cases. Though Dutt faced legal consequences, unequal treatment lingers. It reminds us how societal status shapes justice. For ordinary citizens, the case reinforced the belief that justice favors wealth, fame, or power, making equality before the law a distant ideal.

2.4 VIJAY MALLYA

The saga of Vijay Mallya encapsulates the complex interplay between wealth, influence, and the vulnerabilities of financial systems in holding powerful individuals accountable. Mallya, once the "King of Good Times," fell from grace. His downfall exposed India's fragile banking and regulatory systems. Kingfisher Airlines, Mallya's now-defunct carrier, epitomized opulence. It crumbled under debt, leaving employees unpaid and banks burdened with over ₹9,000 crore ($1.2 billion) in loans.

Mallya's troubles began with the financial collapse of Kingfisher Airlines in 2012, but the roots of the crisis ran deeper. The airline, despite never turning a profit, had managed to secure massive loans from public sector banks. Observers alleged that banks sanctioned these loans without adequate collateral or due diligence, influenced by Mallya's close ties to politicians and banking officials. Reports suggested that his proximity to power allowed him to bend institutional norms, raising troubling questions about how wealth and connections could override prudent financial practices.

As the airline spiraled into insolvency, Mallya's personal life stood in sharp contrast to the company's woes. Lavish parties, yachts, and mansions were hallmarks of his brand, presenting an image of unabashed privilege that fueled public outrage. By the time investigations into his financial dealings gained momentum, Mallya had already left India for the UK in March 2016, triggering a political firestorm. Critics accused the government and regulatory bodies of failing to act decisively, enabling his escape at a critical juncture. How did a man facing vast financial scrutiny leave the country? Critics blamed oversight gaps or systemic leniency for elites.

The legal pursuit of Mallya became a drawn-out affair, underscoring the challenges of prosecuting financial crimes involving global jurisdictions. Indian authorities accused Mallya of willful default and money laundering. Loans for Kingfisher Airlines allegedly funded personal accounts and extravagant acquisitions. Mallya claimed innocence, arguing Kingfisher's failure was a business risk, not a crime. He asserted political targeting.

Efforts to extradite Mallya from the UK became a focal point of the case, emblematic of the hurdles in bringing high-profile offenders to justice. In 2018, after extensive legal proceedings, UK courts approved his extradition, acknowledging that there was a prima facie case of financial wrongdoing. Yet, years later, Mallya remained in the UK, shielded by undisclosed legal maneuvers. The delay eroded public trust further. Many saw it as another example of the wealthy exploiting international law to evade accountability.

The Mallya case struck a nerve in a country grappling with growing economic inequality and rising non-performing assets in its banking sector. His audacity—defaulting on massive loans while continuing to live a life of luxury abroad—became a potent symbol of the perceived impunity enjoyed by India's elite. Ordinary citizens struggling with loans saw Mallya's unscathed status as unjust. His debts, effectively socialized, felt like an affront to justice.

Beyond Mallya's personal culpability, the case exposed systemic flaws in India's financial and regulatory frameworks. How could banks extend such colossal loans without adequate safeguards? Why did regulatory bodies fail to detect or act on early warning signs of financial irregularities? And most critically, why was there no mechanism to prevent a high-profile defaulter from fleeing the country? These questions remain central to the broader discourse on accountability and reform in India's financial ecosystem.

The Vijay Mallya saga is not just about a business tycoon gone rogue. It reflects the vulnerabilities in systems designed to ensure fairness and accountability. It highlights the challenge of prosecuting financial crimes in a globalized world. Borders offer refuge to the powerful while justice moves unevenly. Mallya's case spurred calls for stricter regulations and loan scrutiny. It reminds us how far institutions must go to bridge law and justice against elite influence.

2.5 NIRAV MODI

The Nirav Modi case warns how loopholes, regulatory lapses, and elite privilege enable bold financial crimes under seemingly robust institutions. A celebrated jeweler whose name had become synonymous with luxury, Modi's rise seemed emblematic of entrepreneurial success in a globalized India. In 2018, the glittering facade crumbled. Punjab National Bank (PNB), one of India's largest state-owned banks, revealed a ₹14,000 crore ($2 billion) fraud. The scam, allegedly orchestrated by Modi and his uncle Mehul Choksi, sent shockwaves through India's financial system and sparked a nationwide turmoil.

The mechanics of the fraud were as audacious as they were simple. Modi's companies exploited weaknesses in PNB's systems for years. They secured unauthorized Letters of Undertaking (LoUs), which guaranteed loans from overseas branches of Indian banks. These LoUs, issued without proper authorization or collateral, financed Modi's sprawling diamond empire. The scheme relied on corrupt bank officials' complicity and oversight mechanisms' inertia. These systems failed to detect irregularities in time.

When the scam became public in early 2018, Modi had already fled India, leaving weeks before the scandal erupted. Revealing Modi's escape infuriated the public. It raised questions about how a high-profile figure under financial scrutiny left the country unchallenged. The ease of Modi's departure drew comparisons to Vijay

Mallya's flight to the UK. It reinforced the view that India's elites use wealth and connections to evade accountability.

Modi's flight to the UK initiated a long and winding legal battle. Arrested in London in 2019, he has since fought extradition to India, citing concerns over prison conditions and the fairness of trials in his home country. His defense mirrored that of other fugitives, leveraging international legal frameworks to delay proceedings and exploit the slow gears of global justice. In 2021, UK courts approved Modi's extradition. However, he remains in a British jail, using appeals and legal strategies to avoid Indian authorities.

The fallout from the PNB fraud exposed deep vulnerabilities in India's financial regulatory apparatus. How could a scam of such magnitude persist for years without detection? Critics pointed to systemic issues, including inadequate auditing practices, over-reliance on manual processes, and the complicity of bank insiders. The episode highlighted the urgent need for reforms in India's banking sector, particularly in state-owned institutions where political influence often overrides merit-based decision-making.

The case also intensified scrutiny on how India handles financial fugitives. Modi's flight and subsequent resistance to extradition underscored the challenges of bringing elite offenders to justice in a globalized world. India, like many nations, lacks comprehensive mechanisms to prevent economic offenders from escaping its jurisdiction. India passed the Fugitive Economic Offenders Act in 2018. It allows authorities to seize assets from individuals who refuse to return and face trial. However, its implementation remains nascent, and its effectiveness against wealthy, internationally connected offenders like Modi is yet to be tested fully.

Public reaction to the Nirav Modi case was one of outrage and disillusionment. For ordinary Indians, the elite appeared to exploit systemic gaps with impunity. Society bore the consequences, including bank losses, economic instability, and reduced trust. Farmers and small-business owners struggling to secure modest loans from the same banking system saw Modi's billions as emblematic of the inequities entrenched in the system.

The Nirav Modi scandal is not merely a tale of one man's greed but reveals how the powerful manipulate financial ecosystems. The case revealed fragile checks and balances meant to protect public resources. It underscored the need for transparency and accountability in key institutions. Modi's story underscores a critical challenge. Justice must be blind and equitable, holding elites to the same standards as ordinary citizens.

3. JUSTICE ON DEMAND: VVIP EDITION

The deliberate underfunding and inefficiency of judicial systems are not merely byproducts of bureaucratic inertia but often a feature of elite design. The judiciary, a democratic pillar, should counterbalance power. It allows citizens to challenge oppression, corruption, and inequality. Yet, for elites, a robust and impartial judiciary represents a threat. A judicial system that is swift, transparent, and accessible could hold them accountable for financial malfeasance, abuse of power, or even systemic discrimination. Elites benefit from maintaining a slow, under-resourced judiciary. This ensures justice stays an abstract promise, not a practical reality.

Historically, elites have understood the strategic advantage of a faltering judiciary. Feudal lords monopolized justice systems in medieval Europe, ensuring that courts served their interests, not the serfs'. A peasant seeking redress for a lord's exploitation faced a huge amount of fees, procedural delays, and outright bias. Feudal lords designed these systems not to deliver justice but to entrench hierarchy. Even after the Enlightenment and the rise of constitutional democracies, remnants of this approach persisted. Access to justice became contingent on wealth, with protracted legal battles requiring resources that only the privileged could afford. The same tactics—delays, opaque procedures, and prohibitive costs—now persist in modern democracies, cloaked in the language of legal formalism and administrative backlog.

A slow judiciary is an elite's ally because delay is its own form of denial. In countries like India, for instance, cases can drag on for decades, with some litigants never seeing a resolution within their lifetime. The infamous Babri Masjid land dispute, which spanned more than 70 years, exemplifies how judicial inertia can sap public faith. For ordinary citizens, the complicated process of filing complaints, gathering evidence, and enduring adjournments becomes a deterrent to even approaching the courts. Meanwhile, elites use their vast resources to hire top-tier legal teams, exploit procedural loopholes, and prolong cases until the opposition is financially and emotionally exhausted.

Systemic underinvestment perpetuates this deliberate dysfunction. Governments, often under elite influence, prioritize spending on visible, vote-winning projects over intangible judicial reforms. Building highways or airports may fetch electoral dividends, but upgrading court infrastructure, hiring judges, and digitizing case management systems rarely make for compelling campaign slogans. In India, for instance, the judiciary receives less than 1% of the annual budget, a staggering under-allocation given its caseload. The result is a shortage of judges, overburdened courts, and archaic systems reliant on paper files and manual tracking. In the U.S., better-funded courts still face delays. Elites use financial power to outlast plaintiffs, negotiating settlements that avoid accountability.

The backlog of cases is both symptom and strategy. As of 2023, India had over 40 million pending cases, with some disputes lingering for decades. Family inheritance battles, land disputes, and corporate fraud cases routinely languish, benefiting those who can afford to wait or manipulate delays. The slowness also discourages whistleblowers and victims of systemic injustice from pursuing litigation, as the prospect of years of legal wrangling looms over their quest for justice. Meanwhile, elites enjoy the advantage of inertia, knowing that even if they are eventually found guilty, the punishment may come too late to be meaningful or enforceable.

Technology could revolutionize this system, yet its adoption has been suspiciously slow. Digitizing case records, automating scheduling, and integrating AI to expedite routine processes would dramatically reduce delays and improve transparency. But such reforms threaten the elite playbook. A technologically advanced judiciary would limit their ability to manipulate the system, making it harder to delay proceedings or suppress evidence. Unsurprisingly, reforms remain piecemeal and underfunded, with ambitious projects like e-courts moving at a glacial pace. Elite influence ensures that technological advancements, which could democratize access to justice, remain stifled under the guise of budgetary constraints or bureaucratic feasibility.

The implications of a failed judiciary extend beyond individual cases; they corrode the very fabric of society. When citizens lose faith in the courts, they turn to alternative forms of dispute resolution, often informal and inequitable. In rural India, for example, khap panchayats—traditional village councils—have filled the judicial vacuum, often delivering rulings steeped in patriarchy and caste bias. In urban areas, vigilante justice and public lynchings arise when communities perceive the courts as unwilling or unable to act. These breakdowns in the rule of law serve elites well, as they reinforce social hierarchies and maintain a fragmented populace incapable of challenging systemic injustices.

In maintaining a dysfunctional judiciary, elites ensure that social inequality remains entrenched. The inability of ordinary citizens to challenge exploitative labor practices, environmental degradation, or fraudulent financial schemes perpetuates cycles of poverty and marginalization. When courts are slow or expensive, impunity thrives. Landlords evade rent laws, corporations pollute, and politicians siphon public funds. The same system operates swiftly when elites need to protect their interests, such as securing intellectual property rights or suppressing dissent through defamation suits.

The judiciary's failures are not accidents but deliberate constructs, shaped by those who benefit from a justice system that is both inaccessible and ineffectual. By ensuring that courts remain slow, underfunded, and technologically backward, elites maintain their grip on power while the promise of justice remains a mirage for the masses. This dynamic reveals a broader truth. Inequality is not accidental, but a maintained feature serving top-tier interests.

3.1 JUSTICE ON A BUDGET

The judiciary, a symbol of fairness, faces systemic challenges. It is often called the last bastion of justice but remains elusive for many. Its inefficiencies and inequities are not random flaws but integral components of a complex system, shaped by societal priorities and the dynamics of power. Underfunding shapes a judicial system that struggles to serve the people it aims to protect. Across the world, courts operate in dilapidated buildings, with basic facilities either absent or inadequate. In India, overcrowded courtrooms lack technological resources to handle the daily mountain of paperwork. The sight of clerks manually sifting through stacks of files is emblematic of a system trapped in a bygone era, overwhelmed by modern demands. Neglected infrastructure reveals a disturbing truth. Justice, essential to democracy, is often a secondary concern in national budgets.

This chronic underfunding leads directly to the judiciary's most visible ailment—case backlogs. With millions of cases pending globally, the judiciary risks becoming a caricature of itself, where swift justice is the exception rather than the rule. In India alone, as of 2023, there were over 4.7 crore (47 million) cases awaiting resolution, ranging from petty disputes to high-stakes corporate battles. These numbers aren't just statistics; they represent years, sometimes decades, of lives caught in legal limbo. For a farmer fighting a land dispute or a worker challenging wrongful dismissal, such delays translate into sustained hardship, financial ruin, and emotional exhaustion. These backlogs perpetuate the adage that "justice delayed is justice denied," with the system's sluggishness disproportionately affecting those without the means to sustain prolonged legal battles.

One of the most glaring contributors to these delays is the woefully low judge-to-population ratio in many countries. In India, there are merely 21 judges per million people, a figure that pales in comparison to international recommendations. Such numbers result in judges presiding over hundreds of cases simultaneously, diminishing their ability to give each case the attention it deserves. The sheer volume of cases forces courts to prioritize urgent matters, pushing less sensational or politically inconsequential cases into a seemingly endless queue. Judiciary strain grows because of insufficient support staff and resources. Even diligent judges struggle to maintain efficiency.

Outdated processes exacerbate these issues, with many judicial systems still relying heavily on physical paperwork and manual operations. While the rest of the world embraces digitization, the judiciary lags behind, bound by traditions that hinder progress. In courts across developing nations, case files remain prone to misplacement, tampering, or outright loss—a vulnerability that often serves the interests of those seeking to manipulate outcomes. Digitization, though increasingly recognized as essential, has seen piecemeal implementation at best. Automation and case-tracking technologies, which could revolutionize court efficiency, remain underutilized, stalled by bureaucratic inertia and a lack of political will.

Access to justice is another critical fault line, particularly for marginalized communities. The geographic concentration of courts in urban centers creates a stark urban-rural divide. For individuals in remote areas, reaching a courthouse often involves significant travel, expense, and time—barriers that deter many from seeking redress altogether. Even for those who manage to approach the courts, high legal fees act as another gatekeeper, ensuring that only the well-resourced can afford sustained litigation. A system promising equality often falls short. The judiciary serves those who afford it over those needing it most.

Political and bureaucratic interference frequently compromise the judiciary's independence, a cornerstone of its credibility. In many democracies, delays in judicial appointments—whether deliberate or because of inefficiency—create power vacuums that weaken the judiciary's ability to function effectively. The process of selecting judges often becomes a battleground for political maneuvering, with governments seeking to install individuals who align with their ideologies. Powerful individuals or entities influence prosecutorial decisions, quietly derailing or stalling cases. Eroding judicial autonomy undermines public trust and breeds cynicism about whether justice can prevail against political power.

Perhaps the most insidious challenge facing the judiciary is its susceptibility to elite manipulation. Wealthy and influential individuals have the resources to hire the best legal minds, exploit procedural loopholes, and prolong cases indefinitely. For elites, delay is a strategy, not a setback. Corporations accused of environmental violations delay proceedings for years. Politically connected individuals push hearings into oblivion, making guilty verdicts irrelevant. Litigation's financial and emotional toll wears down less-resourced opponents, often the victims. Circumstances force them to settle or abandon claims altogether.

Underfunding, inefficiency, and systemic bias benefit the well-resourced. Ordinary citizens, however, remain mired in complexities. The judiciary, rather than being a leveling force, becomes yet another arena where power and privilege dictate outcomes. Failing to modernize judicial processes, expand infrastructure, and insulate courts from external pressures ensures that justice remains an aspiration for many rather than a reality. Delays and inequality erode democracy's foundation—accountability, fairness, and the rule of law. The system upholds the status quo instead of challenging it.

3.2 LOBBYISTS RULE THE BENCH

Elites have historically shaped institutions to serve their interests. They ensure accountability mechanisms stay underfunded, outdated, or pliable. The judiciary, ostensibly the guardian of fairness and impartiality, has not been immune to these manipulations. One of the most direct ways elites influence judicial inefficiency is by lobbying governments to deprioritize funding for judicial infrastructure. Cloaked in arguments of fiscal prudence, elites pressure policymakers to allocate resources elsewhere, claiming that investments in education, healthcare, or defense are more urgent. On the surface, these arguments seem reasonable. However, they often aim to maintain an overburdened judicial system incapable of challenging entrenched power. The judiciary remains perpetually starved of resources. Ordinary citizens face delays, while elites exploit the system's cracks.

This resistance extends beyond mere funding to active opposition against modernization initiatives. Technological upgrades, such as digitized case management systems, automated tracking, and virtual hearings, hold the potential to revolutionize judicial efficiency. However, for elites accustomed to exploiting the inefficiencies of paper trails and opaque processes, such advancements represent a threat. Digitization would leave a clearer record, making it harder to manipulate evidence, delay proceedings, or lose critical documents. Transparency initiatives, such as live-streaming court proceedings or creating public databases of judgments, further compound this risk by subjecting judicial processes to unprecedented levels of scrutiny. Elites often use their influence to stall or sabotage such efforts, framing them as costly, unnecessary, or even dangerous to the sanctity of legal traditions. Their aim is clear: to preserve a system that offers them avenues for evasion while ordinary citizens grapple with its inefficiencies.

The influence of elites is perhaps most insidious in the selective manipulation of judicial appointments and case assignments. Behind closed doors, decision-makers appoint judges known for corporate leniency or political alignment to key positions.

Such influence is subtle yet potent, ensuring that rulings align with elite interests with no apparent intervention. For example, in high-stakes corporate disputes or regulatory cases, elites maneuver to have matters heard by judges whose track records suggest favorable outcomes. This is not a phenomenon unique to one country or era but a recurring theme across legal systems worldwide. Judicial appointments subtly reshape the system, creating a judiciary that appears impartial but perpetuates systemic inequality.

Historical cases illustrate how such strategies play out in practice. Whistleblowers exposing fraud often see cases delayed or dismissed because of technicalities. Judges with elite ties frequently oversee these cases. In political corruption cases, key hearings face indefinite delays. Witnesses turn hostile, and evidence is "misplaced," revealing elite influence. High-profile individuals accused of financial crimes often transfer trials to lenient courts. Prolonged deliberations neutralize accountability threats.

These tactics are not just about protecting individual elites but about safeguarding a broader ecosystem of privilege. A sluggish, underfunded, and manipulable judiciary protects mechanisms that accumulate and retain wealth and power, ensuring systemic inequality remains unchallenged. This creates a chilling effect on justice seekers. Marginalized communities and whistleblowers see the judiciary as a web, not a shield. Meanwhile, judges' work hard to maintain the appearance of legal fairness. They make it look like justice is balanced, even though the system remains tilted in favor of elite interests.

Elites actively oppose changes, block modernization, and manipulate judicial processes to keep things as they are. Reforming justice systems is a tough challenge because it must fight against inefficiency and the powerful forces protecting privilege. The judiciary often serves the interests of those who have the most to lose from change. This highlights that the fight for justice is not just about fixing the system—it's both a political and moral struggle.

3.3 RIGGING THE SCALES

The consequences of a dysfunctional judiciary ripple across society, entrenching inequalities, stifling economic growth, and corroding the very foundations of the rule of law. When the scales of justice tilt in favor of the wealthy and powerful, it is not just the marginalized who suffer; the fabric of society itself begins to fray. Elites, with their access to influential lawyers and extensive networks, can navigate legal hurdles with ease. Expensive legal teams, adept at exploiting procedural loopholes, often ensure favorable outcomes for those who can afford them. Meanwhile, ordinary citizens and marginalized communities, often lacking the resources or connections to fight protracted legal battles, find themselves at the mercy of an unyielding system. This disparity perpetuates cycles of poverty, as land rights disputes, labor claims, or instances of discrimination languish unresolved, leaving vulnerable populations without recourse or redress.

Yet the most insidious impact of a broken judiciary lies in the erosion of the rule of law. As delays and inefficiencies mount, citizens begin to lose faith in the system's ability to deliver justice. This loss of trust has far-reaching consequences, fostering a culture where people seek extra-legal means to resolve disputes. Corruption, already a byproduct of bureaucratic inefficiency, normalizes as officials exchange bribes to expedite cases or sway judgments. In extreme cases, vigilante justice emerges. Communities take the law into their own hands, believing the judiciary cannot address their grievances. The rise of vigilante justice signals governance failure. It reflects a social contract breakdown, with institutions driving individuals to bypass them.

Historical examples reveal how these dynamics can lead to long-term instability. Brazil faces a backlog of over 100 million cases. Wealthy corporations manipulate the system, delaying compliance and exhausting opponents. This practice not only weakens trust in the courts but emboldens the powerful to act with impunity. In Mexico, judicial inefficiency and corruption fuel cartel violence. Communities hire militias or endure organized crime's arbitrary rule. These examples underscore the universal consequences of judicial dysfunction: it not only entrenches inequality and stifles development but also erodes the legitimacy of the state itself.

The growing divide between those who can access justice and those who cannot is a moral crisis, not just an administrative failure. A society where law favors the wealthy and connected becomes a plutocracy, not a democracy, regardless of its constitution. Restoring trust in the judiciary means more than clearing backlogs; it requires reaffirming that justice is a right, not a privilege. Without this reform, judicial dysfunction will deepen inequality, harm economies, and weaken the fragile fabric of social cohesion.

Justice is humanity's oldest promise, the assurance that fairness will prevail. Yet in a world where power corrupts and truth is malleable, justice becomes another casualty of dysfunction. Biased courts and corrupted systems overshadow the promise of fairness with the reality of privilege.

But these injustices spread beyond courtrooms. They ripple outward into the geopolitical landscape, explored in Chapter 11: *Nationalism*. When nations exploit rather than uplift, the dysfunction of justice becomes the dysfunction of borders, creating a world where inequality knows no boundaries.

Part IV

Global Dysfunctions

"Divided by Lines, United by Greed, Ready to get Destroyed"

Nationalism sells pride while the globe burns.
This section reveals the contradictions of globalization, the destruction of our planet, and the wars waged to profit the powerful. It's a brutal reminder that our tribal instincts are rewriting the future—a future where survival might depend on whether we grow or annihilate.

11

Nationalism

The quest for natural resources has long been a driving force behind human conflict and global injustice, laying the foundation for systems of exploitation that transcend borders. From the early colonial conquests to modern multinational corporations, elites have sought to control the earth's wealth—its oil, minerals, forests, and fertile lands—through force, coercion, and manipulation. This relentless pursuit of resources often leaves devastation in its wake, erasing traditional ways of life, destabilizing regions, and creating cycles of poverty and dependency. Yet the victims of these systems frequently find no avenue for justice. Courts, governments, and international bodies are meant to mediate disputes and uphold fairness. However, these institutions are often complicit. They are either unable or unwilling to challenge the power of the elites they serve. This systemic failure of justice intensifies inequalities born of resource extraction and exploitation. It sets the stage for globalization. This process becomes a tool for consolidating elite control on a planetary scale.

Consider the colonial resource grabs of the 19th and early 20th centuries, which exemplify this dynamic on a brutal scale. The Congo Free State, under King Leopold II of Belgium, was nominally a humanitarian project but, in reality, a massive plundering operation. Millions of Congolese endured backbreaking labor to extract rubber. The consequences were horrific. Hands were severed as punishment for failing quotas. Colonial forces burned entire villages. An estimated 10 million people died. This stands as one of history's worst atrocities. Yet justice for these crimes was nonexistent. The global powers that might have intervened were themselves complicit in similar exploitative systems, and the international legal frameworks to hold elites accountable simply did not exist. Unchecked resource exploitation echoes into the modern era. Corporations, not monarchs, now wield the power. The violence is subtler but no less destructive.

As globalization intensified in the late 20th century, it brought with it promises of interconnected prosperity and universal progress. However, beneath this optimistic narrative lay a deeper reality: globalization became a tool for elites to extend their control over resources beyond national borders. Multinational corporations, backed by powerful governments and international financial institutions, entered developing nations under the guise of development and investment. The result was often resource extraction on terms that overwhelmingly favored the elites. In Nigeria, for instance, oil companies like Shell and Chevron extracted vast wealth while local communities bore the brunt of environmental destruction. The Niger Delta, once a fertile region, became synonymous with pollution, poverty, and violence. Authorities systematically stymied efforts to seek justice, whether through domestic courts or international mechanisms. Activists like Ken Saro-Wiwa, who led protests against oil exploitation, were silenced—sometimes brutally—as elites protected their interests at all costs.

The failure of justice in these contexts goes beyond legal or institutional shortcomings; it strikes at the heart of what it means to be human. Justice systems, in their ideal form, evolved as mechanisms to ensure fairness and resolve conflicts, fostering trust and cohesion within societies. The social fabric unravels when these systems fail—when they become tools of the powerful rather than safeguards for the powerless. Ingroup-outgroup boundaries harden as people retreat into identities that feel secure amidst chaos. Nationalism emerges as both a shield and a weapon, rallying individuals around a shared identity while creating scapegoats for systemic failures. In resource exploitation, these dynamics are glaring. Elites manipulate nationalist rhetoric to suppress dissent. They frame their actions as defenses of national sovereignty. They sell their countries' wealth to global interests.

This interplay between resource exploitation, justice, and nationalism reveals a paradox at the heart of globalization. Globalization relies on the seamless movement of capital, goods, and resources across borders. Yet, it deepens inequalities. It fractures societies. These fractures fuel nationalist movements that seek to resist globalization. Yet nationalism, in its exclusionary form, rarely provides a solution. Instead, it becomes another tool for elites to consolidate power, diverting attention from the structural issues at the root of injustice. This cycle—global exploitation fueling inequality, leading to nationalist backlash, which elites then manipulate to maintain dominance—defines much of the modern world.

The failure of justice in this context is not just an institutional collapse; it is a betrayal of the evolutionary trait of fairness that underpins human societies. For millennia, fairness has been a cornerstone of social cohesion, guiding communities toward collective survival. Elites undermine this principle, eroding trust and fostering division when they exploit globalization to hoard wealth and power while shielding themselves from accountability. Humanity faces a dual challenge. First, we must address these failures. Second, we need to reimagine systems of justice. These systems must transcend national borders and offer true accountability in an interconnected world. This is the dual-edged sword of globalization and nationalism: while one binds humanity together in a shared destiny, the other tears it apart through exclusion and division. Balancing these forces remains a major challenge. Reconciling our ancient instincts with the demands of a unified future is one of the great questions of our time.

The interplay between globalization and nationalism reveals a profound irony. Globalization promises collective progress. Yet, it often becomes a tool for elites. They manipulate national systems for their own benefit. Nationalism, rather than countering this exploitation, frequently serves as a distraction, channeling public anger toward cultural or external scapegoats instead of addressing the root causes of inequality. This dynamic allows multinational corporations to thrive unchecked, exploiting the very borders they claim to transcend while using national governments as enforcers of their agendas. The result is stark. Global profits flow upward. Policies leave nations and their people grappling with the fallout. Policymakers design these policies to benefit the few.

1. GLOBAL PROFITS, NATIONAL PUPPETS

The mechanisms through which globalization consolidates elite power are intricate and deliberate, often masked behind promises of economic progress, technological innovation, and environmental responsibility. The global trade system lies at the heart of this exploitation. This framework claims to foster prosperity. Yet, it disproportionately serves multinational corporations and the elites who control them. The World Trade Organization (WTO), established in the 1990s, exemplifies this imbalance. Through policies of trade liberalization, the WTO dismantled barriers to global commerce, allowing corporations to operate with unprecedented freedom across borders. On paper, these reforms promised growth for all; in practice, they decimated small businesses in developing nations. Farmers in sub-Saharan Africa, for instance, found themselves competing with heavily subsidized agricultural imports from the United States and Europe, driving many into poverty. Meanwhile, the corporations that lobbied for these policies reaped enormous profits, free from the constraints of tariffs or local regulations. The garment industry in Bangladesh further illustrates this dynamic. Multinational brands outsourced production to exploit cheap labor markets, paying workers a fraction of a living wage while selling their products at massive markups. The 2013 Rana Plaza disaster, in which over 1,100 workers died because of unsafe factory conditions, revealed the human cost of this relentless pursuit of profit. Such tragedies are not anomalies but symptoms of a system designed to prioritize corporate wealth over human lives.

Beyond trade, globalization's mechanisms of exploitation extend into the digital realm, where monopolistic entities increasingly control technological sovereignty. The Facebook-Cambridge Analytica scandal is a telling example of how elites manipulate global tech platforms for their gain. These platforms operate under the guise of connectivity and innovation. They harvest vast amounts of personal data. Governments and corporations weaponized this data to influence elections, sow division, and consolidate political power. The 2016 United States presidential election and the Brexit referendum exposed the power of such manipulation. Targeted misinformation campaigns exploited societal fractures. These campaigns served specific elite agendas. This control over information flows is not limited to elections. Governments and corporations increasingly stifle dissent through algorithmic censorship and surveillance, colluding to maintain their grip on power. In China, surveillance technology integrates with social credit systems. This creates an extreme example. Subtler versions of this control exist worldwide. Silicon Valley dominates digital discourse. Authoritarian regimes use spyware from private firms to suppress opposition.

Even in the realm of climate action—where cooperation and altruism should take precedence—the mechanisms of globalization reveal a darker side. Industrial emissions in developing countries are a stark example of environmental exploitation. Multinational corporations, seeking to evade stringent regulations in developed nations, relocate polluting industries to weaker economies, where lax enforcement ensures minimal accountability. The result is global environmental damage outsourced to vulnerable regions. Textile factories poison rivers in Southeast Asia with dye. Companies raze forests in Indonesia to create palm oil plantations. Skies over Indian cities choke with smog. Meanwhile, elites in developed nations promote greenwashing initiatives to appear progressive. Carbon credit trading, for instance, allows corporations to continue polluting under the guise of offsetting emissions, often by investing in projects that yield questionable environmental benefits. These schemes fail to address the systemic causes of climate change. Instead, they act as public relations tools. They protect the reputations and profits of those responsible for the crisis.

Global institutions, often presented as arbiters of fairness and development, further entrench these dynamics of exploitation. The International Monetary Fund (IMF) and the World Bank were established to stabilize the global economy. Over time, they have become instruments of domination. Wealthy nations and their elites now wield them as tools of control. Through conditional loans, these institutions impose austerity measures on developing countries, forcing governments to cut public spending, privatize essential services, and open their markets to foreign investors. In the 1990s, structural adjustment programs targeted Latin America and Africa. These programs wreaked havoc on social infrastructures. They caused widespread unemployment. Access to healthcare declined. Education standards plummeted. The beneficiaries were foreign corporations that gained access to lucrative markets and resources, as well as local elites who profited by privatizing state assets. For the majority, however, these policies deepened inequality and perpetuated cycles of poverty.

Economic, technological, environmental, and institutional mechanisms function as interconnected facets of a global system that favors a select few. These dynamics reveal a pattern. Globalization is far from neutral or inherently benevolent. It is a tool used by elites. They expand their influence and insulate themselves from accountability. By exploiting the very systems that promise progress, they perpetuate inequalities on a staggering scale, leaving billions to bear the costs of their ambition. This dynamic is not accidental. It is a deliberate strategy. It shapes the contours of modern society. Meanwhile, it hides its true nature behind layers of complexity and rhetoric. The challenge lies in uncovering these truths and reimagining globalization as a force that serves humanity rather than a privileged few.

The global elites, cornered by rising public discontent, found themselves at a crossroads: address systemic failures or deflect the blame. Nationalism emerged as the perfect diversion. It offered a simple, emotionally charged narrative, one that redirected frustration away from power structures and toward convenient scapegoats. This wasn't a solution; it was an escape plan—an ideological smokescreen that obscured accountability while fueling division.

1.1 NATIONALISM: THE ULTIMATE ESCAPE PLAN

Nationalism has long been a potent tool for elites to divert public attention away from systemic inequalities and structural failures. Elites stoke cultural and identity conflicts. They create a convenient "us vs. them" framework. This framework redirects diffuse public anger. It channels hostility against marginalized groups or foreign influences. This tactic was glaringly evident in the aftermath of the 2008 financial crisis, a moment of profound economic disillusionment. The crisis, caused by unchecked greed and reckless practices within elite financial institutions, devastated economies worldwide. Millions lost jobs, homes, and savings, yet the architects of the collapse largely escaped accountability. Political and media elites avoided addressing structural flaws in global capitalism. Instead, they redirected public anger. Immigrants and the forces of globalization became their scapegoats. Anti-immigration rhetoric surged. Populist leaders framed migrants as job stealers and cultural threats. Meanwhile, they ignored systemic deregulation and corporate malfeasance. These were the real roots of the crisis. This polarization deflected scrutiny from the elites. It reinforced their positions of power. Voters became consumed by identity-based conflicts. Systemic change was no longer their focus.

The exploitation of nationalism extends beyond cultural polarization; it also manifests in economic policies that protect elite interests under the guise of patriotic duty. Protectionism, often framed as a defense of national sovereignty, is a recurring theme in this strategy. In Russia, Vladimir Putin's government has masterfully deployed nationalism to consolidate economic power among a select group of oligarchs. By promoting policies that emphasize national strength—such as reclaiming Crimea and challenging Western hegemony—Putin has fostered a sense of Russian exceptionalism. This intense nationalism distracts from the vast economic inequalities within Russia and allows the oligarchs who back his regime to amass wealth without scrutiny. Paradoxically, while these elites publicly champion the nationalist cause, they also benefit from the very globalization they denounce. Russian billionaires invest heavily in global luxury markets. They buy London real estate and deposit in Swiss banks. This ensures their wealth remains insulated. Meanwhile, they exploit nationalist narratives to maintain domestic power.

The media plays a crucial role in amplifying these nationalist agendas, often acting to extend elite interests. Media moguls, like Rupert Murdoch, have demonstrated how controlling public discourse can shape nationalist movements to serve elite goals. Murdoch's empire, spanning newspapers and television networks, was instrumental in promoting the Brexit campaign in the UK. His outlets churned out headlines vilifying the European Union, portraying it as a faceless bureaucracy undermining British sovereignty. This relentless barrage of nationalist propaganda polarized the public, framing the debate as a battle for independence rather than a nuanced discussion about economic and political integration. Murdoch's support for Brexit did not stem from ideological conviction. It arose from strategic interest. EU regulations posed challenges to his media operations. Brexit provided a way to remove those barriers. By aligning his corporate objectives with nationalist rhetoric, Murdoch exemplified how elites manipulate media to advance their agendas while sowing division among the public.

Nationalism's power to shape collective identity also lies in its ability to weaponize historical narratives, creating myths that serve elite interests. India's "Make in India" campaign is a striking example. The government launched the campaign in 2014 to ostensibly foster national pride and self-reliance by promoting domestic manufacturing. It drew heavily on India's colonial history, invoking memories of economic exploitation under British rule to rally support for policies that emphasized independence from foreign domination. However, beneath the surface of this nationalist rhetoric lay a different reality. The campaign actively courted foreign direct investment (FDI) and partnerships with multinational corporations, enabling elites to profit from globalization even as they preached self-sufficiency to the masses. Industrial magnates and political leaders used the campaign to attract foreign capital. They secured lucrative contracts and expanded their influence. They presented themselves as champions of Indian nationalism.

This duality—publicly embracing nationalism while privately benefiting from globalization—reveals the calculated cynicism of elite strategies. By manipulating national identity and historical grievances, elites deflect attention from systemic inequalities and obscure the true beneficiaries of their policies. Nationalism, for all its emotional power, often serves as a mask, concealing the intricate web of global interests that sustain elite dominance. Nationalism employs polarization, propaganda, and the strategic use of history. It becomes a tool of division, not unity. This tool helps maintain the structures it claims to challenge. The interplay between nationalism and globalization is less about conflict and more about collaboration. This carefully orchestrated balance ensures that power remains in the hands of the few.

Nationalism and globalization may seem like opposites, but their power lies in the same source: the human ability to believe in shared myths. Societies construct nations, like markets, as ideas that derive their strength from collective faith. This faith doesn't require truth—it only requires people to act as if the myth is real. Nations, imagined yet fiercely defended, are among humanity's most enduring fictions, reshaping history and human behavior with astonishing force.

1.2 NATIONS: IMAGINED, YET POWERFUL

The concept of a nation, one of the most potent ideas to shape modern humanity, is at once foundational and utterly fabricated. It tells a story so pervasive that it has become invisible, an assumed truth about the world rather than a constructed framework. The nation asserts that land, people, culture, and governance are inextricably bound, that the people of a nation share an unbroken heritage and identity. Yet this idea, which defines who we are and where we belong, is astonishingly recent. For most of human history, people did not live or die for abstract notions like nations; their loyalties lay with families, villages, or religious communities. Nations are inventions—artful, compelling, and deeply consequential—that emerged from specific historical processes to solve specific problems. They are not timeless. They are stories we have collectively chosen to believe, often at great cost.

Take France as an example. The modern idea of France as a nation-state with a shared language, culture, and identity would have been unrecognizable to someone living in the 13th century. The Kingdom of France was a patchwork of feudal territories. Allegiance to a distant king united them. This king collected taxes and waged wars. The vast majority of the population did not consider themselves "French" in any meaningful way. Local dialects, customs, and allegiances rooted their identities. Even language—a cornerstone of modern national identity—fragmented into regional variations. As late as the early 19th century, less than half of France's population spoke what we now call French, and even fewer could read it. Elites deliberately unified language, culture, and governance into a cohesive national identity to consolidate power. Napoleon Bonaparte accelerated this transformation, rallying disparate communities around a shared sense of "Frenchness" through symbols, songs, and wars fought in the name of the nation. He sidelined religion, formerly the great unifying force of European identity, and replaced it with the nation-state as the primary source of loyalty and pride. This shift was profound, but incomplete. France achieved true national unity only in the late 19th or early 20th century. It required mass education, railroads, and centralized government administration to emerge.

The story of nation-building repeats itself across the globe, following similar patterns of invention and consolidation. Italy, according to one of its unification leaders, existed only on maps. After political unification in 1861, the deliberate creation of "Italians" became necessary. Fewer than 3% of its population spoke Italian, and regional identities far outweighed any sense of national belonging. This process took decades and was largely driven by public schooling, national media, and industrialization, which gradually erased regional distinctions in favor of a cohesive Italian identity. Even by the mid-20th century, the task was incomplete; it wasn't until the 1960s, with the spread of national television, that a shared Italian identity became broadly internalized.

Yet nations are not simply benign inventions. Their success as ideas often hinges on their ability to exclude. Nations rose in 19th-century Europe alongside ethnic nationalism. Nationalists believed shared ethnicity, language, and culture should define a nation. This belief contributed to the redrawing of borders after the Napoleonic Wars and again after World War I, as empires fragmented into nation-states. But these borders were rarely neat. Ethnic groups spilled across boundaries, leading to conflicts over who belonged where. The unfulfilled promises of ethnic nationalism fueled grievances and ambitions that would later explode into World War II. The 20th century saw the dark side of nationalism reach its peak. Regimes carried out genocides and ethnic cleansings to preserve or purify national identity. The Holocaust exemplifies this horrific logic, where regimes murdered millions deemed outside the bounds of a constructed national story.

Even outside Europe, the idea of the nation spread with transformative and often violent consequences. Colonial powers carved up Asia, Africa, and the Middle East into artificial nations. They drew borders with little regard for ethnic, linguistic, or cultural realities. In places like India, Kenya, and Vietnam, nationalism became a powerful force for resistance against colonial rule. Anti-colonial leaders appropriated the language of nationhood, rallying their people around the promise of independence and self-determination. Once freed from colonial rule, these nations faced similar dilemmas to those of Europe. They struggled to reconcile the many with the one. Forging a cohesive identity out of diversity often risked exclusion or oppression.

Today, the nation remains both a source of stability and a driver of conflict. It provides a framework for governance, identity, and belonging, yet it also perpetuates divisions and inequities. The nation's claim to permanence and inevitability belies its constructed nature, but that very myth is what gives it power. The borders we fight over, the flags we wave, and the anthems we sing form a powerful narrative. This narrative can unite or divide. It can inspire or oppress. As we face global challenges like climate change, pandemics, and economic inequality, the limitations of the nation-state become increasingly apparent. These problems do not respect borders, yet our solutions remain constrained by them. If we recognize the nation as a flexible human invention, new possibilities emerge. We can imagine ways to organize ourselves beyond the nation-state. These systems could be inclusive, adaptive, and suited to the challenges of globalization.

The promises of globalization—prosperity, innovation, and interconnectedness—have often come at a steep price for those excluded from its rewards. While wealth and opportunity flow seamlessly across borders for a privileged few, vulnerable communities disproportionately bear the localized costs. This imbalance is a deliberate feature, not a flaw. Global gains remain concentrated. Policymakers overlook or dismiss local losses as inevitable collateral damage.

1.3 GLOBAL GAINS, LOCAL LOSSES

Social inequality is not just a byproduct of globalization. It is, in many ways, its intended outcome. Systems concentrate wealth and power among the elite. Economic changes force the majority to bear the burdens. This pattern is most evident in the widening income gap that has become a defining feature of the modern globalized economy. The post-1990s neoliberal era marked a dramatic acceleration of this trend. Deregulation, free trade, and open market policies unleashed a tidal wave of capital across borders. However, the spoils of this wealth were far from evenly distributed. Billionaires emerged as the primary beneficiaries of this global transformation. Figures like Jeff Bezos, who amassed extraordinary wealth through global supply chains and labor practices, exemplify this dynamic. Amazon thrived on low-cost production in developing nations. It also used tax avoidance schemes in developed nations. Meanwhile, warehouse workers and gig economy employees faced precarious conditions, stagnant wages, and little job security. This growing disparity was no accident. It was the outcome of a system rigged to funnel wealth upward. Globalization became a vehicle for elite enrichment. This came at the expense of the working and middle classes.

Privatization has been another tool in the arsenal of elites, often justified as a necessary step for economic modernization. Under the banner of globalization, governments have sold state-owned resources to corporations frequently controlled by a small cadre of well-connected elites. Privatizing Chile's copper industry during Augusto Pinochet's dictatorship is a stark example of this phenomenon. Copper, which accounted for the majority of Chile's export revenues, was a cornerstone of the national economy. Under Pinochet's rule, neoliberal reforms took hold. The "Chicago Boys," a group of United States trained economists, advised these reforms. They transferred assets into private hands, often at prices well below true value. The beneficiaries were not the Chilean people. A select group of domestic and foreign corporations profited immensely. Corporations left local communities to contend with environmental degradation and diminished public revenues. The wealth generated from these resources flowed upward, entrenching inequality and weakening the state's ability to provide for its citizens. The rhetoric of efficiency and global competitiveness masked the reality: privatization served as a mechanism for consolidating elite control over national wealth.

Education, often lauded as the great equalizer, now entrenches inequality. The global education system, particularly its elite institutions, functions less as a ladder for upward mobility and more as a gatekeeping mechanism for maintaining elite dominance. Universities like Harvard, Oxford, and Cambridge operate as both symbols of meritocracy and bastions of exclusivity. They present themselves as open to all through scholarships and diversity initiatives. However, their admissions processes favor legacy applicants, donors' children, and those with access to expensive preparatory education. These institutions not only confer prestige but also form elite networks, where personal connections matter as much as academic achievement. Consider the disproportionate representation of Ivy League graduates in positions of global influence, from corporate boardrooms to political leadership. This system ensures that power and opportunity remain concentrated within a closed circle, perpetuating inequality across generations. The global reach of these institutions further amplifies their role in solidifying elite dominance. Wealthy families from around the world send their children to these universities. This ensures the benefits of globalization stay concentrated among a transnational elite. Policymakers fail to distribute these benefits more broadly.

Together, these dynamics of income disparity, resource privatization, and educational exclusivity reveal a world meticulously structured to maintain and expand elite privilege. The systems underpinning globalization are not neutral. These systems favor those already at the top while appearing to offer opportunity and progress. Social inequality, far from being an unfortunate side effect, is the strategic outcome of policies and practices that prioritize profit and power over equity and fairness. Understanding these mechanisms is the first step. It allows us to challenge the narratives that sustain them. We can then imagine alternatives that distribute globalization's benefits more equitably. Societies could share progress among all, rather than reserving it for the few.

Nationalism's allure lies in its simplicity—it transforms complex systemic failures into digestible narratives of cultural pride and external threats. As a political tool, it channels frustration into loyalty, often leaving voters blind to the contradictions between rhetoric and policy. In doing so, it not only wins elections but also cements elite power under the guise of protecting the people.

1.4 NATIONALISM: THE VOTE MAGNET

Nationalism, often cloaked in the language of pride and sovereignty, has become a powerful shield for elites to protect their interests and consolidate control. It thrives on emotional appeals to heritage and identity, rallying populations around exclusionary ideals while distracting from deeper systemic inequalities. In electoral politics, nationalism becomes a polarizing tool. It ensures debates focus on cultural grievances. Economic structures that disproportionately benefit the elite remain unchallenged. Donald Trump's "America First" campaign exemplifies this strategy. Framing globalization as a threat to American jobs and culture, Trump promised to restore manufacturing and secure the nation's borders. This rhetoric resonated deeply with working-class voters disillusioned by decades of economic stagnation, yet the policies enacted under his administration revealed a different story. Corporate tax cuts disproportionately benefited wealthy individuals and multinational corporations, while deregulation favored industries already entrenched in power. Simultaneously, nationalist themes inflamed cultural divisions, shifting focus away from the very economic disparities that fueled voter discontent. The result was a deeply polarized electorate, primed to view globalization and immigration as existential threats rather than examining the systemic factors that perpetuated inequality.

Elites have also learned to weaponize nationalism by funding allied political parties that align with their interests. Across Europe, wealthy donors and corporate entities have buoyed the rise of far-right nationalist movements through covert and overt support. These parties, which often decry globalization and immigration, frame themselves as defenders of traditional values and national sovereignty. Yet their policies frequently align with elite agendas, such as deregulation and tax reductions for the wealthy. Consider how parties like France's National Rally (formerly the National Front) or Italy's League Party fund their operations. These groups thrive on anti-globalization narratives, often vilifying the European Union as an oppressive bureaucracy. This rhetoric obscures the fact that many of their donors and backers benefit from globalization's structures, whether through multinational trade or tax loopholes. These parties stir nationalist enthusiasm. They create an environment where voters prioritize cultural and identity concerns over economic justice. This allows elites to operate with minimal scrutiny. They enjoy the protections of favorable policies.

Militarization provides another avenue through which nationalism serves elite interests, as it often justifies exorbitant defense spending under the guise of national security. Nationalist rhetoric frames military strength as synonymous with national pride, a narrative that benefits defense contractors and political leaders alike. The aftermath of the September 11, 2001, attacks illustrates this dynamic on a massive scale. In the name of combating terrorism, the United States launched wars in Afghanistan and Iraq, accompanied by an unprecedented surge in defense spending. Companies like Halliburton, once led by former Vice President Dick Cheney, secured billions of dollars in government contracts for reconstruction and logistics. These profits came at a staggering human and financial cost: hundreds of thousands of lives lost, trillions spent, and entire regions destabilized. Yet, the nationalistic framing of these wars—portraying them as battles to defend American freedom and security—shielded these profiteering activities from public scrutiny. The rhetoric of patriotism equated questioning these expenditures or outcomes with disloyalty, allowing elites to amass wealth through defense contracts without accountability.

In 2014, Narendra Modi swept into power, riding a wave of promises and grand visions, his rhetoric wrapped tightly in the fabric of Hindu nationalism. India was weary of corruption scandals, economic stagnation, and policy paralysis under the Congress-led UPA government. Modi presented himself as a transformative leader. He was a "chaiwala" who had risen through sheer merit. His campaign was a spectacle unlike anything India had seen before. Social media blitzes, holographic rallies, and slogans like "Achhe Din Aane Wale Hain" (Good days are coming) powered the campaign. Modi promised to revive the economy, create 20 million jobs annually, tackle black money, and position India as a global superpower. Each pledge carried a narrative of national pride and cultural resurgence. These promises appealed to a broad spectrum of voters. Many saw in Modi not just a leader but a symbol of hope for a rejuvenated India. Yet, as his tenure unfolded, many of these promises began to unravel, exposing a gap between rhetoric and reality that should have sparked widespread disillusionment. Modi relied on Hindu nationalism. This narrative overshadowed critical failures. The government often reframed them as part of a larger, existential battle for the soul of the nation.

One of Modi's most ambitious promises was economic transformation, particularly through job creation. Modi's vision captivated India's youth, a significant portion of the electorate. His plans for a thriving economy included initiatives like "Make in India" and "Skill India." Modi pledged to create 20 million jobs annually, a figure that resonated in a country where unemployment and underemployment have long plagued millions. However, by the end of his first term, job creation had fallen drastically short of these expectations. In fact, according to the Centre for Monitoring Indian Economy, the unemployment rate in 2018 reached a 45-year high of 6.1%. The promised manufacturing boom did not materialize. Many sectors faced stagnation or decline. Small businesses struggled under the twin shocks of demonetization and the rushed implementation of the Goods and Services Tax (GST). Demonetization, a policy ostensibly aimed at rooting out black money and fostering a cashless economy, ended up wiping out cash-dependent informal jobs without delivering significant gains. The Reserve Bank of India revealed that over 99% of demonetized currency notes returned to the banking system. The Reserve Bank of India revealed that the government failed to eradicate black money as promised. Modi's narrative control reframed these economic setbacks as sacrifices for the greater good. This portrayal cast him as a decisive leader willing to take bold steps for the nation.

The promise of bringing back black money stashed in foreign accounts was another cornerstone of Modi's campaign. He claimed that retrieving these illicit funds would yield such massive returns that each Indian citizen could receive a direct payout of ₹15 lakh. The statement, repeated at rallies across the country, became a powerful symbol of his anti-corruption crusade. Yet, once in office, neither the black money nor the promised payouts materialized. When pressed, BJP leaders dismissed the ₹15 lakh claim as a rhetorical flourish, not a literal commitment. This bait-and-switch tactic could have eroded trust in any other leader, but Modi's ability to redirect attention toward cultural and religious issues effectively neutralized these failures. The electorate's focus shifted from unfulfilled economic promises to a larger nationalist project. This project centered on Hindu identity and pride.

Failing to deliver on infrastructural and development promises further highlights this disconnect. Modi's vision of a "Digital India" and "Smart Cities" appealed to urban voters hungry for modernization. However, these programs remained largely aspirational, with limited tangible progress. The "Smart Cities Mission," launched in 2015, promised to develop 100 cities with state-of-the-art infrastructure and technology-driven governance. By 2019, the government had used less than 25% of allocated funds. Many cities on the list saw only cosmetic changes, like beautification projects or small-scale Wi-Fi installations. Similarly, the "Digital India" initiative faced hurdles in rural connectivity, where infrastructure gaps continued to hinder access to high-speed internet. Despite these shortcomings, Modi's carefully cultivated image as a visionary leader endured, bolstered by a sophisticated propaganda machine and the strategic invocation of Hindu nationalism.

One of Modi's most potent tools has been his ability to frame himself as a protector of Hindu identity. This narrative has often overshadowed his economic and developmental shortcomings, as his rhetoric taps into deeply rooted anxieties about cultural and religious identity. Modi positioned himself as the defender of Hindu values. These values stood against perceived threats from Pakistan, secular liberals, or India's Muslim minority. This created a rallying point that overshadowed policy failures. The strategy became clear after controversies like the abrogation of Article 370 in Jammu and Kashmir. Other examples included the Citizenship Amendment Act (CAA) and constructing the Ram Temple in Ayodhya. The government presented each move not as routine politics but as a civilizational triumph. They fulfilled the long-standing aspirations of Hindu nationalist groups like the Rashtriya Swayamsevak Sangh (RSS). Focusing on symbolic victories allowed Modi to shift public discourse. This deflection moved attention from critical issues like income inequality, environmental degradation, and eroding democratic institutions.

The 2019 election campaign demonstrated the power of this narrative strategy. By then, critics noted that Modi had not fulfilled many of his 2014 economic promises. Yet, his campaign centered not on his economic record but on themes of national security and cultural pride. The Pulwama attack and subsequent Balakot airstrikes became rallying cries, reinforcing Modi's image as a decisive leader who would go to any length to protect India's borders. This shift in focus let Modi sidestep scrutiny. Farmer distress, which led to widespread protests and struggles of the informal sector, received little attention. The government mobilized voters around a shared sense of Hindu identity and a perceived need to defend the nation from external and internal threats.

A systematic rewriting of history and divisive narratives promote Modi's ability to harness Hindu nationalism. The government revised educational curricula to emphasize the contributions of Hindu rulers while downplaying or erasing the legacy of Muslim dynasties. The government reshapes historical memory to align with broader attempts to frame India's Muslim population as outsiders, responsible for historical wrongs needing vengeance. A media ecosystem increasingly aligned with the BJP reinforces these narratives. Debates focus on historical grievances and cultural pride, drowning out discussions of pressing economic and social issues.

Combining nationalism and populism has also allowed Modi to deflect criticism by portraying dissent as unpatriotic. The government frequently labels journalists, academics, and activists who challenge its policies or rhetoric as "anti-national," creating an environment where questioning becomes a fraught endeavor. This dynamic ensures that the public rarely subjects Modi's unfulfilled promises to sustained scrutiny.

Instead, the focus remains on his larger-than-life persona and the ideological battle he claims to be fighting on behalf of the Hindu majority.

Remarkably, this strategy has ensured that Modi's failures do not translate into electoral losses. His government's handling of the COVID-19 pandemic, for instance, revealed glaring deficiencies in planning and execution. The sudden announcement of a nationwide lockdown in March 2020 left millions of migrant workers stranded without jobs, food, or transportation. Harrowing images of families walking hundreds of kilometers on foot to return to their villages highlighted the human cost of this decision. The underfunded and overstretched healthcare system struggled to manage the surge in cases. This led to devastating shortages of oxygen and hospital beds during the second wave. Despite these failures, Modi maintained high approval ratings by diffusing or redirecting public anger through narrative control.

Modi's repeated electoral successes underscore a critical feature of contemporary politics: the power of identity-based appeals to override material concerns. Modi tapped into Hindu nationalism to create a new political environment. Voters overlooked unfulfilled promises and governance failures. They prioritized symbolic victories that reaffirmed cultural and religious identity. This dynamic is not unique to India. It reflects broader global trends. Leaders like Donald Trump, Jair Bolsonaro, and Recep Tayyip Erdoğan have also used identity politics to consolidate power. However, in Modi's case, the scale and sophistication of this strategy, combined with the historical context of India's diverse and complex society, make it particularly potent.

Ultimately, Modi's ability to win elections despite his government's mixed record is a testament to the enduring power of nationalism as a political tool. Modi framed himself as both a visionary reformer and a cultural warrior. This strategy helped him maintain a broad base of support that spanned economic and social divides. The dual narrative of development and identity let Modi sidestep accountability. Supporters reframed his failures as temporary setbacks in a larger struggle or simply forgot them. Hindu nationalism continues to resonate with a significant portion of the electorate. As a result, Modi's unfulfilled promises remain secondary. The emotional and ideological appeal of his vision for India overshadows these shortcomings.

In these examples, nationalism is not a genuine defense of the people. Instead, it serves as a carefully orchestrated tool. It diverts attention from systemic inequalities and consolidates elite power. Its emotional appeal is its greatest strength, binding individuals to a collective identity that often prioritizes loyalty over logic. By stoking fears of external threats or internal enemies, elites manipulate nationalist narratives to justify policies that benefit the few at the expense of the many. The result is a society divided along lines of identity and allegiance, incapable of addressing the deeper inequities that sustain elite dominance. The strategic use of nationalism reveals its dual nature. It promises unity but delivers division. It acts as a shield that protects the powerful while leaving others exposed.

Elite strategies, whether cloaked in the rhetoric of globalization or nationalism, often promise transformation but deliver preservation—of their own power. These maneuvers repackage systemic inequities as inevitable or even beneficial, ensuring that public discontent is either redirected or suppressed. The result is a cycle: brief moments of upheaval, like the Arab Spring, followed by restoring structures that perpetuate inequality. The game changes players, but the rules remain the same, leaving the many to bear the weight of the few ambitions.

1.5 ELITE GAMES, PUBLIC PAINS

The consequences of elite manipulation through globalization and nationalism are far-reaching, reshaping societies and destabilizing the very structures they claim to defend. Widening economic inequality has become a defining feature of modern global systems, with elite-driven policies concentrating wealth in ever-fewer hands. This inequity breeds profound social unrest, as the majority bear the burdens of austerity, unemployment, and diminished opportunities. The Arab Spring, which erupted across the Middle East in 2010, serves as a stark illustration of these dynamics. Economic frustration deeply rooted the uprisings, often framed as a spontaneous call for democracy. Decades of elite-dominated governance had created systems that favored the politically connected while leaving ordinary citizens to grapple with rising food prices, unemployment, and stagnant wages. In Tunisia, the revolution's spark ignited against wealth concentrated among a small group of families closely tied to the regime. Mohamed Bouazizi's self-immolation symbolized the despair of those excluded from globalization. Corrupt local officials destroyed the livelihood of a street vendor, sparking broader unrest. Though the Arab Spring toppled several autocrats, it also highlighted how entrenched elite systems resist meaningful reform, often replacing one set of oligarchs with another.

Nationalist tensions further exacerbate global instability, appearing to create conflict between nations while masking underlying collusion among global elites. The rhetoric of the China-United States trade war in recent years illustrates this phenomenon. Political leaders on both sides framed the conflict as a battle for national supremacy, pitting American workers against Chinese manufacturing in a zero-sum game. Yet, beneath the surface, elites in both countries continued to collaborate through interconnected financial markets, supply chains, and technological exchanges.

Multinational corporations reliant on Chinese production and American consumers weathered the storm, often exploiting the nationalist eagerness to justify price increases or labor cuts. This duality—public conflict paired with private cooperation—reveals the calculated use of nationalism to distract populations from systemic inequalities. Political and corporate elites urged workers in Rust Belt towns and Chinese factory cities to see each other as adversaries. Meanwhile, the global elite operated seamlessly across borders. They remained insulated from the consequences of the nationalist rhetoric they had amplified.

Elites wield nationalism to undermine pluralism and suppress dissent, causing a dangerous disintegration of democratic values. In Hungary, Prime Minister Viktor Orbán has become a master of this strategy, using nationalism as a tool to consolidate power and weaken democratic institutions. Orbán's rhetoric frames Hungary as defending Christian values against siege by foreign forces, from European Union bureaucrats to Middle Eastern migrants. This narrative has allowed his government to justify sweeping reforms that erode checks and balances, including restricting judicial independence and curbing press freedom. Orbán's party, Fidesz, has leveraged its control of the media to promote a nationalist agenda that demonizes political opposition as unpatriotic, effectively silencing dissent. Meanwhile, policies ostensibly designed to protect national sovereignty, such as rejecting EU migrant quotas, distract from the regime's economic favoritism toward its own elite allies. The result is a hollowing out of democracy, where elections continue but the playing field is so tilted that meaningful competition becomes impossible.

Economic inequality, global instability, and eroding democratic norms represent interconnected outcomes of elite manipulation. By harnessing the emotional power of nationalism, elites deflect scrutiny from systemic issues and redirect public frustration toward scapegoats. This strategy fractures societies, making collective action against inequality increasingly difficult. The same forces that elites exploit can backfire. This is evident in the social unrest of movements like the Arab Spring. Growing resistance to authoritarian regimes worldwide also reflects this phenomenon. The question remains whether these cracks in the system can be used to create more equitable societies. Alternatively, will they deepen and perpetuate the cycle of manipulation and unrest that defines our age?

The search for alternatives has always been driven by desperation and hope—a desire to escape systems that oppress while dreaming of ones that liberate. Nationalism and communism, though vastly different, both emerged from this dual yearning. While nationalism stoked collective pride to mask inequality, communism offered a bold, almost utopian vision of equality. Yet, as history shows, even the most promising ideologies are vulnerable to the same corruptions they seek to abolish. Each revolution carries within it the seeds of its own disillusionment, as ideals collide with the complexities of power and human ambition.

2. MARXIST BY DAY, CAPITALIST BY NIGHT

Marx's critique of personal wealth and materialism lies at the heart of his revolutionary ideology. He envisioned a society where the means of production were collectively owned. Communist theorists rejected amassing wealth for personal indulgence as exploitation of the working class. To Marx, the bourgeoisie—capitalist elites—were the embodiment of greed, hoarding resources and property while the proletariat labored in deprivation. His philosophy called for a radical rethinking of societal values, promoting communal ownership and equitable distribution as the antidote to capitalist excess. This ideal aimed to prevent wealth from concentrating in the hands of a few. Instead, societies would share it for the collective benefit. This would create a society where materialism no longer defined human worth or purpose.

However, a stark contradiction has emerged in the behavior of many who claim allegiance to Marxist ideals, particularly in modern capitalist democracies. Self-proclaimed Marxist intellectuals and political figures often indulge in the very lifestyles Marx denounced. Luxury cars, sprawling estates, and high-end vacations are not uncommon among these supposed advocates of equality, exposing a dissonance between their rhetoric and their reality. Their wealth, amassed through royalties, speaking engagements, or public office, reflects the capitalist structures they claim to oppose. This hypocrisy undermines their credibility. It also dilutes the power of Marxist critiques. It invites skepticism about the sincerity of those who claim to fight for the working class.

History reveals a more complex relationship between Marxist ideals and personal wealth. Early communist leaders like Lenin and Mao Zedong promoted frugality as a virtue, arguing that true comrades must live modestly to demonstrate solidarity with the proletariat. Lenin, in particular, emphasized the need for leaders to embody the values they espoused. "We must live as the poorest of the poor," he declared. This statement underscored his belief. He held that the success of the revolution depended on the integrity and humility of its leaders. While Lenin himself adhered to these principles, living modestly in a worker's apartment in Moscow, the system he helped create eventually drifted from this ethos. By the mid-20th century, party officials in the Soviet Union enjoyed privileges. These privileges starkly contrasted with the austerity they preached. They included access to exclusive stores and luxury dachas in the countryside.

Mao Zedong similarly positioned himself as a man of the people, donning the iconic Zhongshan suit and rejecting ostentatious displays of wealth. Yet, Mao's own lifestyle became a paradox. Mao championed frugality during campaigns like the Great Leap Forward, where millions starved. Yet, he lived in relative comfort. He had personal chefs and palatial retreats shielded from the devastation experienced by ordinary citizens. The disconnect between rhetoric and reality among Marxist leaders highlights a recurring challenge: the difficulty of reconciling ideological purity with the temptations and practicalities of power.

Modern examples demonstrate that this tension extends beyond historical figures. In contemporary politics, the image of wealthy "socialists" thriving in capitalist systems further illustrates the contradictions within Marxist rhetoric on personal wealth. These figures often argue that their success allows them to fund progressive causes or amplify their platform. However, the optics of opulence undermine the moral authority of their critiques. For Marxism to remain relevant in debates about inequality and materialism, it must address these inconsistencies. The credibility of its advocates depends on their ability to align their actions with their ideals.

The contradictions of modern Marxist advocates highlight a broader dilemma: the inescapable entanglement of ideology with the systems it seeks to critique. In a world where personal brand and public persona have become commodities, even the staunchest critics of capitalism find themselves navigating its mechanisms for visibility and influence. This uneasy coexistence between ideology and commerce reflects significant challenges. It highlights the difficulty of staying ideologically pure. It also underscores the seductive power of a system that rewards those who play by its rules, even as they denounce them.

2.1 MARX MEETS MARKETING

The commodification of the self in modern capitalism is a phenomenon Marx could scarcely have imagined. Yet, it starkly illustrates the contradictions inherent in contemporary practices of ideological branding. Many self-proclaimed Marxists, far from rejecting the capitalist system they critique, have found ways to monetize their own identities, transforming their advocacy into a profitable enterprise. This commodification contradicts the foundational Marxist critique of turning labor into a commodity. It also exposes a deeper paradox. It reveals the challenge of critiquing a system while thriving within its structures. The rise of social media and digital platforms has accelerated this trend. Individuals now sell not just their labor but also their personas, ideologies, and physical appearances for profit. This often funds lifestyles that starkly contrast with the values they espouse.

Influencers and activists who identify as Marxist or socialist while leveraging their political identity for personal gain provide a striking example of this phenomenon. Some use platforms like OnlyFans, Patreon, or YouTube to sell content under the banner of ideological advocacy. They showcase luxury items or lavish lifestyles on social media. Activists turn branded merchandise, premium subscriptions, and exclusive access to their "comradely" thoughts into commodities. This creates a paradox where the critique of commodification itself becomes a product to be bought and sold. The commodification of their Marxist identity often mirrors the strategies of capitalist marketing: carefully curated content, audience engagement metrics, and the monetization of attention. Their followers, drawn by a shared disdain for inequality, unwittingly participate in the same capitalist exchange that these influencers decry.

This practice raises questions of hypocrisy, as these self-styled comrades actively participate in the very system they claim to oppose. Marxism critiques capitalism for commodifying human labor, reducing workers to tools for profit and stripping them of their autonomy. By extension, Marx would have condemned the commodification of the self—turning one's identity, body, or beliefs into products for sale. Yet, modern ideologues frequently justify their actions by claiming that they are using capitalist tools to undermine the system from within. This rationalization, however, often rings hollow. Their actions align more closely with entrepreneurial capitalism than with Marxist principles, as they prioritize personal gain and visibility over collective solidarity or systemic change.

Historically, Marxist movements emphasized solidarity and sacrifice, positioning their leaders and advocates as representatives of the working class rather than as individuals seeking personal enrichment. Lenin's modest living conditions in the early Soviet era reflected an effort to align personal lifestyles with ideological commitments. Similarly, Mao's attempts to embody proletarian aesthetics, despite later contradictions, aimed to achieve the same. The modern commodification of ideology undermines this alignment, as the pursuit of profit often eclipses the drive for collective change. Lavish lifestyles funded by these endeavors stand in stark contrast to the modest existence once championed by traditional Marxist figures. This disparity further erodes the credibility of contemporary advocates.

The commodification of Marxist advocacy reveals a deeper irony: the system being critiqued often becomes the enabler of its critics. As personal brands and ideological messaging thrive within capitalist frameworks, the contradiction becomes sharper.

How does one denounce capitalism's inequities while benefiting from its freedoms and opportunities? This tension is perhaps most vividly embodied in the image of modern Marxists enjoying the trappings of wealth—luxuries made possible by the very structures they oppose. Such contradictions force a reckoning: can Marxism retain its integrity when its advocates inhabit a world shaped by the privileges of the system they aim to dismantle?

2.2 MARXISM WITH A MERCEDES

The paradox of modern self-identified Marxists enjoying the luxuries afforded by democratic, capitalist systems exposes a profound philosophical and practical contradiction. These individuals critique capitalism's excesses and inequalities vocally. However, they often reside in societies where democratic freedoms and capitalist economies allow them to accumulate wealth, own property, and live lavish lifestyles. Communist systems they idealize would restrict or eliminate rights such as freedom of speech, the ability to earn and invest, and access to consumer goods. This dynamic not only highlights a disconnect between ideology and practice but also underscores the irony of criticizing a system while thriving within it.

Consider the stark contrast between the lives of modern "comrades" in democratic nations and the conditions under historical communist regimes. In capitalist democracies, these individuals can purchase luxury cars, live in opulent homes, and enjoy wealth disparities. These realities are antithetical to Marxist principles of equity. The USSR strictly prohibited private ownership of significant assets, with the state controlling housing, distribution of goods, and employment. Party elites may have enjoyed privileges unavailable to ordinary citizens, but even their material benefits paled in comparison to the excesses embraced by today's Marxist influencers. The ability to accumulate wealth in capitalist systems while denouncing the very mechanisms that facilitate their comfort underscores a reliance on what they ostensibly oppose.

This exploitation of freedom is particularly glaring in the philosophical conflict it reveals. Traditional Marxism critiques capitalism for enabling wealth accumulation and creating vast inequalities. Yet, many modern Marxists rationalize their material indulgences as "self-care" or "rewards for hard work," language steeped in the individualism and self-justification typical of capitalist values. Critics often reframe the purchase of luxury items or the pursuit of financial gain. Advocates describe it as necessary to sustain activism or balance the pressures of advocacy. However, such justifications often ring hollow, as they align more closely with the capitalist ethos of personal success than with the collective ideals of Marxist thought.

This contradiction reflects a broader tension within the modern adoption of Marxist principles. In democratic societies, Marxism often functions more as a critique than a practical framework for governance. The freedoms provided by democracy—freedom of expression, association, and economic mobility—allow individuals to espouse revolutionary ideas without the constraints of living under the systems they advocate. This trend creates a space where Marxism becomes performative, transforming into a brand that individuals can adopt and commodify without genuine sacrifice or alignment with its core tenets. The result is an ideological dissonance that weakens the credibility of its advocates and diminishes the potency of its critique.

The historical and philosophical distance between modern "comrades" and the systems they champion raises critical questions about the authenticity of their advocacy. Traditional Marxist leaders like Lenin and Mao grappled with the complexities of implementing egalitarian policies, often with dire consequences. In contrast, today's proponents engage with Marxism more as a rhetorical tool than a lived commitment. Their reliance on capitalist freedoms and privileges highlights capitalism's adaptability in accommodating dissent. It also underscores the challenges of aligning ideology with action in a contradictory world. If Marxism is to remain a relevant critique of inequality, its advocates must address these inconsistencies, demonstrating through their actions a commitment to the values they espouse.

The juxtaposition of Marxist ideals with modern luxuries reveals a profound disconnect between rhetoric and reality. Historical revolutionaries embodied solidarity with the working class through grim lives and collective struggles. In contrast, today's self-styled comrades often live in worlds far removed from those they claim to represent. This contrast exposes not just the adaptability of capitalism but its ability to co-opt even its most vocal critics. For solidarity to be meaningful, it must extend beyond words to actions. It must bridge the gap between advocacy and authenticity. This connection is essential to reconnect with the realities of marginalized individuals.

2.3 SOLIDARITY, BUT MAKE IT LUXURY

The luxurious lifestyles of some self-proclaimed comrades stand in unambiguous contrast to their claimed solidarity with the working class. This reveals a deep and troubling disconnect. For workers struggling to afford basic necessities, such displays of wealth are not only alienating but also deeply insulting. An activist railing against capitalist greed while driving a luxury car or flaunting designer clothing and lavish vacations is demoralizing. It disheartens those who live paycheck to paycheck. This disconnect creates a gap between the rhetoric of equality and the lived reality of those ostensibly represented. It erodes trust and amplifies skepticism about the sincerity of such advocacy.

Historically, revolutionary leaders who genuinely sought to align with the working class understood the symbolic importance of modest living. Che Guevara, who fought alongside Fidel Castro in the Cuban Revolution, famously rejected material wealth. He chose a life of struggle and austerity to sympathize with those he sought to liberate. Ho Chi Minh, the leader of Vietnam's independence movement, lived humbly in a simple stilt house, emphasizing the virtues of sacrifice and shared hardship. These figures recognized that credibility as advocates for equality depended on aligning their personal lifestyles with the principles they championed. Leaders chose modest living not only as a personal choice but to state unity, signaling to workers that they remained connected to their struggles.

Modern self-identified comrades, particularly in Western democracies, often fail to embody this ethos. While they criticize capitalism for fostering greed and inequality, their actions often betray a contradictory pursuit of material comforts. Designer goods, private properties, and extravagant vacations become the trappings of lives lived in contradiction to the ideals they espouse. Social media further exacerbates this dissonance, as activists curate their public personas, showcasing luxury lifestyles while simultaneously decrying the very system that enables such excess. For a struggling worker, this display of hypocrisy creates a sense of betrayal, undermining the connection that might otherwise inspire collective action.

This alienation is not just a matter of optics but a deeper philosophical failure to bridge the gap between advocacy and lived experience. In alienating the workers, they claim to represent, these comrades reinforce the same structures of inequality and detachment that they criticize. Where solidarity should foster trust and mutual effort, ostentatious living creates resentment and division. This dynamic weakens the broader movement for equality. The working class sees in these so-called advocates not allies, but beneficiaries of the system they are fighting against.

The contrast between historical leaders and modern comrades serves as a cautionary tale. While figures like Guevara and Ho Chi Minh understood the power of shared sacrifice, today's luxury-living activists risk reducing worker solidarity to mere rhetoric. If the goal is to inspire meaningful change, the commitment to equality must go beyond speeches and slogans. It must become a way of life that genuinely reflects the movement's values. Anything less risks turning the fight for equality into a hollow performance, devoid of the trust and unity needed to achieve its aims.

The shift from shared sacrifice to curated rebellion marks a turning point in how people perceive Marxist ideals. What was once a call for profound societal change has, for some, become a personal brand. It is now a way to signal dissent while remaining firmly rooted in the comforts of capitalism. This transformation highlights a troubling trend: aestheticizing ideology diminishes its power to inspire collective action, leaving behind a mask of solidarity devoid of substance. In this performance-driven era, even revolution risks becoming just another commodity.

3. US DEMOCRACY VS CHINESE TECHNOCRACY

The 21st century has brought a global race for dominance. Military might and contrasting governance models define this race. Distinct and powerful systems support China's technocracy and the United States' democracy. This competition is not merely ideological; it is a contest for influence, resources, and the future of global governance. On one side stands China, with its centralized technocracy powered by rapid industrialization, advanced surveillance technologies, and a state-directed economy. The United States intertwines its flawed democracy with a formidable military-industrial complex, shaping its foreign policy and geopolitical strategies. Each system leverages its strengths, while simultaneously exposing vulnerabilities, in a high-stakes game that could shape the next century.

China's technocracy has emerged as a force to be reckoned with, combining authoritarian governance with cutting-edge technological capabilities. China has tightly controlled information and resources. This has enabled remarkable feats, including the world's largest high-speed rail network and artificial intelligence for urban planning and surveillance. The state's command over big data allows it to monitor and predict societal trends, enabling precise economic planning and rapid crisis response. During the COVID-19 pandemic, China used contact tracing apps and enforced quarantines. These measures demonstrated the power of its centralized system, though controversies over privacy and human rights persisted. China's technocratic approach extends to its international strategy. The Belt and Road Initiative exemplifies this, using infrastructure investments to expand influence across Asia, Africa, and Europe. However, this model is not without its critics, who argue that its efficiency comes at the cost of individual freedoms and creates dependency among partner nations.

In contrast, the United States' democratic model, though slower and messier in decision-making, wields the immense power of its military-industrial complex as a tool for global influence. A nexus of defense contractors, policymakers, and military leaders drives innovation. These technologies are both commercial and strategic, including the internet and satellite systems. The United States has leveraged this complex to maintain global hegemony. It has military bases in over 70 countries and a defense budget that dwarfs those of its competitors. The wars in Iraq and Afghanistan, though controversial, showcased the extent to which United States democracy and its military-industrial complex work in tandem to project power. Advanced weaponry, private contractors, and alliances such as NATO are all part of a system designed to secure resources, influence international norms, and counter rivals like China.

This race is fueled by fundamentally different tactics. China's approach is long-term and systematic, focusing on economic integration and technological supremacy. It uses soft power tools, such as Confucius Institutes and infrastructure loans, to weave a web of influence while avoiding direct military confrontations. The United States, on the other hand, often employs hard power, using military interventions and defense alliances to assert its dominance. The rise of the Indo-Pacific strategy, aimed at countering China's influence in the region, is a clear example of this approach. It combines military presence with diplomatic efforts to build coalitions among nations like India, Japan, and Australia, creating a counterweight to China's expanding reach.

Yet, both systems face significant vulnerabilities. China's technocracy, for all its efficiency, risks overreach as its centralized model struggles to accommodate the complexities of global partnerships and diverse domestic challenges. Its surveillance state, while a tool of control, breeds resentment and mistrust, both at home and abroad. The United States faces challenges reconciling its democratic values with its military-industrial complex. This complex often operates with opacity, undermining public trust. The wars it engages in, justified in the name of democracy and freedom, frequently lead to unintended consequences, eroding its moral authority on the global stage.

The global race between China and the United States is more than systems competing against each other. This struggle defines how leaders will exercise power in the 21st century. It raises profound questions about the balance between efficiency and freedom, technology and ethics, and hard power versus soft power. The outcome of this contest will shape the geopolitical landscape and the nature of governance. Nations worldwide will look to these superpowers for models on navigating an interconnected and contentious world.

The rivalry between the United States and China is more than a clash of ideologies; it is a contest to define the principles that will govern the global future. As each nation champions its model—democratic pluralism versus technocratic centralization—their influence extends far beyond their borders, shaping the aspirations and strategies of nations worldwide. This struggle is not just about dominance but about the values that will underpin power in the coming decades. With the unipolar era fading, China's vision emerges, marking a tectonic shift and signaling a world increasingly drawn toward the shadow of the dragon.

3.1 DRAGON OVER EAGLE

The world is entering a period of significant transformation, marked by the decline of a United States-dominated unipolar order and the emergence of a rival system spearheaded by China. For much of the post-World War II period, the United States shaped a global framework rooted in liberal democracy, free trade, and a rules-based international system. Institutions like NATO, the United Nations, and the World Trade Organization were created to project Western values globally. They aimed to ensure stability, economic growth, and an unprecedented period of peace among great powers. Yet, this order was never without its contradictions. The United States promoted democracy and human rights. It selectively violated these principles to protect its interests. It toppled democratically elected leaders, supported authoritarian regimes, and justified military interventions under the guise of maintaining order.

As the world's sole superpower following the collapse of the Soviet Union, the United States further entrenched its influence. However, its role as the "global policeman" often came with unintended consequences. Wars in Iraq and Afghanistan showcased the limits of American military power and moral authority, as narratives of liberation gave way to accusations of imperialism. These contradictions fueled global resentment. However, the United States-led order also facilitated unparalleled economic interconnectedness. It lifted millions out of poverty and integrated nations into a tightly woven global economy.

Enter China, a nation that until recently seemed content to operate within this United States-dominated system. Benefiting from globalization, China grew into an economic behemoth, using its state-driven technocratic model to modernize at an unprecedented pace. Today, China has emerged as a challenger, seeking not to adopt the American-led framework but to rewrite the rules entirely. China, through initiatives like the Belt and Road Initiative (BRI), is creating a transactional global order. This order prioritizes infrastructure investments, resource extraction, and strategic alliances over ideological commitments. In March 2023, Chinese President Xi Jinping formalized this vision with the Global Civilization Initiative. He declared that nations should refrain from imposing their values on others, a thinly veiled critique of the United States' approach.

Pragmatism and economic leverage root China's strategy. State-backed investments in Africa, Latin America, and Asia have established deep ties with developing nations, often accompanied by infrastructure loans that, while fostering growth, create dependency. For example, Chinese-funded railways, ports, and power plants in Africa have linked the continent to Beijing's sphere of influence. Trade between China and Africa has ballooned, dwarfing United States engagement in the region. Similarly, China's recent mediation between Saudi Arabia and Iran, a feat long out of reach for American diplomacy, signals its ambition to reshape global geopolitics.

The United States, however, retains formidable advantages, especially through its military-industrial complex and control of global financial systems. The United States dollar remains the cornerstone of international trade. Organizations like the International Monetary Fund (IMF) and World Bank ensure that American economic policies resonate globally. Furthermore, the United States is not retreating quietly. It has responded to China's rise with measures such as restricting Chinese access to advanced technologies and strengthening military alliances in the Indo-Pacific region. Partnerships like AUKUS (Australia-UK-United States) and heightened support for Taiwan signal a strategy of containment, reminiscent of Cold War tactics.

The competition between these two powers is reshaping the global landscape. Unlike the ideological clash of the Cold War, this contest is less about capitalism versus communism and more about differing approaches to power and influence. China offers a model of transactional relationships, where economic cooperation supersedes ideological alignment. Meanwhile, the United States continues to champion a values-based system, albeit one that often bends those values for strategic gain. Both nations are competing for the allegiance of non-aligned countries. Regions like Africa, South America, and South Asia use this rivalry to secure favorable trade and security agreements.

Countries like Brazil, India, and Saudi Arabia exemplify this balancing act. Brazil maintains close ties with the United States while participating in BRICS (Brazil, Russia, India, China, South Africa), a bloc seeking to challenge Western economic dominance. India benefits from United States investments in technology while sourcing arms and oil from Russia. Saudi Arabia, a longtime United States ally, has deepened its economic ties with China, signaling a willingness to pivot away from its traditional reliance on Washington.

As the competition intensifies, the interconnectedness fostered by globalization is beginning to fray. The decoupling of United States and Chinese supply chains marks a significant shift. Parallel economic systems and growing regional powers emerge, signaling the end of an era dominated by a single superpower. In this new multipolar world, nations are adopting a more opportunistic stance, navigating between Beijing and Washington to maximize their interests. Yet, as tensions rise, the pressure to choose sides may become unavoidable.

The unfolding rivalry between the United States and China is not merely a geopolitical contest but a struggle to define the rules of a transforming world. It raises fundamental questions about governance, sovereignty, and the future of globalization. Whether this new era brings greater fragmentation or a balanced global order remains uncertain. One thing is clear: the dynamics of power are shifting, and the world is entering uncharted waters.

The rivalry between the United States and China is no longer confined to trade wars or military posturing; it extends into the realm of symbols and narratives, where even a map becomes an instrument of power. This struggle reveals how nations use tools as ordinary as cartography to assert dominance and reshape both literal and ideological borders. As the world observes this high-stakes contest, the battleground shifts. Subtle yet potent arenas contest influence and draw controversy with the stroke of a pen.

3.2 MAPPING CONTROVERSY

On August 28, 2023, the Chinese government unveiled a new "standard map," sparking a wave of condemnation across Asia and beyond. While ostensibly a routine cartographic update, the map was anything but neutral. It staked claims on disputed territories, projected aggressive geopolitical aspirations, and amplified simmering tensions with China's neighbors. A high-profile media campaign accompanied the release, emphasizing how maps are important for national unity. A map never simply represents geography. It is a tool of power, declaring intent, and, in this case, directly challenging the global order.

The map stretches China's claims from the Himalayas to the South China Sea, reasserting territorial ambitions that have long fueled conflict. The inclusion of contested regions like Arunachal Pradesh (rebranded as "South Tibet"), the Aksai Chin plateau, and Taiwan as part of China provoked a swift backlash. India and other nations strongly opposed this move. Beijing emphasized these territorial assertions with calculated precision, signaling its unyielding stance on these disputes. Notably, the map also added a provocative "10th dash" to its infamous nine-dash line in the South China Sea, further encroaching on the waters near Taiwan. This move reinforced China's historical claims over vast maritime territories, intensifying tensions with Southeast Asian nations and the United States.

The Himalayas, with their jagged peaks and treacherous terrain, have long been a flashpoint for Sino-Indian tensions. The map reasserts China's claim over Aksai Chin, a region seized during the 1962 Sino-Indian War. It also claims Arunachal Pradesh, a territory populated by Indian citizens but declared by Beijing as part of "South Tibet." These contested areas are not merely symbolic; they hold strategic value, serving as critical trade routes and potential military vantage points. Skirmishes along the so-called Line of Actual Control, where Chinese and Indian troops have clashed using improvised weapons, highlight the ongoing volatility. The most recent confrontation in 2020 claimed the lives of 20 Indian soldiers and four Chinese troops, a stark reminder that these disputes remain far from resolved.

To the east, China's cartographic ambitions stretch into the tiny Himalayan nations of Bhutan and Nepal, where Beijing has quietly built infrastructure on contested land. In Bhutan, China has established roads and settlements in the Doklam Plateau. This region holds immense strategic importance because of its proximity to India's "chicken neck," a narrow corridor linking mainland India to its northeastern states. These incursions blur borders and create facts on the ground, leaving smaller nations with little recourse but to acquiesce. Nepal, similarly, has reported Chinese encroachments, though it often downplays these violations to maintain diplomatic ties. Such tactics—building roads, fortifying disputed regions, and changing the narrative through maps—exemplify China's strategy of incremental assertion.

The South China Sea stands as one of the most contentious regions on the new map. Vital for global trade and rich in resources, it has been central to China's territorial ambitions for decades. First introduced in the 1940s, the infamous nine-dash line has since expanded into a 10-dash line, encircling even more territory. China enforced these claims, dismissed as illegitimate by international law, by creating artificial islands and militarized outposts. Satellite images reveal sprawling military installations on reclaimed reefs, complete with airstrips and radar systems. Neighboring countries, from the Philippines to Vietnam, have pushed back against these assertions, often finding themselves outmatched by China's navy and coast guard.

Taiwan, a focal point of China's geopolitical ambitions, is another flashpoint on the map. Despite operating as a de facto independent state for decades, Beijing unequivocally marks Taiwan as Chinese territory. The map's inclusion of the 10th dash further underscores Beijing's readiness to assert control over the island and its surrounding waters. For Taiwan, this is not just a cartographic slight but a reminder of China's long-standing threat to reunify the island by force if necessary. For the United States and its allies, the map serves as a stark signal of Beijing's resolve, prompting increased military presence and diplomatic support for Taiwan.

Maps are, by nature, political instruments, but China's latest cartographic effort takes this to a new level. Its map serves as a bold statement of Beijing's territorial ambitions, signaling to the world that China intends to define the region's borders on its own terms. For its neighbors, the map is a provocation, a reminder of China's growing military and economic power. For the United States and its allies, it is a challenge to the rules-based international order, raising the stakes in an already tense geopolitical rivalry. In every line and border, the map encapsulates China's aspirations and the increasingly fragmented global order it seeks to reshape.

China's territorial ambitions, etched boldly into its maps, extend far beyond borders, manifesting in strategies that blend generosity with control. The same hand that redraws boundaries also offers aid and infrastructure, binding recipients into complex relationships of dependency and influence. Yet, as the African Union scandal revealed, such generosity can come with hidden costs—microphones in the walls, data siphoned under the guise of partnership. This duality—aid as both opportunity and leverage—underscores the intricate and often opaque strategies shaping China's global ascent.

3.3 BUGGED BY GENEROSITY

In January 2017, an IT engineer at the African Union headquarters in Ethiopia noticed something alarming. Chinese engineers installed servers in the headquarters in 2012, and every night, they connected to a server in Shanghai. Emails, audio files, and sensitive internal data were being uploaded—an act of espionage hidden within the infrastructure of a $200 million "gift" from the Chinese government. The African Union IT team investigated and discovered microphones embedded in walls and furniture, confirming that construction-stage bugging compromised the headquarters. This shocking revelation became a stark symbol of China's growing but controversial influence in Africa, raising questions about the intentions behind its largesse.

China's involvement in Africa has expanded dramatically over the past two decades, driven by two primary motives: economics and geopolitics. As China transitioned from a poor agrarian society to a global economic powerhouse, its domestic labor costs rose, and its rapid growth began to slow. Seeking new markets, cheaper labor, and untapped resources, China turned to Africa, investing over $300 billion in infrastructure projects that span the continent. These investments include roads, railways, ports, dams, and even entire government buildings. These projects have provided economic stimulus and modernized infrastructure in many African nations.

However, they have also left countries deeply indebted to Beijing, raising concerns about sovereignty and long-term consequences.

Consider Kenya's Standard Gauge Railway, a $3.6 billion project linking Nairobi to Mombasa. Chinese loans financed it, and Chinese firms constructed it, hailing it as a transformative investment and Kenya's most expensive infrastructure project. Yet, the railway quickly became emblematic of the pitfalls of Chinese investment. Despite its promise to reduce highway congestion, it fell short of its intended impact, cutting through national parks and disrupting ecosystems without delivering substantial economic benefits. Corruption scandals involving Chinese contractors and allegations of poor treatment of local workers further marred the project's reputation. Today, Kenya owes 72% of its national debt to China, and concerns about repayment loom large.

China's Belt and Road Initiative (BRI) exemplifies the country's strategy of using infrastructure development as a tool for geopolitical influence. In Africa, China has built everything from ports in Djibouti and railways in Ethiopia to government buildings in countries like Zimbabwe and Senegal. These projects often come with strings attached. Debt is the most visible tool of leverage. When Sri Lanka failed to repay Chinese loans for the Hambantota Port, Beijing took control of the facility through a 99-year lease. This set a precedent that alarms African nations with similar debt burdens. Critics warn that Africa risks falling into a neocolonial relationship with China, trading political independence for economic dependence.

Beyond economics, China's actions in Africa reflect its geopolitical ambitions. Africa's 54 nations represent a significant voting bloc in international organizations like the United Nations. By funding infrastructure and offering no-strings-attached loans, China has cultivated alliances across the continent, ensuring support for its global initiatives and policies, including the contentious One-China policy. Nearly every African nation, save Eswatini, has severed diplomatic ties with Taiwan, a testament to China's success in leveraging financial aid for political alignment.

However, the costs of these relationships are becoming apparent. The African Union headquarters scandal revealed the extent to which China prioritizes its strategic interests, even at the expense of its allies' sovereignty. Projects touted as mutually beneficial often come with hidden costs, from environmental degradation to unsustainable debt. Critics argue that China's approach undermines local governance by letting Chinese contractors dominate construction and relegating local workers to low-skill jobs. Additionally, Beijing's investments frequently sidestep environmental and labor standards, prioritizing speed and profit over sustainability and social impact.

Despite these challenges, China's influence in Africa is undeniable. In countries like Nigeria, Chinese-built dams have brought electricity to underserved regions, while roads in Lesotho have improved connectivity and commerce. These tangible benefits make China an appealing partner for African nations seeking to modernize. Yet, the long-term implications remain uncertain. Failure to meet debt obligations may force Africa to cede strategic assets to Beijing, mirroring Sri Lanka's experience.

John Adams' observation that "there are two ways to conquer and enslave a country: one is by the sword; the other is by debt" resonates strongly in China's African investments. While the sword is absent, the financial burden imposed by massive loans could erode African sovereignty, making nations beholden to China's strategic ambitions. As Africa grapples with the consequences of these partnerships, the question remains: are these investments a pathway to shared prosperity or a subtle form of economic subjugation?

China's actions in Africa reflect the behavior of a rising superpower using economic leverage to secure geopolitical influence. While its investments have brought undeniable benefits, they also raise pressing questions about the nature of modern global power dynamics and the future of African sovereignty. How Africa navigates this delicate balance will shape not only its future but also the contours of the emerging multipolar world.

China's strategies of influence, from infrastructure projects in Africa to its contested maps, highlight its ambition to shape global power dynamics. Yet, as Beijing extends its reach, nations like Japan respond with strategic countermeasures, turning remote outposts into symbols of resistance. Transforming Magashima into a military hub underscores the shifting balance of power in Asia. In this region, every move—whether through aid or armament—carries the weight of intention and the shadow of looming conflict.

3.4 ISLAND OF INTENTIONS

In January 2023, construction workers arrived on the desolate volcanic island of Magashima, off Japan's southern coast. Their mission was clear: to transform the uninhabited land into a military stronghold. The Japanese government, keenly aware of its strategic significance, even paid local fishermen to steer clear of the island. Soon, Magashima would house runways and ammunition storage facilities, serving both Japanese and American military operations. The base was part of a broader military strategy, a deliberate effort to bolster defenses against a looming threat centered on one specific adversary—China.

Magashima is only one node in a vast web of militarized islands, forming what military planners call the "first island chain." This chain, spanning from Japan through Taiwan and the Philippines, down to the South China Sea, is both a barrier and a beacon of rising tensions. The United States and its allies are reinforcing this chain, deploying troops, missiles, and advanced military equipment. At its core, this strategy seeks to deter aggression, especially concerning Taiwan, an island that has become the focal point of escalating tensions between two global superpowers.

The United States Department of Defense's 2022 National Defense Strategy broke new ground by focusing heavily on China, labeling it the "most consequential strategic competitor" for the coming decades. Highlighting China's military modernization, aggressive maritime claims, and efforts to reshape global norms to suit authoritarian preferences, the report underscores a pressing concern. Such worries from the Pentagon are not without merit. China builds the same amount as an entirely new British Navy every four years. It uses its growing military might to coerce neighbors, enforce territorial claims, and assert dominance in disputed waters like the South China Sea.

The stakes are especially high in Taiwan, a critical hub for global microchip production and a symbolic cornerstone of United States-led democratic ideals. China considers Taiwan a "renegade province" and vows to reunite it with the mainland, using force if necessary. For the United States and its allies', defending Taiwan is both a strategic imperative and a test of their commitment to maintaining the current international order. This tension has catalyzed an arms race, with the United States rapidly reshaping its military posture in the Indo-Pacific.

Japan has emerged as a critical partner in this strategy, transforming its traditionally pacifist stance into a proactive military posture. Along its southern islands, stretching toward Taiwan, Japan is fortifying defenses with anti-ship missiles, long-range cruise missiles, and electronic warfare units. Japan expands its capabilities on Okinawa, where thousands of United States troops station themselves, ensuring seamless integration with American forces. Magashima, along with other fortified islands, forms a missile barrier that any Chinese fleet must consider in its calculus for military action. This island chain not only monitors Chinese movements but also sends an unmistakable message of preparedness.

Further south, the Philippines has become another pivotal player in the chain. Despite a fraught colonial history with the United States, the Philippines has welcomed increased American military access to counter China's aggressive moves in the South China Sea. China's "nine-dash line," an arbitrary claim that swallows nearly the entire sea, has brought conflict to Filipino waters. Chinese naval vessels routinely harass Filipino fishermen, and laser attacks and blockades have become distressingly common.

In response, the Philippines has granted the United States access to nine military bases, strategically positioned to bolster defenses near Taiwan and the South China Sea.

Australia, too, has stepped into the fold, enhancing its alliance with the United States and the UK through the AUKUS pact. This partnership will provide Australia with nuclear-powered submarines capable of extended patrols in the Pacific. United States B-52 bombers, potentially armed with nuclear weapons, will soon have a permanent base in northern Australia. Together, these developments solidify a robust network of allies encircling China, amplifying the strategic pressure.

Yet, this strategy is a double-edged sword. While the island chain aims to deter conflict, it also risks provoking the very aggression it seeks to prevent. From China's perspective, the encirclement is a clear act of containment, reminiscent of Cold War-era strategies. Chinese President Xi Jinping has labeled it a policy of "encirclement and suppression," and his government has vowed to respond. This tit-for-tat dynamic could accelerate the timeline for a Chinese invasion of Taiwan, a move calculated to occur before the United States completes its fortifications.

The paradox of deterrence looms large. While the military buildup aims to avoid war, its sheer scale and visibility could make war seem inevitable. The world watches as the United States and China navigate this precarious balance, their rivalry shaping the contours of a new global order. Whether this militarized island chain prevents or precipitates conflict remains to be seen. It will define the next chapter in the struggle between these two superpowers, with Taiwan as the flashpoint and the Pacific as the battleground.

Globalization and nationalism are two sides of the same coin, each reflecting humanity's ancient instincts for tribalism and expansion. Elites manipulate these forces, turning them into tools of exploitation instead of progress. The dysfunction here is global, touching every corner of society and the planet itself.

This leads us to the ultimate consequence of human dysfunction: climate change, explored in Chapter 12: Climate Change. The same greed that divides nations and hoards resources has pushed the Earth to the brink of collapse. This serves as a stark reminder. Humanity's survival depends on overcoming its oldest instincts.

12

Climate Change

For centuries, the elites of developed nations fueled environmental destruction. They built wealth by exploiting the earth's resources. Pollution became a byproduct of their progress. As these nations grew rich, they ignored the long-term costs. Now, they urge others to stop polluting. The same systems that caused harm are now seen as models. The wealthy call on the developing world to change. Yet, those nations are still struggling to grow. The elites demand sacrifice from those who have less. This chapter examines the irony of this situation.

The energy transition serves as a stark example of how deeply rooted national interests hinder global progress. The coal mines of early 20th century Britain and the oil fields of mid-20th-century Saudi Arabia became symbols of national prosperity and geopolitical leverage. For decades, the exploitation of fossil fuels powered not only industrial revolutions but also narratives of national superiority. Moving away from fossil fuels toward renewable energy now threatens to destabilize the economies and identities that many nations have built. Economic and political realities compound this conflict. The West's push for decarbonization often faces accusations of hypocrisy from developing nations, which argue for their right to industrialize using resources that once enriched Western powers. Historical incidents, such as OPEC's oil embargo in 1973, emphasize how energy politics can fracture global alliances. At the time, nations dependent on imported oil were thrust into crises, spurring inflation and recession. The embargo exposed the fragility of energy systems built on non-renewable resources. It laid the groundwork for today's geopolitical conflicts over rare earth minerals vital for renewable technologies. Even as countries acknowledge the urgency of clean energy transitions, the path remains stuck in competing priorities. These include balancing economic disruption with reducing carbon emissions.

Efforts to manage carbon emissions further reveal the moral and practical complexities of collective action. Carbon markets, hailed as a solution to incentivize reductions, often falter under the weight of greenwashing and inadequate enforcement. Take, for instance, the European Union's Emissions Trading System (ETS), launched in 2005. Initially celebrated as a groundbreaking tool for regulating emissions, it soon became a battleground for corporate manipulation and ethical disputes. Large companies, particularly in energy-intensive industries, exploited loopholes, purchasing cheap offsets from projects with questionable environmental integrity. In some cases, carbon credit schemes led to unintended consequences, such as the displacement of indigenous communities for reforestation efforts that prioritized carbon accounting over human rights. These controversies highlight the tension between creating effective mechanisms for global cooperation and ensuring equity in their implementation. More radical solutions, such as geoengineering, present even graver dilemmas. Proposals to inject aerosols into the atmosphere to reflect sunlight or to seed oceans with iron to promote carbon absorption carry significant risks of ecological disruption. The unintended consequences of these measures may echo past tragedies. For instance, the Dust Bowl of the 1930s arose when misguided agricultural practices transformed fertile land into barren wastelands.

Equity and justice remain central to addressing climate change but are fraught with historical and geopolitical tensions. The idea of climate reparations, for instance, confronts the legacy of industrialization. Wealthy nations, responsible for emitting the lion's share of greenhouse gases since the 19th century, face calls to compensate poorer nations enduring the brunt of climate impacts. The devastation wrought by Typhoon Haiyan in the Philippines in 2013—killing over 6,000 people and displacing millions—illustrates the human cost of climate disasters exacerbated by global warming. Yet, the question of who should pay, and how much remains contentious. Non-binding agreements like the Paris Accord offer aspirational targets but lack enforceable mechanisms, as nations often prioritize domestic political considerations over global commitments. Historical precedents, such as the reparations imposed on Germany after World War I, show how financial penalties can breed resentment and instability if perceived as unjust. Balancing accountability with fairness is essential to avoid deepening divides between developed and developing nations.

Food systems and land use further illustrate the overlap between environmental degradation and resource conflicts. The deforestation of the Amazon rainforest is emblematic of this crisis, driven by global demand for soy, beef, and palm oil. Brazil's successive governments have oscillated between environmental protection and economic exploitation, often under intense international scrutiny. This struggle mirrors agricultural shifts during the mid-20th-century Green Revolution. While alleviating hunger for millions, it entrenched inequalities and led to excessive use of chemical fertilizers and pesticides. Today, the challenge is not just about feeding the planet but doing so without exacerbating climate change. Livestock production alone accounts for nearly 15% of global greenhouse gas emissions, yet attempts to curb meat consumption often encounter cultural resistance. Efforts to promote plant-based diets in Western nations have sparked debates over food sovereignty, particularly in regions where animal agriculture firmly shapes traditions and livelihoods.

Infrastructure and migration reveal the localized consequences of global challenges. Rising sea levels have already begun to displace communities, from the sinking islands of the Pacific to the flooded streets of Jakarta, Indonesia. Historically, mass migrations have shaped civilizations but often triggered conflicts, as with the Great Migration of African Americans in the United States during the early 20th century. While this movement sought refuge from racial oppression in the South, it intensified competition for jobs and housing in northern cities, fueling social tensions. Similarly, today's climate-induced migrations—estimated to reach 200 million people by 2050— test the capacity of nations to adapt. Border policies, such as building walls or enforcing restrictive immigration laws, reflect deep-seated risk aversion and echo past responses to perceived threats from outsiders." Yet, global infrastructure projects, such as China's Belt and Road Initiative, further complicate the picture. These investments, often presented as solutions to development needs, risk locking nations into unsustainable practices while creating dependencies that undermine sovereignty.

The call to save the planet, though vital, carries irony as those who have exploited it the most often lead the rallying cry. This paradox reveals a recurring theme in history. Those at the pinnacle of privilege often set terms for collective action while remaining insulated from the consequences they ask others to face. Wealth shields the affluent from poverty, and beauty redefines standards of acceptance. Similarly, the global climate narrative risks being shaped by those least affected by its immediate dangers. To truly address this crisis, humanity must move beyond these contradictions, recognizing that privilege cannot shape or impose solutions.

1. NATURE EXPLOITERS GO GREEN!

The irony of privilege is as old as civilization itself, a contradiction so ingrained in human society that it often passes unnoticed. It whispers through the lips of the fortunate, their declarations of universality shaped by their unique vantage points. "Money doesn't matter," the wealthy proclaim, as they enjoy the insulation that wealth provides from the hardships of life. "Looks don't matter," say the genetically or surgically blessed, relaxing in the privileges conferred by their appearance. And in the global arena, another refrain echoes: "Save the planet!"—urged most enthusiastically by the very nations whose relentless exploitation of nature secured their prosperity. This call, noble in intent, carries irony. The voices demanding action belong to those who ignited the industrial revolution, sending carbon skyward and reaping wealth from destroyed landscapes. The urgency of climate action is undeniable, but it exposes a deep fracture in the global narrative. History's beneficiaries now seek to dictate terms of environmental salvation.

The historical disparities are stark. Consider Britain, the cradle of the Industrial Revolution, where coal-fueled factories in Manchester and Birmingham transformed it into the workshop of the world. By the mid-19th century, Britain was producing over 80% of the world's coal, feeding a voracious appetite for progress. But this prosperity came at a cost—not just to Britain's landscapes, but to its colonies, which were drawn into a web of resource extraction. British colonizers stripped Indian forests for timber and forced enslaved laborers to toil in Caribbean sugar plantations, enriching the empire's coffers. The United States followed a similar path, with oil fields in Texas and coal mines in Appalachia driving its rise to global dominance. Yet, these nations now spearhead climate summits, urging restraint and sustainability from countries still navigating the path to development. The irony is cutting: the once-exploiters, their wealth secured and their populations insulated, now call on others to tighten their belts.

This disparity is evident in the metrics of carbon debt. Wealthy nations like the United States, Germany, and Japan have historically contributed the lion's share of greenhouse gas emissions. By the time developing nations began industrializing in earnest, much of the atmospheric "budget" for safe levels of carbon dioxide had already been spent. The Paris Agreement, for all its aspirations, struggles to reconcile this injustice. The framework asks developing countries like India and Brazil to curb emissions while lifting millions out of poverty. This expectation is akin to asking a marathon runner to carry weights while competitors sprint unburdened. Historical responsibility is delicate at the negotiating table. It underscores the chasm between those who have reaped industrialization's fruits and those still struggling to plant seeds.

The contradictions become even more poignant in the realm of energy transition. Nations like the U.S. and the E.U. champion renewable energy and decry deforestation, yet their affluence arose from fossil fuels and unrestrained exploitation. When Brazil burns the Amazon to clear land for agriculture, or Indonesia razes rainforests for palm oil plantations, they face global condemnation. History reminds us Britain deforested landscapes centuries ago to build its navy. Industrial agriculture destroyed American plains, depleting bison herds and other resources. The demand for environmental accountability, often levied against developing nations, ignores the precedent set by those now wielding the moral high ground. Urging a clean energy revolution is easier when industrial groundwork is already complete, cities electrified, and populations employed.

This hypocrisy extends to the financial mechanisms touted as solutions. Carbon markets, for instance, enable wealthy nations to offset their emissions by funding projects in poorer countries, such as reforestation or renewable energy installations. Developers frame these schemes as win-win scenarios, but they often perpetuate inequalities. Monoculture plantations designed to maximize carbon absorption displace Indigenous communities and disrupt local ecosystems. Meanwhile, wealthier nations continue emitting, their economies scarcely disrupted. It is a modern-day iteration of colonial resource extraction, where the Global South bears the burdens of conservation while the Global North retains the privileges of consumption.

Even the rhetoric of climate change reveals this imbalance. The term "climate crisis" gained currency only after its impacts began threatening the economies and infrastructures of wealthy nations. Small island nations like Kiribati and the Maldives raised alarms about rising sea levels, but global powers ignored their warnings. It was only when hurricanes devastated New York and wildfires scorched California that the urgency became mainstream. The disparity is striking: while vulnerable nations grapple with existential threats, wealthier ones frame climate action as a challenge to innovation and market efficiency. This selective urgency highlights the enduring power dynamics of a world where privilege dictates whose crises matter most.

The call to "save the planet," then, is not merely a call to action but a mirror reflecting the inequities of history. As nations rally for sustainability, the challenge lies in distributing burdens and benefits equitably. The path forward must confront the ironies of privilege head-on, balancing the moral imperatives of justice with the pragmatic need for collective action. If the global community fails to reconcile these divides, efforts to combat climate change risk becoming another chapter in the long history of exploitation veiled as progress.

The irony of modern sustainability lies in its origins. The nations calling most loudly for global action gained prosperity through unchecked industrialization. This contradiction is not just historical; it is structural, embedded in a system where past pollution built present wealth. As the world tackles climate change, the question is whether those who profited from this legacy will acknowledge responsibility—or let the costs fall again on those left behind.

1.1 ETHICS FOR YOU, EXPORTS FOR US!

"Save the planet!" is a rallying cry that echoes across global forums, environmental summits, and international declarations. The nations shouting loudest often carry the deepest footprints of ecological exploitation. These nations built industrial empires on unrestrained resource extraction and carbon emissions. Historically, these developed countries carved their paths to economic prosperity through practices that scarred the environment: rampant deforestation, uncontrolled industrialization, and exploitation of fossil fuels. Today, they continue to emit significant greenhouse gases through their industries, albeit more covertly, while projecting themselves as stewards of environmental sustainability. Ironically, these same countries quickly criticize developing nations striving to climb the economic ladder through similar means. They conveniently ignore that such growth mirrors their historical journeys. The pledges made at global climate forums often remain unfulfilled, as self-interest repeatedly trumps collective environmental responsibility.

The hypocrisy becomes starker when one considers other arenas of global governance, such as the arms trade, which offers a striking parallel to the climate crisis. Critics chastise developing countries for using arms trade to bolster economies, yet this mirrors the path of many current economic giants. For instance, the arms trade has historically been a cornerstone of economic policy for several developed nations, allowing them to fund their development and secure geopolitical influence. A recent episode involving India and Spain reveals the contradictions within this discourse. In May 2024, Spain denied docking permission to the Danish-flagged cargo ship Marianne Danica, which carried nearly 27 tonnes of explosives from Chennai, India, to Haifa, Israel. The Spanish government justified its decision by citing its policy of not contributing to arms proliferation in conflict zones. Yet, contradictions abound, as Spain's robust arms export industry has fueled its economic growth and global standing.

Between 2019 and 2023, Spain ranked as the world's eighth-largest arms exporter, accounting for 2.7% of global arms exports. This industry is not a minor sector but a major driver of the Spanish economy. In 2023 alone, Spain exported $37 million worth of military weapons, excluding smaller firearms like revolvers and pistols. This marked a 17.5% increase from 2022, showcasing a rapidly growing sector. The economic impact is undeniable; in 2017, arms exports accounted for 1.6% of Spain's total exports. The industry's primary recipients during the 2019-2023 period included Saudi Arabia (21.5%), Australia (20.4%), and Turkey (18.3%), nations with active military engagements and significant geopolitical controversies. In 2022, Spanish arms exports surged by 24% compared to the previous year, achieving one of the highest figures in the country's history. Clearly, Spain's arms trade is not just a footnote in its economic strategy—it is a critical element of its global economic and political clout.

The recipients of Spanish military exports further expose the contradictions in its moral posturing. Saudi Arabia, for instance, has been a significant customer for Spanish arms. This partnership draws controversy due to Saudi Arabia's role in Yemen's conflict, widely criticized for its devastating humanitarian impact. Reports show that combatants used Spanish-made weapons in this conflict, raising ethical concerns about their role in human suffering. Similarly, Turkey, a major Spanish arms recipient, actively fights in Syria and against Kurdish groups. Imported weaponry, including Spanish arms, has been integral to these operations, drawing international scrutiny and criticism.

The case of Ukraine offers another layer of complexity. In 2024, Spain committed to supplying Ukraine with €1 billion worth of military equipment as part of its support amid the ongoing conflict with Russia. This substantial aid underscores Spain's role in supplying arms to nations in active conflict, highlighting a pattern of selective ethics. Spain denied docking permission to a ship carrying explosives from India to Israel. At the same time, it strengthened its role as a major arms supplier to conflict zones, justifying these exports as political alliances and strategic interests. These decisions reveal a duality in Spain's approach. There is an apparent commitment to peace and stability paired with economic reliance on arms exports to war-torn countries.

India's position in the arms trade also warrants examination, particularly in the context of its burgeoning partnership with Israel. Both nations share strategic interests, and their arms trade is an extension of this relationship. Yet, unlike Spain, India is a developing nation seeking to secure its economic and geopolitical aspirations. The denial of docking rights to the Marianne Danica exposes the uneven standards applied to nations at different stages of development. Spain, a developed nation with a long arms trade history, feels entitled to dictate terms to India. Meanwhile, India navigates a complex web of economic and strategic imperatives. This incident exemplifies the broader dynamic of power imbalances in international relations, where developed nations impose standards they themselves routinely fail to meet.

Spain's economy heavily relies on arms trade, a fact that underscores its critical importance. In 2022, Spain exported $599 million in weapons. Major recipients included the United States ($116 million), the United Kingdom ($44.2 million), and Saudi Arabia ($36.3 million). These figures illustrate the scale and reach of Spain's arms industry, which continues to thrive despite ethical questions surrounding its exports. Major destinations for Spanish military weapons that year also included Malaysia ($8.88 million), Pakistan ($7.18 million), and Kuwait ($2.49 million). These transactions further underscore the global nature of Spain's arms trade and its willingness to engage with nations in complex geopolitical contexts.

The broader historical context adds another layer to this analysis. Arms trade revenues have historically financed the industrial and infrastructural development of many developed nations. These revenues have allowed countries to fund technological innovation, build critical infrastructure, and achieve economic stability. Critics often challenge developing nations when they adopt similar arms trade practices. This double standard reflects a deeply ingrained hypocrisy in the international system, where power dynamics and historical privilege shape the narrative.

In conclusion, the interplay between environmental and arms trade hypocrisies reveals a persistent pattern in global governance. Developed nations, having benefited from exploitative practices to achieve their current status, often impose moral and ethical standards on developing nations striving for similar progress. Spain's denial of docking rights to the Marianne Danica while maintaining a thriving arms export industry exemplifies this double standard. This underscores the need for a more equitable and consistent global framework. It must recognize historical injustices and allow developing nations to grow without undue criticism or obstruction. Global calls to "save the planet" or regulate arms trade must be meaningful. They require genuine commitments and a willingness to confront deep-seated hypocrisies. Only then can the world move toward a future that is not just sustainable but also just.

Ethics for you, exports for us. History tells us that the wealthiest nations often impose rules they themselves never followed when building their empires. As we critique the arms trade's role in modern hypocrisy, the broader question looms: how did we get here? The answer lies in smoke-filled skies and the relentless hum of industry.

1.2 FROM EXPLOITATION TO EXPECTATION

The climate crisis carries a profound irony. Nations that plundered the Earth to build empires now stand at podiums, urging restraint from those who seek to survive. Coal mines that choked the air and factories that polluted rivers fueled the industrial revolutions of the US, UK, and Germany. Colonization ensured that resources flowed in one direction—from the Global South to the Global North—leaving behind barren lands and impoverished societies. Today, these same nations, having secured their dominance through environmental exploitation, preach sustainability to countries still climbing the ladder of development. It resembles a consumed feast, where full diners demand austerity from those still waiting to eat.

This imbalance is not merely historical; it persists in every summit, every accord, and every negotiation. Wealthier nations pledge action but often fall short of meaningful commitments. The $100 billion annual climate finance goal, promised over a decade ago, remains unmet. Loans, not grants, account for much of the aid delivered, deepening dependency in vulnerable nations. Hurricanes batter the Caribbean, floods submerge Pakistan, and droughts ravage East Africa. The nation's most responsible offer sympathy but little restitution. The weight of privilege allows them to dictate the terms of global climate action while shielding themselves from the consequences of inaction.

The need for genuine equity and shared responsibility in addressing the climate crisis has never been more urgent. It demands that nations bridge the gap between rhetoric and reality, moving beyond symbolic gestures to enact policies that reflect the interconnectedness of the world's fate. Wealthy nations must reduce emissions aggressively and provide resources for poorer nations to do the same. These resources must come as grants, not loans, and as reparations, not charity. We must dismantle barriers blocking green technologies for developing nations and amplify their voices in decision-making. True equity acknowledges not only the emissions of the past but the inequalities of the present, addressing them with policies that prioritize justice over convenience.

History will not remember the fine print of summits or the intricacies of negotiations. It will remember whether humanity rose to meet the defining challenge of its time. Will privilege perpetuate inequality, or can it drive change as a transformative responsibility? The answer lies in actions, not proclamations, by wealthier nations. These actions must recognize that in a warming world, one's failure is everyone's failure. The challenge is not merely to preach sustainability but to embody it, forging a future where privilege is not a fortress but a foundation for solidarity.

The rhetoric of solidarity often collapses under the weight of historical realities, where progress for some has come at the expense of many. Wealthier nations and elites, having reaped the benefits of exploitation, now champion sustainability while sidestepping the moral debts they owe. This hypocrisy is not new; centuries of economic expansion followed this pattern, where profit ignored its cost. Will we break this cycle? Or will history again see privilege hoarding the spoils of a greener future while others bear the burden?

2. RICH IN PROFITS, POOR IN MORALS

History is the story of exploitation dressed as progress, and nowhere is this more apparent than in the actions of economic elites. For centuries, they have wielded power not as custodians of the Earth but as opportunists seeking profit, often at great social and ecological cost. Colonial conquests stripped Africa, Asia, and the Americas of wealth. Unchecked industrialization ravaged ecosystems. Economic elites thrived by bending natural resources and people to their will. The scramble for oil in the early 20th century offers a vivid example. Western oil companies, under the guise of modernization, extracted vast reserves from the Middle East, often propping up autocratic regimes to secure favorable contracts. The Anglo-Iranian Oil Company (later BP) epitomized this. Britain fueled its empire with Iranian oil while Iran saw little wealth, sparking resentment and nationalization efforts in the 1950s.

This pattern of exploitation has been repeatedly justified under the banner of progress, with international norms often sidelined to serve elite interests. The Gulf of Mexico's infamous Deepwater Horizon disaster in 2010 was not just an environmental catastrophe; it was a glaring symbol of regulatory capture. BP's shortcuts to maximize profit resulted in one of the largest oil spills in history, devastating marine ecosystems and the livelihoods of coastal communities. Yet the fines and apologies that followed barely scratched the surface of the systemic inequality the incident revealed. Local communities suffered while shareholders profited. Economic elites ensured the powerless bore environmental degradation costs while the privileged reaped rewards.

As the world shifts to renewable and nuclear energy, elites position themselves to dominate. These structures reconfigure and preserve fossil fuel inequalities for modern markets. Lithium, often called "white gold" for its role in battery production, has already become a battleground. The Atacama Desert in Chile, rich with lithium reserves, is being drained to feed the global demand for electric vehicles and renewable energy storage. But while multinational corporations reap the profits, indigenous communities in the region face water shortages and ecological destruction. Similarly, the push for nuclear energy, once heralded as a democratizing force, has largely become the domain of powerful state-backed entities and private firms. India builds nuclear power plants on lands forcibly taken from farmers and indigenous peoples. Promises of clean energy become mechanisms for dispossession.

The irony is unmistakable. Those who profited most from fossil fuel extraction now claim to lead sustainability efforts. They often frame themselves as visionaries of a greener future. Yet their investments in renewables and nuclear power rarely align with global equity. Instead, they consolidate patents, control supply chains, and monopolize new technologies, ensuring that energy transitions benefit the few rather than the many. A few nations and corporations dominate the solar industry. Global South countries often must import expensive panels and technologies rather than develop their own industries. This monopolization perpetuates dependence, mirroring the colonial resource flows of the past.

Economic elites influencing energy transitions merely continue historical patterns of control. It is a profound challenge to the idea of equitable progress. As the world faces climate action urgency, a question arises. Will the shift to renewable and nuclear energy dismantle fossil fuel hierarchies or refashion them for a new era? The answer depends on whether humanity can wrest control from those who view the planet as a ledger of extractable value rather than a shared home. For now, history's shadow looms. The forces that dominated oil fields now target deserts, wind currents, and uranium mines for tomorrow.

The transition to renewable and nuclear energy risks repeating an all-too-familiar pattern: the promise of progress masking the exploitation of resources and people. Fossil fuels concentrated wealth and power in a few hands. The new energy economy shows signs of following suit, with deserts, forests, and oceans becoming extraction battlegrounds. The Congo's tragic history reminds us that unchecked resource exploitation leaves scars—on land, people, and the promise of equitable progress. The question is whether humanity will finally break free from this cycle or continue to rob the Earth under the guise of innovation.

2.1 RESOURCES ROBBED

The exploitation of natural resources by economic elites is as old as empire. Its roots lie deep in colonial histories that promised progress but delivered plunder. Few examples capture this duality as starkly as the Congo Rubber Boom of the late 19th and early 20th centuries. Under King Leopold II's "humanitarian project," the Congo Free State became a site of unimaginable brutality. Europe's automotive and industrial demands stripped vast tracts of land of rubber. Colonial powers forced the Congolese into backbreaking labor, threatening mutilation or death, with severed hands as grim compliance tokens. Leopold amassed immense wealth, financing palaces and monuments in Belgium. The Congolese paid the ultimate price: over 10 million lives lost and lush forests decimated. This extraction left the Congo impoverished and destabilized. It illustrates the bitter irony of colonial resource exploitation: vast riches for European elites, environmental ruin, and societal collapse for the colonized.

Oil, the "black gold" of the 20th century, perpetuated this legacy of exploitation, with the Middle East serving as the battleground for corporate and geopolitical greed. Companies like Standard Oil—later fragmented into the "Seven Sisters" of the oil industry—did not merely extract petroleum; they reshaped nations to secure it. Western oil interests used coercive diplomacy, covert interventions, and support for autocratic regimes. They ensured profits flowed northward, leaving local populations mired in poverty. The 1953 CIA-backed coup in Iran, which toppled Prime Minister Mohammad Mossadegh, exemplifies this dynamic. Mossadegh's government had moved to nationalize Iranian oil, challenging British and American control. In response, foreign intelligence agencies orchestrated his removal, reinstating the Shah, whose regime maintained Western access to oil reserves. The coup funneled Iran's wealth to multinational corporations, sacrificing sovereignty for fossil fuel profits.

Even within the Global North, the prioritization of oil profits over environmental and human safety is evident in modern history. The Deepwater Horizon disaster of 2010 epitomized the dangers of unchecked corporate power. BP, one of the world's largest oil conglomerates, had systematically cut corners on safety to reduce costs and maximize shareholder returns. The result was catastrophic: an offshore drilling rig explosion that killed 11 workers and spilled 4.9 million barrels of oil into the Gulf of Mexico. Fisheries, wildlife, and coastal economies suffered irreparable damage as entire ecosystems were devastated. The spill laid bare the dark reality behind the oil industry's promises of responsibility and innovation. Despite fines and public outrage, BP quickly returned to profitability, demonstrating how the financial interests of elites often shield them from the full consequences of their actions.

The extraction and destruction of forests for elite-controlled commodities further illustrate the pervasive exploitation of natural resources. Nowhere is this more evident than in the Amazon Rainforest, where agribusiness giants have clearing millions of acres for cattle grazing and soy production. These activities are often justified by local elites as economic necessities, yet they disproportionately benefit multinational corporations that dominate global supply chains. The Amazon is being deforested to meet demand for cheap beef in fast-food chains and soy for animal feed. This has displaced indigenous communities and accelerated climate change. International appeals to protect the rainforest often falter in the face of these economic interests, as global markets reward the very destruction they condemn. Burning forests choke the skies with carbon emissions. They remind us how the pursuit of wealth by a privileged few endangers the planet.

Historical resource exploitation shows a pattern. Economic elites prioritize immediate gains over long-term stewardship, causing environmental and social devastation. From the rubber trees of the Congo to the oil fields of the Middle East and the vanishing forests of the Amazon, the story is the same. Resource wealth has built empires, powered revolutions, and filled corporate coffers. Yet, it has left scars on land, communities, and global equity. As the planet nears environmental collapse, history warns us. The unchecked greed of the past must not dictate future green transitions.

The exploitation of natural resources may wear new disguises, but its essence remains unchanged: profit for the powerful at the expense of the vulnerable. As global demand shifts from oil to cobalt and coltan, the practices of extraction mirror those of a darker past, where legality is a facade easily bypassed. The rise of sustainable technologies, ironically, fuels unsustainable practices in places like the Congo, highlighting the persistent gap between ideals and realities. Until global systems confront the intersection of legality and profit, the future risks being built on the same foundations of inequity and exploitation as the past.

2.2 ILLEGAL BUT PROFITABLE

Illegal resource extraction echoes colonial exploitation. Profit-driven actions ignore rules protecting people and the planet. In Congo, cobalt and coltan mining highlights how global elites bypass international norms to dominate critical supply chains. Cobalt, indispensable for lithium-ion batteries, powers the smartphones, laptops, and electric cars that define modern convenience. Yet, its extraction often occurs under harrowing conditions. In makeshift mines, workers, including children, labor for hours in dangerous, unregulated environments, earning a pittance for their efforts. The irony is striking: the tech giants that tout their commitment to sustainability rely on a supply chain steeped in exploitation and environmental destruction. International frameworks like the Kimberley Process aim to prevent conflict mineral trade. Yet, loopholes and weak enforcement let violations persist, depriving Congolese people of their mineral wealth.

Oceans, once seen as boundless sources of life, now bear scars from overfishing and exploitation. Fleets from wealthy nations often flout international rules. One striking example is the unchecked overfishing in international waters, particularly near the coasts of developing nations. The UNCLOS aims to regulate maritime activities and protect marine resources. Yet, fishing fleets from China, Spain, and Japan often violate these agreements. In West African waters, illegal and unregulated fishing has decimated fish stocks. This deprives coastal communities of protein and livelihoods. These fleets deploy advanced technologies, enabling them to harvest fish on a massive scale, often leaving local fishermen with empty nets. The imbalance is stark: nations that claim to champion environmental stewardship exploit the oceans with impunity, leveraging their wealth and political clout to avoid accountability. The result is not just environmental degradation but also deepening inequities for the communities left in their wake.

Climate treaty violations exemplify how global powers manipulate international agreements to serve their interests while projecting an image of responsibility. The Paris Agreement, once heralded as a climate milestone, faces undermining by its own champions. Wealthy countries, many of them historical emitters, routinely fail to meet their self-imposed Nationally Determined Contributions (NDCs) for emission reductions. In the United States, fossil fuel companies, backed by powerful lobbies, have successfully diluted climate legislation, ensuring that corporate profits remain untouched even as global temperatures climb. At COP26 in Glasgow, for instance, nations pledged renewed efforts to limit warming to 1.5 degrees Celsius. Yet, behind closed doors, major economies like Australia and Saudi Arabia lobbied to soften language on phasing out coal, undermining the agreement's ambition. Such actions betray collective action. They reveal a global order where power and wealth dictate outcomes, harming vulnerable nations bearing climate change's brunt.

From African conflict minerals to marine resource plundering and treaty subversion, violations show persistent inequality in global governance. Elite actors prioritize short-term gains, rendering equity-promising agreements toothless. The world's poorest bear the disproportionate costs of this exploitation—whether through depleted fisheries, poisoned rivers, or rising seas—while those responsible face few consequences. These violations remind us that without strong enforcement and accountability, international agreements risk becoming facades that mask historical exploitation.

The illegal exploitation of resources reveals a troubling truth: the shift to sustainability often replicates the inequalities it seeks to address. As the world embraces green technologies, the monopolization of critical resources like rare earth elements ensures that power remains concentrated in the hands of a few. This new chapter of exploitation, cloaked in the language of environmentalism, perpetuates the same cycles of harm—this time under the banner of progress. Without a rethinking of global supply chains and accountability, the green revolution risks becoming another story of monopoly and marginalization, rather than a beacon of shared prosperity.

2.3 MONOPOLY GOES GREEN

The shift to renewable energy, seen as humanity's climate solution, is becoming another arena for elite control. Resource monopolization persists under a new guise. At the heart of this shift lie rare earth elements, the lifeblood of wind turbines, solar panels, and electric vehicles. These metals—neodymium, dysprosium, and lanthanum, to name a few—are indispensable for the technologies driving the green revolution. Yet, the extraction and control of rare earth elements tell a story far removed from their green promise. China, for example, dominates global rare earth mining and processing, accounting for over 70% of global production. This monopoly stems from decades of Western outsourcing. Corporations seeking cheaper production moved rare earth extraction's environmental damage and labor abuses overseas. Today, corporations and Chinese elites' benefit, while mining region residents face pollution, poisoned water, and unsafe work. Industries sacrifice their communities in the name of "sustainable progress."

The lithium triangle of South America—spanning Bolivia, Chile, and Argentina—presents a similar picture of exploitation and inequity. Lithium, a critical component for rechargeable batteries, is abundant in this region, yet its extraction often benefits elite-controlled corporations rather than the local populations. In Bolivia, vast reserves of lithium lie beneath the Salar de Uyuni, the world's largest salt flat. Bolivia champions state-led lithium mining to protect its interests. Meanwhile, corporations promised development but often caused environmental damage and displacement. Private companies like SQM exploit Chile's lithium-rich Atacama Desert. Profits flow globally, while indigenous communities face water shortages as mining depletes groundwater. The irony is sharp: the very materials that symbolize a cleaner, greener future perpetuate the same extractive dynamics that renewable energy seeks to replace.

As renewable energy expands globally, privatizing energy infrastructure keeps its benefits beyond the reach of many. Large-scale solar and wind projects are increasingly owned by private investors and energy firms. Private investors price out public utilities and the people they serve. Privatized solar grid installations in Sub-Saharan Africa and parts of Asia have established a two-tiered energy system. Wealthier urban populations enjoy reliable, albeit expensive, access to renewable electricity, while poorer rural communities remain in energy poverty, unable to afford the new infrastructure. This mirrors fossil fuel era inequalities. Elites control resources, ensuring profits flow upward while marginalized communities fend for themselves. Privatizing renewable energy transforms a potential democratizing force into yet another tool for exclusion and profit.

The phenomenon of greenwashing further reveals how elites navigate the renewable energy landscape to maintain power while avoiding accountability. Many corporations, from oil giants to tech firms, prominently advertise their investments in renewable energy projects, claiming a commitment to sustainability. Yet, behind the scenes, these same corporations continue to lobby for fossil fuel subsidies, explore new oil fields, and resist stricter climate regulations. BP, once rebranded as "Beyond Petroleum," epitomizes this duplicity. The company promotes solar and wind while investing billions in oil and gas. Its emissions targets rely on speculative technologies like carbon capture, not reductions. These practices mask ongoing fossil fuel dependence with a superficial illusion of progress and environmentalism.

Renewable energy holds potential to fight climate change. Yet, its trajectory suggests it may replace one inequitable system with another. Rare earth mining, lithium extraction, and corporate greenwashing reveal a grim truth. Without equity and justice, this transition may consolidate elite power further. Will the world seize this moment to create an inclusive and sustainable energy future? Or will it repeat past mistakes, wrapping old hierarchies in the promise of solar panels and wind turbines?

2.4 NUKES AND NATIONS

Nuclear energy, often championed as a clean alternative to fossil fuels, is steeped in dynamics of strategic control, where resource monopolization and geopolitical power converge. At the heart of this industry lies uranium, the critical element fueling nuclear reactors and, by extension, shaping the global distribution of power. Niger, a nation endowed with some of the world's largest uranium reserves, exemplifies the exploitation inherent in this system. For decades, corporations like France's Orano have extracted uranium from Niger's mines. The material powers French cities, while mining regions remain in poverty. Workers in towns like Arlit endure unsafe conditions, often exposed to radioactive waste that contaminates their water and air. The wealth from Niger's uranium rarely benefits the country. The resource powers Paris but leaves local communities in darkness, burdened by environmental and health costs.

Beyond resource extraction, the geopolitics of nuclear energy reflect a deep asymmetry in global power structures. Access to uranium and the ability to refine and utilize it remain concentrated among a handful of nations and elite-controlled corporations, perpetuating dependencies in the Global South. Australia and Canada, with vast uranium reserves, dominate supply chains. Import-reliant nations in Asia and Africa remain tethered to these suppliers. This control extends into the political realm, where uranium-exporting nations often wield disproportionate influence over international energy policies. The strategic importance of uranium has even led to political manipulation and unrest. Struggles over uranium revenues fuel coups and instability in Niger. Elites compete for control, undermining sovereignty and stability.

High costs and safety concerns undermine nuclear energy's potential as a climate solution. Vulnerable communities bear the greatest burdens. The disasters at Chernobyl in 1986 and Fukushima in 2011 remain stark reminders of the dangers of prioritizing profit and efficiency over public safety. Chernobyl's reactor explosion in Soviet Ukraine stemmed from flawed design and poor safety measures. Pressure to meet unrealistic goals worsened the disaster. The fallout, both literal and figurative, devastated surrounding regions, displacing thousands and leaving a legacy of health issues and environmental contamination. Negligence in plant design and oversight exacerbated the Fukushima disaster, triggered by a tsunami. TEPCO, the corporation managing the plant, had cut costs on protective measures despite warnings, prioritizing short-term savings over disaster preparedness. In both cases, the brunt of these failures fell on ordinary citizens, who lost their homes, health, and livelihoods, while elites managing these operations faced minimal accountability.

Promoting nuclear energy as a clean alternative to fossil fuels reveals deep contradictions. While producing no direct carbon emissions, its lifecycle—from uranium mining to waste disposal—inflicts significant environmental and human harm. In places like the Navajo Nation, uranium mining left radioactive contamination, poisoning land and water for decades. Marginalized communities bear these risks, from waste storage to fallout, while elites frame nuclear power as a solution to global warming. This push often reinforces exploitation and inequality. Without equitable benefit distribution, nuclear energy remains a symbol of technological progress overshadowed by injustice.

Climate change is not just a scientific crisis; it is a moral reckoning. The same traits that drove humanity to conquer and exploit now threaten to destroy us. But as the planet warms and resources dwindle, the competition for survival intensifies, leading us to Chapter 13: *War and Conflict*. The dysfunction of humanity finds its most destructive expression on the battlefield, where the fight for survival turns violent.

13

War and Conflict

War, at its core, is the story of humanity's relentless pursuit of resources, land, and power. In the distant past, people often framed conflicts as divine mandates. People invoked gods, spirits, and cosmic forces to justify battles, unite tribes, and compel loyalty. People rallied under sacred banners, believing their wars mirrored celestial struggles. The battlefield became a theater of faith, where victory wasn't just measured in land or wealth, but in proving divine favor.

Yet, as societies grew more complex, the gods began to retreat from the frontlines of human conflict. Empires and nation-states emerged, replacing divine authority with bureaucratic systems, laws, and economies that could mobilize entire populations. By the time of the Industrial Revolution, war was no longer about appeasing deities but securing material dominance. Steel, coal, and oil—these became the new gods, driving conflicts that reshaped the world map.

Today, the landscape of war has transformed again. Technology, data, and ideology now coordinate the machinery of conflict. Satellites pinpoint targets, algorithms predict enemy movements, and cyberspace has become a battlefield where nations wage silent wars over information and influence. The cold logic of AI and the profit motives of corporations have replaced the gods of the past, making modern conflicts less visible but no less ruthless.

As we explore this chapter, we will trace the arc of war from its primal beginnings to its digital future, asking not just how humanity fights, but why. What has driven us to spill blood for millennia, and what does this say about the forces—both visible and unseen—that continue to shape our world?

1. UNITED STATES OF AMBUSH

For the United States, the narrative of counterterrorism has often served as a powerful tool to mask more self-serving ambitions. Powerful entities quickly label local leaders as insurgents, rebels, or terrorists when they recognize and resist the exploitation of their resources—whether oil, minerals, or land. This label transforms their struggle from one of sovereignty to one of global security, instantly justifying United States intervention. The brilliance of this strategy lies in its framing. America portrays itself not as a looter but as a protector of stability, aiding beleaguered governments against so-called "terrorist threats." Often, these governments—many fragile, corrupt, or complicit—embrace the United States narrative, trading their autonomy for military aid, intelligence, and political backing. This dynamic secures American access to wealth and entrenches its influence over local governments. It appears benevolent while tightening its grip on the land's riches. For the United States, counterterrorism becomes not a goal but a method, a malleable tool used to safeguard its interests under the ambush of global peace.

The United States' strategic use of counterterrorism highlights a broader pattern: framing its interventions as moral imperatives while advancing self-serving goals. This narrative mastery extends beyond military campaigns into economic, political, and cultural realms. Post-World War II, the U.S. perfected this skill, shaping a global order that aligned its ambitions with world events. Through institutions like NATO, the IMF, and the UN, it embedded its influence into international systems, presenting itself as a benevolent global leader. This narrative cast the U.S. not just as a participant but as the director of a global cinematic universe, where resources, conflicts, and alliances are choreographed to sustain its dominance. From counterterrorism to economic sanctions, every act reinforces this script, maintaining power while masking exploitation under the guise of promoting freedom, democracy, and global stability.

1.1 AMERICA'S GLOBAL CINEMATIC UNIVERSE

After World War II, the United States emerged not just as a victor but as an architect of a new global order. In the ashes of a devastated Europe and Asia, America used its unmatched economic and military power to reshape the world. This vision was equal parts ideology and pragmatism. But behind the lofty rhetoric of freedom and democracy lay a far more calculated reality. Every war, every coup, and every treaty that touched the global stage in the latter half of the 20th century bore the fingerprints of American ambition. Natural resources—oil, minerals, and fertile land—were no longer just commodities but weapons in a geopolitical game. Planners ambushed, prepared, and executed these operations with precision. They turned conflicts into investments and atrocities into collateral damage for a larger strategy.

The United States understood early that controlling resources meant controlling the future. The Marshall Plan, heralded as a humanitarian effort to rebuild Europe, was also a shrewd maneuver to secure markets and ensure allegiance in the emerging Cold War. In the Middle East, America orchestrated a new era of oil politics, toppling regimes and installing allies to guarantee the flow of black gold. The CIA used Latin America as a testing ground for interventions, overthrowing democratically elected leaders to protect American corporate interests. From Vietnam's jungles to the deserts of Iraq, wars were justified with grand narratives, but often fought for access to resources and influence. Each conflict was not a chaotic eruption but a carefully staged act in a theater where the United States always sought to dictate the script.

This dominance was not only about amassing wealth or power; it was about embedding American interests so deeply into the fabric of global systems that they became inseparable. Creating institutions like the International Monetary Fund (IMF) and the World Bank ensured that economic dependency would replace colonialism as a means of control. Trade routes, energy supplies, and financial markets aligned with American priorities. This positioning made the United States not just a player but the global game's referee. Yet, this ambition came at a cost—wars that ravaged entire regions, coups that stifled local sovereignty, and atrocities justified in the name of stability and progress.

As we unpack these layers, one question arises. Was this orchestrated dominance an inevitable outcome of power or a deliberate choice prioritizing profit over cooperation? The sections ahead will unravel this complicated web, exposing the hidden mechanisms that shaped our world. They will ask whether a system born of ambition can evolve into something equitable.

The narrative of America's global influence reveals a deeper truth: power, once attained, seeks to perpetuate itself through any means necessary. Behind the surface of democracy lies a strategy honed over decades. Regime changes, covert operations, and alliances ensure the world aligns with American interests. These interventions are not anomalies but integral to a superpower's strategy. They script the global order, reshaping regimes to maintain dominance repeatedly.

1.2 REGIMES RELOADED

The tale of American coups, regime changes, and orchestrated interventions is not one of coincidence or reactive measures; this saga reveals calculated moves and relentless ambition, with its fingerprints visible across continents and centuries. From the 20th century to today, the United States has used coups as both scalpel and sledgehammer. These actions carve out a global order aligned with its economic, ideological, and strategic interests. Meticulously planned and executed, these acts were deliberate operations. They reshaped the world map to reflect American priorities.

Take Hawaii in 1893, where the United States military, under the guise of protecting American sugar plantations, arrived with troops to overthrow Queen Liliʻuokalani. The coup was as much about asserting control over the lucrative sugar trade as it was about planting the seeds of annexation. The result was a new government led by Sanford B. Dole—a name that would become synonymous with corporate expansionism—followed by Hawaii's eventual absorption into the United States. This was not an isolated incident but a prototype, a template for future interventions where economic stakes dictated political outcomes.

In 1953, in Iran, Prime Minister Mohammad Mossadegh boldly nationalized the oil industry. This decision challenged the Anglo-Iranian Oil Company's monopoly. In response, the United States, with Britain's urging, orchestrated Operation Ajax, deploying CIA operatives like Kermit Roosevelt to bribe officials, manipulate public opinion, and incite chaos. The operation culminated in Mossadegh's ousting and reinstating the Shah, whose autocratic rule ensured Western access to Iran's oil reserves. Dressed in Cold War justifications, this coup sparked decades of Iranian resentment and turmoil. It ultimately led to the 1979 revolution and the theocratic regime that followed.

In Guatemala in 1954, the script played out similarly. American leaders labeled President Jacobo Árbenz's land reforms as communist threats, accusing them of targeting the United Fruit Company's dominance. The CIA engineered his overthrow, installing a more compliant regime. Decades of instability and violence in Guatemala exposed the enduring costs of this intervention. American interventions plunged the nation into chaos to safeguard their business interests.

The pattern repeated across decades and continents. In 1973, in Chile, the United States backed a coup toppling Salvador Allende, ushering in Augusto Pinochet's brutal dictatorship. In the Congo, assassinating Patrice Lumumba, supported by CIA machinations, ensured that the mineral-rich nation remained under Western influence. Each coup caused more than momentary upheaval. These seismic shifts redirected nations' political and social trajectories, often leaving enduring scars.

Even as the Cold War faded, the logic of intervention persisted. In 2003, invading Iraq was justified by claims of weapons of mass destruction. At its core, it was another regime change operation designed to secure American influence in the Middle East. The toppling of Saddam Hussein unleashed a maelstrom of instability, birthing insurgencies and extremist groups that continue to haunt the region.

What makes these acts particularly harrowing is their predictability. Planners orchestrated each coup with precision, using propaganda, military force, and economic coercion to achieve objectives that rarely aligned with America's proclaimed democratic ideals. Instead, these operations often undermined fledgling democracies, installing authoritarian regimes more amenable to United States interests. The legacy of these actions is a world where the seeds of American ambition have sprouted into forests of distrust, conflict, and instability.

The question is not whether such actions were effective—they often were—but at what cost. As we survey the wreckage of nations reshaped by these interventions, this forces us to grapple with the ethical and historical implications. How does a nation reconcile its ideals with its actions? And in a world increasingly weary of external interference, can the tools of the past continue to serve the ambitions of the present? These are the unresolved dilemmas of an empire built as much on coups as on commerce, as much on ideology as on power.

The legacy of American interventions has often left fractured nations and lasting instability, highlighting the consequences of unchecked ambition and the limits of power. Nowhere is this more evident than in the Middle East, a region reshaped by external influences and internal conflicts. The Iran-Iraq War exemplifies how global superpowers exploited local rivalries, turning them into devastating proxy battles. Fueled by arms supplies and strategic maneuvering from the U.S. and its rivals, the war inflicted immense human and economic costs, deepening regional divisions. This conflict redefined the Middle East's future, entrenching its role as a chessboard for distant empires seeking dominance over vital energy resources. The aftermath continues to echo, perpetuating cycles of instability, power struggles, and the enduring shadow of foreign intervention.

1.3 IRAN-IRAQ WAR

The Iran-Iraq War was one of the most catastrophic conflicts of the modern era, lasting from 1980 to 1988 and reshaping the geopolitics of the Middle East. Later events in the region often overshadow its significance. This war was not just a clash between neighbors. It became a proxy battleground where global superpowers played dangerous games, sowing the seeds of the instability that defines the Middle East today. The conflict claimed over a million lives and displaced millions more. The roles played by the United States and other external powers in the war remain critical and undeniable.

It began in 1979, when Iran was in the throes of a revolution. A mass uprising overthrew the Shah, a monarch installed in the 1950s through a United States- and UK-led coup. Decades of corruption, autocratic rule, and dependence on Western powers had alienated Iranians, leading to the rise of Ayatollah Ruhollah Khomeini and his Shia Islamist regime. This new government established the Islamic Revolutionary Guard Corps to protect the revolution and suppress opposition, both domestic and foreign. Khomeini's Iran openly rejected both Western and Soviet influence, broadcasting revolutionary calls to overthrow regimes in neighboring Arab countries.

This revolutionary fervor sent shockwaves across the Middle East. Sunni leaders in Saudi Arabia, Kuwait, and Iraq saw Khomeini's rhetoric as a direct threat to their rule. In Iraq, Saddam Hussein worried that Iran's Shia majority might inspire Iraq's own Shia population to rise against his Sunni-dominated Ba'athist regime. Saddam also saw an opportunity. Iran's weakened state left its military fractured, its officers purged, and its infrastructure in chaos. Saddam believed a swift invasion would prevent Iranian influence from spreading. He also aimed to seize the disputed Shatt al-Arab waterway, a vital oil export route. Moreover, Saddam hoped that a victory would bolster his image as a pan-Arab leader.

In September 1980, Saddam launched his invasion, sending 10,000 troops across the border and targeting Iranian air bases in a surprise attack. However, these initial strikes failed to achieve the intended shock-and-awe effect, as Iran still had United States-supplied F-14 fighter jets capable of striking back. The invasion sparked fierce resistance from Iran, which quickly unified behind Khomeini. Ironically, the war solidified his control over the country, as factions that had opposed him during the revolution rallied to defend Iran's sovereignty.

Brutal trench warfare, reminiscent of World War I, defined the war's early years. In its fight against Iranian forces, Iraq resorted to using chemical weapons like mustard gas—a blatant violation of international law that met little resistance from global powers supporting Saddam Hussein. To curb Iran's revolutionary influence, the United States provided Iraq with satellite imagery and intelligence on Iranian troop movements. The United States restored official diplomatic ties and allowed American companies to sell Iraq technology that fueled its chemical and biological weapons programs.

Meanwhile, the war spread beyond the battlefield. Saddam targeted Iran's oil tankers in the Persian Gulf to weaken its economy, igniting the so-called "Tanker War." Both sides attacked hundreds of ships, killing over 400 civilian sailors. The United States deployed its Navy to the Gulf to protect Kuwaiti oil tankers, even re-flagging them with American insignia to deter Iranian strikes. In 1988, escalating tensions led to tragedy. The United States Navy shot down Iran Air Flight 655, a passenger jet, killing all 290 civilians on board. The United States claimed it mistook the airliner for a hostile aircraft. However, the incident deepened Iranian distrust and fueled suspicions that the attack was deliberate.

The war also drew in other global players. Israel, despite being an enemy of Iran, sold arms to Tehran, hoping to prolong the conflict and keep both Iraq and Iran weakened. France supplied Iraq with Mirage fighter jets, while China sold weapons to both sides, profiting from the carnage. Saudi Arabia and Kuwait provided billions of dollars in financial aid to Iraq, seeking to counter Iran's revolutionary ambitions.

By the mid-1980s, Iran had gained the upper hand on the ground, launching a series of offensives aimed at capturing the Iraqi city of Basra. These campaigns featured horrific human-wave attacks. Thousands of Iranian soldiers, many teenage volunteers, charged into Iraqi defenses through minefields and barbed wire. The casualties were staggering, but Iran was determined to break Iraq's resolve.

In the north, Kurdish rebels, long suppressed by Saddam's regime, seized the opportunity to rise up. Iran provided support to these Kurdish forces, hoping to further destabilize Iraq. Saddam responded with brutal efficiency, using chemical weapons not only against Iranian forces but also against Kurdish civilians. The 1988 attack on the town of Halabja killed over 5,000 Kurds, most of them women and children. This massacre was part of a broader campaign of genocide against the Kurds, which claimed an estimated 50,000 to 100,000 lives.

Despite these atrocities, the United States and its allies continued to support Saddam. Declassified documents later revealed that Washington was aware of Iraq's chemical weapons program but chose to downplay or ignore it. The United States even blamed

Iran for some of Saddam's actions, demonstrating the extent to which it prioritized geopolitical strategy over human rights.

As the war dragged into its eighth year, both sides were exhausted. Iran's economy was in ruins, its cities devastated by Iraqi missile strikes that killed 16,000 civilians. In Iraq, mounting casualties and economic strain fueled discontent. The UN brokered a ceasefire in 1988, ending the war with no territorial changes but leaving a legacy of destruction. Over a million people had died, and both countries faced decades of recovery.

For Iraq, ending the war signaled the start of new troubles. Burdened with debt and emboldened by his chemical weapons success, Saddam invaded Kuwait in 1990. This move triggered the Gulf War and alienated his former backers in the United States. Iran, meanwhile, emerged more isolated but resolute, its leaders convinced that only nuclear weapons could protect the country from foreign aggression.

The Iran-Iraq War was more than a conflict between the two nations. It symbolized the global power struggles of the late 20th century. The United States, the Soviet Union, and regional players used the Middle East as a chessboard for their ambitions. The scars of this war still shape the region. From the sectarian divisions, it provoked the cycles of violence it perpetuated. It remains a stark reminder of the human cost of geopolitical gamesmanship for natural resources.

The Iran-Iraq War underscored how the pursuit of resources can turn entire regions into battlefields for global powers, leaving behind a legacy of division and instability. This dynamic extends beyond the Middle East, affecting regions globally. Across the Atlantic, in the oil-rich landscapes of Nigeria and Angola, a similar story unfolds—where vast natural wealth becomes both a blessing and a curse. African nations entangled in the global energy economy show how resources can fuel prosperity for some while triggering cycles of corruption and conflict that last generations.

1.4 ARCTIC: A NEW FRONTIER

The Arctic, long regarded as an icy wilderness at the fringes of human endeavor, is rapidly emerging as one of the most contested regions on Earth. Climate change is reshaping its landscape at an unprecedented pace, with rising global temperatures melting vast swathes of sea ice. This transformation is unlocking a treasure trove of opportunities—and dangers—once hidden beneath the frozen expanse. New navigation routes like the Northern Sea Route and the Northwest Passage are opening for longer periods each year. These routes promise to reshape global shipping by dramatically cutting travel distances between major markets. The real prize lies beneath the Arctic seabed. It holds an estimated 13% of the world's undiscovered oil and 30% of its untapped natural gas reserves, along with vast deposits of rare earth minerals. For the United States and other Arctic nations, this is more than a new frontier. It is a high-stakes competition for resources, influence, and security in a region that may define 21st century geopolitics.

The United States, as one of the eight Arctic nations, has been slow to recognize the strategic significance of this evolving landscape. For decades, American engagement in the Arctic was minimal, largely limited to scientific research and environmental monitoring. However, the accelerating pace of ice melt has forced Washington to rethink its priorities. By the 2010s, the Arctic was no longer an isolated backwater but a vital arena where economic, environmental, and security interests converged. The United States Geological Survey's 2008 report estimated the region's massive energy reserves. It acted as a wake-up call, highlighting the Arctic's potential to become a major contributor to global energy markets. Russia, China, and other nations began asserting their presence, setting off a quiet race for dominance in this new frontier.

In terms of resource access, the Arctic's transformation has been staggering. Oil companies like Shell and ExxonMobil have invested billions in exploratory drilling, particularly off the coast of Alaska. Although technical and environmental challenges have delayed large-scale production, the allure of Arctic energy remains undeniable. The potential rewards are immense. Arctic oil and gas reserves could sustain global energy demands for decades, providing a critical buffer as existing fields in the Middle East and elsewhere face depletion. The United States, with its vast Arctic coastline in Alaska, stands to gain significantly if it can successfully exploit these resources. However, this pursuit is fraught with challenges, not least of which is the environmental fragility of the Arctic ecosystem.

The U.S. government balances economic ambition with environmental stewardship in its Arctic strategy, oscillating between these priorities. The Obama administration emphasized climate change, advocating for international agreements to reduce carbon emissions and imposing restrictions on Arctic drilling. Yet, it also prioritized the Arctic's strategic importance, releasing the National Strategy for the Arctic Region in 2015, which called for "responsible stewardship" and competitiveness for resources.

The Trump administration took a different approach, prioritizing resource extraction. In 2017, Trump reversed Obama-era restrictions on offshore drilling, opening Arctic areas to exploration. This sparked opposition from environmental groups and indigenous communities.

Strategic competition in the Arctic extends beyond resource extraction to include military positioning. The melting ice has created new vulnerabilities, as the Arctic's once-impassable ice shield no longer serves as a natural barrier. Russia, which claims nearly half of the Arctic coastline, has aggressively expanded its military presence in the region, reopening Soviet-era bases and deploying advanced weaponry. By 2021, Russia had established more than 50 Arctic military installations, including bases equipped with air-defense systems and nuclear-powered icebreakers.

The United States has begun bolstering its Arctic capabilities, though its efforts lag behind Russia's. The U.S. Coast Guard operates only two icebreakers, one often out of service, compared to Russia's fleet of over 40. Congress has funded new icebreakers, but these will take years to build. Meanwhile, the Pentagon's Arctic strategy emphasizes countering Russian and Chinese ambitions. Joint military exercises with NATO allies, like Norway and Canada, signal a renewed focus on Arctic security.

China's role in the Arctic adds complexity. Despite lacking Arctic territory, China calls itself a "near-Arctic state" and uses its Belt and Road Initiative to gain influence. Chinese investments in Arctic infrastructure, such as ports and research stations, have raised U.S. concerns. In 2018, the United States labeled China a "strategic competitor," highlighting the Arctic's importance in great-power rivalry.

The U.S. Arctic policy reflects a tension between asserting its presence and addressing climate change, which drives the region's transformation. The Biden administration has rejoined climate agreements while facing pressure to expand drilling and mining operations. The Arctic encapsulates global challenges, where resource competition meets sustainability, and geopolitics intersects with environmental change. For the U.S., it is both an opportunity and a test of its ability to lead responsibly in a transforming world.

The Arctic's icy expanse reflects a world in transition, where competition for resources reshapes old boundaries and tests global priorities. But as the cold frontier melts, another battleground heats up—one not of frozen landscapes, but of silicon circuits. From the frigid poles to the humming centers of technological power, the struggle for dominance reveals humanity's unyielding quest to control the future.

1.5 SILICON WAR

The modern world runs on microchips, the intricate and diminutive pieces of silicon that form the bedrock of technological civilization. Their ubiquity belies their significance—found in everything from smartphones to military systems, microchips are the invisible lifeblood of contemporary power structures. Yet, these devices are not merely tools of convenience or commerce; they are the currency of global influence, dictating the trajectory of geopolitics in the 21st century. The escalating rivalry between the United States and China over microchips underscores their importance, as each nation maneuvers to secure dominance over this critical technology.

Microchips, also known as semiconductors, emerged from mid-20th-century breakthroughs in computing. The transistor, developed in 1947, transformed clunky, wire-filled devices into compact machines capable of precise electrical control. By the 1960s, engineers discovered that carving millions of these transistors on silicon chips could exponentially increase computing power, laying the foundation for modern electronics. This innovation fueled an arms race of technological progress. By the 1980s, American companies had cemented their leadership in semiconductor design and production, driven by a fervent "more transistors per chip" ethos. However, as these chips became integral to both civilian and military applications, the stakes around their production and control grew exponentially.

The semiconductor gold rush did not remain confined to the United States. East Asian nations, particularly Japan, Taiwan, and South Korea, quickly recognized the transformative potential of microchips. Japan initially emerged as a formidable competitor, leveraging government subsidies to produce high-quality chips at lower costs. The United States, alarmed by Japan's ascendance, imposed heavy tariffs to protect its domestic industry—a rare deviation from its free-market ethos. This intervention began geopolitics entwining with the semiconductor supply chain.

Among the nations eager to carve a niche in the microchip market, Taiwan's strategic foresight stands out. Understanding that direct competition with American firms could provoke similar punitive measures, Taiwan adopted a collaborative approach. Visionary engineer Morris Chang spearheaded the creation of Taiwan Semiconductor Manufacturing Company (TSMC) as a "pure-play" foundry. Unlike integrated firms that designed and manufactured chips, TSMC specialized in production, solving the increasingly complex and costly challenge of chip fabrication for global clients. With support from the Taiwanese government, TSMC propelled Taiwan to the forefront of the semiconductor industry. It also positioned the nation as a linchpin in the global supply chain, a role now referred to as the "Silicon Shield" against potential Chinese aggression.

As TSMC and other Asian firms advanced, the United States increasingly outsourced chip manufacturing while retaining leadership in design and machinery. By the 2010s, Taiwan produced 92% of the world's most advanced semiconductors, leaving the United States reliant on a single, geographically vulnerable supplier. Meanwhile, China emerged as the largest consumer of semiconductors, purchasing 40% of global supply, but lagging significantly in domestic production capability. This dependence on foreign suppliers created a strategic vulnerability that Beijing sought to address.

China's push for semiconductor self-sufficiency is emblematic of its broader ambitions. China's "Made in China 2025" initiative underscores its determination to dominate critical technologies. These include artificial intelligence, quantum computing, and advanced weaponry—all reliant on high-performance chips. However, despite massive investments and state-backed programs, China's semiconductor industry struggled to close the gap with global leaders. Producing cutting-edge chips demands vast financial resources, intricate expertise, and access to specialized equipment. In these fields, the United States and its allies maintain significant advantages.

The geopolitical stakes of semiconductors became glaringly evident with China's development of hypersonic missiles capable of evading existing defense systems. In 2021, reports revealed that these advancements relied, in part, on American-designed semiconductor technology, highlighting the risks of technological leakage. This revelation catalyzed a decisive shift in United States policy. Viewing microchips as a strategic asset akin to oil in the 20th century, the United States implemented sweeping measures to curtail China's access to advanced semiconductor technology.

The Biden administration's 2022 export controls epitomized this approach, barring Chinese firms from acquiring cutting-edge chips, software, and equipment. These restrictions extended beyond American companies, targeting any entity globally that utilized United States-origin technology. The CHIPS Act followed, channeling $52 billion in subsidies to domestic semiconductor manufacturers to bolster onshore production. This legislation signaled the United States' commitment to reducing reliance on foreign suppliers and safeguarding its technological edge.

Yet, these measures are not without consequences. For American firms like Nvidia and Intel, China represents a critical market. The sudden severance of commercial ties has resulted in substantial revenue losses, highlighting the tension between national security and economic interests. Moreover, the fragmented supply chain exacerbates global vulnerabilities. During the COVID-19 pandemic, disruptions in semiconductor production underscored the fragility of this interconnected system, amplifying calls for diversification and resilience.

Taiwan, at the epicenter of the United States-China microchip rivalry, faces unique challenges. Taiwan's semiconductor industry, a democratic U.S. ally and obstacle to China's goals, is both a deterrent and a target. China's military posturing, including naval exercises near the island, underscores the potential for escalation. An outright invasion of Taiwan remains improbable because of the complexities of chip manufacturing and geopolitical risks. However, Beijing could use tactics like blockades to assert leverage over the global supply chain. Such a scenario would disrupt industries worldwide, from consumer electronics to defense systems.

The microchip war is reshaping international relations in profound ways. The era of globalization, characterized by interdependence and cooperation, is giving way to a landscape of fragmentation and rivalry. As nations prioritize technological sovereignty, geopolitical barriers increasingly obstruct the once seamless flow of goods and knowledge. This transformation extends beyond semiconductors, reflecting broader shifts in the global order. Like oil in the 20th century, microchips have become a strategic resource, their control dictating the balance of power in the 21st century.

In this high-stakes competition, the question is not just who will dominate the microchip industry. It is also about how this contest will shape the future of technology, security, and globalization. The rivalry over silicon, with its complex interplay of innovation, economics, and politics, is not just a battle for technological supremacy. It is a microcosm of the broader struggle to define the rules of a rapidly evolving world. As nations vie for control over the building blocks of the future, the microchip war underscores the profound interconnectedness—and fragility—of modern civilization.

The race for silicon dominance reveals a modern truth: power lies in controlling the intangible foundations of technology. But the drive for resources is as old as civilization itself. Long before circuits and chips, wealth and dominance emerged from the earth, secured through conquest. The spoils of empire included not just land and goods but also the people who tilled, built, and served. In both arenas, the quest for control reshapes the world, forging new hierarchies and reviving ancient strategies.

2. ISRAEL & UKRAINE: POWERED BY PENTAGON

The narratives spun around the conflicts in Gaza and Ukraine reveal a pattern of superficial justifications crafted by global elites to obscure deeper, resource-driven motives. Take, for instance, the United States framing of the conflict between Hamas and Israel. The story told to the world revolves around religious extremism, and the ideological drive. Media portray Hamas's fight as an existential clash against Israel, highlighting its militant tactics and theological rhetoric. Media often depict Hamas as a group striving for an Islamic caliphate, Palestinian rights, and resistance to anti-Semitic oppression. While these narratives carry grains of truth, they are also simplistic reductions that serve to deflect from the underlying reality.

Similarly, Russia frames its war in Ukraine within the language of geopolitics and history. Vladimir Putin speaks of NATO encroachment, the need to protect ethnic Russians, and the so-called "denazification" of Ukraine. By framing the war in ideological and existential terms, Putin distracts effectively.

China, meanwhile, listens to the dog whistle by Russia, positioning itself as a financial backer and arms supplier while watching these conflicts unfold. By purchasing vast amounts of Iranian oil and supplying funds and weapons to Tehran, Beijing indirectly fuels groups like Hamas. These arms flow from Iran to proxies engaged in Israel's perpetual state of conflict. For China, this is not about ideology; it is a strategic maneuver to maintain influence in the Middle East and weaken United States dominance as per Russia's request and get profits in the process.

Do you truly believe in the narratives our beloved elites have been feeding us? After exploring the intricate web of manipulations and natural resource politics in this book, we must ask: Can religious fanatism or defensive postures alone explain these wars?

For readers who have jumped to this section out of sheer curiosity, rest assured, the detailed chapters earlier provide a comprehensive breakdown of these complex geopolitical strategies. But for simplicity, let's distill the essence here: the conflicts are about one thing—natural resources. Human history, despite its ideological and political surfaces, has always pivoted on access to the raw materials that sustain life and power economies.

The urgency of these battles stems from a looming crisis. The United States may deplete its oil reserves between 2034 and 2044 unless it taps into new domestic sources. This would make the United States dependent on foreign oil, destabilizing its economic foundation and undermining the petrodollar. The surge in investments into electric vehicles, such as Elon Musk's Tesla, emphasizes America's race to pivot away from fossil fuels. Simultaneously, Russia could face a similar reckoning between 2044 and 2085 when its oil reserves hit rock bottom. Its proximity to Iran, whose oil reserves may deplete around 2200, and Iraq, with depletion expected around 2110, makes the future course clear. Russia's history of aggressive expansion for resources—recalled earlier in this book—provides the blueprint for its likely ambitions.

The United States, anticipating this, has strategically aligned itself with Saudi Arabia for oil while biding its time. A Russian move on Iran could provide America with a pretext to engage militarily. Seemingly, it would act to protect global stability, but in reality, it could aim to secure Iran's resources by installing an American-favored regime. The Pentagon's billions in military aid to Israel and Ukraine are not acts of altruism; they are maneuvers to position these allies as front lines in containing Russian influence while Russia tries to annex Iran. Ukraine's proximity to Moscow and Israel's ties to Iran's region are pivotal to this grand chess game.

Putin understands this, which is why his aggression towards Ukraine is not just about NATO or historical grievances but an attempt to preempt United States encirclement around Russia. However, these conflicts will persist, with only brief intermissions of ceasefire. The global stage now faces an era of unending proxy wars fueled by the need to control dwindling resources powering human civilization. We can call this geopolitical dynamic the "*Petrocalypse.*"

The conflicts in Ukraine and Palestine reveal a shared truth: global powers often perpetuate local struggles to serve their broader strategic interests. Powerful nations carefully manage these proxy wars—framed as ideological or territorial disputes—to maintain a balance of instability, justifying intervention while avoiding resolution. With Palestine, this dynamic manifests in the grim disparity between landowners and the dispossessed. It echoes through the lives of Palestinian effendi (elites) and Palestinian fellahin (tenants), where power and possession collide under the shadow of global agendas.

2.1 PALESTINIAN JANMI VS TENANT

The Israel-Palestine conflict often unfolds in conversations as a tangled web of morality and legality. We ask: Who holds the historical right to the land? Who has suffered more? Is there a moral high ground in a war that destroys lives on both sides? These debates, almost predictably, lead to calls for empathy—a recognition that both Palestinians and Jews deserve safety, dignity, and peace. The discussion then deflects toward the perennial "solution," often the two-state solution, as if that concept alone could untangle decades of political chess, displacement, and trauma. Yet, behind this narrative is a pattern too deliberate to dismiss as a simple failure of diplomacy. It is a playbook—one masterminded not in the Middle East, but in Pentagon boardrooms. Global powers calibrate these conflicts to keep them simmering, neither resolved nor abandoned, serving purposes beyond the reach of their local actors.

When the United States champions the two-state solution through its puppet, the United Nations, it presents itself as a peacemaker. It claims to be a guiding hand offering balance to a conflict-ridden world. But inquire deeper, and the contradictions unravel the mask. Although superficially reasonable, the two-state proposal is functionally unworkable in a land where infrastructure—roads, hospitals, and water systems—remains as enmeshed as its populations. Seeing the territory sliced into neat halves, each sovereign ignores the logistical impossibilities of such a division. In truth, it is a strategy designed to fail. The more intractable the conflict, the greater the opportunity for the United States military-industrial complex to flourish. Arms deals, technological innovations in warfare, and intelligence-sharing agreements flow abundantly under the guise of "assisting" Israel, ensuring that American influence remains entrenched in the region. This enduring instability aligns perfectly with United States interests. These interests include safeguarding oil futures against the looming specter of a "*petrocalypse*"—a global energy crisis poised to shift power structures worldwide.

Religious rhetoric becomes the smoke screen, a weapon as potent as any missile. The discourse pivots to theological claims, invoking the Bible, the Quran, and the Torah. Rich with allegory and layered interpretations, these texts justify territorial claims and demonize opponents. But religion, while deeply significant to individual and collective identities, is not the engine driving the policies of Washington or Moscow. For the United States, amplifying the religious pretext is a strategic distraction. By framing the conflict as ancient, theological, and immutable, America avoids confronting the material realities—the geopolitical maneuvering and economic dependencies—that perpetuate the crisis.

To understand what is truly at stake, one must strip the conflict of its religious layer and examine it in purely pragmatic terms.

2.1.1 CURRENT GOD'S OWN COUNTRY

Let us take a step back from the conflict-ridden sands of Israel-Palestine. Instead, we journey to a different land—a strip of fertile terrain nestled along the southwestern coast of India, known as Kerala, God's own country. At first glance, the comparison may seem audacious. What does a lush, rain-soaked sliver of the subcontinent have in common with the arid landscapes of the Middle East? Yet, Kerala's geographical shape, a narrow stretch of land bound by sea and hills, mirrors the physical dimensions of Israel. More intriguingly, Kerala once grappled with its own intricate social dynamics over land and identity—issues that were deeply rooted in history, religion, and colonial interference. By exploring Kerala's past and imagining a hypothetical scenario where colonial powers inserted Jews into its socio-political fabric, we might uncover the layered complexities of Israel-Palestine. And, more importantly, this comparative lens could offer insights into solutions far more grounded than the Pentagon-sponsored, UN-endorsed fantasy of a two-state solution.

Kerala's pre-independence social fabric tightly revolved around the Janmi system, a feudal structure shaping land ownership and social hierarchy. At the apex were the janmis—large landowners who held absolute control over vast tracts of agricultural land. Below them were the tenants and agricultural laborers, whose livelihoods depended on cultivating land they would never own. The tenants bore the weight of exorbitant rents, often amounting to over half their produce, while enduring the constant threat of eviction. Rural poverty was not an occasional plight but a generational curse. Families tilled the soil knowing that neither the land nor its fruits would ever truly be theirs. It was a system of exploitation that ensured the wealth and power of the janmis remained intact while the majority lived on the edge of survival.

This feudal order persisted under the princely states of Travancore and Cochin, which governed the region. It also prevailed in the Malabar region, which was administered under the Madras Presidency of British India. British colonial rule entrenched the janmi system by codifying land ownership patterns in a way that protected the elites. While the British collected revenue and maintained control, they were content to let the janmis wield unchecked power over the agrarian economy. In Malabar, the plight of tenant farmers drew some attention. This led lawmakers to enact the Malabar Tenancy Act of 1930, which aimed to regulate rents and prevent arbitrary evictions. However, the act's impact was minimal. Landlords still retained ownership, and the tenants remained mired in insecurity and poverty. The laws were little more than a gesture, a concession to growing unrest rather than a genuine attempt at reform.

When India gained independence in 1947, the nation's leaders faced the daunting task of dismantling centuries-old systems of oppression. For Kerala, this began with merging Travancore and Cochin into the state of Travancore-Cochin in 1949, followed by forming Kerala State in 1956. During this period, tenancy reforms gained momentum as political leaders sought to address rural inequality. Authorities in Travancore and Cochin introduced laws to reduce evictions and provide tenants with security of tenure. Legislators revised the Malabar Tenancy Act, offering modest improvements in tenant rights. The enduring power of the janmis, many of whom held significant influence within the ruling Indian National Congress (INC), stymied these early efforts. Authorities watered down the reforms, leaving meaningful change elusive.

The turning point came in 1957. Kerala elected the first democratically elected Communist government in the world, led by EMS Namboodiripad of the Communist Party of India (CPI). This government introduced the Kerala Agrarian Relations Bill, a bold attempt to dismantle the janmi system altogether. The bill sought to impose strict land ceilings, abolish tenancy, and redistribute surplus land to the landless. It was a revolutionary step, aiming to overturn centuries of feudal exploitation. However, the opposition was fierce. Landlords, the Congress Party, and the Catholic Church— representing Christian landlords—challenged the bill. The courts struck it down as unconstitutional, citing the fundamental right to property enshrined in Article

31 of the Indian Constitution. Ultimately, the central government, controlled by Congress, dismissed the EMS government in 1959, halting its reforms.

A weakened version of land reforms resurfaced under a Congress coalition government in the early 1960s. The Kerala Land Reforms Bill of 1963 aimed to address tenant rights and introduce land ceilings, but it lacked the teeth of its predecessor. Delayed by political resistance and legal challenges, the bill failed to make a substantial impact. It was only under the second Communist government in 1967, led by C. Achutha Menon of the CPI(M), that the land reform agenda regained momentum. Legislators amended the Land Reforms Act of 1963 in 1969, strengthening land ceilings and granting ownership rights to tenants. This time, the government established land tribunals to identify and redistribute surplus land. Officials systematically implemented the reforms over the following decade, despite continued resistance from landlords and delays caused by legal challenges.

By the 1970s, the land reforms in Kerala had achieved remarkable success. Reformers effectively dismantled the janmi system and granted tenants ownership of the land they cultivated. Agricultural laborers and hut dwellers received small plots for housing, fostering a more equitable rural economy. The reforms had far-reaching effects. They reduced rural poverty, empowered marginalized communities, and set the stage for Kerala's transformation into a state known for its social development indicators, such as high literacy rates, healthcare access, and gender equity.

Kerala's success story stands in contrast to the uneven progress of land reforms across India. States like West Bengal, under the Left Front government, and Jammu & Kashmir, under Sheikh Abdullah's administration in the 1950s, also achieved significant reforms. They redistributed land and empowered tenants. Yet, in much of India, land reforms wobbled because of elite resistance, administrative inefficiency, and lack of political will. The legacy of these reforms remains mixed, with a patchwork of outcomes reflecting the political and social dynamics of each state.

Today, outside progressive states like Kerala and West Bengal, land inequality persists. In many regions, elites continue to control significant portions of land, perpetuating rural poverty and social inequities. While the ghosts of the janmi system no longer haunt Kerala, its history offers a blueprint for addressing land-based inequalities elsewhere. By examining Kerala's journey—from feudal oppression to social transformation—we gain insight into the complexities of land reform. This also helps us understand the broader challenge of dismantling entrenched systems of exploitation.

2.1.2 JEWISH GOD'S OWN COUNTRY

Let us reimagine Kerala's pre-independence landscape, but with altered names and an added variable. This mirrors the dynamics of a conflict many know from the history of another land. Elite landowners known as the effendi controlled vast tracts of land, standing at the top of the agrarian hierarchy. Tenant farmers, or fellahin, toiled endlessly on these lands without owning a single parcel, forming the backbone of this social order. While the effendi collected high rents and dictated terms, the fellahin lived in near-complete dependence, trapped by their circumstances. Now, let us introduce a hypothetical twist: what if the British, with their imperial cunning, decided to bring a significant Jewish population into the equation? Imagine a colonial decree akin to the Balfour Declaration, granting the Jewish newcomers legal rights to purchase land in Kerala. How would the effendi and fellahin respond to this disruption? How would such a scenario unfold over time?

At first, the effendi, sensing an opportunity, might welcome the Jewish settlers as potential buyers for their lands. The British, eager to secure loyalty from both sides, would create a legal framework to facilitate these transactions. This framework ensured that the effendi could sell their estates at lucrative prices. The effendi, ever motivated by profit, would sell swathes of land and move on to more urban pursuits. They pocketed their wealth without regard for the fellahin who worked the land. But for the fellahin, the outcome would be catastrophic. The Jewish buyers, keen to create a cohesive and prosperous community, might offer jobs to their own kin instead of the displaced fellahin. Displacement would ripple through the countryside. Landless fellahin migrated, leaving behind a life tethered to the soil they had cultivated for generations.

Years pass, and the Jewish settlers, with access to education, capital, and British support, transform Kerala into a thriving, modernized land. They build infrastructure—roads, schools, factories—and create an advanced civilization, showcasing the fruits of innovation and hard work. Their success, however, does not go unnoticed. The effendi, now detached from rural life and having squandered much of their newfound wealth, begin to resent the prosperity they see. Their envy stirs, particularly as independence movements gain momentum in India. Sensing an opportunity to reclaim their former power, the effendi craft a narrative centered on the plight of the displaced fellahin. They demand the return of the lands sold to the Jews, conveniently ignoring the wealth they had pocketed from those very transactions.

The arguments escalate. The effendi claim to act on behalf of the fellahin, portraying themselves as champions of justice. Yet their demands grow more pointed: the land, now developed and productive, must return to its "original owners." What about the money the Jews paid for the land? The effendi argue that such concerns are irrelevant—what matters is rectifying the historical injustice. But the situation is no longer simple. The lands once sold are no longer barren fields; they are now thriving towns and cities. The Jews have invested generations of effort into creating a modern society. A reversal would not only be legally fraught but also practically unworkable.

Here, the complexities of the issue emerge. Legally, the Jews are in the right. They purchased the land within the framework of the law, transformed it, and contributed to the economic growth of the region. The effendi have no legal claim, having voluntarily sold their holdings. Morally, however, the situation is more nuanced. The fellahin, displaced and impoverished, have the strongest moral claim. Displacement uprooted their livelihoods and left them without alternatives. The effendi, having profited from the sale, hold little moral ground to demand restitution.

Practically, the challenge lies in balancing these historical grievances with the current realities. Undoing the advancements made by the Jewish settlers would lead to chaos and destroy the region's economic progress. A solution must consider justice, coexistence, and pragmatic governance.

To address the plight of the fellahin, land redistribution or resettlement would be essential. Authorities could allocate unused or underutilized land to them, enabling them to rebuild their lives. Where land redistribution is not feasible, financial compensation and integration into the Jewish-led economy—through education, jobs, and infrastructure development—would offer a viable path forward. Communities must reject outright the opportunistic claims of the effendi. However, society could address genuine grievances through collaborative economic initiatives with the Jewish community, fostering shared prosperity rather than division.

The Jewish settlers, now landowners, would need to commit to inclusivity. By opening their advanced economy to the displaced fellahin, they could foster coexistence and stability. Efforts to preserve the cultural identity of the displaced communities would also be vital, ensuring that development does not erase the region's historical fabric.

The government must play a central role, mediating between these groups to facilitate equitable solutions. New land reform policies could prevent future displacements, safeguarding local populations' access to land and resources.

This hypothetical journey through Kerala's past illustrates the intricacies of land ownership, displacement, and societal transformation. It mirrors the struggles of

Israel-Palestine while offering a broader lesson: true resolution requires moving beyond historical blame and focusing on justice, integration, and shared progress. Only by addressing the needs of the displaced, rejecting opportunism, and fostering coexistence can such conflicts find lasting solutions.

2.1.3 GOD'S OWN MIDDLE-EAST

Now let us turn our lens to a hypothetical land, Jewish God's Own Country. Here, we explore the dynamics of the Israel-Palestine conflict through the reimagining of its key actors and circumstances. During the Ottoman and early British Mandate periods, a class of landowners dominated the social and economic landscape of the region now known as Israel-Palestine. Their titles reflected their prestige and control over vast estates. These titles—Effendi, Sheikh, Agha, Bey, and Mulki— denoted a hierarchy of influence and privilege. These individuals often owned vast tracts of agricultural land, which they leased to tenant farmers, the fellahin, who worked the soil under precarious conditions. For simplicity, in this narrative, we will collectively refer to these elite landowners as Hamas and refer to fellahin as Palestinians. In this story, Hamas represents the elite landowners who once controlled vast swathes of land. The Palestinians are the tenant farmers who toiled and lived off the land without ownership, and the land itself is Israel. This framework allows us to unravel the historical threads that shaped the conflict and explore the interplay of legal, moral, and practical claims.

In this reimagining, Hamas, as the powerful elite landowners, initially controlled much of the fertile land. The Palestinians, tenant farmers dependent on this land for survival, existed in a precarious state, cultivating fields they could not claim as their own. Into this tense dynamic entered the British, armed with colonial strategies designed to reshape the region for their benefit. Imagine a Balfour-like Declaration, granting Jewish settlers the legal right to purchase land in Israel. With this mandate, the Jewish community, seeking refuge and a homeland, began to acquire property in the region.

At first, Hamas, motivated by profit, welcomed these new buyers. The British, seeking to placate all sides, created a legal framework to ensure these transactions occurred smoothly. This enabled Hamas to sell large portions of land at attractive prices. Flush with the proceeds, Hamas often moved to urban centers or reinvested in other ventures, leaving behind the lands they once controlled. However, the displacement stranded Palestinians who had lived and worked on these lands for generations. The Jewish buyers, determined to establish a self-reliant community, often chose to hire their own kin instead of the displaced Palestinians, resulting in mass displacement and migration.

Over time, the Jewish settlers, bolstered by education, capital, and British support, transformed the region. The once-agrarian landscape evolved into a modern, industrialized society with advanced infrastructure, thriving cities, and economic prosperity. This success, while beneficial for the settlers, sowed seeds of resentment among Hamas. They observed from a distance as the land they once controlled flourished in others' hands. The displacement of the Palestinians added to this tension, providing a rallying cry for Hamas. They began to position themselves as defenders of the dispossessed Palestinians, demanding the return of the land now under Jewish control.

The arguments escalated. Hamas insisted on returning the lands to their "original owners"—the Palestinians—claiming historical injustice as their justification. When asked about the money they had received from the sales, Hamas dismissed the issue, framing the demand solely in moral terms. Jewish settlers had transformed the land into a modern society, making it unrecognizable from its earlier state. Undoing their achievements would not only be legally untenable but also practically unworkable, threatening chaos and economic collapse.

Here, the complexities of the issue become clear. Legally, the Jewish settlers were in the right—they had purchased the land within the framework of the law, invested in it, and made it productive. Morally, however, the Palestinians—displaced and impoverished—held the strongest claim. Their dependence on the land for survival and their lack of alternatives made their plight undeniable. Hamas, meanwhile, lacked both moral and legal standing, having willingly profited from the transactions that displaced the Palestinians.

A solution must reconcile historical grievances with current realities. For the displaced Palestinians, measures such as land redistribution or resettlement would be critical. Authorities should allocate unused or underutilized land to them to rebuild their livelihoods. Where such redistribution is impractical, financial compensation or integration into the Jewish-led economy through jobs, education, and infrastructure support would offer a path forward. Policymakers should dismiss Hamas's opportunistic claims but could address genuine grievances through cooperative economic ventures that build bridges rather than deepen divisions.

For the Jewish settlers, the path to peace lies in inclusivity and coexistence. They must integrate the displaced Palestinians into the region's prosperity, fostering stability through shared economic and social benefits. Respecting the cultural and historical identity of the displaced populations would also be essential to building a lasting resolution.

This exploration of Jewish God's Own Country offers a lens to understand the intricate interplay of legality, morality, and practicality in the Israel-Palestine conflict. It highlights that while blame and historical narratives often dominate discourse, true resolution lies in creating systems of coexistence and mutual benefit. Only through addressing the needs of the displaced, rejecting opportunistic claims, and fostering pragmatic governance can such a deeply rooted conflict find a sustainable path forward.

The United States and its puppet, the United Nations, have long promoted a two-state solution as the ultimate path to peace. Many people often see it as a resolution to the Israel-Palestine conflict. At first glance, it appears reasonable: two sovereign nations, living side by side in harmony. But peel back the layers, and the flaws in this plan become glaringly obvious. This is not a solution crafted to resolve a deeply entrenched conflict. Instead, it is a convenient fiction designed to placate the world while preserving the interests of global superpowers, particularly the United States. The problem is that such a division, even if achievable on paper, is wholly unworkable in reality. Splitting a land intertwined for decades—economically, socially, and politically—fails to create two functional states. You end up with fragmented enclaves, perpetual instability, and renewed violence.

The better path, though more challenging, is a single, integrated state where Palestinians and Israelis coexist within a unified political and social framework. This solution rejects artificial divisions and instead focuses on inclusion, opportunity, and coexistence. For this to work, authorities must provide Palestinians, particularly the poor and disenfranchised, with pathways to integrate into Israeli society. This isn't just about granting citizenship or symbolic gestures; it's about meaningful opportunities—education, jobs, access to healthcare, and a stake in the prosperity that Israel has built. By empowering the Palestinian population, the unified state would not only address historical grievances but also strengthen itself through diversity and shared progress.

But such integration would require addressing another, often-overlooked obstacle. This includes the elite effendi, represented today by groups like Hamas and other entrenched power structures claiming to speak for the Palestinian people. These elites thrive on division, their influence rooted in the perpetual conflict that keeps ordinary Palestinians marginalized. For these "effendis," peace is not a goal—it's a threat. A united, prosperous society where Palestinians and Israelis coexist would strip them of their power and render their narratives of struggle and resistance obsolete. Thus, society must confront these elites. Whether through political marginalization, mental reconditioning, or the outright dismantling of their structures, reformers must break the grip of the effendi on the Palestinian cause. Society must encourage—or compel—them to adopt a mindset of live and let live, abandoning their exploitative hold over the population they claim to represent.

The single-state solution, of course, is not without challenges. It requires Israelis to confront deep-seated fears and prejudices, to share resources and power with a group often perceived as "the other." It also requires Palestinians to embrace integration, which might feel like surrendering their distinct identity after decades of struggle. Yet, history has shown us that integration, though painful, is possible. The dismantling of apartheid in South Africa, the civil rights movement in the United States, and unifying Germany are all imperfect examples. Yet, they remain powerful examples of societies that chose unity over division.

The alternative—continuing to pursue the mirage of a two-state solution—would only perpetuate the cycle of displacement, poverty, and violence. A divided land cannot create peace. It creates borders, walls, and checkpoints that reinforce the divisions rather than heal them. Worse, it leaves the poor—on both sides—at the mercy of political elites who profit from their suffering. A unified state, though fraught with difficulties, offers the possibility of breaking free from this destructive cycle. It would demand not just political agreements but a cultural shift. This shift would require a shared vision of a future where both Palestinians and Israelis see themselves not as adversaries, but as partners.

The world must abandon its fixation on the two-state solution, a relic of Cold War-era diplomacy that no longer serves the realities of this conflict. Instead, it must embrace the idea of integration, coexistence, and shared opportunity. In doing so, it would not only address the root causes of the conflict but also create a model for resolving other seemingly intractable divisions. In the end, peace is not about drawing new borders—it's about removing the barriers that exist within our minds.

The quest for peace in the Middle East requires bold thinking, much like the transformative ideologies that reshaped societies elsewhere. Just as Kerala reimagined its social fabric by dismantling feudal hierarchies, the Israel-Palestine conflict demands a departure from outdated paradigms. Both cases highlight a universal truth: societies achieve enduring progress not by reinforcing divisions but by addressing the inequities that underpin them. Yet, Kerala's success also serves as a cautionary tale, for even the most revolutionary ideas can stagnate. As communism in Kerala began to falter under the weight of changing times, inefficiencies replaced its idealism. This showed that even the most visionary political ideology must evolve—or risk decay.

2.1.4 ROTTING COMMUNISM

Drawing lessons from unexpected corners of the world becomes useful as we navigate the complexity of the Israel-Palestine conflict. Kerala, a southern state in India, is renowned for its social development and visionary reforms. Kerala's communist leadership, in its early years, championed policies to dismantle feudal hierarchies and address inequalities between elites and tenants. The land reforms initiated by the first communist government in 1957, under the leadership of EMS Namboodiripad, were transformative. They dismantled the oppressive janmi system, redistributed surplus land to the landless, and ensured that tenant farmers could claim ownership of the soil they worked. This ideology, built on equality and justice, was visionary and earned Kerala global recognition as a model of inclusive development.

Yet, as with many great ideologies, communism in Kerala has not been immune to the corrosive effects of time. Over decades, the ideals that once inspired revolutionary change began to rot as leaders evolved into political elites, more concerned with maintaining power than addressing new inequalities. The cracks became evident as vote-bank politics started dictating policy decisions. This trend is not unique to Kerala. Communism also failed in West Bengal, where it collapsed under administrative inefficiency, complacency, and an inability to adapt to changing realities.

Today, Kerala remains the last stronghold of communism in India, but it is a pale shadow of its former self. The current leadership's priorities often reflect political expediency rather than ideological conviction. To consolidate their base, Kerala's communists rely on vote-bank politics. They frequently appease religious communities, including Muslims, instead of addressing systemic issues like unemployment, environmental degradation, or widening economic disparities. This strategy also affects international narratives. The party aligns with elite perspectives on the Israel-Palestine conflict, supporting Hamas and advocating the two-state solution. The reasons are obvious. Endorsing a single-state solution risks alienating a significant portion of their Muslim vote bank, even if it better addresses the realities of the conflict.

This transformation highlights the broader irony of modern communism in Kerala. A movement that once stood for dismantling hierarchies now props up elites and their narratives to secure its political survival. The communists firmly support the two-state solution, despite its impracticality and failure to address coexistence and integration. This mirrors their unwillingness to confront uncomfortable truths at home. The ideology that built Kerala's progressive foundation now deteriorates under political opportunism. This shows how even visionary movements can rot when they lose sight of their purpose.

The lesson is sobering but essential. Ideological rigidity and political self-interest breed stagnation and decay, whether in Kerala's communism or global conflicts like Israel-Palestine. Correct solutions lie not in pandering to elites or appeasing convenient narratives, but in addressing fundamental inequalities and fostering a shared future.

Communism, once a movement that prided itself on rationality and atheism, has undergone a peculiar transformation in Kerala, India. In its early days, Marxist ideology denounced religion as an "opiate of the masses," claiming it dulled the critical faculties of the working class and upheld exploitative structures. The Communists championed reason, modernity, and the eradication of superstition. Yet, over time, the ideological rigidity has eroded, and a paradox has emerged. In the name of tradition and culture, Communists now embrace practices they once dismissed as irrational. Kerala's Communist Party of India (Marxist) often organizes cultural events that prominently feature deeply religious rituals. These include Theyyam, an ancient performance art form that blends devotion and mysticism, where secular Communists are now its loudest promoters.

The scene is familiar yet startling: a family purchases a car, possibly a new sedan or a gleaming SUV. Before the car takes its first ride, the family summons a priest, who chants Sanskrit verses while smearing vermillion and sandalwood paste (thilakam) on the vehicle. The family breaks a coconut, arranges flowers on the dashboard, and lets incense breeze through the air. In a region where communism has long been dominant, such rituals happen with surprising regularity. These acts, claimed to be "cultural" rather than religious, show how deeply contradictions have seeped into Kerala's Communist ethos. The same leaders who once lambasted temple visits now engage in such rituals publicly, citing "tradition" as justification. This selective adoption of religion, cloaked as culture, exposes the hollowness of the Communist claim to secularism. It is no longer the fiery atheism of early Marxists but a softer, compromised stance that veers closer to the practices it once abhorred.

The hypocrisy deepens with events like Theyyam. This art form, where performers take on the persona of deities, often involves walking over fire—a practice loaded with spiritual and ritualistic significance. The CPM, Kerala's ruling Communist party, actively promotes Theyyam, calling it an integral part of local heritage. Theyyam is a traditional ritual art form of Kerala. It is popular in northern districts, like Kannur and Kasaragod. One performance, called "Ember Walk," involves a striking act. Locals call it "Thee Chatti" or "Thee Thullal." In this ritual, the Theyyam performer walks barefoot over glowing embers or burning coal. Critics often raise concerns about health risks from such practices. Some participants suffer burns or even develop severe conditions like gangrene. Despite these issues, party leaders dismiss the criticism with weak justifications. They argue that these superstitions do no harm and are merely expressions of cultural identity. This defense rings hollow when old cases resurface, like villagers losing toes due to untreated burns sustained during fire-walking rituals. The irony is hard to miss. Communists preach scientific temper and mock superstitions. Yet, they now organize, defend, and celebrate such practices. All of this happens in the name of preserving culture.

Communism in Kerala has drifted far from its origins. Instead of challenging entrenched beliefs, it often reinforces them under the guise of respecting local traditions. The party's manifesto once demanded ending practices that subjugate reason, but its current actions suggest a complete reversal. This shift highlights a broader trend—when ideologies lose their ideological anchors, they often morph into the very things they once opposed. The CPM's embrace of rituals is not an isolated phenomenon. They baptize cars or promote Theyyam, claiming it is cultural. This shift reflects the slow decay of an ideology. Communism once sought to liberate minds but now reinforces old practices. Now, it often finds itself tangled in the web of customs and beliefs it previously sought to dismantle.

The decay of rigid ideologies, whether in Kerala's communism or global conflict strategies, underscores the perils of failing to adapt. When narratives serve only to mask deeper inequalities or advance the agendas of elites, they eventually collapse under the weight of their contradictions. This dynamic is evident on the global stage, where the struggle for dwindling resources has turned geopolitics into a theater of manipulation. In Ukraine, the drama unfolds as *Petrocalypse*. Leaders like Zelenskyy play roles shaped more by strategic designs of powerful nations than by autonomy.

2.2 COMIC COMMANDER OF UKRAINE

The narrative of *Petrocalypse*—a world scrambling for dwindling petroleum reserves—remains at the core of the United States' strategic maneuvers, including its involvement in Ukraine. The United States thrives on a legacy of coups and regime changes to secure energy dominance. It often cloaks these actions as efforts to promote democracy. Ukraine, with its strategic position as the gateway to Russia's capital, is the latest chapter in this tale of calculated power plays. By destabilizing Ukraine and installing a sympathetic government, the U.S. strengthens its encirclement of Russia. This ensures Russia stays subdued in the global energy game. Zelenskyy, the charismatic comic commander, often masks his role as a pawn in a geopolitical chessboard. This highlights how the U.S. turns leaders into symbols for its agendas.

Criticism of the Ukraine war often defaults to condemning Vladimir Putin for his aggression in Ukraine. Putin's actions are indefensible. However, this singular focus overlooks the U.S.'s broader pursuit of Iranian oil and other energy resources. Does this mean I support Russia's invasion of Ukraine? Certainly not. My position is simpler yet more transformative: get the United States out of Asia. If the United States lacks oil in the future, pay for it like any other buyer, and allow the nations selling it to prosper without coercion or conflict. Analysts estimate that petroleum in Russia will deplete between 2044 and 2085. This gives the world time to shift focus from war to education, innovation, and equality, preparing for a post-petroleum era. America's relentless pursuit to keep the dollar as the dominant global currency drives its involvement in Asia, fueling conflicts, a truth the people of the United States must recognize and challenge by holding their politicians accountable for this destructive agenda.

This transition requires bold and visionary steps. First, a reformed United Nations, free from the influence of powerful nations, must take charge of global governance. It should focus on educating populations, fostering research, and empowering experts to guide decision-making rather than allowing profit-driven elites to dominate. Governments must cap billionaire wealth and redistribute excess funds to address inequality. This would support education centers and programs to train scientists, engineers, and technologists for sustainable progress. This redistribution is not about punishing success, but about ensuring the well-being of humanity.

As part of this vision, nations must begin the gradual process of demilitarization, redirecting funds from weapons and defense ministries into research and development. By ending the global arms race, we can prioritize finding sustainable alternatives to petroleum. The United States, with its immense influence and military presence, must be "leashed." It should step back from imperialism and let the UN lead cooperative energy transitions and peacebuilding.

In the immediate term, transitioning from petroleum requires diversification of energy sources. Solar, wind, and nuclear energy, along with innovative solutions like geothermal and wave power, offer pathways to sustainability. To overcome the limitations of current battery technologies reliant on scarce minerals, we must invest in alternatives like sodium-ion batteries, flow batteries, and supercapacitors. These advancements, coupled with developing smart grids and decentralized microgrids, can minimize energy storage needs and optimize renewable usage.

A sustainable future also demands a reimagining of how we use energy. By improving efficiency in buildings, transport, and industry, and by adopting direct-use renewable systems like solar thermal heating, we can significantly reduce overall consumption.

Simultaneously, a global push for recycling and sustainable mining practices is crucial. Developing materials that bypass the need for rare minerals will also secure the long-term viability of emerging technologies.

The ultimate goal is ambitious but achievable. It envisions a world where energy is abundant, accessible, and sustainable, while economic power no longer rests in the hands of a few. As petroleum resources diminish, let this be an opportunity—not for conflict, but for collaboration. By focusing on education, innovation, and equity, humanity can break free from the cycles of exploitation and war that defined the petroleum era. This shift can create a legacy of peace and progress for future generations.

The shift away from petroleum dependence offers a chance to rewrite the story of global power, yet the barriers to this transformation remain formidable. At the core of these challenges lies the unchecked dominance of the United States and its intertwined elites. Their vast influence shapes global economic systems, political structures, and military landscapes. As calls for redistribution and demilitarization intensify, a question emerges. Can humanity restrain the forces that perpetuate inequality and conflict, or will America's entrenched power structures and billionaires continue to dominate the global future?

2.2.1 UKRAINE WAR 2022

The war that erupted in Ukraine in February 2022 was not a bolt from the blue. Russia meticulously choreographed the prelude to its full-scale invasion over months, using troop buildups and diplomatic feints to mask its agenda of territorial conquest. In late 2021, satellite imagery revealed alarming movements of Russian forces near Ukraine's borders. Over 150,000 troops, along with armored units and support vehicles, amassed under the pretense of military exercises. The military complemented these buildups with logistical networks, including field hospitals and ammunition depots, signaling preparations for sustained combat. The United States, leveraging its unparalleled intelligence apparatus, repeatedly warned of an impending invasion. By early February 2022, President Joe Biden and senior officials, supported by CIA assessments, publicly announced that Russia planned to strike. However, skepticism lingered among European allies and even within Ukraine, where many believed Moscow's actions were a bluff designed to extract concessions on NATO's eastward expansion.

As the invasion unfolded, the CIA's role in supporting Ukraine became a cornerstone of the resistance effort. In the days leading up to February 24, the CIA had already shared actionable intelligence with Kyiv, detailing Russian attack vectors and logistical preparations. This allowed Ukrainian forces to reposition assets and fortify defenses in key areas, including the capital, Kyiv. The agency's network of assets within Russia, combined with signals intelligence, enabled it to provide granular insights into Moscow's intentions and military plans. This real-time intelligence sharing continued throughout the conflict, allowing Ukraine to anticipate and counter Russian maneuvers. For example, Ukrainian forces thwarted an early Russian attempt to seize Hostomel Airport. This critical objective in Moscow's plan to encircle Kyiv was foiled because of precise intelligence on troop movements and air support operations.

Cybersecurity became another critical front in the war, and the CIA played a pivotal role in safeguarding Ukraine's digital infrastructure. Russian cyberattacks targeting Ukraine's power grids, financial systems, and communication networks were anticipated well in advance. These preparations drew on lessons from the 2015 and 2016 cyberattacks, which had plunged parts of Ukraine into darkness. The CIA, in collaboration with other United States agencies and private-sector partners, provided cybersecurity training and resources to Ukrainian operators. Experts shared tools for detecting malware, countering phishing attempts, and isolating compromised networks to mitigate the impact of Russian cyber aggression. The agency protected Ukraine's government databases and military command systems, ensuring Russian hackers could not access or sabotage vital information.

As the war escalated, the CIA also engaged in high-stakes operations to support Ukraine's leadership and disrupt Russian operations. One of the most critical missions involved evacuation planning for Ukrainian President Volodymyr Zelenskyy and other top officials. The CIA recognized Zelenskyy's survival as crucial for maintaining Ukraine's resistance. The CIA devised contingency plans to extract him and his team to secure locations, either within Ukraine or abroad, if the situation became untenable. Despite the offer, Zelenskyy famously refused to leave Kyiv, stating, "I need ammunition, not a ride." Nevertheless, the planning underscored the lengths to which the CIA was prepared to go to ensure the continuity of Ukraine's government.

Disrupting Russian communication lines became another focus of CIA operations. Drawing on its expertise in signals intelligence, the agency worked to intercept and degrade Russian military communications, which were plagued by inefficiencies and outdated equipment. Russian reliance on unsecured channels, including civilian radios and mobile phones, proved to be a significant vulnerability. Ukrainian forces, armed with CIA-supplied intelligence, exploited this weakness by targeting Russian command posts and supply lines. In the prior weeks of the war, precision strikes killed several high-ranking Russian officers after intercepted communications pinpointed their locations. These operations not only decimated Russian leadership on the battlefield but also sowed confusion and demoralization among their ranks.

One particularly notable operation disrupted a Russian convoy advancing toward Kyiv. Stretching over 40 miles, the convoy was a critical component of Russia's strategy to encircle and capture the capital. Combining satellite imagery, intercepted communications, and local reconnaissance, the CIA and its Ukrainian counterparts identified vulnerabilities in the convoy's logistics. Targeted strikes on fuel trucks and supply depots forced the convoy to stall, buying Ukrainian forces valuable time to reinforce their defenses. This marked a turning point in the battle for Kyiv, as Russia's initial blitzkrieg faltered under logistical strain and unexpectedly fierce resistance.

The CIA's contributions to Ukraine's war effort extended beyond the battlefield. Its efforts to counter Russian propaganda and maintain international support for Ukraine were equally significant. Through strategic leaks and briefings, the agency provided evidence of Russian atrocities, including the deliberate targeting of civilians in places like Bucha and Mariupol. These revelations galvanized global condemnation of Moscow and bolstered the resolve of Western nations to sustain their support for Kyiv.

As the war grinds on, the CIA's role remains pivotal. The agency's adaptability to the conflict's evolving dynamics underscored its central role in modern warfare. In this landscape, intelligence and information proved as critical as tanks and missiles. For Ukraine, the partnership with the CIA has been a lifeline, enabling a smaller, embattled nation to resist a far larger adversary. For the United States, this represents a calculated yet high-stakes gamble to uphold the international order against aggression. Its outcome will shape the geopolitical landscape for decades.

The war in Ukraine, fueled by territorial ambitions and geopolitical rivalries, reveals a deeper, less visible engine driving global conflict: the fight over dwindling resources. In aiding Ukraine, the CIA and its allies are not only defending sovereignty. They are also positioning themselves in a larger contest for control over energy flows that sustain modern power structures. The Ukraine conflict is a skirmish in a larger, silent war—the *Petrocalypse*. This global struggle will only escalate as reserves fueling economies and empires edge closer to depletion.

2.3 PETROCALYPSE CLIMAX

The complexity of global politics and conflicts over past decades reveals a narrative akin to an orchestrated drama. In this story, the CIA acts as the director, while the IDF (Israeli Defense Forces) plays the assistant director. At the heart of this unfolding saga is one central theme: the relentless pursuit of control over diminishing resources, especially petroleum. This commodity is so embedded in modern civilization's lifeblood that its depletion threatens to upend global power structures. The term *"Petrocalypse"* aptly describes the silent axis around which many of the world's most defining conflicts revolve. From the sands of the Middle East to Eastern Europe's frozen battlefronts, every maneuver and proxy war seems scripted. Each undercover operation aims to secure the pathways and profits of oil. Experts project the climax to occur between 2044 and 2085, when they expect Russia's oil reserves to run critically low.

The CIA's role as the central architect of this narrative is unmistakable. Over decades, the agency has woven a narrative spanning continents and generations. It used subterfuge, military interventions, and alliances to secure American dominance in the energy landscape. The plotline has remained consistent. From the 1953 coup in Iran that restored Western control over Iranian oil to recent wars in Iraq, Syria, and now Ukraine, the strategy remains clear. Destabilize regimes threatening U.S. oil access, install friendly governments, and ensure global U.S. influence reigns supreme. The tools of this strategy are diverse, ranging from economic sanctions and propaganda to direct military intervention. But the driving force behind it all is the agency's foresight—it's understanding that as the oil runs out, the geopolitical stakes will rise exponentially.

In this geopolitical theater, Israel's IDF has emerged as the assistant director, playing a critical role in shaping the narrative and providing tactical expertise. Perpetual conflict and resource scarcity have honed Israel's military and intelligence networks to an unparalleled degree of precision. The IDF's role in securing energy routes, countering hostile regimes, and supporting U.S. interests in the region is far from incidental. It is an integral part of the *Petrocalypse* script. Israel's influence extends far beyond its borders, with its intelligence-sharing agreements and military technologies becoming indispensable to the CIA's operations. From joint cybersecurity initiatives to the targeted elimination of adversaries, the IDF's methods are both a model and an asset for the CIA's broader objectives.

Observers view the ongoing conflict in Ukraine as the latest chapter in this unfolding drama. The CIA's orchestration of intelligence sharing, strategic disruptions, and political maneuverings to counter Russia's aggression highlights its ability to adapt its script to new theaters. Meanwhile, Israel's parallel engagements, particularly in managing its position in the Middle East, underscore its role as a co-producer of this global spectacle. Both nations are acutely aware that the *Petrocalypse* is not merely about controlling oil but about managing the transition to a post-petroleum world.

The race is on to secure not just the remaining reserves but also the technological and geopolitical infrastructure that will define the energy order of the future.

The looming climax, expected between 2044 and 2085, will probably involve a convergence of crises. These include the near-depletion of accessible petroleum reserves, intensifying climate change impacts, and the rise of new energy technologies that could shift global power dynamics. The ending scenes of this drama may feature nations scrambling to dominate alternative energy resources like lithium and rare earth minerals. They will confront with the destabilizing effects of an energy-starved global economy. The CIA, with its decades of experience in resource-driven conflict, will undoubtedly remain a central player, scripting new narratives for new energy wars. The IDF, demonstrating proven adaptability and strategic prowess, will continue assisting to secure the interests of its principal ally, the United States.

As the *Petrocalypse* unfolds, the world watches, often unwittingly, as players follow a script, they neither wrote nor fully understand. Yet the ultimate plot twist remains unknown. Will humanity find a way to rewrite the ending, transitioning peacefully to a sustainable and equitable energy future? Will chaos, conflict, and a final showdown define the climactic scenes of this geopolitical thriller? Perhaps it will revolve around the last remnants of the resources that once powered the modern age. Only time will tell, but for now, the camera is still rolling, and the CIA's directorial vision shows no sign of yielding the spotlight.

3. ELITE VS. ELITE CONFLICT

Wars, at their core, have always been battles between elites competing for control over scarce resources. Beneath the patriotic slogans, ideological rhetoric, and calls for justice, lies a stark reality. Competing power structures aim to secure their dominance under the guise of these justifications. Whether it's oil fields, fertile land, water reserves, or mineral-rich territories, the objective remains the same: access to resources that can sustain and grow their influence. The Second World War, for instance, wasn't merely a clash of fascist and democratic ideologies—it was a desperate race for resource supremacy. Japan invaded Manchuria and Southeast Asia in pursuit of oil and rubber. Similarly, Germany aimed to conquer Eastern Europe not only for Lebensraum but also for the wheat fields of Ukraine and the oil wells of the Caucasus. Even modern wars, cloaked in humanitarian or anti-terror justifications, echo this pattern. The United States-led invasions of Iraq and Afghanistan hinted at securing oil reserves and pipelines. Russia ties its incursions into Ukraine to its goal of maintaining access to natural gas routes and industrial regions.

However, the drama does not conclude at the international borders where nations fight wars. Once the victorious nation secures these resources, another battle begins—this time among its elites. How much of the spoils should go to political elites who orchestrated the strategy? What share should the economic elites who financed the war receive? And what of the military-industrial elites who supplied the weapons and logistics? These internal divisions are just as fierce, though often far less visible, as the wars fought on the battlefield. In post-colonial states, for instance, the question of who profits from newly nationalized resources like oil or gold mines often sparks elite infighting. Nigeria, endowed with vast crude oil resources, has witnessed its wealth concentrated among political leaders, corporate executives, and influential tribal elites. Very little of this wealth trickles down to the broader population. This disparity has fueled tensions that sometimes spiral into insurgencies, like those in the oil-rich Niger Delta.

Elites, as we must note, do not form a monolith. They are a kaleidoscope of competing factions, each wielding power in their domains. Political elites, such as government leaders, lawmakers, and bureaucrats, wield state authority. Economic elites, comprising industrial magnates, financiers, and corporate leaders, control the engines of commerce and wealth creation. Cultural elites, like media barons and intellectual leaders, shape narratives and influence public opinion. Military elites, meanwhile, derive their power from controlling the means of force. Conflicts between these groups often play out behind closed doors but have profound consequences for societies. Take Venezuela, where the political elite, embodied by the Chavez and Maduro regimes, nationalized the oil industry, sidelining economic elites. This move created a resource-rich yet cash-strapped state, as political infighting left the oil sector mismanaged and the broader population in extreme poverty.

The competition between elites is most evident when resources are scarce or when the system distributing them is fragile. The fall of the Soviet Union offers a stark example. When the USSR collapsed, vast state-controlled resources—oil fields, gas reserves, and industrial infrastructure—suddenly became available to be claimed. What followed was a chaotic scramble among the newly emerging Russian political and economic elites. The rise of the oligarchs in the 1990s was a direct result of this resource grab. Figures like Boris Berezovsky and Roman Abramovich accumulated massive fortunes by aligning with political leaders who helped them acquire former state assets at absurdly low prices. In return, these oligarchs financed the political elite's campaigns and ensured their grip on power. However, this uneasy alliance eventually fractured. When Vladimir Putin rose to power, he reined in the oligarchs. Some became enemies of the state, while others aligning with his vision gained elevation.

Elite-versus-elite conflicts also manifest globally when overlapping spheres of influence collide. The United States-China trade wars, for example, are more than disputes over tariffs or trade balances; they represent the competing ambitions of American and Chinese economic and political elites. Both sides seek dominance over emerging technologies like AI, semiconductors, and green energy. But even within these nations, internal elite struggles complicate the picture. In the United States, tech moguls in Silicon Valley clash with Washington over data regulations and privacy laws. Wall Street banks lobby fiercely to retain their influence over monetary policy. In China, President Xi Jinping has consolidated power through purges of rival political elites. He has also cracked down on corporate giants like Alibaba's Jack Ma, who dared to challenge the state's authority.

Throughout history, elite conflicts have shaped the contours of nations and empires. In ancient Rome, the Senate, representing the aristocratic elite, clashed with military leaders like Julius Caesar, whose rise threatened the old guard. Historians often describe the American Civil War as a conflict between Northern industrial elites and Southern plantation owners. At its core, it was a battle for control over economic systems tied to slavery. These struggles expose an inescapable truth. Nations never fight wars purely for ideals or survival. Instead, the ambitions and rivalries of those in power deeply intertwine with wars.

Today, as the world faces existential challenges like climate change and dwindling resources, these elite dynamics remain pivotal. Who controls the rare earth minerals necessary for renewable technologies? Which elites will lead the charge—or resist the shift—toward green energy? These questions are not merely academic. They will define the wars, policies, and global alliances of the 21st century. The struggle between elites, whether on the battlefield or in boardrooms, is a drama that continues to drive human history.

3.1 TALIBAN VS. ISIS

The Taliban and ISIS, two of the most infamous Islamist extremist organizations, share a common foundation. Both aspire to establish states governed by rigid interpretations of Sharia law. However, their ideological and operational paths have diverged sharply, leading to animosity and violent conflict between them. To understand their motivations and the role of external powers like the United States, one must examine their histories, ideologies, and the geopolitical struggles that have fueled their rise.

The Taliban emerged in the early 1990s during the Afghan Civil War, rooted in the Pashtun areas of southern Afghanistan and parts of Pakistan. Afghanistan, a nation long scarred by instability, became a theater of Cold War rivalry when the Soviet Union invaded in 1979 to support its allied government. The United States, seeking to counter Soviet influence, covertly armed and funded the Mujahadeen— insurgent fighters who opposed the Communist-aligned regime. Billions of dollars in military aid flowed to the Mujahadeen through the CIA, making Afghanistan one of the most significant fronts of the Cold War. The Mujahadeen, composed of various fragmented groups, waged a guerrilla war against the Soviets, using United States-supplied weapons like Stinger missiles to devastating effect.

After the Soviet withdrawal in 1989, the power vacuum left in Afghanistan led to infighting among the Mujahadeen factions. This chaos provided fertile ground for the rise of the Taliban; a group initially formed by displaced Pashtun students educated in Islamic schools in Pakistan. The Taliban, under the governance of Mullah Mohammed Omar, implemented order according to their stringent understanding of Islamic law. By 1996, the Taliban had seized control of most of Afghanistan, ruling with brutality, particularly toward women and minorities. Public executions, a rollback of women's rights, and strictly enforcing societal controls marked their reign.

The Taliban's harboring of Osama bin Laden and al-Qaeda brought the group into direct conflict with the United States after the September 11, 2001, attacks. The United States-led invasion of Afghanistan in 2001 toppled the Taliban regime. However, they regrouped as an insurgent force and waged a protracted guerrilla war against American and NATO forces for two decades. In 2021, following the United States withdrawal, the Taliban swiftly regained control of Afghanistan, raising concerns as extremist activity resurged in the region.

ISIS, or the Islamic State, took a different trajectory. Abu Musab al-Zarqawi, a Jordanian militant who gained prominence during the Iraq War, traces the origins of this movement. Al-Zarqawi's group, initially aligned with al-Qaeda, adopted an exceptionally violent approach, targeting not only foreign forces but also Shia Muslims and other perceived heretics. After al-Zarqawi's death in 2006, his group evolved into the Islamic State of Iraq (ISI) and later ISIS, expanding its ambitions to establish a global caliphate. In 2014, ISIS shocked the world by seizing large swathes of Iraq and Syria, declaring a caliphate under Abu Bakr al-Baghdadi. Unlike the Taliban, whose focus remained localized, ISIS aimed to export its ideology globally, using sophisticated propaganda to recruit fighters from across the world.

The ideological clash between the Taliban and ISIS became evident as ISIS sought to expand into Afghanistan and Pakistan through its affiliate, ISIS-K (Khorasan Province).

Founded in 2015 by disgruntled former Taliban members and Pakistani militants, ISIS-K adopted an even more extreme interpretation of Islam, openly challenging the Taliban's authority. The two groups clashed repeatedly, with ISIS-K carrying out high-profile attacks against Taliban targets. The Taliban launched offensives to root out ISIS-K fighters, resulting in fierce battles that highlighted their fundamental differences. While both groups adhere to Sunni Islam, the Taliban's Deobandi tradition contrasts with ISIS's Wahhabi-Salafist ideology, further fueling their rivalry.

External powers, particularly the United States, involved themselves in ways that proved a double-edged sword. During the Cold War, United States support for the Mujahadeen inadvertently laid the groundwork for the rise of groups like the Taliban. Later, the United States-led invasion of Iraq in 2003 destabilized the region, creating conditions for ISIS to thrive. Both groups have leveraged their control over resource-rich territories, including opium fields in Afghanistan and oil wells in Iraq and Syria, to fund their operations. However, these resources have also attracted foreign intervention, with the United States and other nations conducting military campaigns to disrupt the financial networks of these groups.

The United States's peace agreement with the Taliban in 2020 underscored the complexities of dealing with such groups. The deal facilitated the United States withdrawal from Afghanistan. However, it left the Taliban in a stronger position, raising fears that Afghanistan could once again become a haven for terrorism. Meanwhile, ISIS, though weakened, continues to operate through affiliates like ISIS-K, exploiting the instability created by the Taliban's return to power.

The rivalry between the Taliban and ISIS illustrates a broader truth about extremist movements. While they may share ideological roots, their pursuit of power often leads to fragmentation and internecine conflict. At their core, these groups are not merely religious movements but actors driven by territorial control, resource acquisition, and the quest for dominance. The landscapes they inhabit—rich in resources like oil, opium, and strategic geography—serve as both battlegrounds and prizes, perpetuating cycles of violence that transcend ideological narratives.

3.2 PRESIDENT VS. BILLIONAIRE

Joe Biden and Elon Musk, two towering figures in the 21st century, embody different facets of American ambition and innovation. Biden, a seasoned statesman with decades of political experience, envisions steady progress. He roots his vision in traditional democratic values, supporting unionized labor, addressing climate change, and revitalizing American infrastructure. Musk, the maverick entrepreneur, disrupts industries and defies norms with his relentless pursuit of technological breakthroughs. These two figures, though aligned on renewable energy and electric vehicles (EVs), have increasingly clashed. Their conflict reflects broader tensions between government institutions and disruptive innovation. Their interactions, or lack thereof, underscore the complexities of aligning public policy with private ambition in a transforming world.

Joe Biden's journey to the presidency is a study in perseverance and pragmatism. With over 36 years as a United States Senator from Delaware and eight years as Vice President under Barack Obama, Biden's career embodies a commitment to middle-class economic growth. It also reflects his dedication to international diplomacy. His legislative legacy includes the Violence Against Women Act and significant contributions to the Affordable Care Act. As President, Biden has focused on tackling climate change through historic investments in renewable energy and infrastructure. His landmark Inflation Reduction Act of 2022 allocated $369 billion toward clean energy initiatives, the largest such investment in United States history. Biden emphasizes unionized labor, evident in his push for domestic EV production by American workers. This ties his environmental agenda to a broader vision of equitable economic growth.

Elon Musk's trajectory contrasts starkly with Biden's. Born in South Africa, Musk emigrated to the United States and quickly established himself as a transformative entrepreneur. His ventures—Tesla, SpaceX, Neuralink, and Twitter—span industries, reshaping transportation, space exploration, and digital communication. Tesla revolutionized the automotive sector. It made EVs mainstream, selling over 1.3 million vehicles in 2022 and achieving a market valuation exceeding $1 trillion at its peak. SpaceX, with its reusable rockets and successful missions to the International Space Station, has brought humanity closer to Mars colonization. Musk's acquisition of Twitter in 2022 for $44 billion added a social media platform to his empire, signaling his ambition to influence public discourse directly. Yet, Musk's unapologetic style—marked by controversial tweets and clashes with regulators—has made him a polarizing figure.

Initially, the paths of Biden and Musk seemed destined to converge on shared goals. Biden's presidency began with an ambitious agenda to transition the United States economy toward clean energy, a vision aligned with Musk's pioneering work at Tesla and SolarCity. Both recognized the existential threat of climate change and the need for technological innovation to address it. Biden's bipartisan Infrastructure Investment and Jobs Act, passed in 2021, earmarked $7.5 billion for EV charging infrastructure. This policy could complement Tesla's Supercharger network expansion, which now includes over 45,000 chargers worldwide. Yet, despite these overlapping interests, direct collaboration between the White House and Musk was conspicuously absent.

The friction between President Joe Biden and Elon Musk embodies a broader struggle over power, influence, and competing visions for America's future. This dynamic is most evident in their interactions—or lack thereof—while EVs evolved alongside labor relations, economic policies, and the contentious world of social media. These conflicts seem rooted in ideological differences but are also deeply personal. Historical tensions between government leaders and industrial magnates, who aim to disrupt the established order, shape their conflicts. By examining key incidents, we can trace how their rivalry has shaped and influenced the defining issues of the 21st century.

Early tensions arose when Tesla, the world's leading electric vehicle manufacturer, faced conspicuous exclusion from White House events celebrating the burgeoning EV industry. These summits, held in 2021 and 2022, highlighted legacy automakers like General Motors and Ford, whose unionized workforces aligned with Biden's pro-labor agenda. Despite producing over 70% of all EVs sold in the United States during this period, Tesla remained excluded. Musk, never one to shy away from controversy, took to Twitter to express his frustration, accusing the Biden administration of ignoring Tesla's contributions to the EV revolution. "No one even invited Tesla," Musk said. "In what universe does that make sense?" Musk tweeted in 2021, sparking a wave of public debate. Biden's aides cited the administration's commitment to unionized manufacturers. However, Musk's supporters noted the irony of excluding the company that made EVs a household name. By 2022, Tesla had sold nearly 2 million EVs globally, cementing its status as the industry leader, yet its relationship with the White House remained strained.

This clash over recognition reflects deeper ideological divides, particularly on the issue of labor. Biden, a lifelong supporter of unions, has framed unionization as a cornerstone of his economic policies. His administration's push for domestic EV production, including incentives in the Inflation Reduction Act for unionized manufacturers, underscored his commitment to organized labor. Tesla, on the other hand, operates with a non-union workforce, a point of pride for Musk, who has repeatedly resisted unionization efforts at the company's factories. In 2018, Tesla faced allegations of anti-union practices. The National Labor Relations Board ruled that Tesla violated labor laws by discouraging union activity at its Fremont, California, plant. Musk's public remarks, including a tweet suggesting that unionizing would result in workers losing stock options, added fuel to the fire. For Biden, Tesla's labor practices challenged his vision of fair economic growth. For Musk, unionization was an outdated model ill-suited to the agility required in a high-tech industry.

Their disagreement extended beyond labor into broader economic policies. Biden's administration championed significant government spending to stimulate the economy, including $1.9 trillion through the American Rescue Plan and hundreds of billions in clean energy investments. These measures, aimed at addressing income inequality and accelerating the green transition, often clashed with Musk's libertarian leanings and skepticism of government intervention. Musk strongly opposed certain regulatory measures in 2021, criticizing proposed tax increases on billionaires as part of Biden's Build Back Better plan. "Eventually, they run out of other people's money, and then they come for you," Musk remarked during a public debate on wealth redistribution. With a net worth fluctuating between $180 billion and $250 billion, Musk became a lightning rod in debates about economic inequality. He symbolized both the promise and peril of extreme wealth in a time of technological disruption.

Tensions escalated further when Musk acquired Twitter in late 2022 for $44 billion. He transformed the platform into a battleground for free speech debates. Musk's stated goal of promoting open dialog resonated with many who felt social media platforms had become overly censored. However, his actions—such as reinstating controversial accounts and loosening content moderation policies—raised alarms about the spread of misinformation. The Biden administration, already concerned about the role of online disinformation in eroding democratic norms, viewed Musk's approach as a potential threat. In 2023, the White House backed increased regulatory oversight of social media platforms. It emphasized the need to combat false narratives about elections, public health, and other critical issues. Musk accused excessive governance, positioning himself as a defender of free expression against what he described as the "censorship-industrial complex."

The intersection of Musk's business ventures with national security issues added another layer of complexity to the relationship. During the Ukraine conflict, SpaceX's Starlink satellite internet service became a vital lifeline for Ukrainian forces and civilians, enabling communication amid Russian cyberattacks and infrastructure damage. Initially provided free, Starlink's continued operation in Ukraine sparked debates over funding. In October 2022, Musk publicly floated the idea of withdrawing support unless the United States government covered the costs, estimated at $20 million per month. The Pentagon eventually negotiated a deal to ensure Starlink's continuity. Musk's open discussion of the matter highlighted the unusual power dynamic between a private entrepreneur and a global superpower. Musk's comments on geopolitical matters, including a controversial peace plan proposal for Ukraine and

Russia, drew criticism. United States officials viewed them as undermining official foreign policy.

Musk's remarks on China-Taiwan relations further exemplified the delicate balance between his global business interests and United States national security concerns. In 2022, Musk suggested that Taiwan could become a "special administrative zone" under Chinese control, a statement that echoed Beijing's rhetoric. United States policymakers viewed Musk's comments with suspicion, given Tesla's reliance on the Chinese market, where it sold over 400,000 vehicles that year. The Biden administration focused on countering China's influence, imposing restrictions on technology exports and increasing its military presence in the Indo-Pacific. Musk's pragmatic engagement with Chinese authorities contrasted sharply with this approach. This divergence underscored the broader challenge of reconciling the interests of multinational corporations with national security imperatives.

The Biden-Musk dynamic is not merely a clash of personalities but a microcosm of larger societal tensions. Their interactions highlight the challenges of governing in a world where private innovation often outpaces public policy. In such a world, the lines between economic ambition and political influence blur, while the stakes of technological and geopolitical leadership grow ever higher. Their rivalry, shaped by historical precedents and modern complexities, offers a lens to examine the evolving relationship between government and industry in the 21st century. As Biden pursues his vision of a fair and sustainable economy, Musk continues to push the boundaries of private enterprise by offering help to the president itself in future that we will see in the next chapter. Their story is far from over—a tale of two titans navigating a transforming world.

War is the ultimate failure of humanity's collective imagination. In this pursuit, our aggression evolves into curiosity. Our defense mechanisms transform into plans for survival beyond Earth, shifting focus from territorial boundaries to the cosmic expanse. It reflects our oldest instincts—competition, domination, and fear—magnified to catastrophic proportions. Yet these same instincts are now propelling us into space, as explored in Chapter 14: Space Exploration. The question remains: will we carry our dysfunctions with us, or will we learn from our past and chart a fresh course among the stars?

Part V

Technology—Savior or Destroyer?

"When Earth Is Done, Billionaires Will Send a Postcard from Mars"

What happens when we break the only home we have?
The ultra-rich plan escape routes to space while the rest of us debate whether
nuclear war powered by AI and Solar Panel will come before or after
environmental collapse.

14

Space Exploration

"The Earth is the cradle of humanity, but mankind
cannot stay in the cradle forever."

– KONSTANTIN TSIOLKOVSKY

Space, once a domain of wonder and mystery, has now transformed into the next frontier of geopolitical competition and elite survival strategies. Throughout history, the race for resources has defined the trajectory of human conflict and progress. During the Cold War, proxy wars in the Middle East served strategic purposes. In 1953, the West orchestrated the United States-backed coup in Iran to secure access to oil. Decades of Soviet-American rivalry revealed a similar focus. Resource control has often been the underlying motive in both cases. Ultimately, the 20th century became a saga of competition for energy, territory, and influence. The stage is shifting upward as the planet faces the twin existential threats of nuclear war and climate change. To advance collective knowledge and foster national pride, humanity explored space in the past. Today, it is increasingly becoming a battlefield. Nations and corporations now maneuver for dominance over untapped celestial resources and the ultimate escape route—colonization of other planets.

The current race for space mirrors the same dynamics that once defined imperial conquests on Earth. European powers once scrambled for colonies in the Americas, Africa, and Asia, often citing trade and exploration as noble motives. However, they exploited native populations and resources. Today's space powers mirror this pattern, cloaking their ambitions in the rhetoric of scientific advancement and human progress. Beneath this surface lies a stark reality. The militarization of space, privatizing satellite networks, and colonizing celestial bodies are not just technological pursuits. They are strategic moves by elites to secure their long-term survival. Earth's environment is destabilizing, and geopolitical tensions are threatening global stability. In this context, controlling orbital paths, asteroid mining, and extraterrestrial outposts is no longer just a matter of technological pride. It has become a matter of existential necessity.

History offers ample examples of how resource scarcity catalyzed human imagination and ruthless competition. Britain's coal-driven industrial revolution in the 19th century spurred global dominance. However, it also led to the subjugation of territories like India. These resources were essential to sustaining British hegemony. Similarly, during the Cold War, control over oil pipelines in Iran and Saudi Arabia became a critical component of the United States strategy against the USSR. These historical episodes demonstrate a recurring pattern. When elites face crises of scarcity or geopolitical shifts, they seek new domains of control. This pursuit often combines innovation with coercion. Space is no different. The key players in this race include state actors like the United States, China, and Russia. Private entrepreneurs such as Elon Musk, Jeff Bezos, and Richard Branson are also competing to secure their claims in this new domain. What makes space unique, however, is its finality. While humans have always fought over finite resources, space appears to offer infinite opportunity—a blank slate where the cycles of exploitation and domination can begin anew.

The militarization of space, though ostensibly forbidden by international treaties, has progressed steadily under the guise of defense and communication needs. World leaders signed the 1967 Outer Space Treaty during the height of the Cold War. It prohibited placing nuclear weapons in orbit. The treaty also declared space a domain for peaceful exploration. Yet, advances in missile technology, anti-satellite weapons, and militarized satellite networks have undermined this noble ideal. The United States, under its Space Force initiative, has openly acknowledged space as a warfighting domain, while China and Russia have conducted tests of satellite-destroying weapons. These developments echo the arms races of previous centuries. Technological advancements, whether the Maxim gun in colonial conquests or intercontinental ballistic missiles during the Cold War, shifted the balance of power. In 2020, the United States tested its X-37B spaceplane, capable of conducting classified missions in orbit. Meanwhile, China's experimental satellite SJ-21 demonstrated its ability to physically alter the orbit of other satellites. These moves signify the creeping weaponization of a domain once heralded as a sanctuary from Earth's conflicts.

Privatization adds another dimension to the space race. State programs dominated space exploration in the mid-20th century. The Soviet Union's Sputnik launch in 1957 and the United States' Apollo moon landings in the 1960s epitomized this era. These were nationalist projects, symbolic of ideological superiority during the Cold War. Today, however, private companies are leading the charge. Elon Musk's SpaceX, Jeff Bezos's Blue Origin, and Richard Branson's Virgin Galactic are not merely commercial enterprises; they are symbols of a new era where private elites aim to monopolize access to space. SpaceX's Starlink program, which aims to deploy tens of thousands of satellites to provide global internet coverage, is already reshaping geopolitical power dynamics. Starlink satellites played a crucial role in maintaining Ukrainian communications during the 2022 Russian invasion, showcasing how private actors can wield strategic influence once reserved for states. Meanwhile, Bezos's vision of O'Neill colonies—massive space habitats designed to house millions—reflects the growing belief among elites that Earth may soon become uninhabitable for human civilization.

The allure of space colonization stems not only from the prospect of survival but also from the promise of untapped resources. Asteroids, rich in precious metals like platinum and gold, hold wealth exceeding Earth's entire economy. NASA estimates that the asteroid belt contains minerals worth quadrillions of dollars, making ventures like Planetary Resources—one of the first asteroid mining companies—more than speculative dreams. However, history warns us of the perils of unchecked resource extraction. The European exploitation of African gold and diamonds fueled centuries of inequality and environmental destruction. Will space mining follow a similar trajectory, where private corporations reap the profits while the rest of humanity bears the ethical and ecological costs? Or will space laws evolve to prevent such disparities?

Underlying all these efforts is the specter of existential risk. The prospect of nuclear war, which loomed over the 20th century, has not disappeared; rather, it has evolved alongside new threats like climate change and global pandemics. Space offers a potential insurance policy—a chance to establish human settlements on Mars or the Moon that could survive even if Earth does not. Musk's oft-repeated mantra of making humanity a "multi-planetary species" reflects this logic. However, it also raises unsettling questions. If humanity devotes resources to colonizing other planets, who will decide who gets to leave? Historical patterns suggest that such decisions would favor the wealthy and powerful, reinforcing existing inequalities rather than addressing them.

As we dream of stepping onto the red sands of Mars, we must confront an uncomfortable truth: the challenges we face on Earth will not vanish with a change of scenery. The very act of venturing into space magnifies these issues, demanding solutions we have yet to find here at home. This is not just a question of technology or willpower; it is a question of readiness. Before we plant flags on alien soil, we must ask ourselves—are we truly prepared to thrive in a new world if we have not yet mastered the art of healing in our own?

1. HEAL HERE, FLY LATER

Humanity's fascination with reaching Mars is not a new chapter in its history of exploration, but extends its enduring ambition to push boundaries. The billions of dollars poured into making Mars habitable are a testament to our inventiveness and vision. Yet, in this passion to colonize another planet, we overlook a crucial question: Are we equipped to sustain human life on Mars? Among the many existential challenges lies a problem we are already grappling with on Earth—cancer. Cancer is a condition that has eluded complete understanding and a definitive cure for centuries. It poses a far greater threat in the harsh environment of Mars. Galactic cosmic radiation bombards every unshielded cell with unrelenting ferocity.

On Earth, life thrives under the protective embrace of the heliosphere—a bubble of magnetic influence generated by the Sun, shielding us from the majority of cosmic radiation. This natural barrier, coupled with the Earth's magnetic field and dense atmosphere, absorbs and deflects high-energy particles, ensuring that only a fraction of radiation reaches the surface. Even this small amount can induce mutations in DNA over time, leading to cancer development. Now imagine the scenario on Mars, a planet without a magnetic field, with a thin atmosphere that offers virtually no protection from cosmic rays. Every second on Mars exposes settlers to levels of radiation that far exceed safety limits on Earth.

Galactic cosmic rays, originating from supernovae and other high-energy astrophysical phenomena, are among the most damaging forms of radiation. These high-energy particles, capable of penetrating deep into tissues, wreak havoc on the human body at a cellular level. These particles generate secondary radiation as they collide with the human body or a spacecraft's material. The result is a cascade of radiation that damages DNA, compromises cellular repair mechanisms, and accelerates degenerative diseases, including cancer.

To mitigate this, scientists have proposed constructing habitats shielded by heavy materials or underground structures on Mars. However, the practicality of transporting the necessary materials across millions of kilometers is prohibitive. Current spacecraft designs, though innovative, lack the shielding required to reduce exposure to galactic cosmic radiation significantly. Even the most optimistic estimates suggest that astronauts on a round-trip mission to Mars would exceed NASA's career radiation limits, with potential lifetime cancer risks spiking dramatically. Building such defenses is an engineering challenge. It also serves as a stark reminder that our understanding of cancer and its mechanisms is far from sufficient to protect life in such environments.

The urgency of solving this problem becomes clear because radiation-induced cancers may not be the only concern. Radiation also weakens the immune system, hinders wound healing, and accelerates aging processes, making the very act of survival on Mars a Herculean task. The current focus on Mars colonization overlooks the critical reality: Without advancements in cancer prevention, detection, and treatment, Mars colonization risks becoming a futile endeavor. Investing billions in rockets and infrastructure might serve humanity better if initially allocated to unraveling cancer's mysteries, including those worsened by radiation.

Investing in cancer research is not just an Earthbound priority; it is an essential step toward sustaining life in extraterrestrial environments. Protecting or repairing DNA from radiation damage, developing therapies to counteract cellular degeneration, and engineering biological resilience are critical goals. These innovations would serve humanity well, both on Earth and beyond. The pursuit of curing cancer aligns with the broader aspirations of space exploration. This ensures that when humanity reaches Mars, it will carry the tools needed not just to land, but to thrive.

The idea of colonizing Mars captures the collective imagination, symbolizing humanity's boundless ambition to explore and conquer new frontiers. Beneath the soaring rhetoric of interplanetary travel lies a stark and unspoken reality. We lack the technology to shield astronauts from the lethal radiation that would bombard them on such a mission. Sustaining life on the Martian surface is even further beyond reach. Current solutions, such as constructing underground tunnels to escape the constant barrage of galactic cosmic rays and solar particles, remain theoretical and prohibitively resource-intensive. Without such protections, prolonged exposure on Mars would lead to catastrophic health outcomes, rendering the dream of colonization not just impractical but potentially suicidal.

Given these unresolved challenges, it is almost certain that NASA—or any other serious governmental space agency—would hesitate to green light a human mission to establish Martian colonies. The sheer scale of the radiation problem is daunting.

Coupled with the ethical implications of knowingly exposing astronauts to such risks, it makes Mars colonization politically and scientifically untenable in the near term. Paradoxically, the United States government continues to endorse Elon Musk's vision of transforming Mars into humanity's second home. This lends credibility to what many scientists and policymakers regard as a fanciful, if not reckless, endeavor. This apparent contradiction begs the question: Why?

The answer may lie not in Mars colonization itself but in what the rhetoric surrounding it allows. The United States government's visible support for Musk's ambitions could be a strategic maneuver to mask a far more terrestrial agenda. Behind the guise of interplanetary exploration lies a dual-purpose strategy. Developing space stations capable of sustaining human life serves as a technological stepping stone toward Mars. It also acts as a contingency plan for United States leadership if a catastrophic nuclear conflict occurs on Earth. This "presidential backup plan" would involve constructing orbital substations—safe havens from which the United States government could operate if global annihilation became imminent.

Were the United States to announce such an intention outright, international opposition would be swift and overwhelming. Rival nations, particularly those with nuclear capabilities, would interpret the move as an aggressive escalation, akin to establishing an orbital throne for unilateral global dominance. The geopolitical fallout would be catastrophic, with other nations racing to establish similar facilities or preemptively targeting American space assets. By leveraging Musk and his private-sector credibility, the United States can pursue these goals under the radar. Advocates present these efforts as the natural progression of space exploration and commercial tourism.

SpaceX's rapid development of reusable rockets and its ambitious Starship program are crucial components of this strategy. On the surface, these technologies promise to revolutionize access to space, enabling everything from satellite launches to interplanetary missions. But their underlying capabilities—long-term habitation, rapid deployment, and payload versatility—align suspiciously well with the requirements for orbital substations. The United States government gains a plausible deniability shield by supporting Musk's ventures. This approach allows it to develop strategic space infrastructure while cloaking its intentions in the aspirational language of Mars colonization and space tourism.

This covert alignment of interests between the United States government and private enterprise mirrors historical patterns of leveraging technological advances for geopolitical advantage. During the Cold War, officials often portrayed rocket technology development as peaceful space exploration. However, it frequently doubled as a means to advance ballistic missile capabilities. Similarly, the Space Shuttle program, celebrated for its scientific contributions, also served as a tool for deploying military satellites and testing defense technologies. The current push for Mars colonization may follow the same template. A public dream masks a strategic gambit, where the survival of a select few trumps the lofty ideal of interplanetary settlement.

2. THE PRESIDENT'S BACKUP

When we hear about space exploration today, the discussion inevitably centers on Mars colonization and the captivating idea of making humanity a "multi-planetary species." Elon Musk's oft-quoted mantra, hailed as visionary and forward-thinking, has become synonymous with the ambitions of spacefaring humanity. Beneath the dazzling rhetoric and sleek prototypes lies a shadowy undercurrent of motivations. It is less about utopian dreams of interplanetary life and more about ensuring the survival of an elite few. Whether Musk himself fully grasps the intricate layers of geopolitical maneuvering behind his endeavors is irrelevant. His vision of Martian colonies, supported and encouraged by the United States, aligns seamlessly with a hidden agenda. Russia and the US have rooted this agenda in the grim realities of the impending "Petrocalypse," a war triggered as fossil fuel reserves deplete.

The elites understand this. They recognize that their survival in the face of these crises will require drastic measures, including decisions that could precipitate mass genocide. The looming depletion of resources cannot sustain the current human population. The elite view a "cleansing" of billions not as an atrocity but as a grim necessity for their survival. Governments and corporations will publicly deny these dark intentions. Yet, their actions tell a different story. The push to accelerate space colonization, the militarization of orbital technologies, and the focus on projects like Musk's Starship betray a long-term plan at play.

Consider the parallels between the functionality of Air Force One and the space faring vessels under development. Air Force One, equipped with advanced communication systems, defensive countermeasures, and aerial refueling capabilities, represents the pinnacle of escape planning. This system protects the United States president during times of crisis. Even with its technological sophistication, the plane is ultimately a stopgap. It is a temporary solution designed to provide a mobile command center during a nuclear exchange or other catastrophic event. Its range, while extended by refueling, is finite. Its capacity to protect those aboard is limited by time and resources. Faced with global annihilation—whether from nuclear war over resource conflicts or the environmental collapse of the petrocalypse—Air Force One offers only a temporary reprieve. It cannot stop the inevitable.

Enter the idea of seeing space as a new frontier. The Starship rocket, initially praised as a passenger vehicle for colonizing Mars, begins to resemble less a vessel of exploration and more an interstellar Ark. With its ability to carry dozens of passengers and massive cargo, it represents a new kind of escape plan. This plan transcends the limitations of Air Force One and Earth's atmosphere itself. The persistent narrative of a "multi-planetary species" becomes less about humanity and more about ensuring the continuity of a select group. The Mars colony isn't being designed to save humanity; it's being designed to save the elites.

To fully grasp the implications, we must consider the timeline and investment priorities. The United States government has quietly provided both implicit and explicit support for Musk's ventures. This includes NASA contracts and regulatory frameworks that favor SpaceX's rapid development and testing cycles. Advocates frame the argument around national interest, innovation, and competition with global rivals like China. But behind the patriotic messaging is a stark truth: these projects are insurance policies for those who hold the reins of power. Millions of displaced, impoverished victims of the petrocalypse will not populate a functioning Martian colony or orbital habitat. It will house the architects of the system that failed to prevent the collapse.

The cruelty of this vision is not unprecedented. Throughout history, the powerful have demonstrated their willingness to abandon the many to save the few. Government officials and military leaders constructed fallout shelters during the Cold War. Meanwhile, authorities left the general population to fend for itself if nuclear war occurred. The same logic is now being applied on a planetary scale. Earth's surface, ravaged by climate change and resource wars, will become a battleground, while the elites retreat to their celestial fortresses. Leaders will distract the masses with illusions of hope—fascinating them with news of Martian colonies and orbital habitats—while executing the real agenda in secrecy.

Starship's passenger rockets, ostensibly intended to ferry colonists to Mars, serve more immediate contingencies. If a *Petrocalypse* driven nuclear war occurs, they provide an escape route that Air Force One could never offer. Unlike planes, which are tethered to fuel supplies and subject to terrestrial hazards, spacefaring vessels offer an unparalleled degree of separation. The rockets, equipped with advanced life-support systems and modular habitats, are essentially lifeboats in the vast ocean of space. The colonization of Mars becomes a convenient narrative—a decoy that obscures the true purpose of these endeavors.

Musk's timeline for Mars colonization aligns ominously with projections for peak oil depletion and escalating global instability. By the mid-21st century, as the

Petrocalypse reaches its zenith, the infrastructure for elite survival in space may already be in place. And while corporations will sell the public stories of human triumph and interplanetary adventure, they will mask an underlying reality of exclusion and abandonment. The question is not whether humanity will become a multi-planetary species, but which humans will—and at what cost to those left behind.

2.1 MARS COLONIZATION

Seeing Mars colonization, with its romanticized allure of red deserts and domed habitats, often feels more like a science fiction dream than a practical goal. Elon Musk and his tireless optimism proclaim humanity's destiny as a "multi-planetary species." However, the scale of technological, logistical, and biological challenges makes the concept laughable to many. Terraforming an entire planet, establishing self-sufficient ecosystems, and ensuring survival in a hostile environment is a daunting task that would require centuries of coordinated effort. This grand vision serves as a smokescreen for a more pragmatic and immediate agenda. It is less about pioneering interplanetary civilization and more about securing an escape plan for Earth's elites. The real focus is not on Mars itself. Instead, it is on building intermediate infrastructure, such as space stations capable of sustaining human life for years. Advocates position these stations as celestial lifeboats in case of global catastrophe.

These so-called "substations," ostensibly being developed as stepping stones for Mars missions, are far from innocent experiments in human ingenuity. They are survival bunkers in orbit—a modern-day ark for those who hold the reins of political and economic power. For the United States, a nation keenly aware of how fragile global stability can be, space development is more than an engineering challenge. It's about building long-term life-supporting stations. Beyond science, it has become a geopolitical necessity. While Musk's SpaceX and NASA openly discuss the potential of these stations as hubs for space exploration, their real purpose is far darker. They are backup plans for when Earth becomes uninhabitable—whether through nuclear war, climate collapse, or resource depletion during the looming Petrocalypse.

The concept of orbital survival stations is not entirely new. During the Cold War, the United States invested heavily in the idea of space as the ultimate strategic high ground. Projects like the MOL (Manned Orbiting Laboratory) in the 1960s aimed to create military outposts in orbit. However, technological and financial constraints forced officials to shelve these efforts. Recent years have brought together private innovation and public desperation. The technology to sustain human life in space has advanced significantly. This includes innovations such as advanced recycling systems for air and water and modular habitats that crews can assemble in orbit. SpaceX's Starship program, with its emphasis on reusability and scalability, is a crucial component of this new strategy. SpaceX officially markets Starship as a platform for interplanetary travel. However, its capacity to carry large payloads and crews to orbit also makes it the perfect vehicle for transporting the elite to these orbital sanctuaries.

Building these stations aligns suspiciously well with projections of global instability. As the petrocalypse looms closer, the strategic importance of having self-sustaining refuges beyond Earth becomes undeniable. The idea is simple yet chilling. If Earth plunges into chaos—be it from nuclear war over shrinking resources, uncontrollable climate disasters, or widespread social unrest—these orbital stations will provide safe havens. However, they will only shelter a select few. The infrastructure being built today under the guise of space exploration is not for humanity at large. The architects of the current system, those with the wealth and power, secure their survival while leaving billions to fend for themselves.

Even Air Force One, the epitome of terrestrial emergency planning, cannot match the strategic advantages of these orbital stations. A well-equipped orbital station offers near-total autonomy from the chaos unfolding on the ground. Powered by solar arrays and equipped with advanced life-support systems, such stations could remain functional for years. These stations would shelter more than just political leaders. They'd house technocrats, scientists, and military personnel—those deemed essential to rebuilding society. Or, at the very least, to maintain power after the dust settles.

The timeline of these developments is telling. SpaceX's Starship has already achieved milestones in payload delivery and orbital testing, with plans for operational missions within this decade. Meanwhile, NASA's Gateway project, a lunar orbital platform, is quietly pioneering the modular technologies necessary for long-term habitation in space. Billions of dollars in government contracts and private investments fund these advancements. They suggest a sense of urgency that aligns uncomfortably well with the ticking clock of Earth's resource crises. While leaders feed the public inspiring narratives of scientific progress and the human spirit, they lay the groundwork for their escape.

These orbital stations will not be lifeboats for humanity. Much like the fallout shelters of the Cold War, these stations will prioritize the survival of a select few. The current system designs them to protect those it deems most valuable. The question of who gets a seat on these celestial arks is not merely logistical, but deeply ideological. This reflects the same hierarchical logic that has governed elite behavior throughout history. It prioritizes preserving power and privilege at all costs, even if it means leaving the majority behind.

When Musk speaks of making life "multi-planetary," it is easy to be swept up in the grandeur of his vision. But the truth lies not in the deserts of Mars but in the space between Earth and its moon, where these substations are quietly being prepared. The future they represent is not one of shared human progress. This vision paints a future defined by stark inequality. Space wouldn't be a frontier for exploration but the ultimate refuge for an elite class. They would have already decided that the rest of humanity is disposable.

3. BOTSTRONAUT

The profound challenges of venturing beyond Earth's protective cradle have always tempered humanity's ambition to explore the cosmos. Among the most significant are the physiological risks posed by the hostile environment of space. Outside Earth's magnetosphere, cosmic rays and solar radiation bombard astronauts at levels far exceeding those on the planet's surface. These high-energy particles can penetrate spacecraft walls and human tissue, causing cellular damage that increases the risk of cancer and other long-term health issues. Acute exposure, such as during a solar flare, could result in radiation sickness, marked by nausea, vomiting, and potentially fatal complications. The Apollo astronauts, who ventured beyond Earth's orbit in the 1960s and 70s, were the first to experience heightened radiation exposure. However, their missions were too short for long-term effects to manifest. Future endeavors, such as missions to Mars, which require months in deep space, will magnify these risks exponentially.

Lacking gravity adds another layer of complexity to human space exploration. In microgravity, the human body undergoes profound changes. These include weakening skeletal muscles and losing bone density at a rate of about 1-2% per month. These effects mimic accelerated aging and can lead to fractures and other complications upon returning to gravity. NASA's twin study involving astronauts Mark and Scott Kelly highlighted additional physiological changes, such as altered gene expression and immune system disruptions. Equally daunting are the psychological challenges. Prolonged isolation and confinement, coupled with the monotony of long-duration space missions, can lead to stress, anxiety, and depression. Even the most meticulously selected and trained crews face challenges. They are not immune to the mental strain of being separated from Earth by millions of miles, with no immediate possibility of rescue.

The technical and logistical hurdles of sustaining human life in space are equally formidable. Life support systems must reliably provide oxygen, water, and food while managing waste over extended periods. Current systems, such as those used on the International Space Station (ISS), rely heavily on recycling technologies, including devices that convert urine into drinkable water. While these systems are effective in low Earth orbit, their reliability over multi-year missions remains unproven. On the surface of planets like Mars, the challenges multiply. Habitats must protect against radiation, micrometeoroids, and extreme temperatures, while also maintaining an atmosphere suitable for human life. Using local resources, such as extracting water from Martian soil or producing oxygen from its carbon dioxide-rich atmosphere, is a promising concept. However, it remains in the experimental stage. The sheer complexity of these systems leaves little room for error, as even minor failures could be catastrophic.

Spacecraft design must also evolve to meet the unique demands of human exploration. Radiation shielding is critical but adds significant weight to spacecraft, increasing launch costs. Protection against micrometeoroids, which travel at speeds of up to 28,000 kilometers per hour, requires innovative materials and engineering solutions. Additionally, the journey to other planets necessitates advanced propulsion technologies to reduce travel time and mitigate the risks of prolonged exposure to microgravity and radiation. Yet, despite decades of innovation, human spaceflight remains fraught with risks that robotic missions avoid entirely.

The economic costs of human space exploration present another formidable challenge. Crewed missions are orders of magnitude more expensive than robotic missions because of the need for life support, safety measures, and return capabilities. For example, the Apollo program, which sent humans to the Moon, cost an estimated $25.4 billion in 1973—equivalent to roughly $160 billion today. In contrast, robotic missions such as NASA's Perseverance rover, which landed on Mars in 2021, cost $2.7 billion, a fraction of the price. These stark differences raise questions about resource allocation. Critics argue that the funds required for human missions could instead be used to advance robotic exploration or address pressing Earth-based issues like climate change and poverty. Proponents argue that the scientific and inspirational value of human exploration justifies the expense. They point to programs like Apollo, which achieved unprecedented milestones and galvanized public interest in science and technology.

Ultimately, the challenges of human space exploration are as much a test of will as they are of technology and economics. Overcoming the physiological risks, technical hurdles, and financial barriers will require not only ingenuity but also a collective determination to push the boundaries of what is possible. Humanity's quest to explore the cosmos reflects our enduring curiosity and resilience at its core. As we prepare to step further into the unknown, we must confront these challenges with a clear-eyed understanding of their gravity. We must also commit to ensuring that the pursuit of the stars does not come at the expense of the world we call home.

The botstronaut represents a turning point in space exploration, but it is only the beginning. Behind its mechanical frame lies the true force driving this revolution: artificial intelligence and robotics. These technologies are not just tools—they are the architects of a future where humanity's reach extends far beyond what was once imaginable.

3.1 AI AND ROBOTICS

The rise of artificial intelligence and robotics marks a transformative moment in human history, akin to the Industrial Revolution or predicting the internet's emergence. AI, powered by machine learning algorithms, has evolved to solve complex problems with precision and speed. These systems can process vast amounts of data, identify patterns, and make autonomous decisions in real-time, even in unpredictable environments. In tandem, robotics has achieved remarkable feats, with machines capable of dexterous manipulation and unprecedented mobility. Boston Dynamics' robots, for example, can navigate rugged terrain, while humanoid robots like NASA's Valkyrie mimic human actions to perform tasks traditionally reserved for astronauts. These advancements, when applied to space exploration, are not merely supplementary; they are revolutionary, expanding humanity's ability to explore the cosmos while mitigating the risks inherent in sending humans to space.

The operational benefits of AI and robotics in space missions are unparalleled. Robots are immune to the physiological challenges that humans face, such as exposure to cosmic radiation, the effects of microgravity, or the psychological toll of isolation. They do not require oxygen, water, food, or sleep, eliminating the need for complex life support systems. This makes robotic missions inherently safer and allows for more streamlined spacecraft designs. Consider the Mars rovers, from Spirit and Opportunity to Perseverance. These machines have operated in extreme environments where human survival would be impossible, enduring freezing temperatures, dust storms, and the relentless bombardment of cosmic rays. Their endurance and efficiency are unmatched: while humans would require rest and resources, these robots function continuously, maximizing the scientific return of every mission.

Robotic missions are also far more cost-effective than their human counterparts. With no life support systems, spacecraft can be lighter and smaller, reducing launch costs significantly. Lacking return requirements further simplifies mission architecture.

For instance, NASA's Perseverance rover cost approximately $2.7 billion, including development, launch, and operations—a fraction of what a crewed Mars mission would require. Moreover, the scalability of robotic missions is transformative. For the cost of one crewed mission, scientists can deploy multiple robotic units to cover a wider area and perform diverse experiments simultaneously. This approach not only enhances scientific output but also reduces the financial risks associated with space exploration.

The applications of AI and robotics in learning and research have already reshaped our understanding of the universe. Robotic explorers like the Hubble Space Telescope and the Voyager probes have provided humanity with unprecedented data. These include high-resolution images of distant galaxies and detailed environmental analyzes of extraterrestrial terrains. In situ instruments, such as Perseverance's SHERLOC (Scanning Habitable Environments with Raman & Luminescence for Organics and Chemicals), can conduct advanced experiments on-site. They relay real-time results back to Earth. The adaptability of these systems is a key advantage. Scientists can update mission parameters based on ongoing discoveries, enabling robots to perform new tasks or explore promising areas without the delays and risks of human intervention.

These missions also drive technological development in ways that reverberate beyond space exploration. AI systems developed for space missions often find applications on Earth, from improving machine learning algorithms in healthcare to optimizing autonomous vehicles. The iterative process of refining AI through space exploration creates feedback loops that enhance their performance in both domains. Similarly, advances in robotics engineering, driven by the demands of space exploration, lead to breakthroughs in materials science, mobility, and autonomous repair systems. For example, robotic arms initially designed for space stations have inspired technologies used in delicate surgical procedures on Earth.

The integration of artificial intelligence and robotics into space exploration represents a profound shift in how humanity engages with the cosmos. These technologies enable safer, more efficient, and more cost-effective missions, expanding our capacity to learn and innovate. As AI and robotics evolve, they will deepen our understanding of the universe and redefine the boundaries of what is possible. This creates a future where exploration is no longer limited by the constraints of human biology or resources. This is not merely a technological advancement—it is a paradigm shift, one that promises to transform humanity's relationship with the stars.

3.2 ASTEROID MINING

The idea of mining asteroids and utilizing space resources has captured the human imagination for decades, blending visions of limitless wealth with the hope of sustainable exploration. Asteroids, relics of the early solar system, are rich in materials that are scarce on Earth. Certain types of asteroids contain platinum-group metals, essential for advanced electronics and industrial applications, in abundant quantities. Experts estimate that a single metallic asteroid, like 16 Psyche, contains metals worth over $10 quintillion—exceeding the global economy's annual output by orders of magnitude. Besides metals, many asteroids harbor water ice, a critical resource for sustaining life and producing rocket fuel through electrolysis. NASA's OSIRIS-REx mission, which successfully returned samples from the asteroid Bennu in 2023, demonstrated the feasibility of extracting extraterrestrial materials, paving the way for future mining operations. The economic potential of asteroid mining is staggering, but it also raises profound questions about distributing benefits and ethically using space resources.

Developing robotic mining operations transforms these ambitions into practical possibilities. Autonomous systems, equipped with AI and advanced robotics, are being designed to extract and process materials on-site, reducing the need for human presence in hazardous environments. Companies like Planetary Resources and Deep Space Industries have spearheaded efforts to develop these technologies, although financial and technical challenges have slowed progress. NASA and ESA have also invested heavily in robotic technologies for mining and In-Situ Resource Utilization (ISRU), with robots capable of drilling, excavating, and refining resources. NASA engineers designed the RASSOR (Regolith Advanced Surface Systems Operations Robot) prototype to extract regolith, which contains valuable elements and converts into building materials. These systems, operating autonomously or with minimal human oversight, promise to lower the risks and costs associated with space mining while accelerating the timeline for resource extraction.

ISRU has emerged as a cornerstone of sustainable space exploration, offering the potential to produce essential resources like water, oxygen, and fuel directly on-site. By converting local materials into usable products, ISRU systems could drastically reduce the need to launch supplies from Earth—a costly and logistically challenging endeavor. Engineers can process lunar regolith, abundant on the Moon's surface, to extract oxygen and construct habitats using 3D printing techniques. Water ice, recently confirmed in permanently shadowed regions of the lunar poles, could serve as both a life-sustaining resource and a component for fuel production. Mars offers similar opportunities: scientists can process its carbon dioxide-rich atmosphere to produce methane fuel for return journeys. Robotic ISRU systems, deployed ahead of human missions, could establish stockpiles of resources, creating the infrastructure necessary for long-term exploration and eventual colonization.

Policymakers and leaders must address the ethical and societal implications of these advancements. One of the most immediate considerations is the balance between human and machine roles in space exploration. Robots excel in hazardous and monotonous tasks, offering a safer alternative to human labor in the extreme environments of space. This ethical imperative to preserve human life aligns with broader societal values, making robotic mining and ISRU systems the logical choice for early-stage resource utilization. However, as robots increasingly take on roles that were once the purview of humans, the cultural narrative of space exploration could shift. Historically, the bravery and ambition of astronauts have captivated the public, symbolizing the human spirit of discovery. The rise of robotic systems, while practical, might challenge this perception, reducing the emotive appeal of space exploration and reframing it as a predominantly technical endeavor.

Economically, the push for mining and resource utilization in space is creating opportunities and disruptions in equal measure. The robotics and AI industries anticipate substantial growth, spurring demand for engineers, scientists, and technicians to develop and maintain space-capable systems. Entire sectors could emerge by producing specialized materials, software, and hardware, driving innovation and job creation on Earth. However, the same technologies that enable these opportunities could displace human roles in space exploration, particularly in manual and operational tasks. This raises concerns about workforce transitions and the need for retraining programs to equip displaced workers with new skills. Leaders must carefully plan how to integrate robots into space industries to ensure a fair distribution of economic benefits, much like during past automation revolutions.

The potential for mining and resource utilization in space represents both an extraordinary opportunity and a profound challenge. It promises to unlock resources that could transform industries, support human exploration, and reshape global economies. Yet, it also demands that humanity grapple with the ethical, cultural, and economic implications of outsourcing the frontier to machines. As we look to the stars for solutions to Earth's challenges, we must ensure that these endeavors reflect our highest values. Society must balance ambition with responsibility and align innovation with equity. The choices made in the coming decades will not only determine the success of space exploration but also define humanity's legacy in the cosmos.

Space is humanity's final frontier, a realm of infinite possibility and infinite risk. But if we cannot overcome the dysfunctions that plague us on Earth, we risk replicating them among the stars. The journey concludes in Chapter 15: Nuclear War, where the specter of nuclear war looms as the ultimate expression of human failure. It serves as a reminder that our survival depends not on escaping our problems but on confronting them.

15

Nuclear war

"The release of atom power has changed everything
except our way of thinking."

– ALBERT EINSTEIN

Resource scarcity often drives the roots of conflict in both humans and our closest evolutionary relatives, primates such as chimpanzees. Among chimpanzees, aggression frequently arises over access to food, territory, or mates. Observational studies, such as those conducted by Jane Goodall in the Gombe Stream National Park during the 1960s, revealed chilling parallels to human conflict. One of her most striking findings was the "Four-Year War" between two chimpanzee groups, the Kahama and Kasakela communities. What began as territorial disputes escalated into coordinated attacks, where males from one group would ambush and kill isolated individuals from the other. This violence, driven by the instinct to secure resources and dominance, mirrors the early conflicts in human societies. Anthropological evidence from pre-agricultural human tribes shows similar patterns. Disputes over fertile land, water sources, or hunting territories often led to skirmishes or raids. These conflicts reflected a primal struggle for survival.

Yet, where chimps rely on their physical strength and social alliances, humans have introduced a profound and terrifying variable—technology. The tools we have created to protect ourselves or secure resources have drastically magnified the scale and consequences of conflict. Technological innovation has transformed how wars occur, from the spears of hunter-gatherer societies to the industrialized weaponry of World War I. This technological trajectory culminated in 1945. The United States dropped atomic bombs on Hiroshima and Nagasaki, killing over 200,000 people. This event ushered in the nuclear age. This moment marked a stark divergence from the primal conflicts of our ancestors. The power to annihilate entire cities—and potentially the planet—elevated human aggression to a level incomprehensible to any other species. The Cold War that followed turned this capability into a geopolitical chess game, where the fear of mutually assured destruction paradoxically maintained a fragile peace.

However, the fundamental difference between humans and other primates lies not in our tools but in our capacity for conscious choice. While chimps act primarily on instinct, humans can reflect, reason, and negotiate. This potential for diplomacy and ethical decision-making introduces a layer of complexity to human conflicts. The Cuban Missile Crisis of 1962 exemplifies this. For thirteen tense days, the world teetered on the brink of nuclear war. The United States and the Soviet Union clashed over deploying missiles in Cuba. Careful negotiation by United States President John F. Kennedy averted what could have ended in catastrophic destruction. Kennedy and Soviet Premier Nikita Khrushchev. Their ability to prioritize survival over dominance highlighted humanity's unique potential to resolve conflicts through cooperation rather than violence.

Yet, this capacity for reflection also brings ethical burdens. Unlike chimps, whose actions are driven by immediate needs, humans grapple with the morality of their choices. Developing nuclear weapons and deciding to use them sparked intense debates among scientists, politicians, and the public. Figures like J. Robert Oppenheimer, who led the Manhattan Project, later expressed deep regret, quoting the Bhagavad Gita: "Now I am become Death, the destroyer of worlds." This duality—the ability to create tools of destruction and the conscience to question their use—defines the human experience of conflict. It is a testament to both our ingenuity and our struggle to transcend our primal instincts.

The competition for resources has always been at the heart of survival and reproduction. It has shaped the trajectory of life on Earth through the relentless sieve of natural selection. From the moment life emerged, the ability to secure food, water, shelter, and mates determined which individuals thrived and which vanished into evolutionary obscurity. In this struggle, resource acquisition became not just a biological imperative but established behavioral strategies. Among these, mate guarding—a behavior observed across species from insects to primates—evolved as a critical mechanism to ensure reproductive success. By protecting access to mates and their offspring, individuals could maximize their genetic legacy, a principle that underscores the very logic of natural selection. In humans, this evolutionary pressure gave rise to cultural practices and conflicts centered on resource control. These ranged from territorial wars to social hierarchies. Each echoed the ancient dance of survival.

Territoriality, a behavior deeply ingrained in the animal kingdom, further illustrates the evolutionary advantages of resource defense. Among chimpanzees, humanity's closest relatives, territorial disputes often escalate into violent confrontations, as documented by Jane Goodall in her groundbreaking studies at Gombe Stream National Park. Male chimps patrol their territories, vigilantly guarding access to food and potential mates while seeking opportunities to expand their domain. These behaviors are not unique to primates. In the Serengeti, lions defend hunting grounds, while birds like the red-winged blackbird aggressively ward off intruders from nesting sites. Across species, territoriality serves a dual purpose: it safeguards vital resources and signals fitness to potential mates. For early humans, tribal societies fiercely defended land and resources, laying the groundwork for modern concepts of ownership and conflict. The parallels between territoriality in animals and human societies highlight a continuum. The evolutionary drive for resource defense transcends species boundaries. It shapes behaviors that persist in contemporary geopolitics.

At the biological level, aggression emerges as an adaptive response to resource scarcity, its roots intertwined with neurological and hormonal systems designed to maximize survival. In mammals, the hypothalamus and amygdala play critical roles in processing threats and triggering aggressive responses, while hormones like testosterone amplify these behaviors. Studies in rodents have shown that increased testosterone levels correlate with heightened territorial aggression, a finding mirrored in primates, including humans. This biological machinery evolved as a response to environments where resources were finite, and competition was intense. In times of abundance, aggression might subside, but scarcity flips the switch, unleashing behaviors designed to secure survival at any cost. During the Pleistocene epoch, when early humans contended with fluctuating climates and limited food sources, these mechanisms likely determined which groups endured and which perished. The same instincts reverberate today in conflicts over water in the Middle East or arable land in Sub-Saharan Africa. Resource scarcity stokes ancient fires of aggression. Modern politics and economics reframe these struggles.

The biological and behavioral underpinnings of resource competition reveal a profound truth about human nature: our capacity for cooperation rivals our propensity for conflict. The same neurological systems that fuel aggression also enable empathy and social bonding, underscoring the duality of our evolutionary inheritance. Understanding these roots provides not just a glimpse into the past, but a framework for addressing the conflicts of the present. Whether the battleground is a patch of forest or a geopolitical hotspot, the forces at play are echoes of a shared evolutionary journey. This journey continues to shape our species in profound and often troubling ways.

Ultimately, the study of primate and human conflict dynamics reveals a spectrum of behavior, from instinct-driven aggression to calculated diplomacy. While technology has amplified the stakes of human conflict, it has also provided the means for resolution, from communication networks to international treaties. The challenge lies in whether humanity can consistently choose reflection over retaliation, cooperation over conquest. In the vast arena of human history, the capacity for ethical choice may prove to be our most powerful tool. It can break the cycles of violence that began in the trees of our ancestors and now threaten the stars.

The fear of annihilation has always been a paradoxical motivator for humanity—driving us toward both destruction and cooperation. Nuclear war, with its existential stakes, forced the world to confront the need for dialog and restraint, leading to frameworks that promised peace but delivered hierarchy. Among these, the Non-Proliferation Treaty stood as both a shield against chaos and a mirror reflecting our deepest inequities. What began as an attempt to control the atom's destructive power soon revealed the fault lines of global power. Disarmament became an illusion, and the powerful redefined justice to suit their needs.

1. NPT: NOW PROHIBITING THEM (NOT US)

Adopting the Non-Proliferation Treaty (NPT) in 1968 marked a monumental step toward preventing the spread of nuclear weapons and fostering global disarmament. At its core, the treaty relies on three pillars. These included preventing nuclear weapons from proliferating to new states, facilitating peaceful uses of nuclear energy, and committing to eventual disarmament by nuclear-armed powers. For its noble intentions and its role in stabilizing Cold War tensions, the NPT earned the 2005 Nobel Peace Prize, celebrated as a beacon for multilateral cooperation. Yet, beneath the surface of this apparent triumph lay a framework riddled with inequities. The treaty entrenches the privileges of nuclear-armed states while constraining the ambitions of others.

The treaty's structure institutionalized a stark double standard. It divided the world into nuclear "haves" and "have-nots." Five states—the United States, the Soviet Union (now Russia), China, the United Kingdom, and France—gained legitimacy for possessing nuclear arsenals. The treaty explicitly forbids others from acquiring such weapons. These five nations gained this status because they conducted nuclear tests before the treaty's cutoff date of January 1, 1967. For the rest of the world, the treaty demanded abstinence, creating an imbalance that critics have long argued perpetuates global inequality. While the treaty obligated nuclear states to pursue disarmament, this clause remained vague, unenforceable, and ultimately ignored. The result was a system where nuclear-armed states maintained their dominance. By denying non-nuclear states the tools that nuclear states claimed were essential for their own security, the treaty highlighted a blunt imbalance.

The inequities became particularly evident during key moments in the treaty's history. India, which refused to sign the NPT, argued that it enshrined an unjust world order by allowing certain states to keep their arsenals indefinitely. India vindicated this sentiment in 1974 by conducting its first nuclear test, calling it a "peaceful nuclear explosion." Similarly, Israel's ambiguous nuclear program, widely believed to have produced weapons by the late 1960s, went unchallenged by the international community. This highlighted the selective enforcement of the NPT's principles. Meanwhile, nations like Iraq and Iran, both signatories of the treaty, faced severe scrutiny and sanctions over their nuclear programs, even when evidence of weaponization was inconclusive.

The NPT's promise of equitable access to peaceful nuclear technology also proved to be a source of contention. Article IV of the treaty ostensibly guaranteed all signatories the right to develop nuclear energy for civilian purposes. In practice, a small group of nations tightly controlled access to advanced nuclear technology. Nations formed the Nuclear Suppliers Group (NSG) in response to India's 1974 test. It imposed additional restrictions on the transfer of nuclear materials and technology. These measures effectively limited the development of nuclear energy in the Global South. Countries like Brazil and South Africa sought to develop independent nuclear programs. They faced significant diplomatic and economic pressure to abandon their ambitions. Meanwhile, nuclear-armed states expanded their arsenals and modernized their warheads.

The Nobel Peace Prize awarded to the NPT in 2005 reflected the global community's hope that the treaty could serve as a cornerstone for disarmament and peace. Yet, the prize committee overlooked the inherent inequalities that critics had pointed out for decades. The treaty succeeded in limiting the number of nuclear-armed states to nine. Without the NPT, this figure might have been much higher. However, it also cemented a world order in which a handful of nations retained the ultimate tools of destruction. This disparity has fueled resentment among non-nuclear states, many of which argue that the NPT perpetuates a system of "nuclear apartheid."

Perhaps the most glaring failure of the NPT lies in the lack of progress toward disarmament. Despite commitments made during the treaty's review conferences, nuclear-armed states have shown little willingness to relinquish their arsenals. The United States and Russia hold over 90% of the world's nuclear weapons. They have reduced their stockpiles since the height of the Cold War. However, they continue to modernize their arsenals. New delivery systems, such as hypersonic missiles, and developing tactical nuclear weapons undermine the treaty's disarmament goals. For non-nuclear states, this hypocrisy underscores the power dynamics that the NPT has failed to address.

The Non-Proliferation Treaty stands as both a testament to humanity's desire to avoid nuclear catastrophe and a symbol of its failure to confront global inequities. While it may have slowed the spread of nuclear weapons, it has also entrenched a system of inequality. Some nations wield ultimate power, while the treaty denies others the means to defend themselves on equal footing. Recognizing the NPT's flaws does not negate its achievements, but it does demand a reexamination of the structures it has created. The challenge for the future is to reconcile the treaty's noble aspirations with the realities of a deeply unequal world.

The NPT sought to freeze the nuclear clock, but time marches on relentlessly. While the treaty attempted to lock power into the hands of a few, technology has refused to sit still. In an era of algorithms and cyber capabilities, the nuclear arsenal of the 20th century has begun its unsettling evolution. Welcome to the age of Nukes 2.0, where the weapons of mass destruction are no longer just bombs, but nodes in a digital network of deterrence—and destabilization.

1.1 NUKES 2.0: NOW WITH WI-FI!

Modernizing nuclear weapons systems has emerged as one of the most contentious issues in contemporary international security. It is a dilemma that exposes the inherent contradictions of nuclear deterrence. Advocates argue that nations must update aging arsenals to ensure reliability and maintain a credible deterrent. They emphasize the need to adapt to evolving threats, particularly with advancements in missile defense and cyber capabilities. Critics, however, see modernization efforts as a dangerous escalation that undermines global disarmament goals and fuels an arms race with catastrophic potential. This tension is not new; it has been a defining feature of the nuclear age. This trend dates back to the early years of the Cold War, when the United States and the Soviet Union continuously upgraded their arsenals to outpace each other.

The United States decided to invest $1.7 trillion over 30 years in modernizing its nuclear triad. This three-pronged system includes land-based intercontinental ballistic missiles (ICBMs), submarine-launched ballistic missiles (SLBMs), and strategic bombers. The decision has drawn sharp criticism from disarmament advocates. They argue that such expenditures contradict the spirit of the 1968 Non-Proliferation Treaty, which obligates nuclear states to pursue disarmament. Yet, supporters contend that these upgrades are essential for maintaining a deterrent capable of addressing emerging challenges, particularly from Russia and China. Observers often cite Russia's deployment of hypersonic glide vehicles, capable of evading missile defenses, as justification for modernization initiatives. Similarly, China's expansion of its nuclear arsenal, including constructing new missile silos, adds to these arguments. However, these developments have also prompted a cycle of escalation, with each modernization effort triggering similar responses from rival powers.

Historical precedent underscores the peril of such arms races. During the 1980s, President Ronald Reagan's Strategic Defense Initiative (SDI) aimed to develop a missile defense system. Derisively nicknamed "Star Wars," it sought to render Soviet ICBMs obsolete. The initiative never fully materialized, but its announcement spurred the Soviet Union to invest heavily in countermeasures, straining its already fragile economy further. This mutual escalation, while arguably contributing to the end of the Cold War, highlighted the fragility of deterrence when paired with technological competition. Today, the same dynamics are at play, with hypersonic weapons and artificial intelligence threatening to destabilize the delicate balance that has prevented nuclear war for decades.

The implications of modernization extend beyond the technical realm into the moral and strategic dimensions of nuclear deterrence. At the heart of the debate lies a paradox: nations maintain nuclear weapons ostensibly to prevent their use. Proponents of deterrence argue that the very existence of these weapons ensures peace by making the cost of conflict unthinkable. This logic, known as mutually assured destruction (MAD), has been held since 1945. The bombings of Hiroshima and Nagasaki showed the world the devastating potential of atomic weapons. However, the same argument has been used to justify the expansion and enhancement of arsenals. This has led to the stockpiling of over 12,500 nuclear warheads globally as of 2023. Critics question whether deterrence justifies perpetuating a system that holds humanity hostage to its own creations.

The tension between maintaining arsenals for deterrence and pursuing disarmament is further complicated by the role of emerging nuclear powers and non-state actors. Nations like North Korea view nuclear weapons as vital to their survival. Since 2006, North Korea has conducted six nuclear tests, citing threats from the United States and its allies. For them, the modernization efforts of established nuclear powers serve as a validation of their own programs. This reasoning creates a dangerous precedent, as other nations may seek to develop or modernize their arsenals under the guise of self-defense. Meanwhile, the specter of nuclear terrorism looms. There are fears that advanced weapons systems could fall into the hands of non-state actors or rogue elements. This makes the goal of disarmament appear increasingly elusive.

Efforts to resolve these tensions have been fraught with challenges. Treaties like the New START agreement between the United States and Russia offer a framework for reducing arsenals. This treaty limits the number of deployed warheads and delivery systems. However, its scope remains limited. In 2019, the United States withdrew from the Intermediate-Range Nuclear Forces (INF) Treaty, citing Russian violations. This decision further eroded trust and raised concerns about a renewed arms race. On the other hand, the Treaty prohibiting Nuclear Weapons (TPNW) represents a bold push for disarmament. Adopted by the United Nations in 2017, over 50 nations actively support it. However, no nuclear-armed state has signed it, underscoring the gulf between rhetoric and reality.

Modernizing nuclear arsenals thus sits at the intersection of existential risk and strategic necessity. It reflects humanity's struggle to reconcile its technological ingenuity with its capacity for self-destruction. As nations navigate this precarious balance, the question remains whether the logic of deterrence can continue to hold in an era of rapid technological change. The stakes could not be higher: the choices made today will determine whether nuclear weapons remain tools of stability or instruments of annihilation.

As nuclear arsenals evolve with digital precision and strategic ambiguity, the traditional rules of deterrence are being redefined. The core contradiction lies not in advancing technology but in the politics governing it. Modernization enhances these weapons, yet it is the double standards of their custodians that fuel global tensions. Nowhere is this hypocrisy clearer than in the United States. While championing non-proliferation abroad, it invests heavily in upgrading its own arsenal, framing these efforts as essential for security. This paradox of deterrence versus dominance undermines trust and exacerbates the risks of a destabilized nuclear landscape.

1.2 NUCLEAR HYPOCRITE

The American stance on nuclear weapons has long exemplified a troubling double standard. It asserts the legitimacy of its own arsenal while aggressively opposing similar capabilities in other nations. This contradiction stems from a belief in its unique role as a global arbiter of security, bolstered by its technological and military dominance. The United States justifies its possession and modernization of nuclear weapons as essential for deterrence. However, it denies the same rationale to nations like Iran and North Korea. It argues that their nuclear ambitions threaten regional and global stability. This policy, grounded in self-interest and a selective application of international norms, has sparked accusations of hypocrisy and fueled tensions across the world.

Iran's nuclear program has been a focal point of these double standards. Since 2002, when officials exposed its clandestine nuclear facilities, Iran has insisted its nuclear activities are peaceful. This is a right enshrined in the Non-Proliferation Treaty (NPT). Yet, the United States and its allies have treated Iran's program with deep suspicion, citing concerns over the potential for weaponization. These fears culminated in the Joint Comprehensive Plan of Action (JCPOA) in 2015. This agreement, brokered by the United States, Iran, and other major powers, aimed to limit Iran's nuclear activities in exchange for sanctions relief. While heralded as a diplomatic triumph, the JCPOA revealed the lopsided expectations imposed on non-nuclear states. Inspectors imposed stringent inspections and constraints on Iran, a country without nuclear weapons. Meanwhile, nuclear-armed nations, including the United States, continued to modernize their arsenals without serious commitments to disarmament.

The double standards became glaringly apparent in 2018 when the Trump administration unilaterally withdrew from the JCPOA, citing Iran's alleged destabilizing behavior in the region. The move, widely criticized internationally, reimposed severe economic sanctions on Iran, pushing its economy into a tailspin. Meanwhile, the United States pressed forward with a $1.7 trillion nuclear modernization plan, developing new warheads and delivery systems. To many observers, this reinforced the perception that the United States seeks to maintain a monopoly on nuclear power. It dictates terms to others while evading scrutiny of its own actions. Iran's subsequent resumption of uranium enrichment underscored the fragility of such one-sided agreements. It raised questions about the viability of a global non-proliferation regime. This regime allows some states to wield ultimate destructive power while denying others the same tools.

North Korea's nuclear program has further exposed these contradictions. In 2006, North Korea conducted its first nuclear test, defying international condemnation and joining the ranks of nuclear-armed states. Unlike Iran, North Korea had never signed the NPT, allowing it to claim a legal—if not moral—justification for its actions. The regime pursues nuclear weapons because it perceives existential threats. These threats come from the United States and its allies, particularly after the United States-led regime changes in Iraq and Libya. For North Korea, the lesson was obvious: nuclear weapons are the ultimate guarantee of sovereignty and survival. This rationale, though frequently dismissed by the United States as propaganda, mirrors the very logic that underpins American nuclear policy.

International responses to North Korea's nuclear tests have oscillated between harsh sanctions and high-stakes diplomacy. The six-party talks in the mid-2000s aimed to denuclearize the Korean Peninsula but collapsed amid mutual mistrust and unmet commitments. In 2018, a historic summit between President Donald Trump and North Korean leader Kim Jong-un briefly raised hopes for a diplomatic breakthrough. However, these talks ultimately failed to produce substantive results, with North Korea continuing to expand its nuclear arsenal. As of 2023, estimates suggest that North Korea possesses between 40 and 50 nuclear warheads, along with missiles capable of reaching the United States mainland. Despite this growing threat, United States efforts to curb North Korea's ambitions have often been reactive and inconsistent. They focus on containment rather than addressing the underlying security concerns driving North Korea's nuclear strategy.

The starkly different approaches to Iran and North Korea reveal the selective logic underpinning United States nuclear policy. Iran, a signatory of the NPT, faced crippling sanctions for activities within the treaty's framework. Meanwhile, North Korea, which withdrew from the NPT in 2003, has faced a mix of sanctions and sporadic engagement. This inconsistency has not gone unnoticed. Critics argue that it undermines the credibility of international norms and highlights the limitations of a non-proliferation regime dominated by nuclear-armed powers. Moreover, the United States's unwillingness to lead by example—by reducing its own arsenal or committing to disarmament—has weakened its moral authority in confronting nuclear proliferation elsewhere.

At its core, the controversy over nuclear double standards reflects a deeper issue: the unequal distribution of power in the global order. By maintaining a vast nuclear arsenal while denying others the same capability, the United States perpetuates a system. This system prioritizes its security at the expense of global equity. This approach not only fosters resentment but also incentivizes states like Iran and North Korea to pursue nuclear weapons as a means of leveling the playing field. As history has shown, such disparities are inherently unstable, and the selective enforcement of non-proliferation norms risks accelerating the arms races it seeks to prevent.

The double standards of nuclear policy highlight a grim truth: those in power rarely relinquish it willingly. As nations wield their arsenals to enforce inequity, the institutions meant to foster global cooperation falter under the weight of their own contradictions. If the current order cannot resolve these disparities, then perhaps it is time to reimagine the very structures that uphold it—beginning with the United Nations itself.

Nuclear conflict represents the ultimate and most devastating outcome of humanity's unchecked evolutionary tendencies. The same instincts that drove our ancestors to guard their mates, dominate their rivals, and pile their resources now threaten to end humankind itself. But amidst this bleak horizon lies a glimmer of hope.

This book is a call to action, a plea for humanity to observe its dysfunctions and learn from them. If we can nurture curiosity, prioritize science, and instill critical thinking in the next generation, we may yet rewrite our fate. The survival of humanity is not a matter of chance—it is a matter of choice. Let us choose wisely.

Conclusion

"The greatest threat to our planet is the belief that
someone else will save it."

– ROBERT SWAN

Humans have always been both the creators and victims of their dysfunctions. We walk a paradoxical path. It has carried us to the heights of extraordinary achievement, yet it also drags us toward the brink of existential collapse. Our evolutionary journey draws from traits specifically designed for survival. Yet, these instincts have outpaced their original purpose. They leave us struggling in a world we've built—one where they no longer serve us. This book explores those dysfunctions—not to condemn humanity, but to understand it. Each chapter has unraveled a thread of this intricate complexity. It traces our failings to their roots while offering hope that awareness can inspire meaningful change.

It begins with relationships, the cornerstone of human connection, but also reflects our deepest insecurities. The mate-guarding trait, an evolutionary mechanism to secure partnerships, has mutated into jealousy, betrayal, and control. From the friction between genders to how love disintegrates, these dynamics emerge from one core truth. They stem from our deep fear of abandonment and loss. And yet, this same trait that fractures partnerships underpins the broader societal clashes we see today. The need to guard and protect goes beyond relationships. It extends to identities, shaping the fault lines of gender and discrimination. Our tribal instincts, once critical for survival, now betray us. Instead of uniting, they divide and turn us against each other.

This division seeps into the mind, creating a battlefield where societal dysfunctions manifest as mental health crises. Shame, loneliness, and the pressures of modern life are not merely personal struggles; they are the echoes of an evolutionary past that prioritized social cohesion at all costs. When shame kept us in line with the group, it was adaptive. Today, it isolates and crushes. A world far too complex for our ancient instincts shapes the demons of the mind. They reflect the larger dysfunctions within the systems we've created. And nowhere is this more evident than in politics.

The dysfunction of governance is an amplification of the insecurities that plague us individually. Leaders, driven by ego and the instinct to dominate, perpetuate cycles of inequality and exploitation. Policies often serve the few at the cost of the many. The systems designed to uphold justice bend under pressure, favoring those in power. Politics is not just a failure of leadership. It reflects the dysfunction deeply ingrained in humanity's collective psyche. This dysfunction seeps into the economy. The drive to hoard resources, a relic of our ancestors' survival instincts, has created staggering inequalities.

Economic systems, designed to manage scarcity, now manufacture it. The relentless pursuit of profit depletes the planet, widening the gap between the elite and everyone else. Technology, which could democratize access and opportunity, instead consolidates power in the hands of the few. This is most evident in agriculture, where industrial farming ravages the Earth in the name of efficiency. And yet, here too, there is hope. Smart farming offers a glimpse of what becomes possible when technology aligns with sustainability. It is a reminder that our dysfunctions are not destiny.

Education should be the great equalizer, a force that lifts everyone up. Instead, it has become a tool to protect privilege. Schools and systems meant to enlighten now suppress critical thinking. They teach obedience instead of curiosity. This dysfunction does more than pass on our problems to future generations. It robs them of the ability to solve those problems. When education fails, institutions withhold knowledge. And when institutions withhold knowledge, health suffers. Healthcare becomes a commodity. Society treats human bodies as profit machines, prioritizing wealth over well-being. This isn't just a systemic failure. It's a moral one—a betrayal of our basic responsibility to care for one another.

Religion, once a source of solace and meaning, often magnifies these dysfunctions. It exploits the same tribal instincts that fuel discrimination. Faith becomes a tool for control, not compassion. Institutions built on spiritual ideals often become tangled in scandals. Their hypocrisies reflect the very flaws they claim to transcend. Even as religion falters, new faiths emerge—in technology, media, and markets. Yet, they replicate the same cycles of manipulation and power.

Media, the storyteller of our age, turns truth into a commodity, eroding trust and fueling division. The narratives it crafts shape our perceptions, often blurring the line between fact and fiction. Justice, too, bends under these forces. Courts and laws favor the privileged while leaving the vulnerable to suffer. The dysfunction here is not just institutional but existential, challenging the very idea of fairness and equality.

Globalization and nationalism, two seemingly opposing forces, reveal the same underlying dysfunction: the drive to dominate. Global systems exploit local vulnerabilities, while nationalism weaponizes identity to consolidate power. This creates a world of winners and losers. The few thrive, but only at the expense of the many. The consequences are most visible in the climate crisis, where humanity's short-sightedness threatens the planet itself.

Climate change is not just a failure of policy but of perspective. It is the ultimate expression of humanity's inability to think beyond immediate gain. The same instincts that drove us to conquer nature now threaten to destroy it. And as resources dwindle, the competition for survival intensifies, escalating into war. Conflict, the most primal of human behaviors, reflects our deepest dysfunctions. This is the result of fear, greed, and the relentless pursuit of power. It serves as a stark reminder of what happens when instincts take control over reason.

In the final frontier, space, we see both the promise and peril of humanity's ingenuity. Our drive to explore and innovate is a testament to human potential. Yet, it risks carrying our earthly dysfunctions into the cosmos, replicating them on a larger scale. The shadow of nuclear war looms large. It serves as a chilling reminder. Our evolutionary traits—mate guarding, tribalism, and the instinct to protect—can spiral out of control, leading to catastrophic outcomes.

The only reason to write this book, to examine these dysfunctions so meticulously, is hope. Hope that by understanding our flaws, we can transcend them. Hope that humanity, as the greatest observer of its own dysfunction, can also become its greatest healer. This book is a call to action. It urges readers to educate their children, instilling curiosity instead of dogma and prioritizing science over superstition. It is a plea to nurture the next generation of thinkers and problem-solvers. Only they can confront the challenges we have left unresolved.

1. TAILORED TECHNOCRACY

The concept of tailored technocracy offers governance envisioning solutions to centralized technocratic model pitfalls while retaining their strengths. This approach decentralizes decision-making while centralized protocols ensure flexibility and coherence. Evidence-based governance forms tailored technocracy. It combines the expertise of global organizations like the United Nations with insights from grassroots leaders. This creates a dynamic interplay between macro and micro perspectives. It operates by establishing constant feedback, public accountability, and real-time data, making it a model that is not only responsive but also inherently adaptable. Unlike rigid centralized systems, tailored technocracy thrives on collaboration, empowering regional actors to address local needs within a broader framework of shared goals.

At the heart of tailored technocracy is the principle of global-local integration. In this system, trained experts operate at every level of governance. They work in international bodies, neighborhood councils, and everywhere in between. Policies reflect global best practices and local realities. Consider managing climate change, a challenge that requires both coordinated global action and localized solutions. Under a tailored technocracy, a global framework might set overarching goals for carbon reduction, while regional experts design strategies tailored to their specific geographies, industries, and cultures. A coastal region prone to flooding, for instance, might prioritize sustainable infrastructure, while an arid area focuses on water conservation. This dual approach aligns global strategies with local relevance, sidestepping one-size-fits-all planning pitfalls.

Decentralization is another cornerstone of this model. Regional experts independently make decisions within defined protocols, swiftly tackling emerging challenges. This flexibility fosters innovation, as local leaders can experiment with solutions that best suit their contexts without waiting for directives from higher authorities. Consider public health emergencies. Decentralized technocracy enables local experts to address regional outbreaks immediately. They would have resources and decision-making authority. Their actions would align with a broader national or international framework. This contrasts sharply with the delays and inefficiencies seen in highly centralized systems, where decision-making bottlenecks often exacerbate crises.

Public accountability is another defining feature of tailored technocracy, distinguishing it from opaque models like China's. In this system, governance is transparent, with open platforms for complaints, feedback, and performance reviews. Citizens play an active role in evaluating policies and officials, creating a culture of trust and participation. This accountability extends to the use of data, which is made accessible to the public to ensure transparency in decision-making. For instance, in urban planning, citizens might have access to real-time updates on infrastructure projects, allowing them to track progress and provide input. Such mechanisms not only enhance trust but also minimize corruption, as public scrutiny acts as a powerful deterrent against malfeasance.

Data-driven governance forms the backbone of tailored technocracy, enabling real-time policy adjustments based on scientific evidence and feedback. Unlike traditional models, where policies are often static and slow to adapt, this approach allows for continuous refinement. Educators can analyze data on student performance and teacher effectiveness. They identify gaps and implement targeted interventions. It ensures the proper allocation of resources to where they are most needed. Similarly, in environmental management, satellite data on deforestation or air quality could inform immediate action, preventing long-term damage. This constant feedback loop ensures that policies remain relevant and effective, adapting to changing circumstances with agility.

Tailored technocracy offers significant advantages over China's centralized model. Its decentralized structure allows for greater flexibility in addressing local problems, empowering regional experts to innovate and respond to unique challenges. Public accountability builds trust and ensures that governance remains transparent and inclusive, avoiding the alienation and inefficiencies that often plague centralized systems. By integrating global expertise with local knowledge, tailored technocracy promotes collaboration rather than control, creating a system that is resilient and adaptive.

Ultimately, tailored technocracy represents a shift toward governance that embraces complexity and diversity. It acknowledges that no single entity can solve the challenges of a globalized world. Varied solutions must match the complexity of the problems they address. By decentralizing decision-making, fostering accountability, and leveraging data, this model holds the potential to address the systemic failures of both capitalist and communist systems. It envisions a future where governance is efficient and equitable. It offers a roadmap for societies striving to balance expertise with inclusivity, and global ambition with local relevance.

The promise of tailored technocracy lies in its ability to adapt and respond, combining the rigor of decentralized expertise with the flexibility of local action. It offers a blueprint for addressing the unresolved issues of governance systems past and present, bridging the gaps left by both capitalism and communism. As we grapple with enduring problems like inequality and alienation, comparing the approaches taken by various systems provides critical insights. By understanding their failures and successes, we move closer to crafting solutions that honor both the complexity of global challenges and the humanity of those they affect.

1.1 NO TAX, JUST WORK

Imagine a world without taxes—where monetizing data and state-led ventures fund public services. This innovative model aligns economic value with sustainability and collaboration, transforming governance into a system that fosters innovation and equity.

This world does not rely on extracting money from its citizens' incomes, purchases, or inheritances. Instead, it thrives on the most abundant and underutilized resource of the modern age: data. Every digital interaction, every scientific breakthrough, every industrial innovation generates data—a raw material so valuable that it now surpasses oil in economic significance. This proposed system recalibrates governance to harness the data economy's potential. Prosperity would stem from what citizens generate, not merely from what they give.

This vision centers on transforming data into currency. For decades, corporations like Google, Facebook, and Amazon have mined user data to generate billions in profits. Meanwhile, individuals have exercised little control over how others use their information. This new model flips the script: citizens own their data, and governments act as custodians. By anonymizing and aggregating this data, governments can monetize it responsibly, selling insights for applications in artificial intelligence, urban planning, healthcare, and more. This process redistributes proceeds as dividends to data owners. This creates a participatory economy where citizens act as stakeholders in their governance. Transparency is paramount, with blockchain technology ensuring every transaction is traceable and every decision is accountable. Governments no longer extract wealth through taxes; they cultivate it through innovation and equitable data management.

This shift extends beyond data alone. Governments also take a more entrepreneurial approach to governance, establishing profit-generating enterprises in sectors that align with national priorities and global demands. Imagine state-owned clean energy companies harnessing wind, solar, and geothermal power to not only meet domestic needs but also export surplus energy to neighboring nations. Governments can invest in sustainable resource management, developing cutting-edge technologies to exploit natural resources responsibly and trade them profitably. By fostering research and development hubs in fields like artificial intelligence, green technology, and pharmaceuticals, governments position themselves as innovators in the global market. These hubs create high-value products that not only contribute to GDP but also reinforce a nation's reputation as a leader in technological progress.

The success of this model depends on collaboration between public and private sectors, but with a redefined relationship. Instead of corporations wielding disproportionate influence over policy for campaign donations or lobbying efforts, they enter into profit-sharing agreements with governments. These partnerships fuel massive projects like renewable energy farms and smart cities. Governments contribute intellectual infrastructure—data, research, and logistical support. In return, they earn royalties or shares in profits. This synergy fosters innovation and distributes benefits equitably among all stakeholders, avoiding concentration in a few hands.

Governance also becomes more service-oriented, adopting a subscription-based model for public benefits. Citizens fund essential services like healthcare, education, and security through minimal fees tied to usage or received benefits. This approach ensures affordability for low-income groups through subsidies while asking wealthier individuals to shoulder a proportionate share of the costs. Unlike the opaque nature of traditional taxation, this model is transparent, giving citizens a direct connection between their contributions and the services they receive. Moreover, eliminating arbitrary taxes and introducing a pay-as-you-use system incentivizes efficiency for both service providers and users.

To stabilize this system, a national blockchain-backed digital currency builds trust and ensures security. Each unit of this currency links to a tangible or intangible resource—natural reserves, data contributions, or productivity metrics—keeping its value stable and grounded. This approach not only safeguards against inflation but also aligns the economy with national priorities. For instance, a currency tied to sustainability metrics incentivizes ecological stewardship, as the economy's value depends on responsible resource management.

The recalibration of GDP in this new governance model reflects a profound shift in societal values. Instead of measuring economic success by consumption—a system that encourages waste and environmental degradation—the new model focuses on value-added contributions through science, technology, and innovation. A "Data Contribution Index" quantifies the quality and impact of data generated for research and industry. A "Productivity Score" measures individual and collective contributions to domestic and global projects, while a "Sustainability Quotient" assesses ecological and technological practices. Revised: Together, such metrics offer a comprehensive view of national progress, prioritizing long-term resilience over short-term gains.

Transitioning to this system requires careful planning and significant investment in infrastructure and education. New legislative frameworks must establish clear guidelines for data ownership, privacy, and monetization. Education systems need to prepare citizens for the demands of a data-driven economy, emphasizing skills in artificial intelligence, data literacy, and sustainable innovation. Governments must build robust technology infrastructure to ensure secure and efficient data collection, storage, and processing. They must guarantee accessibility for all citizens to prevent inequality. Pilot projects in select regions or industries can test the viability of this model, refining it before scaling nationally. On the global stage, forming alliances with like-minded nations ensures shared learning and collective progress toward a data-driven future.

This system, however, is not without challenges. Concerns about data misuse or monopolization loom large. Addressing these requires unwavering transparency, enforced through technologies like blockchain that make every data transaction immutable and auditable. Initial resistance to moving away from taxes may arise, particularly from entrenched interests benefiting from the current system. A gradual phase-out of taxation, paired with clear communication of the new model's benefits, can ease this transition. Bridging inequalities in data access requires targeted initiatives. Universal access programs can equip all citizens with the tools and knowledge to fully participate in the data economy.

Eliminating the archaic "king-tax" model and adopting a productivity-based governance system could yield transformative results. Society would gain greater economic efficiency and foster a stronger connection between citizens and their governments. This new paradigm shifts governance from extraction to cultivation. It focuses on resources, innovation, and collective well-being. This approach reimagines the social contract for the 21st century. It aligns governance with the realities of a digital and interconnected world while addressing past inequities. Such a system could redefine national economies and the global economic framework. Societies would share prosperity and measure progress not by consumption but by contributions.

Data, the modern oil of the digital age, offers untapped potential for driving economic progress. But harnessing this resource requires rethinking governance and equitably sharing its benefits.

1.2 FROM ROCKS TO BYTES

As humanity transitions from physical to intangible wealth, data emerges as the cornerstone of prosperity. From artificial intelligence to personalized medicine, data powers innovation. By treating it as a public asset, governments can create systems that fund societal progress while ensuring ethical and equitable use.

For most of human history, societies anchored wealth in physical resources—gold, land, crops, and later, coal and oil. These assets were tangible, finite, and fought over in countless wars and conquests. But humanity stands on the cusp of a paradigm shift: wealth is becoming intangible, infinite, and boundless. Data, not land or gold, is emerging as the most valuable resource of the 21st century. Unlike physical resources, data is endlessly scalable, capable of being shared and replicated without depletion. Yet our governments, clinging to industrial age paradigms, remain focused on outdated economic systems, blind to the monumental opportunities data presents.

The monetization of data is no longer theoretical—it is a reality, albeit one driven by private enterprises rather than visionary governance. Netflix and Spotify use entertainment data to craft addictive algorithms. Social media platforms like Facebook and TikTok mine user behavior to fuel targeted advertising empires. Fitness apps analyze personal health data, guiding users toward tailored goals while quietly selling insights to insurers and pharmaceutical companies. Scientific data, from genomics to climate models, is driving breakthroughs in fields as diverse as precision medicine and environmental restoration. Yet even as private industries capitalize on this new gold rush, governments lag behind, preoccupied with traditional taxation models and industrial policies that feel increasingly anachronistic.

The potential applications of data far exceed anything currently realized. Entertainment data could evolve into real-time AI-generated films tailored to each viewer's preferences or fully immersive holographic experiences that dissolve the boundary between cinema and reality. Geospatial data, already used for navigation and logistics, could coordinate autonomous vehicles and design climate-resilient smart cities. Healthcare data could usher in personalized medicine, predicting and preventing diseases long before they manifest, and turning aging into a manageable condition.

Agricultural data, often overlooked, holds the key to solving the global food crises. AI systems could monitor global crop yields in real time, optimizing food distribution and minimizing waste. Climate and environmental data could similarly transform disaster response systems, enabling governments to predict and mitigate the impact of floods, wildfires, and hurricanes. Meanwhile, energy data could power AI-managed grids that ensure optimal distribution of renewable energy, reducing waste and accelerating the transition to sustainability.

Even education, long resistant to innovation, could harness data to drive a revolution. Real time learning analytics could create personalized curriculums for every student, while immersive VR classrooms could connect learners across the globe. In the realm of content creation, AI tools already generate art, music, and stories; the next step will be dynamic, interactive works that evolve based on the audience's emotions and preferences. Every sector of society, from transportation to cultural preservation, stands to be transformed by the creative application of data.

Despite these possibilities, leaders and institutions cling to a pre-digital mindset, underutilizing data's potential. Governments see data as a tool for surveillance or a secondary asset, rather than the cornerstone of future economic models. Even worse, governments have ceded control of this vital resource to private corporations. Companies like Google, Amazon, and Tencent shape the data economy without meaningful oversight or public benefit. This abdication reflects both a lack of vision and a failure to grasp wealth's changing nature.

Imagine a world where governments acted as stewards of data, ensuring its ethical use while channeling its value into public goods. Entertainment data could fund arts and culture programs; healthcare data could underwrite universal healthcare systems; agricultural data could subsidize sustainable farming practices. Rather than taxing incomes and stifling innovation, governments could monetize anonymized and aggregated data, sharing the dividends with citizens and investing in the infrastructures of the future. This approach reduces individuals' financial burden while aligning governance with a data-driven world.

Critics might argue that the leap from natural resources to data is implausible, that data cannot "feed the hungry" or "power the grid." But this is a failure of imagination. Data is not an end in itself but a multiplier—a force that, when combined with human ingenuity, transforms every other resource it touches. In the industrial age, coal and oil powered machines in the digital age, data powers intelligence. And intelligence, applied correctly, is the ultimate resource. It can make agriculture more productive, energy more efficient, healthcare more effective, and education more accessible. Rejecting data as the cornerstone of future economies reflects an outdated worldview. It mirrors feudal barons hoarding gold as the world shifted toward industrialization.

The genuine challenge lies not in the feasibility of a data-driven economy but in its governance. Who owns the data? Who decides how to use it? And who ensures the equitable distribution of its value? These are not just technical questions but moral and political ones, demanding a level of foresight and cooperation that humanity has rarely achieved. The stakes are too high to ignore. Failing to use data for collective good turns it into a tool of inequality. It rewards a few while disadvantaging many.

The path forward requires bold imagination and careful planning. Governments must shift their focus from taxing income and consumption to stewarding data and fostering innovation. This involves building robust infrastructures for data collection, storage, and processing, ensuring that these systems are transparent, secure, and accessible to all. It requires educating citizens in data literacy, so they understand their role in this new economy and can hold institutions accountable. And it demands international cooperation to set standards and prevent the monopolization of data by a handful of corporations or states.

In this vision, data underpins a new social contract. Citizens, as the producers of data, are its rightful owners, receiving dividends from its monetization. Governments act as custodians, ensuring ethical data use for public benefit. And the private sector, as the innovator, transforms raw data into tools and technologies that improve lives. This model transcends being a theoretical alternative to taxation. It is essential for a world shaped by digital connections and rapid information growth.

Dismissing data as a mere adjunct to traditional resources ignores history's trajectory. The agricultural revolution transformed land into the basis of wealth. Later, the industrial revolution did the same for coal and oil. Now, the digital revolution transforms data into the most valuable asset of our time. The question is not whether this shift will happen, but whether we will embrace it with the vision and responsibility it demands.

Humanity began with survival-focused data gathering, like tracking seasons or animal migrations. Now, it advances to extracting meaning from dreams, brainwaves, and even the fabric of the cosmos. This shift redefines wealth rather than simply marking a leap forward. The global economy approaches a transformation as profound as the agricultural or industrial revolutions. Prosperity will no longer rely on finite resources like oil or gold. Instead, it will depend on intangible and infinite streams of data. This evolution, however, requires a shift in our understanding of governance, ethics, and innovation—scaling data monetization into a system capable of sustaining entire societies.

The current monetization of data, while groundbreaking, only scratches the surface of its potential. Entertainment platforms mine viewing habits to predict preferences, healthcare apps leverage fitness data to sell insights to insurers, and AI systems process retail behavior to optimize pricing. These applications already contribute significantly to the global economy. However, their impact pales compared to the potential of retooling education and governance to focus on untapped data categories. Emerging technologies, driven by scientists and engineers trained to think beyond traditional disciplines, could unlock streams of value far beyond what today's systems can comprehend.

Imagine neuro data, derived from brain-computer interfaces, allowing us to map emotions, thoughts, and decisions in real time. Such data could create mind-controlled devices or optimize mental health treatments, merging human consciousness with artificial intelligence. Quantum data, born from quantum computers and sensors, could revolutionize cryptography, precision weather forecasting, and molecular modeling, giving rise to industries that don't yet exist. Synthetic biology sits at the crossroads of biology and engineering. It could allow the design of organisms tailored to produce medicines, clean energy, or advanced materials. This shift could steer entire industries toward sustainable production.

Some data categories challenge the boundaries of imagination itself. Consider dream data, which could unlock the subconscious for therapeutic use or create entirely new entertainment formats. Consciousness mapping data might digitize human experience, offering digital immortality and memory preservation while opening new frontiers in virtual storytelling. On a cosmic scale, environmental DNA data could preserve biodiversity by identifying ecosystem changes in real time. Meanwhile, cosmic data from asteroid compositions and interstellar radiation might drive off-world colonization and interplanetary trade.

The scale of wealth generation from these innovations is almost incomprehensible. Health applications could revolutionize diagnostics and preventative care. By leveraging neuro data, biofeedback networks, and nanobot swarms, these innovations could create trillions in value while improving the global quality of life. Energy innovations, based on data streams like planetary energy flux or dark matter interactions, could unlock clean, limitless energy sources, rewriting the rules of industrial economies. Entirely new economies may emerge around immersive markets. Dream analysis, emotional resonance data, and virtual consciousness systems could become the backbone of industries focused on personalized experiences and escapism.

Achieving this vision, however, demands innovations far beyond the technologies themselves. Advanced sensors capable of capturing previously unobservable phenomena—like brain waves or subatomic interactions—will be essential. Quantum computing and next-generation AI systems must process these colossal datasets in real time, converting raw information into actionable insights. Ethical frameworks must evolve to address ownership, privacy, and fair use of emerging data categories. Without global cooperation on issues like biofeedback privacy or consciousness digitization, the risks of exploitation and inequality could outweigh the benefits.

Governments, too, must reimagine their roles. Instead of relying on outdated taxation systems that burden citizens and stifle innovation, they could act as stewards of these emerging data economies. Governments could invest in infrastructure, foster interdisciplinary collaboration, and create public-private partnerships to reinvest wealth from data into societal progress. In this model, citizens act as shareholders in the national data economy. They receive dividends from anonymized data sets' monetization. They benefit from innovations in healthcare, energy, education, and beyond.

Transitioning to this system poses challenges. Educational systems must prepare future generations for this data-centric world, teaching skills in AI, neuroscience, quantum physics, and interdisciplinary thinking. Governments must establish the legislative and technological frameworks to protect individual rights while enabling global-scale data-sharing initiatives. Collaboration between nations, corporations, and research institutions will be essential. This approach ensures breakthroughs benefit all humanity rather than concentrating power among a few.

The potential rewards, however, are staggering. By tapping into these untapped data streams, humanity could move closer to a post-scarcity economy, where innovation rather than exploitation drives prosperity. In this future, data moves beyond targeted advertising and market optimization. It lays the groundwork for a new civilization where wealth is infinite, equitable, and tied to human creativity. The challenge is monumental, yet the possibilities are vast, like the data streams themselves.

Yet, the promise of data-driven economies comes with its own challenges. Storage, energy, and resource limitations threaten this vision's viability, demanding revolutionary solutions.

1.3 BIG DATA, NO SPACE

The rise of data comes at a cost. Current technologies, reliant on finite resources, are unsustainable, risking environmental degradation and resource scarcity. To sustain the digital economy, humanity must embrace breakthroughs in storage, renewable energy, and global cooperation.

The data-driven future we envision brims with possibilities—a world where information fuels governance, powers economies, and shapes innovations that redefine the boundaries of human potential. Beneath this utopian vision lies a critical constraint. Humanity faces physical limits in storing, processing, and managing the vast oceans of data generated every second. Data is intangible, but the infrastructure that supports it is anything but. Rare earth metals, finite resources, and energy-intensive systems form its foundation, stretching toward their breaking point. Without transformative technological breakthroughs, the ambitions of a data-centric society will collapse under the weight of its own infrastructure, limited by the finite resources of our planet.

Consider the scale of the data explosion. Experts predict that by 2025, global data will surpass 200 zettabytes—a number so vast it defies comprehension. Imagine each byte as a grain of rice. Together, they could fill a continent. Current storage technologies, primarily reliant on silicon-based semiconductors and magnetic hard drives, cannot sustainably meet this demand. These devices depend on rare earth metals like neodymium for their magnets, lithium for batteries, and cobalt for cooling systems. Yet these resources are anything but abundant. Mining these resources is environmentally destructive and geopolitically fraught. Most activity occurs in a few regions, like the Democratic Republic of the Congo for cobalt and China for rare earth elements. The scarcity of these materials presents not only a looming crisis but also an imminent bottleneck to progress.

Beyond resource scarcity, energy consumption poses an equally daunting challenge. Data centers, the nerve centers of the digital economy, already consume 2% of global electricity—equivalent to the entire energy usage of some mid-sized countries. Experts project this figure will rise exponentially as artificial intelligence, machine learning, and other data-intensive technologies spread. These centers also rely on massive water resources for cooling, exacerbating water scarcity in regions already under stress. The environmental footprint of storing and processing data threatens to offset the very progress it seeks to achieve, pushing us closer to ecological tipping points.

E-waste compounds the problem. Rapid technological obsolescence results in mountains of discarded electronics, much of it containing toxic materials like lead and mercury. In 2021 alone, global systems generated over 57 million tons of e-waste, recycling less than 20%. This waste poses an environmental hazard and tragically wastes materials that societies could reclaim and reuse. The current trajectory depletes resources faster than replenishment through relentless extraction, consumption, and disposal.

To address these challenges, the world must pivot toward revolutionary storage technologies that minimize reliance on finite resources. One promising avenue is DNA data storage, a method that encodes digital information into synthetic DNA molecules. This technology offers staggering storage density—one gram of DNA can hold 215 petabytes of data. Moreover, DNA is remarkably stable, capable of preserving information for centuries without degradation. However, the technology remains prohibitively expensive, with significant engineering challenges to overcome before it becomes viable at scale.

Quantum storage offers another potential breakthrough. By leveraging quantum states, systems could store data with unparalleled efficiency and minimal material requirements. Yet, quantum systems are still in their infancy, plagued by instability and exorbitant costs. Advances in nanotechnology also hold promise, with the potential to create storage devices at the atomic scale, drastically increasing capacity while reducing resource dependency. These technologies, still conceptual or in development, demand thinking beyond the silicon age.

Sustainability must also be a cornerstone of the data economy. Transitioning data centers to run entirely on renewable energy is an essential step, reducing their carbon footprint and reliance on fossil fuels. Innovations in green cooling technologies, such as liquid immersion cooling or hydrogen-based systems, could mitigate water usage and energy demand. Governments and industries must create robust e-waste recycling programs, harvesting materials from old devices and reintroducing them into production.

But technology alone cannot solve the problem. Societal attitudes toward data generation and consumption must evolve. Today, every click, photo, and video contribute to an ever-expanding digital footprint, much of it unnecessary. A philosophy of data minimization—storing only what is truly valuable and necessary—could alleviate storage demands. Artificial intelligence could play a role here, optimizing data management by identifying and prioritizing critical information while archiving or deleting redundant files.

This transformation requires global coordination. Countries must align on policies that promote sustainable resource use, ethical mining practices, and equitable access to new technologies. A coalition of nations could pioneer a "Data Sustainability Agreement," similar to international climate accords, committing to shared principles for managing the digital economy responsibly. Collaborative research initiatives could accelerate breakthroughs in DNA, quantum, and optical storage, spreading the benefits across borders.

The stakes are high. Failure to address these challenges could choke the digital economy's growth. Progress in areas like artificial intelligence and healthcare innovation would grind to a halt. Worse, the environmental toll of unrestrained data expansion could exacerbate the climate crisis, turning a tool of human advancement into a catalyst for ecological collapse. Conversely, if humanity rises to the occasion, the rewards could be transformative. A sustainable data economy would not only support the ambitions of a connected world but also serve as a model for balancing technological progress with ecological stewardship.

The dream of a data-driven society depends on more than technological prowess. As the digital age unfolds, success hinges on humanity's ability to navigate ethical and environmental challenges. The solutions are within reach, but they demand unprecedented collaboration, innovation, and foresight. The question is not whether we can store tomorrow's data. It is whether we can do so responsibly, without depleting the resources that make progress possible. The answer will shape both the future of technology and humanity itself.

Governance should aim higher than stability or growth; it should strive for peace. "Conflict Zero" envisions dismantling the machinery of war and building a world driven by cooperation.

1.4 CONFLICT ZERO

A world without conflict is no longer a utopian fantasy, but an inevitable milestone in humanity's evolution. Humanity can dismantle the machinery of militarism and reimagine governance through global welfare. This shift could shatter the cycles of violence that have defined its history. Anchored in global technocracy, this vision offers a pragmatic path forward. Collaboration replaces confrontation, and shared prosperity and enduring unity define progress, not power.

Such a system would not rely on charismatic leaders or transient ideologies. Instead, it would depend on a meticulously trained cadre of technocrats. Unified under the United Nations, these experts in science, governance, and ethics would address humanity's most pressing issues, from climate change to resource distribution. Their work could make war obsolete. In such a system, data would ground decisions, free from bias or nationalism, with policies prioritizing global welfare over parochial interests. For all its promises, this vision requires a profound shift in education. Preparing the next generation means fostering critical thinking, systems design, and a shared global identity.

Conflict Zero builds on a forgotten truth: the world operates as an interconnected system. Our economies, supply chains, and technologies transcend borders, but our governance remains fragmented and tribal. The wars of the 20th century—from World Wars to the Cold War—illustrate the cost of fragmentation. The global arms race drained trillions of dollars and left millions dead, all in the name of ideologies that were inherently transient. Even today, military budgets continue to consume resources that could eradicate poverty or fund universal education. Yet history also offers glimpses of what is possible when humanity unites. Global leaders established the United Nations after World War II to acknowledge humanity's shared fate. It aimed to mediate disputes and prevent future conflicts. While imperfect, the UN's peacekeeping missions, international agreements, and global initiatives underscore the power of collective governance. The next step is clear: transform this nascent framework into a true technocracy that spans all nations, eliminating the need for militaries altogether.

Leaders cannot impose on creating a united technocracy from above. The failure of many 20th century ideologies—communism, fascism, and even unchecked capitalism—stemmed from their imposition without addressing the underlying culture of their societies. For a technocracy to succeed, its principles must be deeply ingrained in the minds of future generations. Imagine classrooms that go beyond teaching basic math and science. In these spaces, children would learn to think like systems designers, understanding the intricate web of cause and effect governing our planet. They would study the failures of governance—not to assign blame, but to extract lessons. They would learn that conflict arises not from immutable human nature but from scarcity, miscommunication, and shortsightedness—all solvable problems in a world governed by experts. Embedding this vision into global education systems lays a crucial foundation. It prepares a generation to view the world not as a battleground of competing interests, but as a shared project requiring collective stewardship.

We must also recognize that the barriers to technocracy are not merely practical but psychological. Humans are deeply tribal creatures, evolved to prioritize in-groups and fear outsiders. This instinct, which once helped us survive in small bands, now fuels nationalism, sectarianism, and other divisive forces. Overcoming this requires not just education but a deliberate effort to foster a shared human identity. Programs like international student exchanges, global science competitions, and multilingual curricula can help dissolve the mental walls that separate us. Meanwhile, advances in technology—virtual reality, AI-driven translation, and global media—can create shared experiences that bridge cultural divides. By uniting the next generation around common goals, from curing diseases to colonizing other planets, we can channel humanity's competitive spirit away from warfare and toward progress.

A world without militaries may appear naïve, much like when societies first abolished slavery. For centuries, societies justified slavery as a natural institution using economic and religious arguments. Yet, moral progress, technological innovation, and political reform dismantled it. Technocratic leadership and grassroots movements can unravel the military-industrial complex, which thrives on fear and profit. Imagine redirecting the $2 trillion spent annually on militaries toward renewable energy, advanced healthcare, and poverty alleviation. The benefits of *Conflict Zero* would be immediate and profound. A virtuous cycle would emerge, where reduced conflict leads to greater prosperity and further diminishes the drivers of conflict.

Achieving this future demands genuine commitment toward fostering long-term education. Just as medieval Europe's monasteries preserved knowledge that would later fuel the Renaissance, so too must our schools become the incubators of a future technocracy. Every lesson in data literacy, every experiment in sustainable design, and every debate about ethics brings us closer to a generation capable of realizing *Conflict Zero*. This investment benefits not only children but also humanity's survival and growth. In chapters ahead, we delve into the role of the media in shaping truth and misinformation—a critical battleground where the seeds of technocracy must take root. Without shared reality, even brilliant systems collapse under mistrust and division. How can the media transform from a weapon of manipulation into a tool for progress? The answers lie ahead.

In the 21st century, humanity channels resources disproportionately into a perpetual machine of conflict. Military expenditures worldwide have already surpassed $2 trillion annually, an astonishing figure that represents a staggering misallocation of wealth. Nations divert resources into an endless arms race, competing for supremacy rather than peace, driven by distrust and geopolitical rivalries. The irony is glaring: while millions languish in poverty, lacking basic healthcare, clean water, and education, countries spend fortunes stockpiling weapons designed to destroy. The world's great powers claim commitment to progress but funnel wealth into war technologies. Hypersonic missiles, nuclear arsenals, and autonomous drones take priority over solutions to crises threatening our collective future. If unchecked, this trajectory escalates violence, leading to conflicts deadlier than any humanity has endured.

The specter of resource depletion looms as a harbinger of catastrophic escalation. Petroleum, the lifeblood of the modern economy, is not infinite. Conservative estimates predict severe depletion of reserves in most major oil-exporting regions by the late 22nd century. Analysts project Saudi Arabia, Iraq, Russia, and the United States—all major oil players—will exhaust their accessible reserves by 2150–2200. This depletion's implications extend beyond energy shortages, signaling new conflicts. When scarcity sets in, history teaches us that nations do not negotiate—they compete, often violently. The resource wars of the 20th century offer stark reminders of how scarcity fuels global instability. Oil-fueled Middle Eastern interventions and African conflicts over diamonds and minerals exemplify this. By 2200, dwindling petroleum reserves could turn Venezuela, with the world's largest untapped oil deposits, into the epicenter of a desperate struggle for energy dominance.

If it happens, the battle for Venezuela's oil will escalate beyond a localized skirmish into an unprecedented conflict. With technology advancing at exponential rates, the militaries of the 23rd century would wield weapons inconceivably more destructive than those of today. Artificial intelligence augments nuclear warheads. Hypersonic platforms deliver them at unimaginable speeds. Entire regions vanish in moments, reduced to charred landscapes and lifeless silence. Biological weapons, fine-tuned to target specific populations, could bring devastation unseen in previous wars. These conflicts would cost more than money; they threaten existence itself. Humanity, teetering on the edge of irreversible climate collapse and resource depletion, could well push itself into a downward spiral of destruction. And yet, the seeds of this bleak future are being sown today, as nations cling to their weapons and military industries with an almost religious fervor.

The global arms industry, a multibillion-dollar behemoth, thrives on the perpetual manufacture of conflict. Corporations producing guns, missiles, tanks, and warships depend on war to justify their existence, lobbying governments to maintain bloated military budgets. These companies profit from chaos, supplying weapons to both sides of a conflict, if necessary, while politicians justify ever-increasing military expenditures under the guise of national security. This cycle feeds itself. More arms production fuels conflict, driving demand for deadlier weapons. Breaking this cycle requires a revolutionary shift in priorities. Imagine disbanding every arms manufacturer and redirecting their resources toward education, healthcare, and sustainable development. The trillions now spent on destruction could instead fund the eradication of poverty, the transition to renewable energy, and the universal education of the next generation.

Achieving such a transformation requires unity among nations rather than isolated efforts. A global technocracy, where governance is based on expertise and collective welfare rather than narrow self-interest, offers the only viable path to Conflict Zero. This system would eliminate military forces, replacing them with a unified global body to mediate disputes and allocate resources fairly. Imagine pooling the $2 trillion spent annually on military budgets to develop fusion energy, breaking our dependence on fossil fuels. With strategic investments, humanity could break free from resource wars. This approach would ensure a stable energy supply for centuries without spilling a drop of blood. Educating future generations remains central to this vision. Children must learn to see other nations as partners, not enemies, in a shared survival project. Curricula must emphasize critical thinking, collaboration, and the lessons of history— lessons that show the futility of war and the potential of unity. If society realizes this vision, today's children could grow into tomorrow's leaders. They could dismantle the last remnants of militarism and repurpose its vast infrastructure for humanity's benefit. Schools would become incubators of peace, producing technocrats capable of solving the world's most complex problems without resorting to violence.

The stakes could not be higher. The choice is stark. We can either continue the current path, where unchecked military spending escalates conflicts over dwindling resources, or embrace a global transformation that prioritizes life over destruction. The road to *Conflict Zero* is difficult, but it is necessary. Banish the specter of Venezuela's oil wars. Redirect humanity's resources toward its betterment. To consign war to history's pages, we must act now. The first step envisions a changed world, seeing it not as it is but as it might become. This vision turns tools of war into instruments of peace.

2. CURRICULUM 2.0

The world has changed, but education has not kept pace. Adolescents today face challenges unimaginable to previous generations, from mental health crises to global uncertainties. To prepare for the future, we must rethink what and how we teach. Life skills, emotional intelligence, and critical thinking should be core elements of modern education. This is not just an upgrade—it's a transformation.

Modern youth face vast, interconnected challenges that span education, mental health, and social inclusion. Addressing these issues requires not only targeted strategies but also a holistic reimagining of the systems designed to support young people. Education, which establishes personal and societal growth, must transform to better engage students and prepare them for life's complexities. The traditional model of rote memorization and standardized testing has outlived its usefulness, leaving students disengaged and ill-equipped for the dynamic challenges of the modern world. Reforming curricula to incorporate life skills, critical thinking, and emotional intelligence can breathe new life into the classroom. Historical shifts, such as the introduction of liberal arts into Renaissance education, demonstrate how adapting curricula to the needs of the time can revolutionize learning. Today, similar innovation is required to ensure that education is not just a burden but a bridge to opportunity.

Equally important is preparing educators who serve as the linchpins of this transformation. Schools must equip teachers to address the diverse needs of students, including mental health concerns and dynamics of diversity and inclusion. Professional development programs, focusing on areas like trauma-informed teaching and cultural competence, can empower educators to foster environments where all students feel seen and supported. Lessons from Finland's education system, where teachers receive extensive training and autonomy, highlight the profound impact of investing in those who shape the next generation. This approach, if scaled globally, could transform schools into true havens of growth and understanding.

Mental health, once relegated to the shadows of public discourse, must now take center stage in the conversation about youth well-being. Adolescents today face unprecedented pressures, from the relentless comparisons of social media to the residual anxieties of a post-pandemic world. Schools, as primary spaces where young people spend much of their formative years, must play a proactive role in supporting mental health. Initiatives like school-based counseling programs, peer support groups, and dedicated wellness curricula can provide the scaffolding young people need to navigate their emotional landscapes. Reducing stigma is equally critical; open conversations about mental health, driven by awareness campaigns and inclusive messaging, can dismantle the shame that often prevents students from seeking help. Historical parallels show the potential for societal change. The destigmatization of physical disabilities through 20th century advocacy reminds us that attitudes can shift through compassion and education.

Creating safe, inclusive environments is essential for positive youth development. Bullying, exclusion, and discrimination undermine supportive education, leaving lasting scars. Clear anti-bullying policies and restorative justice practices can foster accountability and empathy. Programs celebrating diversity—such as LGBTQ+ alliances, cultural events, and inclusive curricula—promote unity amid diversity. These efforts are fundamental to shaping a generation that values inclusion.

The challenges young people face are complex, and solutions must be interconnected. Addressing disengagement requires mental health promotion, while fostering inclusivity necessitates safe spaces. Together, these elements create a web of support to help youth thrive.

Action is essential now. Educators, parents, policymakers, and communities must unite to prioritize youth development. Societies investing in young people gain rewards like economic innovation and cultural vitality. Equipping adolescents with understanding helps them navigate challenges and create solutions. With empowerment, this generation holds the potential to build a resilient, hopeful future for all.

2.1 SCRAP RELIGION BY TECHNOCRACY

Transitioning to technocracy requires investing in training technocrats—experts in science, economics, and policy—capable of addressing global challenges with precision. These programs must start with rigorous STEM education and critical thinking, followed by training in advanced fields like AI, biotechnology, and climate science. Institutes like MIT and IIT produce problem-solvers, but scaling these efforts globally with scholarships for underrepresented areas ensures equitable access. Technocrats need training in systems thinking, ethical policymaking, and cross-cultural communication to create solutions suited for diverse societies. By cultivating a global cadre of technocrats, humanity can better confront challenges such as climate change, resource scarcity, and the ethical dilemmas of emerging technologies.

Phasing out religious influence from institutions requires sensitivity to prevent alienating communities. Historical examples demonstrate the challenges and successes of such reforms. In early 20th century Turkey, Mustafa Kemal Atatürk replaced Islamic laws with European-style civil codes to modernize the nation and foster rational governance. While successful in many respects, the abruptness of these changes also sparked resistance, highlighting the need for gradualism in modern efforts. Education systems, for instance, could introduce comprehensive science-based curricula while slowly reducing religious content, ensuring that future generations grow up with a firm foundation in empirical thinking. Similarly, healthcare policies could prioritize evidence-based practices, phasing out the influence of religious dogma in decisions about reproductive rights or end-of-life care. Transitioning policies requires limiting religious lobbying, setting boundaries between personal beliefs and public policy, and ensuring governance driven by data.

Humanism, a secular commitment to individual and community well-being, lies at the heart of the technocratic vision. Unlike ideologies rooted in divine authority or abstract dogmas, humanism focuses on tangible outcomes: reducing suffering, increasing opportunity, and promoting flourishing lives for all. This principle guided many of the Enlightenment-era reforms that gave rise to modern democratic systems, from abolishing feudal privileges to establishing universal education. In technocracy, humanism guides policies, ensuring scientific advancements serve society rather than exploit it. For instance, humanistic technocrats might prioritize the equitable distribution of resources, addressing global disparities in wealth and healthcare access while safeguarding the planet's ecosystems for future generations.

Adopting universal values and ethics is critical for navigating the challenges of a globalized world. Societies should root these values in shared human experiences and principles from scientific understanding rather than sectarian doctrines. Concepts such as empathy, fairness, and sustainability resonate across cultures and can form the foundation for a global ethical framework. The 1948 Universal Declaration of Human Rights reflects an early effort to affirm dignity for all, transcending national and religious boundaries. However, these principles must evolve alongside technological and societal changes. AI and genetic engineering push human capability, necessitating new ethical standards to address autonomy, equity, and humanity's nature. Technocracy, guided by universal ethics, can navigate these frontiers while maintaining a commitment to justice and inclusivity.

Transitioning to technocracy is not merely a logistical challenge but a profound transformation of how societies organize themselves and define progress. Training technocrats, removing ideological biases, and grounding governance in humanism allow humanity to address 21st-century complexities. This shift requires patience, collaboration, and a commitment to reason over dogma, shaping a future driven by collective aspirations, not past divisions.

3. MEDIA 2.0

Imagine governance free from election chaos. A transparent process would select leaders based on measurable expertise and performance, not slogans, charisma, or narratives. This is the promise of a technocratic system, a paradigm in which governance operates like a well-calibrated machine rather than a spectacle of competing ideologies. In such a system, the role of media would undergo a radical transformation. Freed from manipulation, sensationalism, and bias, media could serve as a neutral truth conduit. Experts in information dissemination would monitor and regulate it.

Historically, the media has oscillated between a watchdog role and a tool of influence, often shaped by the interests of those who control it. From the propaganda pamphlets of the Reformation to the 24-hour news cycles of modern cable networks, the media has wielded immense power over public perception. This power, when wielded by political elites, often degenerates into a mechanism for maintaining control rather than enlightening the populace. Think of the 20th century propaganda machines of regimes like Nazi Germany and Stalinist Russia. Media there tightly controlled narratives to justify war, persecution, and repression. These regimes understood that controlling what people believed was as critical as controlling what they ate or where they lived.

But even in democratic systems, media manipulation persists, albeit in subtler forms. Elections have become theaters of public persuasion, fueled by advertising dollars, viral misinformation, and algorithms designed to inflame emotions rather than inform reason. The United States' 2016 presidential election stands as a case study in the vulnerabilities of modern media. Operatives weaponized social media platforms to spread disinformation, including fake news about candidates and divisive propaganda targeting key demographics. Meanwhile, traditional outlets, striving for ratings and clicks, often prioritized sensationalism over substance, creating an environment where truth became malleable and perception trumped reality.

A technocratic government would eliminate the conditions that allow such manipulations to thrive. Without elections, there would be no campaigns to sell, no populist narratives to weave, and no echo chambers to cultivate. A transparent process would vet leaders based on qualifications, using public review and meritocratic evaluation. Performance, not persuasion, would dictate tenure. Media, in such a framework, must become precise and accountable. It would report unvarnished truth, free from profit-driven sensationalism or partisan distortions.

This evolution would necessitate a new class of professionals: technocrats trained specifically to oversee and monitor media. These individuals would not be political appointees or ideologues but experts in fields such as journalism ethics, data analysis, and cognitive psychology. Their role would be to align media output with verifiable facts. They would correct biases and ground public discourse in reality, not conjecture. Algorithms, too, would be subject to scrutiny, re-engineered to prioritize accuracy and context over engagement metrics. Instead of amplifying outrage or tribalism, they would promote nuanced discussions and elevate voices of reason.

Historical moments where media assumed a truly educational role offer a glimpse of what this could achieve. Consider the BBC during World War II, which provided factual updates and morale-boosting content without descending into crude propaganda. Consider 1970s investigative journalism, like The Washington Post uncovering Watergate. It showed how a free press, acting responsibly, could hold power accountable. These examples show that media, when guided by principles rather than profit or politics, can serve as a pillar of informed citizenship.

In a technocratic world, media's accountability would extend beyond the experts monitoring it. Public reviews would play a critical role, much like periodic assessments of government technocrats. With transparent data and unbiased reporting, citizens could evaluate leaders and the mechanisms shaping their understanding of governance. This feedback loop would create a system of mutual accountability, where the media's performance is as subject to scrutiny as the performance of those in office.

Although this model may seem utopian, historical precedents root its core principles in reality. Ancient Athens, for example, relied on citizens' assemblies where informed debate shaped policy, albeit on a smaller and more exclusive scale. The Enlightenment philosophers envisioned a world governed by reason and evidence, not superstition or populism. A technocratic media system would be the modern realization of these ideals, harnessing technology and expertise to create a public square where truth reigns supreme.

Removing electoral distortions and adding media oversight by impartial technocrats could dismantle propaganda and misinformation that has plagued humanity for centuries. In this world, leaders would govern with the clarity of evidence-based policies, reported by a media apparatus dedicated to accuracy rather than influence. The system would deliver governance that prioritizes excellence over rhetoric. Citizens, armed with unassailable truth, could shape their collective destiny.

4. COURTROOM 2.0

Imagine a world where the concept of justice transcends its historical roots in punishment, evolving instead into a mechanism of prevention, rehabilitation, and systemic harmony. A technocratic global system promises progress. Decision-making relies on expertise, data insights, and scientific methods, not tradition or impulse. In this envisioned reality, the judiciary is no longer an isolated pillar of governance, struggling under the weight of inefficiencies and biases. It operates as part of a seamless system. Its mission addresses societal challenges at their roots and minimizes crime through human progress.

For centuries, justice systems have relied on punitive measures, a vestige of times when deterrence through fear and retribution seemed the only path to societal order. Punishment has long been both a tool of control and a symbol of power. It ranges from medieval Europe's public executions to modern prison-industrial complexes. Yet, the effectiveness of this approach has always been questionable. Crime rates rise and fall, not with the severity of punishments but with the underlying conditions that foster deviance—poverty, mental illness, inequality, and systemic neglect. A technocratic judiciary offers a departure from this reactive model, envisioning a system designed not merely to punish but to preempt and rehabilitate.

Central to this vision is the understanding that crime is often a symptom of deeper societal or individual dysfunctions. Drawing on advancements in psychological, neurological, and behavioral sciences, a technocratic judiciary focuses on addressing these root causes. Instead of imprisoning a violent offender, the system would analyze their emotional states. It would identify neural imbalances, trauma histories, or environmental triggers contributing to their actions. The goal is not to absolve culpability but to design interventions that prevent recurrence. This could involve targeted therapies, neural recalibration techniques, or even community-level changes to mitigate the factors that led to the crime. Each case would contribute data to a global repository, enhancing predictive algorithms and refining preventive measures across jurisdictions.

Crime prevention under a technocratic model shifts from reactive enforcement to anticipatory governance. Advanced data monitoring systems, powered by artificial intelligence and global surveillance networks, would detect patterns indicative of potential criminal activity. These systems could identify high risk behaviors or deteriorating social conditions long before they escalate into crime, enabling targeted interventions. Historical examples provide a glimpse of this potential. In the 19th century, investigators eventually traced London's cholera outbreaks to contaminated water sources, catalyzing public health reforms and preventing future epidemics. A technocratic judiciary applies this principle to societal behavior—identifying and addressing the "contaminants" of injustice and inequality that lead to crime.

The integration of judicial functions into a global framework ensures consistency, equity, and coordination on an unprecedented scale. Community-level technocratic units handle local disputes, such as property conflicts or domestic violence cases, using real-time data and behavioral experts. Regional systems manage more complex cases, pooling expertise and resources to resolve multi-jurisdictional challenges like cybercrime or environmental violations. A global technocratic council oversees international issues like climate litigation or human trafficking. It ensures justice aligns with humanity's goals, not fragmented national interests.

This technocratic model envisions a world where justice is no longer a slow-moving, adversarial process but a dynamic, adaptive system. By merging neuroscience with governance, it unlocks the potential to rehabilitate offenders rather than perpetuate cycles of punishment. By integrating advanced analytics into judicial processes, it ensures fairness and transparency, rendering bias and corruption obsolete. And by embedding the judiciary within a unified global framework, it transforms justice from a localized construct into a universal human right.

The technocratic judiciary is not an experiment in utopia but a necessary evolution. This vision promises a future where crime becomes a solvable challenge, not an inevitability. Governance would reflect humanity's ideals of precision, equity, and compassion. This vision faces challenges, yet its pursuit signals a profound shift. Civilizations can transcend history's constraints to build a system serving everyone.

4.1 TECHNOCRATIC JUDICIAL SYSTEM

A technocratic judicial system transforms governance itself. It sheds traditional inefficiencies, embracing data-driven, expertise-oriented, and globally aligned decisions. At the heart of this system lies the principle of integration—a centralized judicial framework seamlessly connected to a global governance structure. Instead of fragmented national legal systems shaped by cultural biases or political influence, a technocratic model would operate under the oversight of a Global Technocratic

Council (GTC). This council, trained and supported by institutions such as the United Nations, would draw on expertise from diverse disciplines: law, neuroscience, behavioral sciences, and cutting-edge technology. The GTC would act as a guiding force, setting universal standards for justice while allowing for regional adaptation through meticulously designed hierarchies.

The hierarchical structure ensures a balance between local responsiveness and global consistency. Local Technocratic Units (LTUs) handle community disputes. They focus on understanding behavioral and societal factors instead of just punishment. Trained mediators, mental health experts, and social scientists would work in tandem to resolve issues through restorative practices, prioritizing community harmony over retribution. These units would employ technology to monitor cases in real-time, identifying patterns and potential escalations that might necessitate intervention from a higher authority. For more complex cases that cross local boundaries or require specialized expertise, Regional Technocratic Authorities (RTAs) would step in. These RTAs would function as hubs of advanced legal and scientific collaboration, equipped with forensic technologies, AI-driven analytics, and multidisciplinary panels to ensure equitable resolutions. At the apex, the Global Technocratic Council (GTC) would address transnational issues—ranging from climate litigation to cybercrime—ensuring that justice transcends borders and aligns with humanity's collective interests.

Central to this system are the technocrats themselves, individuals selected not for political allegiance or charisma but for their demonstrable expertise. LTUs train in traditional law, neuroscience, psychology, and criminology. This prepares them to approach justice with a holistic understanding of human behavior. A technocrat addressing violent crime would use neurological assessments, psychological evaluations and sociological analyzes. Their interventions would target root causes, not symptoms. This approach minimizes recidivism, transforming the judicial system from a punitive institution into one centered on societal healing and prevention.

Collaboration is the lifeblood of this model. Technocrats would not operate in isolation but as part of multidisciplinary teams, working closely with health professionals, data scientists, and governance experts. For example, a technocratic response to corporate fraud might involve forensic accountants, blockchain analysts, and sociologists studying the systemic vulnerabilities that allowed such fraud to flourish. By pooling insights across disciplines, the system not only resolves individual cases but also generates actionable data to inform policy reforms and preempt future infractions.

The integration of neuroscience and technology is particularly revolutionary. Imagine a world where AI algorithms flag potential inconsistencies in a technocrat's decision-making before they finalize rulings. Brain-computer interfaces could help determine a defendant's cognitive state at the time of an offense, distinguishing intent from impulsivity with unprecedented accuracy. Blockchain technology would ensure complete transparency, making every decision traceable and every data point immutable. Such innovations would enhance efficiency and rebuild public trust in judicial processes by rooting decisions demonstrably in evidence and fairness.

Yet, this technocratic system's most transformative feature lies in its ability to scale globally while respecting local nuances. An LTU in rural Kenya addressing land disputes might operate differently from one in urban Japan tackling intellectual property issues. However, both units would adhere to the overarching principles and methodologies established by the GTC, ensuring consistency without imposing cultural homogenization. The global-local balance relies on continuous feedback loops. Data from LTUs and RTAs flows to the GTC, refining protocols and addressing blind spots.

The technocratic judiciary envisions a world where justice is not bound by borders, politics, or outdated traditions. It replaces the chaos of adversarial systems with the clarity of collaborative expertise, ensuring that fairness is no longer an aspiration but a measurable reality. The judicial process evolves into a dynamic ecosystem. It adapts, learns, and grows with humanity's needs, offering precise and compassionate justice.

4.2 CASE MANAGEMENT

In a world governed by technocratic precision, officials would handle complaints and cases differently. This approach would transform the fragmented and opaque systems that define today's judicial processes. A seamless, unified global case management system would replace the chaos of paper trails, jurisdictional conflicts, and human delays, embodying both accessibility and accountability. A centralized complaint registry lies at the heart of this transformation. This digital platform lets citizens worldwide raise grievances as easily as sending a message. Advanced artificial intelligence and blockchain technology would power this system, ensuring that bureaucracy never silences a voice.

A farmer in India, a New York worker, or a Syrian refugee could air grievances. These might include land disputes, unfair wages, or human rights violations. Under the current global framework, their paths to justice diverge sharply. For some, there might be layers of local and national courts to navigate; for others, the concept of accessible justice may be entirely alien. A centralized global complaint registry would erase these disparities. Every complaint, whether submitted via smartphone or through local administrative hubs, would enter a single global portal. Algorithms trained to detect urgency, societal impact, and patterns would triage inputs, ensuring that oversight or inefficiency never delays cases.

The case registry would not merely be a passive repository of complaints. It would act as an active, self-learning organism. AI systems sift through cases, flagging larger systemic issues. These might include recurring workplace discrimination or complaints about environmental damage. This approach echoes the principles of public health surveillance, where identifying the outbreak of a single disease in one locality can prevent pandemics. In the judiciary, this predictive capability would allow authorities to intervene early, addressing issues before they escalate into widespread crises.

The system's architecture would integrate transparency, addressing a perennial challenge in legal systems worldwide. Blockchain technology would anchor the registry. This system would ensure that officials track each registered case throughout its journey. No case could be "lost" or altered without leaving an immutable record, eliminating the shadowy manipulation that has so often plagued the courts of the past. Complainants receive regular updates, from acknowledgment to resolution. This fosters trust in a system serving people, not the powerful. Historical examples underscore how societies prize such transparency. Consider the countless corruption scandals buried under layers of red tape in 20th century democracies or the secretive "disappearances" of political dissidents' cases in authoritarian regimes. A technocratic registry, by design, would make such abuses impossible.

Advanced case assessment systems would investigate into complaints, not merely to resolve them but to understand their root causes. Suppose a surge of cases indicates rising mental health issues leading to family disputes or workplace incidents. Instead of merely adjudicating each case individually, the system would highlight these patterns, recommending societal-level interventions—perhaps reforms in mental health care access or workplace policies. AI flags cases of suspected mental instability for psychological evaluations. Solutions go beyond punishment to address underlying causes.

This vision of a global case management system is not without precedent, albeit on a smaller scale. Post-war Germany's Allied Control Council used centralized systems for denazification. They pooled data and decisions to ensure uniformity in addressing complex issues. While imperfect, the system highlighted the value of coordination and transparency in judicial efforts. A modernized, global version of such a system—amplified by digital technologies—could achieve outcomes far beyond the limitations of its historical predecessors.

In the technocratic framework, the registry would function not only as an administrative tool but as a symbol of empowerment. It would dismantle barriers of geography, wealth, and influence, ensuring that justice is accessible to all and manipulable by none. Elites could once stifle complaints or delay proceedings to their advantage. Now, algorithms and global oversight prevent such distortions. The system would become a monument to fairness, a digital colossus standing firm against the inequities of human history.

4.3 PREVENTION AND REHABILITATION

Technocratic judiciary systems shift justice from punishment to understanding. They mitigate risks and foster transformation by focusing on human behavior. Imagine a world where global data systems observe every societal ripple. They track patterns in interactions or shifts in individual mental states. Such a system would not be dystopian surveillance but an ethically guided, anonymized network designed to flag risks before they manifest into harm. Advanced algorithms would sift through vast pools of data, identifying crime hotspots or individuals exhibiting behavioral instability. Social cues—sudden isolation, extreme language in digital spaces, or spikes in physiological stress markers—would trigger interventions, offering support rather than suspicion. This approach, far from policing thought, would aim to provide resources to those most at risk of harm, whether as potential perpetrators or victims.

The power of predictive analytics would extend beyond vague probabilities to actionable insights. Just as meteorologists predict hurricanes, technocratic systems would map societal fault lines. Historical data, cultural patterns, and individual histories converge into forecasts. These forecasts predict tensions, such as gang activity in urban areas or domestic violence in suburbs. Proactive intervention teams, trained in conflict resolution and mental health, would engage with at risk communities, neutralizing risks through dialog, resource allocation, and targeted support programs. By addressing root causes—poverty, trauma, or social alienation—before they spiral into criminal acts, the technocratic system would aim to reduce the very conditions that breed crime.

Rehabilitation, under this paradigm, would replace punishment as the cornerstone of justice. The journey begins with a neuropsychological assessment, not as a mere formality but as a deep dive into the offender's mental and emotional framework. Scans and assessments would reveal the brain's secrets—an underactive prefrontal cortex indicating poor impulse control or hyperactivity in the amygdala pointing to heightened fear responses. Experts would map emotional histories to uncover scars of childhood abuse, untreated mental illnesses, or systemic neglect. This data would replace the traditional binary of "guilt" and "innocence" with nuanced causality, contextualizing criminal behavior without excusing it.

Psychological and neurological data would shape intensely personalized rehabilitation programs. Medical interventions might include neurostimulation to correct imbalances in brain activity or tailored medication plans to stabilize moods and reduce aggression. Cognitive reformation therapies would work like rewiring circuits—immersing individuals in scenarios that challenge their biases, teach empathy, and enforce ethical reasoning. A convicted fraudster might undergo virtual reality simulations to experience their victims' financial ruin. Violent offenders could join group therapies to foster connections and break cycles of alienation. Rehabilitation would go beyond fixing broken aspects, fostering traits like integrity, responsibility, and accountability.

Behavioral realignment would go beyond clinics or prison cells to create transformative environments. Offenders could live in immersive rehabilitation communities. These small, monitored societies mimic real-life complexities, rewarding cooperation, ethical decisions, and emotional growth. These environments would serve as proving grounds, where individuals could practice reintegrating into the broader society without the stigma of their pasts weighing them down. Success isn't just about lowering recidivism rates. It's measured by offenders' ability to contribute positively to their communities, breaking traditional cycles of crime and punishment.

Through prevention and rehabilitation, the technocratic approach would address crime not as a series of isolated events but as symptoms of deeper societal and individual fractures. This system would address causes, not just effects. It fosters a safer, equitable world where justice heals rather than punishes.

4.4 COURT 2.0 IN ACTION

The British Army abandonment scandal in Kenya exposes systemic issues. Allegations of rape, love affairs, and abandoned children intersect with colonial legacies and power dynamics. Currently, these courts operate in a fragmented collaboration, often hindered by jurisdictional limitations, political influences, and cultural disparities, resulting in delays and partial resolutions. A global technocratic judicial system envisions a seamless framework, handling cases like this with precision, neutrality, and holistic focus. Uniting advanced technologies, interdisciplinary expertise, and global oversight addresses root causes. It sets a higher standard for justice. Through this comparison, we uncover the potential for evolution in delivering accountability and equity on a truly global scale.

A global technocratic judicial system offers a tantalizing vision. Justice could thrive if freed from outdated systems and entrenched power dynamics. Yet, the stark realities of the present judicial framework reveal how far we still have to go. The British Army abandonment scandal in Kenya highlights injustice. Systemic inequalities and diplomatic protections often shield perpetrators. Focusing on the current judiciary reveals persistent failures. Local and international courts struggle to rise above challenges, highlighting the urgent need for reform.

4.4.1 CURRENT JUDICIARY

The British Army abandonment scandal in Kenya reveals the harrowing intersection of colonial legacies, military immunity, and systemic judicial failures. At the heart of this case are countless women and their mixed-race children, left to navigate lives spoiled by ostracization, poverty, and unfulfilled promises of justice. For decades, allegations of rape, abuse, and abandonment by British soldiers stationed in Kenya have surfaced, spanning from the 1950s to the present. Despite the gravity of these claims, both the local judiciary and international bodies have struggled—or outright failed—to deliver meaningful accountability. Entrenched power dynamics make justice inaccessible to the vulnerable. Elite institutions, protected by diplomatic shields, often evade accountability.

Take the story of Marian, a 17-year-old girl born from one such tragic encounter. Marian's mother, Lydia Juma, accused a British soldier of rape but never saw justice in her lifetime. Lydia's attempts to navigate Kenya's shame-based societal norms and judicial inertia culminated in trauma and her untimely death. Marian, left without a father and scorned as a "poor white girl" by her community, takes up the fight. She seeks recognition and accountability where her mother could not succeed. Her story echoes those of other women, such as Generica Namuru, who endured abandonment after consensual relationships with British soldiers. Generica, like many others, has unsuccessfully sought child support, repeatedly stonewalled by both local authorities and British institutions, which collectively sidestep responsibility under legal pretexts.

The judiciary's inadequacies in these cases reveal a grim pattern of systemic neglect and elite interference. In the 1990s and early 2000s, women and human rights groups pursued justice. Britain's Ministry of Defense dismissed over 2,000 allegations from Maasai and Samburu women. The reason? Supposedly unreliable evidence—a conclusion reached without DNA testing for any of the 69 children reportedly born from these abuses. Kenyan government case files mysteriously disappeared, while a Royal Military Police investigation cast doubt on the women's accounts, labeling much of their testimony as fabricated. It was a textbook case of institutional denial, where the combined forces of diplomatic immunity and political apathy shielded the British Army from scrutiny. For the women involved, the British government's refusal to recognize their children as citizens or provide compensation symbolized the erasure of their trauma.

Historical parallels magnify the scale of this injustice. During Britain's colonial presence in Kenya, authorities met similar patterns of abuse with indifference. In the 1970s and 1980s, British courts dismissed claims by rural women accusing officers of rape. Survivors like Toya Len Kanan courageously came forward. They alleged soldier assaults, but colonial-era mistrust undermined their testimonies. Dismissive attitudes persist into the 21st century. Elite power, whether colonial hierarchies or modern diplomacy, continues to obstruct justice.

Elite interference remains a cornerstone of this case's stagnation. The British government pays Kenya $400,000 annually for training access, a financial arrangement that underscores the disparity between economic pragmatism and human rights. Critics argue that this monetary relationship discourages the Kenyan government from pursuing justice too aggressively, for fear of jeopardizing a lucrative agreement. Meanwhile, allegations of witness intimidation and deliberate procedural delays in Kenyan courts further complicate the path to accountability. The power imbalance is stark. Women like Lydia and Generica face barriers, while elite institutions maintain the status quo.

Even today, efforts to revisit these cases face resistance. Marian, now a lead plaintiff, faces a legal battle. She confronts her mother's unresolved trauma and the weight of international bureaucracy. Lawyers like Kelvin Kubai work tirelessly to reintroduce these claims into Kenyan courts, yet the shadow of prior failures looms large. Without a global technocratic judicial system, cases like this struggle. Local corruption and political calculus replace moral clarity.

The British Army abandonment scandal is not just a story of judicial failure; it is a testament to how elite systems, fortified by privilege and power, perpetuate social injustice. The abandoned children, dismissed women, and unfulfilled promises of this case raise serious doubts about the foundations of international accountability. This is not just about whether systems can deliver justice to Marian and others like her. It challenges global frameworks to evolve and prioritize humanity over hierarchy.

The failures illuminated by the British Army abandonment scandal reveal more than just gaps in justice; they expose a systemic inability to confront entrenched power and deliver accountability across borders. These are not just individual failures but symptoms of a larger, outdated framework—one that struggles to navigate the complexities of modern transnational issues. To envision a system where jurisdictional limitations or bureaucratic inertia do not hinder justice, we must look forward. The concept of a Technocratic Judiciary offers a revolutionary alternative, reimagining how justice can function in a world where technology, expertise, and impartial oversight replace outdated processes. In this model, the system would eliminate the inefficiencies and biases that failed Marian and others like her, creating a more equitable framework.

4.4.2 TECHNOCRATIC JUDICIARY

The British Army abandonment scandal, which left behind a trail of broken lives in Kenya, encapsulates the glaring inadequacies of traditional judicial systems. A technocratic judiciary would approach this case with a clinical precision, stripped of the inefficiencies, biases, and geopolitical hesitations that have long plagued such international incidents. The first step is registering all claims in a Unified Global Case Registry. This platform manages complex transnational disputes. The system digitizes each testimony, claim, and piece of evidence. Blockchain technology safeguards them from tampering. Unlike the Kenyan government files that conveniently vanished, this system would ensure a transparent and immutable record. AI algorithms would comb through the registry, flagging high-priority cases, such as unresolved paternity disputes and historical patterns of abuse, for immediate action.

Evidence collection would bypass the sluggish and often compromised processes of local authorities. Court-mandated DNA testing, enforced globally, would definitively establish paternity for the mixed-race children ostracized in their communities. Digital forensic investigations would add clarity. Satellite imagery and archival data confirm British Army deployments during alleged abuses. Witnesses and survivors, silenced by intimidation, would gain anonymity and relocation support. A technocratic protection framework removes the power imbalance deterring them.

The adjudication of such cases would fall to a Global Technocratic Council. This body, immune to nationalistic and military pressures, ensures state interests do not subvert justice. With Kenya and the UK having shared jurisdiction under this system, technocratic investigators and legal experts would work collaboratively to eliminate redundancies and prevent diplomatic standoffs. AI-assisted bias detection systems would further minimize cultural or institutional bias by scrutinizing case proceedings and judgments for historical patterns of elite interference.

Beyond judicial verdicts, the technocratic framework emphasizes restorative justice for victims. A global reparations fund, partly sourced from the UK's annual payment to Kenya for military training rights, would provide immediate financial support to survivors and their families. Counseling programs would address the deep psychological scars left by decades of neglect and abuse. Mixed-race children, often treated as outsiders in their communities, would gain British citizenship. They would also access specialized education and healthcare programs funded by the technocratic system. Such measures would not only compensate for past injustices but also pave the way for genuine reintegration into society.

Trials, conducted in a centralized technocratic court, would avoid the pitfalls of fragmented legal systems. Modern forensic techniques would reevaluate historical claims, such as the 2,000 allegations dismissed by the UK Ministry of Defense in 2007. Automated sentencing algorithms, informed by global legal precedents, would ensure consistent and fair penalties for both individual offenders and systemic failures. The British Army itself would face mandatory reforms, with any personnel found guilty of abuse held accountable regardless of rank.

Systemic reform would extend beyond the courtroom. A technocratic institutional audit system would review the terms of agreements allowing foreign military training in host countries, ensuring compliance with human rights standards. This oversight would prevent future abuses, replacing the permissive "British Boys Behaving Badly" narrative with one of accountability and responsibility. Real-time reporting and surveillance tools in an ongoing monitoring mechanism would provide permanent oversight on military operations, ensuring prompt action on flagged incidents.

A technocratic judiciary would resolve the British Army abandonment scandal. It would transform it from a shameful colonial footnote into a landmark in transnational justice. The system would prioritize evidence and safeguard victims while reforming institutional structures. It would offer a model for addressing global injustices, ensuring no victim is unheard, and no perpetrator escapes accountability.

5. CLIMATE FIX

Technocratic governance offers a compelling response to the challenges of climate change and energy transitions, emphasizing evidence-based decisions and expert leadership. By replacing political gridlock with rational frameworks, it aims to balance global frameworks with local needs. While this model envisions a structured approach to sustainability, it also raises concerns about elitism. Yet, its modern adaptation seeks inclusivity, accountability, and transparency, prioritizing long-term progress over short-term political gains.

At the global level, technocratic governance finds its anchor in institutions like the United Nations, capable of unifying fragmented efforts. A proposed Global Energy Equity Council can align the energy transition with principles of fairness and sustainability, prioritizing the needs of the Global South. Blockchain-based systems could enhance transparency, offering real-time data on emissions, resource use, and renewable projects. These measures not only foster accountability but also empower civil society to monitor compliance with international accords like the Paris Agreement.

For enforcement, specialized task forces could utilize satellite surveillance and AI monitoring to detect and penalize violations, such as illegal fishing or unregulated deep-sea mining. However, achieving universal buy-in remains a challenge. Centralizing authority in a transparent, expert-led system could overcome the shortcomings of fragmented approaches, making global cooperation a survival mechanism rather than a utopia.

Regional frameworks bridge global ambitions with diverse local realities. Training hubs, established under UN oversight, could develop regional expertise tailored to specific challenges. For instance, engineers in Senegal might specialize in solar grids for arid regions, while experts in Poland could focus on wind energy for colder climates.

Ownership models also play a critical role in democratizing clean energy. Germany's energy cooperatives, where communities own and manage renewable assets, provide an inspiring template. These cooperatives generate local income, empower decision-making, and foster energy independence. Scaling similar models in sub-Saharan Africa and South Asia could transform the energy landscape, bypassing traditional monopolies.

Regional cooperation further amplifies impact. Initiatives like the European Green Deal demonstrate how interconnected grids and shared policies can drive unified progress. In Africa, solar farms in Niger could supply energy to industries in Nigeria, creating a continent-wide network of equitable energy distribution. Such systems ensure that renewable energy transitions benefit all, not just the privileged.

At the national level, technocratic governance requires embedding expertise and accountability into energy and climate policies. Training national technocrats to translate global accords into actionable strategies is essential. For example, India could focus on rural solar electrification, while Norway targets decarbonizing hydro-based systems.

Transparency platforms that provide real-time data on emissions and energy usage could rebuild public trust in government initiatives. AI-driven insights could identify inefficiencies and suggest improvements. Public ownership of renewable projects, as seen in Denmark's Middelgrunden Offshore Wind Farm, ensures that profits benefit communities directly, not private corporations. Adapting this model globally would make renewable energy transitions both equitable and effective.

At the grassroots level, local communities are central to sustainable energy transitions. Decentralized renewable projects, such as solar microgrids, empower communities to manage their energy futures. Initiatives like India's Barefoot College, which trains rural women as solar engineers, exemplify how grassroots engagement can electrify underserved areas while addressing social inequities.

Participatory platforms allow communities to have a voice in energy planning, fostering ownership, and accountability. For instance, Ugandan villagers might vote on solar panel placements or track project budgets through digital portals, ensuring that energy transitions reflect their needs and priorities.

Economic empowerment further strengthens grassroots efforts. By linking renewable projects to job creation, communities can thrive on sustainability. In Kenya's Rift Valley, solar farms have created employment opportunities, reducing urban migration and supporting local economies. Prioritizing inclusivity in hiring—such as involving women and marginalized groups—ensures renewable energy becomes a platform for social equity.

Technocratic governance offers a pragmatic path forward, weaving global coordination and local ingenuity into a coherent strategy. From global frameworks to grassroots initiatives, it envisions governance as a tool for equitable progress rather than consolidation of power. This model, by prioritizing expertise, transparency, and inclusivity, transforms the energy transition into a shared journey, ensuring no one is left behind.

6. PHILANTHROPY TO GLOBAL FUND

The staggering accumulation of wealth by the world's elite—those in the top 1%—represents not only an economic anomaly but a profound societal inefficiency. Banks, investment funds, and institutions hold trillions of dollars. These funds serve little purpose beyond securing their holders' positions on Forbes lists or making stock markets appear stable. This wealth, far removed from productive use, becomes self-perpetuating through financial instruments like loans, equity trading, and speculative investments. Unlike wealth generated from tangible resources or human labor, the money created by this financial system feeds on itself, inflating GDP figures without corresponding real-world benefits. In the United States, for example, financial services account for nearly 20% of GDP. Yet, this contribution largely disconnects from producing goods or services that directly improve societal well-being.

A deeper examination reveals a stark imbalance composing GDP. Wealth generated through financial mechanisms increasingly overshadows natural resources and human effort—the foundational components of any economy. For instance, the global derivatives market, valued at over $1 quadrillion, dwarfs the GDP of every nation combined. This virtual wealth exists as numbers on a ledger, cycling between institutions with no connection to the natural or labor-based value it purportedly represents. The inequity is glaring. While vast sums sit idle in corporate coffers or personal accounts, billions of people struggle for access to basic necessities like clean water, education, and healthcare. This accumulation not only entrenches inequality but also perpetuates a system that rewards wealth hoarding over meaningful contribution.

Addressing this imbalance requires a revolutionary approach: capping the wealth of elites across all sectors—business tycoons, artists, politicians, and anyone amassing disproportionate influence. This cap would be dynamic, determined by each country's socioeconomic status, and calculated based on the operational needs of individuals and their ventures. For companies, this means maintaining the funds necessary for day-to-day operations, growth, and research, with a percentage buffer for unforeseen challenges. Experts in economics, management, and industry would determine these thresholds. Any profits exceeding this cap would flow into a United Nations-managed fund, repurposed for global development initiatives. For individuals, the cap would ensure a luxurious but reasonable standard of living, far from asceticism but equally distant from unchecked opulence. This recalibration would channel excess wealth into projects that directly address inequality, starting with the most impoverished regions.

The implementation of such a system must begin with nations whose wealth is most intertwined with global inequalities, particularly the United States, the United Kingdom, and France. The United States, with its immense concentration of corporate and individual wealth, is an obvious starting point. American elites benefit from a global order shaped by centuries of exploitation—colonial legacies, resource extraction, and trade imbalances. By capping wealth here first, the system could generate a compelling portfolio to showcase the feasibility and benefits of this redistribution model. Once established, the initiative would expand to authoritarian nations, offering them a blueprint for adopting similar structures while transitioning to technocratic governance systems. Governance bodies would build these systems on expertise rather than patronage, fostering stability and trust.

Expansion to other countries would follow, tailored to their unique socio-economic landscapes. Governance bodies could deploy the capped funds in resource-rich but governance-poor nations to create robust educational institutions, infrastructure, and localized governance frameworks. For instance, in Africa, a continent with immense potential yet marred by systemic underdevelopment, the funds could establish universities designed to train technocrats for regional governance. By showcasing the tangible benefits of such systems, these models could convince even authoritarian rulers to participate. This is especially true if these models demonstrate enhanced stability and economic growth without threatening their control.

Resistance to such a paradigm shift is inevitable. Elites will argue that capping wealth stifles innovation, entrepreneurship, and growth. Policymakers can address these concerns by ensuring that operational needs and research funding receive full consideration within the caps. Tax havens and illicit financial flows would pose significant challenges, requiring international cooperation and robust enforcement mechanisms. The United Nations, bolstered by its newly centralized funding, could create specialized financial task forces to monitor compliance and close loopholes. Public campaigns emphasizing the societal benefits of redistribution—better healthcare, education, and infrastructure—would build grassroots support, countering elite resistance with popular demand.

Opposition from powerful nations, particularly those reliant on financial dominance, would be another obstacle. Diplomatic efforts must emphasize the collective benefits of reducing inequality, framing the initiative not as a punitive measure, but as a pathway to sustainable global stability. Economic incentives could also play a role, offering participating nations preferential access to the resources and expertise funded by the capped wealth. For authoritarian regimes, the promise of improved governance models that reduce internal dissent and enhance international legitimacy could be a compelling argument.

The journey to implement such a system will not be without setbacks, but the potential rewards far outweigh the challenges. By capping wealth and redirecting excess funds toward global development, humanity can address the root causes of inequality, insecurity, and conflict. This approach not only challenges the status quo, but redefines what prosperity means. It envisions a world where societies equitably distribute resources, ensure universal access to education, and drive governance through expertise rather than privilege. The ultimate vision—a world free of nuclear weapons, governed by cooperative technocracies, and united by shared purpose—may seem utopian. But history has shown that transformative ideas often begin as impossibilities until they become inevitabilities.

If progress demands dismantling the monopolies of power and privilege, then it must also challenge the engines that sustain them. Wealth, unchecked and concentrated, has become not a tool for societal advancement but a fortress against it. To cap the money is not to limit ambition, but to redirect it. It shifts focus away from hoarding and toward building a world where prosperity belongs to all, not just the few perched at its peak.

The idea of capping wealth may seem radical. At its core, it aligns with a principle already embraced by many of the world's wealthiest individuals: redistributing excess for the greater good. The difference lies in the method. Philanthropy offers voluntary, selective, and often self-directed generosity. In contrast, a wealth cap represents a systemic approach. It ensures that the resources of the few are consistently and equitably directed toward the needs of the many. In this light, philanthropy begins to resemble a softer, more palatable version of a wealth cap. It achieves similar ends while leaving the underlying inequalities untouched.

6.1 CAP THE MONEY

Capping elite wealth is not merely an economic adjustment; it is a seismic shift that challenges deeply entrenched structures in global economies and governance. At its core, wealth capping disrupts the existing dynamics of financial systems that revolve around the accumulation and reinvestment of capital by the wealthiest individuals and institutions. Today, the top 1% of the world's population holds over 45% of global wealth, a concentration that drives inequality and stifles opportunities for broader societal advancement. Billionaires often tie their vast fortunes to speculative financial instruments, real estate, or corporate equity. These assets rarely contribute to productive investments that create jobs or innovate industries. This system is driven by the pursuit of shareholder value above all else. It reinforces a cycle where wealth begets more wealth, while much of society struggles to access basic resources. Capping this accumulation, therefore, confronts not just individual fortunes but the very mechanisms that sustain economic inequality.

The consequences of such a policy ripple across different fields of the economy. In the financial sector, limiting the wealth of elites would challenge the model of hyper-leveraged growth. This model relies on vast amounts of capital borrowed against the assets of the wealthy to fuel speculative ventures. This could initially create instability in markets that rely heavily on the liquidity provided by billionaire-driven hedge funds and private equity firms. However, redirecting capped wealth can mitigate this instability. The United Nations or sovereign wealth funds could manage these resources to prioritize long-term investments in infrastructure, education, and green technologies. By broadening the base of wealth distribution, these funds can stabilize markets through diversified, socially productive investments, reducing the dependence on volatile speculative capital.

Governance systems would also face significant challenges when implementing wealth caps. Existing structures often serve the interests of the elite, with lobbying, campaign financing, and regulatory capture ensuring that wealth remains concentrated. The political resistance to wealth capping would likely be fierce, with elites leveraging their influence to frame such policies as anti-growth or anti-freedom. To counter this, governance frameworks must emphasize transparency and equity. Independent commissions of economists, sociologists, and legal experts could be established to set dynamic wealth caps. Experts would adjust these caps to reflect the operational needs of industries and the socio-economic conditions of different regions. For instance, a tech entrepreneur in Silicon Valley might face a different cap than an agricultural magnate in sub-Saharan Africa. These differences reflect disparities in costs and contributions to local economies.

To implement wealth capping, a phased approach is essential. The first step involves identifying the operational needs of individuals and ventures to ensure their productivity and innovation thrive. Experts could calculate a threshold for businesses, directing excess profits to global funds. For instance, if a company needs $1 billion annually for operations, growth, and contingency reserves, any profits above this cap could flow into UN-managed programs. Individuals, too, would benefit from a cap that allows for a luxurious but finite lifestyle, with surplus wealth supporting initiatives to combat poverty, improve education, and tackle climate change. Governments would enforce these caps using robust financial tracking systems enhanced by emerging technologies like blockchain to ensure transparency and prevent evasion.

The United States would be the logical starting point for such a policy. It is the world's largest economy and home to over 700 billionaires, with a combined wealth of $4.7 trillion as of 2023. By implementing wealth caps domestically and channeling excess funds into global development initiatives, the United States could set an example. This approach could inspire other nations, particularly in Europe, like the UK and France, where similar disparities exist. Once democratic nations with transparent governance systems establish these policies, leaders could adapt them for more complex contexts, such as authoritarian regimes. In these cases, the success of capped wealth redistribution in fostering stability and economic growth could serve as a compelling argument for adoption.

Resistance to wealth capping will undoubtedly be significant, ranging from legal challenges to outright attempts at tax evasion or capital flight. To address this, international cooperation will be crucial. Nations could establish agreements akin to the Paris Climate Accord, committing to wealth capping as a shared strategy to reduce inequality and foster sustainable development. Enforcement mechanisms, including penalties for non-compliance and incentives for participation, would ensure adherence. Leaders must cultivate public support through education campaigns. These campaigns would highlight the benefits of wealth redistribution and emphasize how capped funds directly improve lives through better healthcare, education, and infrastructure.

Wealth capping is not a panacea, but it represents a profound opportunity to address the systemic inequalities that define the modern world. By dismantling the structures that allow wealth to pool indefinitely at the top, societies can unlock resources for the collective good. This would foster a global economy that prioritizes equity, innovation, and resilience. The challenges are immense, but so are the stakes. If humanity can implement such a system, it would mark a turning point. It would demonstrate that societies can resolve the age-old struggle between individual ambition and collective welfare in favor of a more just and sustainable future.

6.2 PHILANTHROPY: A FANCY WEALTH CAP

The paradox of elite philanthropy in the face of growing inequality is one of the most striking contradictions of our age. On one hand, some of the world's wealthiest individuals dedicate significant portions of their fortunes to charitable causes. They establish foundations to combat poverty, cure diseases, and address climate change. Bill Gates and Warren Buffett's Giving Pledge have inspired over 240 billionaires to commit to giving away at least half of their wealth. Elon Musk has pledged billions to climate initiatives, while Jeff Bezos has allocated substantial funds to combating global warming through the Bezos Earth Fund. Yet, as these acts of generosity unfold, the systemic inequalities that created the fortunes enabling such philanthropy remain unaddressed. These same elites dismiss the wealth cap—a theoretical policy that could limit extreme capital accumulation and redistribute resources to serve humanity more equitably—outright. The contradiction lies not in their intentions, which may be noble, but in their reluctance to relinquish the structures that perpetuate their dominance.

Imagine a world where capped wealth directs the excess to a centralized, technocratic governance reserve designed to fund humanity's collective betterment. Instead of relying on individual goodwill and discretionary philanthropy, organizations could systematically pool, transparently monitor, and effectively disburse resources. A wealth cap could redistribute the financial power concentrated among a handful of individuals. It could address global challenges, from healthcare innovation to clean energy infrastructure. The economic structures that favor accumulation over redistribution deeply entrenched resistance to such policies. The notion of elite control is central to this resistance. Philanthropy allows the wealthy to dictate the terms of their contributions, often funding initiatives that align with their personal values and interests. This contrasts sharply with a capped-wealth system, where expert panels accountable to humanity at large would collectively make decisions about resource allocation.

The irony is that the mechanisms of wealth capping and philanthropy could achieve similar outcomes in theory, yet the difference lies in control and accountability. When an individual like Musk donates millions to carbon capture technologies, the funding process reflects his priorities. It does not necessarily align with a broader consensus on what the world needs most urgently. If a wealth cap collected those same funds, the decision-making process would shift. A governance body resembling a Y Combinator for global development would allocate these resources. Y Combinator, a well-known startup accelerator, evaluates ideas based on their potential for impact and scalability, offering funding and guidance to entrepreneurs. A similar model, scaled for global governance, could pool capped wealth into a reserve managed by interdisciplinary experts. These panels could identify the most pressing issues. Whether it's funding vaccine research, developing clean energy solutions, or advancing space exploration technologies, they would allocate resources to where they are most needed. Such a system would not only democratize access to funding, but also ensure that investments are driven by collective priorities rather than individual preferences.

One compelling example of how this model could work is the story of SpaceX. Founded by Elon Musk, SpaceX has revolutionized space exploration. It has reduced the cost of rocket launches by orders of magnitude and made strides toward humanity's goal of becoming a multi-planetary species. Yet, a mix of private funding and substantial government support has built the venture's success. NASA has awarded SpaceX billions of dollars through contracts for commercial crew and cargo missions. These funds, derived from taxpayer contributions, demonstrate the power of public investment in private innovation. However, under a wealth cap and governance reserve system, organizations could initiate similar ventures without relying on individual billionaires to set the agenda. An expert panel could identify space exploration as a priority. They would allocate resources to companies and research institutions, ensuring that these endeavors equitably share their benefits.

This approach would address one of the core issues with philanthropy: its inherent unpredictability and lack of accountability. While billionaires can choose to fund climate change mitigation or space research, there is no guarantee that their priorities align with the most urgent needs. Furthermore, the very act of philanthropy often comes with strings attached, from branding opportunities to policy influence. The Gates Foundation, for example, has earned praise for its contributions to global health. However, it has also faced criticism for promoting specific technological solutions that align with its founders' interests. A governance reserve would operate with clear mandates and transparent criteria, ensuring that rigorous evaluation allocates resources rather than individual whims.

Critics of wealth caps argue that such policies would stifle innovation and deter accumulating capital necessary for large-scale investments. Yet history suggests otherwise. The mid-20th century was a period marked by relatively high taxation on the wealthy, particularly in countries like the United States. This era coincided with some of the greatest technological and societal advancements, from the space race to expanding public education and healthcare systems. Wealth capping would not eliminate incentives for innovation, but would redirect excess resources toward collective goals. Entrepreneurs and innovators would still have the opportunity to profit from their ventures. However, a system designed to prioritize humanity's broader needs would temper the scale of their personal wealth accumulation.

Philanthropy, for all its virtues, is inherently a reactive mechanism. It addresses problems only after identifying them, often seeking to mitigate the symptoms of systemic issues rather than their root causes. A wealth cap and governance reserve system, on the other hand, could proactively address global challenges, funding initiatives that prevent crises before they arise. For instance, investments in renewable energy infrastructure could reduce the likelihood of climate-related disasters. Policymakers could steer advancements in artificial intelligence toward solving logistical challenges in food distribution rather than exacerbating inequalities. Such a system would operate with a foresight that philanthropy, bound by individual priorities and market trends, cannot consistently provide.

The role of governments in this vision is crucial. A governance reserve would require robust oversight, transparency, and accountability to function effectively. Governments could adopt the Y Combinator model, convening panels of experts from diverse fields—science, technology, economics, and ethics—to evaluate proposals and allocate funding. These panels would ensure that resources target projects with the greatest potential for impact. This approach resembles how venture capital firms invest in startups with scalable solutions. By leveraging the expertise of multidisciplinary teams, this approach would combine the agility of private innovation with public governance, ensuring accountability.

Such a transformation would also redefine the relationship between individuals and society. In a world where societies pool capped wealth for collective use, the emphasis would shift from individual accumulation to collective progress. This is not merely a utopian ideal but a practical necessity in an era defined by global challenges that transcend borders, from pandemics to climate change. Redistributing wealth through a governance reserve would enable humanity to tackle these challenges. With the necessary resources and coordination, societies could advance progress without the constraints of individual philanthropy or market forces.

Ultimately, the question is not whether humanity can afford to adopt such a system, but whether it can afford not to. The stakes are too high to rely on the goodwill of a few to address the needs of the many. By capping wealth and pooling resources into a technocratic governance reserve, humanity can build a better future. In this future, innovation thrives, societies prioritize equity, and everyone shares in the benefits of progress. The transformation may require a shift in mindset and the dismantling of entrenched power structures. However, the potential rewards—both for individuals and for humanity—are immeasurable.

7. NUKE TO NURTURE

The solution to avoiding nuclear war lies not in weapons reduction alone but in addressing the deeper instincts that drive conflict—our innate tribalism and mate-guarding tendencies. These traits, while once essential for survival, now amplify modern dangers, especially in an interconnected world where power and aggression can have catastrophic consequences. To transcend these primal impulses, we must focus on shaping human behavior from the earliest stages of life. This involves fostering empathy, understanding, and cooperative instincts. This change begins at home, with parents playing a pivotal role. Broader societal measures must actively reinforce it. Governments could implement mandatory parenting classes. These classes would teach couples how to nurture children in ways that discourage aggression and promote empathy. By doing so, we emotionally equip the next generation to handle conflicts constructively.

Imagine a child coming to their parent after being stung by a bee, tears streaming down their face. The parent's reaction to this small yet significant event becomes a lasting lesson. It imprints on the child's developing brain and forms the foundation for how they will navigate relationships and challenges in the future. Consider two possible scenarios. In one, the parent roots their response in anger and vengeance: "Did the bee sting you? Where is it? I'll kill it! How dare it hurt my baby!" This reaction inadvertently teaches the child that harm always demands retaliation. Experiences like this actively strengthen neural pathways associated with anger, revenge, and retribution, creating a mindset that seeks payback whenever wronged. Over time, this child grows into an adult who views the world through a lens of conflict and dominance, potentially escalating disputes rather than resolving them.

Now, consider an alternative response. The parent, while comforting the child, takes a moment to provide perspective: "Oh no, did it hurt? Bees don't know it hurts you—they're just protecting themselves. Be careful next time when you see a bee. Don't go too close, or come home if you see one. They only sting when they feel threatened." This approach instills a sense of understanding and respect for other creatures, even when they cause pain. The child learns that not all harm is malicious and that sometimes, giving space and moving on is the best course of action. Experiences actively strengthen neural pathways associated with empathy, patience, and self-regulation, fostering a personality inclined toward compassion and thoughtful problem-solving.

Now, imagine how these two children, shaped by such different upbringings, might respond to conflicts as adults. The first, trained to seek revenge, might react to a colleague's slight with anger, creating friction that escalates. The second, having learned empathy and perspective, might instead recognize that the colleague's behavior stems from stress or insecurity and choose to de-escalate the situation, preserving harmony. Scaled up to global conflicts, the implications are profound. Leaders raised with empathy are more likely to seek diplomatic solutions, recognizing the humanity in their adversaries, while those shaped by vengeance are more prone to rash, destructive decisions.

This is why parenting is not just a personal responsibility but a societal one. Governments should invest in training programs that equip parents with the tools to raise emotionally intelligent children. Such initiatives, though seemingly far removed from issues like war and peace, address the root causes of conflict by reshaping the instincts that drive human behavior. Over time, a world populated by empathetic individuals could steer humanity away from the brink of destruction. These individuals, raised to prioritize understanding over dominance, would create a future where cooperation prevails over conflict

8. WHO IS GOD?

The irony lies in how humans themselves answer this question. Throughout history, great thinkers and reformers have boldly declared, "There is no God." They argued that humans alone are the architects of their own destiny. Yet, over time, we raise these very individuals to divine status. Their ideals turn into doctrines, and followers worship their images as gods. Take Sree Narayana Guru, who preached equality and the oneness of humanity, rejecting rigid notions of divinity. Consider Buddha, who encouraged self-realization and dismissed the need for a supreme deity. Today, people worship him and his teachings as divine. Even rational minds, like Socrates or modern revolutionaries, face the same fate. Those who once followed their words immortalize and worship them.

While we elevate humans to godhood, the all-loving God we speak of remains silent. God becomes merely a witness to dysfunction. Wars rage, inequalities deepen, and suffering persists, yet the divine does not intervene. But is it truly God who remains passive, or is it us? The principle of Tat Tvam Asi, "Thou art That"—teaches us that we and the divine are one. If so, then the silence is ours. We stand as mute observers of chaos, waiting for someone—or something—to save us.

Perhaps this is the truth: no God will descend from the skies to mediate. The divine already resides within us. God is not separate from humans. The question isn't whether God or humans are the greatest observers of dysfunction. It is whether we will remain silent or awaken to realize our role. The moment we accept this truth, we stop waiting for miracles. Instead, we become the force of transformation that the world so desperately needs.

We stand on the cliff of extinction. The question isn't whether humanity will survive—it's whether we will evolve. Will we continue to be slaves to our instincts like Mate guarding, which spirals us dangerously close to the edge of nuclear war. Will we rise above it? And in this quest for survival and understanding, two question remains:

Does GOD exist or not?

If GOD does exist, that being would be the greatest observer of dysfunction.

Who is GOD?

Greatest Observer of Dysfunction

Afterword

To the reader,

Thank you for journeying through the pages of *Greatest Observer of Dysfunction*. By choosing to read this book, you've done something extraordinary—you've lit the flame of awareness within yourself. This flame isn't just for you; it's part of a greater torch, one that has been passed from those who dared to see the world's dysfunctions and sought to inspire change. Now, it's in your hands.

Now, I humbly ask for your help to carry this message further. If this book has resonated with you, please take a moment to share your thoughts. Leaving a review is a small yet impactful way to amplify its reach and encourage others to pick it up.

Here's how you can contribute:

1. Scan the QR code below or visit the store where you purchased this book.
2. Leave an honest review. Every word counts in helping the message reach more readers.
3. Share your experience with others. Recommend the book to friends, family, or anyone who might benefit from its insights.
4. Spread the word on social media, tagging us so we can share in the journey you've started.

Your voice has power. With it, you can help inspire others to pick up the torch and ignite meaningful change in their lives and communities.

Thank you for being part of this mission. Together, we can keep the flame alive and spread its light further than we ever imagined.

The road may be long, and the challenges great, but change begins with one person daring to hold the torch and carry it forward. Let this be your moment. Take what you've learned here and keep the flame alive. Together, we can pass this light through the darkness and illuminate a better future for all.

With gratitude and hope,
Human

About the Author

Writing under the pen name Human, the author steps forward not as an individual but as a collective voice—a voice for all of humanity grappling with the dysfunctions that threaten our survival. The name "Human" is a deliberate choice, stripping away divisions of identity, nationality, and privilege, and focusing on the shared experience of being part of a fragile and interconnected species.

This book, *Greatest Observer of Dysfunction*, is not just a critique of the world's systems but an act of survival—a survival guide for humankind to recognize the forces pulling us apart and to take action before it's too late. The author sees writing this book as their personal act of rebellion against apathy, a step toward the change we all desperately need.

The journey to write this book began with a stark realization: the same systems that claim to protect and guide us are often the ones creating the dysfunctions we face daily. Whether through manipulation by elites, exploitation of resources, or the commodification of humanity itself, these systems perpetuate inequality, suffering, and division. But recognizing these truths isn't enough—the author believes action starts with awareness, and that awareness must be shared.

"I chose to write as 'Human' because the dysfunctions I'm addressing affect all of us. This is not a story about me—it's about us. We are all responsible for the world we inherit and the one we leave behind."

The author's ultimate hope is that this book will spark a global awakening. It aims to empower readers to see through the false narratives of those in power, to reclaim their agency, and to act. The message is clear: the first step to fixing a broken system is acknowledging its cracks, and this book is here to help you see them.

Through this survival guide, Human invite you to join a collective effort to turn awareness into action. After all, survival is a shared responsibility, and the time to act is now.

Stay Connected:

Email: booksbyhuman@gmail.com
X(Twitter):   @BooksbyHuman
Instagram: @booksbyhuman

Abbreviation

ADHD	Attention Deficit Hyperactivity Disorder
AGM	Air-to-Ground Missile
AI	Artificial Intelligence
AIDS	Acquired Immunodeficiency Syndrome
AIG	American International Group
AIS	Androgen Insensitivity Syndrome
AK	Avtomat Kalashnikova(AK-47)
ALEC	American Legislative Exchange Council
AT	Anti-Tank
ATACMS	Army Tactical Missile System
AUKUS	Australia-United Kingdom-United States
AWACS	Airborne Warning and Control System
AZT	Azidothymidine (Zidovudine)
BBC	British Broadcasting Corporation
BJP	Bharatiya Janata Party
BP	British Petroleum
BRI	Belt and Road Initiative
BRICS	Brazil, Russia, India, China, South Africa
CAA	Citizenship Amendment Act
CAG	Comptroller and Auditor General
CAH	Congenital Adrenal Hyperplasia
CBN	Christian Broadcasting Network
CE	Common Era
CEO	Chief Executive Officer
CHIPS	Creating Helpful Incentives to Produce Semiconductors
CIA	Central Intelligence Agency
CLU	Command Launch Unit
CNN	Cable News Network
COVID	Coronavirus Disease
CPI	Communist Party of India
CPM	Communist Party of India(Marxist)
CT	Computed Tomography
DNA	Deoxyribonucleic Acid
DRC	Democratic Republic of the Congo
DSM	Diagnostic and Statistical Manual of Mental Disorders
EHR	Electronic Health Record
EITI	Extractive Industries Transparency Initiative
EMS	Elamkulam Manakkal Sankaran
ESA	European Space Agency
ETS	Emissions Trading System
EU	European Union
EV	Electric Vehicle
FARC	Fuerzas Armadas Revolucionarias de-Colombia
FBI	Federal Bureau of Investigation
FDI	Foreign Direct Investment
FEC	Federal Election Commission
FGM	Female Genital Mutilation
GAD	Generalized Anxiety Disorder
GDP	Gross Domestic Product
GDPR	General Data Protection Regulation
GI	GI Bill(Servicemen's Readjustment Act)
GOP	Grand Old Party (Republican Party)
GST	Goods and Services Tax
GTC	Global Technocratic Council
GVK	GVK Group
HARM	High-speed Anti-Radiation Missile
HGH	Human Growth Hormone
HIMARS	High Mobility Artillery Rocket System
HIV	Human Immunodeficiency Virus
HR	Human Resources
HSBC	Hong Kong and Shanghai Banking Corporation
HUR	Main Directorate of Intelligence, Ukraine
ID	Identification
IDF	Israel Defense Forces
IDR	Indonesian Rupiah
IEA	International Energy Agency
IIT	Indian Institutes of Technology
IMF	International Monetary Fund
IMS	Information Management Services
INC	Indian National Congress
INF	Intermediate-Range Nuclear Forces Treaty
IQVIA	International Quantitative Ventures in Analytical Health
ISI	Inter-Services Intelligence
ISIS	Islamic State of Iraq and Syria
ISRU	In-Situ Resource Utilization
ISS	International Space Station
IT	Information Technology
IVF	In Vitro Fertilization
JCPOA	Joint Comprehensive Plan of Action
JDAM	Joint Direct Attack Munition
KBR	Kellogg Brown & Root
KG	Krishna Godavari Basin D6
LAPD	Los Angeles Police Department
LGBTQ	Lesbian, Gay, Bisexual, Transgender, and Queer
LGBTQIA	Lesbian, Gay, Bisexual, Transgender, Queer, Intersex, and Asexual
LOL	Laugh Out Loud
LSD	Lysergic acid diethylamide
LTU	Local Technocratic Units
LVMH	Louis Vuitton Moët Hennessy
MAD	Mutually Assured Destruction
MDMA	3,4-Methylenedioxymethamphetamine

MERS	Middle East Respiratory Syndrome
MIT	Massachusetts Institute of Technology
MLRS	Multiple Launch Rocket System
MOL	Manned Orbiting Laboratory
MRI	Magnetic Resonance Imaging
MSNBC	Microsoft and the National Broadcasting Company
NAFTA	North American Free Trade Agreement
NASA	National Aeronautics and Space Administration
NASAMS	National Advanced Surface-to-Air Missile System
NASDAQ	National Association of Securities Dealers Automated Quotations
NATO	North Atlantic Treaty Organization
NBC	National Broadcasting Company
NDA	National Democratic Alliance
NDTV	New Delhi Television
NFL	National Football League
NHS	National Health Service
NICE	National Institute for Health and Care Excellence
NIE	National Intelligence Estimate
NITI	National Institution for Transforming India
NPT	Nuclear Non-Proliferation Treaty
NRA	National Rifle Association
NSG	Nuclear Suppliers Group
OECD	Organisation for Economic Co-operation and Development
OPEC	Organisation of the Petroleum Exporting Countries
OSIRIS	Origins, Spectral Interpretation, Resource Identification, and Security-Regolith Explorer
PCOS	Polycystic Ovary Syndrome
PIL	Public Interest Litigation
PNB	Punjab National Bank
PT	Perseroan Terbatas
PTO	Paid Time Off
PTSD	Post-Traumatic Stress Disorder
RASSOR	Regolith Advanced Surface Systems Operations Robot
RIL	Reliance Industries Limited
RSS	Rashtriya Swayamsevak Sangh
SARS	Severe Acute Respiratory Syndrome
SAT	Scholastic Assessment Test
SBC	Southern Baptist Convention
SBI	State Bank of India
SBU	Security Service of Ukraine
SDI	Strategic Defense Initiative
SEC	Securities and Exchange Commission
SHERLOC	Scanning Habitable Environments with Raman & Luminescence for Organics and Chemicals
SIGAR	Special Inspector General for Afghanistan Reconstruction
SJ	Shijian (Experimental Satellite)
SMA	Spinal Muscular Atrophy
SQM	Sociedad Química y Minera de Chile
START	Strategic Arms Reduction Treaty
STEM	Science, Technology, Engineering, and Mathematics
STOCK	Stop Trading on Congressional Knowledge Act
SUV	Sport Utility Vehicle
TADA	Terrorist and Disruptive Activities (Prevention) Act
TARP	Troubled Asset Relief Program
TBN	Trinity Broadcasting Network
TEPCO	Tokyo Electric Power Company
TPNW	Treaty on the Prohibition of Nuclear Weapons
TSMC	Taiwan Semiconductor Manufacturing Company
UBI	Universal Basic Income
UCC	Union Carbide Corporation
UCIL	Union Carbide India Limited
UK	United Kingdom
UN	United Nations
UNCLOS	United Nations Convention on the Law of the Sea
UNESCO	United Nations Educational, Scientific and Cultural Organization
UNICEF	United Nations International Children's Emergency Fund
UPA	United Progressive Alliance
US	United States
USA	United States of America
USS	United States Ship
USSR	Union of Soviet Socialist Republics
VR	Virtual Reality
VVIP	Very Very Important Person
WHO	World Health Organization
WIV	Wuhan Institute of Virology
WPATH	World Professional Association for Transgender Health
WTO	World Trade Organization